PRENTICE HALL

SCIENCE EXPLORER

Physical Science

Prentice
Hall

Needham, Massachusetts
Upper Saddle River, New Jersey
Glenview, Illinois

PRENTICE HALL
SCIENCE EXPLORER

Physical Science

Print Resources

Student Edition
Annotated Teacher's Edition
Unit Resource Books, including:
- Chapter Project Support
- Lesson Plans
- Section Summaries
- Review and Reinforce Worksheets
- Enrich Worksheets
- Student Edition Lab Worksheets
- Complete Answer Keys

Chapter and Unit Tests
Performance Assessment
Standardized Test Preparation Book
Laboratory Manual, Student Edition
Laboratory Manual, Teacher's Edition
Inquiry Skills Activity Book
Student-Centered Science Activity Books
Guided Study Workbook
Reading in the Content Area with Literature Connections
Science Explorer Interdisciplinary Explorations
Prentice Hall Interdisciplinary Explorations series
Product Testing Activities by Consumer Reports™
How to Manage Instruction in the Block
How to Assess Student Work

Media and Technology

Interactive Student Tutorial CD-ROM
Computer Test Bank with Dial-A-Test®
Resource Pro® (Teaching Resources on CD-ROM)
Lab Activity Video Library
Internet Site at www.phschool.com (includes www.PlanetDiary.com)
Color Transparencies
Section Summaries on Audio CD
Spanish Section Summaries on Audio CD and Book
Science Explorer Video Library
Science Explorer Spanish Video Library
Science Explorer Videodisc Library (English/Spanish)
Odyssey of Discovery (CD-ROMs for Life and Earth Science)
Mindscape CD-ROMs
A.D.A.M. CD-ROM
Interactive Earth CD-ROM
Interactive Physics Software

Materials Kits

Consumable Materials Kit
Nonconsumable Materials Kit
Materials List CD-ROM

Acknowledgments

Excerpt on page 137 from *The Iron Peacock* by Mary Stetson Clarke. Copyright © 1966 by Mary Stetson Clarke.

ISBN 0-13-050623-0
4 5 6 7 8 9 10 05 04 03 02 01

Prentice
Hall

Cover: The 13-kilometer-long San Francisco–Oakland Bay Bridge is actually a series of bridges. The towers soar 150 meters above the bay.

Program Authors

Michael J. Padilla, Ph.D.
Professor
Department of Science Education
University of Georgia
Athens, Georgia

Michael Padilla is a leader in middle school science education. He has served as an editor and elected officer for the National Science Teachers Association. He has been principal investigator of several National Science Foundation and Eisenhower grants and served as a writer of the National Science Education Standards.

As lead author of *Science Explorer,* Mike has inspired the team in developing a program that meets the needs of middle grades students, promotes science inquiry, and is aligned with the National Science Education Standards.

Ioannis Miaoulis, Ph.D.
Dean of Engineering
College of Engineering
Tufts University
Medford, Massachusetts

Martha Cyr, Ph.D.
Director, Engineering
   Educational Outreach
College of Engineering
Tufts University
Medford, Massachusetts

Science Explorer was created in collaboration with the College of Engineering at Tufts University. Tufts has an extensive engineering outreach program that uses engineering design and construction to excite and motivate students and teachers in science and technology education.

Faculty from Tufts University participated in the development of *Science Explorer* chapter projects, reviewed the student books for content accuracy, and helped coordinate field testing.

CHAPTER PROJECT

Book Authors

David V. Frank, Ph.D.
Head, Department of
   Physical Sciences
Ferris State University
Big Rapids, Michigan

John G. Little
Science Teacher
St. Mary's High School
Stockton, California

Steve Miller
Science Writer
State College, Pennsylvania

Jay M. Pasachoff, Ph.D.
Professor of Astronomy
Williams College
Williamstown, Massachusetts

Camille L. Wainwright, Ph.D.
Professor of Science Education
Pacific University
Forest Grove, Oregon

Contributing Writers

Rose-Marie Botting
Science Teacher
Broward County School District
Fort Lauderdale, Florida

Mary Sue Burns
Science Teacher
Pocahontas County High School
Dunmore, West Virginia

John Coffey
Science/Mathematics Teacher
Venice Area Middle School
Venice, Florida

Edward Evans
Former Science Teacher
Hilton Central School
Hilton, New York

Mark Illingworth
Teacher
Hollis Public Schools
Hollis, New Hampshire

Peter Kahan
Former Science Teacher
Dwight-Englewood School
Englewood, New Jersey

Thomas L. Messer
Science Teacher
Cape Cod Academy
Osterville, Massachusetts

Linda Shoulberg
Science Teacher
Millbrook High School
Raleigh, North Carolina

Thomas R. Wellnitz
Science Teacher
The Paideia School
Atlanta, Georgia

Reading Consultant

Bonnie B. Armbruster, Ph.D.
Department of Curriculum
   and Instruction
University of Illinois at Urbana
Champaign, Illinois

Interdisciplinary Consultant

Heidi Hayes Jacobs, Ed.D.
Teachers College
Columbia University
New York, New York

Safety Consultants

W. H. Breazeale, Ph.D.
Department of Chemistry
College of Charleston
Charleston, South Carolina

Ruth Hathaway, Ph.D.
Hathaway Consulting
Cape Girardeau, Missouri

Content Reviewers

Activity Field Testers

Nicki Bibbo
Russell Street School
Littleton, Massachusetts

Connie Boone
Fletcher Middle School
Jacksonville Beach, Florida

Rose-Marie Botting
Broward County School District
Fort Lauderdale, Florida

Colleen Campos
Laredo Middle School
Aurora, Colorado

Elizabeth Chait
W. L. Chenery Middle School
Belmont, Massachusetts

Holly Estes
Hale Middle School
Stow, Massachusetts

Laura Hapgood
Plymouth Community
    Intermediate School
Plymouth, Massachusetts

Sandra M. Harris
Winman Junior High School
Warwick, Rhode Island

Jason Ho
Walter Reed Middle School
Los Angeles, California

Joanne Jackson
Winman Junior High School
Warwick, Rhode Island

Mary F. Lavin
Plymouth Community
    Intermediate School
Plymouth, Massachusetts

James MacNeil, Ph.D.
Concord Public Schools
Concord, Massachusetts

Lauren Magruder
St. Michael's Country
    Day School
Newport, Rhode Island

Jeanne Maurand
Glen Urquhart School
Beverly Farms, Massachusetts

Warren Phillips
Plymouth Community
    Intermediate School
Plymouth, Massachusetts

Carol Pirtle
Hale Middle School
Stow, Massachusetts

Kathleen M. Poe
Kirby-Smith Middle School
Jacksonville, Florida

Cynthia B. Pope
Ruffner Middle School
Norfolk, Virginia

Anne Scammell
Geneva Middle School
Geneva, New York

Karen Riley Sievers
Callanan Middle School
Des Moines, Iowa

David M. Smith
Howard A. Eyer Middle School
Macungie, Pennsylvania

Derek Strohschneider
Plymouth Community
    Intermediate School
Plymouth, Massachusetts

Sallie Teames
Rosemont Middle School
Fort Worth, Texas

Gene Vitale
Parkland Middle School
McHenry, Illinois

Zenovia Young
Meyer Levin Junior
    High School (IS 285)
Brooklyn, New York

Contents

Physical Science

Introduction to Physical Science . . . . **xxii**

Unit 1 Chemical Building Blocks

Chapter 1 **Introduction to Matter** **16**
1 Describing Matter 18
2 Measuring Matter 24
3 Particles of Matter 31
4 Integrating Earth Science: Elements From Earth 36

Chapter 2 **Solids, Liquids, and Gases** **44**
1 States of Matter 46
2 Gas Behavior 51
3 Integrating Mathematics: Graphing Gas Behavior 58
4 Changes in State 64

Chapter 3 **Atoms and the Periodic Table** **74**
1 Inside an Atom 76
2 Organizing the Elements 81
3 Metals 89
4 Nonmetals and Metalloids 98
5 Integrating Space Science: Elements From Stardust 106

Chapter 4 **Chemical Bonds** **112**
1 Ionic Bonds 114
2 Covalent Bonds 121
3 Integrating Earth Science: Crystal Chemistry 128

Interdisciplinary Exploration:
Soap—The Dirt Chaser **134**

Unit 2   Chemistry in Action

Chapter 5   **Chemical Reactions** **142**
1 Observing Chemical Reactions 144
2 Writing Chemical Equations 152
3 Controlling Chemical Reactions 160
 4 Integrating Health: Fire and Fire Safety 168

Chapter 6   **Acids, Bases, and Solutions** **176**
1 Understanding Solutions 178
2 Concentration and Solubility 184
3 Describing Acids and Bases 192
4 Acids and Bases in Solution 198
5 Integrating Life Science: Digestion and pH 206

Chapter 7   **Carbon Chemistry** **212**
1 Chemical Bonding, Carbon Style 214
2 Carbon Compounds 219
3 Integrating Life Science: Life With Carbon 227

Chapter 8   **Exploring Materials** **242**
1 Polymers and Composites 244
2 Integrating Technology: Metals and Alloys 255
3 Ceramics and Glass 260
4 Radioactive Elements 265

Unit 3 Motion, Forces, and Energy

Nature of Science: Sonic Booms 276

Chapter 9 **Motion** **280**
    1 Describing and Measuring Motion 282
    2 Integrating Earth Science:
       Slow Motion on Planet Earth 296
    3 Acceleration 302

Chapter 10 **Forces** **310**
    1 The Nature of Force 312
    2 Force, Mass, and Acceleration 320
    3 Friction and Gravity 323
    4 Action and Reaction 332
    5 Integrating Space Science: Orbiting Satellites 338

Chapter 11 **Forces in Fluids** **344**
    1 Pressure 346
    2 Transmitting Pressure in a Fluid 354
    3 Floating and Sinking 358
    4 Integrating Technology:
       Applying Bernoulli's Principle 365

Chapter 12 **Work and Machines** **372**
    1 What Is Work? 374
    2 Mechanical Advantage and Efficiency 378
    3 Simple Machines 386
    4 Integrating Life Science:
       Machines in the Human Body 400

Chapter 13 **Energy and Power** **406**
    1 The Nature of Energy 408
    2 Energy Conversion and Conservation 416
    3 Energy Conversions and Fossil Fuels 422
    4 Integrating Mathematics: Power 426

Chapter 14 **Thermal Energy and Heat** **434**
    1 Temperature and Thermal Energy .436
    2 The Nature of Heat 439
    3 Integrating Chemistry:
       Thermal Energy and States of Matter 449
    4 Uses of Heat 455

Interdisciplinary Exploration:
       Bridges—From Vines to Steel **462**

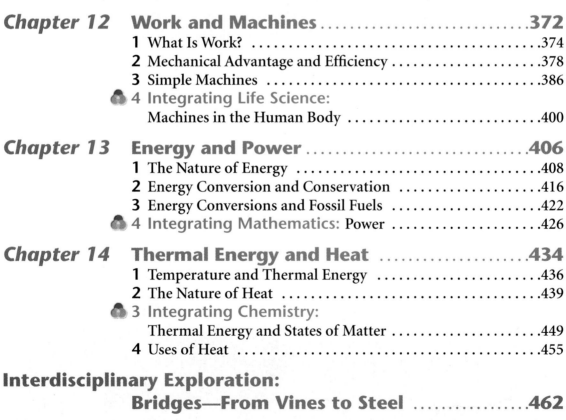

Unit 4   Sound and Light

Chapter 15   Characteristics of Waves **470**
   1 What Are Waves? 472
   2 Properties of Waves 476
   3 Interactions of Waves 482
   4 Integrating Earth Science: Seismic Waves 490

Chapter 16   Sound **496**
   1 The Nature of Sound 498
   2 Properties of Sound 504
   3 Combining Sound Waves 510
   4 Integrating Life Science: How You Hear Sound 520
   5 Applications of Sound 524

Chapter 17   The Electromagnetic Spectrum **532**
   1 The Nature of Electromagnetic Waves 534
   2 Waves of the Electromagnetic Spectrum 538
   3 Producing Visible Light 548
   4 Integrating Technology: Wireless Communication 554

Chapter 18   Light **568**
   1 Reflection and Mirrors 570
   2 Refraction and Lenses 575
   3 Color 581
   4 Integrating Life Science: Seeing Light 587
   5 Using Light 591

Interdisciplinary Exploration:
      The Magic of the Movies **604**

Unit 5   Electricity and Magnetism

Chapter 19   Magnetism and Electromagnetism 610
1 The Nature of Magnetism 612
2 Integrating Earth Science: Magnetic Earth 622
3 Electric Current and Magnetic Fields 628
4 Electromagnets 636

Chapter 20   Electric Charges and Current 642
1 Electric Charge and Static Electricity 644
2 Circuit Measurements 654
3 Series and Parallel Circuits 662
4 Integrating Health: Electrical Safety 666

Chapter 21   Electricity and Magnetism at Work 674
1 Electricity, Magnetism, and Motion 676
2 Generating Electric Current 682
3 Using Electric Power 690
4 Integrating Chemistry: Batteries 697

Chapter 22   Electronics 708
1 Electronic Signals and Semiconductors 710
2 Electronic Communication 718
3 Computers 726
4 Integrating Technology: The Information Superhighway 736

**Interdisciplinary Exploration:
    Edison—Genius of Invention** 744

Reference Section
Skills Handbook 750
    Think Like a Scientist 750
    Making Measurements 752
    Conducting a Scientific Investigation 754
    Thinking Critically 756
    Organizing Information 758
    Creating Data Tables and Graphs 760
Appendix A: Laboratory Safety 763
Appendix B: Using a Laboratory Balance 766
Appendix C: List of Chemical Elements 767
Appendix D: Periodic Table of the Elements 768
Glossary 770
Index 782
Acknowledgments 794

PRENTICE HALL
SCIENCE EXPLORER
PHYSICAL SCIENCE

Activities

....

Inquiry Activities

CHAPTER PROJECT
Opportunities for long-term inquiry

Chapter 1: Comparing Brand X 17
Chapter 2: A Story of Changes in Matter ...45
Chapter 3: Getting Organized 75
Chapter 4: Model Compounds 113
Chapter 5: Keep a Chemical Change Log ..143
Chapter 6: Make Your Own Indicator 177
Chapter 7: Check Out the Fine Print 213
Chapter 8: Polymer Profiles 243
Chapter 9: Speeds à la Carte 281
Chapter 10: Newton Scooters 311
Chapter 11: Staying Afloat 345
Chapter 12: The Nifty Lifting Machine ...373
Chapter 13: Roller Coaster! 407
Chapter 14: In Hot Water 435
Chapter 15: Over and Over
            and Over Again 471
Chapter 16: Music to Your Ears 497
Chapter 17: You're on the Air 533
Chapter 18: What a Sight! 569
Chapter 19: Electromagnetic Fishing Derby ..611
Chapter 20: Cause for Alarm 643
Chapter 21: Electrical Energy Audit 675
Chapter 22: Bits and Bytes 709

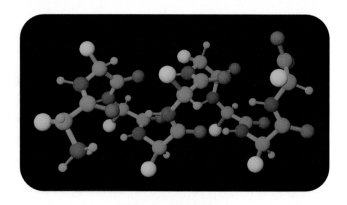

DISCOVER
Exploration and inquiry before reading

What Properties Help You Sort Matter? 18
Which Has More Mass? 24
What's in the Box? 31
How Can You Separate Bolts From Sand? 36
What Are Solids, Liquids, and Gases? 46
How Can Air Keep Chalk From Breaking? ...51
What Does a Graph of Pressure and
    Temperature Show? 58
What Happens When You Breathe
    on a Mirror? 64
How Far Away Is the Electron? 76
Which Is Easier? 81
Why Use Aluminum? 89
What Are the Properties of Charcoal? 98
Can Helium Be Made From Hydrogen? 106
How Do Ions Form? 114
Why Don't Water and Oil Mix? 121
How Small Do They Get? 128
What Happens When Chemicals React? 144
Do You Lose Anything? 152
Can You Speed Up or Slow Down
    a Reaction? 160
How Does Baking Soda Affect a Fire? 168
What Makes a Mixture a Solution? 178
Does It Dissolve? 184
What Colors Does Litmus Paper Turn? 192
What Can Cabbage Juice Tell You? 198
Where Does Digestion Begin? 206
Why Do Pencils Write? 214
What Do You Smell? 219
What Is in Milk? 227
What Did You Make? 244
Are They Steel the Same? 255
Does It Get Wet? 260

How Much Goes Away? 265
How Fast and How Far? 282
How Slow Can It Flow? 296
Will You Hurry Up? 302
What Changes Motion? 312
How Do the Rocks Roll? 320
Which Lands First? .323
How Pushy Is a Straw? 332
What Makes an Object Move in a Circle? . . .338
Can You Blow Up a Balloon in a Bottle? 346
How Does Pressure Change? 354
What Can You Measure With a Straw? 358
Does Water Push or Pull? 365
What Happens When You Pull at an Angle? . .374
Is It a Machine? 378
How Can You Increase Your Force? 386
Are You an Eating Machine? 400
How High Does a Ball Bounce? 408
What Would Make a Card Jump? 416
What Is a Fuel? 422
Is Work Always the Same? 426
How Cold Is the Water? 436
What Does It Mean to Heat Up? 439
What Happens to Heated Metal? 449
What Happens at the Pump? 455
How Do Waves Travel? 472
How Can You Change a Wave? 476
How Does a Ball Bounce? 482
Can You Find the Sand? 490
What Is Sound? 498
How Does Amplitude Affect Loudness? 504
How Can You Produce Patterns of Sound? . .510
Where Is the Sound Coming From? 520
How Can You Use Time to Measure
    Distance? 524

How Does a Beam of Light Travel? 534
What Is White Light? 538
How Do Light Bulbs Differ? 548
How Can Radio Waves Change? 554
How Does Your Reflection Wink? 570
How Can You Make an Image
    Appear on a Sheet of Paper? 575
How Do Colors Mix? 581
Can You See Everything With One Eye? 587
How Does a Pinhole Viewer Work? 591
What Do All Magnets Have in Common? . . .612
Can You Use a Needle to Make a Compass? . .622
Are Magnetic Fields Limited to Magnets? . . .628
How Do You Turn a Magnet On and Off? . . .636
Can You Move a Can Without Touching It? .644
How Can Current Be Measured? 654
Do the Lights Keep Shining? 662
How Can You Blow a Fuse? 666
How Does a Magnet Move a Wire? 676
Can You Produce Electric Current
    Without a Battery? 682
How Can You Make a Bulb Burn
    More Brightly? 690
Can You Make Electricity
    With Spare Change? 697
Can You Send Information
    With a Flashlight? 710
Are You Seeing Spots? 718
How Fast Are You? .726
How Important Are Computers? 736

Sharpen your *Skills*

Practice of specific science inquiry skills

Inferring 22
Developing Hypotheses 52
Classifying 83
Observing 91
Interpreting Data 117
Designing Experiments 123
Calculating 156
Interpreting Data 164
Designing Experiments 182
Graphing 187
Classifying 223
Classifying 250
Predicting 267
Calculating 269
Predicting 297
Calculating 328
Developing Hypotheses 348
Measuring 359
Inferring 376
Classifying 395
Graphing 423
Inferring 440
Observing 452
Observing 483
Graphing 501

Designing Experiments 525
Observing 549
Classifying 572
Developing Hypotheses 583
Observing 614
Measuring 623
Classifying 632
Drawing Conclusions 646
Calculating 658
Predicting 664
Classifying 685
Observing 693
Communicating 715
Calculating 728

TRY THIS

Reinforcement of key concepts

Bubble Time 25
As Thick as Honey 49
Balloon Test 54
Show Me the Oxygen 101
Crystal Shapes 118
Mostly Cloudy 145
Still There 155
Scattered Light 181
pHone Home 200
Dry or Wet? 221
Alphabet Soup 231
A Bright Idea 263
Sunrise, Sunset 284
Around and Around 316
Spinning Plates 325

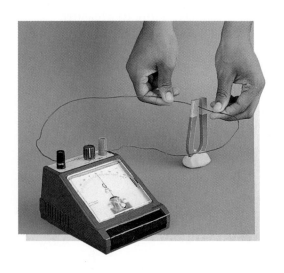

Colliding Cars 336
Dive! 362
Going Up 381
Modeling a Screw 389
Pendulum Swing 419
Feel the Warmth 442
Shake It Up 456
Standing Waves 485
The Short Straw 506
Pipe Sounds 508
Plucking Rubber Bands 512
Listen to Sounds 521
How Do Light Beams Behave? 536
What Does a Bee See? 545
Produce Electromagnetic Interference 556
Disappearing Glass .576
True Colors 589

What a View! 592
How Attractive! 618
Spinning in Circles .625
Sparks Are Flying 648
Down the Tubes 657
Keeping Current 684
What a Web You Weave 738

Skills Lab

In-depth practice of inquiry skills

Making Sense of Density 30
It's a Gas 62
Melting Ice 70
Alien Periodic Table 104
Shape Up! 120
Shedding Light on Chemical Bonds 126
Where's the Evidence? 150
Speedy Solutions 190
How Many Molecules? 218
That's Half-Life! 272
Inclined to Roll 294
Forced to Accelerate 318
Sink and Spill 360
Seesaw Science 384
Soaring Straws 414
Just Add Water 446
Wavy Motions 478
Making Waves 488
The Speed of Sound 503
Looking at Images .580
The Versorium 652
Electricity Grows on Trees 702
The Penny Computer 734

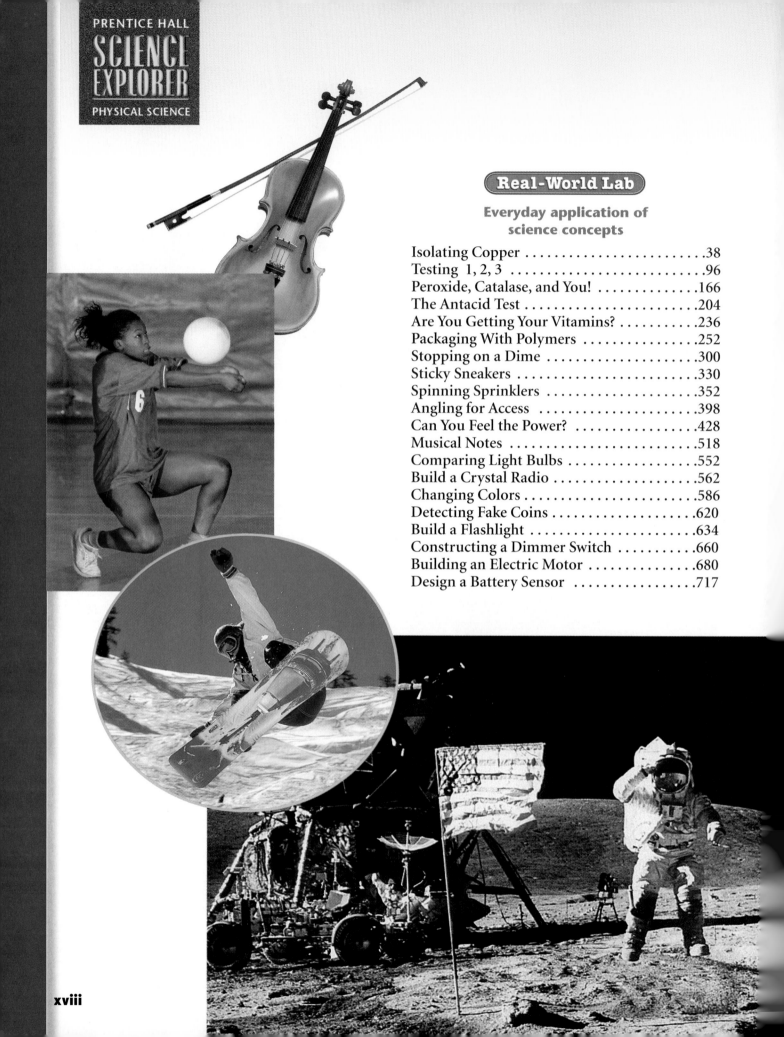

Real-World Lab

Everyday application of science concepts

Isolating Copper 38
Testing 1, 2, 3 96
Peroxide, Catalase, and You! 166
The Antacid Test 204
Are You Getting Your Vitamins? 236
Packaging With Polymers 252
Stopping on a Dime 300
Sticky Sneakers 330
Spinning Sprinklers 352
Angling for Access .398
Can You Feel the Power? 428
Musical Notes 518
Comparing Light Bulbs 552
Build a Crystal Radio 562
Changing Colors 586
Detecting Fake Coins 620
Build a Flashlight 634
Constructing a Dimmer Switch 660
Building an Electric Motor 680
Design a Battery Sensor 717

Science at Home

**Family involvement in
science exploration**

Density Demonstration 29
What Gives? 50
News Data 61
Atoms on Display 80
Halogens in the Home 103
Piling Up 130
Comparing Reaction Rates 165
Family Safety Plan 171
Passing Through 183
A Warming Trend 189
Liquid Layers 226
Metal Inventory 259
Fingernail Growth 299
Coin Inertia 317
Swing the Bucket 340

Under Pressure 351
Atomizer 368
Household Machines .383
Finger Force 402
Hot Wire 421
Room Temperature 438
Freezing Air 454
Waves in a Sink 487
Sounds Solid 492
Ear to the Sound 502
Sound Survey 522
Sunglasses 537
Buying Bulbs 551
Pencil Bending 579
Optical Illusion 590
House Magnets 627
Standing on End 651
Circuit Diagrams 670
Recharge Your Batteries 701
Remote Controls 725
Computer Age 739

Interdisciplinary Activities

Science and History
Measurement Systems .26
Models of Atoms 78
The Development of Polymers 248
The Speed of Transportation 288
Engineering Marvels 392
Wireless Communication 558
Optical Instruments .596
The History of Electric Power 694
The Development of Computers 730

Science and Society
Cleaning Up Metal Contamination 95
Transporting Hazardous Chemicals 172
Natural or Artificial—A Sweet Dilemma . . .238
Grocery Bags: Paper or Plastic? 254
Automation in the Workplace—Lost Jobs or
    New Jobs? 397
Insulation—And a Breath of Clean Air 448
Keeping It Quiet 523
Food Irradiation 547
Disposing of Batteries—Safely 704
When Seeing ISN'T Believing 740

Math Toolbox
Ratios 20
Constant Ratios 33
Ratios and Subscripts 153
Converting Units 285
Area 347
Percents 383
Squared Numbers 410
Calculating With Units 480

Connection
Language Arts 34
Social Studies 66
Language Arts 86
Language Arts 124
Social Studies 162
Language Arts 194
Language Arts 228
Language Arts 247
Social Studies 270
Social Studies 286
Language Arts 314
Social Studies 355
Visual Arts 390
Visual Arts 420
Language Arts 451
Music 513
Social Studies 539
Visual Arts 584
Language Arts 626
Social Studies 668
Social Studies 678
Music 712

EXPLORING

Visual exploration of concepts

Matter at the Beach .... .21
Changes of State .... .68
The Periodic Table .... .84
Ionic Bonds .... .116
Evidence for Chemical Reactions .... .146
Uses of Acids .... .195
Uses of Bases .... .196
The Molecules of Life .... .233
Alloys and Metals in Aircraft .... .257
Motion Graphs .... .290
Combined Forces .... .315

Wings .... .367
The Three Classes of Levers .... .391
Levers in the Body .... .401
Energy Conversions .... .424
A Four-Stroke Engine .... .457
Interactions of Waves .... .486
Making Music .... .514
The Electromagnetic Spectrum .... .542
Uses of Lasers .... .599
Electric Circuits .... .631
Static Electricity .... .649
Energy Resources .... .686
Computer Hardware .... .728

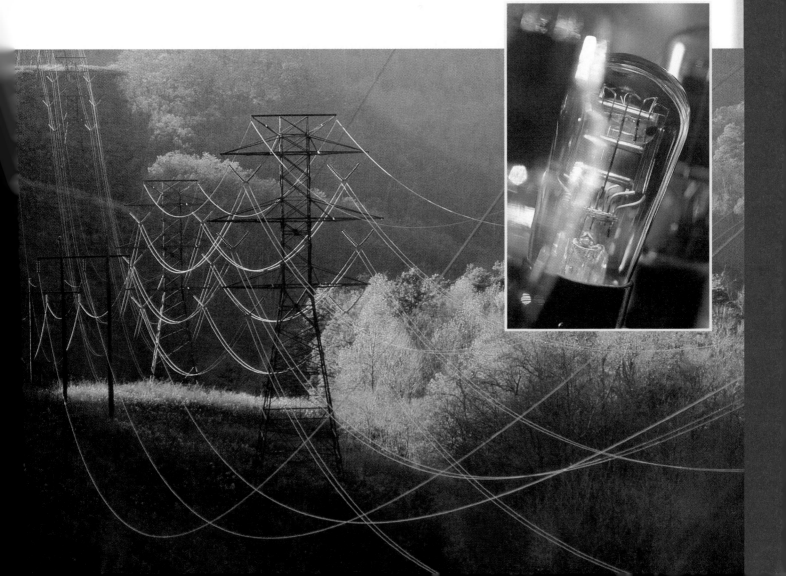

SAVING THE OZONE LAYER

As a child growing up in Mexico, long before he won a Nobel Prize in chemistry, Mario Molina enjoyed playing with science. "I was always interested in chemistry sets or toy microscopes. With the microscope in front of me, I'd take a piece of lettuce, put it in water, and let it rot and really stink. To see the life teeming in a drop of water—that for me was fascinating. Even then I realized it would be great if I could become a research scientist."

What Mario wanted to do, he decided, was "actually use science for things that affect society." Mario Molina began by looking at the chemicals people put into the air.

Dr. Mario Molina Born in Mexico City, chemist Mario Molina is now a Professor of Earth, Atmospheric, and Planetary Sciences at the Massachusetts Institute of Technology in Cambridge, Massachusetts. In 1995, Professor Molina, F. Sherwood Rowland, and Paul Crutzen won the Nobel Prize in Chemistry for their work on CFCs and the ozone layer.

Cycle of Ozone Destruction

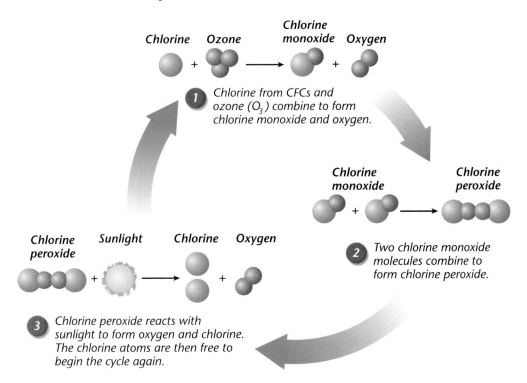

Chlorine + **Ozone** → **Chlorine monoxide** + **Oxygen**

1 Chlorine from CFCs and ozone (O_3) combine to form chlorine monoxide and oxygen.

Chlorine monoxide + **Chlorine monoxide** → **Chlorine peroxide**

2 Two chlorine monoxide molecules combine to form chlorine peroxide.

Chlorine peroxide + **Sunlight** → **Chlorine** + **Oxygen**

3 Chlorine peroxide reacts with sunlight to form oxygen and chlorine. The chlorine atoms are then free to begin the cycle again.

Asking Simple Questions

In the early 1970s, one of Dr. Molina's co-workers, F. Sherwood Rowland, heard about a group of compounds called chlorofluorocarbons, or CFCs. CFCs were used in air conditioners, refrigerators, and aerosol spray cans, but leaked into the air. "It is something that is not natural, but is now in the atmosphere all over the planet." What happens to these compounds in the air, Rowland and Molina wondered, and what do they do to the air?

"We didn't know ahead of time if CFCs were doing damage or not," Dr. Molina explains. "So what we did was study what was going on. We learned that CFCs aren't changed much down near Earth. But we expected that if they got high enough in the atmosphere, solar radiation would destroy them."

Radiation is how energy from the sun reaches Earth. Ultraviolet (UV) rays, a form of radiation, break compounds apart and change them. "Above a certain altitude, everything falls apart. We had to learn how high CFCs went and how long it took them to get there. Then we asked: What does it mean that CFCs are up there?"

A Protective Shield in the Sky

In his laboratory, Dr. Molina studied how ultraviolet light changes CFCs. "It became clear that these molecules would be destroyed by UV rays in the stratosphere—the upper atmosphere, where the ozone layer is. At the time, I didn't even know what the ozone layer was."

But Mario Molina learned fast. The ozone layer is a thin layer of the atmosphere that contains ozone, a form of oxygen. The ozone blocks out UV rays from the sun. UV rays would be dangerous to living things if they reached Earth's surface.

In a 1987 international treaty, the United States and other industrial nations agreed to reduce the use of CFCs in spray cans and other products.

Changes in the ozone layer over Antarctica, 1979 to 1993

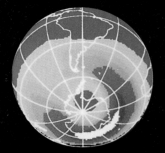 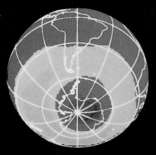 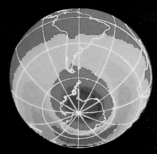 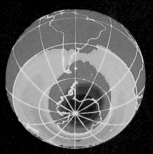

In 1979, thinning of the ozone layer was visible in satellite images.

In 1985, a hole in the ozone layer was clearly visible.

In 1989, the hole in the ozone layer was expanding.

In 1993, the damage to the ozone layer was even worse.

← Less ozone   More ozone →

These images of the South Pole, taken by satellite between 1979 and 1993, show a hole developing in the ozone layer of the atmosphere. The changing size and color of the image over the pole represent how quickly the hole increased.

Dr. Molina learned something very disturbing. When the sun's rays break CFCs apart, chlorine forms. A chain of chemical changes that destroys ozone then begins. "Very small amounts of CFCs can have very big effects on ozone."

A Scary Prediction Comes True

Mario Molina and his co-workers made a frightening prediction. If CFCs can reach the stratosphere, they will eventually damage the protective ozone layer. Other scientists thought Mario Molina was wrong or exaggerating. But more and more evidence came in. Researchers sent balloons up into the stratosphere with scientific instruments to measure chlorine formed by CFCs. They found that CFCs were in the stratosphere and that the sun's rays were breaking them down.

Was the ozone layer being hurt? Yes. Over Antarctica, there was an

"ozone hole," an opening in the ozone layer. The hole lets in harmful radiation from the sun. "That was a surprise to us and to everybody. It was a very large effect that we hadn't predicted. Some scientists thought the ozone hole was natural, but we thought it was caused by CFCs. We checked it out by doing experiments from Antarctica. In a couple of years it became very clear that this hole was a result of the CFCs."

Scientist and Speaker

Dr. Molina now had to persuade people to stop making and using CFCs. "We were lucky that the effect

Shown here is the ER-2 aircraft, which was used to measure gases in the ozone hole over Antarctica. ▶

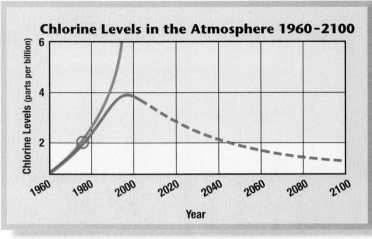

Chlorine Levels in the Atmosphere 1960-2100

Chlorine Levels (parts per billion)

Year

— Predicted levels without controls
— Actual levels with controls
○ Antarctica ozone hole found
– – Predicted levels with controls

The graph shows that the level of chlorine in the atmosphere would have increased rapidly if controls on CFCs had not been passed. With controls in place, the amount of chlorine in the atmosphere should gradually decrease to levels in the light blue region of the graph. The ozone hole should then close.

over Antarctica was so large. That made it easy to measure and test. But similar effects exist everywhere. As scientists, we had to inform the public and the government. If you're convinced that you're right and that something dangerous is going to happen, you need to risk speaking out."

Mario Molina went to the U.S. Senate and to other governments. He was able to show how UV radiation was causing damage. "There was damage to some crops, damage to growing fish, damage that we can already see and measure today."

Finally, the world listened. Through the United Nations, an agreement was signed by most industrial nations to stop using CFCs by the year 2000.

Work Still to Do

"Everybody has to work together," chemist Molina says. He has done more than his share. He gave $200,000 of his Nobel Prize money to help train scientists from Latin America and other developing countries. "There is a need to understand our planet, and we need very good minds to work on these problems. There are big challenges out there," he says with a confident smile, "but fortunately science is fascinating."

In Your Journal

Mario Molina particularly wants to know how chemicals made by people get into the atmosphere and change it. Take a walk in your neighborhood. Make a list of ways you can observe—or think of—that people put chemicals into the air. Remember that smoke is a mixture of chemicals.

WHAT IS SCIENCE?

GUIDE FOR READING

◆ What skills do scientists use in their work?

◆ How may a scientific hypothesis be tested?

◆ Why are safe laboratory practices important?

Reading Tip

Before you read, make a list of the boldfaced terms on pages 4–9. As you read, write a definition in your own words for each term.

Mario Molina's road to the Nobel Prize in Chemistry began with simple curiosity. As a child, he asked questions and observed the world around him. When he grew up, Dr. Molina applied his curiosity to his environment. He wondered how certain chemicals released into the air affected the atmosphere. To answer the questions he raised, Dr. Molina used the methods of science.

Some people wonder whether science is a body of knowledge or a process. It's really both. **Science** is a way of learning about the natural world through observations and logical reasoning. Science also includes a body of information that can grow and change as new ideas are explored.

Another term for the ongoing process of discovery in science is **scientific inquiry.** It refers to the various organized methods of investigating problems and answering questions. In this book, you will take part in science inquiry through laboratory investigations and other activities. In the process, you will find out about **physical science**—the study of matter, energy, and the changes that matter and energy undergo.

Figure 1 You use scientific inquiry to solve all sorts of problems. A simple challenge might be figuring out how to make a row of dominoes collapse.

Thinking Like A Scientist

Dr. Molina used scientific inquiry to study the effects of certain chemicals in the atmosphere. His work depended on a variety of skills. **Some of the skills used by scientists include posing questions, making observations and inferences, developing hypotheses, and conducting experiments.** You can use these same skills as you make discoveries yourself.

Look at the picture of the boy on the bike. How did he get into mid-air? Where was his starting point? What will happen when he lands? If you ask questions about objects or events you observe, you are thinking like a scientist. You have begun the process of scientific inquiry.

Posing Questions Are you curious? Curiosity drives scientific inquiry by leading people to think about a question or a problem. Dr. Molina wondered, "What do CFCs do to the atmosphere?" You may have questions about the natural world as well. For example, if you've tried to take good photographs, you may have had problems with shadows. Perhaps you've started to wonder, "How do I control the shadows appearing in my photos? What makes shadows larger or smaller?"

Observing In order to learn more about shadows, you use the skill of observation. **Observation** involves using all five senses—sight, hearing,

touch, smell, and sometimes taste—to gather information. You may observe, for example, that shadows on a wall can change in height. The facts, figures, and other evidence that you learn through observation are called **data.** Scientists usually record their observations in order to have a permanent account of their data.

Figure 2 Flying through the air isn't the usual way to ride a bike. Unusual sights or events often lead to asking questions.

✓ *Checkpoint* *What senses can the skill of observation involve?*

Figure 3 Photographers make use of shadows to create artistic works. *Posing Questions Think of some questions about light and shadows that a photographer would want to investigate to take photographs like these?*

Inferring An observation is important, but it's only one part of a larger process. Observations usually lead to inferences. An **inference** is a logical interpretation based on observations or prior knowledge.

You may infer, for example, that the height of an object's shadow depends on how near the object is to the light.

Developing Hypotheses

Scientific inquiry moves forward when ideas can be tested. In doing so, scientists often work from one or more hypotheses. A **hypothesis** is a possible explanation for observations that relate to a scientific question. **In science, a hypothesis must be testable by observation or experiment.** In this way, information may be collected that may or may not support the hypothesis.

In your study of shadows, you might develop the following hypothesis: *The distance between an object and a light source affects the size of the object's shadow.* You could then set up an experiment to test this idea. You might even make a prediction about the outcome. Perhaps you would think the object's shadow gets smaller as the light source is moved farther from it.

Designing Controlled Experiments

To test a hypothesis, scientists examine all the factors that can change during an experiment. Such factors are called **variables.** The variable that a scientist changes is called the **manipulated variable,** or independent variable. The variable that is expected to change because of the manipulated variable is the **responding variable,** or dependent variable.

The manipulated variable for the hypothesis above is the distance between the light and the object. The responding variable is the height of the shadow. See the setup for this experiment in Figure 5.

To be sure that changes in the manipulated variable are causing the changes in the responding variable, scientists test, or change, only one variable at a time. All other variables must be controlled—that is, kept constant. In the example, some of the variables that must be controlled are the height and angle of the light, and the distance between the object and the wall. An investigation in which all variables except one remain the same is called a **controlled experiment.**

Figure 4 The position of a light source can affect the size of an object's shadow.
Inferring How would you explain the length of the shadows in this photograph?

Collecting Data Scientific data may include both qualitative and quantitative descriptions. Qualitative data are descriptions, such as color, odor, or sound, that don't involve measurements or numbers. Quantitative data are measurements made using standard units, such as temperature in degrees Celsius (°C) or speed in meters per second (m/s). To make it easier to share data, scientists take measurements in a standard way. They use a system of measurement called the International System of Units (SI). SI is based on the metric system used in many countries around the world. By using SI, scientists from all over the world can communicate their findings with one another.

Notice that the data for the shadow experiment are measured in the SI unit centimeters. Before you conduct any experiments, learn more about making measurements with SI on pages 752–753 of the Skills Handbook.

☑ *Checkpoint* How do qualitative data differ from quantitative data?

Interpreting Data Scientists interpret data, or find out what they mean, by identifying trends or patterns. Data are often organized in tables or graphs. Figure 6 shows a table and graph for the shadow experiment. To learn more about tables and graphs, look at pages 760–762 in the Skills Handbook.

Figure 5 In this experiment, the distance between the flashlight and the ruler is the manipulated variable.
Applying Concepts Why is the height of the ruler's shadow the responding variable?

Distance Between Object and Light (cm)	Height of Shadow (cm)
10	32
15	27
20	25
25	23
30	22
35	21
40	20

Figure 6 The distances in this table are examples of quantitative data. When the data are graphed, the result is a curved line.

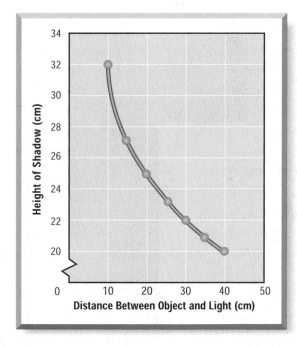

Drawing Conclusions After interpreting the data, you are ready to draw a conclusion. A conclusion states whether the data supported the hypothesis or showed it to be false. For example, based on the data in Figure 6, you would conclude that the size of a shadow does decrease as the light is moved farther away.

Scientists in Action Sometimes people think that scientific inquiry always happens in a set order of steps. Not necessarily so. Often, inquiry begins with a creative guess, or a surprising observation. New information may spring from an accidental discovery. Then a scientist's path takes a different turn. Work may go forward or even backward—testing a hunch to see where it leads or fitting a new idea with already existing ones.

In the example, the data supported the hypothesis. However, experimental data often show a hypothesis to be false. Does this mean that the investigation was a failure? Quite the contrary. What may be most surprising to you is that failure is often an important step in the scientific process! What looks like a dead end can lead to new questions that need to be investigated further. Then the process of inquiry begins all over again. When answers come, they may increase scientific knowledge in small steps. Or, they may lead to a giant leap of understanding.

Figure 7 An understanding of light and shadows helps artists and performers create visual effects that delight and surprise the viewer. *Predicting If the photographer wanted to make the shadow of the musician look larger, how would the light source have to change?*

8

Communicating Information

You may recall that an important step in Dr. Molina's work involved communication, the sharing of ideas and experimental data with others. First, Dr. Molina explained his hypothesis to other scientists. Many of them thought his idea was wrong. When the data supported his hypothesis, Dr. Molina communicated his prediction about the ozone layer to government agencies and the United Nations.

Scientists often communicate by writing articles in scientific journals and speaking at scientific meetings. The Internet is also extremely useful for communicating ideas and gathering information.

Developing Scientific Laws and Theories

As a body of knowledge, science is built up cautiously. Scientists do not accept a new hypothesis with just a few successful experiments. Instead, it is tested repeatedly by different scientists. Some hypotheses have

become so well established that they are called laws. A **scientific law** is a statement that describes what scientists expect to happen every time under a particular set of conditions. One law you will learn about describes how objects fall toward Earth in a certain way.

Sometimes a large body of related information can be explained by a single major idea. If that idea is supported by many tests, it may develop into a theory. A **scientific theory** is a well-tested idea that explains and connects a wide range of observations. For example, the theory that matter is made of atoms helps explain a huge number of observations related to changes in matter. It is possible that a scientific theory will be contradicted by new evidence, however. If that happens, scientists will change the theory or abandon it.

✓ *Checkpoint* **How does a scientific hypothesis become well-established?**

Figure 8 Gravity causes a ball to fall downward when it is released. Gravity also affects a hang glider, but other conditions that can be investigated slow the descent. *Developing Hypotheses State at least one hypothesis to explain why the hang glider does not fall to Earth as rapidly as the ball. How would you test your hypothesis?*

SWING TIME

You can study the movement of a pendulum by hanging an object—the bob—on a string.

Problem

Does the swing of a pendulum take longer for an object of greater mass?

Materials

stand with clamp	string, 50 cm in length
large paper clip	5 metal washers
ruler	stopwatch

Procedures

1. Read the whole procedure. Write a hypothesis describing how the mass of the bob will affect the speed of its swing. Then create a data table like the one shown.
2. Tie one end of a string to a clamp on a stand. Tie the other end to a large paper clip. Pull out one side of the paper clip to serve as a hook.
3. Place a metal washer on the hook, and let it hang down. If necessary, raise the clamp so that the bob swings freely.
4. Pull the bob back so that the string makes an angle of about 45° with the stand. Have your partner measure the height of the bob above the table top. Record this height as the starting position of the bob.

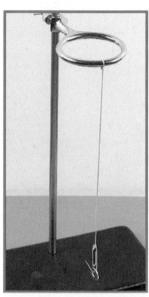

5. Release the bob gently, without pushing it. During a complete swing, the bob will move from its starting position and back again. Your partner should time 10 complete swings.
6. Record the time for 10 swings to the nearest tenth of a second. Then divide that time by 10 to find the average time for one swing.
7. Repeat Steps 5 and 6, increasing the mass of the bob each time by adding a washer. Make sure you always start the bob at the same height.

Analyze and Conclude

1. Graph your results. (*Hint:* Place the number of washers on the horizontal axis and the average time per swing on the vertical axis.)
2. Use the graph to decide if your data support your hypothesis.
3. What conclusion can you draw from this experiment?
4. **Think About It** How did this experiment enable you to test your hypothesis?

DATA TABLE

Number of washers	Time for 10 swings	Average time per swing
1		
2		

Design an Experiment

Design an experiment to test how the average time for a pendulum swing changes when the mass is constant but the length of the string changes. Obtain your teacher's approval before carrying out this experiment.

Laboratory Safety

You will carry out experiments and other activities as you learn about physical science. During these investigations, be sure to observe safe laboratory practices. Always follow your teacher's instructions, and show respect and courtesy to your teacher and classmates. Before you begin an activity, make sure you understand every step of the procedure and the accompanying safety information. Handle all laboratory materials carefully.

Before conducting any experiment or activity, read and learn the rules for laboratory safety and the meaning of each safety symbol in Appendix A: Laboratory Safety on pages 763–765. The safety symbols alert you to necessary precautions, such as wearing a lab apron or heat-resistant gloves. **Remember, safe laboratory practices will not only protect you and your classmates from injury but also make your observations more accurate.**

Physical Science in Daily Life

Physical science is divided into two main areas. The first, chemistry, is the study of the particles that make up everything around you and the ways these particles interact. Dr. Molina, for example, needed an understanding of chemistry to study CFCs and their effects on the ozone layer. The first two units of this book cover key topics in chemistry.

The second topic in physical science is physics, covered in Units 3, 4, and 5. You will see how and why objects move, the characteristics of sound and light, and how electricity and magnetism work.

You may think that physical science will be important only if you want to become a chemist or a physicist. The fact is that you use physical science all the time. You may discover that the principles of physical science explain many everyday events that have puzzled you.

Figure 9 Following laboratory safety rules keeps scientists safe and makes experiments more successful.
Observing What steps has this student taken to protect himself while carrying out this experiment?

EXPLORING Careers in Physical Science

Physical scientists study topics as varied as the structure of tiny atoms and the forces that move spaceships. People who work in the field of physical science study how changes in matter and energy affect their world, and how to make use of those changes.

▼ Pollution Control Officer

Environmental chemists study the chemicals found in air, soil, and water. The chemist shown here is measuring the oxygen content of river water. Her data is important in tracking changes in the water that may affect its drinking quality or the organisms that live in the river.

Musician ▶

An understanding of the nature of sound is essential for musicians and sound technicians. Often, technicians produce music and other sound effects electronically and then manipulate the sounds using computer programs.

Electrical Engineer ▶

Electrical engineers study and control electrical energy and put it to use in helpful ways. Electrical engineers design technologies for such diverse uses as satellite communications, computer systems, radio, TV, and other audiovisual components, delivering electricity to consumers, and designing and building electrical systems for airplanes and other vehicles.

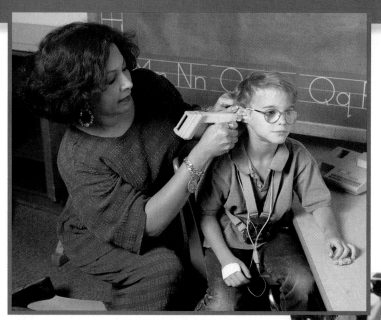

◄ Audiologist

Audiologists test hearing ability through the use of specialized equipment. Many school systems employ audiologists to test students' hearing yearly. In this way, a hearing loss may be identified and addressed before it can interfere with a child's progress in school. Audiologists also help diagnose the degree of hearing impairment in adults who have had hearing loss.

Chemical Researcher ►

Chemists play an important role in the development of new medicines. This chemist is testing the effect of a new drug on living tissue. The results of such research lead to the manufacture of safe and effective products that can be used in health care.

Physicist ▲

Physicists are interested in understanding the way the world really works—from the smallest particles of matter to the most powerful forces of nature. Physicists conduct research and do experiments in areas such as motion, forces, and energy. The work of physicists has allowed people to light the night, keep warm in the cold, and fly to the moon.

Architect ►

Architects design buildings using their knowledge of materials and loads. Loads are the forces that act on buildings, such as the weight of people and materials, and the effects of weather and earthquakes. Architects must know about physical properties of building materials and apply this knowledge to the building design.

Study Guide

Key Ideas

◆ Science is an organized way of learning about the natural world. Through observations and logical reasoning, scientists investigate problems and look for answers to questions.

◆ Scientists use many specific skills, including posing questions, making observations, making inferences, developing hypotheses, designing experiments, and communicating information.

◆ A scientific hypothesis states an idea in a way that can be tested.

◆ In a controlled experiment, the manipulated variable is changed in order to see how the responding variable changes. All other variables are kept constant.

◆ Data from an experiment are analyzed to determine whether or not they support the hypothesis being tested.

◆ All laboratory activities must be conducted by following safe laboratory procedures.

Key Terms

science
scientific inquiry
physical science
observation
data
inference
hypothesis

variable
manipulated variable
responding variable
controlled experiment
scientific law
scientific theory

Reviewing Content

 For more review of key concepts, see the Interactive Student Tutorial CD-ROM.

Multiple Choice

Choose the letter of the best answer.

1. A logical interpretation based on observations or prior knowledge is called
   a. scientific inquiry.
   b. an inference.
   c. communication.
   d. an observation.

2. The scientific skill in which the senses are used to gather information is
   a. posing questions. b. drawing conclusions.
   c. observing.   d. developing hypotheses.

3. A statement that is tested through scientific experiments is called a
   a. conclusion.   b. variable.
   c. law.   d. hypothesis.

4. In an experiment in which you change only the temperature, temperature is the
   a. responding variable.
   b. manipulated variable.
   c. hypothesis.
   d. controlled variable.

5. A well-tested idea that explains and connects a wide range of observations is a
   a. scientific law.
   b. scientific theory.
   c. hypothesis.
   d. conclusion.

True or False

If the statement is true, write true. If it is false, change the underlined word or words to make the statement true.

6. A <u>hypothesis</u> sums up what was learned from an experiment.

7. The observations made during an experiment are called <u>data</u>.

8. A factor that can change during an experiment is called a <u>variable</u>.

9. A <u>scientific theory</u> describes what is always expected to happen under a given set of conditions.

10. <u>Scientific inquiry</u> is the process of sharing information with other scientists.

Checking Concepts

11. Explain the difference between an observation and an inference.
12. Why is controlling variables an essential part of a scientific experiment?
13. How does a hypothesis guide a scientist in setting up an experiment?
14. Why is it an advantage for scientists to use one system of measurement when collecting data?
15. List ways in which scientists communicate about their work.
16. **Writing to Learn** The process of science usually begins with one or more questions. Write a question that you have about the physical world. Then write a plan describing how you might find an answer to your question.

Thinking Critically

17. **Making Generalizations** A friend tells you that science is all the information found in this textbook. Do you agree with that statement? Why or why not?
18. **Applying Concepts** You are about to conduct an experiment in which you drop a ball from different heights in order to find out how high the ball bounces. Create a table to show the data you might record. (You can refer to Creating Data Tables and Graphs in the Skills Handbook on pages 760–762.)
19. **Problem Solving** Suppose a company advertises a piece of sports equipment that's "guaranteed to improve your game." How could you use the idea of a controlled experiment to safely test that claim?
20. **Making Judgments** Why does everyone involved in science activities have to take responsibility for the class's safety?

Test Preparation *Use these questions to prepare for standardized tests.*

Read the information below. Then answer Questions 21–24.

Three students wanted to find out whether the mass of an object affects how fast it falls. They designed an experiment in which different stacks of washers would be released from the same height. They tied the washers together and determined how long each stack took to reach the ground. Here is their data.

Number of Washers	Time (s)			
	Trial 1	Trial 2	Trial 3	Average
2	2.9	2.8	3.3	3.0
10	3.0	2.9	3.1	3.0
20	2.9	2.9	3.2	3.0

21. What is the manipulated variable?
    a. number of trials   b. starting height
    c. number of washers   d. time of the drop
22. What is the responding variable?
    a. number of trials   b. starting height
    c. number of washers   d. time of the drop

23. Which of the following could be the hypothesis for this experiment?
    a. If the distance of the drop is increased, then the dropped object will fall faster.
    b. If an object has a greater mass, then it will fall faster than an object having less mass.
    c. If objects take the same time to drop, then the objects have the same mass.
    d. If two objects land at the same time, then they were dropped from the same height.
24. Based on the results of this experiment, what can you conclude about objects dropped from the same height?
    a. Objects having greater mass will drop faster than objects with less mass.
    b. Objects having less mass will drop faster than objects with greater mass.
    c. All objects take the same time to drop.
    d. The mass of an object has no effect on the rate at which it falls.

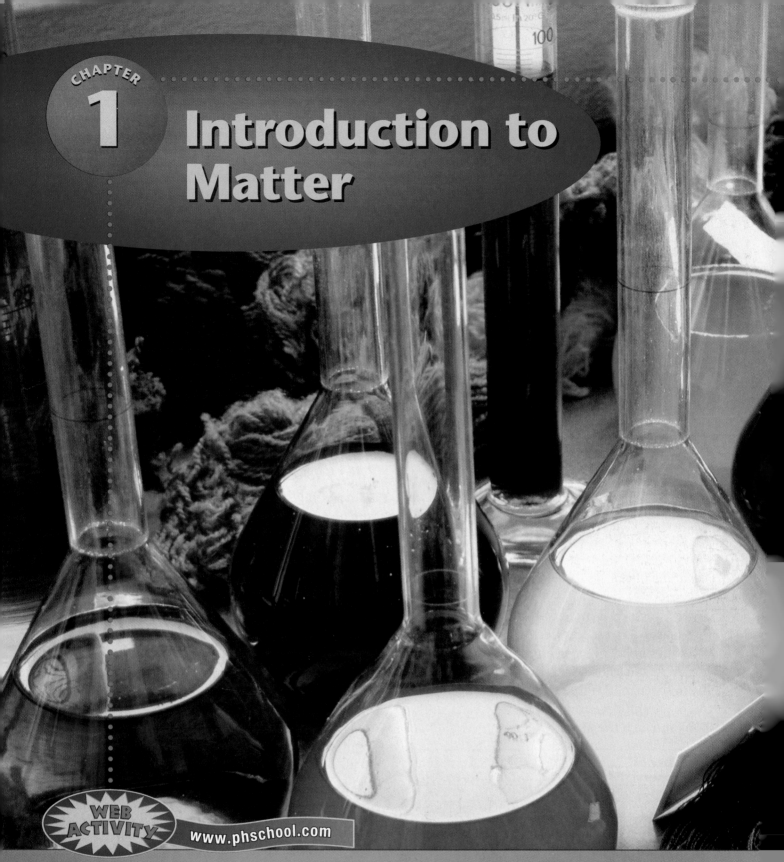

CHAPTER

1 Introduction to Matter

WEB ACTIVITY
www.phschool.com

SECTION
1 **Describing Matter**

Discover What Properties Help You Sort
   Matter?
Sharpen Your Skills Inferring

SECTION
2 **Measuring Matter**

Discover Which Has More Mass?
Try This Bubble Time
Skills Lab Making Sense of Density
Science at Home Density Demonstration

SECTION
3 **Particles of Matter**

Discover What's in the Box?

Comparing Brand X

Before you get dressed, you probably spend time picking out clothes that go together. Your clothes can come in a huge variety of colors. That's because researchers have developed many different dyes. Fibers, cloth, dyes, and water are just some examples of the materials that make up our world. The scientific name for these materials is matter. Every object in this photograph—actually, every object in the world—is an example of matter. Also, materials have different properties, such as color, shape, and hardness. It's the properties of a particular material that determine whether it is useful for a specific purpose.

Your Goal Compare a property of matter in three different brands of a consumer product.

To complete the project you will
- design a comparison test on the products and collect data
- provide a procedure for a partner to follow
- conduct the comparison test designed by a partner
- compare the data you and a partner obtained
- follow the safety guidelines in Appendix A

Get Started As a class, brainstorm a list of different products to compare. For each product, write down several properties that could be compared. For example, paper towels may absorb different amounts of water or adhesive bandages may have different strengths. Review Designing an Experiment in the Skills Handbook.

Check Your Progress You'll be working on this project as you study this chapter. To keep your project on track, look for Check Your Progress boxes at the following points.
Section 1 Review, page 23: Design an experiment.
Section 3 Review, page 35: Perform the procedure.
Section 4 Review, page 40: Trade procedures with your partner.

Present Your Project At the end of the chapter (page 43), you and your partner will try to repeat each other's procedures.

Dyes give fibers and other materials their distinctive colors.

Integrating Earth Science

SECTION 4 Elements From Earth

Discover How Can You Separate Bolts From Sand?
Real-World Lab Isolating Copper

1 Describing Matter

DISCOVER •••ACTIVITY•••

What Properties Help You Sort Matter?

1. Carefully examine the ten objects that your teacher provides. Write a brief description of each object. What properties are unique to each object? What properties do some objects have in common?

2. Which objects appear to be made of a single substance? Which objects appear to be mixtures of different substances?

3. Divide the objects into small groups so that the objects in each group share one of the properties you identified.

Think It Over

Classifying Share your observations and grouping with your classmates. How do the ways your classmates grouped the objects compare with the way you grouped the objects? Think of at least one other way to group the objects.

GUIDE FOR READING

◆ How can an unknown substance be identified?

◆ Why are elements called the building blocks of matter?

◆ What are two basic ways that matter can change?

Reading Tip Before you read, use the headings to outline the section. As you read, add information to your outline.

You have probably heard the word *matter* used in lots of ways. "It doesn't matter!" "As a matter of fact, . . ." "Hey, what's the matter?"

In science, however, the word *matter* has a specific meaning. Matter is the "stuff" that makes up everything in the universe. Fruit, baseballs, statues, milk, books, flowers: These and every other object are examples of matter. Even air is matter. Air may be invisible, but you know it is there when you feel a cool breeze or watch trees bend in the wind.

What exactly is matter? This question is not so easy to answer! You can begin by looking at some of its properties.

Properties of Matter

Matter can have a variety of properties, or characteristics. A material can be hard or soft, rough or smooth, round or square, hot or cold. Some materials catch fire easily, while others do not

Figure 1 Surrounded by snow, a geyser gives off hot water and steam—small droplets of hot liquid water in air. It also gives off water vapor, a gas you cannot see. These events display just a few of water's properties. *Predicting How will the snow change if its temperature increases above 0°C?*

burn. Matter may be any color—or have no color at all. Hardness, texture, shape, temperature, flammability, and color are all examples of properties of matter.

Each specific substance has its own combination of properties that can be used to identify the substance. For example, you could tell whether or not a particular substance is water by its properties. Water is a clear, colorless liquid at room temperature. At temperatures of 0°C or lower, water changes into ice. At temperatures of 100°C or higher, water changes into water vapor, an invisible gas. Investigating properties like these is one of the jobs that chemists do. **Chemistry** is the study of the properties of matter and how matter changes.

Kinds of Matter

Take an imaginary walk through your neighborhood and notice the buildings. It's easy to tell the difference between a gas station, an office building, and a supermarket. Yet they are built of just a few kinds of materials. Bricks, wood, glass, stone, concrete, and steel are among the most common. Using the same materials, people make many different structures.

Elements Just as many different buildings are made from just a few kinds of materials, all the different kinds of matter in the universe are made from about 100 different substances, called elements. An **element** is a substance that cannot be broken down into any other substances by chemical or physical means. **Elements are called the building blocks of matter because all matter is composed of elements.** Each element is made up of tiny particles called **atoms.**

Ratios

A ratio compares two numbers. It tells you how much you have of one item in comparison to how much you have of another. For example, a recipe for cookies calls for 2 cups of flour for every 1 cup of sugar. You can write the ratio of flour to sugar as:

2 to 1 or 2 : 1

The elements in a compound are present in a specific ratio. If two compounds contain the same elements in different ratios, such as CO and CO_2, they are different compounds.

You are already familiar with some elements, such as aluminum in foil or copper in a penny. Others, such as tungsten, may be new to you. Each element has its own symbol. That **symbol** is usually one or two letters that represent the element. Examples include aluminum (Al), carbon (C), copper (Cu), hydrogen (H), gold (Au), iron (Fe), and oxygen (O).

Compounds Elements can exist in an uncombined or a combined form. For example, most of the oxygen present in the air is not combined with another element. In nature, however, most elements are found combined with one or more elements in a compound. A **compound** is a substance made of two or more elements chemically combined in a specific ratio. For example, the carbon dioxide gas (CO_2) you give off when you breathe is a compound made of carbon atoms and oxygen atoms in a 1 to 2 ratio.

Each compound is represented by a formula that uses symbols to identify which elements are present. A **formula** shows the ratio of elements in the compound. You may know that water has the formula H_2O. That tells you that the ratio of hydrogen atoms to oxygen atoms is 2 to 1. If you see a compound with a different formula, such as H_2O_2, you know that the compound cannot be water. H_2O_2 is hydrogen peroxide, a medicine used to clean cuts and scrapes. H_2O_2 and H_2O each have their own set of properties.

☑ *Checkpoint* *How do compounds differ from elements?*

Mixtures Most matter that you find in the environment occurs as mixtures. A **mixture** is made from two or more substances—elements, compounds, or both—that are together in the same place but are not chemically combined into a new substance. For example, in nature water is not found in a pure state. Instead, it is found as a mixture that contains dissolved oxygen, salts, and other substances.

Figure 2 The element silver (above) is sometimes found in a wiry, treelike form. The paints (right) are mixtures of several compounds. Those compounds that give paints their colors are called pigments.

EXPLORING *Matter at the Beach*

You can find all sorts of matter at an ocean beach, including sand, sea shells, grasses and other plants, and sea water. Many types of beach sand are made up of small rocks and other particles that are washed ashore by the ocean's waves.

Mixture
Some beach sand is a mixture of a substance called quartz and tiny fragments of sea shells. The color of the beach sand varies with its shell content.

Compounds
Sea shells contain different calcium compounds, including calcium carbonate. Quartz is formed from a compound called silicon dioxide.

Calcium carbonate

Silicon dioxide

Elements
The compounds in beach sand are made mostly of four elements: silicon, oxygen, calcium, and carbon. Like most substances, beach sand shares few properties with the elements that compose it!

Silicon

Oxygen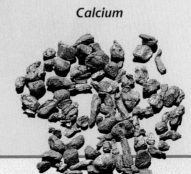

Calcium

Carbon

ACTIVITY

1. Obtain a mixture of sand and iron filings. Place the mixture in the center of a piece of paper.
2. Examine the mixture carefully. Predict the effect a magnet would have on it.
3. Hold a magnet below the paper under the mixture. Move the magnet toward the edge of the paper.
4. Use the magnet to separate as much of the mixture as you can.
5. Was your prediction in Step 2 correct? What property allowed you to separate parts of the mixture?

Mixtures differ from compounds in two ways. First, the substances in a mixture keep their individual properties. Soil, for example, is a mixture of sand, clay, water, and other materials. If you look closely at soil, you can see the sand particles. Second, the parts of a mixture are not necessarily present in specific ratios. Different soils contain different amounts of sand and clay.

☑ *Checkpoint* **Why is soil a mixture and not a compound?**

Changes in Matter

Imagine going to a costume party and seeing someone dressed as a clown. Could it be someone you know? How can you tell?

Physical Change Putting on a costume can make someone look quite different, but the person hasn't changed. So it is with changes in matter that do not produce a new substance. A change that alters the form or appearance of a material but does not make the material into another substance is called a **physical change.** Examples of physical changes include chopping wood, bending copper wire into new shapes, and changes in state.

Matter has three principal states—solids, liquids, and gases. A substance, such as water, can change from one state to another when the temperature changes. But water remains the same substance, whether it's in the form of a solid, a liquid, or a gas. It is still made of two parts hydrogen and one part oxygen (H_2O).

Investigating changes of state is one way chemists study matter. For example, under ordinary conditions, some substances are solids, while others are liquids or gases. And some of these substances change state with just a small amount of heating or cooling, while others require intense heat or extreme cold. Chemists try to explain those differences.

Figure 3 When you make a giant soap bubble, you cause a physical change to occur. The bubble is a thin film of liquid that surrounds a body of air.

Chemical Change A change in matter that produces new substances is called a **chemical change,** or a **chemical reaction.** The new substances are made of the same elements as the original substances, but the atoms are rearranged in new combinations. In a chemical change, elements may combine to form compounds, or compounds may be broken down into elements, or compounds may change into other compounds. Some familiar examples of chemical changes include the rusting of iron and the burning of gasoline in a car engine.

Physical changes and chemical changes are the two basic ways that matter can change. To illustrate the difference between these two changes, think of elements as letters and compounds as words. Just as a word is made of certain letters in a specific combination, a compound is made of certain elements in a specific combination.

A physical change is like printing the same word in a different style of type without changing the word:

$$\text{stampedes} \rightarrow \textit{stampedes}$$

A chemical change is like rearranging the letters of the original word to make one or more new words:

$$\text{stampedes} \rightarrow \text{made} + \text{steps}$$

The new substances formed during a chemical change always have their own set of properties.

Figure 4 In this explosive chemical change, the elements sodium (Na) and bromine (Br) combine to form the compound sodium bromide.

Section 1 Review

1. Name several properties of matter that help you identify an unknown substance.
2. What substances are the building blocks of matter?
3. Explain the difference between a physical change and a chemical change.
4. How does a chemical formula differ from a symbol?
5. **Thinking Critically** **Applying Concepts** You see a solid that looks like an ice cube, but it does not melt at room temperature. Can the solid be frozen water? Explain.

Check Your Progress

CHAPTER PROJECT

Choose which product and property you will test. Design a procedure to test your chosen property of a product. Decide which variables you will keep constant. Describe how you will measure and organize the data you will collect. Work with a partner to discuss ideas for your procedure. Answer your partner's questions about the procedure, listen to any comments offered, and incorporate appropriate comments into your plan.

SECTION
2 Measuring Matter

DISCOVER

ACTIVITY

Which Has More Mass?

1. Your teacher will provide you with some small objects, such as a rock, a plastic drinking cup, an aluminum can, and a pencil. Look at the objects, but do not touch them.

2. Predict which object is lightest, which is second lightest, and so on. Record your predictions.

3. Use a triple-beam balance to find the mass of each object.

4. Based on your results, list the objects from lightest to heaviest.

Think It Over

Drawing Conclusions How did your predictions compare to your results? Are bigger objects always heavier than smaller objects? Why or why not?

GUIDE FOR READING

◆ What is the difference between weight and mass?

◆ How is density calculated?

Reading Tip Before you read, define mass, volume, and density in your own words. Then revise your definitions as you read.

Figure 5 If you stood on this scale on the moon, it would show your weight is less there than on Earth.

Here's a riddle for you: Which weighs more, a pound of feathers or a pound of bricks? If you answered "the pound of bricks," think again. Both weigh exactly the same—one pound!

There are all sorts of ways of measuring matter, and you use these measurements every day. Scientists rely on measurements as well. In fact, scientists work hard to make sure that their measurements are as accurate as possible.

Mass

A veterinarian wants an updated weight for a dog at its annual check-up. To find the weight, the owner steps on the scale, holding the dog. Their combined body weight presses down on springs inside the scale. The more the girl or her dog weighs, the more the springs compress and the higher the reading. Subtract the owner's weight from the total, and the vet has his answer.

However, a scale would not indicate the same weight if you were on the moon. Step on a scale on the moon, and the springs inside it wouldn't compress as much as they did on Earth. You would weigh less on the moon.

24

Weight or Mass? Why does your weight change when you travel away from Earth? The reason is that your **weight** is a measure of the force of gravity on you. On Earth, all objects are attracted downward by Earth's gravity. On other planets, the force of gravity may be more or less. On the moon, the force of gravity is much weaker than on Earth. You weigh less.

In everyday life, weight is a useful measurement of how much matter an object contains. But scientists rely on a property that is constant wherever the object may be. This property is called mass. The **mass** of an object is the measurement of how much matter it contains. An object's weight will change if you move it from Earth to the moon or to other planets, but its mass will stay the same.

Units of Mass To measure the properties of matter, scientists use a system of units called the **International System of Units.** The system is abbreviated "SI," after its French name, Système International. For mass, the SI unit is the kilogram (kg). If you weigh 90 pounds on Earth, then your mass is approximately 40 kilograms.

Although you sometimes will see kilograms used in this textbook, usually you will see a smaller unit—the gram (g). There are exactly 1,000 grams in a kilogram. A nickel has a mass of about 5 grams, the mass of a baseball is about 150 grams, and the water in a medium-sized glass has a mass of about 200 grams.

☑ *Checkpoint* *What is the SI unit for mass?*

Volume

The amount of space that matter occupies is called its **volume.** It's easy to see the volume that solid and liquid objects take up. But gases have volume, too. Watch a balloon as you blow into it. You're actually increasing its volume with your breath.

TRY THIS

Bubble Time

Do gases have volume? **ACTIVITY**

1. Fill a large container with water. Completely submerge a clear plastic cup, right side up, in the container.
2. Mark the water level with a piece of tape on the outside of the container.
3. Turn the cup upside down underwater, without letting any air bubbles enter the cup.
4. Insert the short end of the straw into the water and up into the cup. Then blow into the straw.

Inferring Did blowing air into the cup change the water level in the container? Explain your observations.

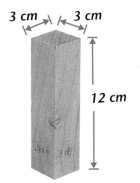

3 cm 3 cm

12 cm

Figure 6 Volume is measured in several units. Those that scientists commonly use include liters (L), milliliters (mL), and cubic centimeters (cm³).

 **INTEGRATING MATHEMATICS** For rectangular objects such as a block of wood, the volume is found by multiplying the measurements of length, width, and height.

$$Volume = Length \times Width \times Height$$

When you multiply the three measurements, you must multiply the units as well as the numbers. So, just as $2 \times 2 \times 2 = 2^3$, $cm \times cm \times cm = cm^3$. If a block of wood has a length of 3 centimeters, a width of 3 centimeters, and a height of 12 centimeters, then the volume would equal the product of those values.

$$Volume = 3\,cm \times 3\,cm \times 12\,cm = 108\,cm^3$$

SCIENCE & History

Measurement Systems

Like so much else in science, systems of measurement developed gradually over time in different parts of the world.

1400 B.C.

Egypt

The ancient Egyptians developed the first known weighing instrument, a simple balance with a pointer. Earlier, they had been the first to standardize a measure of length. The length, called a cubit, was originally defined as the distance between the elbow and the tip of the middle finger.

1500 B.C.	1000 B.C.	500 B.C.	A.D. 1

640 B.C.

Lydia

Merchants in the Middle East and Mediterranean used units of weight to be sure that they received the correct amount of gold and silver and to check the purity of the metal. A *talent* was about 25 kilograms and a *mina* about 500 grams. The Lydians minted the first true coins to have standard weight and value.

200 B.C.

China

Shih Huang Ti, the first emperor of China, set standards for weight, length, and volume. Even earlier, the Chinese were the first to use decimal notation, the number system based on 10 digits. This is the system most people use today.

The name for cm³ is the cubic centimeter, and it is a common unit of volume. Other units of volume include the liter (L) and the milliliter (mL), both of which are often used to measure liquids. A milliliter is exactly 1 cubic centimeter. There are 1,000 milliliters in one liter.

How can you measure the volume of an object with an irregular shape, such as a piece of fruit or a rock? One way is to put the object in a graduated cylinder containing water and measure the change in the volume of the water.

☑ *Checkpoint* *How can you calculate the volume of a rectangular object like a shoebox?*

In Your Journal

Although scientists rely on SI units, people use other measurement units for many different purposes. Research the units used in diamond cutting, horse breeding, sailing, or other activities that interest you. Write a brief essay to present your findings.

A.D. 789
Central Europe

The foot of Charlemagne, emperor of most of central Europe, was set as the standard unit of length. The standard unit of weight was the *Karlspfund,* translated as "Charlemagne's pound."

A.D. 1714
Germany

Gabriel Fahrenheit invented the thermometer, a temperature-measuring device that relies on the expansion of mercury with heat. His name later came to be used as the name for a unit of temperature.

A.D. 500	A.D. 1000	A.D. 1500	A.D. 2000

A.D. 700   England

During the reign of Ethelbert II in England, the term *acre* was in common use as a measurement of area. An acre was defined as the amount of land that two oxen could plow in one day.

A.D. 1983
France

The International Bureau of Weights and Measures defines a single set of units that is the same everywhere. In 1983, the meter was defined as the distance light travels in a fraction of a second.

Common Units and Conversions			
Quantity	SI/Metric Units	Other Units	Conversions
Mass	Kilogram (kg) Gram (g)		1 kilogram = 1,000 grams
Volume	Cubic meter (m³) Liter (L) Milliliter (mL) Cubic centimeter (cm³)	Quart Gallon	1 liter = 1,000 milliliters 1 milliliter = 1 cm³
Distance	Meter (m) Kilometer (km) Centimeter (cm)	Foot Mile Inch	1 kilometer = 1,000 meters 1 centimeter = 0.01 meter

Density

Different substances may have the same mass, but they don't necessarily fill the same volume. Remember the riddle about the bricks and the feathers? A kilogram of bricks takes up a much smaller volume than the same mass of feathers. This is because bricks and feathers have different densities—a very important property of matter. **Density** is the measurement of how much mass is contained in a given volume. **To calculate the density of an object, divide its mass by its volume.**

$$Density = \frac{Mass}{Volume}$$

A unit of density is always a unit of mass, such as grams, divided by a unit of volume, such as cubic centimeters. One typical unit of density is written as "g/cm³," which is read as "grams per cubic centimeter." The word *per* means "for each," which in mathematics is the same as "divided by." For liquids, density is often stated in grams per milliliter, or g/mL. The density of water is 1.0 g/mL, which is the same as 1.0 g/cm³.

Figure 8 An object sinks or floats in water depending, in part, on its density. This stone statue remains on the sea floor where it was placed. A statue of solid wood, with a density less than that of water, would float.

Sometimes you can compare the densities of substances just by observing them. For example, suppose you have a solid block of wood and a solid block of gold. When you drop each block into a tub of water, the wood floats and the gold sinks. You know the density of water is 1.0 g/cm³. You can conclude that the wood has a density lower than 1.0 g/cm³. In contrast, the density of the gold is greater than 1.0 g/cm³. In the same way, you can conclude that the density of the solid stone statue in Figure 8 is greater than the density of the water around it.

Sample Problem

A small block of wood floats on water. It has a volume of 25 cubic centimeters and a mass of 20 grams. What is the density of the wood?

Analyze. You know the mass and the volume. You want to find the density.

Write the formula.

$$\text{Density} = \frac{\text{Mass}}{\text{Volume}}$$

Substitute and solve.

$$\text{Density} = \frac{20\ g}{25\ cm^3}$$

$$\text{Density} = 0.8\ g/cm^3$$

Think about it. The answer shows mass per unit volume. The correct unit is g/cm^3.

Practice Problems

1. A sample of liquid has a mass of 24 grams and a volume of 16 milliliters. What is the density of the liquid?
2. A metal sample has a mass of 43.5 grams and a volume of 15 cubic centimeters. What is its density?

Watch a bottle of oil-and-vinegar salad dressing after it's been shaken. You will see oil droplets rise toward the top of the bottle. Eventually, the oil forms a separate layer above the other ingredients. What can you conclude? You're right if you said the oil is less dense than the rest of the liquid dressing.

The density of a substance is the same for all samples of that substance. For example, all samples of pure gold have a density of 19.3 g/cm^3. Measuring the density of a shiny yellow material is one way to test whether or not that material is gold.

Section 2 Review

1. How are mass and weight different measurements?
2. What two quantities do you need to know in order to calculate density?
3. Describe how you could measure the volume of an object with an irregular shape.
4. **Thinking Critically Problem Solving** The density of aluminum is 2.7 g/cm^3. A metal sample has a mass of 52.0 grams and a volume of 17.1 cubic centimeters. Could the sample be aluminum? Explain your answer.

Science at Home

Density Demonstration Label two cups A and B and place a cup of water in each. Stir 3 small spoonfuls of salt and several drops of food coloring into Cup B. Dip a clear straw into Cup A to a depth of about 2 cm. Place your finger on the end of the straw and dip it into Cup B to a depth of about 4 cm. Remove your finger from the straw and then replace it. Remove the straw from the cup. Explain to your family what densities have to do with the results.

MAKING SENSE OF DENSITY

Skills Lab

In this lab you will investigate whether an object's density changes when its size changes.

Problem

Does the density of a substance change if it is broken into pieces?

Materials

balance   water   paper towels
wooden stick, approximately 6 cm long
ball of modeling clay, approximately 5 cm wide
crayon with paper covering removed
graduated cylinder, 100 mL

Procedure

1. Use a balance to find the mass of the wooden stick. Record the mass in a data table like the one at the right.
2. Add enough water to a graduated cylinder that the stick can be completely submerged. Measure the initial volume of the water.
3. Place the stick in the graduated cylinder. Measure the new volume of the water.
4. The volume of the stick is the difference between the water levels in Steps 2 and 3. Calculate this volume and record it.
5. The density of the stick equals its mass divided by its volume. Calculate and record the density.
6. Thoroughly dry the stick with a paper towel. Then carefully break the stick into two pieces. Repeat Steps 1 through 5 to calculate the density of each of the two pieces.
7. Repeat Steps 1 through 6 using the clay rolled into a rope.
8. Repeat again using the crayon.

Analyze and Conclude

1. For each of the three objects you tested, compare the density of the whole object with the densities of the pieces of the object.
2. Use your results to explain how density can be used to identify a substance.
3. Why did you dry the objects in Step 6?
4. **Think About It** Predict the results of this experiment if you had used a pencil that had an eraser on one end instead of a wooden stick. Explain your prediction.

More to Explore

Wrap the modeling clay around the wooden stick and predict the density of the object you created. Then measure mass and volume and calculate the density to see if your prediction was correct.

DATA TABLE

Object	Mass (g)	Volume Change (cm³)	Density (g/cm³)
Wooden Stick			
Whole			
Piece 1			
Piece 2			
Modeling Clay			
Whole			
Piece 1			
Piece 2			
Crayon			
Whole			
Piece 1			
Piece 2			

SECTION 3 Particles of Matter

DISCOVER ·· ACTIVITY

What's in the Box?

1. Your teacher will give you a sealed box that contains one or more objects. Without opening the box, try to find out as much as you can about its contents. Try tilting, turning, shaking, or tapping the box.

2. Ask yourself questions such as these: Are the objects inside round or flat? Do they slide or roll? How many objects are there?

3. Make a list of your observations about the objects in the box.

4. Trade boxes with another group of students and repeat the activity.

Think It Over

Inferring Try to imagine what familiar objects would fit your observations. Make a sketch showing what you think the contents look like. How is it possible to make an inference from indirect evidence?

Glance at the painting below and you see people enjoying an afternoon in the park. Look again and notice that some people are in the sunlight and others are in the shade. How did the artist make your eyes see bright light, dark shadows, and shades in between? You can find the answer by looking closely at the circled detail of the painting. The artist used thousands of small spots of color.

Are you surprised that such a rich painting can be created from lots of small spots? Matter is like that too. The properties you can observe are produced by tiny objects and events that you cannot see.

GUIDE FOR READING

◆ What are the smallest particles of an element?

◆ What did Dalton conclude about atoms?

Reading Tip As you read, take notes on the main points under each heading.

◀ "Sunday Afternoon on the Island of La Grande Jatte," by Georges Seurat, at the Art Institute of Chicago

Chapter 1 **31**

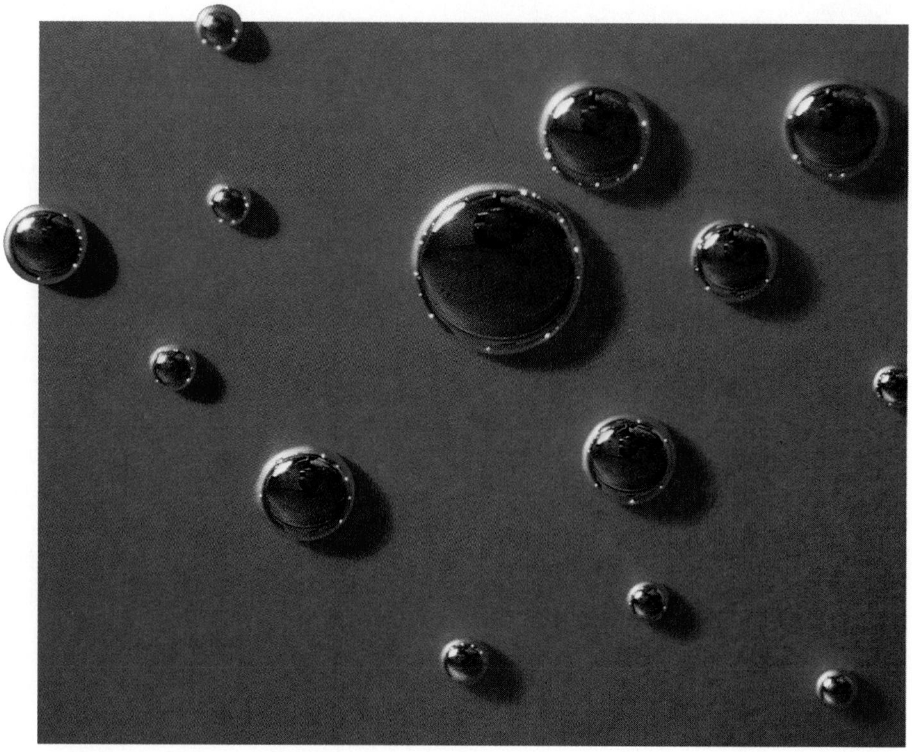

Figure 9 A drop of spilled mercury breaks into droplets. (Don't do this at home. The element mercury is poisonous and can cause brain damage.) Although these droplets are small, they are not the smallest particles of mercury possible. *Applying Concepts What is the smallest particle of an element?*

Early Ideas About Atoms

What's the smallest possible piece of an element? Think of tearing a sheet of aluminum foil in half, and then tearing the halves into quarters, and the quarters into eighths. Could you keep tearing forever, producing smaller and smaller pieces? Or would you eventually reach the smallest possible piece of aluminum? And if matter is made of such tiny pieces, what are those pieces like? How can they explain the properties of matter that you observe? Philosophers and scientists have asked these kind of questions for more than 2,000 years.

One of the first people known to have thought that matter is formed of small pieces was Democritus, a Greek philosopher who lived about 440 B.C. He thought that you could cut matter into ever smaller pieces until you got to its smallest piece, which couldn't be divided any further. Democritus called this smallest piece *atomos*, which is Greek for "uncuttable." Does that word look familiar? Of course! It's where the word *atom* comes from. **Today scientists use the word *atom* for the smallest particle of an element.**

Dalton's Ideas About Atoms

A major step in understanding atoms occurred in 1802 when a British school teacher, John Dalton, proposed an atomic theory. No one knows how much Dalton was influenced by the ideas of Democritus. Unlike Democritus and the ancient Greeks, Dalton tested his ideas by carrying out experiments.

Based on the evidence that Dalton found, he inferred that atoms had certain characteristics. Here are his main conclusions.

- *Atoms can't be broken into smaller pieces.* **Dalton imagined atoms to be like tiny marbles, or rigid spheres that are impossible to break.**

- *In any element, all the atoms are exactly alike.* This idea explains why an element always has the same properties.

- *Atoms of different elements are different.* This idea explains why different elements have their own set of properties.

- *Atoms of two or more elements can combine to form compounds.* Compounds can be broken down into elements, so Dalton concluded that compounds had to be made of atoms as well.

- *Atoms of each element have a unique mass.* Dalton and other scientists of his day were not actually able to measure the mass of individual atoms, however.

- *The masses of the elements in a compound are always in a constant ratio.* Water is a compound composed of hydrogen atoms and oxygen atoms. In any two samples of water that have nothing else mixed in with them, the ratio of the mass of hydrogen to the mass of oxygen is always the same.

Today, scientists have identified some important exceptions to Dalton's statements. Even so, Dalton's ideas form the basis of our understanding of atoms.

☑ *Checkpoint* *What were two of Dalton's ideas about atoms?*

Math TOOLBOX

Constant Ratios

A ratio is two quantities represented as a fraction. If two pairs of numbers produce the same ratio, the ratio is constant. Suppose you want to compare the ratio of 16 to 2 with the ratio of 24 to 3.

1. Write the first fraction, then reduce it to smallest whole-number values.

$$\frac{16}{2} = \frac{8}{1}$$

2. Now do the same with the other pair of numbers.

$$\frac{24}{3} = \frac{8}{1}$$

3. Both fractions produce the same ratio, so the ratio is constant.

In any sample of a compound, the ratio of the masses of two elements in the compound is always constant.

Figure 10 The compound calcium oxide is part of mortar, the "glue" that holds bricks together. In this compound the ratio of the mass of calcium to the mass of oxygen is always 5 to 2.

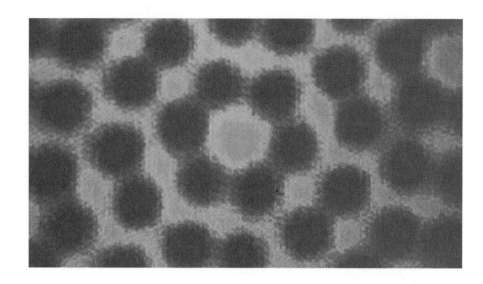

Figure 11 Here you can see something scientists once thought no one would ever see—atoms! This image of silicon atoms was produced by a scanning tunneling microscope.

Language Arts
CONNECTION

In Isaac Asimov's science fiction story *Fantastic Voyage*, people are shrunk down to the size of a single cell. Their experiences inside the body of a full-sized person are "fantastic" reading. Imagine what it would be like to shrink down to the size of a single atom!

In Your Journal

Write a one-page story about what you would see and experience as you shrink down to the size of an atom. Explore your new world, describing the other atoms and molecules around you. What happens as you grow back to normal size?

Ideas About Atoms Today

Atoms are so small that for many years no one expected to see them. Just how small? Compare the size of atoms to some everyday objects.

One grain of sand on a typical beach contains more atoms than there are grains of sand on the entire beach.

There are 2,000,000,000,000,000,000,000 (that's 2,000 billion billion) atoms of oxygen in one drop of water—and twice as many atoms of hydrogen!

Newspaper pictures are made from tiny dots of ink. Each dot contains about a billion billion atoms! (That's a 1 followed by 18 zeros!)

Despite their tiny size, there is now a tool that gives a glimpse of what atoms look like. A scanning tunneling microscope can magnify matter so much that it can actually capture images of atoms. Figure 11 shows an example of what this microscope can reveal.

Atoms and Molecules

An atom can frequently be linked with one or more other atoms. The force that holds two atoms together is a **chemical bond.** A combination of two or more atoms that are bonded together is called a **molecule.** Some molecules are made of atoms that are alike, as in the oxygen gas (O_2) that you breathe. Most molecules, though, are made of more than one type of atom. Water molecules have 2 hydrogen atoms combined with 1 oxygen atom (H_2O). Acetic acid, the compound that gives vinegar its sharp odor and sour taste, has 2 carbon atoms, 4 hydrogen atoms and 2 oxygen atoms ($C_2H_4O_2$). Molecules can be huge. Some molecules in your body contain millions of atoms.

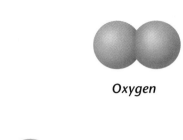

Oxygen

Acetic acid

Water

Figure 12 Each sphere is a model of an atom. The molecule on the right shows a small part of the DNA in living cells. (This computer image of DNA was made using a color code for atoms different from the code used in this book.) *Classifying Which one of these models shows an element? How do you know?*

The Atom as a Model

Look at the atoms in Figure 11 again. From that image, you cannot really see what atoms look like or discover how they might work. Like a person trying to imagine what's in a box by shaking it, scientists studying atoms must make inferences about them based on observations.

Thus atoms are actually models, mental pictures that explain how matter works. In Chapter 3, you will investigate the atomic model in detail. You will see how it explains the properties of matter and events that you observe every day.

Section 3 Review

1. What would you get if you could break an element into its smallest particles?
2. What did Dalton visualize atoms to be like?
3. An ice cube consists of molecules of water (H_2O). Could you continue, forever, to break an ice cube into smaller and smaller pieces of ice? Explain your answer.
4. **Thinking Critically Interpreting Diagrams** Examine the model of acetic acid ($C_2H_4O_2$) in Figure 12. Which elements are represented by each of the three colors? How do you know? What does the model tell you about the way the different atoms are arranged?
5. **Thinking Critically Calculating** A sample of a compound contains 64 grams of copper and 16 grams of oxygen. What is the ratio of the mass of copper to the mass of oxygen? If another sample of the same compound has 40 grams of copper, how much oxygen is there in the second sample?

SECTION 4 Elements From Earth

How Can You Separate Bolts From Sand?

1. Mix dry sand with a few small metal bolts. Place the mixture in a tray or pie pan.

2. Think of a way to separate the sand and the bolts. You may not use a magnet, but may use water, a bowl, paper towels, and other supplies available in your classroom.

3. With your teacher's permission, try your procedure.

Think It Over

Designing an Experiment What properties of matter did you use to separate the sand and the bolts? How successful was your procedure?

GUIDE FOR READING

◆ What property of gold allows it to be panned?

◆ What must be done to obtain an element from one of its compounds?

Reading Tip As you read, list the ways that people obtain elements from the forms in which they are found in nature.

Gold! In 1848, several gold nuggets were found in the American River in northern California near a mill owned by John Sutter. Thousands of people rushed to California with pans, pickaxes, and shovels. They searched the riverbanks and stream beds hoping to find more nuggets or even gold flakes.

Some people got rich, but many went home empty-handed. Perhaps the most disappointed of all were those who found pyrite, a substance that looks like gold. Pyrite is actually a compound of iron and sulfur. Can you tell why pyrite is also called "fool's gold"?

A gold miner pans for gold in Northern California. ▶

Gold and Density

During the California gold rush, miners needed a way to remove the precious metal from a mixture that also contained dirt and sand. **Gold can be separated from other materials in a mixture because of its density.** As you saw in Section 2, gold has a density of 19.3 g/cm^3. This is much higher than the density of most other materials, including fool's gold, which has a density of only 5.0 g/cm^3.

Figure 13 Gold nuggets contain only the element gold.

The miners used a technique called panning. They put the mixture of gold, dirt, and sand into a shallow pan and covered it with water. They then swirled the contents around and carefully poured off the water. The water carried the less dense dirt and sand with it. The more dense gold sank and was left behind. The miners repeated this process until only gold remained in the pan.

Today, gold mining is done on a much larger scale using machines called dredges. But the basic process of separating gold by its density is the same. The dredge scrapes up large amounts of dirt and sand, washes the mixture, and separates the gold in a way that's similar to panning.

☑ *Checkpoint* *What could you do to tell the difference between real gold and fool's gold?*

Copper and Electrolysis

In nature, finding an element that's not part of a compound is unusual. Most elements, including those people use for industrial purposes in great amounts, are usually found as compounds. For example, copper compounds are most often found in certain kind of ore. An ore is any rock that contains a metal or other economically useful material.

The process of obtaining copper from one of its compounds is more complicated than panning for gold. **To obtain an element from its compound, it is necessary to cause a chemical reaction to take place.** In that chemical change, the copper atoms must be separated from the other atoms in the compound.

Figure 14 Ores contain useful elements that are combined with other substances. **A.** Malachite contains copper. **B.** Iron pyrite contains iron.
Applying Concepts Why do ores have different properties from the elements that they contain?

A method that's commonly used to break down a copper compound is called **electrolysis,** which literally means "electric cutting." First, the copper compound is dissolved in water to form a mixture called a solution. Two metal strips called **electrodes** are placed in the copper compound solution. Each electrode is attached to a wire, and the wires are connected to a source of electric current such as a battery.

Isolating Copper

In nature, copper is usually found in compounds with other elements. In this investigation, you will perform an electrolysis to isolate copper from a compound called copper chloride.

Problem

How can copper be isolated from a compound by electrolysis?

Skills Focus

observing, inferring

Materials

glass jar, about 250 mL   6-volt battery
two paper clips   index card
wires with alligator clips or battery holder with
    wires
copper chloride solution (0.6 *M*), 50–100 mL

Procedure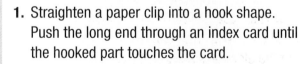

1. Straighten a paper clip into a hook shape. Push the long end through an index card until the hooked part touches the card.

2. Repeat Step 1 with another paper clip so that the clips are about 2–3 cm apart. The paper clips serve as your electrodes.

3. Pour enough copper chloride solution into a jar to cover at least half the length of the paper clips when the index card is set on top of the jar. **CAUTION:** *Copper chloride solution can be irritating to the skin and eyes. Do not touch it with your hands or get it in your mouth. The solution can stain your skin and clothes.*

4. Place the index card on top of the jar. If the straightened ends of the paper clips are not at least half-covered by the copper chloride solution, add more solution.

When the electric current is turned on, one electrode attracts the copper, and the other electrode attracts the other materials. The first electrode becomes coated with copper, which can be scraped off and used as needed. In a laboratory, electrolysis produces only small amounts of copper. In the copper industry, however, electrolysis is used on a huge scale to produce large amounts of copper metal.

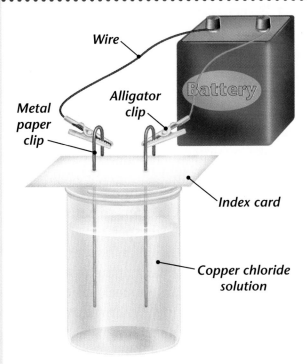

Wire

Battery

Alligator clip

Metal paper clip

Index card

Copper chloride solution

5. Attach a wire to each pole of a battery. Attach the other ends of the wires to a separate paper clip. See the drawing. Prevent the paper clips from touching each other.

6. Predict what you think will happen if you allow the current to run for 2–3 minutes. (*Hint:* What elements are present in the copper chloride solution?)

7. Let the setup run for 2–3 minutes or until you see a deposit forming on one of the electrodes. Also look for bubbles.

8. Remove the index card. Bring your face close to the jar and gently wave your hand toward your nose. Try to detect any odor.

9. Note if the color of the solution has changed since you began the procedure.

10. Disconnect the wires. Note the color of the tips of the electrodes.

Analyze and Conclude

1. Make a labeled diagram of your experimental setup. Indicate which electrode is connected to the positive side of the battery and which is connected to the negative side.

2. On which electrode was the copper produced? On which electrode was the chlorine produced?

3. If the color of the solution changed, how can you explain the change?

4. Compare the properties of copper, chlorine, and copper chloride solution.

5. Describe the changes in matter that you observed. Classify them as physical changes or chemical changes.

6. **Apply** Using your observations of this procedure as evidence, explain why you think copper chloride is a compound, and not a mixture.

More to Explore

Suppose you were to reconnect the wires with the positive and negative sides reversed. Predict how your results would differ under these conditions. With your teacher's permission, carry out the electrolysis with the connections reversed. Was your prediction correct?

Figure 15 Industry uses large-scale chemical reactions to produce useful materials. This blast furnace is used to react carbon with iron ore to produce iron metal. The source of the carbon is coke, a substance produced from coal.

Iron and the Blast Furnace

Iron is another element that industry needs in huge amounts. Like copper, iron is usually found in an ore in the form of a compound. And also like copper, the element iron must be separated from its compounds by a chemical reaction.

Iron ores usually contain compounds formed of iron and oxygen. In order to release the iron, chunks of iron ore are placed in a hot fire along with coke, a source of carbon. In the intense heat of a blast furnace like the one in Figure 15, the carbon reacts with the oxygen. The element iron is left behind.

After leaving the blast furnace, iron is often combined with other materials to produce mixtures having specific properties. For example, iron may be combined with carbon and other metals to produce steel, which is stronger than iron alone. Adding chromium and nickel makes stainless steel, which resists rusting. Iron, copper, and gold are just three examples of useful elements that are extracted from Earth's surface.

Section 4 Review

1. Describe how panning for gold takes advantage of a specific property of gold.
2. What kind of change must take place to remove an element from its compound? Explain.
3. What happens to the elements in iron ore when the ore is mixed with carbon and heated?
4. **Thinking Critically** **Making Judgments** Planet Earth contains a limited supply of all metals. Predict whether programs to recycle aluminum, iron, and other metals will become more important in the future.

Check Your Progress CHAPTER PROJECT

Trade your written procedure and product samples with a new partner. Repeat this partner's procedure, following the directions as exactly as you can. Share your results with your partner. Think of ways to improve both your procedure and your partner's procedure to make them clearer to follow.

SECTION 1 Describing Matter

Key Ideas

◆ Matter makes up everything in the universe. Matter can have a variety of properties.

◆ Each specific substance has its own set of properties. These properties can be used to identify the substance.

◆ Matter is made up of elements. Elements can be chemically combined in compounds. Elements and compounds may also be together as mixtures.

◆ Physical changes alter the form of a substance, but not its identity. Chemical changes result in one or more new substances.

Key Terms

chemistry   compound   physical change
element   formula   chemical change
atom   mixture   chemical reaction
symbol

SECTION 2 Measuring Matter

Key Ideas

◆ Mass is a measurement of how much matter an object contains. If you move an object away from Earth, its weight changes but its mass stays the same.

◆ The density of an object equals its mass divided by its volume. A unit of density is always a mass unit divided by a volume unit, such as grams per cubic centimeter (g/cm^3).

Key Terms

weight   volume
mass   density
International System of Units (SI)

SECTION 3 Particles of Matter

Key Ideas

◆ Atoms are the smallest particles of an element.

◆ Dalton stated that atoms are unbreakable, rigid spheres. He also said that atoms of different elements are different from one another.

◆ Atoms can be combined into molecules, which are held together by chemical bonds.

Key Terms

chemical bond   molecule

SECTION 4 Elements From Earth

INTEGRATING EARTH SCIENCE

Key Ideas

◆ Gold, which is usually found in nature as an element, can be separated from other materials because of its density.

◆ Earth contains deposits of many elements in the form of compounds. A chemical reaction is needed to remove an element from its compound.

Key Terms

electrolysis   electrode

Organizing Information

Concept Map Copy the concept map about classifying matter onto a separate sheet of paper. Then complete the map and add a title. (For more on concept maps, see the Skills Handbook.)

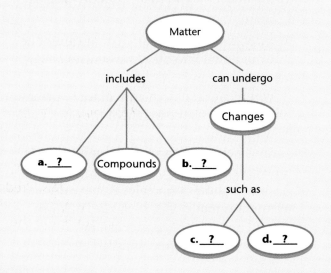

Reviewing Content

 For more review of key concepts, see the Interactive Student Tutorial CD-ROM.

Multiple Choice

Choose the letter of the answer that best completes the statement or answers the question.

1. The building blocks of matter are called
   a. mixtures.   b. elements.
   c. compounds.   d. properties.
2. A formula shows the ratio of elements in
   a. a mixture.   b. matter.
   c. a compound.   d. a chemical change.
3. The density of an object equals
   a. the product of its length, width, and height.
   b. its volume divided by its mass.
   c. the product of the mass and volume.
   d. its mass divided by its volume.
4. Dalton imagined atoms to be
   a. rigid, unbreakable spheres.
   b. all exactly alike.
   c. always joined together in compounds.
   d. of equal mass.
5. A method used to release iron metal from its ore involves
   a. heating the ore and carbon together.
   b. cooling the ore in an ice bath.
   c. breaking the ore into small pieces.
   d. panning.

True or False

If the statement is true, write true. If it is false, change the underlined word or words to make it true.

6. <u>Compounds</u> are substances that cannot be broken down into other substances by any chemical means.
7. If you move an object from place to place in the universe, the <u>weight</u> of the object will stay the same.
8. Grams per milliliter (g/mL) is an example of a unit of <u>volume</u>.
9. One of Dalton's principles is that each element is made of its own kind of <u>atom</u>.
10. Useful amounts of copper can be isolated during a process called <u>electrolysis</u>.

Checking Concepts

11. When a piece of paper is torn into two pieces, has it undergone a chemical change or a physical change? Explain.
12. How could you find the volume of a small rock, using only a graduated cylinder and water?
13. What can you infer about the density of a substance if a block of that substance floats in water?
14. How are atoms related to molecules in a sample of a compound?
15. **Writing to Learn** In a novel or short story, the author describes the properties of objects he or she is writing about. These details add interest to the story. Select at least six different kinds of objects. You might include objects from nature as well as objects made by people. List the properties of each object. Now use that list to write the first paragraph of a story.

Thinking Critically

16. **Problem Solving** How can you show that salt water is a mixture and not a compound? First compare the properties of the solution to the properties of the individual components. Then come up with a plan to separate the solution into its components.
17. **Comparing and Contrasting** Compare and contrast atoms and molecules. What do the two kinds of particles have in common? How are they related? Give an example that shows this relationship.
18. **Applying Concepts** How can you use Dalton's atomic theory to explain why every sample of a particular substance has the same properties?
19. **Inferring** Solid gold has a greater density than liquid gold. What must happen to the volume of a given mass of solid gold when it becomes a liquid? Explain.

Applying Skills

*Use the table below to answer Questions 20–22.
The table lists the mass and volume of six coins.*

Coin	Mass (g)	Volume (cm³)
A	3.1	0.41
B	4.0	0.50
C	8.6	1.2
D	8.0	0.95
E	9.8	1.1
F	5.0	0.67

20. Calculating Based on the data in the table, calculate the density of Coins A–F.

21. Interpreting Data In Altrusia, all coins are made of a mixture of copper and zinc that has a density of 8.42 g/cm³. Which coins could be from Altrusia?

22. Drawing Conclusions The density of copper is 8.92 g/cm³ and the density of zinc is 7.14 g/cm³. If you assume that only copper and zinc were used to make the coins, can any of the coins be pure copper? Can any be pure zinc? Explain.

Performance ▽CHAPTER PROJECT Assessment

Present Your Project Work with your second partner to show the data each of you collected. The data should be presented so that other students can see whether your procedures produced similar results. Briefly present your procedure and results to the class.

Reflect and Record In your journal, record the results of your experiment and describe any conclusions you reached. Are you satisfied that your conclusions are accurate? If you could repeat the experiment, what improvements would you make to your procedure?

Test Preparation
Use these questions to prepare for standardized tests.

Use the diagram to answer Questions 23–26.

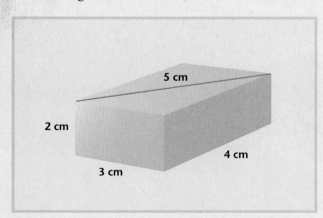

Alexander found a solid block of an unknown material. He used a metric ruler to measure the size of the block. The measurements he recorded are shown in the diagram.

23. What is the volume of the block?
    a. 9 cm   **b.** 24 cm²
    c. 24 cm³   **d.** 60 cm³

24. Which measurement shown in the diagram was not needed to find the volume of the box?
    a. length (4 cm)   **b.** height (2 cm)
    c. width (3 cm)   **d.** diagonal (5 cm)

25. Alexander knows that the density of the material from which the block is made is 2 g/cm³. Knowing this, what is the mass of the block?
    a. 4.8 g   **b.** 48 g
    c. 480 g   **d.** 4,800 g

26. If the block could be molded into a flatter and longer shape, then the
    a. mass, volume, and density all would change.
    b. volume would change, but the mass and density would remain the same.
    c. mass and volume would change, but the density would remain the same.
    d. mass, volume, and density all would remain the same.

CHAPTER

2 Solids, Liquids, and Gases

www.phschool.com

WEB ACTIVITY

Integrating Mathematics

SECTION **1** **States of Matter**

Discover **What Are Solids, Liquids, and Gases?**
Try This **As Thick as Honey**
Science at Home **What Gives?**

SECTION **2** **Gas Behavior**

Discover **How Can Air Keep Chalk From Breaking?**
Sharpen Your Skills **Developing Hypotheses**
Try This **Balloon Test**

SECTION **3** **Graphing Gas Behavior**

Discover **What Does a Graph of Pressure and Temperature Show?**
Science at Home **News Data**
Skills Lab **It's a Gas**

44

A Story of Changes in Matter

This river is a story of changing matter. In winter, the surface of the river froze solid. Now it's spring, and the ice has begun melting. The ice around each rock is the last to melt. The river water flows downstream, and plants, such as the green moss on the rocks, begin their spring growth.

If you could look very closely at ice, water, rock, and moss, you would be able to see that all matter is made up of small particles. In this chapter, you will learn how the behavior of these small particles explains the properties of solids, liquids, and gases. Your project is to model what happens to particles of matter as they change from a solid to a liquid to a gas.

Your Goal Create a skit or cartoon that demonstrates how particles of matter behave as they change from a solid to a liquid to a gas and then from a gas to a liquid to a solid.

To complete the project, you must
- describe what happens to the particles during each change of state
- outline your skit or cartoon in a storyboard format
- illustrate your cartoon or produce your skit

Get Started With a group of classmates, brainstorm a list of the properties of solids, liquids, and gases.

Check Your Progress You'll be working on this project as you study this chapter. To keep your project on track, look for Check Your Progress boxes at the following points.

Section 2 Review, page 57: Describe the particles in solid, liquid, and gas, and begin preparing a storyboard.

Section 4 Review, page 69: Finish your cartoon or skit.

Present Your Project At the end of the chapter (page 73), you will present your skit or cartoon to the class.

SECTION
4 **Changes in State**

Discover What Happens When You Breathe on a Mirror?
Skills Lab Melting Ice

Ice formations on Bridal Veil Creek, Columbia River Gorge National Scenic Area, Oregon

DISCOVER

ACTIVITY

What Are Solids, Liquids, and Gases?

1. Break an antacid tablet (fizzing type) into three or four pieces. Place them inside a large, uninflated balloon.

2. Fill a 1-liter plastic bottle about halfway with water. Stretch the mouth of the balloon over the top of the bottle, taking care to keep the pieces inside the balloon.

3. Jiggle the balloon so that the pieces fall into the bottle. Observe what happens for about two minutes.

4. Remove the balloon and examine its contents.

Think It Over

Forming Operational Definitions Identify examples of the different states of matter—solids, liquids, and gases—that you observed in this activity. Define each of the three states in your own words.

GUIDE FOR READING

◆ How are shape, volume, and particle motion useful in describing solids, liquids, and gases?

Reading Tip Before you read, list properties that you think characterize solids, liquids, and gases. Revise your list as you read.

I f you visit the annual Winter Carnival in St. Paul, Minnesota, you will see some unusual structures. To celebrate the cold winter weather, people carve huge sculptures out of ice. Over the years, the carnival has featured giant snow figures and ice palaces like the one shown here.

Even in Minnesota, anything made of snow and ice won't last beyond winter. When the temperature rises, snow figures and ice palaces melt into liquid water. And unlike frozen water, liquid water is a poor building material.

Your world is full of substances that can be classified as solids, liquids, or gases. Those substances may be elements, compounds, or mixtures. Gold is an element. Air is a mixture of gases. Water is a compound you've seen as both a solid and a liquid. The states of matter are not defined by what they are made of, but mainly by whether or not they hold their volume and shape.

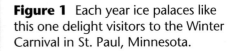

Figure 1 Each year ice palaces like this one delight visitors to the Winter Carnival in St. Paul, Minnesota.

Figure 2 In the tanks on their backs these scuba divers carry air to breathe. *Classifying Find an example of each state of matter in this photograph.*

Solids

What if you were to pick up a solid object, such as a pen or a comb, and move it from place to place around the room? What would you observe? Would the object ever change its size or shape as you moved it? Would a pen become larger if you put it in a bowl? Would a comb become flatter when you place it on a tabletop? Of course not. A **solid** has a definite volume and a definite shape. If your pen has a volume of 6 cm³ and a cylindrical shape, then it will keep that volume and shape in any position and in any container.

Particles in a Solid The particles that make up a solid are packed very closely together, as shown in Figure 3A. In addition, each particle is tightly fixed in one position. This makes it hard to separate them. **Because the particles in a solid are packed tightly together and stay in fixed positions, a solid has a definite shape and volume.**

Are the particles in a solid completely motionless? No, not really. The particles vibrate, meaning they move back and forth slightly. This motion is similar to a person running in place. Or, you can think of the particles in a solid as something like a group of balls connected by tight springs. Like the balls in Figure 3B, the particles that make up a solid stay in about the same position. However, the individual pieces are still able to vibrate back and forth in their places.

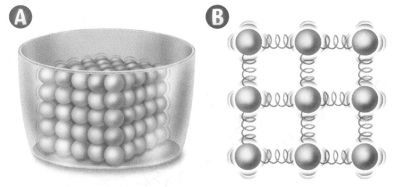

Figure 3 The balls represent the particles in a solid. **A.** A solid keeps its own shape. It doesn't take the shape of a container. **B.** The particles vibrate back and forth within the solid.

Figure 4 When you heat an amorphous solid such as this butter, it softens before it melts.

Types of Solids In many solids, the particles form a regular, repeating pattern. These patterns create crystals. Solids that are made up of crystals are called **crystalline solids** (KRIS tuh lin). Salt, sugar, sand, and snow are examples of crystalline solids. When a crystalline solid such as snow is heated, it melts at a distinct temperature called its **melting point.**

In other solids the particles are not arranged in a regular pattern. These solids are called **amorphous solids** (uh MAWR fus). Plastics, rubber, and glass are amorphous solids. Unlike a crystalline solid, an amorphous solid does not have a distinct melting point. Instead, when it is heated it becomes softer and softer as its temperature rises. You have probably noticed this property in plastic items that have been out in the sun on a hot day. The plastic gradually melts. In fact, the word *plastic* means "able to be molded into many shapes."

✓ *Checkpoint* *How do crystalline and amorphous solids differ?*

Liquids

Unlike a solid, a **liquid** has no shape of its own. Instead, a liquid takes on the shape of its container. Without a container, a liquid spreads into a wide, shallow puddle.

However, liquids are like solids in that they do not easily compress or expand. If you tried to squeeze water between your palms, for example, the water might change its shape, but its volume would not decrease or increase.

What if you have 100 mL of water? If you pour it into another container, the water still fills 100 mL. It has the same volume no matter what shape its container has.

Figure 5 Although a liquid's volume does not change, it takes the shape of whatever container you pour it into.
Comparing and Contrasting How do the particles of a liquid differ from the particles of a solid?

Figure 6 You can think of the particles of a liquid as somewhat like the people in this train station. They remain near one another but move from place to place.

Particles in a Liquid The particles in a liquid are packed almost as closely as in a solid. However, the particles in a liquid move around one another freely. **Because its particles are free to move, a liquid has no definite shape. However, it does have a definite volume.** You can compare a liquid to the rush-hour crowd at a train station. Like particles in a liquid, the people in the crowd move around the platform that contains them, but they stay in close contact with one another.

Viscosity Because particles in a liquid are free to move around one another, a liquid can flow from place to place. Some liquids flow more easily than others. The resistance of a liquid to flowing is called **viscosity** (vis KAHS uh tee). Liquids with high viscosity flow slowly. Cold molasses is an example of a liquid with a particularly high viscosity. Liquids with low viscosity flow quickly. Water, rubbing alcohol, and vinegar have relatively low viscosities.

INTEGRATING EARTH SCIENCE The viscosity of lava that erupts from a volcano can reflect the type of volcanic eruption. Some volcanos that erupt quietly have thin, runny lava—that is, lava with low viscosity. High-viscosity lava, which is thick and sticky, is typical of some volcanos that erupt explosively.

Gases

Unlike solids and liquids, a **gas** can change volume very easily. If you put a gas in a sealed container, the gas will spread apart or squeeze together to fill that container. The volume and shape of a gas is the volume and shape of its container. To illustrate this principle, take a deep breath. Your chest expands. Can you feel the air coming through your nose and mouth? Air is a mixture of

As Thick as Honey

Here's how you can compare the viscosity of two liquids.

ACTIVITY

1. Place on a table a clear plastic jar almost filled with honey and another clear plastic jar almost filled with vegetable oil. Make sure that the tops of both jars are tightly closed.
2. Turn the jars upside down at the same time. Observe what happens.
3. Turn the two jars right-side up and again watch what happens.

Observing Which liquid has a greater viscosity? What evidence leads you to this conclusion?

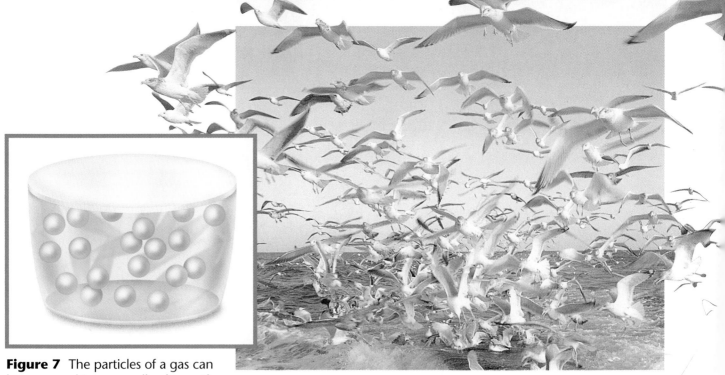

Figure 7 The particles of a gas can be squeezed into a small volume. If allowed to, they will spread out without limit, somewhat like this flock of gulls.

gases that acts as one gas. When you breathe in, air moves from your mouth to your windpipe to your lungs. In each place, the air changes shape and volume. When you breathe out, the changes happen in reverse. If you hold your hand in front of your mouth, you can feel the air move around and past your fingers.

If you could see the individual particles that make up a gas, you would see tiny particles flying at high speeds in all directions. **Gas particles spread apart, filling all the space available to them. Thus, a gas has neither definite shape nor volume.** You can compare a gas to the flock of gulls shown in Figure 7. Like gas particles, these gulls fly very quickly in different directions. They can spread out to "fill" any available space.

Section 1 Review

1. Describe how particles in a solid are arranged.
2. How does the movement of particles in a liquid help to explain the shape and volume of liquids?
3. Use what you know about the particles in a gas to explain why a gas has no definite shape and no definite volume.
4. **Thinking Critically Relating Cause and Effect** Glass is an amorphous solid. How can you use that information to help explain why a glassblower can bend and shape a piece of glass that has been heated?

Science at Home

What Gives? Show your family how liquids and gases differ. Completely fill the bulb and cylinder of a turkey baster with water. Hold it over the sink. While you seal the end with your finger, have a family member squeeze the bulb. Now let the water out of the turkey baster. Again, seal the end with your finger and have a family member squeeze the bulb. Was there a difference? Use what you know about liquids and gases to explain the observations.

SECTION 2 Gas Behavior

DISCOVER .... ACTIVITY

How Can Air Keep Chalk From Breaking?

1. Standing on a chair or table, drop a piece of chalk onto a hard floor. Observe what happens to the chalk.

2. Wrap a second piece of chalk in wax paper or plastic food wrap. Drop the chalk from the same height used in Step 1. Observe the results.

3. Wrap a third piece of chalk in plastic bubble wrap. Drop the chalk from the same height used in Step 1. Observe the results.

Think It Over

Inferring Compare the results from Steps 1, 2, and 3. What properties of the air in the bubble wrap accounted for the results in Step 3?

Every Thanksgiving, the people of New York City gather to watch a big parade. Maybe you have seen this parade on television, or even in person. The parade is famous for its large, floating balloons, like the one shown on this page. The balloons float because they are filled with helium, a gas that is less dense than air.

If you were in charge of a parade balloon, you would be faced with many different questions. How large is the balloon? How much helium should you put inside the balloon? Does the balloon behave differently in warm weather than in cold weather? To answer these questions and others like them, you would need to understand the properties of gases.

GUIDE FOR READING

◆ How are the volume, temperature, and pressure of a gas related?

Reading Tip Before you read, change each heading into a question. Write a brief answer to each question as you read.

Figure 8 A helium balloon of Clifford, the Big Red Dog, floats past Central Park in New York City.

Figure 9 The helium gas in this tank is kept under high pressure within the volume set by the thick steel walls. *Predicting What happens to the helium atoms as they move into the balloons?*

Sharpen your Skills

Developing Hypotheses

1. Pour soapy water into a large pan. Add a little glycerin, if available. **ACTIVITY**

2. Bend the ends of a wire or long pipe cleaner into a circle.

3. Dip the wire circle into the soapy water and then blow into the wire shape to make several bubbles. Observe the bubbles that you produce.

4. What factors seem to change the volume of the soap bubbles? How could you test your hypothesis?

Measuring Gases

How much helium is in the tank in Figure 9? You may think that measuring the volume of the tank will give you an answer. But gases easily squeeze together or spread out. To fill the tank, helium was compressed, or pressed together tightly. When the helium is used, it fills a total volume of inflated balloons much greater than the volume of the tank. The actual volume you get, however, depends on the temperature and air pressure that day. So what exactly do measurements of volume, pressure, and temperature mean?

Volume You know volume is the amount of space that matter fills. Volume is measured in cubic centimeters, milliliters, liters, and other units. Because gases fill the space available, the volume of a gas is the same as the volume of its container.

Temperature Hot soup, warm hands, cool breezes—you should be familiar with matter at different temperatures. But what exactly does temperature measure? Recall that in any substance—solid, liquid, or gas—the particles are constantly moving. **Temperature** is a measure of the average energy of motion of the particles of a substance. The faster the particles are moving, the greater their energy and the higher the temperature. You might think of a thermometer as a speedometer for molecules.

Even at ordinary temperatures, the average speed of particles in a gas is very fast. At 20°C, which is about room temperature, the particles in a typical gas travel about 500 meters per second!

Pressure Because gas particles are moving, they constantly collide with one another. They also collide with the walls of their container. As a result, the gas exerts an outward push on the walls of the container. The **pressure** of the gas is the force of its outward push divided by the area of the walls of the container. Pressure is measured in units of kilopascals (kPa).

$$Pressure = \frac{Force}{Area}$$

The firmness of an object inflated with a gas, such as a soccer ball, comes from the pressure of the gas. If the gas (in this case, air) leaks out of the ball, the pressure decreases and the ball becomes softer. But why does an inflated ball leak when punctured? A gas flows from an area of high pressure to an area of low pressure. The air inside the ball is at a higher pressure than the air outside. Gas particles inside the ball hit the hole more often than gas particles outside the hole. Because more inside particles hit the hole, they have a better chance of getting out of the ball. Thus, many more particles go out than in. The pressure inside drops until it is equal to the pressure outside.

✓ Checkpoint *What are three properties of a gas that you can measure?*

Figure 10 The gas particles are in constant motion, colliding with each other and with the walls of their container.

Relating Pressure and Volume

Pressure is also related to the volume of a container. For example, imagine that you are operating a bicycle pump. By pressing down on the plunger, you force the gas inside the pump through the rubber tube and out the nozzle into the tire. What will happen if you close the nozzle and then push down on the plunger?

Figure 11 What will happen when this bicyclist operates the pump she is attaching? She will decrease the volume of air in the cylinder and increase its pressure. As a result, air will be forced into the bicycle tire and the tire will inflate.

Figure 12 As weights are added on top, the same number of particles occupies a smaller volume. The pressure of the gas increases. This relationship is called Boyle's law.

Balloon Test

ACTIVITY

What happens when you change the volume of a gas?

1. Hold the open end of a paper cup on the side of a partly inflated balloon.

2. Inflate the balloon until it presses against the cup and then let go of the cup. What happens?

Developing Hypotheses Use what you know about pressure and volume to write a hypothesis that explains the behavior of the cup after you let it go. How could you test your hypothesis?

The answer to this question comes from experiments with gases done by the English scientist Robert Boyle. In the 1600s, Boyle measured the volumes of gases at different pressures as he experimented with ways to improve air pumps. He saw that gases behave in a predictable way. **Boyle found that when the pressure of a gas is increased at constant temperature, the volume of the gas decreases. When the pressure is decreased, the volume increases.** This relationship between the pressure and volume of a gas is named **Boyle's law.**

 **INTEGRATING EARTH SCIENCE** Boyle's law plays an important role in research done with some high-altitude balloons. These balloons are made from lightweight plastic. They are filled with only a small fraction of the helium they could hold. Why is that? As a balloon rises through the atmosphere, the air pressure around it decreases steadily. As the air pressure decreases, the helium inside the balloon expands, stretching the balloon to a greater and greater volume. If the balloon were fully filled at takeoff, it would burst before it got very high.

Boyle's law also applies to situations in which the *volume* of a gas is changed. Then the *pressure* changes in the opposite way. For example, if you squeeze an inflated balloon, you are decreasing its volume. You should be able to feel the increased pressure of the gas inside it. The bicycle pump described earlier is a similar case. As you push on the plunger, the volume of air inside the pump gets smaller and the pressure increases.

✓ *Checkpoint* What is Boyle's law?

Relating Pressure and Temperature

If you pour a bucketfull of sand onto your skin, it will not hurt at all. But suppose you are caught in a sandstorm. Because the sand grains are flying very fast, they will hurt a great deal! The faster the grains are traveling, the harder they will hit your skin.

Raising Temperature Raises Pressure

Although gas particles are much smaller and lighter than sand grains, a sandstorm is a good model for a gas. Like sand in a sandstorm, gas particles travel individually and at high speeds. Remember that pressure is a measure of how much gas particles push on the walls of a container. The greater the speed of the gas particles, the more collisions will occur. The more collisions there are, the greater the pressure will be.

Temperature is a measure of the average speed of the particles of a gas. The higher the temperature of a gas, the faster the gas particles are moving. Now you can state a relationship between temperature and pressure. **When the temperature of a gas at constant volume is increased, the pressure of the gas increases. When the temperature is decreased, the pressure of the gas decreases.** A constant volume means a closed, rigid container.

Pressure and Temperature in Action Have you ever looked at the tires of an 18-wheel truck? Because these tires need to support a lot of weight, they are large, heavy, and stiff. The inside volume of these tires doesn't vary much.

On long trips, especially in the summer, a truck's tires can get very hot. As the temperature increases, so does the pressure of the air inside the tire. If the pressure becomes higher than the tire can hold, the tire will burst apart. For this reason, truck drivers need to monitor and adjust tire pressure on long trips.

Figure 13 Particles of a gas are like the sand blown by the wind in this sandstorm. When a gas is heated, the particles move faster and collide more with one another and the sides of their container. *Relating Cause and Effect Why does the pressure of the gas increase when the number of collisions increases?*

Relating Volume and Temperature

If the temperature of the gas in a balloon is increased, its volume will change. Will the volume increase or decrease? If you answered "increase," you are right. Gases increase in volume when the temperature increases. As the temperature decreases, the volume decreases. People in charge of the large balloons used for parades need to understand the effect temperature has on volume so that the balloons can be inflated properly. The same principle applies to the smaller balloons at a party.

Charles's Law   In the late 1700s, a French scientist named Jacques Charles examined the relationship between the temperature and volume of a gas kept at a constant pressure. He measured the volume of a gas at various temperatures in a container whose volume could change. **Charles found that when the temperature of a gas is increased at constant pressure, its volume increases. When the temperature of a gas is decreased its volume decreases.** This principle is called **Charles's law.** Remember that at higher temperatures, the particles move faster. As a result, they collide more often with the walls around them. As long as the volume of the container can change, the total push of the collisions results in the gas taking up more space. The volume of the gas increases.

Charles's Law in Action   Picture a basketball game with a player dribbling the ball down the floor of the gym past the opposing team. Each time she dribbles the ball, it responds with a lively bounce. Then, when the game is over, she takes the ball home but leaves it outside her front door. Overnight the temperature drops to −4°C.

Figure 14 If the temperature is increased, the same number of particles of gas will occupy a greater volume. This relationship is called Charles's law.

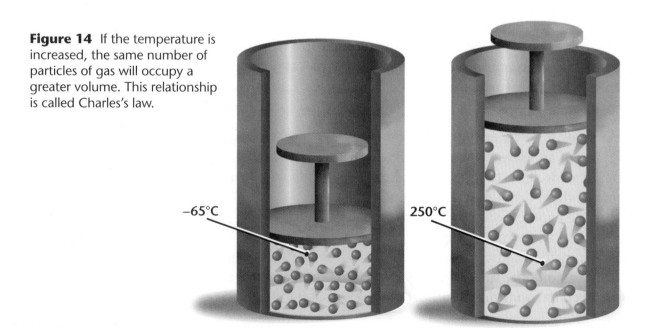

−65°C

250°C

Figure 15 It is 26°C inside the gym where this basketball game is being played. Outside it is –4°C.
Predicting How might the basketball change if it were left outside in the playground?

The next morning, the player picks up the ball and decides to shoot a couple of baskets in the playground outside. Again, she starts to dribble the ball. When the ball hits the ground, it doesn't bounce as high as it did. Why did the ball become soft since the game the night before? A basketball is inflated with air, but no air leaked out of the ball. You can use Charles's law to explain. The ball lost its bounce because the volume of the air inside decreased, chilled by the cold winter air. The same amount of a gas occupies a smaller volume at a lower temperature. Can the ball recover its bounce? Yes, the ball will return to its full volume in the warmth of the school gym.

Section 2 Review

1. Describe the relationship between the pressure and volume of a gas.
2. If you change the temperature of a gas but keep the volume the same, how does the pressure change?
3. What is Charles's law?
4. **Thinking Critically Applying Concepts** Suppose it is the night before Thanksgiving, and you are in charge of inflating a balloon for the Thanksgiving Day parade. You just learned that the temperature will rise 15°C by the time the parade starts. How will this information affect the way you inflate your balloon?

Check Your Progress

CHAPTER PROJECT

With the members of your group, write a description of how particles behave in each of the three states of matter. Next, think of different ways to model each state, using drawings and words. Decide if you want to demonstrate a change of state as cartoon pictures or by acting out the motion of particles in a skit. (*Hint:* Prepare a storyboard. A storyboard is a series of simple drawings and captions that outline the action of a story.)

SECTION 3 Graphing Gas Behavior

DISCOVER

What Does a Graph of Pressure and Temperature Show?

Temperature (°C)	Pressure (kPa)
0	8
5	11
10	14
15	17
20	20
25	23

1. In an experiment, the temperature was varied for a constant volume of gas. Gas pressure was measured after each 5°C change. You now need to graph the data in this table.

2. Show temperature on the horizontal axis with a scale from 0°C to 25°C. Show pressure on the vertical axis with a scale equally spaced from 0 kPa to 25 kPa.

3. For each pair of measurements, draw a point on the graph.

4. Draw a line to connect the points.

Think It Over

Graphing Use the graph to describe the relationship between the pressure and temperature of a gas.

GUIDE FOR READING

◆ What do graphs for Charles's law and Boyle's law look like?

Reading Tip As you read about the experiments in this section, refer to the graphs in Figures 19 and 21.

The population of a town is increasing. The schools are becoming more crowded, and the people need to decide whether to build more schools. Newspapers illustrate their articles about the problem with graphs.

How could a graph help tell this story? **Graphs** are diagrams that tell how two variables, or factors, are related. Graphs show how changes in one variable result in changes in a second variable. You can use graphs to make predictions. For example, according to the graph in Figure 16, the town might have a population of 32,000 in 2020. That assumes, of course, that population continues to grow at the same rate. In this section, you will learn how to interpret graphs that relate properties of gases.

Figure 16 This graph shows that population in the town is growing steadily. The dashed line predicts what the population would be if the current growth rate continues.

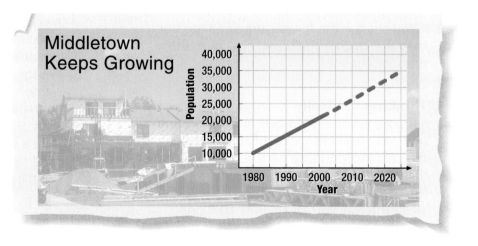

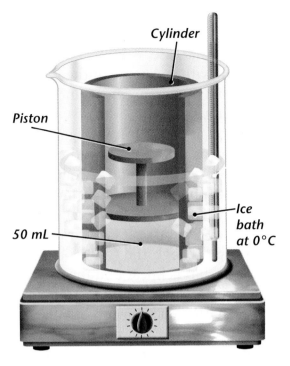

Temperature		Volume
(°C)	(K)	(mL)
0	273	50
10	283	52
20	293	54
30	303	56
40	313	58
50	323	60
60	333	62
70	343	63
80	353	66
90	363	67
100	373	69

Figure 17 As the temperature of the water bath increases, the gas inside the cylinder is warmed by the water. The data from the experiment are recorded in the table. Celsius temperature measurements are converted to kelvins by adding 273 to each value.

Temperature and Volume

Recall from Section 2 that Charles's law relates the temperature and volume of a gas kept at a constant pressure. You can examine this relationship by doing an experiment in which you change the temperature of a gas and measure its volume. Then you can graph the data you have recorded and look for a relationship.

Collecting Data As you can see from the cutaway view in Figure 17, the gas in the experiment is in a cylinder that has a movable piston. The piston moves up and down freely, which allows the gas to change volume and keep the same pressure. To control the temperature, the cylinder is placed in a water bath.

The experiment begins with an ice-water bath at 0°C, and the gas volume at 50 mL. Then the water bath is slowly heated. Very gradually, the temperature increases from 0°C to 100°C. Each time the temperature increases by 10°C, the volume of the gas in the cylinder is recorded.

You'll notice a second set of temperatures listed in the table in Figure 17. Scientists often work with gas temperatures in units called kelvins. To convert from Celsius degrees to kelvins, you add 273. The kelvin temperatures will be used to graph the data.

Graphing the Results A graph consists of a grid set up by two lines—one horizontal and one vertical. Each line, or axis, is divided into equal units. The horizontal, or x-, axis shows the manipulated variable, in this case, temperature. The vertical,

Figure 18 The horizontal, or x-, axis and the vertical, or y-, axis are the "backbone" of a graph. *Interpreting Diagrams Which variable is placed on the x-axis?*

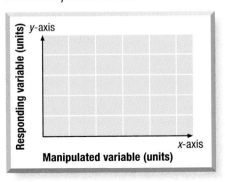

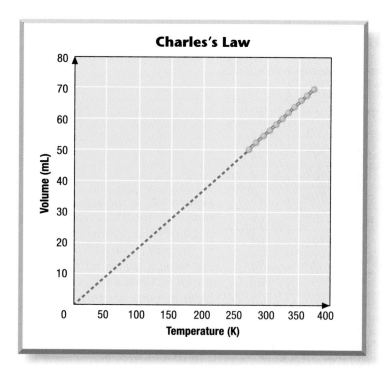

Charles's Law

Figure 19 This graph of the data from Figure 17 shows the linear relationship between temperature and volume known as Charles's law. The dotted line predicts how the graph would look if the gas could be cooled to lower temperatures.

or *y*-, axis shows the responding variable, in this case, volume. Each axis is labeled with the name of the variable, the units of measurement, and a range of values.

Look at the graph in Figure 19. It appears as if the line would continue downward if data could be collected for lower temperatures. Such a line would pass through the point (0, 0). When a graph of two variables is a straight line passing through the (0, 0) point, the relationship is linear and the variables are said to be **directly proportional** to each other. **The graph of Charles's law shows that the volume of a gas is directly proportional to its kelvin temperature under constant pressure.**

☑ *Checkpoint* On which axis of a graph do you show the responding variable?

Pressure and Volume

You can perform another experiment to show how pressure and volume are related when temperature is kept constant. Recall that the relationship between pressure and volume is called Boyle's law.

Figure 20 By pushing on the top of the piston, you compress the gas and thereby increase the pressure of the gas inside the cylinder. The data from the experiment are recorded in the table.
Predicting What would happen if you pulled up on the piston?

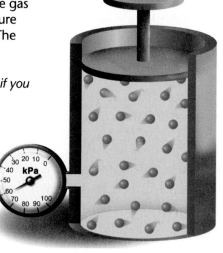

Volume (mL)	Pressure (kPa)
100	60
90	67
80	75
70	86
60	100

Collecting Data The gas in this experiment is also contained in a cylinder with a movable piston. In this case, however, a pressure gauge indicates the pressure of the gas inside.

The experiment begins with the volume of the gas at 100 mL. The pressure of the gas is 60 kilopascals. Next, the piston is slowly pushed into the cylinder, compressing the gas, or shrinking its volume. The pressure of the gas is recorded after each 10-mL change in volume.

Graphing the Results To observe the relationship of the pressure and volume of a gas, it helps to display the data in another graph. In the pressure-volume experiment, the manipulated variable is volume. Volume is shown on the scale of the horizontal axis from 60 mL to 100 mL. The responding variable is pressure. Pressure is shown on the scale of the vertical axis from 60 kPa to 100 kPa.

As you can see in Figure 21, the points lie on a curve. Notice that the curve slopes downward from left to right. Also notice that the curve is steep close to the vertical axis and becomes less steep close to the horizontal axis. When a graph of two measurements forms this kind of curve, the relationship is nonlinear and the measurements are said to **vary inversely** with each other. **The graph for Boyle's law shows that the pressure of a gas varies inversely with its volume at constant temperature.** In other words, the pressure of a gas decreases as its volume increases.

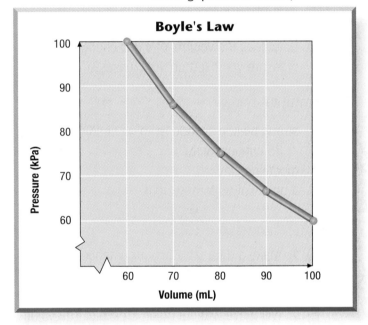

Figure 21 This graph of the data from Figure 20 shows the nonlinear relationship between pressure and volume known as Boyle's law. (The broken lines between 0 and 60 show gaps in the scales.)

Section 3 Review

1. Describe a graph of Charles's law.
2. Describe a graph of Boyle's law.
3. How can you tell the difference between a graph in which one variable is directly proportional to another and a graph in which two variables vary inversely?
4. **Thinking Critically** **Interpreting Graphs** Suppose the temperature of the gas in the experiment illustrated in Figure 17 was increased to 400 K (127°C). Use Figure 19 to predict the new volume of the gas.

Science at Home

News Data Look for graphs in your newspaper or in news magazines. Point out to members of your family which variable is the manipulated variable and which is the responding variable for each graph. Then compare any line graphs you have found to the graphs in this section. Which of your graphs show two variables that are directly proportional to each other? Do any show variables that vary inversely?

Skills Lab

Y ou can use a syringe as a model of an air pump. In this lab, you will determine how the amount you press on a syringe is related to the volume of the air inside it.

Problem

How does the volume of a gas change as the pressure you exert on it increases?

Materials

strong plastic syringe (with no needle), at least 35 cm³ capacity
modeling clay
4 books of uniform weight

Procedure

1. Make a data table in your notebook like the one below.
2. Lift the plunger of the syringe as high as it will move without going off scale. The volume inside the syringe will then be as large as possible.
3. Seal the small opening of the syringe with a piece of clay. The seal must be airtight.

4. Hold the syringe upright with the clay end on the table. With the help of a partner, place a single book on top of the plunger. Balance the book carefully so it does not fall.
5. Read the volume indicated by the plunger and record it in your data table.
6. Predict what will happen as more books are placed on the syringe.
7. Place another book on top of the first book. Read the new volume and record it in your data table.

DATA TABLE			
Adding Books		Removing Books	
Number of Books	Volume (cm³)	Number of Books	Volume (cm³)
0		4	
1		3	
2		2	
3		1	
4		0	

8. One by one, place each of the remaining books on top of the plunger. After you add each book, record the volume of the syringe in your data table.
9. Predict what will happen as books are removed from the plunger one by one.
10. Remove the books one at a time. After you remove each book, again record the volume of the syringe in your data table.

Analyze and Conclude

1. Make a line graph of the data obtained from Steps 5, 7, and 8. Show volume in cubic centimeters (cm^3) on the vertical axis and number of books on the horizontal axis. Title this Graph 1.
2. Make a second line graph of the data obtained from Step 10. Title this Graph 2.
3. Did the results you obtained support your predictions in Steps 6 and 9? Explain.

4. Describe the shape of Graph 1. What does the graph tell you about the relationship between the volume and pressure of a gas?
5. Compare Graph 2 with Graph 1. How can you explain any differences in the two graphs?
6. **Think About It** Did the volume change between the addition of the first and second book? Did it change by the same amount between the addition of the second book and third book? Between the third and fourth book? What is happening to the gas particles in air that could explain this behavior?

Design an Experiment

How could you use ice and warm water to show how the temperature and volume of a gas are related? Design an experiment to test the effect of changing the temperature of a gas. With your teacher's approval, conduct this experiment.

4 Changes in State

DISCOVER • ACTIVITY

What Happens When You Breathe on a Mirror?

1. Obtain a hand mirror. Clean it with a dry cloth. Describe the mirror's surface.

2. Hold the mirror about 15 cm away from your face. Try to breathe against the mirror's surface.

3. Reduce the distance until breathing on the mirror produces a visible change. Record what you observe.

Think It Over

Developing Hypotheses What did you observe when you breathed on the mirror held close to your mouth? How can you explain that observation? Why did you get different results when the mirror was at greater distances from your face?

GUIDE FOR READING

◆ When thermal energy is transferred, in what direction does it flow?

◆ How does the energy of a substance change when it changes state?

Reading Tip As you read, make an outline that includes the headings and main ideas of the section.

Think of what happens to an ice cream cone on a hot summer day. The ice cream quickly starts to drip onto your hand. You're not surprised. You know that ice cream melts if it's not kept cold.

Energy and Changes in State

Under different conditions, a substance may be at different temperatures. At a warmer temperature, the particles of the substance have a higher average energy of motion than at a cooler temperature. The energy that the particles of a substance have is called **thermal energy.** The amount of thermal energy in a substance depends partly on its temperature and the way its particles are arranged.

Thermal energy is transferred from one substance to another as heat. **Thermal energy always flows from a warmer substance to a cooler substance.** When heat flows into a substance, its particles gain energy and move faster. When heat flows from a substance, its particles lose energy and move more slowly. So thermal energy is involved when a substance changes state.

64

Figure 22 A jeweler melts silver before pouring it into a mold. *Predicting What happens to the silver particles as the melted silver cools down?*

You saw that the arrangement and motion of the particles of a substance determine whether the substance is a solid, a liquid, or a gas. The particles of a solid have the least thermal energy. They simply vibrate in a fixed position. The particles of a liquid have more thermal energy. They move around one another freely, although they remain close to one another and are confined to a definite volume. The particles of a gas have the most thermal energy. They are separated from one another and move around in all directions at high speeds. **A substance changes state when its thermal energy increases or decreases by a sufficient amount.**

Changes Between Liquid and Solid

Each specific substance changes states at temperatures that are typical for that substance. But the overall pattern for the way substances change state is the same.

Melting The change in state from a solid to a liquid is **melting.** In Section 1, you saw that a crystalline solid melts at a specific temperature, called the melting point. The melting point of a substance depends on how strongly its particles attract one another.

Think of an ice cube taken from the freezer. The energy to melt comes from the air in the room. At first, the added thermal energy makes the water molecules vibrate faster, raising their temperature. At 0°C, the water molecules are vibrating so fast that they break free from their positions in ice crystals. For a time, the temperature of the ice stops increasing. Instead, the added energy changes the arrangement of the water molecules from ice crystals into liquid water. This is the process you observe as melting.

✓ *Checkpoint* *What happens to the particles of a solid as it gains more and more thermal energy?*

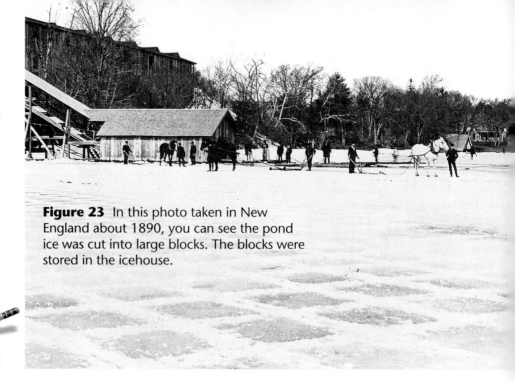

Figure 23 In this photo taken in New England about 1890, you can see the pond ice was cut into large blocks. The blocks were stored in the icehouse.

Freezing   Now suppose you put the liquid water from the melted ice cube into a freezer. After a while, the water will freeze back into ice. **Freezing** is the change of state from liquid to solid—just the reverse of melting.

When you put liquid water into the freezer, the water loses energy to the cold air in the freezer. At first, the water molecules move more slowly. When the temperature reaches 0°C, the molecules are moving so slowly that they form regular patterns. These patterns are the crystals that form ice. When water freezes, the temperature stays at 0°C until freezing is complete. (This is the same temperature at which ice melts.)

Changes Between Liquid and Gas

Have you ever wondered how clouds form, or why rain falls from clouds? And why do puddles dry up after a rain shower? To answer these questions, you need to look at the ways that water changes between the liquid and gas states.

Vaporization   The change from liquid water into water vapor is an example of **vaporization** (vay puhr ih ZAY shuhn). Vaporization occurs when a liquid gains enough energy to become a gas. There are two main types of vaporization.

The first kind, called **evaporation** (ee vap uh RAY shun), takes place only on the surface of a liquid. A drying puddle is an example. The water in the puddle gains energy from the ground, the air, or the sun. The energy enables the molecules on the surface of the puddle to escape into the air. Evaporation also occurs when you sweat. Sweat evaporates as it gains thermal energy from your skin, cooling you down on a hot day or when you exercise.

Figure 24 During evaporation, particles leave the surface of a liquid.

Figure 25 During boiling, groups of particles form bubbles of gas at many locations throughout the liquid. These bubbles rise to the surface, where the particles escape. *Applying Concepts What happens to the boiling point of water when the air pressure increases?*

The second kind of vaporization, called **boiling,** takes place inside a liquid as well as at the surface. Each liquid boils at a specific temperature called its **boiling point**. Like the melting point of a solid, the boiling point of a liquid depends on how strongly the particles of the substance are attracted to one another.

Boiling Point and Air Pressure The boiling point of a substance depends on the pressure of the air above a liquid. The lower the air pressure above the liquid, the less energy that liquid molecules need to escape into the air. As you go up in elevation, air pressure decreases. At the air pressure in places close to sea level, the boiling point of water is 100°C. In the mountains, however, air pressure is lower and so is the boiling point of water.

The city of Denver, Colorado, is 1,600 meters above sea level for example. At this elevation, the boiling point of water is 95°C. When a recipe calls for boiling water, cooks in Denver have to be careful. Food doesn't cook as quickly at 95°C as it does at 100°C.

Condensation The opposite of vaporization is called condensation. **Condensation** occurs when gas particles lose enough thermal energy to become a liquid. Clouds typically form when water vapor in the atmosphere condenses into liquid droplets. When the droplets get heavy enough, they fall to the ground as rain.

You can observe condensation by breathing onto a mirror. When warm water vapor in your breath reaches the cooler surface of the mirror, the water vapor condenses into liquid droplets. The droplets then evaporate into water vapor again.

Remember that when you observe steam from boiling water, clouds, or mist, you are not seeing water vapor, a gas that's impossible to see. What you see in those cases are tiny droplets of liquid water suspended in air.

☑ *Checkpoint* *How are vaporization and condensation related?*

Changes Between Solid and Gas

If you live where the winters are cold, you may have noticed that snow seems to disappear even when the temperature stays well below freezing. This happens because of sublimation. **Sublimation** occurs when the surface particles of a solid gain enough energy to become a gas. Particles do not pass through the liquid state at all. Some solids, such as naphthalene (moth balls), sublime more easily than others, such as table salt.

EXPLORING Changes of State

What changes occur as you slowly heat a beaker of ice from −10°C to 110°C?

Ⓐ **Solid**
Below 0°C, water exists in its solid state—ice. Although the water molecules in ice crystals stay in fixed positions, they do vibrate. As the molecules are heated, they vibrate faster and the temperature rises.

Ⓑ **Melting**
When more energy is added to ice at 0°C, the molecules overcome the forces that keep them in ice crystals. The ice melts or turns to liquid water. As ice melts, the molecules rearrange but do not move faster. Thus, the temperature of the ice stays at 0°C.

Ⓒ **Liquid**
Water must be liquid before its temperature can rise above 0°C. As liquid water is heated, the molecules move faster and the temperature rises again.

Ⓓ **Vaporization**
When more energy is added to liquid water at 100°C, molecules escape the liquid state and become a gas. This process is called vaporization. When water boils, the molecules overcome the forces that hold them together as liquids, but they do not move faster. Thus, the temperature stays at 100°C.

Ⓔ **Gas**
Water must be in its gas state—called water vapor—before its temperature can rise above 100°C. As water vapor is heated, the molecules move faster and the temperature rises again.

Figure 26 shows a common example of sublimation, the change in dry ice. "Dry ice" is the common name for solid carbon dioxide (CO_2). At ordinary air pressures, carbon dioxide cannot exist as a liquid. So instead of melting, solid carbon dioxide changes directly into a gas. As it changes state, it absorbs thermal energy, so it keeps materials near it cold and dry. For this reason, it's an excellent way to keep temperatures low when a refrigerator is not available. Recall that you cannot see the gas that dry ice forms. The fog around it results when water vapor from the nearby air cools and forms tiny droplets.

Figure 26 Dry ice is solid carbon dioxide. It changes directly to gaseous carbon dioxide in the process of sublimation. The energy absorbed in this change of state cools the water vapor in the air, creating fog. *Inferring Describe what happens to the carbon dioxide particles during sublimation.*

Identifying Substances Through Changes of State

Chemists sometimes face the problem of identifying unknown materials. In Chapter 1, you learned that the combination of properties a substance has can be used to identify it. To make such identification possible, chemists have built up a data bank of information about the properties of substances. As a result, comparing melting points and boiling points can be important steps in identifying an unknown material.

Suppose, for example, that chemists are trying to identify three clear, colorless liquids. One is water, another is chloroform (once used to cause sleep during surgery), and a third is ethanol (a type of alcohol). You already know the melting and boiling points of water. Chloroform melts at –64°C and boils at 61°C. Ethanol melts at –117°C and boils at 79°C. You can thus see how testing for these properties would help researchers identify them.

Section 4 Review

1. If an object at 50°C is placed in ice water, how will the object's temperature change? Explain.
2. What is happening to the particles of a liquid as it changes into a gas?
3. What's the main difference between boiling and evaporation?
4. Explain what happens to dry ice when it is left standing at room temperature.
5. **Thinking Critically Applying Concepts** If you are stranded in a blizzard and are trying to stay warm, why should you melt snow and then drink it instead of just eating snow?

Check Your Progress CHAPTER PROJECT

Use the information you learned in this section to revise your storyboard, if necessary. Then if you are creating a cartoon, draw the cartoon and write the captions. If you are presenting a skit, write a script and stage directions. Rehearse the skit with the members of your group.

MELTING ICE

I n this experiment, you will measure temperature as you explore the melting of ice.

Problem

How does the temperature of the surroundings affect the rate at which ice melts?

Materials

thermometer   stopwatch or timer
2 plastic cups, about 200 mL each
2 stirring rods, preferably plastic
ice cubes, about 2 cm on each side
warm water, about 40°C to 45°C
water at room temperature

Procedure

1. Read Steps 1–8. Based on your own experience, predict which ice cube will melt faster.
2. In your notebook, make a data table like the one below.
3. Fill a cup halfway with warm water (about 40°C to 45°C). Fill a second cup to the same depth with water at room temperature.
4. Record the exact temperature of the water in each cup.
5. Obtain two ice cubes that are as close to the same size as possible.
6. Place one piece of ice in each cup. Begin timing with a stopwatch. Gently stir each cup with a stirring rod until the ice cubes melt.
7. Observe both ice cubes carefully. At the moment one of the ice cubes is completely melted, record the time and the temperature of the water in the cup.
8. Wait for the second ice cube to melt. Record its melting time and the water temperature.

Analyze and Conclude

1. Was your prediction in Step 1 supported by the results of the experiment? Explain why or why not.
2. In which cup did the water temperature change the most? Explain this result.
3. When the ice melted, its molecules gained enough energy to overcome the forces holding them together as solid ice. What is the source of that energy?
4. **Think About It** How well could you time the exact moment that each ice cube completely melted? How might errors in measurements affect your conclusions?

Design an Experiment

When a lake freezes in winter, only the top layer turns to ice. Design an experiment to model the melting of a frozen lake during the spring. With your teacher's approval, carry out your experiment. Be prepared to share your results with the class.

DATA TABLE

	Beginning Temperature (°C)	Time to Melt (s)	Final Temperature (°C)
Cup 1			
Cup 2			

Skills Lab

70

States of Matter

Key Ideas
◆ Solids have a definite shape and volume because the particles in a solid are packed tightly together and stay in fixed positions.
◆ Particles in a liquid are move freely around one another. A liquid has no definite shape, but it does have a definite volume.
◆ The particles of a gas spread apart to fill all the space available to them. Thus, a gas has neither definite shape nor definite volume.

Key Terms
solid   liquid
crystalline solid   viscosity
melting point   gas
amorphous solid

 Gas Behavior

Key Ideas
◆ At constant temperature, when the volume of a gas decreases, its pressure increases.
◆ In a rigid container, raising the temperature of a gas increases its pressure.
◆ In a flexible container, raising the temperature of a gas increases its volume.

Key Terms
temperature   Boyle's law pressure
Charles's law

 Graphing Gas Behavior
INTEGRATING MATHEMATICS

Key Ideas
◆ A graph shows that the volume of a gas and its kelvin temperature are directly proportional at constant pressure.
◆ A graph shows that the volume of a gas at constant temperature varies inversely with its pressure.

Key Terms
graph   vary inversely
directly proportional

 Changes in State

Key Ideas
◆ The particles of a substance gain thermal energy as the temperature increases.
◆ Changes of state can occur when a substance gains or loses thermal energy.

Key Terms
thermal energy   boiling
melting   boiling point
freezing   condensation
vaporization   sublimation
evaporation

Organizing Information

Compare/Contrast Table Copy the compare/contrast table about the states of matter onto a separate sheet of paper. Then complete it and add a title. (For more on compare/contrast tables, see the Skills Handbook.)

State of Matter	Shape	Volume	Example (at room temperature)
a. _?_	Definite	b. _?_	Diamond
Liquid	c. _?_	Definite	d. _?_
Gas	e. _?_	Not definite	f. _?_

Reviewing Content

 For more review of key concepts, see the Interactive Student Tutorial CD-ROM.

Multiple Choice

Choose the letter of the answer that best completes each statement.

1. A substance whose particles are close together but move freely around one another is a(n)
   a. crystalline solid. **b.** liquid.
   c. gas. **d.** amorphous solid.
2. Unlike solids and liquids, a gas will
   a. keep its volume in different containers.
   b. keep its shape in different containers.
   c. expand to fill the space available to it.
   d. have its volume decrease when the temperature rises.
3. Boyle's law states that the volume of a gas increases when its
   a. pressure increases.
   b. pressure decreases.
   c. temperature falls.
   d. temperature rises.
4. The vertical axis of a graph shows the
   a. responding variable.
   b. manipulated variable.
   c. constant factors.
   d. same variable as the *x*-axis.
5. When a liquid freezes, its particles
   a. move more rapidly.
   b. escape from its surface more quickly.
   c. vibrate faster.
   d. slow down and form patterns.

True or False

If the statement is true, write true. If it is false, change the underlined word or words to make it a true statement.

6. Rubber and glass become softer and softer over a wide range of temperatures. They are examples of <u>crystalline</u> solids.
7. The energy from the movement of particles is measured by the <u>temperature</u> of a substance.
8. If a gas is contained in a rigid container, raising its temperature will increase its <u>volume</u>.
9. Charles's law states that the volume of a gas varies <u>inversely</u> with its temperature.
10. The boiling point of a liquid is <u>lower</u> at sea level than on a mountain.

Checking Concepts

11. Describe the motion of particles in a solid.
12. Compare and contrast liquids with high and low viscosities.
13. How is the temperature of a substance related to the energy of movement of the particles in the substance?
14. What happens to the gas particles when the air in an inflated ball leaks out?
15. What happens during condensation?
16. What happens to water molecules when water is heated from 90°C to 110°C?
17. Compare the processes of melting and freezing.
18. **Writing to Learn** Imagine you are Robert Boyle or Jacques Charles at the time you described the law that came to be known by your name. Tell the story of your experiments and results as you think Boyle or Charles would if either one could talk to the students in your class today. Write down exactly what you would say.

Thinking Critically

19. **Relating Cause and Effect** Explain why placing a dented table tennis ball in boiling water is one way to remove a dent in the ball. Assume it has no holes.
20. **Comparing and Contrasting** Using diagrams, show the gas particles in an air mattress before you lie down on it and while you are lying on it.
21. **Applying Concepts** Describe what happens when an ice cube and solid carbon dioxide are each placed in a warm room. Why do you think the solid carbon dioxide is called "dry ice"?
22. **Inferring** When snow on the ground undergoes sublimation, where does the necessary energy come from?

Applying Skills

After each 10°C change in temperature, the mass of a compound dissolved in 100 mL of water was measured. Use this data to answer Questions 23–25.

Temperature (°C)	Mass of Compound Dissolved (g)
0	37
10	47
20	56
30	66
40	75

23. Graphing Graph the data for mass dissolved at each temperature. Label the horizontal axis from 0°C to 60°C and the vertical axis from 0 grams to 100 grams.

24. Interpreting Data What does the graph show about the effect of temperature on the amount of the compound that will dissolve in water?

25. Predicting Assume the amount of the compound dissolved continues to increase as the water is heated. Predict how many grams dissolve at 50°C.

Performance   *CHAPTER PROJECT*   Assessment

Present Your Project If you prepared a cartoon, read the captions to the class and discuss the illustrations. If you prepared a skit, perform the skit in front of the class. After you finish your presentation, invite the class to ask questions about your project. Be prepared to share the decisions you made in creating your presentation.

Reflect and Record In your journal, describe the strengths and weaknesses of the way you modeled changes of state. How successful was your model? How well did your classmates understand your cartoon or skit? Describe what you learned from observing the projects of your classmates.

Test Preparation   *Use these questions to prepare for standardized tests.*

Read the information below. Then answer Questions 26–29.

A scientist measured the pressure of a sample of a gas at various volumes. The temperature of the gas was kept constant. The data are shown below.

Volume (cm^3)	Pressure (kPa)
15	222
21	159
31	108
50	67

26. At which volume was the pressure the highest?
   a. 15 cm^3
   b. 21 cm^3
   c. 31 cm^3
   d. 50 cm^3

27. If a measurement was taken when the volume was 25 cm^3, the pressure would be
   a. about 25 kPa.
   b. about 70 kPa.
   c. about 130 kPa.
   d. about 240 kPa.

28. What will happen to the pressure if the volume is increased to 75 cm^3?
   a. The pressure will increase.
   b. The pressure will decrease.
   c. The pressure will remain the same.
   d. There is no way to predict the pressure.

29. If you were to construct a graph with volume on the horizontal axis and pressure on the vertical axis, what would your graph look like?
   a. a straight line slanting up from left to right
   b. a curve slanting down from left to right
   c. a straight horizontal line
   d. a U-shaped line

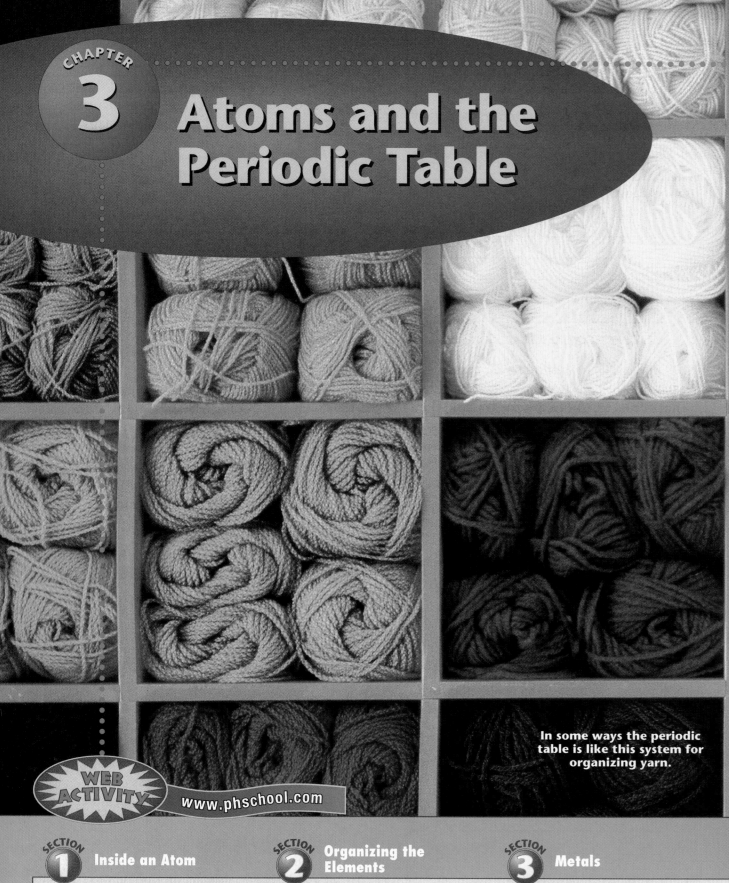

3 Atoms and the Periodic Table

In some ways the periodic table is like this system for organizing yarn.

WEB ACTIVITY
www.phschool.com

SECTION
1 Inside an Atom

Discover **How Far Away Is the Electron?**
Science at Home **Atoms on Display**

SECTION
2 Organizing the Elements

Discover **Which is Easier?**
Sharpen Your Skills **Classifying**

SECTION
3 Metals

Discover **Why Use Aluminum?**
Sharpen Your Skills **Observing**
Real-World Lab **Testing 1, 2, 3**

Getting Organized

Imagine searching for matching skeins of yarn if all the yarn had been tossed randomly into a large bin. Luckily, the owner of the store has grouped the yarn by color and by the thickness of the yarn strands. You may have seen similar systems of organization in other stores or in your own home. Chemists also have a system of organization—a system for organizing the elements. There are more than 100 elements. As you will learn in this chapter, about 80 elements are classified as metals. In this project, you will examine the properties of different metals more closely.

Your Goal To survey the properties of several metal samples.

To complete the project you must
◆ interpret what the periodic table tells you about your samples
◆ design and conduct experiments that will allow you to test at least three properties of your metals
◆ compare and contrast the properties of your sample metals
◆ follow the safety guidelines in Appendix A

Get Started Begin by brainstorming with your classmates about metals. How do you think metals differ from nonmetals? Your teacher will assign samples of metals to your group. You will be observing their properties in this project.

Check Your Progress You'll be working on this project as you study this chapter. To keep your project on track, look for Check Your Progress boxes at the following points.

Section 2 Review, page 88: Extract information from the periodic table.

Section 3 Review, page 94: Design experiments to test for properties.

Section 5 Review, page 108: Conduct tests on all samples.

Present Your Project At the end of the chapter (page 111), you will prepare a presentation comparing and contrasting the expected and observed properties of the metals you investigated.

SECTION 4 **Nonmetals and Metalloids**

Discover **What Are the Properties of Charcoal?**
Try This **Show Me the Oxygen**
Skills Lab **Alien Periodic Table**
Science at Home **Halogens in the Home**

Integrating Space Science
SECTION 5 **Elements From Stardust**

Discover **Can Helium Be Made From Hydrogen?**

SECTION 1 Inside an Atom

DISCOVER ··· ACTIVITY····

How Far Away Is the Electron?

1. On a piece of paper, make a small circle no bigger than a dime. The circle represents the nucleus, or center, of a model atom.

2. Measure the diameter of the circle in centimeters.

3. Now predict where you think the outer edge of this model atom will be. For example, will the outer edge be within the edges of the paper? Your desk? The classroom? The school building?

Think It Over

Making Models The diameter of an actual atom can be 100,000 times the diameter of its nucleus. Calculate the diameter of your model atom. How close was your prediction in Step 3 to your calculation? (*Hint:* To compare your result to the real world, change the units of your prediction from centimeters to meters.)

GUIDE FOR READING

◆ What is the structure of an atom?

◆ What role do valence electrons play in forming chemical bonds?

Reading Tip As you read, make a table listing the particles found in an atom. Include the name of each particle, its charge, and where in an atom the particle is located.

Picture this: It's –5°C. Two white solids—ice and salt—are side by side. You slowly heat the materials. At 0°C, the ice melts, making liquid water. It then boils into a gas at 100°C. The salt doesn't change until it's at 801°C, when it begins to melt. It boils away at 1,413°C. These differences are caused by the kinds of chemical bonds holding the atoms together. To understand chemical bonds, you need to know more about atoms.

Structure of an Atom

If you could look into an atom, what might you see? Theories about the shape and structure of atoms have changed over the last 200 years and continue to change even now. But some ideas about atoms are well understood.

Three Kinds of Particles Although atoms are extremely small, they are made of even smaller parts. **An atom consists of a nucleus surrounded by one or more electrons.** The **nucleus** (NOO clee us) (plural *nuclei*) is the tiny, central core of an atom. Nuclei contain particles called protons and neutrons. **Protons** have a positive electric charge (indicated by a plus symbol, +). **Neutrons** have no charge. They are neutral. (Could you guess that from their name?) A third type of particle moves in the space around the nucleus. These are very energetic particles, called **electrons,** which move rapidly in all directions. Electrons carry a negative charge (indicated by a negative symbol, –).

Ice   Rock salt ▼

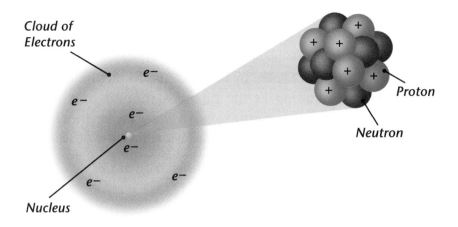

Cloud of Electrons

e^-

e^-

e^-

e^-

e^-

e^-

Nucleus

Proton

Neutron

Figure 1 An atom's tiny nucleus contains protons and neutrons. The electrons move in the space around the nucleus.
Applying Concepts Is this carbon atom negatively charged, positively charged, or neutral overall?

Atomic Number Every atom of a particular element contains the same number of protons. For example, every carbon atom contains six protons. Thus, an element's **atomic number**—the number of protons in its nucleus—is a unique property that identifies that element. And in an atom, the number of protons and the number of electrons are equal, making the atom neutral.

Atomic Mass Atoms cannot be measured with everyday units of mass because they are so small. For this reason, scientists have created the **atomic mass unit (amu)** to measure the particles in atoms. The mass of a proton or a neutron is about one atomic mass unit. Electrons have a much smaller mass. It takes almost 2,000 electrons to equal one atomic mass unit. That means that most of an atom's mass is in its nucleus. An atom that contains 6 protons, 6 neutrons, and 6 electrons has a mass of about 12 atomic mass units.

Although atoms of any particular element always have the same number of protons, the number of neutrons they contain may vary. Carbon atoms, for instance, always have six protons. But they may have five, six, seven, or eight neutrons. That means that the mass of atoms of an element can vary. However, the neutrons do not play a role in chemical reactions. The atoms of a particular element all have the same chemical properties despite their different masses.

✓ *Checkpoint* *Which particles in an atom are in the nucleus?*

The Role of Electrons

Electrons move around the nucleus so fast that it is impossible to know exactly where any electron is at a particular time. Think about the blades of a moving fan. They go too fast to be seen. As electrons move around the nucleus, the effect is like the fan blades, but in three dimensions. The space around the nucleus is like a spherical cloud of negatively charged electrons.

Figure 2 Like a fan's fast-moving blades, electrons cannot be seen as they move around the nucleus of an atom.

Little Particles, Big Spaces Most of an atom's mass comes from its protons and neutrons. But most of an atom's volume is the space in which the electrons move. That space is huge compared to the space occupied by the nucleus. To picture the difference, imagine standing at the pitcher's mound in a baseball stadium. If the nucleus were the size of a pencil eraser, the electrons could be in the outfield or as far away as the top row of seats!

☑ *Checkpoint* *Where are the electrons in an atom?*

Models of Atoms

For over two centuries, models of atoms have helped scientists understand why matter behaves as it does. As scientists have learned more, the model of the atom has changed.

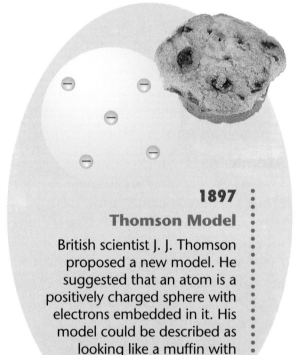

1808

Dalton Model

British chemist John Dalton published his *New System of Chemical Philosophy,* explaining that each element is made of small atoms and that different elements have atoms of different mass. Dalton imagined atoms as tiny, solid balls.

1897

Thomson Model

British scientist J. J. Thomson proposed a new model. He suggested that an atom is a positively charged sphere with electrons embedded in it. His model could be described as looking like a muffin with berries scattered through it.

1800

1900

For almost 100 years, not much ▲ new information was learned about atoms.

1904 Nagaoka Model

Japanese physicist Hantaro Nagaoka proposed a model of the atom that had a large sphere in the center with a positive charge. His model showed the electrons revolving around this sphere like the planets around the sun.

5+

Valence Electrons The electrons in an atom are not all the same distance away from the nucleus. Those farthest away from the nucleus, called **valence electrons** (VAY luns), are involved in the formation of chemical bonds.

A chemical bond forms between two atoms when valence electrons move between them. The valence electrons may be transferred from one atom to another, or they may be shared between atoms. In either case, the change causes the atoms to become connected, or bonded.

In Your Journal

Find out more about one of the scientists who worked on models of the atom. Write an imaginary interview with this person in which you discuss his work with him.

1911
Rutherford Model

British physicist Ernest Rutherford concluded that the atom is mostly empty space. Electrons orbit randomly around a small, positively charged nucleus.

1932
Chadwick Model

British physicist James Chadwick discovered the neutron, a particle having about the same mass as the proton but with no electrical charge. The existence of the neutron explained why atoms were heavier than the total mass of their protons and electrons.

| 1910 | 1920 | 1930 | 1940 | 1950 |

1913
Bohr Model

Danish physicist Niels Bohr determined that electrons aren't randomly located around the nucleus. His model showed electrons moving in specific layers, or shells. He said that atoms absorb or give off energy when the electrons move from one shell to another.

Cloud of electrons

1920s to Present
Modern Model

The current model of the atom came from the work of many scientists from the 1920s to the present. It shows the electrons as forming a negatively charged cloud around the nucleus. It is impossible to determine exactly where an electron is at any given time.

Figure 3 In these electron dot diagrams, each dot represents a valence electron. The total number of dots around the symbol shows the number of valence electrons the element has.
Interpreting Diagrams Which two elements in this diagram have the same number of valence electrons? Which element has the largest number of valence electrons?

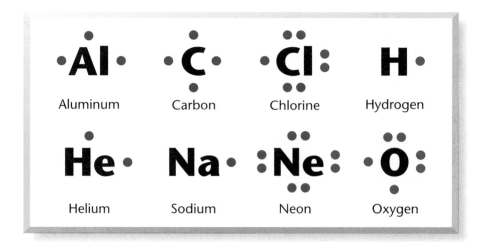

Aluminum   Carbon   Chlorine   Hydrogen

Helium   Sodium   Neon   Oxygen

The number of valence electrons in an atom can range from one to eight. Each element has a typical number of valence electrons. Oxygen has six valence electrons, for example. Carbon has four. Hydrogen's single electron is considered a valence electron.

Chemists often represent valence electrons with simple diagrams like those in Figure 3. An **electron dot diagram** is made up of the symbol for an element surrounded by dots. Each dot stands for one valence electron.

When an atom forms a chemical bond, one of two things usually happens. Either the number of valence electrons increases to a total of eight, or all the valence electrons are given up. When atoms end up with eight or zero valence electrons, the atoms become more stable—or less reactive—than they were before. Later in this chapter, you will learn which elements are likely to give up electrons and which are likely to gain electrons. In Chapter 4, you will find out how valence electrons determine the kind of compound that particular elements form.

 Section 1 Review

Science at Home

Atoms on Display
Draw sketches or construct models of atoms to show your family. The models can be made of clay, beads, string, and other simple materials. Explain what makes the atoms of different elements different from each other. Emphasize that everything in your home is made of about 100 atoms.

1. Describe the parts of an atom and tell where each is found.
2. Explain why the electrical charge on an atom is zero, or neutral.
3. What happens to valence electrons during the formation of chemical bonds?
4. Explain why electrons make up much of an atom's volume but not much of its mass.
5. **Thinking Critically Applying Concepts** What information can you get from an electron dot diagram?

SECTION 2 Organizing the Elements

DISCOVER • ACTIVITY • • •

Which Is Easier?

1. Make 4 sets of 10 paper squares, using a different color for each set. Number the squares in each set from 1 through 10.

2. Place all of the squares on a flat surface, numbered side up. Don't arrange them in order.

3. Ask your partner to name a square by color and number. Have your partner time how long it takes you to find this square.

4. Repeat Step 3 twice, choosing different squares each time. Calculate the average value of the three times.

5. Rearrange the squares into four rows, one for each color. Order the squares in each row from 1 to 10.

6. Repeat Step 3 three times. Calculate an average time.

7. Trade places with your partner and repeat Steps 2 through 6.

Think It Over

Inferring Which average time was shorter, the one produced in Step 4 or Step 6? Why do you think the times were different?

You wake up, jump out of bed, and start to get dressed for school. Then you ask yourself a question: Is there school today? To find out, you check the calendar. There's no school today because it's Saturday.

The calendar arranges the days of the month into horizontal periods called weeks and vertical groups called days of the week. Just as Monday always starts the school week, Saturday always starts the weekend. The calendar is useful because it organizes the days of the year. In the same way that days can be organized into a calendar, the elements can be organized into something like a calendar. As you'll discover in this section, the name of the "chemists' calendar" is the periodic table.

Looking for Patterns in the Elements

By 1830, 55 elements had been discovered. These elements displayed a wide variety of properties. A few were gases. Two were liquids. Most were metals. Some reacted explosively as they formed compounds. Others reacted more slowly. Still others did not form compounds at all.

GUIDE FOR READING

◆ How was the periodic table developed?

◆ What information does the periodic table present?

◆ How are valence electrons related to the periodic table?

Reading Tip As you read this section, refer to *Exploring the Periodic Table* on pages 84–85. Look for patterns.

Chapter 3 **81**

Figure 4 The shiny orange of this copper bowl will gradually turn to dull blue-green, like the tarnished copper sculpture. Mendeleev realized that several metals share with copper the property of tarnishing when exposed to air.
Classifying Is tarnishing a physical or chemical property?

Scientists of the 1800s suspected that the growing number of known elements could be organized in a useful way. (During this time, no one knew about atomic numbers.) One investigator found that some groups of elements, such as those in Figure 5, followed a pattern: The average of the atomic masses of the first and third elements roughly equaled the mass of the middle element. However, this system did not work for most elements.

By the 1860s, a Russian scientist had discovered a system that applied to all the elements. His name was Dimitri Mendeleev (men duh LAY ef). Like any good detective, Mendeleev studied the evidence, considered each clue, and looked for patterns.

Along with other scientists of his time, he observed that some elements have similar chemical and physical properties. Fluorine and chlorine, for example, are both gases that irritate your lungs if you breathe them. Silver and copper are both shiny metals that gradually tarnish if exposed to air. Mendeleev was convinced that these similarities were important clues to a hidden pattern.

To help him find that pattern, he wrote facts about the elements on individual cards. He noted all the properties he knew about an element, including its melting point, density, and color. He included two especially important properties: atomic mass and the number of chemical bonds an element could form. The **atomic mass** of an element is the average mass of one atom of the element. In Mendeleev's day, scientists figured out atomic masses in comparison to hydrogen, the lightest element. They found the number of bonds an element can form by studying the compound each element formed with oxygen.

The Periodic Table

Mendeleev liked to play Patience, a solitaire card game, so he had practice in seeing patterns. He tried arranging his cards on the elements in various ways. **Mendeleev noticed that patterns appeared when the elements were arranged in order of increasing atomic mass.**

Figure 5 In the 1800s, scientists tried different ways to organize the elements. They found that some groups of three elements displayed curious patterns.
Calculating When you average the atomic masses of calcium and barium, how closely does the result come to the atomic mass of strontium? Do the densities follow the same pattern?

Three Similar Elements				
Element	**Description**	**Chemical Properties**	**Atomic Mass**	**Density (gm/cm³)**
Calcium	silvery metal	Reacts readily with oxygen and water	40.1	1.55
Strontium	silvery metal	Reacts readily with oxygen and water	87.6	2.6
Barium	silvery metal	Reacts readily with oxygen and water	137	3.5

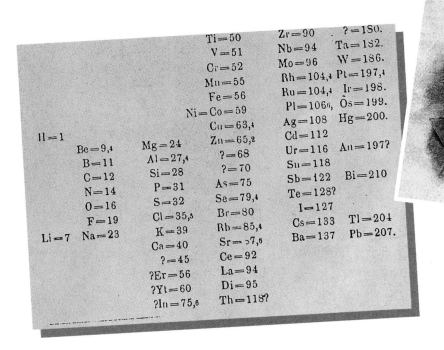

Ti=50   Zr=90   ?=180.
V=51   Nb=94   Ta=182.
Cr=52   Mo=96   W=186.
Mn=55   Rh=104,4 Pt=197,4
Fe=56   Ru=104,4 Ir=198.
Ni=Co=59 Pl=106,6 Os=199.
         Cu=63,4 Ag=108   Hg=200.
H=1   Cd=112
    Be=9,4 Mg=24 Zn=65,2 Ur=116 Au=197?
    B=11   Al=27,4 ?=68   Sn=118
    C=12   Si=28   ?=70   Sb=122 Bi=210
    N=14   P=31   As=75   Te=128?
    O=16   S=32   Se=79,4 I=127
    F=19   Cl=35,5 Br=80   Cs=133 Tl=204
Li=7 Na=23 K=39   Rb=85,4 Ba=137 Pb=207.
           Ca=40   Sr=87,6
           ?=45   Ce=92
           ?Er=56 La=94
           ?Yt=60 Di=95
           ?In=75,6 Th=118?

Figure 6 Mendeleev (above) published this first periodic table in 1869. He left question marks in some places. Based on the properties of surrounding elements, he predicted that new elements with specific characteristics would be discovered.

Mendeleev's Periodic Table Mendeleev discovered a repetition of properties. After fluorine, for instance, the next heaviest element he knew was sodium. (Neon had not yet been discovered.) Sodium (Na) bonded in the same way that lithium (Li) and potassium (K) did. So he placed the cards for these elements into a group. He did the same with other similar elements.

However, Mendeleev discovered that arranging the known elements strictly by increasing atomic mass did not always produce similar groups. So he moved his element cards into groups where they fit best. Doing this left three blank spaces. Mendeleev was confident enough of his discovery to predict that the blank spaces would be filled by elements that had not yet been discovered. He even predicted the properties of those new elements!

Mendeleev published the first periodic table, shown in Figure 6, in 1869. Within 16 years, chemists discovered the three missing elements, named scandium, gallium, and germanium. Their properties are close to what Mendeleev had predicted.

The Modern Periodic Table The word *periodic* means "a regular, repeated pattern." In the modern **periodic table,** the properties of the elements repeat in each period—or row—of the table. Since Mendeleev's time, new discoveries have required a few changes in the periodic table. The most important came in the early 1900s, when scientists learned about atomic number. Also, new elements were added as they were discovered. An up-to-date version of the table appears on the next two pages.

☑ *Checkpoint* What does "periodic" mean?

Classifying ACTIVITY

Choose any 10 elements and assign them letters *A* through *J*. On an index card for each element, write the letter for the element and list some of its properties. You may list properties that you learned in this chapter, or list properties presented in an encyclopedia or other reference source.

Exchange cards with a classmate. Can you identify each element? Which properties are the most helpful in identifying elements?

EXPLORING the Periodic Table

The periodic table has grown to include over 100 elements. Once you understand how the periodic table is organized, you can predict an element's properties from its position in the table.

C	Solid
Br	Liquid
H	Gas

Period
A row of the periodic table is called a period. Notice that the table becomes wider at periods 2, 4, and 6.

Symbol
One- or two-letter symbols identify most elements. Some periodic tables also list the names of the elements.

Atomic Mass
Atomic mass is the average mass of an element's atoms. Usually, atomic mass increases with atomic number.

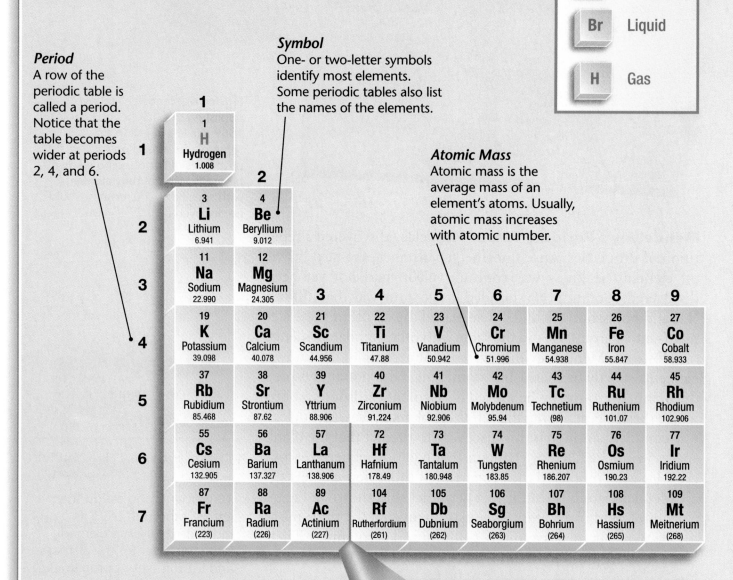

To make the table easier to read, elements 58–71 (the lanthanides) and elements 90–103 (the actinides) are printed below the rest of the table. Follow the blue line to see how they fit in the table.

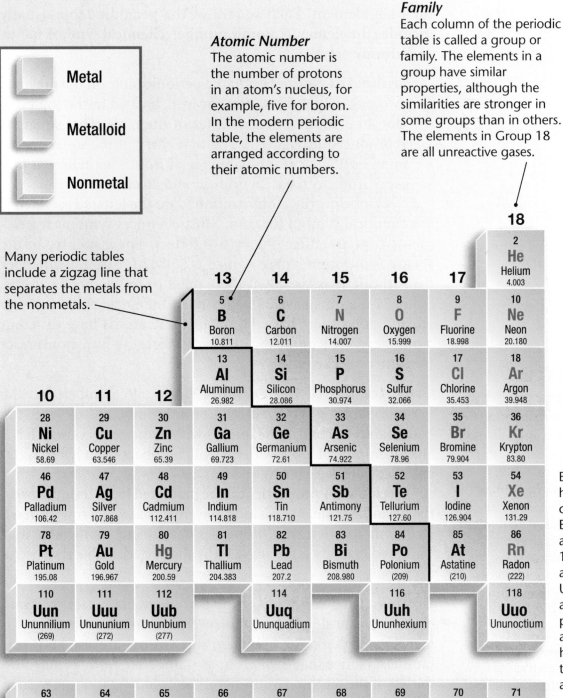

Metal

Metalloid

Nonmetal

Atomic Number
The atomic number is the number of protons in an atom's nucleus, for example, five for boron. In the modern periodic table, the elements are arranged according to their atomic numbers.

Family
Each column of the periodic table is called a group or family. The elements in a group have similar properties, although the similarities are stronger in some groups than in others. The elements in Group 18 are all unreactive gases.

Many periodic tables include a zigzag line that separates the metals from the nonmetals.

18
2 **He** Helium 4.003

13	14	15	16	17	
5 **B** Boron 10.811	6 **C** Carbon 12.011	7 **N** Nitrogen 14.007	8 **O** Oxygen 15.999	9 **F** Fluorine 18.998	10 **Ne** Neon 20.180
13 **Al** Aluminum 26.982	14 **Si** Silicon 28.086	15 **P** Phosphorus 30.974	16 **S** Sulfur 32.066	17 **Cl** Chlorine 35.453	18 **Ar** Argon 39.948

10	11	12						
28 **Ni** Nickel 58.69	29 **Cu** Copper 63.546	30 **Zn** Zinc 65.39	31 **Ga** Gallium 69.723	32 **Ge** Germanium 72.61	33 **As** Arsenic 74.922	34 **Se** Selenium 78.96	35 **Br** Bromine 79.904	36 **Kr** Krypton 83.80
46 **Pd** Palladium 106.42	47 **Ag** Silver 107.868	48 **Cd** Cadmium 112.411	49 **In** Indium 114.818	50 **Sn** Tin 118.710	51 **Sb** Antimony 121.75	52 **Te** Tellurium 127.60	53 **I** Iodine 126.904	54 **Xe** Xenon 131.29
78 **Pt** Platinum 195.08	79 **Au** Gold 196.967	80 **Hg** Mercury 200.59	81 **Tl** Thallium 204.383	82 **Pb** Lead 207.2	83 **Bi** Bismuth 208.980	84 **Po** Polonium (209)	85 **At** Astatine (210)	86 **Rn** Radon (222)
110 **Uun** Ununnilium (269)	111 **Uuu** Unununium (272)	112 **Uub** Ununbium (277)		114 **Uuq** Ununquadium		116 **Uuh** Ununhexium		118 **Uuo** Ununoctium

Elements 93 and higher have been created artificially. Elements with atomic numbers 114, 116, and 118 are the newest. Until chemists agree on permanent names, a few elements have Latin names that relate to their atomic numbers.

63 **Eu** Europium 151.965	64 **Gd** Gadolinium 157.25	65 **Tb** Terbium 158.925	66 **Dy** Dysprosium 162.50	67 **Ho** Holmium 164.930	68 **Er** Erbium 167.26	69 **Tm** Thulium 168.934	70 **Yb** Ytterbium 173.04	71 **Lu** Lutetium 174.967
95 **Am** Americium (243)	96 **Cm** Curium (247)	97 **Bk** Berkelium (247)	98 **Cf** Californium (251)	99 **Es** Einsteinium (252)	100 **Fm** Fermium (257)	101 **Md** Mendelevium (258)	102 **No** Nobelium (259)	103 **Lr** Lawrencium (262)

Reading the Periodic Table

The periodic table contains over 100 squares, one separate square for each element. **Each square of the periodic table usually includes the element's atomic number, chemical symbol, name, and atomic mass.**

Inside the Squares On the periodic table on the previous two pages, find the square for iron, located in the top position in column 8 in the center of the table. That square is reproduced in Figure 7. The first entry in the square is the number 26, the atomic number of iron. That tells you that every iron atom has 26 protons and 26 electrons.

Just below the atomic number are the letters Fe, which is the chemical symbol for iron. Most chemical symbols for elements contain either one or two letters. The last entry in the square is the atomic mass, which is 55.847 for iron. Remember that atomic mass is the average mass of an element's atoms. Some iron atoms have 29 neutrons in the nucleus, others have 30, and still others have 31. All of these atoms have different atomic masses. Despite the different masses, all iron atoms react the same way chemically.

Organization of the Periodic Table Remember that the periodic table is arranged by atomic number. Look over the entire table, starting at the top left with hydrogen (H), which has atomic number 1. Follow the atomic numbers from left to right, and read across each row.

An element's properties can be predicted from its location in the periodic table. As you look at elements across a row or down a column, the elements' properties change in a predictable way. This predictability is the reason why the periodic table is so useful to chemists.

Groups The main body of the periodic table is arranged into eighteen vertical columns and seven horizontal rows. The elements in a column are called a **group.** Groups are also known as **families.** Notice that each group is numbered, from Group 1 on the left of the table to Group 18 on the right. Typically, the group is given a family name based on the first element in the column. Group 14, for example, is the carbon family. Group 15 is the nitrogen family.

The elements in each group, or family, have similar characteristics. The elements in Group 1 are all metals that react violently with water. The metals in Group 11 all react with water slowly or not at all. Group 17 elements react violently with elements from Group 1, while Group 18 elements rarely react at all.

Figure 7 Four important facts about an element are supplied in each square of the periodic table.

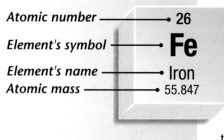

Atomic number — 26
Element's symbol — Fe
Element's name — Iron
Atomic mass — 55.847

Language Arts
CONNECTION

You are learning science in the English language. But in other centuries, the language of science was Greek or Latin or even Arabic. This is why the names and chemical symbols of many elements don't match modern names. For example, the symbol for iron (Fe) comes from the Latin *ferrum.*

In Your Journal

List some of the elements that have puzzling chemical symbols, such as sodium (Na), potassium (K), tin (Sn), gold (Au), silver (Ag), lead (Pb), and mercury (Hg). Look up these names and symbols in the dictionary to learn the original names of these elements.

Periods Each horizontal row across the table is called a **period.** A period contains a series of different types of elements from different families, just as a week on a calendar has a series of different days. Unlike the elements in a family, the elements in a period have very different properties. In fact, as you move across a period from left to right, those properties not only change, they change according to a pattern.

In the fourth period, for example, the elements change from very reactive metals, such as potassium (K) and calcium (Ca), to relatively unreactive metals, such as nickel (Ni) and copper (Cu), to metalloids and nonmetals, such as arsenic (As) and bromine (Br). The last element in a period is always a particularly inactive gas. In this period, that element is krypton (Kr). Krypton bears no relationship to the fictional substance Kryptonite, which is the only thing feared by Superman!

As you can see, there are seven periods of elements. Periods have different numbers of elements. Period 1 has only two elements, hydrogen (H) and helium (He). You can count that Periods 2 and 3 each have 8 elements. Periods 4 and 5 each have 18 elements.

You will also notice that some elements of Period 6 and some elements of Period 7 have been separated out of the table. These elements are part of the periodic table, even though they appear as rows below its main section. The elements are shown separately to keep the table from becoming too wide. Imagine what it would look like if Periods 6 and 7 were stretched out to show all 32 elements in a row.

✓ *Checkpoint* *What is the name for a column of elements in the periodic table?*

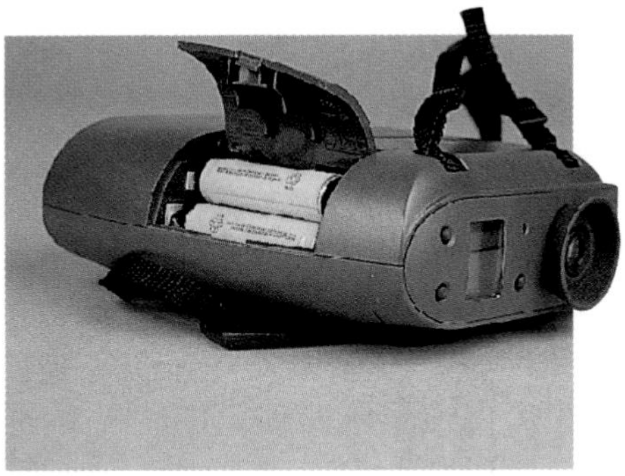

Figure 8 You can find the names of elements in the names of some common products, such as the ni-cad batteries in this camera. *Inferring What is one of the metals you would expect to find in a ni-cad battery?*

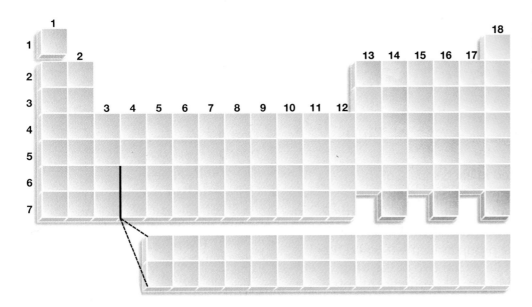

Figure 9 The columns in the periodic table are called groups or families. The rows are called periods.

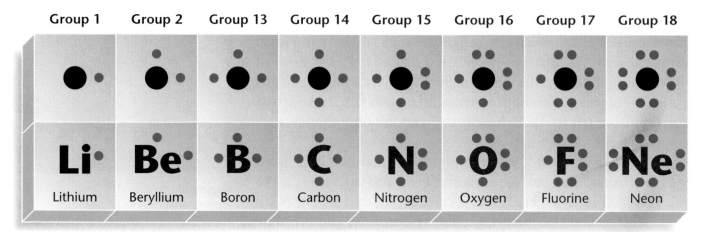

Group 1	Group 2	Group 13	Group 14	Group 15	Group 16	Group 17	Group 18
Li	Be	B	C	N	O	F	Ne
Lithium	Beryllium	Boron	Carbon	Nitrogen	Oxygen	Fluorine	Neon

Figure 10 In a row of eight elements, the number of valence electrons follows the pattern shown in the first row of this diagram. The circle represents the inner part of the atom. *Predicting The atomic number of neon is 10. The atomic number of sodium (Na) is 11. What will the electron dot diagram of sodium look like?*

Why the Periodic Table Works

Although Mendeleev successfully used the periodic table to predict new discoveries, he could not explain why the table works. **The periodic table works because it's based on the structure of atoms, especially the valence electrons.** Look at the electron dot diagrams in Figure 10 to see why.

Think of how atoms change from left to right across a period. You know that from one element to the next, the atomic number increases by one. That means that an element has one more valence electron than the element to its left. And since the first element in a period has one valence electron, the number of valence electrons in a row of eight increases from one to eight. As a result, the properties across a period change in a regular way.

By contrast, the elements in a family all have the same number of valence electrons. The elements in Group 1 have one valence electron. The elements in Group 2 have two. The elements in Group 17 have seven valence electrons, and Group 18 elements have eight. Because the valence electrons within a family are the same, the elements in that group have similar properties.

 Section 2 Review

1. How did Mendeleev organize the elements into the periodic table?
2. What information is listed in each square of the periodic table?
3. Why do elements in a group have similar properties?
4. **Thinking Critically Comparing and Contrasting** Element A is in the same group as element B and the same period as element C. Which two of the three elements are likely to have similar properties? Explain your answer.

Check Your Progress ···CHAPTER PROJECT···
Find the squares in the periodic table for each metal that you have been assigned. Prepare a chart in which to record the chemical symbol, group number, atomic number, and atomic mass of the metals, as well as their characteristic properties. Record data from the periodic table in your chart.

3 Metals

Why Use Aluminum?

1. Examine several objects made from aluminum, including a can, a disposable pie plate, heavy-duty aluminum foil, foil wrapping paper, and aluminum wire.

2. Compare the shape, thickness, and general appearance of the objects.

3. Observe what happens if you try to bend and unbend each object.

4. For what purpose is each object used?

Think It Over

Inferring Use your observations to list as many properties of aluminum as you can. Based on your list of properties, infer why aluminum was used to make each object. Which objects do you think could be made from other metals? Explain your answer.

M etals are all around you. The cars and buses you ride in are made of steel, which is mostly iron. Airplanes are made of aluminum. Many coins are combinations of zinc with copper, nickel, or silver. Copper wires carry electricity into table lamps, stereos, and computers. It's hard to imagine life without metals.

What Is a Metal?

Look at the periodic table, either in Section 2 or in Appendix D. Most of the elements are metals, found to the left of the zigzag line in the periodic table. The other elements are classified as nonmetals and metalloids. You'll learn more about nonmetals and metalloids in the next section.

Physical Properties What is a metal? Take a moment to describe a familiar metal, such as iron, tin, gold, or silver. What words did you use—hard, shiny, smooth? **Chemists classify an element as a metal based on physical properties such as hardness, shininess, malleability, and ductility.** Polished silver (Ag) is a good example of shininess. A **malleable** material is one that can be pounded into shapes. A **ductile** material is one that can be pulled out, or drawn, into a long wire. Copper sheeting and copper wires can be made because of copper's malleability and ductility.

GUIDE FOR READING

◆ What are the properties of metals?

◆ How can you characterize each family of metals?

Reading Tip As you read, list the name of a new metal or group of metals and record its location on the periodic table.

Robot handling metal heart valves ▶

Figure 11 Because it is shiny and slow to react, chromium is ideal for car bumpers. Other metals are magnetic, like the iron in these paper clips.

Most metals are called good **conductors** because they transmit heat and electricity easily. Several metals are attracted to magnets and can be made into magnets. Thus, iron (Fe), cobalt (Co), and nickel (Ni) are described as **magnetic.**

Most metals are solids at room temperatures. This is because most metals have the property of very high melting points. In fact, you would need to raise the temperature of some metals as high as 3,400°C to melt them. An exception is mercury (Hg), which is a liquid at room temperature.

Chemical Properties **Metals show a wide range of chemical properties.** Some metals are very reactive. They combine with other elements and compounds quickly, giving off energy. For example, sodium (Na) and potassium (K) will react explosively if exposed to air or water. To prevent reactions, they must be stored under oil in sealed containers.

By comparison, gold (Au) and chromium (Cr) are unreactive. Gold is valued because it is rare and also because it stays shiny instead of reacting with air. Chromium is plated on objects left outdoors, such as automobile trim, because it is extremely slow to react with air and water.

Other metals fall somewhere between sodium and gold in the ease and speed of their reactions. They react slowly with oxygen in the air, forming metal oxides. For example, if iron is left unprotected, its surface will slowly turn to reddish-brown rust. A metal can actually wear away as the soft metal oxide flakes off. This process of reaction and wearing away is called **corrosion.**

Figure 12 When water is dripped onto sodium metal, the reaction is explosive.

☑ *Checkpoint* *How do reactive metals behave?*

Alloys

As you learned in Chapter 1, a mixture consists of two or more substances mixed together but not chemically changed. Do metals form useful mixtures? Think about the steel in an automobile, the brass in a trumpet, and the bronze in a statue. Each of these materials is made of different metals mixed together.

A mixture of metals is called an alloy. Useful alloys combine the best properties of two or more metals into a single substance. For example, copper is a fairly soft and malleable metal. But mixed with tin, it forms bronze, which can be cast into statues that last hundreds of years. Brass is an alloy of copper and zinc. Pure iron rusts very easily, but when mixed with carbon, chromium, and vanadium, iron forms stainless steel. Knives and forks made of stainless steel can be washed over and over again without rusting.

Metals in the Periodic Table

The metals in a group, or family, have similar properties, and these family properties change gradually as you move across the table. Metals tend to become less reactive as you move from left to right across the periodic table.

Alkali Metals The metals in Group 1, from lithium to francium, are called the **alkali metals.** They are the most reactive metals of all. They are never found uncombined in nature. In other words, they are never found as elements but only in compounds. In the laboratory, however, scientists have been able to isolate the uncombined forms. As elements, the alkali metals are very soft and shiny. They are so soft, in fact, that you could cut them with a plastic knife!

Why are the alkali metals so reactive? Think of their location on the far left of the periodic table. Elements of Group 1 have atoms with one valence electron that is easily transferred to other atoms during a chemical change. When that valence electron is gone, the part of the atom that remains is much more stable.

The two most important alkali metals are sodium and potassium. Sodium compounds are found in large amounts in sea water and salt beds. Your diet includes many compounds that contain sodium and potassium, both of which are essential for life. Lithium compounds are used in batteries and certain drugs.

Figure 13 The bronze of this statue is an alloy of copper and tin. *Classifying Is an alloy an element, compound, or mixture?*

Sharpen your Skills

Observing **ACTIVITY**

1. Find a penny from 1983 or later. Rub one edge on sandpaper to scrape away the copper. Place the penny in a foam cup. Add vinegar to a depth of 1–2 cm.

2. Wait 24 hours. Then describe any changes. What property of metals have you demonstrated?

1	2
3 **Li** Lithium 6.941	4 **Be** Beryllium 9.012
11 **Na** Sodium 22.990	12 **Mg** Magnesium 24.305
19 **K** Potassium 39.098	20 **Ca** Calcium 40.078
37 **Rb** Rubidium 85.468	38 **Sr** Strontium 87.62
55 **Cs** Cesium 132.905	56 **Ba** Barium 137.327
87 **Fr** Francium (223)	88 **Ra** Radium (226)

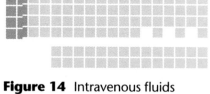

Figure 14 Intravenous fluids (above center) must provide elements, such as potassium and sodium, that are important to living cells. Calcium is part of the compound that makes up the limestone of these cliffs (above right). *Interpreting Diagrams To which families do the metals potassium, sodium, and calcium belong?*

Alkaline Earth Metals Group 2 of the periodic table contains the **alkaline earth metals.** While not as reactive as the metals in Group 1, these elements are more reactive than most metals. They are never found uncombined in nature. Each is fairly hard, gray white, and a good conductor of electricity.

The two most common alkaline earth metals are magnesium and calcium. Magnesium was once used in flash bulbs because it gives off a very bright light when it burns. Magnesium also combines with aluminum, making a strong but lightweight alloy. This alloy is used to make ladders, airplane parts, and other products. Calcium is an essential part of teeth and bones, and it also helps muscles work properly. You get calcium from milk and other dairy products, as well as green, leafy vegetables.

Each atom of an alkaline earth metal has two valence electrons. Like the alkali metals, the alkaline earth metals easily lose their valence electrons in chemical reactions. Each alkaline earth metal is almost as reactive as its neighbor to the left in the periodic table.

Transition Metals The elements in Groups 3 through 12 are called the **transition metals.** The transition metals form a bridge between the very reactive metals on the left side of the periodic table and the less reactive metals and other elements on the right side. The transition metals are so similar to one another that differences between nearby columns are often difficult to detect.

The transition metals include most of the familiar metals, such as iron, copper, nickel, silver, and gold. Most of the transition metals are hard and shiny. Gold, copper, and some other transition metals have unusual colors. All of the transition metals are good conductors of electricity.

The transition metals are fairly stable, reacting slowly or not at all with air and water. Ancient gold coins and jewelry are as beautiful and detailed today as they were thousands of years ago. Even when iron reacts with air and water, forming rust, it sometimes takes many years to react completely, not at all like the violent reactions of the alkali metals.

INTEGRATING LIFE SCIENCE Would you believe that you use transition metals inside your body? In fact, you would not survive very long without one of the transition metals— iron. Iron is an important part of a large molecule called hemoglobin, which carries oxygen in your bloodstream. Hemoglobin also gives blood its bright red color.

Metals in Mixed Groups Groups 13 through 16 of the periodic table include metals, nonmetals, and metalloids. The metals in these groups to the right of the transition metals are not nearly as reactive as those on the left side of the table. The most familiar of these metals are aluminum, tin, and lead. Aluminum is the lightweight metal used in beverage cans and airplane bodies. A thin layer of tin is used to coat steel to protect it from corrosion in cans of food. Lead is a shiny, blue-white metal that was once used in paints and water pipes. But lead is poisonous, so it is no longer used for these purposes. Now its most common use is in automobile batteries.

☑ *Checkpoint* **Which groups are considered transition metals?**

Figure 15 Transition metals are used to make colorful paints, including cobalt blue, zinc white, cadmium red, and chromium oxide green.

3	4	5	6	7	8	9	10	11	12
21 **Sc** Scandium 44.956	22 **Ti** Titanium 47.88	23 **V** Vanadium 50.942	24 **Cr** Chromium 51.996	25 **Mn** Manganese 54.938	26 **Fe** Iron 55.847	27 **Co** Cobalt 58.933	28 **Ni** Nickel 58.69	29 **Cu** Copper 63.546	30 **Zn** Zinc 65.39
39 **Y** Yttrium 88.906	40 **Zr** Zirconium 91.224	41 **Nb** Niobium 92.906	42 **Mo** Molybdenum 95.94	43 **Tc** Technetium (98)	44 **Ru** Ruthenium 101.07	45 **Rh** Rhodium 102.906	46 **Pd** Palladium 106.42	47 **Ag** Silver 107.868	48 **Cd** Cadmium 112.411
57 **La** Lanthanum 138.906	72 **Hf** Hafnium 178.49	73 **Ta** Tantalum 180.948	74 **W** Tungsten 183.85	75 **Re** Rhenium 186.207	76 **Os** Osmium 190.23	77 **Ir** Iridium 192.22	78 **Pt** Platinum 195.08	79 **Au** Gold 196.967	80 **Hg** Mercury 200.59
89 **Ac** Actinium (227)	104 **Rf** Rutherfordium (261)	105 **Db** Dubnium (262)	106 **Sg** Seaborgium (263)	107 **Bh** Bohrium (262)	108 **Hs** Hassium (265)	109 **Mt** Meitnerium (266)	110 **Uun** Ununnilium (269)	111 **Uuu** Unununium (272)	112 **Uub** Ununbium (272)

58	59	60	61	62	63	64	65	66	67	68	69	70	71
Ce	Pr	Nd	Pm	Sm	Eu	Gd	Tb	Dy	Ho	Er	Tm	Yb	Lu

90	91	92	93	94	95	96	97	98	99	100	101	102	103
Th	Pa	U	Np	Pu	Am	Cm	Bk	Cf	Es	Fm	Md	No	Lr

Figure 16 The actinide metal named americium is used in smoke detectors like this one. *Interpreting Diagrams What is the atomic number of americium?*

Lanthanides and Actinides At the bottom of the periodic table are the **lanthanides** (LAN thuh nydz), in the top row, and **actinides** (AK tuh nydz), on the bottom. These elements, called the rare earth elements, fit in Periods 6 and 7 between the alkaline earth metals and the transition metals. They are placed below the periodic table for convenience.

Lanthanides are soft, malleable, shiny metals with high conductivity. They are used in industry to make various alloys. Different lanthanides are usually found together in nature. They are difficult to separate from one another because all of them have very similar properties.

Of the actinides, only thorium (Th) and uranium (U) exist on Earth in any significant amounts. You may already have heard of uranium, which is used to produce energy in nuclear power plants. All of the elements after uranium in the periodic table were created artifically in laboratories. The nuclei of these elements are unstable, meaning that they break apart into smaller nuclei. In fact, many of these synthetic elements are so unstable that they last for only a fraction of a second after they are made.

Section 3 Review

1. List four properties of most metals.
2. Compare the way the metals on the left side of the periodic table react to the way metals on the right side of the periodic table react.
3. If you point to an element in the periodic table at random, is it more likely to be a metal, a nonmetal, or a metalloid? Explain your answer.
4. **Thinking Critically** **Predicting** Element 119 has not yet been made or discovered. If this element existed, however, where would it be placed in the periodic table? (*Hint:* Start at the square for element 112.) Would you expect it to be a metal, a nonmetal, or a metalloid? What properties would you predict for this element? Explain your answer.

Check Your Progress
Observe your samples for properties such as shininess, hardness, and color. Record these observations in your chart. Plan how to test other properties of metals such as electrical and heat conductivity, density, and reactions with acids and oxygen. Remember that you need to compare the properties of your metal samples. Have your teacher approve your experimental plan.

CHAPTER PROJECT

SCIENCE AND SOCIETY

Cleaning Up Metal Contamination

Metals are an important resource. For example, mercury is used in thermometers, medicines, and electrical equipment. Cadmium and lead are used to make batteries, and lead was used to make paints. However, these metals are poisonous, or toxic, to humans who are exposed to them over a long period of time.

Years of manufacturing have left factory buildings and the surrounding soil contaminated with toxic metals. Until 1980, no one was required to clean up property contaminated with toxic metals. Then the federal government passed the Superfund law, which made landowners or previous users of properties responsible for toxic cleanups.

The Issues

Should People Clean Up and Build on Contaminated Land? About 450,000 factories, mines, and dumps in the United States have been closed because of contamination with toxic metals. One cleanup method is to scrape off the contaminated layer of soil and take it to a landfill specially constructed for hazardous wastes. Another common method is to cover the contaminated land with a thick layer of clean soil or a substance that water can't penetrate. The idea is to stop the spread of contamination.

Health experts say the worst sites should be cleaned up to keep people from being exposed to toxic metals. Or at least, sites need to be fenced off. They do not want the sites used again.

Builders, on the other hand, want to clean up the land and build new factories, offices, and houses on it. Some public officials also favor building on the land because construction provides jobs.

How Much Cleanup Is Necessary? Some people only want to clean up sites where people live. They say that contact with toxic metals in

homes is more dangerous than contact in workplaces since people spend more time at home than at work. These people favor complete cleanup of building sites for homes but less complete cleanup of factory and office sites. Limiting the amount of cleanup also reduces the cost.

Other people favor a complete cleanup of all contaminated sites. Toxic metals in the soil of industrial sites could spread to nearby homes or seep into groundwater. People also might build their homes near contaminated sites in the future.

Who Is Responsible for Cleanups? Taking down contaminated buildings, removing soil, and covering sites is expensive. And, determining who is responsible for long-abandoned sites is complicated. The Superfund law, other federal laws, and laws of the individual states differ as to whether current owners or past users are responsible. For some sites, federal or state money may be required to pay for cleanups.

You Decide

1. Identify the Problem
In your own words, explain the problem of sites contaminated with toxic metals.

2. Analyze the Options
How could people benefit by building on contaminated lands? How might people be hurt?

3. Find a Solution
Suppose you are a builder, a factory worker, a landowner, or someone living next to a contaminated site. State and defend your opinion on building on that site.

Testing 1, 2, 3

What materials make the best plumbing pipes? Or the best electrical wiring? Or the best lead for a pencil? A materials scientist answers questions such as these. Materials scientists work to find the best materials for different products. To understand materials, you need to know their basic properties. In this lab, you will be comparing the properties of a copper wire and a sample of graphite. Graphite is a form of the element carbon.

Problem

How does copper compare to graphite?

Skills Focus

observing, interpreting data, classifying

Materials

1.5-V dry cell	hot plate
200-mL beaker	water
stopwatch	

flashlight bulb and socket
3 lengths of insulated wire
thin copper wire with no insulation, about 5–6 cm long
2 graphite samples (lead from a mechanical pencil), each about 5–6 cm long

Procedure

1. Fill a 200-mL beaker about three-fourths full with water. Heat it slowly on a hot plate. Let the water continue to heat as you complete Part 1 and Part 2 of the investigation.

Part 1 Physical Properties

2. Compare the shininess and color of your two samples. Record your observations.
3. Bend the copper wire as far as possible. Next, bend one of the graphite samples as far as possible. Record the results of each test.

Part 2 Electrical Conductivity

4. Place a bulb into a lamp socket. Use a piece of insulated wire to connect one pole of a dry cell battery to the socket, as shown in the photo below.
5. Attach the end of a second piece of insulated wire to the other pole of the dry cell battery. Leave the other end of this wire free.
6. Attach the end of a third piece of insulated wire to the other pole of the lamp socket. Leave the other end of this wire free.

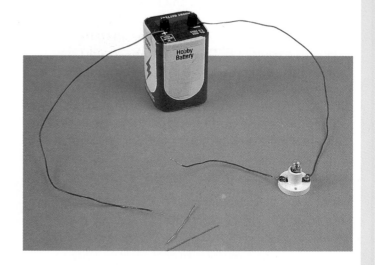

7. Touch the free ends of the insulated wire to the ends of the copper wire. Record your observations of the bulb.
8. Repeat Step 7 using a graphite sample instead of the copper wire.

Part 3 Heat Conductivity

9. Turn off the hot plate.
10. Hold one end of a graphite sample between the fingertips of one hand. Hold one end of the copper wire between the fingertips of the other hand.
11. Dip both the graphite and copper wire into the hot water at the same time. Allow only about 1 cm of each piece to reach under the water's surface. From your fingertips to the water, the lengths of both the graphite sample and the copper wire should be approximately equal.
12. Time how long it takes to feel the heat in the fingertips of each hand. Record your observations.

Analyze and Conclude

1. Compare the physical properties of copper and graphite that you observed.
2. Describe the results of the electrical conductivity and heat conductivity tests that you performed.

3. Based on the observations you made in this lab, explain why copper is classified as a metal and carbon is not classified as a metal.
4. In Step 11, why was it important to use equal lengths of copper wire and graphite?
5. **Apply** Based on your observations and conclusions from this lab, for what products might copper and graphite be best suited?

Design an Experiment

The density of metals is generally greater than the density of nonmetals. Design a procedure that would compare the density of copper and graphite. With your teacher's approval, conduct your investigation.

SECTION 4 Nonmetals and Metalloids

DISCOVER ···ACTIVITY···

What Are the Properties of Charcoal?

1. Break off a piece of charcoal and roll it between your fingers. Record your observations.

2. Rub the charcoal on a piece of paper. Describe what happens.

3. Strike the charcoal sharply with the blunt end of a butter knife or fork. Describe what happens.

4. When you are finished with your investigation, return the charcoal to your teacher and wash your hands.

Think It Over

Classifying Charcoal is a form of the element carbon. Would you classify carbon as a metal or a nonmetal? Use your observations from this activity to explain your answer.

GUIDE FOR READING

◆ Where are nonmetals and metalloids located on the periodic table?

◆ What are the properties of nonmetals and metalloids?

Reading Tip As you read about each family of nonmetals, make a list of their properties.

Think of ten objects that do not contain metal. Some of the objects might be soft and smooth, such as an animal's fur, a blade of grass, or a silk shirt. But you may have thought of objects that are much harder, such as the bark or wood of a tree or the plastic case of a computer. You might also have thought of liquids, such as water and gasoline, or gases, such as the nitrogen and oxygen gases that make up the atmosphere.

Your world is full of materials that contain little or no metal. What's more, these materials have a wide variety of properties, ranging from soft to hard, from flexible to breakable, and from solid to gaseous. To understand these properties, you need to study another important category of the elements: the nonmetals.

What Is a Nonmetal?

Nonmetals are the elements that lack most of the properties of metals. **There are 17 nonmetals, each located to the right of the zigzag line in the periodic table.** As you will discover, many of the nonmetals are very common elements, as well as extremely important to all living things on Earth.

Figure 17 Living organisms, like this raccoon and these reeds, are made up mostly of nonmetals, such as the elements carbon, hydrogen, oxygen, and nitrogen.

Physical Properties Many of the nonmetal elements are gases at room temperature, which means they have low boiling points. The air you breathe is made mostly of two nonmetals, nitrogen (N) and oxygen (O). Other nonmetal elements, such as carbon (C) and iodine (I), are solids at room temperature. Bromine (Br) is the only nonmetal that is liquid at room temperature.

In general, the physical properties of nonmetals are opposite to those that characterize the metals. Most nonmetals are dull, unlike shiny metals. Solid nonmetals are brittle, meaning they are not malleable and not ductile. If you pound on most solid nonmetals with a hammer, they break easily or crumble into a powder. Nonmetals usually have lower densities than metals. Nonmetals are also poor conductors of heat and electricity.

Figure 18 Nonmetal solids, such as this sulfur, tend to be crumbly when hit with a hammer. *Comparing and Contrasting What would you expect to happen if you hammered a metal such as copper or gold?*

Chemical Properties Most nonmetals readily form compounds. But the Group 18 elements hardly ever do. The difference has to do with valence electrons. Atoms of the Group 18 elements do not gain, lose, or share electrons. For this reason, the Group 18 elements do not react with other elements.

The rest of the nonmetals have atoms that can gain or share electrons. In either case, the atoms of these nonmetals can react with other atoms, leading to the formation of compounds.

Compounds of Nonmetals When nonmetals and metals react, valence electrons move from the metal atoms to the nonmetal atoms. Group 17 elements react easily this way. For example, common table salt (NaCl) is formed from sodium (Na) and chlorine (Cl). Other groups of nonmetals form compounds with metals, too. Rust is a compound made of iron and oxygen (Fe_2O_3). It's the reddish, flaky coating you might see on an old piece of steel or an iron nail.

Nonmetals can also form compounds with other nonmetals. The atoms share electrons and become bonded together into molecules, such as carbon monoxide (CO) and carbon dioxide (CO_2). When the molecules contain only two atoms, they are called **diatomic molecules.** Some nonmetal elements also form diatomic molecules. These elements include oxygen (O_2), nitrogen (N_2), and hydrogen (H_2).

Figure 19 When a metal, such as sodium, reacts with a nonmetal, such as chlorine, a valence electron is transferred from each sodium atom to a chlorine atom. When two identical atoms of a nonmetal react, they share electrons.

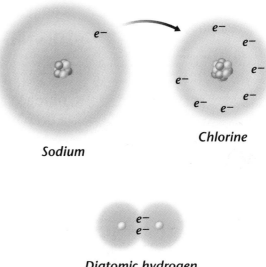

Sodium

Chlorine

Diatomic hydrogen

☑ *Checkpoint* *In which portion of the periodic table do you find nonmetals?*

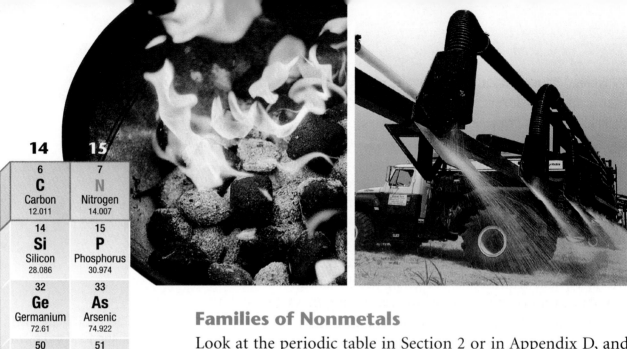

14	15
6 **C** Carbon 12.011	7 **N** Nitrogen 14.007
14 **Si** Silicon 28.086	15 **P** Phosphorus 30.974
32 **Ge** Germanium 72.61	33 **As** Arsenic 74.922
50 **Sn** Tin 118.710	51 **Sb** Antimony 121.75
82 **Pb** Lead 207.2	83 **Bi** Bismuth 208.980

Figure 20 Charcoal (above center) is composed mostly of the element carbon. Farmers provide their growing plants with fertilizers (above right) that include the element nitrogen. *Applying Concepts Which has the greater mass, an atom of carbon or an atom of nitrogen? How can you tell?*

Families of Nonmetals

Look at the periodic table in Section 2 or in Appendix D, and notice the groups that contain nonmetals. Only Group 18 contains nonmetals exclusively. Other groups, such as Groups 14 and 15, contain three classes of elements: nonmetals, metals, and a third class of elements called metalloids. For this reason, the elements in Groups 14 and 15 are not as similar to one another as are elements in other groups.

The Carbon Family Group 14 is also known as the carbon family. Each element in the carbon family has atoms with 4 valence electrons. Only one of the elements is a nonmetal, and that element is carbon itself. (The next two elements, silicon and germanium, are metalloids. Tin and lead are metals.)

What makes carbon especially important is its role in the chemistry of life. All living things contain compounds that are made of long chains of carbon atoms. Scientists have identified millions of these compounds, some of which have more than a billion atoms. You will learn much more about carbon and its compounds in the next chapter.

The Nitrogen Family Group 15, the nitrogen family, contains

INTEGRATING LIFE SCIENCE elements that have 5 valence electrons in their atoms. The two nonmetals in the family are nitrogen and phosphorus. To introduce yourself to nitrogen, take a deep breath. The atmosphere is almost 80 percent nitrogen gas. Nitrogen (N_2) gas does not readily react with other elements, however, so you breathe out as much nitrogen as you breathe in.

Living things do use nitrogen, but most living things are unable to use the nitrogen gas in the air. Only certain kinds of bacteria—tiny, microscopic creatures—are able to combine the nitrogen in the air with other elements, a process called nitrogen fixation. Plants can then take up the nitrogen compounds formed in the soil by the bacteria. Farmers also add nitrogen compounds to the soil in the form of fertilizers. Like all animals, you get the nitrogen you need from the food you eat—from plants, or from animals that ate plants.

Phosphorus is the other nonmetal in the nitrogen family. Unlike nitrogen, phosphorus is not stable as an element. So, phosphorus in nature is always found in compounds. Phosphorus is used to make matches and flares partly because it is so reactive.

☑ *Checkpoint* **Which elements are in Group 15?**

The Oxygen Family Group 16, the oxygen family, contains elements that have 6 valence electrons in their atoms. An atom in Group 16 typically gains or shares 2 electrons when it reacts. The three nonmetals in the oxygen family are oxygen, sulfur, and a rarer element named selenium.

You are using oxygen right now. With every breath, oxygen travels through your lungs and into your bloodstream, which distributes it all over your body. You could not live long without a steady supply of oxygen. The oxygen you breathe is a diatomic molecule (O_2). In addition, oxygen sometimes forms a triatomic (three-atom) molecule, which is called ozone (O_3). Ozone collects in a layer in the upper atmosphere, where it screens out harmful radiation from the sun.

Oxygen is very reactive, and can combine with almost every other element. It also is the most abundant element in Earth's crust and the second most abundant element in the atmosphere.

Sulfur is the other common nonmetal in the oxygen family. If you have ever smelled the odor of a rotten egg, then you are already familiar with the smell of many sulfur compounds. These compounds have a strong, unpleasant odor. You can also find sulfur in rubber bands, automobile tires, and many medicines.

Show Me the Oxygen

How can you test for the presence of oxygen? **ACTIVITY**

1. 🔥🥽 Pour about a 3-cm depth of hydrogen peroxide (H_2O_2) into a test tube.

2. Add a pea-sized amount of manganese dioxide (MnO_2) to the test tube.

3. Observe the test tube for about 1 minute.

4. 🔥 When instructed by your teacher, set a wooden splint on fire.

5. Blow the splint out after 5 seconds and immediately plunge the glowing splint into the mouth of the test tube. Avoid getting the splint wet.

Observing Describe the change in matter that occured in the test tube. What evidence indicates that oxygen was produced?

16

8
O
Oxygen
15.999

16
S
Sulfur
32.066

34
Se
Selenium
78.96

52
Te
Tellurium
127.60

84
Po
Polonium
(209)

Figure 21 The making of modern rubber depends on the element sulfur. *Interpreting Diagrams Which element is above sulfur in the periodic table?*

The Halogen Family Group 17 contains fluorine, chlorine, bromine, iodine, and astatine. It is also known as the **halogen family.** All but one of the halogens are nonmetals, and all share similar properties. A halogen atom has 7 valence electrons and typically gains or shares one electron when it reacts.

All of the halogens are very reactive, and most of them are dangerous to humans. But many of the compounds that halogens form are also quite useful. Fluorine, the most reactive of all the nonmetals, is found in nonstick cookware and compounds that help prevent tooth decay. Chlorine is already familiar to you in one form—ordinary table salt is a compound of sodium and chlorine. Other salts of chlorine include calcium chloride, which is used to help melt snow. Bromine reacts with silver to form silver bromide, which is used in photographic film.

The Noble Gases The elements in Group 18 are known as the **noble gases.** In some cultures, "noble" individuals held a high rank and did not work or mix with "ordinary" people. The noble gases do not ordinarily form compounds with other elements. This is because atoms of noble gases do not gain, lose, or share their valence electrons. As a result, the noble gases are chemically very stable and unreactive.

All the noble gases exist in Earth's atmosphere, but only in small amounts. Because of the stability and relative scarcity of the noble gases, most were not discovered until the late 1800s. Helium was discovered by a scientist who was studying, not the atmosphere, but the sun.

Have you ever come in contact with a noble gas? You have if you have purchased a balloon filled with helium. Noble gases are also used in glowing electric lights. These lights are commonly called neon lights, even though they are often filled with argon, xenon, or other noble gases.

Hydrogen Alone in the upper left corner of the periodic table is hydrogen. Hydrogen is the simplest element—usually each of its atoms contains only one proton and one electron. Because the chemical properties of hydrogen differ very much from those of the other elements, it really cannot be grouped into a family.

Figure 22 The halogen fluorine is found in the nonstick surface of this cookware. Fluorine is a very reactive element, unlike the noble gas neon in these brightly lit signs. *Relating Cause and Effect What makes the element neon so stable?*

Figure 23 The tiny atoms of the element hydrogen are very reactive.

Although hydrogen makes up more than 90 percent of the atoms in the universe, it makes up only 1.0 percent of the mass of Earth's crust, oceans, and atmosphere. Hydrogen is rarely found on Earth as an element. Most of it is combined with oxygen in water. When an electric current is passed through water, bonds are broken and diatomic hydrogen (H_2) gas molecules are formed.

✓ *Checkpoint* *Which elements are called halogens?*

The Metalloids

On the border between the metals and the nonmetals are seven elements called metalloids. The **metalloids** have some of the characteristics of metals and some of the characteristics of non-metals. The most common metalloid is silicon (Si). Silicon combines with oxygen to form a number of familiar substances, including sand, glass, and cement. You also may have encountered boron, which is used in some cleaning solutions. You would not want to encounter arsenic, which is a poison.

 INTEGRATING PHYSICS **The most useful property of the metalloids is their varying ability to conduct electricity.** Whether or not a metalloid conducts electricity can depend on temperature, exposure to light, or the presence of small amounts of impurities. For this reason, metalloids such as silicon and germanium (Ge) are used to make semiconductors. **Semiconductors** are substances that under some conditions can carry electricity, like a metal, while under other conditions cannot carry electricity, like a nonmetal. Semiconductors are used to make computer chips, transistors, and lasers.

Figure 24 As this close up view shows, a silicon computer chip is so small it can fit through the eye of a needle.

Section 4 Review

1. Which elements in the periodic table are nonmetals and which are metalloids?
2. What properties identify nonmetals?
3. How do the noble gases differ from the other elements?
4. Describe an important use of metalloids.
5. **Thinking Critically Interpreting Diagrams** Find the following elements in the periodic table: iodine, xenon, selenium. What properties of these elements are indicated by their positions in the periodic table?

Science at Home

Halogens in the Home Make a survey of compounds in your home that contain halogens. Look at labels on foods, cooking ingredients, cleaning material, medicines, cosmetics, and pesticides. The presence of a halogen is often indicated by the prefixes *fluoro-, chloro-, bromo-, and iodo-.* Show your family examples of substances in your home that contain halogens and describe the properties of the halogen family. ☠

ALIEN PERIODIC TABLE

Imagine that scientists have made radio contact with life on a distant planet. The planet is composed of many of the same elements as are found on Earth. But the inhabitants of the planet have different names and symbols for the elements. The radio transmission gave data on the known chemical and physical properties of 30 elements that belong to Groups 1, 2, 13, 14, 15, 16, 17, and 18. You need to place the elements into a blank periodic table based on these properties.

Problem

Where do the alien elements fit in the periodic table?

Materials

ruler
periodic table from text for reference

Procedure

1. Copy the blank periodic table below into your notebook.
2. Listed below are data on the chemical and physical properties of the 30 elements. Place the elements in their proper position in the blank periodic table.

   ◆ The noble gases are bombal (Bo), wobble (Wo), jeptum (J), and logon (L). Among these gases, wobble has the greatest atomic mass and bombal the least. Logon is lighter than jeptum.

   ◆ The most reactive group of metals are xtalt (X), byyou (By), chow (Ch), and quackzil (Q). Of these metals, chow has the lowest atomic mass. Quackzil is in the same period as wobble.

   ◆ Apstrom (A), vulcania (V), and kratt (Kt) are nonmetals whose atoms typically gain or share one electron. Vulcania is in the same period as quackzil and wobble.

Alien Periodic Table

- The metalloids are ernst (E), highho (Hi), terriblum (T), and sississ (Ss). Sissis is the metalloid with the greatest atomic mass. Ernst is the metalloid with the lowest atomic mass. Highho and terriblum are in Group 14. Terriblum has more protons than highho. Yazzer (Yz) touches the zigzag line, but it's a metal, not a metalloid.
- The lightest element of all is called pfsst (Pf). The heaviest element in the group of 30 elements is eldorado (El). The most chemically active nonmetal is apstrom. Kratt reacts with byyou to form table salt.
- The element doggone (D) has only 4 protons in its atom.
- Floxxit (Fx) is important in the chemistry of life. It forms compounds made of long chains of atoms. Rhaatrap (R) and doadeer (Do) are metals in the fourth period, but rhaatrap is less reactive than doadeer.
- Magnificon (M), goldy (G), and sississ are all members of Group 15. Goldy has fewer total electrons than magnificon.
- Urrp (Up), oz (Oz), and nuutye (Nu) all gain 2 electrons when they react. Nuutye is found as a diatomic molecule and has the same properties as a gas found in Earth's atmosphere. Oz has a lower atomic number than urrp.

- The element anatom (An) has atoms with a total of 49 electrons. Zapper (Z) and pie (Pi) lose two electrons when they react. Zapper is used in flashbulbs.

Analyze and Conclude

1. List the Earth names for the 30 alien elements in order of atomic number.
2. Were you able to place some elements within the periodic table with just a single clue? Explain using examples.
3. Why did you need two or more clues to place other elements? Explain using examples.
4. Why could you use clues about atomic mass to place elements, even though the table is now based on atomic number?
5. **Think About It** Which groups of elements are not included in the alien periodic table? Do you think it is likely that an alien planet would lack these elements? Explain.

More to Explore

Notice that Period 5 is incomplete on the alien periodic table. Create names and symbols for each of the missing elements. Then, compose a series of clues that would allow another student to identify these elements. Make your clues as precise as possible.

SECTION 5 Elements From Stardust

Can Helium Be Made From Hydrogen?

1. Every hydrogen atom consists of a nucleus of 1 proton surrounded by an electron. Most hydrogen nuclei do not contain neutrons, but some contain 1 or 2 neutrons. Draw models of each of the three kinds of hydrogen atoms.

2. All helium atoms have 2 protons and 2 electrons, and almost all have 2 neutrons. Draw a model of a typical helium atom.

Think it Over

Developing Hypotheses How might hydrogen atoms combine to form a helium atom? Draw a diagram to illustrate your hypothesis. Why would hydrogen nuclei with neutrons be important for this process?

GUIDE FOR READING

◆ How do new elements form inside stars?

Reading Tip Before you read, think of questions to pose about what happens inside stars like the sun. Then read to find answers to your questions.

Have you wondered where the elements come from? Would you like to know why some elements are common here on Earth, while others are much rarer?

To answer questions such as these, scientists have looked in a place that might surprise you: the inside of stars. By studying the sun and other stars, scientists have formed some interesting hypotheses about the origins of matter here on Earth.

Atomic Nuclei Collide

Like many other stars, the sun is made mostly of one element—hydrogen. This hydrogen exists at tremendously high pressures and hot temperatures. How hot is it? The temperature in the sun's core is about 15 million degrees Celsius.

At the high pressures and hot temperatures found inside the sun and other stars, hydrogen does not exist as either a solid, liquid, or gas. Instead, it exists in a state called plasma. In the **plasma** state of matter, atoms are stripped of their electrons, and the nuclei are packed close together.

Remember that atomic nuclei contain protons, which means that nuclei are positively charged. Normally, positively charged nuclei repel one another. But inside stars, where matter is in the plasma state, nuclei are close enough and moving fast enough to collide with one another.

When colliding nuclei have enough energy, they can join together in a process called nuclear fusion. In **nuclear fusion,** atomic nuclei combine to form a larger nucleus, releasing huge amounts of energy in the process. **Inside stars, nuclear fusion combines smaller nuclei into larger nuclei, thus creating heavier elements.** For this reason, you can think of stars as "element factories."

✓ *Checkpoint* *What does "nuclear fusion" mean?*

Elements From the Sun

What are the steps of nuclear fusion in the sun and other stars? To answer this question, you need to take a close look at the nuclei of hydrogen atoms. A hydrogen nucleus always contains one proton. However, different types of hydrogen nuclei can contain 2 neutrons, 1 neutron, or no neutrons at all.

Inside the sun, hydrogen nuclei undergo a nuclear fusion reaction that produces helium nuclei, as illustrated in Figure 26. Notice that the reaction requires a type of hydrogen nuclei that contains neutrons. This form of hydrogen is rare on Earth, but it is much more common inside the sun.

As two hydrogen nuclei fuse together, they release a great deal of energy. In fact, this reaction is the major source of the energy that the sun now produces. In other words, hydrogen is the fuel that powers the sun. Although the sun will eventually run out of hydrogen, scientists estimate that the sun has enough hydrogen to last another 5 billion years.

As more and more helium builds up in the core, the sun's temperature and volume also change. These changes allow different nuclear fusion reactions to occur. Over time, two or more helium nuclei combine to form the nuclei of slightly heavier elements. First, two helium nuclei combine, forming a beryllium nucleus. Then, another helium nucleus can join with the beryllium nucleus, forming a carbon nucleus. And yet another helium

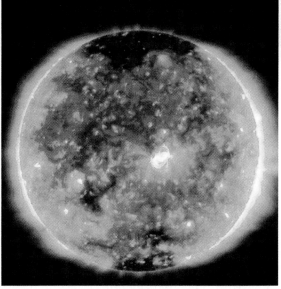

Figure 25 Without the nuclear fusion inside the sun, no sunlight would reach Earth. *Predicting What might happen in 5 billion years when all the hydrogen in the sun's core is used up?*

Figure 26 In the process of nuclear fusion, hydrogen nuclei combine, producing helium and tremendous amounts of energy.

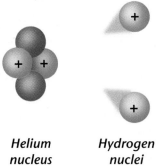

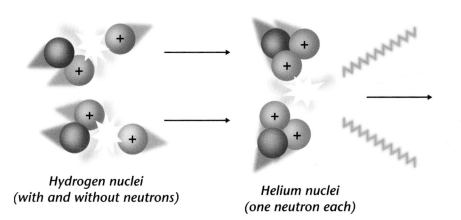

Hydrogen nuclei (with and without neutrons)

Helium nuclei (one neutron each)

Helium nucleus

Hydrogen nuclei

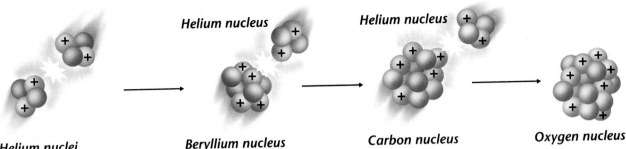

Helium nucleus   Helium nucleus

Helium nuclei   Beryllium nucleus   Carbon nucleus   Oxygen nucleus

Figure 27 A series of nuclear fusion reactions forms nuclei larger than helium. *Interpreting Diagrams Which elements are being formed?*

nucleus can join with the carbon nucleus, forming oxygen. But stars the size of the sun do not contain enough energy to produce elements heavier than oxygen.

Elements From Large Stars

As they age, larger stars become even hotter than the sun. These stars have enough energy to produce heavier elements, such as magnesium and silicon. In more massive stars, fusion continues until the core is almost all iron.

How are elements heavier than iron produced? In the final hours of the most massive stars, scientists have observed an event called a supernova. A **supernova** is a tremendous explosion that breaks apart a massive star, producing temperatures up to one billion degrees Celsius. A supernova provides enough energy for the nuclear fusion reactions that create the heaviest elements.

Figure 28 When massive stars explode in a supernova, enough energy is released to form the heavier elements.

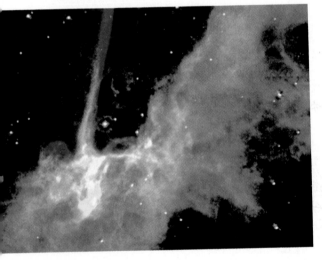

Most astronomers agree that the matter in the sun and the planets around it, including Earth, originally came from a gigantic supernova that occurred billions of years ago. If this is true, it means that everything around you was created in a star. So all matter on Earth is a form of stardust.

Section 5 Review

1. How does nuclear fusion produce new elements?
2. What nuclear fusion reaction occurs in stars like the sun?
3. How do the fusion reactions in the sun compare to the fusion occurring in larger stars and supernovas?
4. **Thinking Critically Inferring** Plasma is not found naturally on Earth. Why do you think this is so?

Check Your Progress
CHAPTER PROJECT

With your teacher's approval, begin testing the metal samples. Record the results of each test. If you cannot measure a property with exact numbers, use a more general rating system. For example, you could describe each metal as showing a particular property very well, somewhat, poorly, or not at all.

SECTION 1 — Inside the Atom

Key Ideas

◆ An atom consists of a nucleus of protons and neutrons, surrounded by electrons.

◆ Chemical bonds form when electrons are transferred or shared between atoms.

Key Terms

nucleus	atomic number
proton	atomic mass unit (amu)
neutron	valence electron
electron	electron dot diagrams

SECTION 2 — Organizing the Elements

Key Ideas

◆ Mendeleev developed the first periodic table of the elements. An element's properties can be predicted from its location in the table.

◆ Each square of the periodic table may contain the atomic number, chemical symbol, name, and atomic mass of an element.

Key Terms

atomic mass	family
periodic table	period
group	

SECTION 3 — Metals

Key Ideas

◆ Most elements are metals, found to the left of the zigzag line in the periodic table.

◆ Metals are usually shiny, ductile, malleable, and good conductors of heat and electricity.

Key Terms

malleable	alkali metal
ductile	alkaline earth metal
conductor	transition metal
magnetic	lanthanide
corrosion	actinide

SECTION 4 — Nonmetals and Metalloids

Key Ideas

◆ Nonmetals, found to the right of the zigzag line, are often gases or dull, brittle solids with low melting points.

◆ Metalloids have characteristics of both metals and nonmetals.

Key Terms

nonmetal	noble gas
diatomic molecule	metalloid
halogen family	semiconductor

SECTION 5 — Elements From Stardust

INTEGRATING SPACE SCIENCE

Key Ideas

◆ Nuclear fusion inside stars produces the nuclei of different light elements, such as helium.

◆ Elements heavier than iron are produced in a supernova, the explosion of a very massive star.

Key Terms

plasma	nuclear fusion	supernova

Organizing Information

Concept Map Copy the concept map about the periodic table onto a separate sheet of paper. Then complete it and add a title. (For more on concept maps, see the Skills Handbook.)

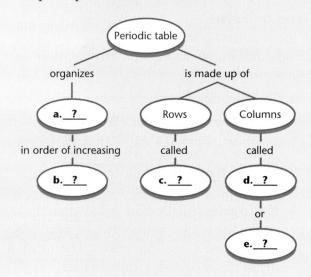

Reviewing Content

 For more review of key concepts, see the Interactive Student Tutorial CD-ROM.

Multiple Choice

Choose the letter of the answer that best completes the statement or answers the question.

1. The atomic number of an atom is determined by the number of
   a. protons.
   b. electrons.
   c. neutrons.
   d. valence electrons.
2. In the current periodic table, elements are arranged according to
   a. atomic mass.
   b. atomic number.
   c. their melting and boiling points.
   d. the number of neutrons in their nuclei.
3. Of the following, the group which contains the most reactive elements is the
   a. alkali metals.
   b. alkaline earth metals.
   c. transition metals.
   d. noble gases.
4. Unlike metals, many nonmetals are
   a. good conductors of heat and electricity.
   b. malleable and ductile.
   c. gases at room temperature.
   d. shiny.
5. Inside the sun, nuclear fusion creates helium nuclei from
   a. oxygen nuclei.
   b. neon nuclei.
   c. carbon nuclei.
   d. hydrogen nuclei.

True or False

If the statement is true, write true. If it is false, change the underlined word or words to make it a true statement.

6. The particles that move around outside an atom's nucleus are underlined{electrons}.
7. Dmitri Mendeleev is credited with developing the first underlined{periodic table}.
8. The underlined{alkali metals} include iron, copper, silver, and gold.
9. Noble gases usually exist as underlined{compounds}.
10. At the hot temperatures of stars, electrons are stripped away from nuclei. This forms a dense phase of matter called a underlined{gas}.

Checking Concepts

11. Why did Mendeleev leave three blank spaces in his periodic table? How did he account for the blank spaces?
12. Why do elements in a group of the periodic table have similar properties?
13. List five different metals. Give examples of how each metal is used.
14. List five different nonmetals. Give examples of how each nonmetal is used.
15. Why would you expect to find the element argon in its pure, uncombined form in nature?
16. **Writing to Learn** Imagine that you are Dmitri Mendeleev, and you have just published the first periodic table. Write a letter to a fellow scientist describing the table and its value.

Thinking Critically

17. **Interpreting Diagrams** An atom contains 74 protons, 74 electrons, and 108 neutrons. Which element is it?
18. **Comparing and Contrasting** Draw one electron dot diagram for an alkali metal and another for a halogen. What do the two diagrams have in common? How are they different?
19. **Drawing Conclusions** A chemistry student claims to have isolated a new element. The student states that the new element has properties similar to fluorine and chlorine, and he argues that it should be placed between fluorine and chlorine in the periodic table. Could the student have discovered a new element? Explain.
20. **Making Models** Draw a model of a carbon nucleus (6 protons, 6 neutrons) fusing with a helium nucleus (2 protons, 2 neutrons). Assuming all the protons and neutrons combine into the new nucleus, what is the identity of the new element?

Applying Skills

The table on the right lists properties of five elements. Use the information to answer Questions 21–26.

Properties of Five Elements			
Element	Appearance	Atomic Mass	Conducts Electricity
A	Invisible gas	14.0	No
B	Invisible gas	39.9	No
C	Hard, silvery solid	40.0	Yes
D	Silvery liquid	200.6	Yes
E	Shiny, bluish-white solid	207.2	Slightly

21. **Classifying** Classify each element in the table as a metal or nonmetal. Explain your answers.

22. **Inferring** Both elements B and C have an atomic mass that is close to 40. Why can two different elements have very similar atomic masses?

23. **Drawing Conclusions** Use the periodic table to identify the five elements.

24. **Predicting** Would you expect elements A and B to have similar chemical properties? Why or why not?

25. **Predicting** Would you expect to find element C uncombined in nature? Explain.

26. **Designing Experiments** Which of the metals you identified is the most reactive? Describe an experiment that would support your answer.

Performance ▼ Assessment

Present Your Project Display the chart showing the metals you studied. Be ready to discuss which properties are common to all metals. Try to predict the types of questions that others might ask you.

Reflect and Record In your journal, describe other properties of metals you could not test. List all the properties that could be used to find out whether an unknown element is a metal.

Test Preparation
Use these questions to prepare for standardized tests.

Use the diagram to answer Questions 27–32.

27. What is the atomic number for zinc (Zn)?
   a. 12   **b.** 30
   c. 15   **d.** 65.39

28. How many electrons does a zinc atom contain?
   a. 0   **b.** 15
   c. 30   **d.** 60

29. In what group of the periodic table is zinc located?
   a. 3   **b.** 4
   c. 11   **d.** 12

30. In what period of the table is zinc located?
   a. 3   **b.** 4
   c. 11   **d.** 12

31. In what way is zinc similar to cadmium (Cd), which is located just below it in the periodic table?
   a. They have the same number of electrons.
   b. They have the same number of valence electrons.
   c. They have the same number of protons.
   d. They are members of the same period.

32. From their location in the periodic table, you know that zinc and cadmium are
   a. alkali metals.   **b.** lanthanides.
   c. noble gases.   **d.** transition metals.

WEB ACTIVITY

www.phschool.com

SECTION
1 Ionic Bonds

Discover **How Do Ions Form?**
Sharpen Your Skills **Interpreting Data**
Try This **Crystal Shapes**
Skills Lab **Shape Up!**

SECTION
2 Covalent Bonds

Discover **Why Don't Water and Oil Mix?**
Sharpen Your Skills **Designing Experiments**
Skills Lab **Shedding Light on Chemical Bonds**

Integrating Earth Science

SECTION
3 Crystal Chemistry

Discover **How Small Do They Get?**
Science at Home **Piling Up**

Model Compounds

Because atoms are very tiny, it can be hard to imagine how they join to form compounds. Models can help you understand what happens at the atomic level. The models can be made from common materials or made with computer software.

In this chapter, you will learn why atoms react with one another. You will also learn about the different types of chemical bonds that can hold atoms together. In your project, you can use familiar materials to show how atoms bond to form two different types of compounds.

Your Goal To make models showing how atoms bond in compounds that contain ionic and covalent bonds.

To complete the project you must
- ◆ select materials that can be used to represent atoms of different elements
- ◆ design ways to show the ionic and covalent bonds that form between atoms
- ◆ make and compare models of compounds that contain ionic and covalent bonds

Get Started Brainstorm with some of your classmates about materials you can use to represent atoms and chemical bonds. You may want to look ahead in the chapter to preview covalent and ionic bonding.

Check Your Progress You'll be working on this project as you study this chapter. To keep your project on track, look for Check Your Progress boxes at the following points.
Section 1 Review, page 119: Build models of ionic compounds.
Section 2 Review, page 125: Build models of compounds that contain covalent bonds.

Present Your Project At the end of the chapter (page 133), you will present and explain your models to the class.

A computer-made model of a protein shows the many atoms that are bonded together in the molecule.

1 Ionic Bonds

DISCOVER .... ACTIVITY....

How Do Ions Form?

1. Place three pairs of checkers (three red and three black) on your desk. The red represent electrons and the black represent protons.

2. Place nine pairs of checkers (nine red and nine black) in a separate group on your desk.

3. Move a red checker from the smaller group to the larger group.

4. Count the number of positive charges (protons) and negative charges (electrons) in each group.

5. Now sort the checkers into a group of four pairs and a group of eight pairs. Repeat Steps 3 and 4, this time moving two red checkers from the smaller group to the larger group.

Think It Over

Forming Operational Definitions What is the total charge on each group before you moved the red checkers (electrons)? What is the charge on each group after you moved the checkers? Based on this activity, what do you think happens to the charge of an atom when it loses electrons? When it gains electrons?

GUIDE FOR READING

◆ How does an atom become an ion?

◆ What are the properties of ionic compounds?

◆ How are the ions in an ionic compound held together?

Reading Tip As you read, make an outline describing the characteristics of compounds containing ionic bonds.

Imagine you are walking down the street with your best friend. A market has a bin of apples for sale. A sign says that they cost 40 cents each. You both want an apple, but your friend has only 35 cents while you have 45 cents. What can you do? It doesn't take you long to figure out that if you give your friend a nickel, you can each buy an apple. Transferring the nickel to your friend gets both of you what you want. Your actions model, in a simple way, what can happen between atoms.

Electron Transfer

Like your friend who needs a few cents to buy an apple, atoms with five, six, or seven valence electrons don't have quite enough electrons to total the stable number of eight. On the other hand, an atom with one, two, or three valence electrons has a few it can lose. When atoms have fewer than four valence electrons, they can transfer these to other atoms that have more than four. In this way, atoms either gain electrons or lose electrons, becoming more stable.

An **ion** (EYE ahn) is an atom or group of atoms that has become electrically charged. **When an atom loses an electron, it loses a negative charge and becomes a positive ion. When an atom gains an electron, it gains a negative charge and becomes a negative ion.**

Forming an Ionic Bond

Consider what can happen to sodium and chlorine atoms. Note how many valence electrons each atom has. Suppose sodium's valence electron is transferred to chlorine. The transfer changes both atoms into ions. The sodium atom becomes a positive ion (Na^+). The chlorine atom becomes a negative ion (Cl^-). Negative and positive electric charges attract each other, so the oppositely charged Na^+ and Cl^- ions come together. They form sodium chloride, which you know as table salt.

$$Na\bullet + \bullet \overset{\bullet\bullet}{\underset{\bullet\bullet}{Cl}}\bullet \rightarrow Na^+ \overset{\bullet\bullet}{\underset{\bullet\bullet}{Cl}}\bullet^-$$

An **ionic bond** is the attraction between two oppositely charged ions. This attraction is similar to the attraction between the opposite poles of two magnets. When the two ions come together, the opposite charges cancel out. Every sodium ion (with a charge written as 1+) is balanced by a chloride ion (with a charge written as 1−). The formula for sodium chloride, NaCl, shows you this 1 : 1 ratio.

Compounds are electrically neutral. When ions come together, they do so in a way that balances out the charges on the ions. Figure 2 lists some common ions. Look at the charge of the magnesium ion. How many chloride ions would be needed to cancel out the 2+ charge of magnesium in the compound magnesium chloride? The formula for magnesium chloride, $MgCl_2$, tells you the answer is two. *Exploring Ionic Bonds* on page 116 reviews how ionic bonds are formed.

Figure 2 Positively charged ions have lost one or more electrons. Negatively charged ions have gained one or more electrons. *Classifying Which ions in the table are positively charged and which are negatively charged?*

Ions and Their Charges		
Name	**Charge**	**Symbol or Formula**
Lithium	1+	Li^+
Sodium	1+	Na^+
Potassium	1+	K^+
Ammonium	1+	NH_4^+
Calcium	2+	Ca^{2+}
Magnesium	2+	Mg^{2+}
Aluminum	3+	Al^{3+}
Fluoride	1−	F^-
Chloride	1−	Cl^-
Iodide	1−	I^-
Bicarbonate	1−	HCO_3^-
Nitrate	1−	NO_3^-
Oxide	2−	O^{2-}
Sulfide	2−	S^{2-}
Carbonate	2−	CO_3^{2-}
Sulfate	2−	SO_4^{2-}
Phosphate	3−	PO_4^{3-}

EXPLORING *Ionic Bonds*

Reactions between metals and nonmetals often form ionic compounds. These reactions occur easily between the metals in Group 1 and the halogens in Group 17. Review what happens when an ionic bond forms between a sodium atom and a chlorine atom.

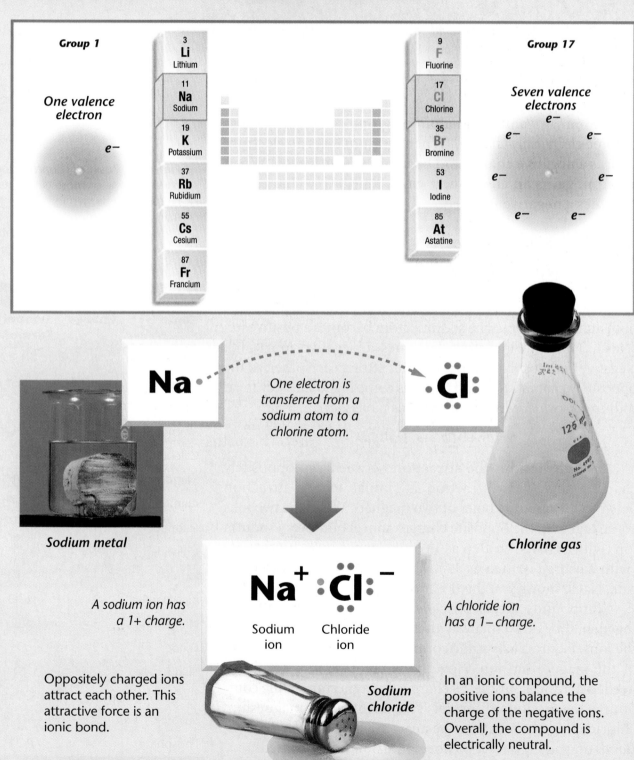

Group 1

| 3 | Li | Lithium |

One valence electron

e^-

| 11 | **Na** | Sodium |

| 19 | **K** | Potassium |

| 37 | **Rb** | Rubidium |

| 55 | **Cs** | Cesium |

| 87 | **Fr** | Francium |

| 9 | F | Fluorine |

| 17 | **Cl** | Chlorine |

| 35 | **Br** | Bromine |

| 53 | **I** | Iodine |

| 85 | **At** | Astatine |

Group 17

Seven valence electrons

e^- e^- e^- e^- e^- e^- e^-

Na· · · · · · **·Cl:**

One electron is transferred from a sodium atom to a chlorine atom.

Sodium metal

Chlorine gas

Na⁺ :Cl:⁻

Sodium   Chloride
ion   ion

A sodium ion has a 1+ charge.

A chloride ion has a 1– charge.

Sodium chloride

Oppositely charged ions attract each other. This attractive force is an ionic bond.

In an ionic compound, the positive ions balance the charge of the negative ions. Overall, the compound is electrically neutral.

Figure 3 What do seashells, chalk, limestone, and eggshells have in common? They all contain calcium carbonate, which is an ionic compound made of Ca^{2+} and CO_3^{2-} ions.

Polyatomic Ions

Some ions are made of more than one atom. Ions that are made of more than one atom are examples of **polyatomic ions** (pahl ee uh TAHM ik). The prefix *poly* means "many," so the word *polyatomic* means "many atoms." You can think of a polyatomic ion as a group of atoms that react as one. Each polyatomic ion has an overall positive or negative charge. If a polyatomic ion combines with another ion of opposite charge, an ionic compound forms. Think, for example, about the carbonate ion (CO_3^{2-}). It is made of one carbon atom and three oxygen atoms and has an overall charge of 2–. This ion can combine with a calcium ion (Ca^{2+}) to form calcium carbonate ($CaCO_3$). Calcium carbonate is the main compound in limestone.

Naming Ionic Compounds

Calcium chloride, potassium iodide, sodium oxide—where do these names come from? For an ionic compound, the name of the positive ion comes first, followed by the name of the negative ion. The name of the positive ion is usually the name of a metal. It may also be the name of a positive polyatomic ion, such as ammonium. If the negative ion is an element, the end of its name changes to *-ide*. For example, MgO is magnesium oxide. If the negative ion is polyatomic, its name is unchanged. For example, the chemical name for washing soda (Na_2CO_3) is sodium carbonate.

✓ *Checkpoint* *What kind of atom has a name change when it becomes an ion?*

Sharpen your Skills

Interpreting Data

ACTIVITY

Look at the list of compounds below. Use the periodic table and Figure 2 to identify the charges of the ions in each compound. Then write the formula for each compound.

◆ sodium fluoride
◆ lithium oxide
◆ magnesium sulfide
◆ boron chloride
◆ aluminum sulfide

How did you know how many of each atom to write in the formula?

Crystal Shapes

Compare the shapes of crystals of different ionic compounds.

ACTIVITY

1. Use a spoon to place a small amount of halite crystals (NaCl) on a piece of black paper.

2. With a hand lens, carefully examine the structure of the crystals.

3. On a separate piece of paper, draw and label a picture of what you see.

4. Repeat Steps 1–3 with samples of other crystals provided by your teacher.

Observing Do the shapes of the crystals vary within a sample? Do the shapes vary from one sample to another? Explain.

Properties of Ionic Compounds

Do you think table salt, iron rust, baking soda, and limestone are very much alike? If you answer no, you're right. If you answer yes, you're right, too! You wouldn't want to season your food with rust, or construct a building out of baking soda. But despite their differences, these compounds share some similarities because they all contain ionic bonds. **The characteristic properties of ionic compounds include crystal shape, high melting points, and electrical conductivity.**

Crystal Shape The object in Figure 4 that looks like a glass sculpture is really a chunk of halite, or table salt. Halite is an ionic compound. All halite samples have sharp edges, corners, and flat surfaces. These properties result from how the ions are arranged. In solid sodium chloride, the Na$^+$ and Cl$^-$ ions come together in an alternating pattern, as shown in the diagram. The ions form an orderly, three-dimensional arrangement called a **crystal.**

In an ionic compound, every ion is attracted to ions near it that have an opposite charge. Positive ions tend to be near negative ions and farther from other positive ions. As a result, a positive sodium ion doesn't bond with just one negative chloride ion. It bonds with ions above, below, and to all sides. Because chloride ions bond with sodium ions in the same way, a crystal forms. This pattern continues no matter what the size of the crystal. In a single grain of salt, the crystal can extend for millions of ions in every direction. The number of sodium ions and chloride ions in the crystal is equal. The formula for sodium chloride, NaCl, represents this 1 : 1 ratio.

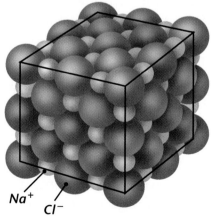

Na$^+$

Cl$^-$

Figure 4 A halite crystal contains sodium and chloride ions in an alternating pattern.
Making Generalizations What general characteristics of crystals can you observe in the photograph of halite?

High Melting Points What happens when you heat an ionic compound such as table salt? Remember, the ions are held together in a crystal by attractions between oppositely charged particles. When the particles have enough energy to overcome the attractive forces between them, they break away from each other. It takes a temperature of 801°C to reach this energy for table salt. Ionic bonds are strong enough to cause all ionic compounds to be solids at room temperature.

Electrical Conductivity When ionic compounds dissolve in  water, the solution conducts electricity. Electricity is the flow of electric charge, and ions have electric charges. However, if you connect wires from a salt crystal to a battery and a light bulb, don't expect anything to happen. A *solid* ionic compound does not conduct electricity very well. The ions in the crystal are tightly bound to each other. If the charged particles do not move, electricity does not flow. But what if the ions are broken apart? When ionic compounds dissolve in water, the ions separate. These ions then move freely, and the solution conducts electricity.

Melting ionic compounds also allows them to conduct electricity. Can you figure out why? Think about the difference between the particles in a solid and a liquid. In a solid, the particles do not move from place to place. But in a liquid, the particles slip and slide past each other. As long as the ions can move around, electricity can flow.

Figure 5 A conductivity tester shows that a solution of salt in water conducts electricity. The bulb lights up because the ions in the salt solution complete the circuit for the flow of electricity.

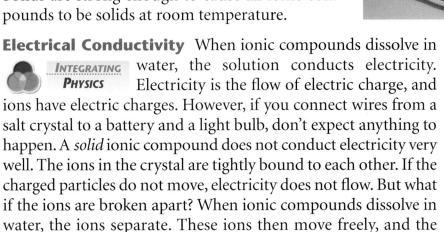

Section 1 Review

1. How does an ion form from an atom?
2. What properties may be used to identify ionic compounds?
3. Why are ions in an ionic compound attracted to each other?
4. Name these compounds: NaF, BeI_2, K_2SO_4, CaO, H_2S, $MgCO_3$.
5. Solid table salt does not conduct electricity. How does dissolving salt in water allow electricity to flow?
6. **Thinking Critically** **Problem Solving** The metal scandium (Sc) has three valence electrons. What is the formula of the ionic compound formed when scandium reacts with iodine?

CHAPTER PROJECT

Check Your Progress

Use your materials to make models of compounds containing ionic bonds, such as sodium chloride (NaCl), magnesium chloride ($MgCl_2$), or potassium oxide (K_2O). (*Hint:* Figure out whether each atom forms a positive or negative ion. Then use combinations that result in a neutral compound.)

Skills Lab

Shape Up!

A s an ionic solid, table salt—sodium chloride—is a crystal. In this lab, you will investigate the structure of that crystal.

Problem

What is the structure of sodium chloride crystals?

Materials

sodium chloride
plastic spoon, small
Petri dishes, 2
black paper
100-mL graduated cylinder
250-ml beaker
water (80°C)
hand lens

DATA TABLE

Substance	Observations
Original NaCl crystals	
NaCl solution	
New NaCl crystals	

Procedure

1. Read the procedure, and write a prediction about the appearance of the crystals in Step 7. Then create a data table like the one above.
2. Your teacher will give you a sample of sodium chloride. Use a spoon to sprinkle some grains of the salt in a Petri dish. Put the dish on black paper. Observe the salt with a hand lens. Record your observations, and draw what you see.
3. Pour 100 mL of hot water (80°C) into a 250-mL beaker. Add about half a spoonful of salt to the water and stir until it dissolves. Observe the solution, and record your observations.
4. Add the rest of the salt and stir well. Let any undissolved salt particles settle at the bottom of the beaker.
5. Carefully pour off 50 mL of the solution into a Petri dish labeled with your name.
6. Let the uncovered Petri dish sit overnight, or until all the water has evaporated.
7. Put the Petri dish on black paper and observe the new crystals with a hand lens. Record your observations, and draw what you see.

Analyze and Conclude

1. How did the appearance of the sodium chloride change between Steps 2 and 3? Explain that change in terms of the ions that make up the compound.
2. Describe the shapes of the crystals you observed in Step 7, along with any patterns you see within any of the crystals.
3. Compare and contrast the crystals you observed in Step 2 and Step 7.
4. Use what you know about ionic compounds to explain the shapes of the new crystals. Would you expect all sodium chloride crystals to have the same shapes? Explain.
5. **Think About It** Could you use the results of this experiment to draw conclusions about the crystals formed by other ionic compounds? Explain.

Design an Experiment

Does the original temperature of the sodium chloride solution affect crystal formation? Design a safe experiment comparing solutions of ice water, tap water, and hot water. Obtain your teacher's approval before trying this experiment.

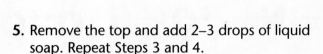

DISCOVER

Why Don't Water and Oil Mix?

1. Pour water into a small jar that has a tight-fitting top until the jar is about a third full.

2. Add an equal amount of vegetable oil to the water and cover the jar tightly.

3. Shake the jar with vigor for about 15–20 seconds. Observe.

4. Allow the jar to sit undisturbed for about 1 minute. Observe again.

5. Remove the top and add 2–3 drops of liquid soap. Repeat Steps 3 and 4.

Think It Over

Inferring Describe how adding soap affected the mixing of the oil and water. How might what you observed depend on chemical bonds in the soap, oil, and water molecules?

R emember the market with apples selling for 40 cents each? On another day, the apples are put on sale at two for 70 cents. You and your friend check your pockets and find 35 cents each. What can you do? You could give your friend a nickel to make enough money for one apple. Then you would have only 30 cents, not enough to get one for yourself. But if you share your money, together you can buy two apples.

Electron Sharing

Just as you and your friend can buy apples by sharing money, atoms can become more stable by sharing valence electrons. A chemical bond formed when two atoms share electrons is called a **covalent bond.**

Unlike ionic bonds, which form between metals and nonmetals, covalent bonds often form between two or more nonmetals. Oxygen, carbon, nitrogen, and the halogens are examples of elements that frequently bond to other nonmetals by sharing electrons.

The element fluorine forms molecules made of two fluorine atoms. Each fluorine atom shares one of its seven valence electrons with the other atom. When you count the number of electrons on one atom, you count the shared pair each time. By sharing, both atoms have eight valence electrons. **In a covalent bond, both atoms attract the two shared electrons at the same time.**

GUIDE FOR READING

◆ What happens to electrons in a covalent bond?

◆ Why do some atoms in covalent bonds have slight negative or positive charges?

◆ How are polar and nonpolar compounds different?

Reading Tip Before you read, preview the illustrations in the section. Predict how covalent bonds differ from ionic bonds.

Figure 6 The shared pair of electrons in a molecule of fluorine is a single covalent bond.

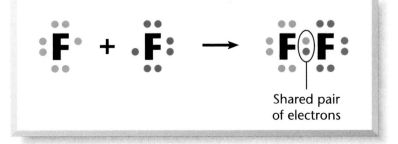

Shared pair of electrons

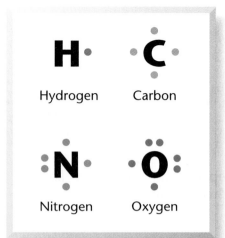

Figure 7 The electron dot diagrams for hydrogen, carbon, nitrogen, and oxygen (left) show the number of valence electrons for each. The diagrams of molecules (right) show how the electrons are shared in covalent bonds.
Interpreting Diagrams How many bonds does each nitrogen atom form?

Figure 8 Molecular compounds have much lower melting points than ionic compounds.

Melting and Boiling Points of Some Molecular Compounds

Compound	Formula	Melting Point (°C)	Boiling Point (°C)
Water	H_2O	0	100
Methane	CH_4	–182	–164
Carbon dioxide	CO_2	—	–78.6*
Ammonia	NH_3	–77.7	–33.6
Rubbing alcohol	C_3H_7OH	–89.5	82.4
Sugar	$C_{12}H_{22}O_{11}$	185–186	(decomposes)

*Carbon dioxide changes directly from a solid to a gas.

How Many Bonds?

Look at the electron dot diagrams for oxygen, nitrogen, and carbon atoms in Figure 7. Count the dots on each atom. The number of bonds these atoms can form equals the number of valence electrons needed to make a total of eight.

For example, oxygen has six valence electrons, so it can form two covalent bonds. In a water molecule, oxygen forms one covalent bond with each hydrogen atom. Since nitrogen has five valence electrons, it can form three bonds. In ammonia (NH_3), a nitrogen atom bonds with three hydrogen atoms.

Next, compare water to a molecule of oxygen. Can you find the two covalent bonds? This time *two* pairs of electrons are shared between the oxygen atoms, forming a **double bond.** In a carbon dioxide molecule, carbon forms a double bond with each oxygen atom. Elements such as nitrogen and carbon can even form triple bonds in which *three* pairs of electrons are shared.

Count the electrons around any atom in the molecules in Figure 7. Remember that shared pairs count for both atoms forming a bond. You'll find that each atom has eight valence electrons. The exception is hydrogen, which can have no more than two electrons and forms one bond.

Properties of Molecular Compounds

Molecular compounds consist of molecules having covalently bonded atoms. Such compounds have very different properties from ionic compounds.

Look at Figure 8, which lists the melting and boiling points for some molecular compounds. Quite a difference from the

122

801°C and 1,413°C described for table salt! In molecular solids, the molecules are held close to each other. But the forces holding them are much weaker than those holding ions together in an ionic solid. Less heat is needed to separate molecules than is needed to separate ions. Some molecular compounds, such as sugar and water, do form crystals. But these compounds, like other molecular solids, melt and boil at much lower temperatures than ionic compounds do.

Most molecular compounds are poor conductors of electricity. No charged particles are available to move, and electricity does not flow. That's why molecular compounds, such as plastic and rubber, are used to insulate electric wires. Even as liquids, molecular compounds are poor conductors. Pure water, for example, does not conduct electricity. Neither does water with sugar dissolved in it.

☑ *Checkpoint* **Why are molecular compounds poor conductors?**

Unequal Sharing of Electrons

Have you ever played tug of war? If you have, you know that if both teams have equal strength, the contest is a tie. But what if the teams pull on the rope with unequal force? Then the rope moves closer to one side or the other. The same is true of electrons in a covalent bond. **Some atoms pull more strongly on the shared electrons than other atoms do. As a result, the electrons move closer to one atom, causing the atoms to have slight electrical charges.** These charges are not as strong as the charges on ions. But the unequal sharing is enough to make one atom slightly negative and the other atom slightly positive. A covalent bond in which electrons are shared unequally is **polar.**

Figure 9 The unequal sharing of the electrons in a polar covalent bond is like a tug of war in which one atom is slightly stronger than the other atom.

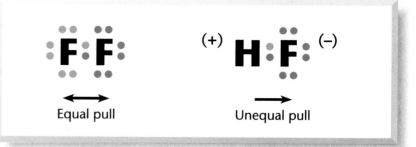

Figure 10 In the nonpolar bond in F_2, the two fluorine atoms pull equally on the shared electrons. In the polar bond in HF, fluorine pulls more strongly on the shared electrons than hydrogen does.

Equal pull

Unequal pull

If two atoms pull equally on the electrons, neither atom becomes charged. This is the case when the two atoms are identical, as in fluorine gas (F_2). The valence electrons are shared equally and the bond is **nonpolar.** Compare the bond in F_2 with the polar bond in hydrogen fluoride (HF) in Figure 10.

Nonpolar Molecules Keep tug of war in mind as you look at the carbon dioxide (CO_2) molecule in Figure 11. Oxygen attracts electrons much more strongly than carbon, so bonds between oxygen and carbon are polar. But the two oxygen atoms are pulling with equal strength in opposite directions. In a sense, they cancel each other out. Overall, a carbon dioxide molecule is nonpolar even though it has polar bonds. A molecule is nonpolar if it contains polar bonds that cancel each other. As you might guess, molecules that contain only nonpolar bonds are also nonpolar.

Polar Molecules Water molecules are polar. As you can see in Figure 11, the shape of the molecule leaves the two hydrogen atoms more to one end and the oxygen atom toward the other. The oxygen atom pulls electrons closer to it from both hydrogen atoms. Overall, the molecule is polar. It has a slightly negative charge at the oxygen end and a slightly positive charge near the hydrogen atoms.

✓ *Checkpoint* **What makes a covalent bond polar?**

Attractions Between Molecules

If you could shrink small enough to move among a bunch of water molecules, what would you find? The negatively charged oxygen ends and positively charged hydrogen ends behave like poles of a bar magnet. They attract the opposite ends of other water molecules. These attractions between positive and negative ends pull water molecules toward each other.

What about carbon dioxide? There is no pulling between these molecules. Remember, carbon dioxide molecules are nonpolar. No oppositely charged ends means there are no strong attractions between the molecules.

CO_2 molecule (nonpolar)

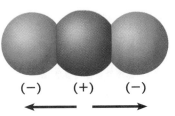

(−)   (+)   (−)

Opposite pulling
cancels

H_2O molecule (polar)

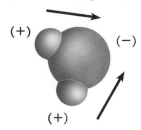

(+)

(−)

(+)

Electrons pulled
towards oxygen

Figure 11 CO_2 molecules are nonpolar, and H_2O molecules are polar. Attractions between the slightly positive and slightly negative ends of water molecules pull the molecules toward each other (below).

Differences in the attractions between molecules lead to different properties in polar and nonpolar compounds. For example, water and vegetable oil don't mix. Oil is nonpolar, and nonpolar compounds do not dissolve well in water. The polar water molecules are attracted more strongly to each other than to the molecules of oil. Water stays with water and oil stays with oil. These differences in attractions come in handy when you wash laundry. Many kinds of dirt—for example, grease—are nonpolar compounds. Their molecules won't mix with plain water. So how can you wash dirt out of your clothes?

INTEGRATING TECHNOLOGY

As you found if you did the Discover activity, adding soap helped the oil and water to mix. When you do laundry, detergent causes the nonpolar dirt to mix with the polar water. Soaps and detergents have long molecules. One end of a soap molecule is polar, and the other end is nonpolar. Soaps and detergents dissolve in water because the polar ends of their molecules are attracted to water molecules. Meanwhile, their nonpolar ends mix easily with the dirt. When the water washes down the drain, the soap and the dirt go with it.

Section 2 Review

1. How are valence electrons involved in the formation of a covalent bond?
2. How do atoms in covalent bonds become slightly negative or slightly positive?
3. Explain how attractions between molecules could cause water to have a higher boiling point than carbon dioxide.
4. **Thinking Critically Comparing and Contrasting** In terms of electrons, how is a covalent bond different from an ionic bond?

Check Your Progress   **CHAPTER PROJECT**
Use your materials to build molecules with single covalent bonds. Also make models of molecules containing double or triple bonds. (*Hint:* After you make bonds, each atom should have a total of eight valence electrons or, in the case of hydrogen, two valence electrons.)

Shedding Light on Chemical Bonds

Electricity is the flow of electric charges. In this lab, you will interpret data about which compounds conduct electricity in order to determine the nature of their bonds.

Problem

How can you use a conductivity tester to determine whether a compound contains ionic or covalent bonds?

Materials

2 1.5-V dry cells
small beaker
plastic spoon
sodium chloride
small light bulb and socket
4 lengths of wire for connections with insulation
    scraped off ends
100-mL graduated cylinder
additional substances supplied by your teacher

DATA TABLE	
Sample	Observations
Water	
Sodium chloride in water	

Procedure

1. Make a conductivity tester by following the instructions below. After you have constructed it, make a data table in your notebook similar to the one above.
2. Pour about 50 mL of water into a small beaker. Place the free ends of the two wires of the conductivity tester into the water. Be sure the ends are close but not touching each other. Record your observations.

Making a Conductivity Tester

A. Use wire to connect the positive terminal of a dry cell to a lamp socket. **CAUTION:** *The bulb is fragile and can break.*

B. Use another wire to connect the negative terminal to the positive terminal of a second dry cell.

C. Connect a third wire to the negative terminal of the second dry cell.

D. Connect a fourth wire to the other terminal of the lamp socket.

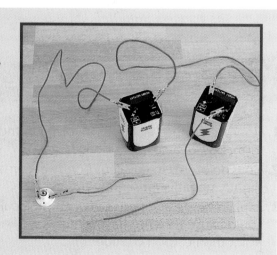

3. Remove the conductivity tester and add a small spoonful of sodium chloride to the water in the small beaker. Stir with the spoon until mixed.
4. Repeat the conductivity test and record your observations in your data table.
5. Rinse the beaker, spoon, and wire ends with clear water. Then repeat Steps 3 and 4 for each substance provided by your teacher.
   ◆ If the substance is a solid, mix a small spoonful of it with about 50 mL of fresh water. Test the resulting mixture.
   ◆ If a substance is a liquid, simply pour about 50 mL into the beaker. Test it as you did the mixtures of solid in water.

Analyze and Conclude

1. Why did you test plain water first?
2. Based on your observations, add a column to your chart indicating whether each substance tested contained ionic or covalent bonds.
3. Explain why one substance is a better conductor of electricity than another.
4. Did all the substances that conducted electricity show the same amount of conductivity? How do you know?
5. **Think About It** How might varying the amount of each substance added to the water have affected your results? How could you better control the amount of each substance?

Design an Experiment

Design another experiment to compare a different property of compounds containing ionic and covalent bonds. You might want to examine properties such as the ability to dissolve in water or in some other liquid. Present your experimental plan to your teacher before proceeding.

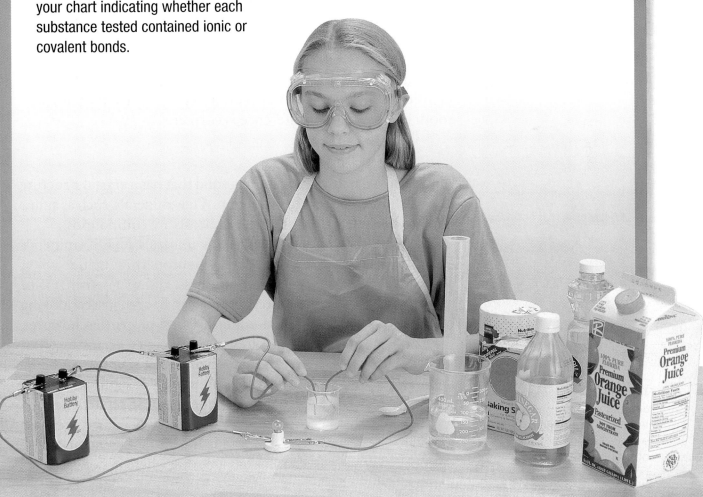

SECTION 3 Crystal Chemistry

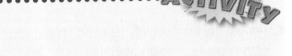

DISCOVER ·············· ACTIVITY ····

How Small Do They Get?

1. Place a piece of rock salt on a hard surface. Make a rough sketch of the shape of your sample.

2. Put on your goggles. Cover the salt with a paper towel. Then break the salt sample into several smaller pieces with the back of a metal spoon.

3. Look at these smaller pieces with a hand lens. Then draw a picture of the shapes you see.

4. Crush a few of these smaller pieces with the spoon. Repeat Step 3.

Think It Over
Predicting What would the crystals look like if you crushed them into such small pieces that you needed a microscope to see them?

GUIDE FOR READING

◆ How are the properties of a mineral related to chemical bonds?

Reading Tip As you read, make a list of the ways in which a mineral can be described or identified.

A class of earth science students gathers rock samples on a field trip. They want to know whether the rocks contain any of the minerals they have been studying. The teacher takes a hammer and strikes one rock. It cracks open to reveal a few small crystals peeking out of the new surface. The crystals are mostly the same shape and have a metallic shine. The teacher tries to scratch one crystal, first with her fingernail and then with a copper penny. Only the penny leaves a mark. By now, the students have enough information to make an inference about the identity of the crystals. They'll do more tests back in their classroom to be sure their inference is correct.

Mineral Properties

A **mineral** is a naturally occurring solid that has a crystal structure and a definite chemical composition. A few minerals, such as sulfur and gold, are elements. But most minerals are compounds.

Mineralogists, scientists who study minerals, identify minerals by looking at certain properties. These properties include color, shininess, density, crystal shape, hardness, and magnetism. Color and shininess can be seen just by looking at a mineral. Other properties, however, require measurements or testing. For example, scientists rate a mineral's hardness by comparing it with something harder or softer. You can scratch the softest mineral, talc, with your fingernail. Diamond is the hardest mineral. Other minerals are somewhere in between.

Figure 12 The mineral sulfur (above) is a pure element. The mineral galena (right) is a compound of sulfur and lead.

Another key property is the way a mineral breaks apart. Some minerals break into regular shapes. Mica, for example, splits easily along flat surfaces and at sharp angles. Crystals also grow in characteristic shapes. All the properties of a mineral depend on its chemical composition. Since each mineral has a different composition, its properties will not be exactly like those of any other mineral.

☑ *Checkpoint* *What is a mineral?*

Bonding in Mineral Crystals

Every mineral has a crystal structure. The repeating pattern of particles creates a shape that may be visible to your eye. Or, you may have to look under a microscope to see it. Either way, the structure of the crystal is a characteristic property of the mineral.

Mineral crystals may be made of ions, or they may contain atoms that are covalently bonded together. **The arrangement of particles in a mineral and the kind of bonds holding them together determine properties such as crystal shape, hardness, and the way the crystal breaks apart.**

An Ionic Crystal In Section 1, you read about halite, a mineral made of sodium chloride (NaCl). You can easily scratch halite with a steel knife. If you put a crystal of halite into water, it would dissolve. The oppositely charged sodium and chloride ions in a halite crystal alternate in every direction, making a pattern something like a three-dimensional checkerboard. This arrangement affects the shape into which halite crystals grow.

If you break a piece of halite, the smaller pieces of halite have the same shape as the bigger piece. When bonds in an ionic crystal break, they break along a line of ions. A blow or crushing action shifts the ions slightly so that positive ions are next to other positive ions and negative ions are next to other negative ions. The effect is the same as bringing the

Figure 13 Mica's flakes **(A)** are a result of how the mineral splits when it breaks. The crystals of fluorite **(B)** and tourmaline **(C)** grew into the shapes you see. *Observing How do the shapes of fluorite crystals and tourmaline crystals differ?*

Figure 14 The particles in an ionic crystal such as halite can shift because of a blow or pressure.

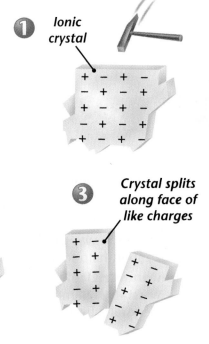

1 Ionic crystal

2 Ions shift

3 Crystal splits along face of like charges

north ends of two magnets together. It creates a weakness in the crystal. The ions push each other away, breaking bonds along a flat surface or face. The result is that the smaller crystals retain the cube shape that is characteristic of halite.

A Molecular Crystal If you picked up a handful of sand, most likely you would be holding some quartz. Quartz is a common mineral made of silicon and oxygen atoms covalently bonded together (SiO_2). The covalent bonds in quartz are much stronger than the ionic bonds in halite. Quartz won't dissolve in water. You can't scratch it with a knife. In fact, you could use quartz to scratch steel! Because of its strong bonds, a quartz crystal doesn't have clear lines of weakness. You can't crush it into predictable shapes with a hammer. Instead, it breaks into smaller pieces with irregular shapes. The broken surfaces have shell-like ridges similar to chipped glass. These features help identify the mineral as quartz.

Figure 15 The uneven surfaces on this crystal are typical of broken quartz.
Comparing and Contrasting How does the way quartz breaks compare to the way mica breaks?

Comparing Crystals

Not all mineral crystals made of ions have the same properties as halite. Similarly, not all minerals made of covalently bonded atoms are like quartz. Properties such as hardness, for example, depend on the strength of the bonds in a crystal. The stronger bonds of quartz make it harder than halite. But other crystals with covalently bonded atoms are stronger than quartz. Still others have weaknesses in their bonds that cause the minerals to break apart the same way every time.

Experienced mineralogists can usually identify a mineral just by looking at it. But when there is a question, they test the sample for characteristics such as hardness and the way the crystals break. The results give the answer.

Section 3 Review

1. Name two properties of minerals that depend on chemical bonds.
2. What property of a mineral can be determined by scratching it?
3. How does the way in which a mineral crystal breaks apart help to identify it?
4. **Thinking Critically Comparing and Contrasting** Name three ways in which a halite crystal differs from a quartz crystal.

Science at Home

Piling Up Construct a model of an ionic crystal. Place round objects of two different sizes (such as balls of clay) in a checkerboard pattern to make the first layer. Now place one smaller object on top of each larger one and vice versa to make the second layer. Continue until the first layer is completely covered. Construct a third layer in a similar way. Explain to your family how your model represents an ionic crystal.

SECTION 1 Ionic Bonds

Key Ideas
◆ When atoms lose or gain electrons, they become positively or negatively charged ions.
◆ In an ionic compound, the ions are arranged in a three-dimensional structure called a crystal. Each ion in the crystal is attracted to nearby ions of opposite charge.
◆ Characteristic properties of ionic compounds include crystal shape, high melting points, and electrical conductivity.

Key Terms
ion
ionic bond
polyatomic ion
crystal

SECTION 2 Covalent Bonds

Key Ideas
◆ In covalent bonds, pairs of electrons are shared between atoms.
◆ In polar covalent bonds, the shared electrons are attracted more to one atom than the other.
◆ Attractions between polar molecules are stronger than attractions between nonpolar molecules, leading to differences in properties.

Key Terms
covalent bond
double bond
molecular compound
polar
nonpolar

SECTION 3 Crystal Chemistry
INTEGRATING EARTH SCIENCE

Key Ideas
◆ Minerals have characteristic properties, such as hardness, density, color, crystal shape, and the way the crystal breaks.
◆ The properties of a mineral depend on its chemical composition and its bonding. Mineral crystals may contain ions or covalently bonded molecules.
◆ The stronger the chemical bonds in a mineral crystal, the harder the crystal is.

Key Term
mineral

Organizing Information

Venn Diagram Copy the Venn diagram comparing ionic and molecular compounds onto a separate sheet of paper. Then complete the diagram and add a title. (For more on Venn diagrams, see the Skills Handbook.)

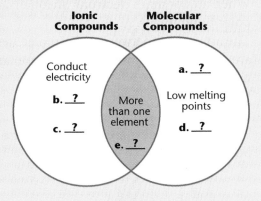

Ionic Compounds / Molecular Compounds

Conduct electricity
b. ?
c. ?
More than one element
e. ?
a. ?
Low melting points
d. ?

Reviewing Content

 For more review of key concepts, see the Interactive Student Tutorial CD-ROM.

Multiple Choice
Choose the letter of the best answer.

1. When an atom loses an electron, it
   a. becomes a negative ion.
   b. becomes a positive ion.
   c. forms a covalent bond.
   d. gains protons.
2. Which of these is a property of an ionic compound?
   a. low melting point
   b. poor conductor of electricity
   c. crystal shape
   d. shared electrons
3. A bond in which a pair of electrons is shared between two atoms is called
   a. ionic.   b. covalent.
   c. polyatomic.   d. triple.
4. Fluorine atoms cannot form a double or triple bond because fluorine
   a. is a nonmetal.
   b. strongly attracts electrons.
   c. has 7 valence electrons.
   d. is a gas at room temperature.
5. An ionic crystal splits along a face of
   a. like charges.   b. molecules.
   c. unlike charges.   d. random ions.

True or False
If the statement is true, write true. If it is false, change the underlined word or words to make the statement true.

6. When a chlorine atom gains an electron, it becomes a <u>positive ion</u>.
7. When atoms share electrons unequally, a <u>polar</u> bond forms.
8. The attractions between polar molecules are <u>weaker</u> than those between nonpolar molecules.
9. <u>Hardness</u> is determined by how easily a mineral can be scratched.
10. The bonds in halite are <u>weaker</u> than the bonds in quartz.

Checking Concepts

11. Explain how the number of valence electrons an element has affects the type and number of bonds it can form.
12. Use the periodic table to identify what type of chemical bond is involved in each of these compounds: NaF, NO_2, CBr_4, MgS. Explain your reasoning.
13. How is a covalent bond between two atoms affected when each atom attracts electrons equally?
14. Of all the elements, fluorine atoms attract electrons most strongly. When fluorine atoms form covalent bonds with other kinds of atoms, are the bonds polar or nonpolar?
15. **Writing to Learn** Imagine you are a chlorine atom. Write a first-person description of the changes you undergo when forming an ionic bond with sodium. Compare these with what happens when you form a covalent bond with another chlorine atom.

Thinking Critically

16. **Applying Concepts** Use the periodic table to find the number of valence electrons for calcium (Ca), aluminum (Al), rubidium (Rb), oxygen (O), sulfur (S), and iodine (I). Then use that information to predict the formula for each of the following compounds: calcium oxide, aluminum iodide, rubidium sulfide, and aluminum oxide.
17. **Inferring** Element Z is a yellow solid that melts at about 100°C and does not conduct electricity. What type of bond holds the element's atoms together? Explain the reasoning for your answer.
18. **Relating Cause and Effect** Explain why a solid ionic compound does not conduct electricity, but the compound will do so when melted or dissolved in water.
19. **Problem Solving** Suppose you were given two mineral crystals that looked alike. How would you determine the identity of each?

Applying Skills

Element X exists as a nonpolar molecule made of two identical atoms. When individual atoms of element X react with sodium, they form ions with a 2– charge. Use the periodic table in Appendix D to answer Questions 20–24.

20. **Classifying** To what group of elements does element X belong?
21. **Inferring** How many valence electrons does an atom of element X have?
22. **Predicting** Sodium can react with element X to form a compound. How many atoms of sodium are needed for each atom of element X? Write the formula for the compound.
23. **Calculating** How many covalent bonds can element X form?
24. **Posing Questions** In order to identify element X, what additional questions would you need to ask?

Performance ▼ CHAPTER PROJECT Assessment

Present Your Project Before you present your models to the class, use an index card for each model to make a key telling what each part of the model represents. Explain why you chose particular items to model the atoms and the chemical bonds. How are your models alike or different from models of the same compounds made by other students?

Reflect and Record In your journal, compare your models containing ionic bonds with those containing covalent bonds. Which were easier to show? Why? What more would you like to know about bonding that could help improve your models?

Test Preparation

Use these questions to prepare for standardized tests.

Use the diagram to answer Questions 25–28.

H·   ·Ċ·   Na·

Hydrogen   Carbon   Sodium

:N̈·   ·Ö: ·C̈l:

Nitrogen   Oxygen   Chlorine

25. When one nitrogen atom joins with another nitrogen atom forming a molecule of nitrogen gas, the atoms are held together by a(n)
    a. single bond   **b.** double bond
    c. triple bond   **d.** ionic bond

26. When nitrogen and hydrogen combine, the ratio of hydrogen atoms to nitrogen atoms in a molecule of the resulting compound is
    a. 2 to 1
    b. 3 to 1
    c. 1 to 3
    d. 1 to 1

27. Atoms of which pair of elements are most likely to form a polar covalent bond?
    a. H and O
    b. Na and O
    c. Na and Cl
    d. Cl and Cl

28. The correct symbol for an ion of oxygen is
    a. O^+
    b. O^{2+}
    c. O^-
    d. O^{2-}

SOAP
The Dirt Chaser

What slippery substance . . .
- makes things cleaner, fresher, brighter?
- can you put on your head and on your floors?
- greases parts of equipment that might stick?
- rids your hands of germs?

It's soap, which is a cleaner made from materials that are found in nature. People figured out how to make soap by heating natural fats or oils, alkali (a chemical they got from wood ashes), and water. Detergent is also a cleaner. It's similar to soap, but made from manufactured materials.

The average American uses about 11 kilograms of soap per year just to keep clean! Some of that soap is used for baths and showers. Soap is also used by medical experts to clean wounds and prevent infection.

In your home you use soaps and detergents to clean dishes, laundry, windows, floors, and much more. Even factories use soaps in the process of making products such as rubber, jewelry, aluminum, antifreeze, leather, and glossy paper.

So, if you lived without soap, you and your surroundings would be a lot dirtier! You would look and feel quite different. You may just owe your way of life to soap!

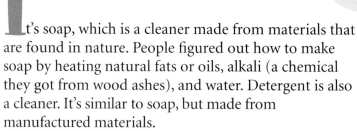

Soapsuds are at work in a baby's bath (top), when washing a dog (middle), and at a car wash (bottom).

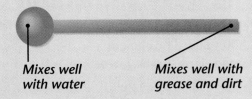

Mixes well with water

Mixes well with grease and dirt

How Soap Works

You rub shampoo and water into your hair.

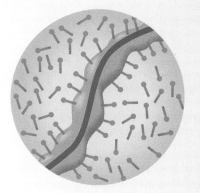

Soap molecules in shampoo loosen the grease and dirt on your hair.

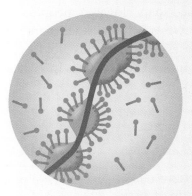

Soap molecules break the dirt into tiny pieces.

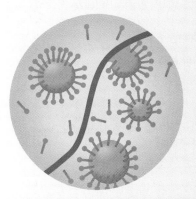

Water carries away the dirt surrounded by soap molecules.

Wash the Dirt Away

Soap manufacturers claim that their products can wash away the dirt from the dirtiest clothes. How does that work? First, you need to wet the clothes with water that contains soap. The soap then spreads out and soaks into the material.

Each molecule of soap is shaped like a tiny tadpole. The tail-like end is similar to a hydrocarbon molecule. It mixes poorly with water, but it mixes well with dirt and grease. The large end, on the other hand, mixes well with water. When you wash, the soap molecules surround the dirt and break it up into tiny pieces that water can wash away.

Some dirt is difficult to dissolve. It takes longer for the soap molecules to loosen it. In these cases rubbing, scrubbing, and squeezing may help to lift the dirt.

Some water, called hard water, has minerals dissolved in it—calcium, magnesium, and iron. In hard water, soap forms deposits, called scum. Scum doesn't dissolve and is difficult to wash away. It keeps clean hair from being shiny and leaves a "bathtub ring."

The invention of detergents helped solve the problem of scum and stubborn stains. For many cleaning tasks, detergent is more effective than soap. Detergent also dissolves in cold water more easily than soap.

The Development of Soap

People have made soap for at least 2,300 years. The ancient Babylonians, Arabs, Greeks, Romans, and Celts made and sometimes traded it. The English word comes from "saipo," the Celts' name for soap. But these early cultures used soap primarily as a hair dye or a medicine, not as a cleaner! Only in the period from A.D. 100–199 did soap become known as a cleaning agent.

Soapmaking in western Europe began about A.D. 100. First France was a leading producer, then Italy by 700, and Spain by 800. England didn't begin making soap until about 1200. But even then, most people didn't use soap for bathing.

Around 1790, Nicolas Leblanc, a French scientist, discovered that alkali could be made from common table salt and water. After that, soap could be made more easily and sold for profit.

In North America beginning around 1650, colonists made their own soap. Families would make up to a year's supply for their own use. Then around 1800, some people started collecting waste fats and ashes from their neighbors and making soap in large quantities. Soon bars of soap were sold from door to door.

In 1806, William Colgate, a soap and candle maker, started a business called Colgate and Company. His company produced soap and another cleaner, toothpaste. Today, nearly all soap is made in factories using large machinery.

In the boiling room of a French soapmaking factory in the 1870s, workers stir and ladle hot soap.

The first detergent was produced in Germany around 1916, during World War I. Because fats were in short supply, detergent was meant to be a substitute for fat-based soap. However, people found that detergent was a better cleaner than soap for many purposes. The first household detergents appeared in the United States in 1933.

Social Studies Activity

Create a time line of important events in the history of soapmaking. Find photos or make illustrations for the time line. Include the following events:

◆ early uses and users of soap
◆ beginning of the soapmaking industry
◆ early North American soapmaking
◆ first detergent

Before they discovered soap, what do you think people in earlier times used as a cleaner?

Colonial Soapmaking

Making soap in North America in the 1600s was an exhausting, unpleasant process. For months, colonists saved barrels of ashes from their wood fires. Then they poured hot water over the ashes. An alkali solution, called lye, dripped out of a spigot in the bottom of the barrel.

In a large kettle over a roaring outdoor fire, they boiled the alkali solution with fat, such as greases, which they had also saved. They had to keep the fire high and hot and stir the mixture for hours. When it was thick, they ladled the liquid soap into shallow boxes. Families made soap in the spring and sometimes again in the fall.

The following passage is from the novel *The Iron Peacock* by Mary Stetson Clarke. The story takes place in 1650 in Massachusetts Bay Colony. In the passage, two large supports hold a crossbar where the pot is hung over the fire. The women stir the pot with a homemade tool.

Soapmaking in colonial times was an all-day process done at home.

The next morning was fair, the air washed sparkling clear. Duncan built a fire under the framework. Maura measured the grease, adding a quantity of lye. Ross and Duncan placed the crossbar under the handle of the pot and raised it until it rested on the supports. Maura took up a long wooden bar with a shorter one set at right angles to it, and began stirring the contents of the pot.

"We'll be back at noon to lend you a hand," said Duncan.

Maura and Joanna took turns stirring the soap. When Maura judged it to be of the right consistency, they let the fire die down.

After the men had lifted the pot off the fire, Joanna and Maura ladled the thick brown liquid into boxes lined with old pieces of cloth. It cooled quickly into thick cream-colored slabs. Maura would cut it into cakes in a few days, when it was solid enough to handle. Then she would stack the bars in a dry place where the air could circulate around them until the soap had seasoned enough for use.

Language Arts Activity

Reread the passage and list the steps for making soap. Think of a process or activity that you know well. It can be packing for a trip or preparing for a party. Jot down the steps and number them. Then, write a description of the process. Include steps and details so that a reader unfamiliar with your activity would know how to do it.

Chemistry of Soap

How is soap made? It's the product of heating two types of compounds—an acid and a base. Acids and bases are compounds that have physical and chemical properties opposite to each other. An acid tastes sour. Grapefruits, pickles, and vinegar have acids in them. A base has properties that make it taste bitter and feel slippery. Bases and acids combine to neutralize each other.

Natural fats and oils are the source of the acids in soapmaking. Fats and oils are made of three fatty acid monomers and an alcohol called glycerol. In soapmaking, the fatty acids combine with an alkali solution (made of bases). The mixture is processed using water and heat. The resulting chemical reaction is called saponification. Saponification produces the main material of soaps, called "neat" soap. The glycerol left over, also called glycerin, is pumped away.

The difference between solid and liquid soaps depends on the alkali that's added. In a solid soap, the alkali solution is the base sodium hydroxide. In liquid soaps, the alkali solution is the base potassium hydroxide.

Making Soap Using the Continuous Process

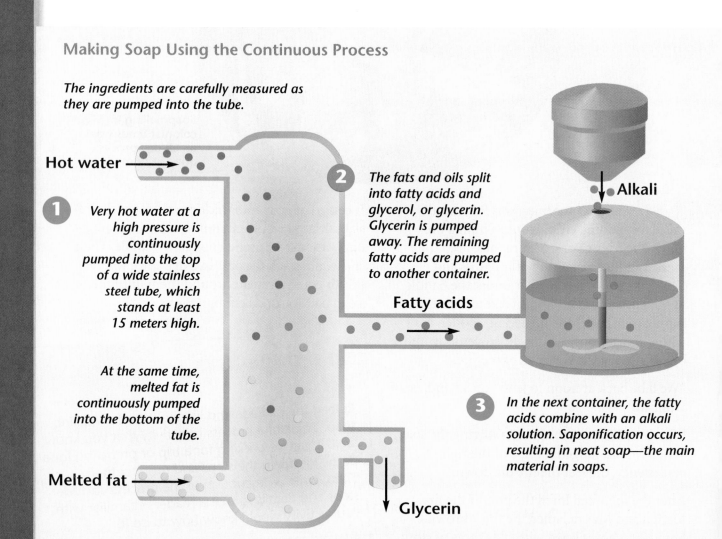

The ingredients are carefully measured as they are pumped into the tube.

Hot water

1 Very hot water at a high pressure is continuously pumped into the top of a wide stainless steel tube, which stands at least 15 meters high.

At the same time, melted fat is continuously pumped into the bottom of the tube.

Melted fat

2 The fats and oils split into fatty acids and glycerol, or glycerin. Glycerin is pumped away. The remaining fatty acids are pumped to another container.

Fatty acids

Alkali

3 In the next container, the fatty acids combine with an alkali solution. Saponification occurs, resulting in neat soap—the main material in soaps.

Glycerin

Soapmaking

After saponification occurs, neat soap is poured into molds. Other ingredients are sometimes added at this stage. Then the bars are stamped with a brand name or designed and wrapped for shipment.

To make cosmetic soaps, an additional process called milling is needed. The neat soap is poured into large slabs instead of into molds. When the slab cools, several sets of rollers press and crush it. This process makes finer, gentler soaps that people can use on their face and hands.

At this stage, a variety of other ingredients can be added, such as scents, colors, or germicides (to kill bacteria). Air can be whipped into soap to make it float. Soapmakers compete to find the combination of ingredients that will be most attractive and smell pleasant to customers.

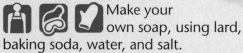

Science Activity

Make your own soap, using lard, baking soda, water, and salt.

◆ Prepare a solution of baking soda by dissolving 5 grams in 10 milliliters of water.

◆ Mix the baking soda solution with 20 grams of lard in a 400-milliliter glass beaker.

◆ Boil gently on a hot plate for 20 minutes. Stir continuously while the mixture is boiling.

◆ Let the mixture cool. Transfer to a plastic beaker. Place in an ice water bath for 5–10 minutes. Stir.

◆ Make a saturated salt solution by dissolving 20 grams in 25 milliliters of water. Add to the mixture. Stir.

◆ Remove soap curdles by pouring through cheesecloth. Drain any liquid. Put soap into a dish to dry and harden.

◆ Put a portion of soap into warm water and stir. Observe the bubbles.

◆ Test with litmus paper to see if it is acid or base. (Blue litmus paper turns red in an acid. Red litmus paper turns blue in a base.)

4 *Neat soap is poured into molds and allowed to harden. Before neat soap is made into bars, flakes, or powdered soap, other optional ingredients such as abrasives (scrubbing agents) can be added.*

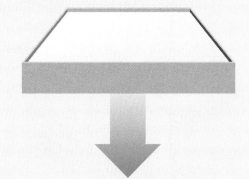

5 *Cosmetic soaps require an additional process. After the neat soap cools, it goes through the milling process. The soap is fed through rollers that crush it. Perfumes and other ingredients can be added at this stage.*

6 *The finished soap is pressed, cut, stamped, and wrapped for shipment.*

A Year of Soap

What would you do if you had to make a year's supply of your own soap, using modern ingredients? You probably buy the soap you use from a store. But it is still possible to make soap yourself by using the right ingredients and following specific instructions.

Soap recipes are as varied and numerous as food recipes. You can make soap using the oil from avocados, hazelnuts, or sunflower seeds. To add natural scents, you might include rose, cinnamon, cloves, lavender, lemon, mint, grapefruit, pine, rose, vanilla, or something else.

Colors might come from beetroot, cocoa, goldenrod, licorice, paprika, or even seaweed. You can even include "scrubbers" such as cornmeal, oatmeal, or poppy seeds!

Here is the ingredient list for one kind of soap. This recipe makes one bar of soap with a mass of 141.75 grams.

Recipe for Soap

16.8 grams alkali

45.4 grams water

42.2 grams olive oil

36.2 grams coconut oil

42.2 grams palm oil

Math Activity

Use the list of ingredients to find the answers to these questions:

◆ What is the ratio of alkali to oil in this recipe? Round to the nearest hundredth.

◆ If you made a large batch with a total mass of 1.701 kg, how many bars of soap would you get in that batch?

◆ How much of each ingredient would you need to make this batch?

◆ If your family used two bars of soap per month, how many batches of soap would you make to provide one year's supply?

◆ How many batches would you make if your family used four bars of soap per month through the summer (June, July, and August), two bars per month through the winter (December, January, and February), and three bars per month during the rest of the year?

Tie It Together

Soap Study

Organize a class project to survey and test soaps and soap products that are on the market today. Work in small groups. Choose one kind of cleaner to study, such as bar soaps, dishwashing detergents, laundry detergents, or another cleaner.

As your group investigates one kind of product, answer these questions:

◆ Look at the labels. What kinds of oils and other ingredients are listed?

◆ What do the makers claim these ingredients do? What language do they use to make these claims?

◆ How many kinds of surfaces can you clean with this product?

Next, collect several brands. Design an experiment to help you decide which brand works best.

◆ Decide what you will test for, such as how well the brand cleans grease.

◆ Develop a grading scale for rating the products.

◆ Before you begin, predict what your results will be.

◆ Keep all variables the same except for the brand.

◆ Perform the tests, collect data, and take careful notes.

Decide how to present your results to the class. You might include photographs of the test results, create a graph, or write a report describing and summarizing the results.

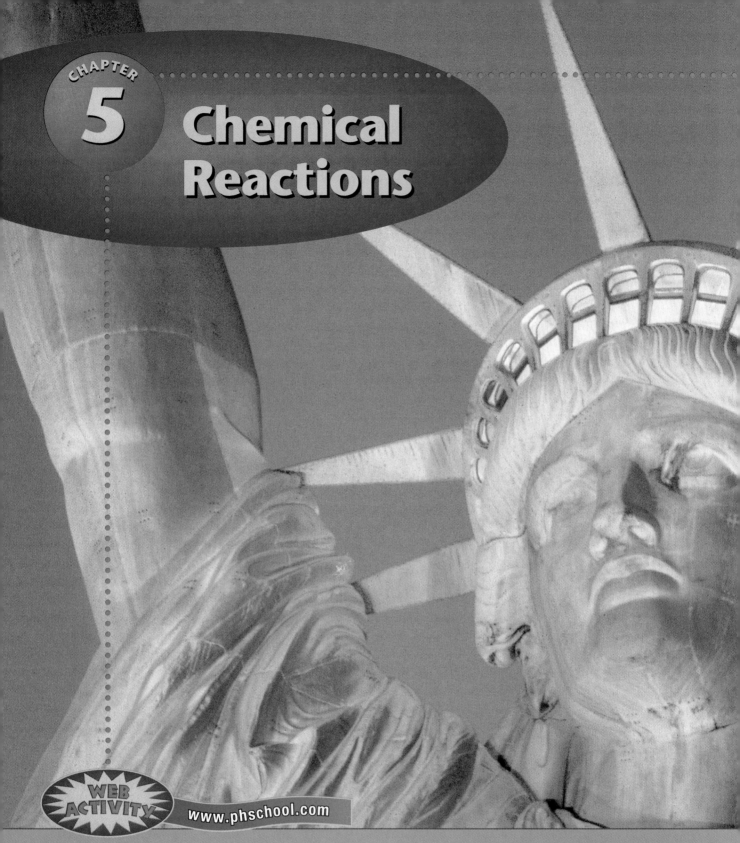

CHAPTER

5 Chemical Reactions

 WEB ACTIVITY www.phschool.com

 SECTION 1 **Observing Chemical Reactions**

Discover What Happens When Chemicals React?
Try This Mostly Cloudy
Skills Lab Where's the Evidence?

 SECTION 2 **Writing Chemical Equations**

Discover Do You Lose Anything?
Try This Still There
Sharpen Your Skills Calculating

SECTION 3 **Controlling Chemical Reactions**

Discover Can You Speed Up or Slow Down a Reaction?
Sharpen Your Skills Interpreting Data
Real-World Lab Peroxide, Catalase, and You!

Keep a Chemical Change Log

Look around. All sorts of changes are taking place. Some changes involve growth. For example, you and your classmates are growing. Other changes produce something that wasn't there before. A factory turns raw materials into desirable products, for instance. Rust coats the surface of a once-silvery fence. Even the green color of the Statue of Liberty comes from a change to the statue's copper metal covering. All of these changes are the result of chemistry, or more specifically, of the reactions between two or more chemicals.

In this chapter, you will learn more about the changes in matter that result from chemical reactions. Your project involves keeping a log of chemical changes occurring around you.

Your Goal To identify and observe chemical changes in your daily life and to record evidence for those changes.

To complete the project you must
◆ determine what evidence indicates that a chemical change has taken place
◆ record observations of the different chemical changes you notice in your life during one week
◆ classify the types of chemical changes you observe
◆ follow the safety guidelines in Appendix A

Get Started Begin by previewing the chapter to learn what a chemical change is. With a group, discuss some changes you observe regularly. Try to decide if each change is a chemical change.

Check Your Progress You'll be working on this project as you study this chapter. To keep your project on track, look for Check Your Progress boxes at the following points.
Section Review 1, page 149: List evidence of chemical changes.
Section Review 2, page 159: Construct a table for observations.

Present Your Project At the end of the chapter (page 175), you will compare your table of chemical changes with those of your classmates and classify the changes.

Integrating Health

SECTION 4
Fire and Fire Safety

Discover How Does Baking Soda Affect a Fire?
Science at Home Family Safety Plan

The copper-covered Statue of Liberty has stood in Upper New York Bay for over 100 years.

EXPLORING Evidence for Chemical Reactions

Chemical reactions produce new substances. The signs of a reaction vary, but many reactions include one or more of the following types of evidence.

Precipitation Two clear solutions react when mixed, forming a red precipitate. The presence of the precipitate tells you a chemical change has taken place.

Color Change A color change often is a sign that a chemical reaction has occurred. The brilliant colors of fall foliage result when green chlorophyll in leaves breaks down. Then colors of other substances in the leaves become visible.

Gas Production Oxygen bubbles formed during photosynthesis collect on the leaves of this underwater plant. Oxygen is a product of the reaction between carbon dioxide and water inside the cells of the plant.

Changes in Temperature The burning of natural gas (a chemical reaction) supplies heat to boil water (a physical change). A temperature change can result from the changes in energy during a chemical reaction.

Changes in Properties Baking turns flour, water, and other ingredients into light, flaky bread. The loaf of bread with its crunchy crust has very different properties from the soft dough that went into the oven.

Changes in Energy From your everyday experience, you know about various types of energy, such as light and electricity. As matter changes, it can either absorb or release energy. **The second observable characteristic of a chemical reaction is a change in energy. Some reactions absorb energy, while others release energy.** One common indication that energy has been absorbed or released is a change in temperature.

If you did the Discover activity on page 144, you observed that the mixture became colder. When baking soda (sodium bicarbonate) reacts with vinegar, the reaction takes heat from the solution, making it feel cooler. This kind of reaction, which absorbs energy, is called an **endothermic reaction** (en doh THUR mik). The reaction that occurs in the cold pack in Figure 2 is another example of an endothermic reaction.

In contrast, the reaction between fuel and oxygen in an airplane engine releases the energy that lifts the plane off the ground and keeps it in the air. Some energy is also given off as heat. A reaction that releases energy in the form of heat is called an **exothermic reaction** (eks oh THUR mik). You will learn more about energy and chemical changes in Section 3.

☑️ *Checkpoint* *How are endothermic reactions different from exothermic reactions?*

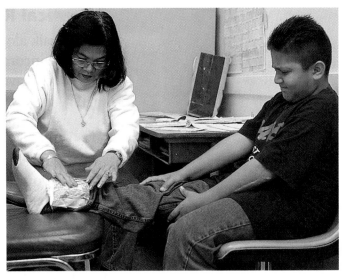

Figure 2 When this cold pack was squeezed, a reaction between water and another compound occurred and the temperature of the pack decreased. The resulting cooling effect reduces pain in the injured ankle and speeds up the healing process. *Classifying Is this reaction exothermic or endothermic? Explain.*

Figure 3 Burning airplane fuel releases a huge amount of energy. This exothermic reaction keeps a supersonic transport plane moving fast enough to remain in the air.

Where's the Evidence?

Chemical reactions occur all around you. In this lab you will observe different types of evidence of chemical reactions.

Problem

What are some signs that a chemical reaction has taken place?

Materials

4 small plastic cups   birthday candles
2 plastic spoons   sugar
tongs   clay
matches
sodium carbonate (powdered solid)
graduated cylinder, 10 mL
aluminum foil, about 10-cm square
dilute hydrochloric acid in a dropper bottle
copper sulfate solution
sodium carbonate solution

Procedure

Preview the steps for each reaction and copy the data table into your notebook.

Part 1

1. Put a pea-sized pile of sodium carbonate into a clean plastic cup. Record the appearance of the sodium carbonate in the data table.
2. Observe a dropper containing hydrochloric acid. Record the appearance of the acid. **CAUTION:** *Hydrochloric acid can burn you or anything else it touches. Wash spills with water.*
3. Predict what you might observe when acid mixes with the powdered solid. Record your prediction.
4. Add about 10 drops of hydrochloric acid to the sodium carbonate. Swirl to mix the contents of the cup. Record your observations during and after the reaction.

Part 2

5. Fold up the sides of the aluminum foil square to make a small tray.
6. Use a plastic spoon to place a pea-sized pile of sugar into the tray.
7. Carefully describe the appearance of the sugar in your data table.

DATA TABLE				
Reaction	Observations Before Reaction	Predictions	Observations During Reaction	Observations After Reaction
1. Sodium carbonate (powder) + hydrochloric acid				
2. Sugar				
3. Copper sulfate + sodium carbonate solutions				

8. Secure a small candle on your desktop in a lump of clay. Carefully light the candle with a match only after being instructed to do so by your teacher. **CAUTION:** *Tie back long hair and loose clothing.*

9. Predict what you might observe when you heat the sugar. Record your prediction.

10. Use tongs to hold the aluminum tray. Heat the sugar slowly by moving the tray gently back and forth over the flame. Make observations while the sugar is heating.

11. When you think there is no longer a chemical reaction occurring, blow out the candle.

12. Allow the tray to cool for a few seconds and set it down on your desk. Record your observations of the material left in the tray.

Part 3

13. Put about 2 mL of copper sulfate solution in one cup. **CAUTION:** *Copper sulfate is poisonous and can stain your skin and clothes. Do not touch it or get it in your mouth.* Put an equal amount of sodium carbonate solution in another cup. Record the appearance of both liquids.

14. Predict what you might observe when the two solutions are mixed. Record your prediction.

15. Combine the two solutions and record your observations. **CAUTION:** *Dispose of the solutions as directed by your teacher.*

16. Wash your hands when you have finished working.

Analyze and Conclude

1. How do the results of each reaction compare with your predictions for that reaction?

2. How did you know when Reaction 1 was over?

3. Was the product of the reaction in Part 1 a solid, a liquid, or a gas? How do you know?

4. How are the properties of the material remaining after the reaction in Part 2 different from those of the sugar?

5. Was the product of the reaction in Part 3 a solid, a liquid, or a gas? How do you know?

6. How do you know if new substances were formed in each reaction?

7. **Think About It** What senses did you use to make observations during this lab? How might you use scientific instruments to extend your senses in order to make more observations?

More to Explore

Use your observation skills to find evidence of chemical reactions involving foods in your kitchen. Look for production of gases, color changes, and changes in properties. Share your findings with your classmates.

2 Writing Chemical Equations

DISCOVER ●●●●●●●●●●●●●●●●●●●●●●●●●●●●●●●●●●●●●● ACTIVITY●●●●

Do You Lose Anything?

1. Place about two dozen coins on a table. Sort them into stacks of pennies, nickels, dimes, and quarters.

2. Count and record the number of coins in each stack. Calculate and record the value of each stack and the total of all stacks combined.

3. Mix all the coins together and then divide them randomly into four unsorted stacks.

4. Again calculate the value of each stack and the total amount of money. Count the total number of each type of coin.

5. Repeat Steps 3 and 4.

Think It Over

Making Models What happened to the total value and types of coins in this activity? Did rearranging the coins change any individual coin? If you think of the coins as representing different types of atoms, what does this model tell you about chemical reactions?

GUIDE FOR READING

◆ What does a chemical equation tell you?

◆ How does mass change during a chemical reaction?

◆ What are three categories of chemical reactions?

Reading Tip As you read, describe how each boldfaced vocabulary word relates to a chemical reaction.

Suppose you were to take a walk in a foreign country where the language is unfamiliar to you. Think of the signs you might see—two doors with drawings of a man and a woman, the receiver of a telephone, a drawing of a bicycle, and a picture of a trash can with something dropping into it. You would have no trouble figuring out what these signs mean.

Symbols express a concept in a shorter form. "Hydrogen molecules react with oxygen molecules to form water molecules," is a sentence that describes the reaction between hydrogen and oxygen. But writing it is slow and awkward. A **chemical equation** is a shorter, easier way to show chemical reactions, using symbols instead of words.

Figure 6 Symbols are short and easy-to-recognize ways of saying something. *Inferring What information does each of these symbols tell you?*

Formulas of Some Familiar Compounds

Compound	Formula	Compound	Formula
Water	H_2O	Fool's gold (pyrite)	FeS_2
Hydrogen peroxide	H_2O_2	Propane	C_3H_8
Ammonia	NH_3	Rubbing alcohol	C_3H_8O
Aspirin	$C_9H_8O_4$	Rust	Fe_2O_3
Baking soda	$NaHCO_3$	Sodium chloride	$NaCl$
Bleach	$NaClO$	Sugar (sucrose)	$C_{12}H_{22}O_{11}$
Carbon dioxide	CO_2	Sulfur dioxide	SO_2
Carbon monoxide	CO	Washing soda	Na_2CO_3
Hemoglobin	$C_{3032}H_{4816}O_{780}N_{780}S_8Fe_4$		

Figure 7 Formulas for compounds tell you what elements as well as how many atoms of each element are present. *Observing How many oxygen atoms are present in water, carbon dioxide, and sugar?*

Understanding Chemical Equations

You may be surprised to learn that though chemical equations are shorter than sentences, they contain more information. That's partly because equations use chemical formulas and other symbols instead of the words. Also, equations follow a common structure that all chemists understand.

Writing Chemical Formulas You have already seen many chemical formulas, such as H_2O and H_2O_2. You know the letter symbols stand for specific elements. (You can review those symbols in the periodic table in Appendix D.) If you think of these symbols as being like the letters of the alphabet, a formula is a "word" that represents a compound. Figure 7 shows you the formulas for some common compounds.

Besides identifying the elements in a compound, a formula also shows the ratio of the different atoms that make up that substance. In the case of molecular compounds, the formula shows the number and kind of atoms in a molecule. You can see at a glance which atoms make up a molecule of table sugar, $C_{12}H_{22}O_{11}$. For ionic compounds, the formula shows the ratio of the different ions that are present. In aluminum chloride, $AlCl_3$, there are 3 chloride ions for every 1 aluminum ion.

Notice that the numbers in a formula are written smaller and lower than the letter symbols. These numbers are subscripts. **Subscripts** show the ratio of the atoms of different elements in a formula. If a letter symbol in a chemical formula doesn't have a subscript, the number 1 is understood. For example, a carbon dioxide molecule, CO_2, has one carbon atom and two oxygen atoms. How many atoms in total does the molecule H_2O have? Since the absence of a subscript means that there is one oxygen atom, there are three atoms altogether.

Ratios and Subscripts

A ratio compares two numbers. In a chemical formula, subscripts show the ratio of one kind of atom to another. $CaBr_2$ for instance, shows that there are 2 bromide atoms for every 1 calcium atom. Write a formula for a compound that has atoms in the following ratios:

- Twice as many silver atoms as carbon atoms
- Three times as many oxygen atoms as carbon atoms

In this formula, show the elements in this order: silver (Ag), carbon (C), and oxygen (O).

Structure of an Equation

A chemical equation summarizes a reaction. It tells you the substances you start with and the substances you get at the end. The materials you have at the beginning are called the **reactants.** When the reaction is complete, you have different materials, called the **products** of the reaction. **A chemical equation uses symbols to show the reactants and the products of a reaction.**

Chemical equations have a definite structure. The formulas for the reactants are written on the left, followed by an arrow. You read the arrow as "yields." The products are written on the right. When there are two or more reactants—or two or more products—they are separated from each other by plus signs.

$$\text{Reactant} + \text{Reactant} \rightarrow \text{Product} + \text{Product}$$

The number of reactants and products can vary. Some reactions have only one reactant or product. Other reactions have two, three, or more reactants or products. Find the number of products that result when limestone ($CaCO_3$) is heated.

$$\underset{\text{Reactant}}{CaCO_3} \rightarrow \underset{\text{Product}}{CaO} + \underset{\text{Product}}{CO_2}$$

Conservation of Mass

No matter how many reactants and products are involved, all the atoms present at the start of a reaction are present at the end. Think about what happens when classes change at your school. A class is made up of a group of students and a teacher together in a room. When the bell rings, people from each class move from room to room, ending up in new and different classes. The number of students and teachers in the school has not changed. But their arrangement is different and the new groups interact differently.

Figure 8 When iron filings and sulfur are mixed and heated, the product is the compound iron sulfide. *Interpreting Diagrams How do you know that mass has been conserved in the reaction?*

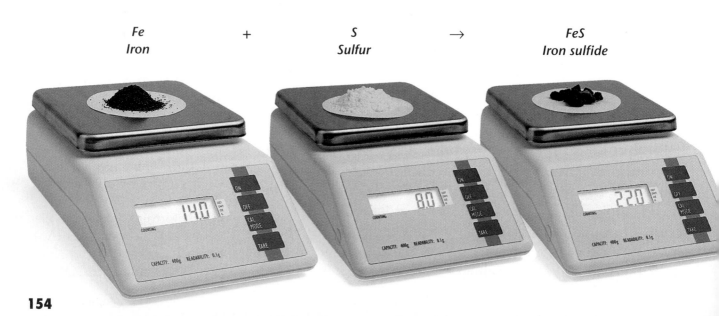

$$\underset{\text{Iron}}{Fe} + \underset{\text{Sulfur}}{S} \rightarrow \underset{\text{Iron sulfide}}{FeS}$$

Problem Solving When wood burns, it reacts with oxygen in the air. What masses would you need to measure before and after the fire to show conservation of mass?

Now imagine that all the students and teachers are atoms, and each class is a molecule. At the end of a reaction (similar to a class change), the same atoms are present, but they are grouped together in different molecules. **The amount of matter involved in a chemical reaction does not change. The total mass of the reactants must equal the total mass of the products.** This principle, called the **conservation of mass,** means that during a chemical reaction, matter is not created or destroyed.

At first glance, some reactions seem to violate the principle of conservation of mass. If you measured the cooled ash left from a wood fire, for example, it wouldn't have the same mass as the wood that had been burned. What happened to the missing mass? It has escaped into the air as carbon dioxide gas and water vapor. If you could trap and measure these gases, you'd be able to prove that the mass didn't change.

✓ *Checkpoint* *How do the masses of the atoms in the reactants of a chemical reaction compare with the atoms in the products?*

Balancing Chemical Equations

How does the principle of conservation of mass relate to a chemical equation? It indicates that the same number of atoms exist in the products as were present in the reactants. So to describe a reaction accurately, a chemical equation must show the same number of each type of atom on both sides of the equation. When that happens, chemists say the equation is balanced. To balance an equation, begin by looking at the formulas.

$$H_2 + O_2 \rightarrow H_2O$$

How many atoms does the hydrogen molecule have? How about oxygen? How many of each kind of atom are present in one water molecule?

Still There

Use nuts and bolts to model the principle of conservation of mass.

1. Measure the mass of a collection of bolts, each with a nut attached to it.
2. Remove all the nuts from the bolts. Measure the total mass of the nuts. Then do the same with the bolts. Add these values.
3. Rearrange your collection, putting two or three nuts on one bolt, one nut on another bolt, and so on. You can even leave a few pieces unattached.
4. Measure the total mass again. Compare this figure with the totals from Steps 1 and 2.

Making Models How are the nuts and bolts similar to atoms and molecules in a chemical reaction? How do your observations model conservation of mass?

Calculating ACTIVITY

Each chemical formula below is written just as it might be in a balanced chemical equation. For each formula, calculate the number of each kind of atom.

$$3\ H_2O$$
$$2\ H_2SO_4$$
$$4\ Fe_2O_3$$
$$6\ NaCl$$
$$NO_2$$

When a coefficient is in front of a formula, how do you find the total number of atoms of one kind? What do you do if there is no coefficient?

Look at the chemical equation and models for the reaction:

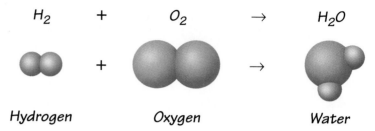

Count the number of atoms of each element on each side of the equation. You find 2 atoms of oxygen in the reactants but only 1 atom of oxygen in the products.

How can you get the number of oxygen molecules on both sides to be the same? You might be tempted to balance the oxygen by changing the formula for water to H_2O_2. Don't even think about it! Remember that H_2O_2 is the formula for hydrogen peroxide, a completely different compound.

To balance the equation, use a coefficient. A **coefficient** (koh uh FISH unt) is a number placed *in front of* a chemical formula in an equation. It tells you how many atoms or molecules of each reactant and product take part in the reaction. If the coefficient is 1, you don't need to write it. Balance the number of oxygen atoms by writing the coefficient 2 for water. That's like saying "2 × H_2O." Now there are 2 oxygen atoms in the product.

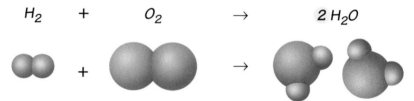

Okay, you've balanced the oxygen atoms. But now there are 2 hydrogen atoms in the reactants and 4 in the product. How can you balance the hydrogen? Try doubling the number of hydrogen atoms on the left side of the equation by changing the coefficient for hydrogen to 2. That's it!

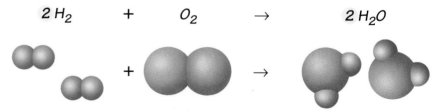

Now there are 4 hydrogen atoms and 2 oxygen atoms on each side. The equation is balanced. It tells you that 2 molecules of hydrogen react with 1 molecule of oxygen to yield 2 molecules of water. Count the atoms in the final diagram. Prove to yourself that the balanced equation is correct.

Sample Problem

When magnesium metal, Mg, reacts with oxygen, O_2, the product of the reaction is magnesium oxide, MgO. Write a balanced equation for this reaction.

Write the word equation.	*Magnesium + Oxygen → Magnesium oxide*	
Write the chemical equation.	$Mg + O_2 \rightarrow MgO$	
Count the number of atoms of each element on each side of the equation.	Mg one O two	Mg one O one
Choose coefficients to balance the equation.	$2\,Mg + O_2 \rightarrow 2\,MgO$	
Think about it.	The answer shows 2 magnesium atoms and 2 oxygen atoms on each side, so the equation is balanced.	

Practice Problems

1. Balance the equation: $C + Cl_2 \rightarrow CCl_4$
2. Balance the equation: $Al_2O_3 \rightarrow Al + O_2$

Classifying Chemical Reactions

Chemical reactions can be classified by what happens to the reactants and products. Substances may add together to make a more complex substance. They may break apart to make simpler substances. Or substances may even exchange parts. In each case, new materials form. **Many chemical reactions can be classified in one of three categories: synthesis, decomposition, or replacement.** As you read about each of these kinds of reactions, look at the examples. Compare the reactants and the products to see how they change.

Synthesis Have you ever listened to music from a synthesizer? You can hear many different notes and types of musical sounds. The synthesizer combines these sounds to make a complicated piece of music. When two or more substances (elements or compounds) combine to make a more complex substance, the process is called **synthesis** (SIN thuh sis). To synthesize is to put things together. Look back at the reaction of hydrogen and oxygen to make water. You should see now that this is a synthesis reaction—two elements come together, making a compound.

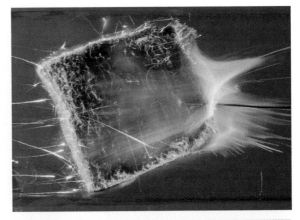

Figure 10 Iron combines with oxygen (top) to form iron oxide, or rust (bottom). This reaction is an example of synthesis.

Acid rain is a product of synthesis reactions. In one case, sulfur dioxide, oxygen, and water combine to make sulfuric acid. Look at the equation for the reaction. Can you find the 8 oxygen atoms on each side of the equation?

$$2\,SO_2 \quad + \quad O_2 \quad + \quad 2\,H_2O \quad \rightarrow \quad 2\,H_2SO_4$$
Sulfur dioxide   Oxygen   Water   Sulfuric acid

Sulfur dioxide comes from car engines or from power plants that burn coal. Oxygen and water vapor are in the air. Together they produce sulfuric acid, which causes rainwater to become corrosive. This acid water then eats away at stone and metal, and can damage living organisms.

Decomposition While a synthesis reaction builds compounds from simpler reactants, a process called **decomposition** breaks down compounds into simpler products. Many people keep a bottle of hydrogen peroxide to clean cuts. If you keep such a bottle for a very long time, you'll have water instead. The hydrogen peroxide decomposes into water and oxygen gas.

$$2\,H_2O_2 \rightarrow 2\,H_2O + O_2$$

The oxygen that is produced escapes into the air.

☑ *Checkpoint* *How do synthesis and decomposition differ?*

Figure 11 Safety airbags in cars inflate as a result of a decomposition reaction. On impact, a detonator cap inside the air bag explodes. The explosion causes a compound made of sodium and nitrogen to decompose. One product is a large quantity of nitrogen gas.
Applying Concepts *Why would quick inflation of airbags be important?*

Replacement When one element replaces another in a compound, or when two elements in different compounds trade places, the process is called **replacement.** Copper metal, for example, can be obtained by heating rock containing copper oxide in the presence of charcoal. The carbon of the charcoal takes the place of copper in the copper oxide.

$$2\,CuO + C \rightarrow 2\,Cu + CO_2$$

Medications for an upset stomach may contain calcium carbonate. Notice how this replacement reduces the amount of stomach acid (HCl).

$$CaCO_3 + 2\,HCl \rightarrow CaCl_2 + H_2CO_3$$

Not all reactions can be classified as synthesis, decomposition, or replacement, however.

Figure 12 Copper metal can be chemically obtained from copper ore. Copper oxide (in the ore) reacts with carbon in a replacement reaction.

Section 2 Review

1. What information do you need in order to write a chemical equation?
2. What is the principle of conservation of mass?
3. List and define three categories of chemical reactions.
4. **Thinking Critically** **Applying Concepts** Balance the following chemical equations by adding coefficients:
   a. $HCl + NaOH \rightarrow H_2O + NaCl$
   b. $Fe_2O_3 + C \rightarrow Fe + CO_2$
   c. $SO_2 + O_2 \rightarrow SO_3$
5. **Thinking Critically** **Classifying** Classify each of the following reactions as synthesis, decomposition, or replacement:
   a. $2\,NH_4NO_3 \rightarrow 2\,N_2 + O_2 + 4\,H_2O$
   b. $2\,Al + Fe_2O_3 \rightarrow Al_2O_3 + 2\,Fe$
   c. $P_4O_{10} + 6\,H_2O \rightarrow 4\,H_3PO_4$

> **CHAPTER PROJECT**
>
> **Check Your Progress**
> Prepare a table to keep track of the chemical changes you observe. Have your teacher check your table to be sure it contains the proper headings. Record the different chemical changes you observe for a week. Make sure you can describe the evidence for each chemical change. If possible, classify each reaction as a synthesis, decomposition, or replacement reaction. Also classify it as occurring in a living or nonliving setting.

Controlling Chemical Reactions

Can You Speed Up or Slow Down a Reaction?

1. Put on your safety goggles and lab apron.

2. Obtain about 125 mL each of three solutions of vitamin C and water—one at room temperature, one at about 75°C, and one chilled to between 5° and 10°C.

3. Add three drops of iodine solution to each container and stir each with a clean spoon. Compare changes you observe in the solutions.

4. Clean up your work area and wash your hands.

Think It Over

Inferring What conclusion can you make about the effect of temperature on the reaction of iodine and vitamin C?

GUIDE FOR READING

◆ How is activation energy related to the start of chemical reactions ?

◆ How can you control the rate of a chemical reaction?

Reading Tip As you read, make a list of factors affecting reaction rate.

Figure 13 Building demolition requires a good understanding of chemical reactions.

Y ou are working on an engineering team that tears down buildings. "3, 2, 1 . . . Let it go!" You push a button and suddenly a loud rumbling sound starts. The ground shakes, and clouds of dust pour into the street. In 15 seconds, a tall building is reduced to a pile of rubble. Careful control of energy in the explosion is critical to collapse the building without even breaking a window next door. If the demolition expert on your team doesn't understand the chemical reactions used, people could be injured or property damaged.

Although you may never demolish a building, you do use energy from controlled chemical reactions every day. Every time your body converts your lunch into the energy to play sports or you go for a ride in a car, you are using controlled reactions.

Getting Reactions Started

If you have watched someone start a wood fire, you may have seen that it's not easy to do. Yet once wood begins to burn, it gives off a steady supply of heat and light. Why is it so hard to start some chemical reactions?

Activation Energy The rock at the top of the hill in Figure 14 contains stored energy because of its position. Yet it remains motionless until it's pushed over the small hump. After that, it falls down the hill rapidly, releasing its stored energy.

Every chemical reaction is like that rock. The reaction won't begin until the reactants get the energy needed to push them "over the hump." **Chemical reactions need a certain amount of energy to get started.** For example, energy is needed to break existing chemical bonds. Once that energy is available, the atoms begin to form the new chemical bonds that create the products. The minimum amount of energy needed to start a chemical reaction is called the **activation energy** of the reaction.

Consider the reaction in which hydrogen and oxygen form water. This chemical change gives off tremendous amounts of energy. But if you simply mix the two gases together, the mixture can remain unchanged for years. For the reaction to start, a tiny amount of activation energy—just a spark—is needed. Once a few molecules of hydrogen and oxygen react, the rest will follow because each reaction provides activation energy for new reactions. So every chemical reaction needs activation energy to begin. But do reactions also need energy to keep going? That depends on whether the reaction is exothermic or endothermic.

Social Studies CONNECTION

In the early 1900s, people sometimes traveled in airships called dirigibles. On May 6, 1937, the airship *Hindenburg* came in for a landing over Lakehurst, New Jersey. Somehow the ship caught fire, killing 36 people. The *Hindenburg* was a tragic example of how much energy could be released during a chemical reaction.

In Your Journal

Pretend you are a reporter on the scene. Write a brief news article explaining how chemical reactions affected the *Hindenburg* disaster.

Figure 14 The rock at the top of this hill cannot roll down the hill until a small push gets it going. *Making Models How is this cartoon a kind of model for the role of activation energy in a chemical reaction?*

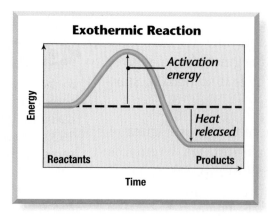

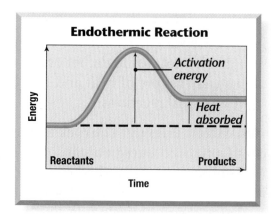

Figure 15 Every chemical reaction needs a certain amount of energy to get started.
Interpreting Diagrams Tell where increases and decreases in energy are shown in each diagram.

Energy and Types of Reactions In Section 1, you learned that an exothermic reaction is one that gives off energy. Most chemical reactions are exothermic. They follow the pattern shown in Figure 15 in the graph on the left. Notice that a dotted line marks the energy level of the reactants before the reaction.

Like all reactions, exothermic reactions need activation energy to get started. But additional energy is not needed to complete the reaction. Instead, energy is given off as the reaction takes place. As a result, the energy level of the products is lower than the energy level of the starting materials. An example of an exothermic reaction is the burning of fuel to produce heat.

Now examine the graph of an endothermic reaction in Figure 15. Like all chemical reactions, endothermic reactions need activation energy to get started. But they also need a supply of energy to keep going. Because the materials absorb energy as the products are formed, the energy level of the final materials is higher than that of the starting materials.

That's what happens when baking soda and vinegar react in the Discover activity on page 144. Thermal energy already present in the solution is enough to start the reaction. As the reaction keeps going, it continues to draw the energy it needs from the solution. Another example of an endothermic reaction is baking bread. Bread dough won't bake in cool temperatures.

☑ *Checkpoint* *Why do exothermic reactions need activation energy?*

Rates of Chemical Reactions

Chemical reactions don't all occur at the same rate. Some, like explosions, are very fast. Others, like the rusting of metal, are much slower. Also, a particular reaction can occur at different rates depending on the conditions. A reaction's speed depends in part on how easily the particles of the reactants can get together.

If you want to make a chemical reaction happen faster, you need to get more reactant particles together more often. To slow down a reaction, you need to do the opposite—get fewer particles together less often. **Chemists can control the rates of reactions by changing factors such as concentration, temperature, and surface area, and by using substances called catalysts and inhibitors.**

Figure 16 Bubbles of hydrogen form when magnesium reacts with an acid. The test tube on the left has a lower concentration of acid than the test tube on the right.
Relating Cause and Effect How does the concentration of acid affect the rate of the reaction?

Concentration One way to increase the rate of a reaction is to increase the concentration of the reactants. **Concentration** is the amount of one material in a given amount of another material. For example, adding a small spoon of sugar to a glass of lemonade will make it sweet. But adding a large spoon of sugar makes the lemonade a lot sweeter! The glass with more sugar has a greater concentration of sugar molecules.

Increasing the concentrations of the reactants makes more particles available to react. Compare the test tubes in Figure 16. In the test tube on the right, the greater concentration of acid means that more acid particles are present to react with the magnesium metal. You can see evidence for the increased rate of reaction in the greater number of bubbles that are produced.

Temperature Another way to increase the rate of a reaction is to increase its temperature. When you heat a substance, its particles move faster. Faster-moving particles increase the reaction rate in two ways. First, the particles come in contact more often, which

Figure 17 Unrefrigerated foods quickly spoil from the chemical reactions carried out by microorganisms. Keeping foods cold slows these changes.

Sharpen your Skills

Interpreting Data

ACTIVITY

1. Measure the length and width of a face of a gelatin cube.
2. Calculate the area of that face of the cube.
   Area = length × width
   Repeat for each of the other five faces. Then add the six values together to get the total surface area.
3. Using a plastic knife, cut the cube in half and repeat Steps 1 and 2 for each piece of gelatin. Add the surface areas of the two pieces to get a new total.

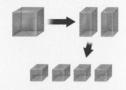

4. How did the total surface area of the cube before it was cut compare with the total after it was cut?
5. Predict what would happen to the total surface area if you cut each cube in two again. If you have time, test your prediction.

Figure 18 The concrete walls of this grain elevator in Kansas were blown apart by an explosion when grain particles and oxygen above the stored wheat exploded. Grain dust has a much greater surface area exposed to air than the top surface of a pile of grain does.

means there are more chances for a reaction to happen. Second, faster-moving particles have more energy. This energy helps the reactants get over the activation energy "hump."

At home, you often use temperature to control reaction rates. Suppose that you forget to put milk back into the refrigerator before you leave for school. When you come home, the milk may smell sour. Milk contains bacteria, which carry out thousands of chemical reactions as they live and reproduce. At room temperature, those reactions happen more quickly. Some of the reactions cause food to spoil. Keeping foods cold slows down those reactions, so your food stays fresh longer.

Surface Area When a chunk of solid material reacts with a liquid or a gas, only the particles on the surface of the solid can come in contact with the other reactant. Now suppose you break the solid into smaller pieces. What happens? You've increased the surface area of the solid. More particles of the material are exposed, so the reaction happens faster. That's also what happens when you chew your food. Chewing breaks food into smaller pieces. Your digestive juices can then work more quickly to change the food into nutrients your body can use.

Catalysts Another way to control the rate of a reaction is to change the activation energy. If you decrease the activation energy, the reaction happens faster. A **catalyst** (KAT uh list) is a material that increases the rate of a reaction by lowering the activation energy. Although catalysts help change a reaction's rate, they are not permanently changed in the reaction. Thus they themselves are not considered reactants.

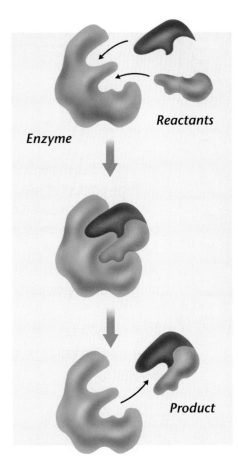

INTEGRATING LIFE SCIENCE Many chemical reactions happen at temperatures that would be deadly to living things. Yet, some of these reactions are necessary for life. The cells in your body (as in all living things) contain biological catalysts called **enzymes** (EN zymz). Your body contains thousands of different enzymes. Each one is specific. That means it affects only one particular chemical reaction.

Enzymes provide a surface on which reactions take place. The surface helps reactions happen at lower temperatures because it lowers activation energy. In this way, enzymes safely increase the reaction rates of chemical reactions necessary for life. After the reaction, the enzyme breaks away unchanged.

Inhibitors Sometimes a reaction is more useful when it can be slowed down rather than speeded up. A material used to decrease the rate of a reaction is called an **inhibitor.** Inhibitors work in many different ways.

The discovery of one inhibitor had an important effect on the construction industry. Nitroglycerin is a powerful liquid explosive that decomposes quickly, releasing tremendous energy. An explosion can be caused just by shaking the bottle! In the 1860s, Alfred Nobel tried adding certain solid materials, such as wood pulp, to the nitroglycerin. The solids absorbed the liquid and kept it from reacting until it was detonated. This mixture could be handled more safely and still be used for blasting. Nobel's discovery is the more easily controlled material known as dynamite.

Figure 19 Enzyme molecules are shaped in ways that help reactant molecules come together.

Section 3 Review

1. What would happen if the activation energy for a particular chemical reaction was not available?
2. Describe three ways to increase the rate of a chemical reaction.
3. Which has greater surface area: a sugar cube or an equal mass of sugar crystals? Explain.
4. **Thinking Critically** **Relating Cause and Effect** Copy and complete the table below to show how some factors increase, decrease, or have no effect on the rate of a reaction.

Changes	Effect on Reaction Rate
Decreased concentration	
Increased surface area	
Heat added	
Catalyst	

Science at Home

Comparing Reaction Rates Place an iron nail in a plastic cup. Add enough water to almost cover the nail. Place a small piece of fine steel wool in another cup and add the same amount of water. Ask family members to predict what will happen overnight. The next day, examine the nail and steel wool. Compare the amount of rust on each. Were your family's predictions correct? Explain how the reaction rates are affected by the surface areas.

Peroxide, Catalase, & You!

Hydrogen peroxide is a poisonous waste product of reactions in living cells. An enzyme called catalase, found in the blood, speeds up the breakdown of hydrogen peroxide into harmless water and oxygen gas. In this lab, you will explore the action of catalase under changing conditions.

Problem

How does temperature affect the action of an enzyme?

Skills Focus

measuring, controlling variables, drawing conclusions

Materials

forceps   stopwatch
test tube with a one-hole stopper
0.1% hydrogen peroxide solution
filter paper disks soaked in liver preparation (catalase enzyme) and kept at four different temperatures (room temperature, 0–4°C, 37°C, and 100°C)
container to hold water (beaker or bowl)

Procedure

1. Form a hypothesis that predicts how the action of the catalase enzyme will differ at the different temperatures to be tested.
2. Make a data table like the one below. Get the room temperature from your teacher.
3. Fill a container with water. Then fill a test tube with 0.1% hydrogen peroxide solution until the test tube is overflowing. Do this over a sink or the container of water.

DATA TABLE

Temperature (°C)	Time (sec)	Average Time for Class (sec)
0		
(room temperarure)		
37		
100		

3. Make a data table similar to the one shown.

4. Moisten the small end of a one-hole stopper with water.

5. Using forceps, remove a filter paper disk soaked in liver preparation (catalase enzyme) that has been kept at room temperature. Stick it to the moistened end of the one-hole stopper.

6. Your partner should be ready with the stopwatch for the next step.

7. Place the stopper firmly into the test tube, hold your thumb over the hole, and quickly invert the test tube. Start the stopwatch. Put the inverted end of the test tube into the container of water, as shown in the photograph, and remove your thumb.

8. If the hydrogen peroxide breaks down, oxygen will be produced. Oxygen bubbles will cling to the disk and cause it to float. Record the time it takes for the disk to rise to the top. If the disk does not rise within 30 seconds, record "no reaction" and go on to Step 9.

9. Rinse the test tube and repeat the procedure with catalase enzyme disks kept at 0°C, 37°C, and 100°C. **CAUTION:** *When you remove the disk kept in the hot water bath, do not use your bare hands. Avoid spilling the hot water.*

Analyze and Conclude

1. Calculate the average time for each temperature based on the results of the entire class. Enter the results in your data table.

2. Make a line graph of the data you collected. Label the horizontal axis (*x*-axis) "Temperature" with a scale from 0°C to 100°C. Label the vertical axis (*y*-axis) "Time" with a scale from 0 to 30 seconds. Plot the class average time for each temperature.

3. What evidence do you have that your hypothesis from Step 1 is either supported or not supported?

4. How is the time it takes the disk to rise to the top of the tube related to the rate of the reaction?

5. What can you conclude about the activity of the enzyme at the various temperatures you tested? (*Hint:* Enzyme activity is greater when the rate of reaction is faster.)

6. Make a prediction about how active the enzyme would be at 10°C, 60°C, and 75°C. Give reasons to support your prediction.

7. **Apply** Oxygen kills many kinds of bacteria that can cause infection. Explain why hydrogen peroxide is often used as a treatment on cuts and scrapes.

Design an Experiment

The activity of an enzyme also depends upon the concentration of the enzyme. Design an experiment that explores the relationship between enzyme activity and enzyme concentration. (Your teacher can give you disks soaked with different enzyme concentrations.)

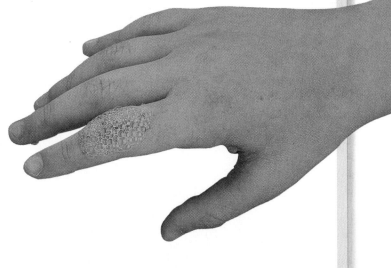

SECTION 4 Fire and Fire Safety

DISCOVER •• ACTIVITY

How Does Baking Soda Affect a Fire?

1. Put on your safety goggles.

2. Secure a small candle in a holder or some clay. After instructions from your teacher, use a match to light the candle.

3. Place a beaker or glass next to the candle. Measure one spoonful of baking soda into the beaker. Add about 60 mL of water and stir. Add 60 mL of vinegar.

4. As soon as the mixture stops foaming, tip the beaker as if you are pouring something out of it onto the flame. **CAUTION:** *Do not pour any liquid on the candle.*

5. Observe what happens to the flame.

Think It Over

Developing Hypotheses The gas produced in the beaker was carbon dioxide. Based on the results of this experiment, develop a hypothesis to explain what you observed in Step 5.

GUIDE FOR READING

◆ What are the three things necessary to maintain a fire?

◆ How does water stop combustion?

Reading Tip Before you read, predict what conditions contribute to the start of a fire. Revise your predictions as you read.

What picture comes to mind when you hear the word *fire?* Do you think of a warm campfire on a cold night or a house reduced to a pile of ashes? All fires are chemically similar, but a fire can be useful or disastrous depending on whether or not it is controlled. You can keep fires under control, but only if you understand fire as a chemical reaction.

Understanding Fire

Fire is the result of **combustion,** a rapid reaction between oxygen and a substance called a fuel. A **fuel** is a material that releases energy when it burns. Some fuels you probably know about are oil, coal, wood, gasoline, and paper. Combustion of these types of fuel always produces carbon dioxide and water. Sometimes products such as smoke and poisonous gases may form from incomplete combustion or the presence of other materials.

The Fire Triangle Although a combustion reaction is very exothermic and fast, a fire cannot start unless conditions are right. **Three things are necessary to start and maintain a fire—fuel, oxygen, and heat.**

Where does oxygen come from? You probably know the answer is the air. About 20 percent of the air around you is composed of oxygen gas. If air can reach the fuel, so can oxygen. A large fire can actually draw oxygen toward it. As other gases in the air around the flame are heated, they move rapidly away from the fire. Cooler air flows toward the fire, bringing a fresh supply of oxygen. If you stand in front of a fire in a fireplace, you can often feel the flow of air to the fire.

The third part of the fire triangle is heat. Fuel and oxygen can be together, but they won't react until something provides enough activation energy to start the combustion reaction. This energy can come from a lighted match, an electric spark, lightning, or the heat from a stove. Once the reaction starts, the heat released by the combustion can keep the reaction going.

Once a fire has started, it can continue a long time, as long as all three components of the fire triangle are available. Coal in abandoned mines underneath the town of Centralia, Pennsylvania, started burning in 1962 and continues to burn. Many old ventilation shafts lead into the tunnels, but they have never been mapped. Since all the shafts cannot be located and sealed, air (containing oxygen) continues to flow into the mines, supporting the fire. Heat and poisonous gases coming up from the fire through cracks in the ground made living in Centralia difficult. Everyone eventually moved away. No one knows how long this fire will continue to burn.

✓ *Checkpoint* *What is necesssary to start a fire?*

Controlling Fire Use your knowledge of chemical reactions to think of ways to control a fire. What if you remove one part of the fire triangle? For example, you can get the fuel away from the flames. You can also keep oxygen from getting to the fuel, or cool the combustion reaction. Any of these actions may help bring a fire under control.

Think about how firefighters put out a fire in a building. They use large hoses to spray huge amounts of water on the flaming part of the building.

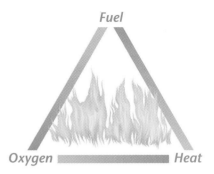

Figure 20 If any point of the fire triangle is missing, a fire will not continue. *Applying Concepts How does putting a lid over a burning pot of food affect the fire triangle?*

Figure 21 Firefighters use water to cool a fire and prevent oxygen from reaching the fuel.

Water removes two parts of the fire triangle. First, water covers the fuel, which keeps it from coming into contact with oxygen. Second, evaporation of the water uses a large amount of heat, causing the fire to cool. Without heat, there isn't enough energy to continue the combustion, so the reaction stops.

Home Fire Safety

Every year, fire claims thousands of lives in the United States. If you know how to prevent fires in your home and what to do if a fire starts, you are better prepared to take action. You may save your home or even your life!

Common Sources of Fires The two most common sources of home fires are small heaters and fires that start in the kitchen during cooking. Another common cause is faulty electrical wiring. The fires that cause the most deaths start from carelessness with cigarettes.

Figure 22 Families can take several steps to prevent fire and to be ready for action if one should start. *Making Judgments Which of these fire safety aids do you think are most important for a home to have?*

Fighting Fires You can fight a small fire by using what you know about the fire triangle. For example, carbon dioxide gas can be used to smother a fire by preventing contact between the fuel and oxygen in the air. If a small fire should start on the stove,

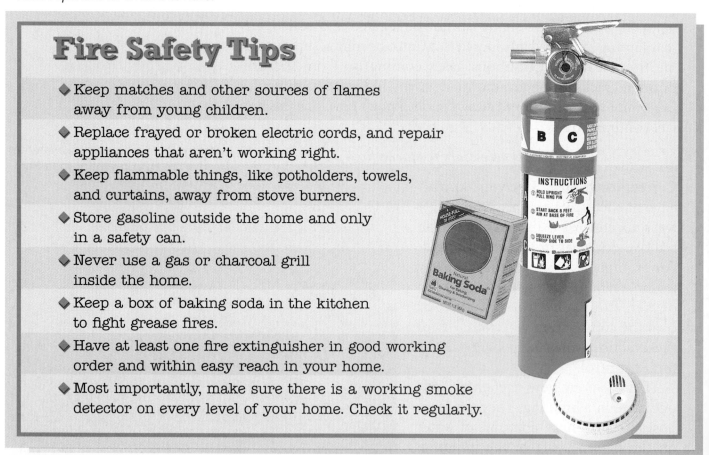

Fire Safety Tips

- Keep matches and other sources of flames away from young children.
- Replace frayed or broken electric cords, and repair appliances that aren't working right.
- Keep flammable things, like potholders, towels, and curtains, away from stove burners.
- Store gasoline outside the home and only in a safety can.
- Never use a gas or charcoal grill inside the home.
- Keep a box of baking soda in the kitchen to fight grease fires.
- Have at least one fire extinguisher in good working order and within easy reach in your home.
- Most importantly, make sure there is a working smoke detector on every level of your home. Check it regularly.

covering it with baking soda may put the fire out. Liquids in food will react with baking soda to produce carbon dioxide. The baking soda itself will help smother the fire, too.

The smaller a fire is, the easier it is to control. You can cool a match enough to stop combustion just by blowing on it. A small fire in a trash can may be doused with a pan of water. If the fire spreads to the curtains, however, even a garden hose might not deliver enough water to put it out.

One of the most effective ways to fight a small fire is with a fire extinguisher. Extinguishers designed for home use are effective when used properly. But a fire that is growing as you fight it is out of control. If this happens, there is only one safe thing to do—get away from the fire and let the fire department handle it.

Preventing Trouble The best form of fire safety is fire prevention. With your family, check your home for fire hazards and fire-fighting aids. Figure 22 shows some things you can do. Fires can be dangerous and deadly, but many fires can be prevented if you are careful. Understanding the chemistry of fire gives you a way to reduce risk and increase your family's safety.

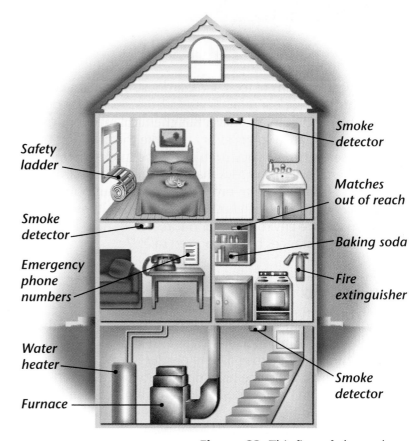

Figure 23 This fire-safe house has many of the fire-prevention features listed in Figure 22.
Interpreting Illustrations Which of those safety features can you find in the picture?

Section 4 Review

1. What are the three points of the fire triangle?
2. Why is water a good tool for fighting most fires?
3. List some of the products of combustion.
4. How does adding carbon dioxide gas to cover a fire control or stop it? Use the fire triangle in your answer.
5. **Thinking Critically Making Judgments** Why is fire prevention one of the best ways to fight fires?

Science at Home

Family Safety Plan Work with your family to formulate a fire safety plan. How can fires be prevented in your home? How can fires be put out if they occur? Is there a functioning smoke detector on each floor of the home, especially near the bedrooms? How can the fire department be contacted in an emergency? Design a fire escape route. Make sure all family members know the route as well as a meeting place outside.

SCIENCE AND SOCIETY

Transporting Hazardous Chemicals

Each year, millions of tons of hazardous substances criss-cross the country by truck and rail. These substances can be poisonous, flammable, and even explosive. But chemical reactions using these materials are also necessary to make the products that people use every day. They even make the trucks themselves run.

The chemical industry says that the transport of hazardous substances is safe and that problems are rare. But public health officials are worried. When accidents do happen, these compounds can damage the environment and threaten human lives. How can hazardous substances be transported safely?

The Issues

Why Do People Transport Hazardous Substances? Transporting hazardous substances can be dangerous. Useful products are made, however, from the hazardous materials that trucks and trains carry. Would people give up cars, computers, and CDs?

For example, CDs are made from plastics. To produce these plastics, manufacturers use compounds such as benzene and styrene. Benzene fumes are poisonous and flammable. Styrene can explode when exposed to air. Public health experts say it is important to find safe substitutes for dangerous substances. But finding alternatives will be difficult and expensive.

What Are the Risks? Serious accidents are rare. But in the United States in a recent year, there were over 300 accidents involving hazardous chemical releases. Public health experts say that some substances are too hazardous to transport on roads and railroads. An accidental release of these substances near a city could harm many people.

Some people say that vehicles carrying chemically reactive or hazardous substances should be restricted to isolated roads. However, many factories that use the chemical compounds are located in cities. Chemicals often must be transported from where they are made to where they are used. In the case of gasoline, cars are everywhere. Trucks and trains must transport the fuel to every neighborhood and region of the country.

How Should Transportation Be Regulated? Manufacturers that use hazardous chemicals say that there already are adequate laws. The Hazardous Materials Transportation Act (1975, revised 1994) requires carriers of hazardous substances to follow strict labeling and packaging rules. They must keep records of what they carry and where they travel. Local emergency officials in communities near transportation routes must also be trained to handle accidents involving these substances.

On the other hand, public health experts say there are not enough inspectors to check all trucks and trains and make sure rules are followed. But hiring more inspectors would cost additional tax money.

You Decide

1. Identify the Problem
In your own words, explain the problem of safely transporting hazardous substances.

2. Analyze the Options
Examine the pros and cons of greater regulation of the transport of hazardous substances. In each position, consider the effects on chemical industries and on the general public.

3. Find a Solution
Suppose there is a chemical factory in your city. You are the emergency planning director. Create regulations for transporting hazardous substances through your community.

SECTION 1 Observing Chemical Reactions

Key Ideas

◆ A chemical reaction produces materials that have different properties than the starting materials had. Each reaction either absorbs or releases energy.

◆ Color change, production of a gas or a precipitate, a change in temperature, or a change in the properties of a substance are all clues that a chemical reaction has taken place.

◆ Chemical reactions occur when chemical bonds are formed or broken.

Key Terms
precipitate   exothermic reaction
endothermic reaction

SECTION 2 Writing Chemical Equations

Key Ideas

◆ A chemical equation uses symbols to show the reactants and products of a chemical reaction.

◆ Matter is neither created nor destroyed during a chemical reaction.

◆ Chemical reactions may be classified by the types of changes in reactants and products.

Key Terms
chemical equation   coefficient
subscript   synthesis
reactants   decomposition
products   replacement reaction
conservation of mass

SECTION 3 Controlling Chemical Reactions

Key Ideas

◆ Every chemical reaction needs activation energy to get started. Endothermic reactions need energy to continue.

◆ The rate of a chemical reaction can be controlled by such factors as concentration, surface area, temperature, and use of a catalyst or inhibitor.

Key Terms
activation energy   catalyst   inhibitor
concentration   enzyme

SECTION 4 Fire and Fire Safety

INTEGRATING HEALTH

Key Ideas

◆ Fuel, oxygen, and heat are needed to start and maintain a fire.

◆ Water stops fire by cooling the materials and keeping oxygen from the fuel.

Key Terms
combustion   fuel

Organizing Information

Concept Map Copy the chemical reactions concept map onto a separate sheet of paper. Then complete it and add a title. (For more on concept maps, see the Skills Handbook.)

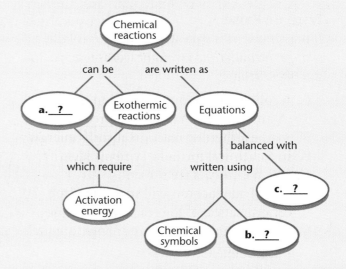

Reviewing Content

For more review of key concepts, see the Interactive Student Tutorial CD-ROM.

Multiple Choice

Choose the letter of the best answer.

1. Which one of the following does NOT indicate a chemical change?
   a. formation of a precipitate
   b. change of color
   c. change in surface area
   d. production of a gas

2. You can balance a chemical equation by changing the
   a. coefficients.   b. products.
   c. reactants.   d. formulas.

3. The reaction between sulfur trioxide and water ($SO_3 + H_2O \rightarrow H_2SO_4$) is called
   a. replacement.
   b. synthesis.
   c. decomposition.
   d. combustion.

4. The rate of a chemical reaction can be increased by all the following, except:
   a. increasing temperature.
   b. decreasing activation energy.
   c. decreasing concentration.
   d. increasing surface area.

5. To extinguish a fire, do *not*
   a. remove fuel.
   b. add oxygen.
   c. reduce heat.
   d. add baking soda.

True or False

If the statement is true, write true. If it is false, change the underlined word or words to make the statement true.

6. A solid that falls out of solution during a chemical reaction is called a <u>precipitate</u>.

7. A(n) exothermic reaction <u>absorbs</u> energy.

8. In a chemical formula, <u>symbols</u> identify which elements are present.

9. Chemical reactions will speed up if the concentration of the reactants <u>decreases</u>.

10. The three parts of the fire triangle are fuel, <u>carbon dioxide</u>, and heat.

Checking Concepts

11. Why can't you balance a chemical equation by changing the subscripts?

12. You find the mass of a piece of iron metal, let it rust, and measure the mass again. The mass has increased. Does this violate the law of conservation of mass? Explain.

13. A fire starts in a frying pan in your kitchen. You throw baking soda into the pan. Bubbling and foaming occur, and the fire goes out. What is the evidence that a chemical reaction has occurred?

14. **Writing to Learn** Imagine that you are asked to write for a community Internet site titled "Fire Safety in Your Neighborhood." For the home page, you must write at least five simple guidelines. Then write the text for at least three links that explain why your guidelines are important.

Thinking Critically

15. **Applying Concepts** Balance the following equations and tell whether they are synthesis, decomposition, or replacement reactions.
    a. $Fe + HCl \rightarrow FeCl_2 + H_2$
    b. $N_2 + O_2 \rightarrow N_2O_5$
    c. $H_2CO_3 \rightarrow H_2O + CO_2$
    d. $CuO + H_2SO_4 \rightarrow CuSO_4 + H_2O$

16. **Problem Solving** Steel that is exposed to water and salt rusts quickly. If you were a shipbuilder, how would you protect a new ship? Explain why your idea works.

17. **Relating Cause and Effect** Firefighters open doors very carefully, because sometimes a room will explode into flames when the door is opened. Based on your knowledge of reaction rates and the fire triangle, why does this happen?

18. **Applying Concepts** Gasohol is a fuel made up of gasoline and alcohol. When gasohol burns, it releases fewer pollutants than pure gasoline. The chemical reaction is:
    $C_2H_5OH + 3O_2 \rightarrow 2CO_2 + 3H_2O$
    Is this equation balanced correctly? How do you know? Why do chemists classify this reaction as combustion?

Applying Skills

Use the energy diagram to answer Questions 19–21.

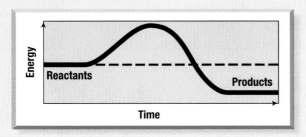

19. **Interpreting Data** How does the energy of the products compare with the energy of the reactants?
20. **Classifying** Tell whether this reaction is exothermic or endothermic.
21. **Predicting** What would happen to the graph if a catalyst were added to the reaction? Would adding heat to the reaction change the height of the curve? Explain.

Performance ▽ Assessment
CHAPTER PROJECT

Present Your Project Compare the reactions in your chemical change log with those of your classmates. How many of the same processes did you observe? Defend your opinions as to whether or not your observations were chemical changes. Together make a list of the types of evidence you observed, and classify the reactions as endothermic or exothermic.

Reflect and Record In your journal, answer these questions. What evidence of chemical change is easiest to detect? What types of chemical reactions did you observe most frequently? Give an example of a chemical reaction you suspect was taking place, but for which you could not find direct evidence.

Test Preparation

Use these questions to prepare for standardized tests.

Read the information below. Then answer Questions 22–26.

A laboratory assistant was experimenting with chemical reactions when she combined a small amount of zinc (Zn) with hydrochloric acid (HCl). She discovered that zinc chloride ($ZnCl_2$) and hydrogen (H_2) were produced.

22. Which of the following substances are the reactants?
    a. $Zn + HCl$
    b. $ZnCl_2 + H_2$
    c. $Zn + H_2$
    d. $ZnCl_2 + HCl$

23. Which of the following substances are the products?
    a. $Zn + HCl$
    b. $ZnCl_2 + H_2$
    c. $Zn + H_2$
    d. $ZnCl_2 + HCl$

24. Which equation correctly describes this reaction?
    a. $Zn + HCl \rightarrow ZnCl_2 + H_2$
    b. $ZnCl_2 + H_2 \rightarrow Zn + 2 HCl$
    c. $Zn + 2HCl \rightarrow ZnCl_2 + H_2$
    d. $2 Zn + 2 HCl \rightarrow 2 (ZnCl_2 + H_2)$

25. How should the assistant classify this reaction?
    a. synthesis   b. decomposition
    c. replacement   d. combustion

26. Which of the following actions would probably speed up the reaction between zinc and hydrochloric acid?
    a. making sure the masses of the reactants and the products are the same
    b. cooling down the reactants before combining them
    c. adding an inhibitor
    d. breaking up the zinc into smaller pieces

WEB ACTIVITY www.phschool.com

SECTION 1 Understanding Solutions

Discover What Makes a Mixture a Solution?
Try This Scattered Light
Sharpen Your Skills Designing Experiments
Science at Home Passing Through

SECTION 2 Concentration and Solubility

Discover Does it Dissolve?
Sharpen Your Skills Graphing
Science at Home A Warm Welcome
Skills Lab Speedy Solutions

SECTION 3 Describing Acids and Bases

Discover What Colors Does Litmus Paper Turn?

Make Your Own Indicator

These delicious looking fruits are more than just nutritious, juicy treats. Many fruits are acidic. And some fruits contain chemicals that change color in an acid or a base. Such chemicals are called acid-base indicators. These natural indicators can be found in different parts of many plants. You can find them in flowers, leaves, or the skins of some fruits.

As you learn about acids and bases in this chapter, you can make your own solutions that will tell you if a substance is an acid or a base. Then you can use your solutions to test for acids and bases among substances found in your home.

Your Goal To remove acid-base indicators from plants and use them to test for acids and bases.

To complete the project you must
◆ make one or more acid-base indicators
◆ use your indicators to test a number of substances
◆ compare your indicators to a standard pH scale
◆ rank the tested substances based on their pH values
◆ follow the safety guidelines in Appendix A

Get Started Brainstorm with your classmates about foods, spices, flowers, or other plant materials that have definite, deep colors. Think about fruits and vegetables you may find in a supermarket. These materials are good candidates for your indicators.

Check Your Progress You'll be working on this project as you study this chapter. To keep your project on track, look for Check Your Progress boxes at the following points.
Section Review 3, page 197: Prepare the indicators.
Section Review 4, page 203: Perform the tests.
Section Review 5, page 208: Compare with pH paper.

Present Your Project At the end of the chapter (page 211), you will demonstrate your indicators and rank the tested substances by acidity.

Fruits and fruit juices often contain weak acids.

SECTION 4
Acids and Bases in Solution

Discover **What Can Cabbage Juice Tell You?**
Try This **pHone Home**
Real-World Lab **The Antacid Test**

SECTION 5
Integrating Life Science
Digestion and pH

Discover **Where Does Digestion Begin?**

SECTION 1 Understanding Solutions

•• ACTIVITY •••

What Makes a Mixture a Solution?

1. Put about 50 or 60 milliliters of water into a plastic cup. Add a spoonful of pepper and stir well.

2. To a similar amount of water in a second cup, add a spoonful of table salt. Stir well.

3. Compare the appearance of the two mixtures.

Think It Over

Observing What is the difference between the two mixtures? What other mixtures have you seen that are similar to pepper and water? That are similar to table salt and water?

GUIDE FOR READING

◆ How does a solution differ from other mixtures?

◆ What happens to the particles of a solute when a solution forms?

◆ How do solutes affect the freezing point and boiling point of a solvent?

Reading Tip As you read, list the properties of solutions, suspensions and colloids.

Imagine a hot summer day. You've been outdoors and now you're really thirsty. A tall, cool glass of just plain water would taste great. Or would it? Have you ever tasted distilled water? It tastes flat. Distilled water is "plain water." To make it, you boil tap water until it becomes water vapor. Then you cool the vapor and recollect it as a liquid. This process separates the water from dissolved materials that give it flavor.

Tap water is a mixture of pure water (H_2O) and a variety of other substances, such as chloride, fluoride, and metallic ions. Gases, such as oxygen and carbon dioxide, are also dissolved in water. As with all mixtures, the composition of tap water can vary. The water coming out of the tap can differ from one home to the next, across a town, or from state to state. Tap water is an example of a kind of mixture called a solution.

Solutions and Suspensions

What happens if you make a mixture of water and pepper? Not much. No matter how much you stir pepper and water, the two never really seem to "mix." When you stop stirring, you can still see pepper flakes floating on the water's surface and collecting at the bottom of the cup. You could scoop them out if you wanted to. Pepper and water make a suspension. A **suspension** (suh SPEN shun) is a mixture in which particles can be seen and easily separated by settling or filtration. If you tasted the pepper suspension, you might find that one mouthful of it tastes more peppery than another mouthful. Such a mixture is not evenly mixed.

On the other hand, if you stir table salt into water, the salt disappears. Water and salt form a **solution**—a well-mixed mixture. If you taste a salt solution, any sip tastes just as salty as the next. **Unlike a suspension, a solution has the same properties throughout. Solutions and suspensions also differ in the size of their particles and the way the parts of the mixtures can be separated.** Dissolved particles are much smaller than suspended particles. They do not settle out of solution, and they pass through a filter. However, salt can be separated from water by boiling. Letting the water evaporate also works.

Solvents and Solutes

All solutions have at least two parts: the solvent and one or more solutes. The **solvent** is the part of a solution present in the largest amount. It dissolves the other substances. A substance that is present in a solution in a smaller amount and dissolved by the solvent is a **solute.** In a solution of table salt and water, the solvent is water and the solute is salt.

Water as a Solvent In many common solutions, the solvent is water. Sugar in water, for example, is the starting solution for flavored soft drinks. Adding food coloring gives the drink color. Dissolving carbon dioxide gas in the mixture produces a soda. Water dissolves so many substances that it is often called the "universal solvent."

INTEGRATING LIFE SCIENCE Life depends on water solutions. Nutrients used by plants are dissolved in water in the soil. Sap is a solution that carries sugar to tree cells. Water is the solvent in blood, saliva, and tears. Reactions in cells take place in solution. To keep cells working, you must replace the water you lose in sweat and urine—two other water solutions.

Figure 1 Glitter mixes with the water when you shake the paperweight, but settles out later. *Classifying Are the glitter particles in solution or in suspension?*

Figure 2 When air bubbles are blown through a fish tank, oxygen gas dissolves in the water. Fish take in this oxygen through their gills. Without oxygen, the fish would die.

Examples of Common Solutions		
Solute	**Solvent**	**Solution**
Gas	Gas	Air (oxygen and other gases in nitrogen)
Gas	Liquid	Soda water (carbon dioxide in water)
Liquid	Liquid	Antifreeze (ethylene glycol in water)
Solid	Liquid	Dental filling (silver in mercury)
Solid	Liquid	Ocean water (sodium chloride and other compounds in water)
Solid	Solid	Brass (zinc in copper)

Solutions Without Water Many solutions are made with solvents other than water. For example, gasoline is a solution of several different liquid fuels. You don't even need a liquid solvent to make solutions. A solution may be made of combinations of gases, liquids, or solids.

Particles in a Solution

Why do solutes seem to disappear when you mix them with water? If you had a microscope powerful enough to look at the particles in the mixture, what would you see? **Whenever a solution forms, particles of the solute leave each other and become surrounded by particles of the solvent.**

Ionic Solids in Water Figure 4 shows what happens when an ionic solid mixes with water. The positive and negative ions are attracted to polar water molecules. Water molecules surround each ion as it leaves the surface of the crystal. As each layer of the solid is exposed, more ions can dissolve.

Figure 4 Water molecules surround and separate positive and negative ions as an ionic solid dissolves. Notice that sodium ions attract the oxygen ends of the water molecules.

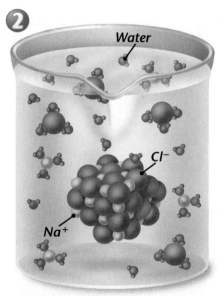

Molecular Solids in Water Not every substance breaks into ions when it dissolves in water. A molecular solid, such as sugar, breaks up into individual neutral molecules. The polar water molecules attract the slightly polar sugar molecules. This causes the sugar molecules to move away from each other. But covalent bonds within the molecules are not broken. Like ions, the sugar molecules become surrounded by water.

Solutions and Conductivity You have a water solution, but you don't know if the solute is salt or sugar. How could you use what you know about particles to find out? (Remember, a smart scientist never tastes chemicals!) Think about what you learned about the electrical conductivity of compounds. A solution of ionic compounds in water conducts electricity, but a water solution of molecular compounds may not. You could test the conductivity of the solution. If no ions were present (as in a sugar solution), electricity would not flow.

☑ *Checkpoint* *How do ionic and molecular solids differ from each other in solution?*

Colloids

Have you ever made a gelatin dessert? To do so, you stir powdered gelatin in hot water until the two substances are uniformly mixed. The liquid looks like a solution, but it's not. It isn't a suspension either. Gelatin is a colloid. A **colloid** (KAHL oyd) is a mixture with small undissolved particles that do not settle out. A colloid has properties that differ from both solutions and suspensions.

Solutions and colloids differ in the size of their particles and how they affect the path of light. Unlike a solution, a colloid contains particles large enough to scatter a light beam. These particles, however, are not as large as those in a suspension. Other colloids include mayonnaise, shaving cream, and whipped cream.

Figure 5 Milk bought in most grocery stores is a colloid. It has been processed to make the particles of water, proteins, and fats small enough to remain uniformly mixed.

Figure 6 The freezing point and boiling point of water are affected by solute particles, which interfere with changes in state.

Effects of Solutes on Solutions

Have you ever made ice cream? First you mix cream, sugar, and other ingredients. Then you freeze the mixture by packing it in ice and water. But ice water by itself is not cold enough to do the job. Cream freezes at a temperature lower than the freezing point of water (0°C). Adding rock salt to the ice water creates a mixture that is several degrees cooler. This salt-ice-water mixture is cold enough to freeze the cream. Mmm!

Salt can affect boiling, too. When cooking spaghetti, people often add table salt to the water. As a result, the water boils at a temperature higher than 100°C, the boiling point of pure water. One small spoonful of salt in a quart of water will raise the boiling point about 0.25°C. A few large spoonfuls of salt in a quart of water could increase the boiling temperature by about 0.5 degrees. This change will cause the spaghetti to cook slightly faster.

Why does salt make cold water colder when it freezes and hot water hotter when it boils? The answer to both parts of this question depends on solute particles.

Lower Freezing Points **Solutes lower the freezing point of a solvent.** When liquid water freezes, the molecules stop moving about. Instead, they form crystals of solid ice. Look at Figure 6 to compare the particles in pure water with those in a saltwater solution. Notice that pure water is made only of water molecules. In the salt solution, solute particles are present, too. In fact, they're in the way. The solute particles make it harder for the water molecules to form crystals. The temperature must drop lower than 0°C for a solid to form.

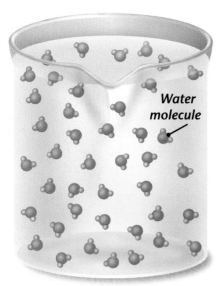

Water molecule

Pure liquid water

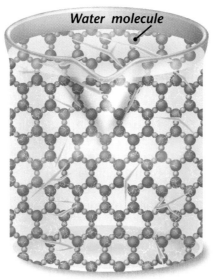

Water molecule

Ice

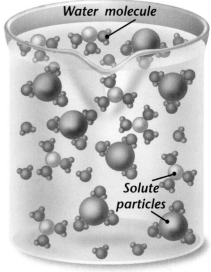

Water molecule

Solute particles

Salt water

Higher Boiling Points Solutes raise the boiling point of a solvent. To see why this happens, think about what you learned in Chapter 2 about vaporization. As a liquid evaporates, molecules from its surface leave the liquid and enter the air above. If the temperature goes up, more evaporation takes place. When the temperature is high enough, bubbles of gas actually form within the liquid. That is, you see the liquid boil. Now, suppose you add solute particles to the liquid. The more solute particles added, the fewer solvent molecules there are exposed to the surface. So fewer escape to the air. As a result, the temperature must go higher for the solution to boil. In the case of water, that would be higher than 100°C.

Figure 7 The coolant in a car radiator is a solution.
Predicting On a very cold day, what might happen to a car that had only water in the radiator?

INTEGRATING TECHNOLOGY Car manufacturers make use of the effects of solutes to protect engines from heat and cold. The coolant in a car radiator is a solution of water and another liquid called antifreeze. Often the antifreeze is ethylene glycol, which freezes at –13°C and boils at 176°C. The mixture of the two liquids has a lower freezing point and higher boiling point than either liquid alone. This solution can absorb more of the heat given off by the running engine. Risk of damage to the car from overheating is greatly reduced. So is the risk of damage from freezing in very cold weather.

Section 1 Review

1. List three ways to tell the difference between a solution and a suspension.
2. Describe what happens to the molecules of a solid, such as a sugar cube, when it dissolves in water. How does the process differ for an ionic compound, such as table salt?
3. Why does salt sprinkled on icy roads cause the ice to melt?
4. **Thinking Critically Relating Cause and Effect** Why is the temperature needed to freeze ocean water lower than the temperature needed to freeze the surface of a freshwater lake?

Science at Home

Passing Through With your family, mix together a spoonful each of sugar and pepper in about 100 mL of water in a plastic container. Pour the mixture through a coffee filter into a second container. Have a family member guess what happened to the sugar. Let the water evaporate overnight. Explain to your family the difference between a solution and a suspension. Also explain why the sugar was in the second container.

2 Concentration and Solubility

Does It Dissolve?

1. Put on your safety goggles.

2. Put half a spoonful of soapflakes into a small plastic cup. Add about 50 mL of water and stir. Observe whether or not the soap flakes dissolve in the water.

3. Clean out the cup. Repeat the test for a few other solids and liquids, such as chalk dust, baking soda, powdered sugar, hand cream, vegetable oil, vinegar, and apple juice.

4. Classify the items you tested into two groups: those that dissolved in water easily and those that did not dissolve easily.

Think It Over

Drawing Conclusions Based on your observations, does the physical state (solid or liquid) of a substance affect whether or not it dissolves in water? Explain.

GUIDE FOR READING

◆ How is concentration measured?

◆ What factors affect the solubility of a substance?

Reading Tip As you read, make a list of questions you would ask in order to review the ideas of this section.

Suppose you make two cups of hot herbal tea for yourself and a friend. Your friend likes the tea "weak" and asks you to leave the tea bag in the cup for only fifteen seconds. You put another tea bag in your cup for a few minutes. When you're done, the tea in your cup is darker than the tea in your friend's cup. The cups may hold the same amount of liquid, but logic tells you that your cup holds more "tea."

Concentration

The two cups of tea differ in their concentrations. That is, they differ in the amount of solute (tea) dissolved in a certain amount of solvent (water). Chemists describe the first mixture as a **dilute solution** because only a little solute is dissolved in the water. By comparison, the darker tea is a **concentrated solution** because it has more solute dissolved in the water.

Figure 8 "Weak" tea is a dilute solution—one that actually contains several solutes that make up tea. "Strong" tea is a more concentrated solution of the same substances.

184

Figure 9 The sap (**a**) from sugar maple trees has almost no flavor. Much of the water must be boiled away (**b**) to produce the thick, sweet syrup people pour on pancakes (**c**).

You can change the concentration of a solution by adding more solute. You can also change the concentration by adding or removing solvent. For example, fruit juices are sometimes packaged and sold as concentrates. When you add water, you make a more dilute solution. You replace the water that was removed to make the concentrate.

Measuring Concentration

You know that one solution in Figure 8 contains more concentrated tea than the other. But you do not know the actual concentration of either solution. **To measure concentration, you compare the amount of solute to the amount of solvent or to the total amount of solution.** Often, the method used to describe concentration depends on the type of solution. You can measure the mass of a solute or solvent in grams. You can measure the volume of a solute or solvent in milliliters or liters. You can report concentration as the percent of solute in solution by volume or mass.

☑ *Checkpoint* *How do a dilute solution and a concentrated solution made from the same solute and solvent differ?*

Sample Problem

Rubbing alcohol sold in grocery stores is a mixture of isopropyl alcohol and water. The concentration of a 473.0-mL sample is 70% alcohol by volume. Find the volume of alcohol in the solution.

Analyze. If the solution is 70% alcohol, then 70% of 473.0 mL is alcohol. Written as a decimal, 70% is equal to 0.70, or 0.7.

Write the equation. *volume of alcohol = 0.7 x volume of solution*

Substitute and solve. *? mL = 0.7 x 473 mL = 331.1 mL*

Think about it. Check your answer by calculating the volume of water in the sample (30% of 473.0 mL). Your two answers should add up to 473.0 mL.

Practice Problems

1. The concentration of hydrogen peroxide in stores is 3% by volume in a water solution. How many milliliters of hydrogen peroxide are there in a 237-mL sample?
2. You dilute a 60-mL can of frozen grape juice concentrate with enough water to make a total of 240 mL. What is the concentration of juice in percent by volume in the final mixture?

Solubility

If a substance dissolves in water, a question you might ask is, "How well does it dissolve?" Suppose you add sugar to a glass of iced tea. You could add half a spoonful to make the tea taste slightly sweet. Or, you could add two spoonfuls to make it sweeter. Is there a limit to how "sweet" you can make the tea? The answer is yes. At the temperature of iced tea, several spoonfuls of sugar are about all you can add. At some point, no matter how much you stir the tea, no more sugar will dissolve. **Solubility** is a measure of how well a solute can dissolve in a solvent at a given temperature.

Saturated and Unsaturated Solutions When no more sugar dissolves in the tea, you have a saturated solution. A **saturated solution** contains as much dissolved solute as possible at a given temperature. Adding more sugar to a saturated solution of iced tea does not change the concentration of sugar in the solution. The extra sugar just settles to the bottom of the glass. If, however, the sugar you add continues to dissolve, you have an unsaturated solution. An **unsaturated solution** does not hold as much of a solute as is possible at the given temperature.

Working with Solubility The solubility of a substance tells you how much solute you can add before a solution becomes saturated. Solubility is given for a specific solvent (such as water) under certain conditions (such as temperature). Look at Figure 10. It compares the solubility of some familiar compounds. In this case, the solvent is water and the temperature is 0°C. From the table, you can see that 6.9 grams of baking soda will dissolve in 100 grams of water at 0°C. But the same mass of water at the same temperature will dissolve 180 grams of table sugar!

Figure 10 Each compound listed in the table dissolves in water, but they have different solubilities.
*Comparing and Contrasting
Which compound is the most soluble? Which is the least soluble?*

Solubility in 100 g Water at 0°C	
Compound	**Solubility (g)**
Table salt (NaCl)	35.7
Baking soda (NaHCO$_3$)	6.9
Carbon dioxide (CO$_2$)	0.348
Sugar (C$_{12}$H$_{22}$O$_{11}$)	180

Figure 11 You would need far less baking soda than sugar to get a saturated solution in 100 grams of water at 0°C.

*Baking Soda
6.9g*

*Sugar
180g*

Solubility is a characteristic property of a compound. As with properties such as density and boiling point, you can use solubility to help identify a compound. Suppose you had a white powder that looked like table salt or sugar. You don't know for sure that the powder *is* salt or sugar. And you wouldn't use taste to identify it. Instead, you could measure its solubility in water at 0°C and compare the results to the data in Figure 10.

☑ *Checkpoint* *Why doesn't solute added to a saturated solution dissolve?*

Changing Solubility

Which holds more sugar: iced tea or hot tea? You have already read that there is a limit on solubility. An iced tea and sugar solution quickly becomes saturated. Yet a hot, steaming cup of the same tea can hold much more sugar before the limit is reached. Later, if the solution is cooled, the solubility of sugar decreases. Sugar crystals may form. The solubilities of sugar and other solutes change when conditions change. **Among the factors that affect the solubility of a substance are temperature, pressure, and type of solvent.**

Temperature For most solids, solubility increases as the temperature increases. That is why the temperature is reported when solubilities are listed. For example, the solubility of table sugar in 100 grams of water changes from 180 grams at 0°C to 231 grams at 25°C to 487 grams at 100°C.

Cooks use this increased solubility of sugar when they make desserts such as hard candy, fudge, or peanut brittle, To make peanut brittle, you start with a mixture of sugar, corn syrup, and water. At room temperature, not enough of the required sugar can dissolve in the water. The mixture must be heated until it begins to boil. Nuts and other ingredients are added before the mixture cools. Some recipes call for temperatures above 100°C. Because the exact temperature can affect the result, cooks use a candy thermometer to check the temperature.

Figure 12 Hard candies are made by cooling a sugar water solution to which different flavors and colorings are added.

Figure 13 Has this ever happened to you? Opening a bottle of soda water can sometimes produce quite a spray as dissolved gas comes out of solution. *Relating Cause and Effect* Why does more gas escape from a warm bottle of soda water than from a cold bottle?

When heated, a solution can hold more solute than it can at cooler temperatures. If you allow a heated, saturated solution to cool slowly, sometimes the extra solute will remain dissolved. A **supersaturated solution** has more dissolved solute than is predicted by its solubility at the given temperature. If you disturb a supersaturated solution by dropping in a crystal of the solute, the extra solute will come out of solution.

Unlike most solids, gases become less soluble when the temperature goes up. For example, more carbon dioxide will dissolve in cold water than in hot water. Carbon dioxide makes soda water fizzy when you pour it into a glass. If you open a warm bottle of soda water, carbon dioxide escapes the liquid in greater amounts than if the soda water had been chilled. Why does warm soda taste "flat"? It contains less gas. If you like soda water that's very fizzy, open it when it's cold!

Pressure Pressure affects the solubility of gases. The higher the pressure, the more gas can dissolve. To increase the carbon dioxide concentration in soft drinks, the gas is added under high pressure. Opening a bottle or can reduces the pressure. Even with a cold drink, you hear the sound of the gas escaping.

Figure 14 Divers must keep track of their depth and the effects of pressure. When ascending, they must rise no faster than 18 meters per minute to avoid "the bends."

Scuba divers are aware of the effect of pressure on gases. Air is 80 percent nitrogen. When divers breathe from tanks of compressed air, nitrogen from the air dissolves in their blood in greater amounts as they descend. This occurs because the pressure underwater increases with depth. If the divers return to the surface too quickly, nitrogen bubbles come out of solution and block blood flow. Divers double over in pain, which is why this condition is sometimes called "the bends."

Solvents If you've ever shaken a bottle of salad dressing, you've seen how quickly water and oil separate. (The vinegar in salad dressing is mostly water.) Oil and water separate because water is polar and oil is nonpolar. Polar compounds and nonpolar compounds do not mix very well. For liquid solutions, the solvent affects how well a solute dissolves. The expression "like dissolves like" gives you a clue to which solutes are soluble in which solvents. Ionic and polar compounds usually dissolve in polar solvents. Nonpolar compounds do not usually dissolve in polar solvents. If you work with paints, you know that water-based (latex) paints can be cleaned up with just soap and water. But cleaning up oil-based paints may require a nonpolar solvent, such as turpentine.

INTEGRATING TECHNOLOGY Vitamins are compounds that you need to keep your body working. There are two types of vitamins. Vitamins A, D, E, and K are soluble in fat and can be stored in your body. All the other vitamins, including vitamin C, are soluble in water. Water-soluble vitamins are not stored by your body. They are removed with waste products and must be replaced each day.

Sometimes vitamins are added to foods. For example, milk often contains extra vitamin D. If you eat lots of vegetables and fruits, you probably get enough vitamins to stay healthy. People who take vitamin pills need to consider the total amount of vitamins they get from all sources. Believe it or not, too much of a vitamin, especially vitamins A or D, can be almost as harmful as too little.

Figure 15 This house painter must clean her used brushes with a solvent that will dissolve the paint. *Applying Concepts* *What is one factor that helps her determine the kind of brush cleaner to use?*

Section 2 Review

1. What quantities are compared when the concentration of a solution is calculated?
2. Why would an ionic compound be more likely to dissolve in water than in oil?
3. How does a saturated solution differ from an unsaturated solution?
4. **Thinking Critically** **Relating Cause and Effect** When you heat tap water on the stove, you can see tiny bubbles of oxygen form. They rise to the surface long before the water begins to boil. Explain what causes these bubbles to appear.

Science at Home

A Warming Trend With your family, make a saturated solution of baking soda in water. Add one small spoonful of baking soda to about 250 mL of cool water. Stir until the baking soda dissolves. Continue adding baking soda in this manner until no more dissolves. Keep track of how much baking soda you use. Then ask your family to predict what would happen if you used warm water instead. Test their predictions and compare the results with those of the first test.

Speedy Solutions

I n this lab, you will design an experiment to find out how a chosen variable affects the speed at which salt dissolves in water.

Problem

How can you control the rate at which salt dissolves in water?

Suggested Materials

spoon	solid stoppers, #4
thermometers	hot plate
balance	stirring rods
ice	timer or watch
test tube rack	test tubes, 25×150 mm
coarse, rock, and table salt	
graduated cylinders and beakers, various sizes	

Design a Plan

1. Make a list of all the variables you can think of that could affect the speed with which salt dissolves in water.
2. Compare your list with your classmates' lists, and add other variables.
3. Choose one variable from your list to test.
4. Write a hypothesis predicting the effect of your chosen variable on the speed of dissolving.
5. Decide how to work with your choice.
   ◆ If you choose temperature, you might perform tests at 10°C, 20°C, 30°C, 40°C, and 50°C.
   ◆ If you choose stirring, you might stir for various amounts of time.
6. Plan at least three tests for whichever variable you choose. Remember to control all other variables.

7. Write down a series of steps for your procedure and safety guidelines for your experiment. Be quite detailed in your plan.
8. As part of your procedure, prepare a data table in which to record your results. Fill in the headings on your table that identify your manipulated variable and the responding variable. (*Hint:* Remember to include units.)
9. Have your teacher approve your procedure, safety guidelines, and data table.
10. Perform the experiment.

DATA TABLE			
Manipulated Variable	Dissolving Time		
	Test 1	Test 2	Test 3

Analyze and Conclude

1. Which is the manipulated variable in your experiment? Which is the responding variable? How do you know which is which?

2. List three variables you held constant in your procedure. Explain why controlling these variables makes your data more reliable.

3. Make a line graph of your data. Label the horizontal axis with the manipulated variable. Label the vertical axis with the responding variable. Use an appropriate scale for each axis and label the units.

4. Study the shape of your graph. Write a conclusion about the effect of the variable you tested on the speed of salt dissolving in water.

5. Does your conclusion support the hypothesis you wrote in Step 4? Explain.

6. How do your results relate to what you have learned about particles and solubility?

7. What advantage would there be in running your tests a second or third time?

8. **Think About It** If you switched procedures with another student who tested the same variable as you, do you think you would get the same results? Explain why or why not.

More to Explore

Choose another variable from the list you made in Steps 1 and 2. Repeat the process with that variable. Of the two variables you chose, which was easier to work with? Explain.

Describing Acids and Bases

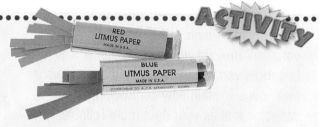
GUIDE FOR READING

◆ What properties can you use to identify acids?

◆ What properties can you use to identify bases?

Reading Tip Before you read, preview *Exploring Uses of Acids* and *Exploring Uses of Bases.* List examples of acids and bases you are already familiar with.

Did you have any fruit for breakfast today—perhaps an orange, an apple, or fruit juice? If so, an acid was part of your meal. The last time you washed your hair, did you use shampoo? If your answer is yes, then you may have used a base.

You use many products that contain acids and bases. Manufacturers, farmers, and builders depend on acids and bases in their work. The chemical reactions of acids and bases even keep you alive! What are acids and bases? How do they react, and what are their uses? In this section you will start to find out.

Properties of Acids

What is an acid and how do you know when you have one? Test its properties. **Acids** are compounds that share characteristic properties in the kinds of reactions they undergo. **An acid is a substance that tastes sour, reacts with metals and carbonates, and turns blue litmus paper red.**

Sour Taste If you've ever tasted a lemon, you've had firsthand experience with the sour taste of acids. Can you think of other foods that sometimes taste sour, or tart? Citrus fruits—lemons, grapefruits, oranges, and limes—are acidic. They all contain citric acid. Other fruits (cherries, tomatoes, apples) contain acids also. The vinegar used in salad dressing is made from a solution of water and acetic acid. Tea is acidic, too. So is spoiled milk, but you might not want to drink it!

Figure 16 A sour taste often means that food is acidic.

Although sour taste is a characteristic of many acids, it is not one you should use to identify a compound as an acid. Scientists never taste chemicals in order to identify them. Though acids in sour foods may be safe to eat, many other acids are not.

Reactions With Metals Do you notice bubbles in Figure 18? Acids react with certain metals to produce hydrogen gas. Not all metals react this way, but magnesium, zinc, and iron do. When they react, the metals seem to disappear in the solution. This observation is one reason acids are described as corrosive, meaning they "eat away" at other materials.

INTEGRATING TECHNOLOGY The metal plate in Figure 18 is being etched with acid. Etching is one method of making printing plates that are then used to print works of art on paper. To make an etching, an artist first coats a metal plate with an acid-resistant material—often beeswax. Then the design is cut into the beeswax with a sharp tool, exposing some of the metal. When the plate is treated with acid, the acid eats away the design in the exposed metal. Later, ink applied to the plate collects in the grooves made by the acid. The ink is transferred to the paper when the etching is printed.

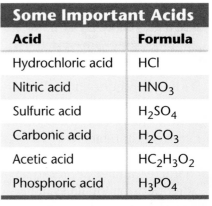

Some Important Acids	
Acid	**Formula**
Hydrochloric acid	HCl
Nitric acid	HNO_3
Sulfuric acid	H_2SO_4
Carbonic acid	H_2CO_3
Acetic acid	$HC_2H_3O_2$
Phosphoric acid	H_3PO_4

Figure 17 The table lists the names and formulas of some common acids.

Figure 18 Metal etching takes advantage of the reaction of an acid with a metal. Lines are cut in the wax coating on the plate. Here, hydrochloric acid eats away at the exposed zinc metal, forming bubbles you can see in the close-up. *Applying Concepts What gas forms in this reaction?*

CONNECTION

Putting someone to the "acid test" has nothing to do with litmus. The phrase is a figure of speech. It refers to a situation that tries someone's character, ability, courage, or other personal qualities. It comes from an old use of nitric acid to test the purity of gold. Many metals react with acid, but gold does not. Fake gold corrodes, while the value and quality of real gold are revealed.

In Your Journal

Write about a time you or someone you know went through an "acid test." What was hard about the situation? What did you learn from it about yourself or the other person?

Reactions With Carbonates Acids also react with carbonate ions in a characteristic way. Carbonate ions contain carbon and oxygen atoms bonded together. They carry an overall negative charge (CO_3^{2-}). When acids react with carbonate compounds, a gas forms. In this case, the gas is carbon dioxide.

INTEGRATING EARTH SCIENCE Geologists, scientists who study Earth, use the reaction of acids with carbonates to identify limestone. Limestone is made of calcium carbonate ($CaCO_3$). If a dilute solution of hydrochloric acid (HCl) is poured on a limestone rock, bubbles of carbon dioxide appear. Look at the equation for this reaction.

$$2\ HCl + CaCO_3 \rightarrow CaCl_2 + CO_2 + H_2O$$

Many forms of limestone come from organisms that live in the ocean. Coral rock, for example, comes from coral reefs. These are large structures made of the skeletons of millions of tiny sea animals that produce an outer layer of calcium carbonate. Another kind of limestone is chalk. It forms from the hard parts of microscopic sea animals deposited in layers on the sea floor. In time, the layers are pressed together and harden into chalk.

Reactions With Indicators If you did the Discover activity, you used litmus paper to test several substances. Litmus is an example of an **indicator,** a compound that changes color when in contact with an acid or a base. Vinegar and lemon juice turn blue litmus paper red. In fact, acids always turn litmus paper red. Sometimes chemists use other indicators to test for acids, but litmus is one of the easiest to use.

Checkpoint *What is the purpose of using an indicator?*

Figure 19 Hydrangea flowers are natural indicators. They may range in color from bright pink to blue, depending on the acidity of the soil in which the bush grows.

EXPLORING Uses of Acids

Acids play important roles in the chemistry of living things. Acids also are used to make valuable products for homes, farms, and industries.

Acids and food
Many of the vitamins in the foods you eat are acids.

Oranges and tomatoes contain ascorbic acid, or vitamin C.

Folic acid, needed for healthy cell growth, is found in green leafy vegetables.

Acids in the body
Acids are useful in the body and are also waste products of cell processes.

Acid in the stomach helps to digest protein.

During exercise, lactic acid builds up in hard-working muscles.

Acid

In solution, acids often look just like water, but they react very differently. A concentrated acid can burn a hole in metal, cloth, skin, wood, and other materials.

Acids in the home
People often use dilute solutions of acids to clean brick and other surfaces. Hardware stores sell muriatic (hydrochloric) acid, which is used to clean bricks and metals.

Acids and industry
Farmers and manufacturers depend on acids for many uses.

Sulfuric acid is used in car batteries, to refine petroleum, and to treat iron and steel.

Nitric acid and phosphoric acid are used to make fertilizers for crops, lawns, and gardens.

EXPLORING *Uses of Bases*

The reactions of bases make them valuable raw materials for a range of products.

Bases and food
Baking soda reacts with acids to produce carbon dioxide gas in baked goods. Without these gas bubbles, this delicious variety of breads, biscuits, cakes, and cookies would not be light and fluffy.

Bases in the home
Ammonia solutions are safe to spray with bare hands, but gloves must be worn when working with drain cleaners.

Drain cleaners contain sodium hydroxide (lye).

You can't mistake the odor of household cleaning products made with ammonia.

In solution, bases sometimes look like water, or they may be cloudy white. Some bases can burn your skin.

Base

Bases and industry
Mortar and cement are manufactured using the bases calcium oxide and calcium hydroxide. Gardeners sometimes add calcium oxide to soil to make the soil less acidic for plants.

Bases and health
Bases such as milk of magnesia (magnesium hydroxide) and calcium carbonate help ease effects of too much stomach acid.

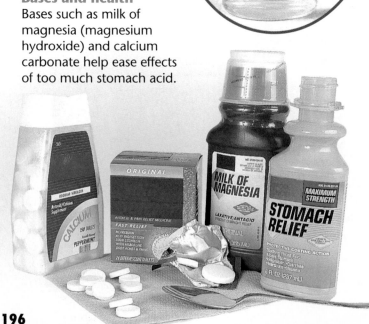

196

Properties of Bases

Bases are another group of compounds that can be identified by their common properties. **A base is a substance that tastes bitter, feels slippery, and turns red litmus blue.** Bases often are described as the "opposites" of acids.

Bitter Taste Have you ever tasted tonic water? The slightly bitter taste is caused by the base quinine. Bases taste bitter. Soaps, some shampoos, and detergents taste bitter too, but you wouldn't want to identify bases by taste!

Slippery Feel Picture yourself washing your hands. You reach for a bar of soap and rub it between your hands underwater. Think about how slippery your hands feel. This slippery feeling is another characteristic of bases. But just as you avoid tasting a substance to identify it, you wouldn't want to touch it. Strong bases can irritate or burn your skin. A safer way to identify bases is by their other properties.

Reactions With Indicators As you might guess, if litmus paper can be used to test acids, it can be used to test bases too. Bases turn red litmus blue. Like acids, bases react with other indicators. But litmus paper gives a reliable, safe test. An easy way to remember which color litmus turns for acids or bases is to remember the letter *b*. **B**ases turn litmus paper **b**lue.

Reactions of Bases Unlike acids, bases don't react with carbonates to produce carbon dioxide. At first, you may think it is useless to know that a base doesn't react with certain chemicals. But if you know what a compound *doesn't* do, you know something about it. For example, you know it's not an acid. Another important property of bases is how they react with acids. You will learn more about these reactions in Section 4.

Some Important Bases

Base	Formula
Sodium hydroxide	$NaOH$
Potassium hydroxide	KOH
Calcium hydroxide	$Ca(OH)_2$
Magnesium hydroxide	$Mg(OH)_2$
Aluminum hydroxide	$Al(OH)_3$
Ammonia	NH_3
Calcium oxide	CaO

Figure 20 The table lists the names and formulas of some common bases.
Predicting What color would any of these compounds turn litmus paper?

Section 3 Review

1. How can you use litmus paper to distinguish an acid from a base?
2. How can you tell if a food may contain an acid or a base as one of its ingredients?
3. Name at least two ways that acids and bases are useful around your home.
4. **Thinking Critically Comparing and Contrasting** Make a table that compares at least three properties of acids and bases.

Check Your Progress
Select sources for your indicators. Explore ways to crush each material and squeeze out its juice. You may have to add some water and remove any solid. (*Hint:* Refrigerate any samples you are not going to use immediately.) Write down your procedure and get your teacher's approval before preparing your indicators.

CHAPTER PROJECT

4 Acids and Bases in Solution

DISCOVER • ACTIVITY • • •

What Can Cabbage Juice Tell You?

1. Using a dropper, put five drops of red cabbage juice into each of three separate plastic cups.

2. Add 10 drops of lemon juice (an acid) to one cup. Add 10 drops of ammonia cleaner (a base) to another. Keep the third cup for comparison. Record the colors you see.

3. Now add ammonia, one drop at a time, to the cup containing lemon juice. Keep adding ammonia until the color no longer changes. Record all color changes you see.

4. Add lemon juice a drop at a time to the ammonia until the color no longer changes. Record the changes you see.

Think It Over
Forming Operational Definitions
Based on your observations, how could you expand your definitions of acids and bases?

GUIDE FOR READING

◆ **What kinds of ions do acids and bases form in water?**

◆ **What does pH tell you about a solution?**

◆ **What happens in a neutralization reaction?**

Reading Tip As you read, write one sentence to summarize the main idea discussed under each heading.

Figure 21 You can find at least one hydrogen atom in the formula of each of these acids.

Acid Formulas	
Name	**Formula**
Hydrochloric acid	HCl
Nitric acid	HNO_3
Sulfuric acid	H_2SO_4
Acetic acid	$HC_2H_3O_2$

A chemist pours hydrochloric acid into a beaker. Then she adds sodium hydroxide to the acid. The mixture looks the same, but the beaker becomes warm. If she tested the solution with litmus paper, what color would the paper turn? Would you be surprised if it did not turn color at all? If *exactly* the right amounts and concentrations of the acid and the base were mixed, the beaker would hold nothing but salt water! How could those two corrosive chemicals produce something harmless to the touch? In this section, you will find the answer.

Acids in Solution

What do acids have in common? Notice that each formula in Figure 21 begins with hydrogen. The acids you will learn about in this section contain hydrogen. They react with water to produce hydrogen ions. A **hydrogen ion** (H^+) is an atom of hydrogen that has lost its electron. When hydrochloric acid, for example, reacts with water, hydrogen ions and chloride ions form.

$$HCl \xrightarrow{\text{water}} H^+ + Cl^-$$

If another acid were used, the negative ion would be different. It could be another simple nonmetal ion. Or, it could be a polyatomic ion such as nitrate (NO_3^-), which forms from nitric acid. However, hydrogen ions would be produced in each case. These hydrogen ions are the key to the reactions of acids.

Figure 22 Acids share certain chemical and physical properties when dissolved in water. Most acids are very soluble.

Now you can add to the definition of acids you learned in Section 3. **An acid is any substance that produces hydrogen ions (H^+) in water.** It is the hydrogen ions that cause the properties of acids you can see. For instance, when you add certain metals to an acid, hydrogen ions interact with the metal atoms. One product of the reaction is hydrogen gas (H_2). Hydrogen ions also react with blue litmus paper, turning it red. That's why every acid gives the same litmus test result.

Bases in Solution

The formulas of bases give you clues to what ions they have in common. Look at Figure 23. Many bases are made of positive ions combined with hydroxide ions. The **hydroxide ion (OH^-)** is polyatomic, made of oxygen and hydrogen. It has a negative charge.

When bases like those in Figure 23 dissolve in water, the positive ions and hydroxide ions separate. Look, for example, at what happens to sodium hydroxide:

$$NaOH \xrightarrow{water} Na^+ + OH^-$$

Not every base contains hydroxide ions. For example, the gas ammonia (NH_3) does not. But in solution, ammonia is a base that reacts with water to form hydroxide ions.

$$NH_3 + H_2O \rightarrow NH_4^+ + OH^-$$

Notice that in both reactions, there are negative hydroxide ions. These examples give you another way to define bases. **A base is any substance that produces hydroxide ions (OH^-) in water.** Hydroxide ions are responsible for the bitter taste and slippery feel of bases. Hydroxides also turn red litmus blue.

☑ *Checkpoint* *What is a hydroxide ion made of?*

Figure 23 Many, but not all, bases dissolve well in water.
Making Generalizations What do all of the base formulas in the table have in common?

Base Formulas	
Name	**Formula**
Sodium hydroxide	NaOH
Potassium hydroxide	KOH
Calcium hydroxide	Ca(OH)$_2$
Magnesium hydroxide	Mg(OH)$_2$

Figure 24 In a solution of a strong acid, all the acid molecules break up into ions. In a solution of a weak acid, however, fewer molecules do so.

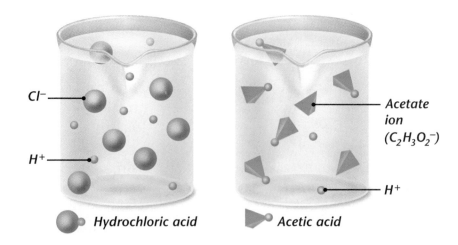

Cl^-

H^+

Hydrochloric acid

Acetate ion $(C_2H_3O_2^-)$

H^+

Acetic acid

pHone Home

ACTIVITY

Find out the pH of familiar substances in your home.

1. Put on your safety goggles and apron.

2. Select substances such as fruit juices, soda water, coffee, tea, or antacids.

3. Predict which substances are most acidic or most basic.

4. If the sample is solid, dissolve some in a cup of water. Use a liquid as is.

5. Using a plastic dropper, transfer a drop of each sample onto a fresh strip of paper for testing pH.

6. Compare the color of the strip to the pH values on the package.

7. Repeat for all your samples. Remember to rinse the dropper between tests.

Interpreting Data List the samples from lowest to highest pH. Which results, if any, surprised you?

Strengths of Acids and Bases

Acids and bases may be strong or weak. Strength refers to how well an acid or a base produces ions in water. With a strong acid, most of the molecules react to form ions in solution. With a weak acid, fewer molecules do. At the same concentration, a strong acid produces more hydrogen ions (H^+) than a weak acid does. Examples of strong acids include hydrochloric acid, sulfuric acid, and nitric acid. Most other acids, such as acetic acid, are weak acids.

Strong bases react in a water solution in a similar way to strong acids. A strong base produces more hydroxide (OH^-) ions than does an equal concentration of a weak base. Ammonia is a weak base. Lye, which is sodium hydroxide, is a strong base.

Strength determines, in part, how safe acids and bases are to use. For example, all the acids that are safe to eat, such as acetic acid and citric acid, are weak. Ammonia cleaner may irritate your hands slightly if you use it. But the same concentration of drain cleaner, which contains sodium hydroxide, would burn your skin.

People often say that a solution is weak when they mean it is dilute. This could be a dangerous mistake! Even a dilute solution of hydrochloric acid can eat a hole in your clothing or sting your skin. An equal concentration of acetic acid would not.

☑ *Checkpoint* *How would a weak base differ from an equal concentration of a strong base in solution?*

Measuring pH

Knowing the concentration of hydrogen ions is the key to knowing how acidic or basic a solution is. To describe the concentration of ions in a convenient way, chemists use a numeric scale called pH. The **pH scale** is a range of values from 0 to 14. It expresses the concentration of hydrogen ions in a solution.

Figure 25 shows where some familiar substances fit on the pH scale. Notice that the most acidic substances are at the low end of the scale. At the same time, the most basic substances are at the high end of the scale. You need to remember one important point about pH. **When the pH is low, the concentration of hydrogen ions is high.** If you keep this idea in mind, you can make sense of how the scale works.

You can find the pH of a solution by using indicators. The student in Figure 25 is using indicator paper that turns a different color for each pH value. Matching the color of the paper with the colors on the test scale tells how acidic or basic the solution is. A pH lower than 7 is acidic. A pH higher than 7 is basic. If the pH is 7, the solution is neutral. That means it's neither an acid nor a base. Pure water has a pH of 7.

A concentrated solution of acetic acid can have a lower pH than a very dilute solution of hydrochloric acid. In order to handle acids and bases safely, you need to know both their pH and their strength.

Figure 25 The pH scale classifies solutions as acidic or basic. Indicator paper turns a different color for each pH value.
Interpreting Diagrams If a solution has a pH of 9, is it acidic or basic? What can you say about a solution with a pH of 3?

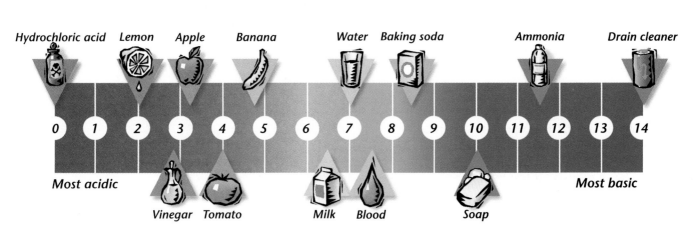

Hydrochloric acid   Lemon   Apple   Banana   Water   Baking soda   Ammonia   Drain cleaner

0   1   2   3   4   5   6   7   8   9   10   11   12   13   14

Most acidic   Most basic

Vinegar   Tomato   Milk   Blood   Soap

Figure 26 The trees in this forest show the damaging effects of acid rain.

Acid Rain

INTEGRATING
ENVIRONMENTAL SCIENCE

Normal rainfall is slightly acidic, with a pH of approximately 5.5. This acidity comes from carbon dioxide in the air. Carbon dioxide dissolves in rainwater, producing carbonic acid, a weak acid.

$$H_2O + CO_2 \rightarrow H_2CO_3$$

Acid rain is more acidic than normal rainwater. It has a pH as low as 3.5 to 3.0. The extra acidity comes from nitrogen oxides and sulfur oxides. These gases are released into the air as pollutants from industry and motor vehicles. These oxides react with water in the air to produce acids, including nitric acid and sulfuric acid. Rainwater containing these acids has more hydrogen ions. It has a lower pH and is more corrosive. Acid rain can damage statues and buildings, destroy forests, and kill fish in lakes.

Acid-Base Reactions

The story at the start of this section describes a chemist who mixed hydrochloric acid with sodium hydroxide. She got a solution of table salt (sodium chloride) and water.

$$HCl + NaOH \rightarrow H_2O + Na^+ + Cl^-$$

If you tested the pH of the mixture, it would be close to 7, or neutral. In fact, a reaction between an acid and a base is called a **neutralization** (noo truh lih ZAY shun). As a result of neutralization, an acid-base mixture is not as acidic or basic as the individual starting solutions were.

Sometimes an acid-base reaction results in a neutral solution. But not always. The final pH depends on such factors as the volumes, concentrations, and identities of the reactants. For example, some acids and bases react to form products that are not neutral. Also, common sense tells you that if only a small amount of strong base is reacted with a much larger amount of strong acid, the solution will remain acidic.

Figure 27 The solution on the left is acidic. The solution on the right is basic. When mixed, these solutions produced the neutral solution in the center.
Interpreting Photos What tells you if the solution is an acid, a base, or neutral?

Acidic   Neutral   Basic

Some Salts and Their Uses		
Salt	Formula	Uses
Sodium chloride	NaCl	Food flavoring; preservative
Potassium iodide	KI	Additive in "iodized" salt that prevents iodine deficiency (goiter)
Calcium chloride	$CaCl_2$	De-icer for roads and walkways
Potassium chloride	KCl	Salt substitute in foods
Calcium carbonate	$CaCO_3$	Found in limestone and sea shells
Ammonium nitrate	NH_4NO_3	Fertilizer; active ingredient in some cold packs

Figure 28 Each salt listed in this table can be formed by the reaction between an acid and a base.

Products of Acid-Base Reactions

"Salt" may be the familiar name of the stuff you sprinkle on food. But to a chemist, the word refers to a specific group of compounds. A **salt** is any ionic compound that can be made from the neutralization of an acid with a base. A salt is made from the positive ion of a base and the negative ion of an acid. Look at the equation for the reaction of nitric acid with potassium hydroxide:

$$HNO_3 + KOH \rightarrow H_2O + K^+ + NO_3^-$$

One product of the reaction is water. The other product is potassium nitrate (KNO_3), a salt. Potassium nitrate is written in the equation as separate K^+ and NO_3^- ions because it is soluble in water. **A neutralization reaction produces water and a salt.** Some salts, such as potassium nitrate, are soluble. Others form precipitates because they are insoluble.

Figure 29 These salt flats were left behind in Death Valley, California, when the water in which the salts were dissolved evaporated.

Section 4 Review

1. What ions would you expect to find when an acid dissolves in water? What ions would you expect to find when a base dissolves in water?
2. If the pH of a solution is 6, would you expect to find more or fewer hydrogen ions (H^+) than in a solution with a pH of 3? Explain why.
3. What does the term *salt* mean to a chemist, and how may a salt form?
4. **Thinking Critically** **Predicting** What salt would form from a reaction between hydrochloric acid, HCl, and calcium hydroxide, $Ca(OH)_2$? Explain your answer.

Check Your Progress

CHAPTER PROJECT

Use each indicator to test for acids and bases in familiar substances. For example, try vinegar, household ammonia, lemon juice, milk, and soapy water. (*Hint:* Use small amounts of indicator and test samples. Watch for a color change, especially where the sample comes in contact with the indicator. If you do not see a color change, add a few more drops of the sample.) Summarize your results in a table.

The Antacid Test

Consumers see or hear ads for antacids on television, radio, and in magazines. Each product claims to "neutralize excess stomach acid" best. You can experiment to see whether some antacids really do work better than others.

Problem

Which antacid neutralizes more stomach acid?

Skills Focus

designing experiments, measuring, interpreting data

Materials

3 plastic droppers   small plastic cups
dilute HCl, 50 mL
methyl orange solution, 1 mL
liquid antacid, 30 mL of each brand tested

Procedure

Part 1

1. Using a plastic dropper, put 10 drops of hydrochloric acid, HCl, into one cup.
   CAUTION: *Hydrochloric acid is corrosive. Rinse spills and splashes immediately with water.*

2. Use another plastic dropper to put 10 drops of liquid antacid into another cup.

3. In your notebook, make a data table like the one below. Record the colors of the HCl and the antacid.

4. Add two drops of methyl orange solution to each cup. Record the colors you see.

5. Test each of the other antacids. Discard all the solutions and cups as directed by your teacher.

Part 2

6. Methyl orange changes color at a pH of about 4. Predict the color of the solution you expect to see when an antacid is added to a mixture of methyl orange and HCl.

7. Design a procedure for testing the reaction of each antacid with HCl. Decide how many drops of acid and methyl orange you need to use each time.

DATA TABLE		
Substance	Original Color	Color With Indicator
HCl		
Antacid Brand A		
Antacid Brand B		

8. Devise a plan for adding the antacid so that you can detect when a change occurs. Decide how much antacid to add each time and how to mix the solutions to be sure the indicator is giving accurate results.
9. Make a second data table to record your observations.
10. Carry out your procedure and record your results.
11. Discard the solutions and cups as directed by your teacher. Rinse the plastic droppers thoroughly.
12. Wash your hands thoroughly when done.

Analyze and Conclude

1. What is the function of the methyl orange solution?
2. Do your observations support your predictions from Step 6? Explain why or why not.
3. Why do you think antacids reduce stomach acid? Explain your answer, using the observations you made.
4. Why is it important to use the same number of drops of HCl in each trial?

5. Which antacid neutralized the HCl with the smallest number of drops? Give a possible explanation for the difference.
6. If you have the same volume (number of drops) of each antacid, which one can neutralize the most acid?
7. Did your procedure give results from which you could draw conclusions? Explain why or why not. What would you do differently if you were to do the tests again?
8. **Apply** If you want to buy an antacid, what information do you need in order to decide which brand is the best buy?

Getting Involved

Look for antacids in a local grocery store or drug store. Check the ingredient lists of several brands. What are some of the different bases used in commercial antacids? (*Hints:* Look for compounds containing "hydroxide." Check out any compound identified as the "active ingredient.") Compare the advertised strengths of several brands.

SECTION 5 Digestion and pH

DISCOVER ·ACTIVITY· · · ·

Where Does Digestion Begin?

1. Obtain a bite-sized piece of crusty bread.
2. Chew the bread for about one minute. Do not swallow until after you notice a change in taste.

Think It Over

Inferring How did the bread taste before and after you chewed it? How can you explain the change in taste?

GUIDE FOR READING

◆ Why is it necessary for your body to digest food?

◆ How does pH affect digestion?

Reading Tip Before you read, preview Figure 32. List the organs of the digestive system in the order in which food passes through them.

You may have seen the following commercial: A man has a stomachache after eating spicy food. A voice announces that the problem is excess stomach acid. The remedy is an antacid tablet.

Ads like this one highlight the role of chemistry in digestion. You need to have acid in your stomach. But too much acid is a problem. Other parts of your digestive system need to be basic. What roles do acids and bases play in the digestion of food?

What Is Digestion?

Foods are made mostly of water and three groups of compounds: carbohydrates, proteins, and fats. Except for water, your body can't use foods in the forms you eat. **Foods must be broken down into simpler substances that your body can use for raw materials and energy.** The process of **digestion** breaks down the complex molecules of foods into smaller molecules.

Digestion has two parts—mechanical and chemical. **Mechanical digestion** is a physical process in which large pieces of food are torn and ground into smaller pieces. The result is similar to what happens when a sugar cube is hit with a hammer. The sugar powder still has the same chemical composition as the cube. **Chemical digestion** is a set of reactions that change large molecules into smaller ones. Some of the products of digestion are used by the body to get energy. Others become building blocks for muscle, bone, skin, and other organs.

Figure 30 The foods in this sandwich will move through areas of the digestive system that have different pH values.

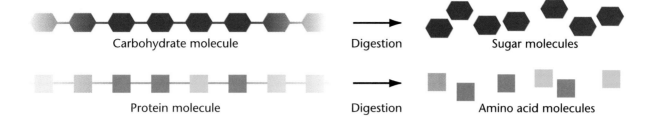

Carbohydrate molecule   Digestion   Sugar molecules

Protein molecule   Digestion   Amino acid molecules

Chemical digestion takes place with the help of enzymes. Enzymes are catalysts that speed up reactions in living things. Enzymes require just the right conditions to work, including temperature and pH. **For some digestive enzymes, the pH must be low. For others, the pH must be high or neutral.**

☑ *Checkpoint* *What happens to foods in your body?*

Figure 31 Carbohydrates and proteins are large molecules that must be broken down by digestion. *Interpreting Diagrams What smaller molecules result in each case?*

pH in the Digestive System

A bite of sandwich is about to take a journey through your digestive system. What pH changes will affect the food molecules along the way? Figure 32 shows the main parts of the human digestive system. As you read, trace the food's pathway through the body.

Your Mouth The first stop in the journey is your mouth. Immediately, your teeth chew and mash the food. The food also is mixed with a watery fluid called saliva. Have you ever felt your mouth water at the smell of something delicious? The odor of food can trigger production of saliva.

What would you expect the usual pH of saliva to be? Remember that saliva tastes neither sour nor bitter. So you're correct if you think your mouth has a pH near 7, the neutral point.

Saliva contains amylase (AM uh lays), an enzyme that helps break down the carbohydrate starch into smaller sugar molecules. Amylase works best when the pH is near 7. You can sense the action of this enzyme if you chew a piece of bread. After about two minutes in your mouth, the carbohydrate is broken into sugars. This makes the bread taste sweet.

Your Stomach Next, the food is swallowed and arrives in your stomach. This muscular organ starts the chemical digestion of foods that contain protein, such as meat, fish, and beans. Cells in the lining of your stomach release enzymes and hydrochloric acid. Rather than the near-neutral pH of your mouth, the pH drops to a very acidic level of about 2. This pH is even more acidic than the juice of a lemon.

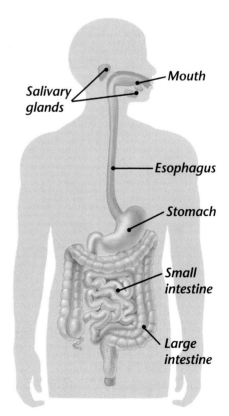

Figure 32 The pH changes as food moves through the digestive system.

Figure 33 Shrimp contains protein. Rice and pea pods contain carbohydrates.

The low pH in your stomach helps digestion take place. One enzyme that works in your stomach is pepsin. It helps break down proteins into small molecules called amino acids. Most enzymes work best in a solution that is nearly neutral. But pepsin is different. It works most effectively in acids.

Your Small Intestine Your stomach empties its contents into the small intestine. Here, other digestive fluids surround the food. One fluid contains the bicarbonate ion (HCO_3^-). This ion creates a slightly basic solution, with a pH of about 8. In the small intestine, other enzymes complete the breakdown of carbohydrates, fats, and proteins. All of these enzymes work best in a slightly basic solution. Most chemical digestion ends in the small intestine.

The large food molecules from the sandwich have been split up into smaller ones by now. These smaller molecules pass through the walls of the small intestine into your bloodstream and are carried to the cells that will use them.

Figure 34 The pH varies greatly throughout the digestive system. *Relating Cause and Effect Why do certain digestive enzymes work only in certain parts of the digestive system?*

pH Changes During Digestion	
Organ	**pH**
Mouth	7
Stomach	2
Small intestine	8

Section 5 Review

1. How are foods changed by your digestive system?
2. How does pH differ in your mouth, your stomach, and your small intestine? Why are the differences important?
3. What two processes of digestion begin in the mouth? How do they differ?
4. **Thinking Critically** **Predicting** How would the digestion of food be affected if your stomach did not produce hydrochloric acid?

CHAPTER PROJECT

Check Your Progress
Use indicator paper to find the pH of each substance you tested earlier with homemade indicators. Add these pH values to your data table. Compare the data you collected with your indicators with the data from the pH tests.

CHAPTER 6 STUDY GUIDE

SECTION 1 Understanding Solutions

Key Ideas

◆ A solution is a well-mixed mixture, having smaller particles than a suspension or a colloid.
◆ When a solution forms, particles of solute are surrounded by particles of solvent.
◆ Solutes lower the freezing point and raise the boiling point of a solvent.

Key Terms

suspension   solute
solution   colloid
solvent

SECTION 2 Concentration and Solubility

Key Ideas

◆ Concentration compares the amount of solute to the amount of solvent or amount of solution.
◆ Solubility can be affected by temperature, pressure, and type of solvent.

Key Terms

dilute solution
concentrated solution
solubility
saturated solution
unsaturated solution
supersaturated solution

SECTION 3 Describing Acids and Bases

Key Ideas

◆ An acid tastes sour, reacts with metals and carbonates, and turns litmus red.
◆ A base tastes bitter, feels slippery, and turns litmus blue.
◆ An indicator is a substance that turns different colors in an acid or a base.

Key Terms

acid
indicator
base

SECTION 4 Acids and Bases in Solution

Key Ideas

◆ An acid produces hydrogen ions (H^+) when it dissolves in water.
◆ A base produces hydroxide ions (OH^-) when it dissolves in water.
◆ pH describes the acidity of a solution. The lower the pH, the higher the concentration of hydrogen ions.
◆ When a base reacts with an acid, water and a salt form.

Key Terms

hydrogen ion (H^+)   acid rain
hydroxide ion (OH^-)   neutralization
pH scale   salt

SECTION 5 Digestion and pH

INTEGRATING LIFE SCIENCE

Key Ideas

◆ Digestion breaks down foods into small molecules that are used for energy and raw materials.
◆ The pH at which digestive enzymes work best varies from very acidic to slightly basic.

Key Terms

digestion   chemical digestion
mechanical digestion

Organizing Information

Concept Map Use key terms and ideas you learned in this chapter to construct a concept map about solutions. (For more on concept maps, see the Skills Handbook.)

Reviewing Content

For more review of key concepts, see the Interactive Student Tutorial CD-ROM.

Multiple Choice

Choose the letter of the best answer.

1. Sugar water is an example of a
   a. suspension.   b. solution.
   c. solute.   d. colloid.

2. A solution in which more solute may be dissolved is a(n)
   a. neutral solution.
   b. supersaturated solution.
   c. unsaturated solution.
   d. saturated solution.

3. When salt is added to an ice and water mixture at 0°C,
   a. the temperature of the mixture drops.
   b. more of the water freezes.
   c. more of the water evaporates.
   d. there is no noticeable change.

4. Bubbles form when washing soda (Na_2CO_3) is mixed with
   a. tap water
   b. salt water
   c. ammonia cleaner
   d. lemon juice.

5. Which of the following compounds is a base?
   a. HNO_3 c. $MgCl_2$
   b. $Ca(OH)_2$ d. CH_4

True or False

If the statement is true, write true. If it is false, change the underlined word or words to make the statement true.

6. The solubility of a gas in water goes up if you <u>increase</u> the temperature.

7. The slightly sour taste of lemonade tells you that it may contain <u>a base</u>.

8. The gas produced when an acid reacts with a carbonate is <u>oxygen</u>.

9. Dilute hydrochloric acid is an example of a <u>strong</u> acid.

10. Amylase, the enzyme in saliva that helps break down carbohydrates into simple sugars, works best in a <u>neutral</u> solution.

Checking Concepts

11. Describe at least two differences between a dilute solution and a concentrated solution of sugar water.

12. The concentration of an alcohol and water solution is 25% alcohol by volume. What is the volume of alcohol in 200 mL of the solution?

13. Explain how you could tell the difference between a solution and a clear colloid.

14. Explain how an indicator helps you distinguish between an acid and a base.

15. What combination of acid and base can be used to make the salt potassium chloride, KCl?

16. **Writing to Learn** Some of the limestone on the outside of buildings in an area looks as if it is being gradually eaten away. As an investigator for the local air pollution agency, write a brief memo explaining what may be causing the problem.

Thinking Critically

17. **Developing Hypotheses** Some power plants release hot wastewater into nearby rivers or streams. Fish living in these waters sometimes die from lack of oxygen. Write a hypothesis to explain what has happened to the oxygen in the water.

18. **Drawing Conclusions** You have two clear liquids. One turns litmus red and one turns litmus blue. If you mix them and retest with litmus, no color changes occur. Describe the reaction that took place.

19. **Comparing and Contrasting** Compare the types of particles formed in a water solution of an acid with those formed in a water solution of a base.

20. **Predicting** Suppose a person took a dose of antacid greater than what is recommended. Predict how this action might affect the digestion of certain foods.

Applying Skills

The diagram below shows the particles of an unknown acid in a water solution. Use the diagram to answer Questions 21–23.

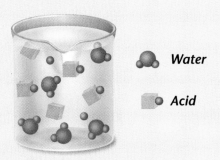

Water

Acid

21. **Interpreting Data** How can you tell from the diagram that the solution contains a weak acid?
22. **Making Models** Suppose another unknown acid is a strong acid. Make a diagram to show the particles of this acid dissolved in water.

23. **Drawing Conclusions** Explain how the pH of a strong acid compares with the pH of a weak acid of the same concentration.

Performance CHAPTER PROJECT Assessment

Present Your Project Demonstrate the indicators you prepared. Make a list of the substances you tested in order from most acidic to least acidic.

Reflect and Record In your journal, discuss whether or not you would use the same materials as indicators if you did this project again. Explain why. Describe how acid-base indicators could be useful for farmers and gardeners. Would you recommend that they use any of the indicators you made? Why or why not?

Test Preparation

Use these questions to prepare for standardized tests.

Study the graph showing solubilities of four compounds. Then answer Questions 24–27.

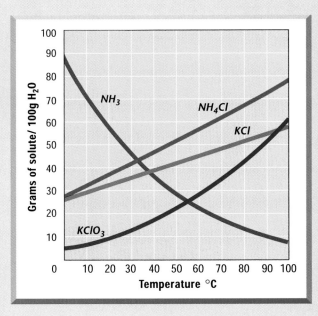

24. At 70°C, about how many grams of ammonium chloride (NH_4Cl) can dissolve in 100 grams of water?
    a. 40 g   **b.** 50 g
    c. 60 g   **d.** 70 g
25. If 30 grams of potassium chloride (KCl) are dissolved in 100 grams of water at 50°C, the solution can be best described as
    a. saturated   **b.** supersaturated
    c. unsaturated   **d.** soluble
26. Which one of the compounds becomes less soluble with increasing temperature?
    a. NH_4Cl **b.** NH_3
    c. KCl   **d.** $KClO_3$
27. At about what temperature is the solubility of ammonia (NH_3) the same as the solubility of potassium chlorate ($KClO_3$)?
    a. 0°C   **b.** 55°C
    c. 85°C   **d.** 100°C

Carbon Chemistry

WEB ACTIVITY
www.phschool.com

SECTION
1 Chemical Bonding, Carbon Style

Discover Why Do Pencils Write?
Skills Lab How Many Molecules?

SECTION
2 Carbon Compounds

Discover What Do You Smell?
Try This Dry or Wet?
Sharpen Your Skills Classifying
Science at Home Liquid Layers

Integrating Life Science
SECTION
3 Life With Carbon

Discover What's in Milk?
Try This Alphabet Soup
Real-World Lab Are You Getting Your
   Vitamins?

Check Out the Fine Print

When you look at a bottle of milk, do you think about a mixture of compounds? Probably not. But all substances—the milk as well as its plastic bottle—are made of chemicals. The milk and its bottle even have something in common chemically. The plastic and many of the compounds in milk contain the element carbon. In fact, all the foods you eat and drink contain carbon compounds. In this project, you will look closely at the labels on various food packages to find carbon compounds.

Your Goal To identify carbon compounds found in different foods.

To complete the project you must
- collect at least a dozen labels with lists of ingredients and nutrition facts
- identify the carbon compounds listed, as well as substances that do not contain carbon
- interpret the nutrition facts on labels to compare amounts of substances in each food
- classify compounds in foods into the categories of polymers found in living things

Get Started Brainstorm with your classmates about what kinds of packaged foods you want to examine. For which types of food will it be easy to obtain nutrition labels?

Check Your Progress You'll be working on this project as you study this chapter. To keep your project on track, look for Check Your Progress boxes at the following points.
Section 1 Review, page 217: Collect food labels and locate nutrition facts.
Section 3 Review, page 235: Identify and classify compounds found in foods.

Present Your Project At the end of the chapter (page 241), you will present a chart of your findings about the chemicals in foods.

Both the plastic bottles in this bottling plant and the milk in them include carbon compounds.

SECTION
1 Chemical Bonding, Carbon Style

DISCOVER 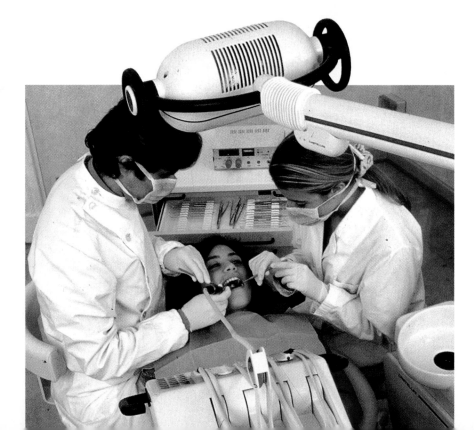·············· ACTIVITY····

Why Do Pencils Write?

1. Tear paper into pieces about 5 cm by 5 cm. Rub two pieces back and forth between your fingers.

2. Now rub pencil lead (graphite) on one side of each piece of paper. Try to get as much graphite as possible on the paper.

3. Rub the two pieces of paper together with the sides covered with graphite touching.

4. When you are finished, wash your hands.

Think It Over

Observing Did you notice a difference in what you observed in Step 1 and Step 3? How could the property of graphite you observed be used for purposes other than pencil lead?

GUIDE FOR READING

◆ Why can carbon form a huge variety of different compounds?

◆ What are the different forms of pure carbon?

Reading Tip Before you read, list characteristics of the element carbon you already know. Add to your list as you read.

O pen your mouth and say "aah." Uh-oh, you have a small cavity. Do you know what happens next? Your tooth needs a filling. But first the dentist's drill clears away the decayed part of your tooth.

Why is a dentist's drill hard and sharp enough to cut through teeth? The answer begins with the element carbon. The tip of the drill is made of diamond—a form of carbon and the hardest substance on Earth. Because it has a diamond tip, a dentist's drill stays sharp and useful. To understand why diamond is such a hard substance, you need to take a close look at the carbon atom and the bonds it forms.

Figure 1 The tip of a dentist's drill is made of diamond, a form of carbon.

214

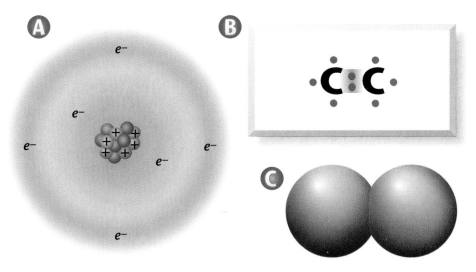

Figure 2 **A.** Only four of the six electrons in a carbon atom are valence electrons. **B.** Electron dot structures show just the valence electrons. Orange shading highlights a shared pair of electrons between two carbon atoms. **C.** Spherical models represent two carbon atoms bonded together.
Interpreting Diagrams How many valence electrons are involved in one bond?

The Carbon Atom and Its Bonds

If you look at a periodic table, you will see that the atomic number of carbon is 6. You may remember that this means a carbon atom has six protons in its nucleus. Outside the nucleus are six electrons. Four of these are valence electrons—the ones involved in forming chemical bonds.

Carbon atoms usually form covalent bonds. Do you remember that covalent bonds occur when two atoms share one or more pairs of electrons? Good for you! Then you may also remember that having four valence electrons means a carbon atom can form four covalent bonds. In comparison, atoms of hydrogen, oxygen, and nitrogen form one, two, or three covalent bonds.

Carbon atoms can form bonds with other carbon atoms. The atoms may bond together in straight chains or chains with branches. They even may form rings. As you can see in Figure 3, it is possible to arrange the same number of carbon atoms in different ways. (Try thinking about the possible shapes you could construct, using seven or eight carbon atoms instead of the six shown in the figure.)

Carbon atoms also form bonds with atoms of other elements. If you think of atoms as small plastic building blocks, you can imagine how many different ways the atoms could be put together. **Carbon can form many compounds because its atoms can bond with each other and with atoms of other elements in different ways.**

☑ *Checkpoint* How many bonds can a carbon atom form?

Figure 3 These carbon chains and rings form the backbones for molecules. In these molecules, atoms of other elements are bonded to the carbons.

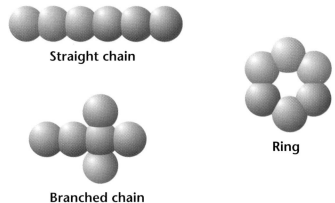

Straight chain

Branched chain

Ring

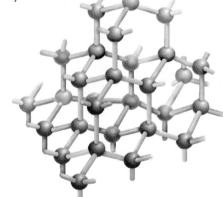

Figure 4 The carbon atoms in a diamond are arranged in a crystal structure. The diamonds in this photo have not yet been cut and polished by a jeweler.

Figure 5 Carbon atoms in graphite are arranged in layers. The weak bonds between the layers are not shown.
Applying Concepts How can you explain the slipperiness of graphite?

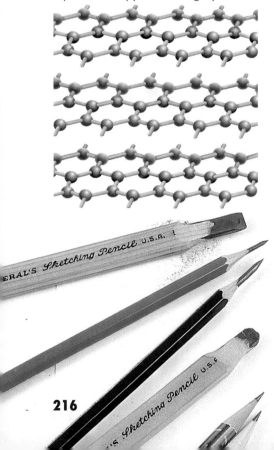

Forms of Pure Carbon

Because of the ways carbon forms bonds, the pure element can exist in different forms. **Diamond, graphite, and fullerene are three forms of the element carbon.**

Diamond The hardest mineral—**diamond**—forms deep within Earth. At very high temperatures and pressures, carbon atoms form diamond crystals. Each carbon atom is bonded strongly to four other carbon atoms. The result is a solid that is extremely hard and unreactive. The melting point of diamond is over 3,500°C. That's as hot as the surface temperatures of some stars.

INTEGRATING EARTH SCIENCE

Diamonds are prized for their brilliance and clarity when cut as gems. They can have color if there are traces of other elements in the crystals. Industrial chemists are able to make diamonds artificially, but these diamonds are not beautiful enough to use as gems. Like many natural diamonds, artificial ones are used only in industry. Diamonds work well in cutting tools, such as drills.

Graphite Every time you write with a pencil, you leave a layer of carbon on the paper. The "lead" in a lead pencil is actually **graphite,** another form of the element carbon. In graphite, each carbon atom is bonded tightly to three other carbon atoms in flat layers. However, the bonds between atoms in different layers are very weak, so the layers slide past one another easily.

Run your fingers over pencil marks, and you can feel how slippery graphite is. If you did the Discover activity, you have observed this property. Because it is so slippery, graphite makes an excellent lubricant in machines. Graphite reduces friction between the moving parts. In your home, you might use a graphite spray to help a key work better in a sticky lock.

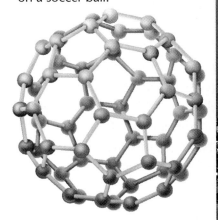

Figure 6 The arrangement of the carbon atoms in fullerenes resembles the structure of a geodesic dome or the pattern on a soccer ball.

Fullerenes In 1985, scientists at Rice University in Texas made a third form of the element carbon, a form that no one had identified before. The new form of carbon consists of carbon atoms arranged in a repeating pattern similar to the surface of a soccer ball. This form is called buckminsterfullerene, or **fullerene** (FUL ur een) for short, in honor of the architect Buckminster Fuller. Fuller designed dome-shaped buildings, called geodesic domes, which the fullerene resembles. Because of their shape, fullerenes have been given the nickname "buckyballs."

Chemists are looking for ways to use fullerenes. Because fullerenes enclose a ball-shaped open area, they may be able to carry substances inside them. Someday, fullerenes may be used to carry medicines through the body or to house very tiny computer circuits.

Section 1 Review

1. What bonding properties of carbon allow it to form so many different compounds?
2. List three different forms of pure carbon.
3. Identify and describe the type of chemical bond that forms between carbon atoms.
4. **Thinking Critically Comparing and Contrasting** How can you use differences in carbon bonds to explain why graphite and diamonds have different properties?

Skills Lab

HOW MANY MOLECULES?

Carbon atoms are found in an amazing variety of compounds. Some carbon compounds have just a few carbon atoms in each molecule; others have thousands. In this lab you will use gumdrops to represent atoms and toothpicks to represent bonds.

Problem

How many different ways can you put the same number of carbon atoms together?

Materials

48 toothpicks
Three colors of gumdrops:
   36 of one color
   15 of a second color
   4 or 5 of a third color (optional)

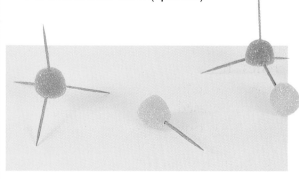

Procedure

1. You will need gumdrops of one color to represent carbon atoms and gumdrops of another color to represent hydrogen atoms. When building your models, always follow these rules:
   - Each carbon atom forms four bonds.
   - Each hydrogen atom forms one bond.
2. Make a model of CH_4 (methane).
3. Now make a model of C_2H_6 (ethane).

4. Make a model of C_3H_8 (propane). Is there more than one way to arrange the atoms in propane? (*Hint:* Are there any branches in the carbon chain or are all the carbon atoms in one line?)
5. Now make a model of C_4H_{10} (butane) in which all the carbon atoms are in one line.
6. Make a second model of butane with a branched chain.
7. Compare the branched-chain model with the straight-chain model of butane. Are there other ways to arrange the atoms?
8. Predict how many different structures can be formed from C_5H_{12} (pentane).
9. Test your prediction by building as many different models of pentane as you can.

Analyze and Conclude

1. Did any of your models have a hydrogen atom between two carbon atoms? Why or why not?
2. How does a branched chain differ from a straight chain?
3. How many different structures have the formula C_3H_8? C_4H_{10}? C_5H_{12}? Use diagrams to explain your answer.
4. If you bend a straight chain of carbons, do you make a different structure? Why or why not?
5. **Think About It** Compare the information you can get from models to the information you can get from formulas like C_6H_{14}. How does using models help you understand the structure of a molecule?

More to Explore

Use a third color of gumdrops to model an oxygen atom. An oxygen atom forms two bonds. Use the rules in this lab to model as many different structures for the formula $C_4H_{10}O$ as possible.

② Carbon Compounds

DISCOVER ● ACTIVITY

What Do You Smell?

1. Wave your hand toward your nose over the top of each of the containers provided by your teacher.

2. Try to identify each of the odors.

3. After you record what you think is in each container, compare your guesses to the actual substance.

Think It Over

Developing Hypotheses Make a hypothesis to explain the differences between the smell of one substance and the smell of another.

I magine that you are heading out for a day of shopping. Your first purchase is a red cotton shirt. Then you go to the drug store, where you buy a bottle of shampoo and a pad of writing paper. Your next stop is a hardware store to buy propane, a fuel used in camping stoves and lanterns. Your final stop is the grocery store, where you buy cereal, meat, and vegetables.

What do all of these purchases have in common? They all are made of carbon compounds. Carbon atoms act as the backbone or skeleton for the molecules of these compounds. Carbon compounds include gases (such as propane), liquids (such as olive oil), and solids (such as wax and cotton). Mixtures of carbon compounds are found in foods, paper, and shampoo. In fact, more than 90 percent of all known compounds contain carbon.

GUIDE FOR READING

◆ What properties do many organic compounds have in common?

◆ What kinds of carbon chains are found in hydrocarbons?

◆ What are some examples of substituted hydrocarbons?

Reading Tip Before you read, use the headings to make an outline of the different categories of organic compounds. As you read, add information to your outline.

Organic Compounds

Carbon compounds are so numerous that they are given a specific name. With some exceptions, a compound that contains carbon is called an **organic compound.** The word *organic* means "of living things." Scientists once thought that organic compounds could be produced only by living

Figure 7 Did you know that when you buy a shirt you are buying carbon compounds?

Figure 8 All living things contain organic compounds. Organic compounds include the oils used to fry foods, the plastic wrap and foam tray in which these apples are packaged, and even the apples themselves. *Inferring What does the dog have in common with the cooking oil, apples, plastic wrap, and tray?*

organisms. Organic compounds are indeed part of the solid matter of every living thing on Earth. Products made from living things, such as paper made from the wood of trees, are also organic compounds. However, not all organic compounds come from recently living things. Petroleum, or crude oil, comes from the remains of plants that lived millions of years ago. Plastics, fuels, cleaning solutions, and many other such products are made from petroleum.

Many organic compounds have similar properties, such as low melting points and low boiling points. As a result, these compounds are liquids or gases at room temperature. Organic liquids often have strong odors. They also do not conduct electricity. Many organic compounds are nonpolar. You may recall that nonpolar compounds do not mix well in water. Vegetable oil, for example, is a mixture of organic compounds. It forms a separate layer in a bottle of salad dressing.

Hydrocarbons

Scientists classify organic compounds into different categories. The simplest organic compounds are the hydrocarbons. A **hydrocarbon** (hy droh KAHR bun) is a compound that contains only the elements carbon and hydrogen. **The carbon chains in a hydrocarbon may be straight, branched, or ring-shaped.**

You might already recognize several common hydrocarbons. Methane, the main gas in natural gas, is used to heat homes. Propane is used in portable stoves and gas grills and to provide heat for hot-air balloons. Butane is the fuel in most lighters. Gasoline is a mixture of several different hydrocarbons. And paraffin wax is a hydrocarbon that is used to make candles.

Properties of Hydrocarbons All hydrocarbons are flammable, which means that they burn easily. When hydrocarbons burn, they release a great deal of energy. This is why they are used as fuels to power stoves and heaters, as well as cars, buses, and airplanes.

Like most other organic compounds, hydrocarbons mix poorly with water. Have you ever been at a gas station during a rainstorm? If so, you may have noticed a thin rainbow-colored film of gasoline or oil floating on a puddle.

Formulas of Hydrocarbons Hydrocarbon compounds differ in the number of carbon and hydrogen atoms in each molecule. You can show how many atoms there are of the elements that make up each molecule of a compound by writing a formula. A **molecular formula** includes the chemical symbols of the elements in each molecule of a compound, as well as the number of atoms of each element.

The simplest hydrocarbon is methane. Its molecular formula is CH_4. The number 4 indicates the number of hydrogen atoms (H). Notice that the 4 is a subscript. Remember that subscripts are written lower and smaller than the letter symbols of the elements. Notice that the symbol for carbon (C) in the formula is written without a subscript. This means that there is one carbon atom in the molecule.

A hydrocarbon with two carbon atoms is ethane. The formula for ethane is C_2H_6. The subscripts in this formula show that an ethane molecule is made of two carbon atoms and six hydrogen atoms. A hydrocarbon with three carbon atoms is propane (C_3H_8). How many hydrogen atoms does the subscript indicate? If you answered eight, you are right.

✓ *Checkpoint* What is a hydrocarbon?

Dry or Wet? ACTIVITY
Petroleum jelly is manufactured from hydrocarbons.

1. Carefully coat one of your fingers in petroleum jelly.
2. Dip that finger in water. Also dip a finger on your other hand in water.
3. Inspect the two fingers, and note how they feel.
4. Use a paper towel to remove the petroleum jelly, and then wash your hands thoroughly.

Inferring Compare how your two fingers looked and felt in Steps 2 and 3. What property of hydrocarbons does this activity demonstrate?

Figure 9 The natural gas burning at the top of this oil well is composed of hydrocarbons.

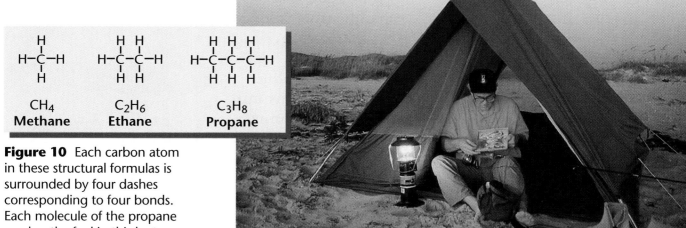

Figure 10 Each carbon atom in these structural formulas is surrounded by four dashes corresponding to four bonds. Each molecule of the propane used as the fuel in this lantern has 3 carbon atoms.

CH₄
Methane

C₂H₆
Ethane

C₃H₈
Propane

Figure 11 C₄H₁₀ has two isomers, butane and isobutane.
Interpreting Diagrams Which isomer is a branched chain?

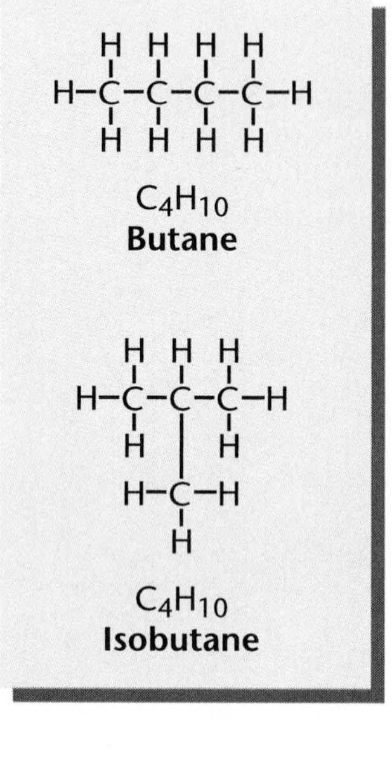

C₄H₁₀
Butane

C₄H₁₀
Isobutane

Straight Chains and Branches

If a hydrocarbon has two or more carbons, the carbon atoms can form a single line, or a straight chain. In hydrocarbons with four or more carbons, it is also possible to have branched arrangements of the carbon atoms.

Structural Formula To show how atoms are arranged in the molecules of a compound, chemists use a structural formula. A **structural formula** shows the kind, number, and arrangement of atoms in a molecule. Figure 10 shows the structural formulas for molecules of methane, ethane, and propane. Each dash (—) represents a bond. In methane, each carbon is bonded to four hydrogen atoms. In ethane and propane, each carbon is bonded to at least one carbon atom as well as to hydrogen atoms. As you look at structural formulas, notice that every carbon atom forms four bonds. Every hydrogen atom forms one bond. There are never any dangling bonds, or dangling dashes.

Isomers Structural formulas come in handy when you study organic compounds. Consider the compound butane, which has the molecular formula C_4H_{10}. The formula doesn't tell you how the atoms are arranged in the molecule. But look at Figure 11. From the structural formulas, you can see there are two ways to arrange the carbon atoms in C_4H_{10}. Compounds that have the same molecular formula but different structural formulas are called **isomers** (EYE soh murz). Each isomer is a different substance with unique properties.

Notice that one isomer of butane is a straight chain. The other isomer, called isobutane, is branched. This one difference in the arrangements of their atoms leads to different properties. For example, butane and isobutane have different melting points and boiling points.

✓ *Checkpoint* *How do structural and molecular formulas differ?*

222

Double Bonds and Triple Bonds

So far in this section, you have seen structural formulas of molecules with only single bonds between any two carbon atoms. One bond, one dash. However, two carbon atoms can form a single bond, a double bond, or a triple bond. A carbon atom can also form a single or double bond with an oxygen atom. Structural formulas represent a double bond with a double dash (C=C). You might think of the two atoms as doubly hooked together. A triple bond is indicated by a triple dash (C≡C). Bonds beyond triple bonds are not found in nature.

Saturated and Unsaturated Hydrocarbons

Hydrocarbons can be classified according to the types of bonds between the carbon atoms. If a hydrocarbon has only single bonds, it has the maximum number of hydrogen atoms possible on its carbon chain. These hydrocarbons are called **saturated hydrocarbons.** You can think of each carbon as being "saturated," or filled up, with hydrogens. Hydrocarbons with double or triple bonds have fewer hydrogen atoms for each carbon atom than a saturated hydrocarbon does. They are called **unsaturated hydrocarbons.**

Notice that the names of methane, ethane, propane, and butane end with the suffix -ane. Any hydrocarbon with a name that ends in -ane is a saturated hydrocarbon. If the name of a hydrocarbon ends in -ene or -yne, it is unsaturated.

The simplest unsaturated hydrocarbon with one double bond is ethene (C_2H_4), commonly known as ethylene. Many fruits, such as bananas, produce ethene gas. Ethene gas helps the fruit to ripen.

The simplest hydrocarbon with one triple bond is ethyne (C_2H_2), which is commonly known as acetylene. Acetylene torches are used in welding.

Sharpen your Skills

Classifying ACTIVITY

Which of the following hydrocarbons contain single, double, or triple bonds? (*Hint:* Remember that carbon forms four bonds and hydrogen forms one bond.)

C_2H_6	C_2H_4
C_2H_2	C_3H_8
C_3H_6	C_3H_4
C_4H_{10}	

Figure 12 Unsaturated hydrocarbons have double and triple bonds. Ethene gas causes fruits such as bananas to ripen.

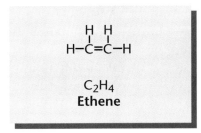

C_2H_4
Ethene

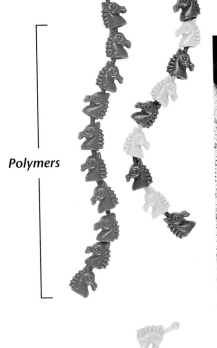

Polymers

Monomers

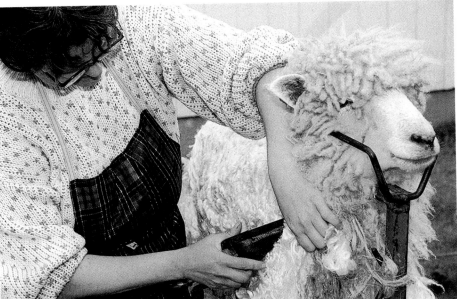

Figure 16 Chains of monomers that make up polymer molecules are somewhat like these chains of plastic beads. Natural polymers include the wool being sheared from this sheep.
Comparing and Contrasting
How do polymer molecules differ from monomer molecules?

Polymers

Organic compounds, such as alcohols, esters, and others, can be linked together to build huge molecules with thousands or even millions of atoms. A very large molecule made of a chain of many smaller molecules bonded together is called a **polymer** (PAHL ih mur). The smaller molecules—the links that make up the chain—are called **monomers** (MAHN ih mur) The prefix *poly-* means "many," and the prefix *mono-* means "one."

Some polymers are made by living things. For example, sheep make wool, cotton plants make cotton, and silkworms make silk. Other polymers, called **synthetic** polymers, are manufactured, or synthesized, in factories. If you are wearing clothing made from polyester or nylon, you are wearing a synthetic polymer right now! And any plastic item you use is most certainly made of synthetic polymers. You will learn more about polymers in the next chapter.

Section 2 Review

1. List properties common to many organic compounds.
2. Describe the different kinds of carbon chains that are found in hydrocarbons.
3. What is a substituted hydrocarbon? List four examples of substituted hydrocarbons.
4. **Thinking Critically** **Problem Solving** You are given two solid materials, one that is organic and one that is not organic. Describe three tests you could perform to help you decide which is which.

Science at Home

Liquid Layers You can make a simple salad dressing to demonstrate one property of organic compounds. In a transparent container, thoroughly mix equal amounts of a vegetable oil and a fruit juice. Stop mixing, and observe the oil and juice mixture for several minutes. Explain your observations to your family.

SECTION 3 Life With Carbon

• ACTIVITY • • •

What Is in Milk?

1. Pour 30 mL of milk into a plastic cup.

2. Pour another 30 mL of milk into a second plastic cup. Rinse the graduated cylinder. Measure 15 mL of vinegar and add it to the second cup. Swirl the two liquids together and let the mixture sit for a minute.

3. Set up two funnels with filter paper, each supported in a narrow plastic cup.

4. Filter the milk through the first funnel. Filter the milk and vinegar through the second funnel.

5. What is left in each filter paper? Examine the liquid that passed through each filter paper.

Think It Over

Observing Where did you see evidence of solids? What do you think was the source of these solids?

Have you ever been told to eat all the organic compounds on your plate? Have you heard how eating a variety of polymers and monomers contributes to good health? What? No one has ever said either of those things to you? Well, maybe what you really heard was something about eating all the vegetables on your plate. Or that you need to eat a variety of foods to give you a healthy balance of carbohydrates, proteins, fats, and other nutrients. Organic compounds are the building blocks of all living things. Foods provide organic compounds, which the cells of living things use or change.

◆ What are the four main classes of organic compounds in living things?

◆ How are the organic compounds in living things different from each other?

Reading Tip Before you read, rewrite each heading as a question. Then read to answer your questions.

Figure 17 This salad bar offers several tasty mixtures of organic compounds that you can eat.

Nutrients From Foods

Nutrients (NOO tree unts) are substances that provide the energy and raw materials the body needs to grow, repair worn parts, and function properly. Most of the nutrients in foods are organic compounds. **The four classes of organic compounds found in all living things are carbohydrates, lipids, proteins, and nucleic acids.** Many nutrients are polymers—large, chainlike molecules made of smaller molecules linked together.

In order for the body to make use of nutrients, they first must be broken down into smaller parts. The process of breaking these large molecules into smaller ones involves chemical reactions that occur during digestion.

After food is digested, the body carries out chemical reactions that change the smaller molecules again. Some small molecules are broken down even further. This process releases energy the body can use. The body also reassembles certain small molecules into larger ones that have specific functions.

✓ *Checkpoint* How does your body use nutrients?

Carbohydrates

A **carbohydrate** (kahr boh HY drayt) is an energy-rich organic compound made of the elements carbon, hydrogen, and oxygen. The word *carbohydrate* is made of two parts: *carbo-* and *-hydrate*. *Carbo-* means "carbon" and *-hydrate* means "combined with

Figure 18 Carbohydrates and other organic compounds in foods are sources of the energy for these cross-country runners. Glucose is a simple carbohydrate.
Interpreting Diagrams What elements make up a glucose molecule?

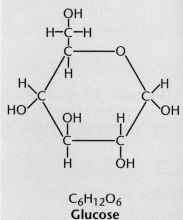

$C_6H_{12}O_6$
Glucose

Figure 19 Grapes and honey contain sugars.

water." If you remember that water is made up of the elements hydrogen and oxygen, then you should be able to remember the three elements in carbohydrates.

Simple Carbohydrates The simplest carbohydrates are sugars. You may be surprised to learn that there are many different kinds of sugars. The sugar listed in baking recipes, which you can buy in bags or boxes at the grocery store, is only one kind. Other sugars are found naturally in fruits, milk, and some vegetables.

One of the most important sugars in your body is **glucose.** Its molecular formula is $C_6H_{12}O_6$. Glucose is sometimes called "blood sugar" because the body circulates glucose to all body parts through the blood. The structural formula for a glucose molecule is shown in Figure 18.

The name of the white sugar that sweetens cookies, candies, and many soft drinks is sucrose. It is a more complex molecule than glucose and has a molecular formula of $C_{12}H_{22}O_{11}$.

Complex Carbohydrates When you eat plants or food products made from plants, you are often eating complex carbohydrates. Each molecule of a simple carbohydrate, or sugar, is relatively small compared to a molecule of a complex carbohydrate. A **complex carbohydrate** is made of long chains of simple carbohydrates bonded to one another. Just one molecule of a complex carbohydrate may have hundreds of carbon atoms.

Two of the complex carbohydrates assembled from glucose molecules are starch and cellulose. **Starch and cellulose are both polymers built from glucose, but the glucose molecules are arranged differently in each case.** So starch and cellulose are different compounds. They serve different functions in the plants that form them. The body also uses starch from foods very differently from the way it uses cellulose.

Figure 20 Starchy foods (left) provide energy. Foods high in cellulose (right) provide fiber. *Interpreting Photographs Name examples of foods high in starch and foods high in cellulose.*

Starch Plants store energy in the form of the complex carbohydrate **starch.** You can find starches in food products made from wheat grains, such as bread, cereal, and pasta. Starches are also found in rice, potatoes, and other vegetables. The body digests the large starch molecules from these foods into individual glucose molecules. Later, the body breaks down the glucose into even smaller molecules, releasing energy.

Cellulose Plants build strong stems and roots with the complex carbohydrate **cellulose** and other polymers. If you imagine yourself crunching on a stick of celery, you will be able to imagine what cellulose is like. Most fruits, vegetables, and nuts are high in cellulose. So are food products made from whole grains. Even though the body can break down starch, the body cannot break down cellulose into individual glucose molecules. Therefore the body cannot use cellulose as a source of energy. In fact, when you eat foods with cellulose, the molecules pass right through you undigested. However, this undigested cellulose helps keep your digestive track active and healthy. Cellulose is sometimes called fiber.

☑ *Checkpoint* What is cellulose?

Proteins

If the proteins in your body suddenly disappeared, you would not have much of a body left! Your muscles, hair, skin, and fingernails are all made of proteins. A bird's feathers, a spider's web, a fish's scales, and the horns of a rhinoceros are also made of proteins.

Proteins are nutrients made of carbon, hydrogen, oxygen, nitrogen, and sometimes sulfur. In living things, proteins are needed for growth and repair. Proteins also play key roles in the chemical reactions within cells.

Chains of Amino Acids Proteins are polymers formed from smaller molecules called **amino acids.** There are 20 kinds of amino acids found in living things. **Different proteins are made when different sequences of amino acids are linked into long chains.** Since proteins can be made of combinations of hundreds of amino acids, a huge variety of proteins are possible.

The structure of one amino acid, valine, is shown in Figure 21. Each amino acid molecule has a carboxyl group (—COOH). You might have just guessed that the *acid* part of the term *amino acid* comes from this part of the molecule. An amine group, with the structure —NH_2, is the source of the *amino* half of the name. The other parts of the molecule differ for each kind of amino acid.

Food Proteins Become Your Proteins Some of the best sources of protein include meat, fish, eggs, and milk or milk products. Some plant products such as beans are good sources of protein as well. If you did the Discover activity, you used vinegar to separate proteins from milk.

The body uses proteins from food to build and repair body parts. But first the proteins must be digested. Just as starch is broken down into glucose molecules, proteins are broken down into amino acids. Then the body reassembles those amino acids into thousands of different proteins that can be used by cells.

TRY THIS

Alphabet Soup

Here's how you can model **ACTIVITY** the rearrangement of amino acids in your body.

1. Rearrange the letters of the word *proteins* to make a new word or words. (Don't worry if the new words don't make sense together.)

2. Choose three other words with ten or more letters. Repeat the activity.

Making Models What words did you make from *proteins*? What new words did you make from the words you chose? How does this activity model the way your body uses proteins in food to make new proteins?

Valine

Figure 21 These foods are all good sources of protein. Proteins are built from long chains of amino acids. Valine is one example of an amino acid.

Figure 22 The labels on some bottles of cooking oil tell you that they are low in saturated fats or high in polyunsaturated oils. These foods (right) are high in animal fats or vegetable oils. *Classifying Which class of organic compounds includes the fats and oils?*

Lipids

The third class of organic compounds in living things is lipids. Like carbohydrates, **lipids** are energy-rich compounds made of carbon, oxygen, and hydrogen. Lipids include fats, oils, waxes, and cholesterol. **Gram for gram, lipids release twice as much energy in your body as do carbohydrates.** Lipids behave somewhat like hydrocarbons—the compounds of carbon and hydrogen you read about in Section 2. They mix poorly with water.

Fats and Oils Have you ever gotten grease on your clothes from foods that contain fats or oils? Fats are found in foods such as meat, butter, and cheese. Oils in foods include those such as corn oil, sunflower oil, peanut oil, and olive oil.

Fats and oils have the same basic structure. Each fat or oil is made of three **fatty acids** and one alcohol named glycerol, as shown in *Exploring the Molecules of Life.* There is one main difference between fats and oils, however. Fats are usually solid at room temperature, whereas oils are liquid. You have to heat butter, for example, to make it melt. The temperature at which a fat or oil becomes a liquid depends on the chemical structure of its fatty acid molecules.

You may hear fats and oils described as "saturated" or "unsaturated." Like saturated hydrocarbons, the fatty acids of saturated fats have no double bonds between carbon atoms. Unsaturated fatty acids are found in oils. Monounsaturated oils have fatty acids with one double bond. Polyunsaturated oils have fatty acids with many double bonds. (Remember that *mono* means "one" and *poly* means "many.") Saturated fats tend to have higher melting points than unsaturated oils do.

Cholesterol Another important lipid is **cholesterol** (kuh LES tuh rawl), a waxy substance found in all animal cells. The body builds cell structures from cholesterol and uses it to form compounds that serve as chemical messengers. The body produces the cholesterol it needs from

INTEGRATING HEALTH

Figure 23 Cholesterol deposits in this artery (shown in cross section) have narrowed the space available for blood to flow through.

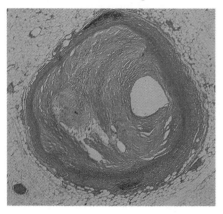

other nutrients. But foods that come from animals—cheese, eggs, and meat—also provide cholesterol. Foods from plant sources, such as vegetable oils, never contain cholesterol.

Although cholesterol is often found in the same foods as saturated fats, they are different compounds. An excess level of cholesterol in the blood can contribute to heart disease. But saturated fats can affect the level of cholesterol in the blood. For this reason it is wise to limit your intake of both nutrients.

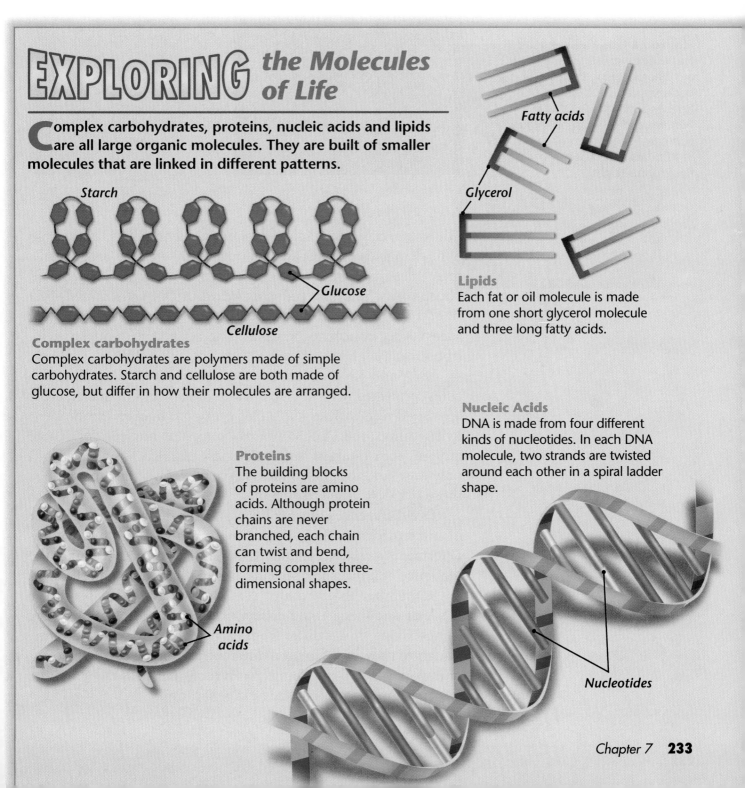

EXPLORING *the Molecules of Life*

Complex carbohydrates, proteins, nucleic acids and lipids are all large organic molecules. They are built of smaller molecules that are linked in different patterns.

Starch

Glucose

Cellulose

Complex carbohydrates
Complex carbohydrates are polymers made of simple carbohydrates. Starch and cellulose are both made of glucose, but differ in how their molecules are arranged.

Fatty acids

Glycerol

Lipids
Each fat or oil molecule is made from one short glycerol molecule and three long fatty acids.

Proteins
The building blocks of proteins are amino acids. Although protein chains are never branched, each chain can twist and bend, forming complex three-dimensional shapes.

Amino acids

Nucleic Acids
DNA is made from four different kinds of nucleotides. In each DNA molecule, two strands are twisted around each other in a spiral ladder shape.

Nucleotides

Figure 24 This hummingbird and the flower it is visiting (left) are different living things because their DNA differs. Scientists who study DNA in humans and other living things compare the patterns of bands in test data called DNA fingerprints (right).

Nucleic Acids

The fourth class of organic compounds in living things is made up of nucleic acids. **Nucleic acids** (noo KLEE ik) are very large organic molecules made up of carbon, oxygen, hydrogen, nitrogen, and phosphorus. You have probably heard of **DNA,** the initials that stand for one type of nucleic acid, called deoxyribonucleic acid (dee ahk see ry boh noo KLEE ik). The other type of nucleic acid, ribonucleic acid (ry boh noo KLEE ic), is called **RNA.**

DNA and RNA are made of different kinds of small molecules connected in a pattern. The building blocks of nucleic acids are called **nucleotides** (NOO klee oh tydz). In even the simplest living things, the DNA contains billions of nucleotides! There are only four kinds of nucleotides in DNA. RNA is also built of only four kinds of nucleotides. Three nucleotides are the same as those in DNA. One is different.

The differences among living things depend on the order of nucleotides in their DNA. The order of DNA nucleotides determines a related order in RNA. That, in turn, determines the sequence of amino acids in proteins made by a living cell.

Remember that proteins regulate cell activities. Since the DNA of one living thing differs from the DNA of other living things, living things differ from each other. The cells in a hummingbird grow and function differently from the cells in a flower or in you. When living things reproduce, they pass DNA and the information it carries to the next generation.

Other Nutrients in Foods

Carbohydrates, proteins, lipids, and nucleic acids are not the only compounds your body needs. Your body also needs vitamins, minerals, and salts. Unlike the nutrients discussed so far, vitamins and minerals are needed in only small amounts. They do not directly provide you with energy or raw materials.

Vitamins are organic compounds that serve as helper molecules in a variety of chemical reactions in your body. For example, vitamin C, or ascorbic acid, is important for keeping your skin and gums healthy. Vitamin D helps your bones and teeth develop and keeps them strong.

Minerals are elements needed by your body. Unlike the other nutrients discussed in this chapter, minerals are not organic compounds. You may remember the names of some of the minerals from the periodic table—for example, the elements sodium, calcium, iron, iodine, and potassium.

If you eat a variety of foods, you will probably get the vitamins and minerals you need. Food manufacturers add some vitamins and minerals to packaged foods to replace vitamins and minerals lost in food processing. Such foods say "enriched" on their labels. Sometimes manufacturers add extra vitamins and minerals to foods to "fortify," or strengthen, the nutrient qualities of the food. For example, milk is usually fortified with vitamins A and D.

Figure 25 Vitamins and minerals occur naturally in foods, but food manufacturers also sometimes add vitamins and minerals.
Interpreting Photos What do the packages of these food products tell you about the addition of vitamins and minerals ?

Section 3 Review

1. List an example of each of the four classes of compounds that living things make and use.
2. Compare the building blocks of complex carbohydrates and those of proteins.
3. How do lipids and carbohydrates compare as energy-rich molecules?
4. How does the DNA differ for different living things?
5. What nutrients do you need besides the main classes of organic compounds?
6. **Thinking Critically** **Making Judgments** Would it matter if you ate foods that provide only carbohydrates but not proteins? Explain your answer.

Check Your Progress

CHAPTER PROJECT

Review the compounds mentioned in this section, and try to find as many as you can on each food label you collected. Prepare a table that will organize your data. Be sure to include entries for carbohydrates (including sugars), proteins, and lipids (including fats, oils, and cholesterol.) Also include entries for vitamins and minerals (for example, the element sodium). You may also want to keep track of ingredients you cannot identify. (*Hint:* Manufacturers may add compounds to improve the flavor or texture of a food, prevent it from spoiling, or give it a longer shelf-life.)

SCIENCE AND SOCIETY

Natural or Artificial—A Sweet Dilemma

Do you have a sweet tooth? Many people do. But there is a price to be paid for sweetness. Excess energy from sugars is easily stored by the body in the form of fat. The bacteria that cause tooth decay use sugars in the mouth as food. And for people who have the disease diabetes, sugary foods can raise blood sugar to a life-threatening level.

Food scientists have developed three organic compounds that taste sweet but provide few calories—saccharin, cyclamate, and aspartame. Aspartame, for example, is 200 times as sweet as the sugar sucrose. Gram for gram, aspartame and sucrose have equal calories. But it takes much smaller amounts of aspartame to give the same sweetness. Unfortunately, saccharin, cyclamate, and aspartame all have health risks associated with their use.

The Issues

Why Use Artificial Sweeteners? Artificial sweeteners allow people with diabetes to enjoy sweet foods and beverages safely without raising their blood sugar level. But most people who consume artificial sweeteners want to lose weight. Advertising has glamorized being thin. In addition, being overweight can lead to serious health conditions, such as heart disease and high blood pressure.

What Are Possible Dangers? Studies of cyclamate have shown that large doses can lead to cancer and birth defects in lab animals. The U.S. Food and Drug Administration (FDA) has banned cyclamate, but some people think that cyclamate would be safe in moderate amounts.

In similar studies of saccharin, large doses seem to cause cancer in lab animals. Long-term studies with people have not provided clear results. Some people think any risk is too much. The FDA, therefore, requires all products containing saccharin to have labels warning of possible health risks.

Early tests on aspartame showed it to be safe. But long-term studies suggest some problems with heavy use. More testing is needed. For about one in every ten thousand people, the use of aspartame can be very dangerous. If a person has the genetic disorder called phenylketonuria (PKU), then one of the amino acids in aspartame can interfere with normal development. These people must avoid aspartame, especially as infants.

How Much Is Too Much? Different people have different health concerns. Thus the question of how much sugar or artificial sweetener is too much depends on the individual. For some people, no artificial sweeteners is the answer. For others, moderate amounts, such as one or two servings a day, may be safe. But more scientific evidence must be collected to answer how much is too much.

You Decide

1. Identify the Problem
In your own words, explain the issues about the use of artificial sweeteners.

2. Analyze the Options
List the pros and cons for using artificial sweeteners as well as the pros and cons for using sugar.

3. Find a Solution
You are planning refreshments for a school event. Should you provide artificially sweetened soft drinks? Write a brief statement supporting your opinion.

Chemical Bonds, Carbon Style

Key Ideas
◆ Carbon atoms can form bonds with one another and with atoms of other elements to form a large number of different compounds.
◆ The element carbon exists in different forms. Diamond crystals are the hardest mineral formed in Earth. Graphite is a slippery form of carbon. Fullerenes have an open, spherelike shape.

Key Terms
diamond
graphite
fullerene

 Carbon Compounds

Key Ideas
◆ Many organic compounds have properties in common with one another.
◆ Carbon chains in hydrocarbons can be straight, branched, or ring-shaped.
◆ Isomers are different from one another because of their differing structural formula.
◆ Substituted hydrocarbons, which are related to other hydrocarbons, include halogen compounds, alcohols, and organic acids.
◆ Polymers are formed from many monomers linked together.

Key Terms
organic compound	hydroxyl group
hydrocarbon	alcohol
molecular formula	organic acid
structural formula	carboxyl group
isomer	ester
saturated hydrocarbon	polymer
unsaturated hydrocarbon	monomer
substituted hydrocarbon	synthetic

 Life With Carbon

INTEGRATING LIFE SCIENCE

Key Ideas
◆ Nutrients provide your body with energy and raw materials. Many nutrients are organic compounds made of large molecules.
◆ The four main classes of organic compounds in living things are carbohydrates, proteins, lipids, and nucleic acids.
◆ Complex carbohydrates are built from sugars. The building blocks of proteins are amino acids. Fats and oils are made from fatty acids and glycerol. Nucleic acids are made from nucleotides.
◆ Vitamins and minerals are other nutrients that contribute to a healthy diet.

Key Terms
nutrient	fatty acid
carbohydrate	cholesterol
glucose	nucleic acid
complex carbohydrate	DNA
starch	RNA
cellulose	nucleotide
protein	vitamin
amino acid	mineral
lipid	

Organizing Information

Venn Diagram Copy the Venn diagram about proteins and nucleic acids onto a separate sheet of paper. Then complete it and add a title. (See the Skills Handbook for more on Venn diagrams.)

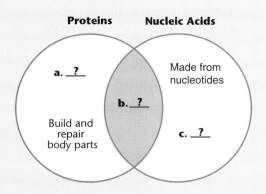

Reviewing Content

 For more review of key concepts, see the Interactive Student Tutorial CD-ROM.

Multiple Choice
Choose the letter of the best answer.

1. The number of valence electrons for each carbon atom is
   a. one.   b. two.
   c. three.   d. four.
2. All organic compounds contain
   a. oxygen.
   b. carbon.
   c. halogens.
   d. carboxyl groups.
3. The group —COOH is characteristic of
   a. an organic acid.
   b. an alcohol.
   c. a halogen compound.
   d. a hydrocarbon.
4. The smaller molecules from which complex carbohydrates are made are
   a. sugars.
   b. amino acids.
   c. nucleotides.
   d. fats.
5. Cholesterol is a type of
   a. nucleic acid.
   b. carbohydrate.
   c. lipid.
   d. cellulose.

True or False
If the statement is true, write true. If it is false, change the underlined word or words to make the statement true.

6. Because the bonds between layers of carbon atoms are weak, layers of <u>fullerenes</u> slide easily past one another.
7. Hydrocarbons that contain only single bonds are said to be <u>unsaturated</u>.
8. An organic acid is characterized by one or more groups of atoms symbolized by the formula <u>—OH</u>.
9. A <u>monomer</u> is a long chain of <u>polymers</u>.
10. Proteins are made up of long chains of <u>amino acids</u>.

Checking Concepts

11. What happens to the electrons when one carbon atom forms a single bond with another carbon atom?
12. What do diamonds, graphite, and fullerenes have in common?
13. How would you notice the presence of esters in a fruit such as a pineapple or banana?
14. Starches and cellulose are both complex carbohydrates. How does your body handle these compounds differently?
15. Compare and contrast the fatty acids in fats that are solid at room temperature with fatty acids in oils that are liquids.
16. Why is the order of nucleotides in DNA important?
17. **Writing to Learn** Write at least ten riddles for different forms of carbon and for organic compounds. Riddles are problems or puzzles usually worded as a question. For example, "What is made of carbon atoms and shaped like a soccer ball?" Write each riddle on the front of an index card and the correct answer on the back. Share your riddles with your classmates and see if they can solve them.

Thinking Critically

18. **Relating Cause and Effect** What features of the element carbon allow it to form the "backbone" of such a varied array of different compounds?
19. **Applying Concepts** Why must unsaturated hydrocarbons have a minimum of two carbons?
20. **Classifying** Classify each of the following compounds as a hydrocarbon, an alcohol, an organic acid, or a halogen compound: $C_{12}H_{20}COOH$, C_7H_{16}, C_2H_5Cl, C_4H_7OH.
21. **Posing Questions** Glucose and fructose are both simple carbohydrates with the formula $C_6H_{12}O_6$. What else do you need to know about glucose and fructose to decide if they should be considered different compounds?

Applying Skills

Use the following structural formulas to answer Questions 22–25.

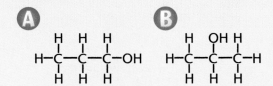

A

B

22. Classifying Which type of substituted hydrocarbons are compounds A and B? What information in the structural formulas did you use to decide your answer?

23. Observing What is the correct subscript for the carbon atoms (C) in the molecular formula that corresponds to each structural formula?

24. Inferring Are compounds A and B isomers? How can you tell?

25. Predicting Would you expect these two compounds to have identical properties or different properties? Explain why.

CHAPTER PROJECT

Performance ▽ **Assessment**

Present Your Project Display your data table classifying compounds in foods, along with the labels from which you collected your data. Point out the nutrients that are found in almost all foods and the nutrients found in only a few foods.

Reflect and Record In your journal, list any questions that you were unable to answer in your research. What would you like to learn more about? How could you learn more about substances used in various food products?

Test Preparation

Use these questions to prepare for standardized tests.

Study the table. Then answer Questions 26–28.

Name	Molecular Formula
Methane	CH_4
Ethane	C_2H_6
Propane	C_3H_8
Butane	C_4H_{10}
Pentane	C_5H_{12}
Hexane	C_6H_{14}
Heptane	C_7H_{16}
Octane	C_8H_{18}
Nonane	C_9H_{20}
Decane	$C_{10}H_{22}$

26. What information does this table provide about each hydrocarbon?
  a. shape
  b. number of branches
  c. number of carbon and hydrogen atoms in each molecule
  d. number of existing isomers

27. Based on the information in the table, what is the relationship between the number of hydrogen atoms and the number of carbon atoms in each hydrocarbon?
  a. There are twice as many hydrogen atoms as carbon atoms.
  b. There are twice as many carbon atoms as hydrogen atoms.
  c. The number of hydrogen atoms is three times the number of carbon atoms minus two.
  d. The number of hydrogen atoms is twice the number of carbon atoms plus two.

28. Propene is a hydrocarbon with six hydrogen atoms in its molecular formula. Based on the names in the table, what is the subscript for carbon in propene's molecular formula?
  a. 1
  b. 2
  c. 3
  d. 4

CHAPTER

8 Exploring Materials

WEB ACTIVITY

www.phschool.com

Integrating Technology

SECTION 1 Polymers and Composites

Discover What Did You Make?
Sharpen Your Skills Classifying
Real-World Lab Packaging With Polymers

SECTION 2 Metals and Alloys

Discover Are They Steel the Same?
Science at Home Metal Inventory

SECTION 3 Ceramics and Glass

Discover Does It Get Wet?
Try This A Bright Idea

242

Polymer Profiles

A spider's delicate web glistens in the early morning sunshine. It was spun overnight from silken fibers produced by the spider's body. These fibers, much of the spider itself, and the flower stems that support the web are made from polymers—one of the types of materials you will study in this chapter. In your project, you will survey different polymers found around you. You will learn about the properties of these materials and see how their uses depend on their properties.

Your Goal To collect and investigate different polymers.

To complete your project you must
- collect at least eight polymer samples from at least three different locations
- investigate the chemical and physical properties of the polymers by performing at least three tests
- create an informative display about these polymers
- follow the safety guidelines in Appendix A

Get Started Brainstorm with your classmates what you already know about polymers. Make a list of items you think are made of polymers. Look in Section 1 to get some hints about materials to investigate. Begin to think about how different polymers are used in everyday life, and why.

Check Your Progress You will be working on this project as you study this chapter. To keep your project on track, look for Check Your Progress boxes at the following points.

Section 1 Review, page 251: Collect samples of polymers and record data about their sources and uses.

Section 3 Review, page 264: Devise procedures to test properties of the polymers.

Section 4 Review, page 271: Carry out your tests and organize your results in your data table.

Present Your Project At the end of the chapter (page 275), you will present a showcase of polymers to the class.

SECTION
4 **Radioactive Elements**

Discover **How Much Goes Away?**
Sharpen Your Skills **Predicting**
Sharpen Your Skills **Calculating**
Skills Lab **That's Half-Life!**

This spider's web and the mountain thistle stems that support it are made of natural polymers.

SECTION 1 Polymers and Composites

DISCOVER ·· ACTIVITY····

What Did You Make?

1. Look at a sample of borax solution and write down properties you observe. Do the same with white glue.

2. Measure about 2 large spoonfuls of borax solution into a paper cup.

3. Stir the solution as you add about one spoonful of white glue to the cup.

4. After 2 minutes, record the properties of the material in the cup. Wash your hands when you are finished.

Think It Over
Observing What evidence of a chemical reaction did you observe? How did the materials change? What do you think you made?

GUIDE FOR READING

◆ How does a polymer form?

◆ Why are composite materials often more useful than single polymers?

Reading Tip As you read, make a list of properties of polymers. Write one sentence describing each property.

Figure 1 The clothing, boots, goggles, and helmet worn by this climber are all made of polymers. So is the rope that protects her from falling off this frozen waterfall in Colorado.

Did you ever step into tar on a hot summer day? Tar is a thick, smelly, black goo that sticks to your shoes. Tar, from crude oil or coal, can be made into rope, insulating fabric for clothes, and safety gear. Manufacturers use tar to make countless products ranging from sports equipment and automobile parts to plastic housewares and toys.

Look around the room. How many things can you see that are made of plastic? What materials do you think people made these items from before plastic was invented? Many things that were once made of metal, glass, paper, or wood have been replaced by plastic materials.

Carbon's Strings, Rings, and Other Things

Plastics and the cells in your body have something in common. They are made of organic compounds. Organic compounds contain atoms of carbon bonded to one another and to other kinds of atoms. Carbon is present in more than two million known compounds, and more are being discovered or invented every day.

You may recall that carbon's unique ability to form so many compounds comes from two properties. Carbon atoms can form four covalent bonds. They can also bond to one another in chains and ring-shaped groups. These structures form the "backbones" to which other atoms attach.

Hydrogen is the most common element found with carbon in its compounds. Other elements include oxygen, nitrogen, phosphorus, sulfur, and the halogens, especially chlorine.

Carbon Compounds Form Polymers

Molecules of some organic compounds can hook together, forming larger molecules. A polymer is a large, complex molecule built from smaller molecules joined together. The smaller molecules from which polymers are built are called monomers. **Polymers form when chemical bonds link large numbers of monomers in a repeating pattern.** A polymer may consist of hundreds or even thousands of monomers.

Many polymers consist of a single kind of monomer that repeats over and over again. You could think of these monomers as linked like the identical cars of a long passenger train. In other cases, two or three monomers may join in an alternating pattern. Sometimes links between monomer chains occur, forming large webs or netlike molecules. The chemical properties of a polymer depend on the monomers from which it is made.

☑ *Checkpoint* *What are the patterns in which monomers come together to form polymers?*

Building a Polymer

One kind of monomer

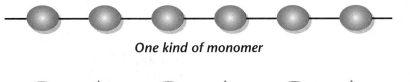

Two kinds of monomers

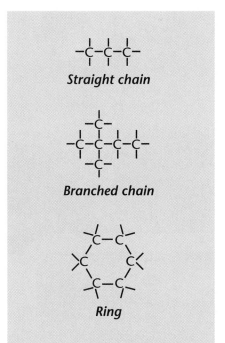

Figure 2 Carbon atoms can form straight chains, branched chains, and rings. In these drawings, lines represent covalent bonds that can form between atoms.
Interpreting Diagrams How many covalent bonds are shown for each carbon atom?

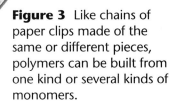

Figure 3 Like chains of paper clips made of the same or different pieces, polymers can be built from one kind or several kinds of monomers.

Natural Polymers

![Integrating Life Science] Polymers have been around as long as life on Earth. Plants, animals, and other living things produce the polymers they need from nutrients and other materials in the environment.

Plant Polymers Look closely at a piece of coarse paper, such as a paper towel. You can see that it is made of long strings, or fibers. These fibers are bundles of cellulose. Cellulose is a flexible but strong natural polymer that gives shape to plant cells. Cellulose is made in plants when sugar molecules (made earlier from carbon dioxide and water) are joined into long strands. The cellulose then forms cell structures.

Animal Polymers Gently touch a spider web and feel how it stretches without breaking. It is made from chemicals in the spider's body. These chemicals mix and react to form a silken polymer that is one of the strongest materials known. Spiders spin webs, egg cases, and traps for prey from these fibers. You can wear polymers made by animals. Silk is made from the fibers of silkworm cocoons. Wool is made from sheep's fur. These polymers can be woven into thread and cloth.

Your own body makes polymers. Tap your fingernail on a tabletop. Your fingernails and the muscles that just moved your finger are made of proteins. Proteins are polymers. Within your body, proteins are assembled from combinations of smaller molecules (monomers), called amino acids. The properties of a protein depend on which amino acids are used and in what order. One combination builds the protein that forms your fingernails. Another combination forms the protein that carries oxygen in your blood. Yet another forms the hair that grows on your head.

☑ *Checkpoint* **What are two examples of natural polymers from plants and animals?**

Figure 4 Both animals and plants make polymers. **A.** The leaves and stems of these desert plants are made of cellulose and other polymers. **B.** A cotton plant is a source of polymers that people make into thread and cloth. **C.** These silk fabrics were made from the threads of silkworm cocoons. *Comparing and Contrasting What do the polymers shown in these photos have in common?*

Synthetic Polymers

Many polymers you use every day are synthesized from simpler materials. Recall that a synthesis reaction occurs when elements or simple compounds combine to form complex compounds. The starting materials for most polymers come from coal or oil. **Plastics,** which are synthetic polymers that can be molded or shaped, are the most common products. But there are many others. Carpets, clothing, glue, and even chewing gum can be made of synthetic polymers.

Figure 5 lists just a few of the hundreds of polymers people use. Although the names seem like tongue-twisters, see how many you recognize. You may be able to identify some polymers by their initials printed on the bottoms of plastic bottles.

Compare the uses of polymers listed in Figure 5 with their characteristics. Notice that many products require materials that are flexible, yet strong. Others must be hard or lightweight. When chemical engineers design a new product, they have to think about how it will be used. Then they synthesize a polymer with properties to match.

Synthetic polymers are often used in place of natural materials that are too expensive or wear out too quickly. Polyester and nylon fabrics, for example, are used instead of wool, silk, and cotton to make clothes. Laminated countertops and vinyl floors replace wood in many kitchens. Other synthetic polymers have uses for which there is no suitable natural material. Compact discs, computer parts, artificial heart valves, and even your bicycle tires couldn't exist without synthetic polymers.

Language Arts CONNECTION

Many words in the English language use prefixes from Greek or Latin. In Greek, *mono-* means "one" and *poly-* means "many." These prefixes tell you that the molecules are made of either one or many parts.

In Your Journal

Make a list of words with other prefixes that tell you "how many," for example, the *tri-* in triangle. Tell what number the prefix indicates. Extend your list to include units of measurement, such as the millimeter. In each case, tell what information the prefix gives.

Figure 5 You can find many applications of synthetic polymers in your own home.

Some Synthetic Polymers You Use

Name	Characteristics	Uses
Low-density polyethylene (LDPE)	Flexible, soft, melts easily	Plastic bags, squeeze bottles, electric wire insulation
High-density polyethylene (HDPE)	Stronger than LDPE; higher melting temperatures	Detergent bottles, gas cans, toys, milk jugs
Polypropylene (PP)	Hard, keeps its shape	Toys, car parts, bottle caps
Polyvinyl chloride (PVC)	Tough, flexible	Garden hoses, imitation leather, piping
Polystyrene (PS)	Lightweight, can be made into foam	Foam drinking cups, insulation, furniture, "peanut" packing material
Nylon	Strong, can be drawn into flexible thread	Stockings, parachutes, fishing line, fabric
Teflon (polytetrafluoroethylene)	Nonreactive, low friction	Nonstick coating for cooking pans

Composites

Every substance has its advantages and disadvantages. What would happen if you could take the best properties of two substances and put them together? **Composites** combine two or more substances as a new material with different properties. **By combining the useful properties of two or more substances in a composite, chemists can make a new material that works better than either one alone.** Many composite materials include one or more polymers.

![SCIENCE & History]

The Development of Polymers

The first synthetic polymers were made by changing natural polymers in some way. Later, crude oil and coal became the starting materials. Now new polymers are designed in laboratories every year.

1869 Celluloid

Made using cellulose, celluloid became a substitute for ivory in billiard balls and combs and brushes. It was later used to make movie film. Because celluloid is very flammable, other materials have replaced it for almost all purposes, except table-tennis balls.

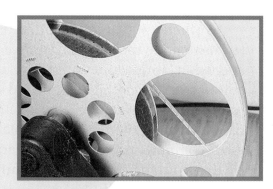

1825 ———————————————————————— **1875**

1839 Synthetic Rubber

Charles Goodyear invented a process that turned natural rubber into a hard, stretchable polymer. It did not get sticky and soft when heated or become brittle when cold, as natural rubber does. Bicycle tires were an early use.

1909 Bakelite

Bakelite was the first commercial polymer made from compounds in coal tar. Bakelite doesn't get soft when heated, and it doesn't conduct electricity. These properties made it useful for handles for pots and pans, telephones, and for parts in electrical outlets.

A Natural Composite The idea of putting two different materials together to get the advantages of both comes from the natural world. Many synthetic composites are designed to imitate a common natural composite—wood. Wood is made of long fibers of cellulose, held together by another plant polymer called lignin. Cellulose fibers are flexible and can't support much weight. At the same time, lignin is brittle and would crack under the weight of the tree branches. But the combination of the two polymers makes a strong tree trunk.

In Your Journal

Find out more about the invention of one of these polymers. Write a headline for a newspaper, announcing the invention. Then write the first paragraph of the news article telling how the invention will change people's lives.

1989 LEP

Light-emitting polymers (LEP) are plastics that give off light when exposed to low-voltage electricity. Research on LEPs points toward their use as flexible and more easy-to-read viewing screens in computers, digital camera monitors, watch-size phones, and televisions.

1934 Nylon

A giant breakthrough came with a synthetic fiber that imitates silk. Nylon replaced expensive silk in women's stockings and fabric for parachutes and clothing. It can also be molded to make objects like buttons, gears, and zippers.

1925 **1975** **2025**

1952 Fiberglass Composite

Fiberglass is mixed with polymers to form a material with the strength of glass fibers and the moldability of plastic. Fiberglass composite is useful for boat and airplane parts because it is much lighter than metal, and it doesn't rust.

1971 Kevlar

Kevlar is five times as strong as the same weight of steel. This polymer is tough enough to substitute for steel ropes and cables in offshore oil-drilling rigs, but light enough to use as parts for spacecraft. Kevlar is also used in protective clothing for firefighters and police officers.

Figure 6 Fiberglass makes a snowboard (left) both lightweight and strong. The composites in a fishing rod (right) make it so flexible that it will not break when pulling in a large fish.

Classifying ACTIVITY

Sit or stand where you have a clear view of the room you are in. Slowly sweep the room with your eyes, making a list of the objects you see. Do the same sweep of the clothes you are wearing. Check off those items on your list made (completely or partly) of natural or synthetic polymers. What percent of the items were *not* made with polymers?

Synthetic Composites The idea of combining the properties of two substances to make a more useful one has led to many new products. Fiberglass composites are one example. Strands of glass fiber are woven together and strengthened with a liquid plastic that sets like glue. The combination makes a strong, hard solid that may be molded around a form to give it shape. These composites are lightweight, but strong enough to be used as a boat hull or car body. Fiberglass also resists corrosion. It will not rust as metal does.

Other composites made from strong polymers combined with lightweight ones have many uses. Bicycles, automobiles, and airplanes built from such composites are much lighter than the same vehicles built from steel or aluminum. Some composites are used to make fishing rods, tennis racquets, and other sports equipment that need to be flexible but strong.

Too Many Polymers?

INTEGRATING ENVIRONMENTAL SCIENCE It is difficult to look around without seeing something made of synthetic polymers. They have replaced many natural materials for several reasons. First, polymers are inexpensive to make. Second, they are strong. Finally, they last a long time.

But synthetic polymers have caused some problems, too. Many of the disadvantages of using plastics come from the same properties that make them so useful. It is often cheaper to throw away plastic materials and make new ones than it is to reuse them. As a result, they increase the volume of trash. Most plastics don't

Figure 7 These rulers are just one product made from recycled plastic bottles.
Drawing Conclusions What would have happened to these bottles if they weren't recycled?

react very easily with other chemical compounds. This means they don't break down into simpler materials in the environment. In contrast, natural polymers do. Some plastics are expected to last thousands of years. How do you get rid of something that lasts that long?

Is there a way to solve these problems? One solution is to use waste plastics as raw material for making new plastic products. You know this idea as recycling. Recycling has led to industries that create new products from discarded plastics. Bottles, fabrics for clothing, and parts for new cars are just some of the many items that can come from waste plastics. A pile of empty soda bottles can even be turned into synthetic wood. Look around your neighborhood. You may see park benches or "wooden" fences made from recycled plastics. Through recycling, the disposal problem is eased and new, useful items are created.

Section 1 Review

1. How are monomers related to polymers?
2. What advantage does a composite have over the individual materials from which it is made?
3. Why is it possible for carbon atoms to form chains and rings with other carbon atoms?
4. Make a list of polymers you can find in your home. Classify them as natural or synthetic.
5. **Thinking Critically Making Judgments** Think of something plastic that you have used today. Is there some other material that would be better than plastic for this use?

Check Your Progress CHAPTER PROJECT
Collect a variety of different polymers. You might look in tool chests, kitchen cabinets, closets or drawers, art classrooms, hardware stores, or outdoors. Be sure to record where you found the polymer and what its function is. Record any information on labels or packaging. Try to identify each polymer as natural or synthetic. Organize this information into a list.

Packaging With Polymers

You need to mail some breakable items to a friend in another state. There are a variety of different polymer materials that you could use to package these items for mailing. In this lab, you will design an experiment to find out more about these materials. Then you will decide which one you would use.

Problem

Which polymer material or combination of materials should you choose for packaging?

Skills Focus

designing experiments, controlling variables, drawing conclusions

Suggested Materials

water   hand lens   weights (or books)
scissors   tape   thermometers
balance   clock or timer
containers (beakers, trays, plastic cups)
iodine solution, 1% solution
hard-boiled eggs (optional)
polymers used in packaging (paper, Tyvek, plastic foam, ecofoam, cardboard, fabric, popcorn, sawdust, wood shavings, or plastic)

Procedure

1. Write a hypothesis about the ideal properties a polymer should have if it is to be used for packaging.
2. Make a list of all the ways you can think of to test the properties of polymers. Think about properties including, but not limited to, the following:
   ◆ ability to protect a fragile object
   ◆ reaction to water   ◆ appearance
   ◆ heat insulation   ◆ strength
   ◆ reaction to iodine   ◆ mass
   (*Note:* Iodine turns a dark blue-black color when starch is present. Starch may attract insects or other pests.)

DATA TABLE

	Brief Description of Test 1	Brief Description of Test 2	Brief Description of Test 3	Brief Description of Test 4
Polymer A				
Polymer B				
Polymer C				

3. Select a property you wish to test. Choose a method that you think would be the best way to test that property.

4. Design a step-by-step procedure for the test. Do the same for each of the other properties you decide to investigate. Be sure that you change only one variable at a time. Include any safety directions in your procedure.

5. Predict which polymers you think will perform best in each test you plan.

6. After your teacher has approved your procedure, perform the tests on a sample of each polymer.

7. Record your observations in a table similar to the one on the left.

Analyze and Conclude

1. Describe the similarities and differences that you discovered among your samples.

2. Review the different tests that you used. Which worked well? Are there any tests you would do differently if you were to do them another time?

3. Which polymer, or polymers, would you use to package your items for mailing? Explain your reasons for this choice.

4. Which polymer, or polymers, would you not want to use? Why?

5. **Apply** Tyvek costs more than paper. Ecofoam costs more than plastic foam. How would this information influence your decision on which material to use?

Design an Experiment

A vending machine must be able to drop a cookie a distance of 1.5 m without breaking it. Design an experiment to determine how you could make a package that is strong, cheap, and environmentally friendly. With your teacher's approval, perform the experiment.

SCIENCE AND SOCIETY

Grocery Bags: Paper or Plastic?

Americans use more than 32 billion grocery bags each year. About 80 percent of the bags are plastic. The other 20 percent are paper. Plastic bags are made from crude oil, a resource that cannot be replaced. Paper bags, on the other hand, are made from trees. Trees are a renewable resource, but it takes time to grow them.

Both paper and plastic grocery bags end up in the trash. Although some bags are incinerated, or burned, most end up buried in landfills. You need a way to carry groceries home. Which bag should you choose at the grocery store—paper or plastic?

The Issues

Should People Choose Paper Bags?
Paper bags can hold more items than plastic. A typical paper bag can hold about 12 items. A plastic bag might hold half as many.

A mature tree can yield about 700 bags. But just one large supermarket can use 700 bags in less than an hour! Most trees that are used to make paper come from forests. Only about 20 percent come from tree farms.

Hazardous chemicals are used in making paper bags. Wood and certain poisonous chemical compounds are heated. The mixture is cooked into a mush of wood fibers, which is pressed into paper.

Usually, paper bags are biodegradable, which means that decay organisms break them down. But in tightly packed landfills, even paper bags don't break down easily.

Should People Choose Plastic Bags?
Plastic bags are lightweight, compact, and waterproof. They take up 80 percent less space in landfills than an equal number of paper bags. But most plastic bags are not biodegradable. They cannot be broken down by natural processes. They can last a long time in landfills.

Some plastic bags end up in the ocean. There they are a danger to sea birds and animals who may eat or get caught in them.

Plastic bags are made from a compound that's left over when crude oil is made into fuel. This waste product used to be discarded or burned.

Most plastic can be recycled. Unfortunately, only about 10 percent of all plastic products are recycled today. Most people are just not recycling.

Which Is the Right Choice?
Some people want laws that would require manufacturers to make all bags—paper and plastic—out of recycled materials. Paper manufacturers say, however, that the fibers in recycled paper are too short to make bags that are strong enough.

The right choice of bags may depend on how your community handles trash. Does it collect paper or plastic or both to be recycled?

Both paper and plastic bags can be reused in many ways, such as for storage or trash containers liners. But the best choice may be neither paper nor plastic. One reusable cloth bag could replace hundreds of paper and plastic bags.

You Decide

1. Identify the Problem
In your own words, explain the problems in choosing paper or plastic bags.

2. Analyze the Options
List the pros and cons of using plastic and paper bags. In each case, who will benefit? Who might be harmed?

3. Find a Solution
Your community wants to pass a law to regulate the kind of grocery bags that stores should offer. Take a stand. Defend your position.

SECTION 2 Metals and Alloys

DISCOVER
ACTIVITY

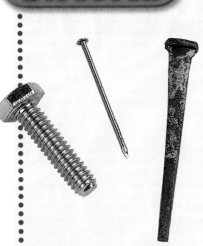

Are They Steel the Same?

1. Wrap a cut nail (low-carbon steel), a wire nail (high-carbon steel) and a stainless steel bolt together in a paper towel.

2. Place the towel in a plastic bag. Add about 250 mL of salt water and seal the bag.

3. After one or two days, remove the nails and bolt. Note any changes in the metals.

Think It Over

Developing Hypotheses What happened to the three types of steel? Which one changed the most, and which changed the least? What do you think accounts for the difference?

Over 6,000 years ago, people learned to make copper knives and tools that were sharper than stone tools. Later, they discovered that they could also use tin for tools. But these metals are soft, so they bend easily and are hard to keep sharp. About 5,000 years ago, metal makers discovered a way to make better tools. Copper and tin mixed together in the right amounts make a stronger, harder metal that keeps its sharp edge after long use. This discovery was the beginning of the Bronze Age. It also was the invention of the first alloy. An **alloy** is a substance made of two or more elements that has the properties of metal. In every alloy, at least one of the elements is a metal.

GUIDE FOR READING

◆ What properties make alloys useful?

Reading Tip Before you read, rewrite the headings in the section as *how, why,* or *what* questions. As you read, look for answers to these questions.

Properties of Metals

You know a piece of metal when you see it. It's hard and usually shiny. At room temperature all metallic elements (except mercury) are solids. Metals share other properties, too. They can conduct electricity. They also can be drawn out into thin wire. Copper, for example, made into wire, is used to carry electric current to the outlets in your home. Metals can be hammered into a sheet. Aluminum, rolled flat, makes aluminum foil. You wouldn't be able to do that with a piece of glass!

Gold leaf dome of City Hall in Savannah, Georgia ▶

Figure 8 Stainless steel is the iron alloy used to make the spaghetti lifter and pot. The coins and chain of this necklace are made from alloys of gold.
Applying Concepts Why are alloys used to make these objects rather than the pure metals?

Properties of Alloys

The properties of an alloy can differ greatly from those of its individual elements. Bronze, for example, is an alloy of copper and tin. It was a much better material for early toolmaking because it was harder than either element alone.

Pure gold is soft and easily bent. Gold jewelry and coins are made of an alloy of gold with another metal, such as copper or silver. These gold alloys are much harder than pure gold but still let its beauty show. Even after thousands of years, objects made of gold alloys still look exactly the same as when they were first made.

Alloys are used much more than pure metals because they are generally stronger and less likely to react with air or water. You have seen iron objects rust when they are exposed to air and water. But forks and spoons made of stainless steel can be washed over and over again without rusting. Stainless steel is an alloy of iron, carbon, nickel, and chromium. It does not react as easily with air and water as iron does. *Exploring Alloys and Metals in Aircraft* shows how other properties of alloys may be put to use.

☑ *Checkpoint* *Why is bronze more useful for tools than copper or tin?*

Making Alloys

Many alloys are made by melting metals and mixing them together in carefully measured amounts. Since the beginning of the Bronze Age, this technique has been used to make copper alloys. Some modern alloys are made by mixing the elements as powders and then heating them under high pressure. This process uses less energy because the metals blend at lower temperatures. The material then can be molded into the desired shape immediately. Another recent technique, called ion implantation, involves firing a beam of ions at a metal. A thin layer of alloy then forms on the metal's surface. Titanium, for example, may be bombarded with nitrogen ions to make a strong alloy for artificial bone and joint replacements.

EXPLORING Alloys and Metals in Aircraft

Much of the structure of an aircraft is made of metals. Engineers often design alloys with specific characteristics to fit the needs of the different parts of the aircraft.

Gold

A thin layer of pure gold coats the polymer (plastic) windshield. An electric current through the gold provides enough heat to keep the windshield frost-free. Gold works well for this purpose because it does not react with air and water.

Iron Alloys

The structural supports that hold the airplane together must be extremely strong. Steel made of iron with carbon and other metals is the best choice for these parts.

Aluminum Alloys

The outside of the plane has to be strong, light, and resistant to corrosion. The airplane's "skin" is aluminum, which is alloyed with magnesium, copper, and traces of other metals to increase strength.

Titanium Alloys

Landing gear must be strong enough to hold the wheels of the airplane and support its great mass. Alloys of titanium with vanadium, iron, and aluminum are strong as steel but much lighter in weight.

Nickel Alloys

The turbine blades found inside jet engines like this one have to spin around thousands of times per minute without changing shape. They also must withstand temperatures up to 1,100°C. Nickel alloyed with iron, carbon, and cobalt does the job.

Common Alloys

Alloy	Elements	Properties	Uses
Brass	Copper, zinc	Strong, resists corrosion, polishes well	Musical instruments, faucets, decorative hardware, jewelry
Bronze	Copper, tin	Hard, resists corrosion	Marine hardware, screws, grillwork
Stainless steel	Iron, carbon, nickel, chromium	Strong, resists corrosion	Tableware, cookware, surgical instruments
Carbon steel	Iron, carbon	Inexpensive, strong	Tools, auto bodies, machinery, steel girders, rails
Plumber's solder	Lead, tin	Low melting point	Seal joints and leaks in metal plumbing
Sterling silver	Silver, copper	Shiny, harder than pure silver	Jewelry, tableware
Dental amalgam	Mercury, silver, tin, copper, zinc	Low melting point, easily shaped	Dental fillings
Pewter	Tin, antimony, copper*	Bright or satin finish, resists tarnish	Tableware, decorative objects
Wood's metal	Bismuth, lead, tin, cadmium	Low melting point	Fire sprinklers, electric fuses

*Pewter containing lead cannot be used with food.

Figure 9 Alloys have a wide variety of uses.
Making Generalizations How do the properties of each alloy make it well-suited for its uses?

Using Alloys

When you want to describe something very hard or tough, you may use the expression "hard as steel." Steel is an alloy of iron with other elements. It is used for its strength, hardness, and resistance to corrosion. Without steel, suspension bridges, skyscrapers, and surgical knives would not exist. Neither would artificial joints that replace damaged knees and hips.

Steels Not all steel is alike. Its properties depend on which elements are added to iron. High-carbon steel, for example, consists of about 0.5 percent manganese and up to 0.8 percent carbon. Carbon steel is stronger and harder than wrought iron, which is almost pure iron. Tools, knives, machinery, and appliances are just some of the uses for carbon steel. Steels with less than 0.8 percent carbon are more ductile and malleable. They may be used for nails, cables, and chains.

There are hundreds of different types of steel. Usually carbon is added to the iron plus one or more of the following metals: chromium, manganese, molybdenum, nickel, tungsten, and vanadium. Steel made with these metals is generally stronger and harder than carbon steel, and usually more corrosion-resistant. Depending on their properties, these steels may become bicycle frames, train rails, steel tubing, and construction equipment.

Other Alloys Bronze, brass, and solder (SAHD ur) are just a few examples of other kinds of alloys. These materials are used to make items ranging from plumbing materials and sprinkler systems to tableware and doorknobs. Even your dentist uses alloys. Have you ever had a cavity in a tooth? A mixture of mercury with silver or gold (called an amalgam) makes a pasty solid. It rapidly hardens, filling the hole in your tooth. Look at Figure 9 and see how many of the examples listed in the table are alloys you have seen or used.

Section 2 Review

1. Name two properties of alloys that make them more useful than pure metals.
2. Describe one way in which alloys are made.
3. What advantage does stainless steel cookware have over cookware made of iron?
4. **Thinking Critically** Applying Concepts What properties would you look for to find out if an object was made of metal?
5. **Thinking Critically** Problem Solving The purity of gold is expressed in units called karats. A piece of 24-karat gold is pure gold metal. A piece of 12-karat gold is one half gold and one half another metal, often silver or copper. What fraction of the metal in a piece of 18-karat gold jewelry is actually gold?

Science at Home

Metal Inventory Find items in your home that are made from metals or alloys. Look for cooking utensils, tools, toys, sports equipment, appliances, and other household items that are made with these materials. Discuss with members of your family how properties of the metals or alloys relate to the uses of the objects.

SECTION 3 Ceramics and Glass

DISCOVER ● ACTIVITY ● ● ● ●

Does It Get Wet?

1. Find the masses of a glazed pottery flowerpot and an unglazed one of similar size. Record both values.
2. Place both pots in a basin of water for ten minutes.
3. Remove the pots from the water and blot dry gently with paper towels.
4. Find and record the masses of both flowerpots again.
5. Calculate the percent of change in mass for each pot.

Think It Over

Inferring Which pot gained the most mass? What can you infer about the effect that glazing has on the pot?

GUIDE FOR READING

◆ What properties of ceramics make them useful?

◆ How may glass be changed to make it useful?

Reading Tip Before you read, make a list of ceramic or glass items you use. As you read, look for reasons why these materials are well suited for their uses.

Picture yourself on a warm day, walking through a slow-flowing stream. The mud at the bottom is soft. It squishes up between your toes. When you pick it up and shape it with your hands, it holds its form. If you let it dry in the sun, it becomes hard. This material is clay. You could also shape the clay into blocks, add some straw to make a composite material, and let the blocks dry. If you live where there is not much rain, you could use the blocks to build a house. In fact, people have used this type of brick to build sturdy homes. The Pueblo homes of the Southwest, for example, were built this way over a thousand years ago. Some of them are still standing today.

Making Ceramics

A discovery made thousands of years ago increased the usefulness of dried clay objects. Heating clay to about 1,000°C makes it harder and stronger. **Ceramics** are hard, crystalline solids made by heating clay and other mineral materials to high temperatures. Clay is made of very small mineral particles containing silicon, aluminum, and oxygen. Other elements, such as magnesium and iron may be present in clay, too. Clay forms when the minerals in

◀ **Pueblo homes in Taos, New Mexico**

rock are broken down. Unheated clay also contains water. When a clay object is heated, much of the water present on its surface evaporates, and the particles of clay stick together.

This process forms the hard ceramic pottery used for bricks and flowerpots. Once cooled, these materials have tiny spaces in their structure that absorb and hold water. If you grow a plant in this kind of pot, you can feel the moisture in the outer surface of the clay after you water the plant. When pottery is brushed with a layer of silicon dioxide and heated again, a glassy coating, called a glaze, forms. This glaze is shiny and waterproof. You might see glazed pottery used to serve or store food. Potters often use colorful glazes to create artistic designs on their work.

☑ *Checkpoint* *How does a glaze change the properties of a ceramic?*

Figure 11 Wet clay takes shape in the hands of a potter. *Predicting What will happen to the water in the clay when the potter heats it in a kiln, or hot oven?*

Properties and Uses of Ceramics

Have you ever heard the phrase "a bull in a china shop"? Imagine the damage. A bull in a bronze shop just wouldn't be as dramatic! The phrase comes from the fact that ceramics are brittle and can shatter when struck. Despite their tendency to break, ceramics have several properties that make them useful. **Ceramics resist moisture, do not conduct electricity, and can withstand temperatures higher than molten metals.**

Ceramic pottery has been used for thousands of years to store food, protecting it from moisture and animals. Roofing tiles, bricks, and sewer pipes are all long-standing uses of ceramics. Ceramics are also used as insulators in electric equipment and light fixtures.

Figure 12 Some ceramics, such as these roof tiles (left), have practical uses. Other ceramics (right) are valued for their delicate beauty.

New uses for ceramics continue to be developed. The walls of ovens for making steel and other metal products are made of a type of brick that does not melt at the temperature of red-hot iron. And ceramic tiles are the only materials that can withstand the temperatures of over 1,600°C that build up on the bottom of the space shuttle during its reentry into the atmosphere. These tiles insulate the shuttle and protect the astronauts.

Figure 13 Before the space shuttle *Columbia* can be launched again, tiles damaged during its last reentry must be replaced. *Predicting What would happen to the spacecraft if many of the tiles were missing?*

☑ *Checkpoint* **What are some uses of ceramics?**

Making Glass

Have you ever looked closely at a handful of sand, or watched the varied grains as they slipped through your fingers? Thousands of years ago people learned that sand mixed with limestone can be melted into a thick, hot liquid. Most sand consists of tiny, hard pieces of quartz, a mineral made of silicon dioxide. When sand is heated to about 1,600°C, it flows like thick molasses. If this liquid cools quickly, it forms a clear, solid material with no crystal structure called **glass.**

The first glass objects were formed on clay molds that were chipped away after the glass hardened. Then about 2,000 years ago, glassmakers in ancient Persia invented glassblowing. The

Figure 14 Glass objects made in ancient Rome are on display at the Corning Museum in Corning, New York.

Figure 15 The lenses in this microscope are made from lead oxide glass. *Applying Concepts* How do the microscope lenses help this girl view a small object?

glassmaker put a blob of melted glass on the end of an iron pipe. By blowing air through the pipe, the glassmaker could produce a hollow glass vessel. If the glass was blown inside a wooden mold, jars and vases in beautiful patterns and shapes could be created.

Different materials may be added to glass to make it useful for particular purposes. Early glassmakers added calcium (as limestone) and sodium (as sodium carbonate) to the melting sand. This mixture melts at a lower temperature than sand alone, so it is easier to work with. Window glass and the bottles and jars you use every day are still made with this type of glass.

Substituting lead oxide for the limestone makes a glass that bends light in useful ways. This kind of glass is used to make lenses for eyeglasses, telescopes, and microscopes. Adding boron oxide creates a glass that resists heat better than ordinary glass. It is used for cookware and laboratory glassware that must be heated. Colored glass is made by adding minerals containing various metals to the molten glass. Selenium and gold produce red glass. Cobalt makes beautiful, deep blue glass.

Communication Through Glass

INTEGRATING PHYSICS There's a good chance that the next time you make a phone call, your message will travel through glass. An **optical fiber** is a threadlike piece of glass (or plastic) that can be used for transmitting light. Light shining into one end of the fiber travels through the glass to the other end. The effect is similar to electrons that carry a signal in copper wire. When you speak into a telephone, the signal created by your voice is converted to light signals that travel through the glass fiber. At the other end, the light may be converted into electronic signals that can then be converted to sound.

A Bright Idea

Can you communicate **ACTIVITY** using an optical fiber?

1. Construct a barrier between you and a partner so that you cannot see each other.
2. Run a plastic optical fiber past the barrier.
3. Bring the bulb of a penlight flashlight close to your end of the fiber.
4. Using a single flash for "yes" and two flashes for "no," send your partner a message by responding to a series of yes and no questions he or she asks.
5. Change roles so that your partner has a chance to send signals in response to your questions.

Observing What happened when you and your partner sent signals to each other?

Figure 16 Even if optical fibers are twisted into a loop, the light moves within the fibers.
Making Generalizations How can this property of optical fibers be useful?

You know that light can pass through glass from one side to the other. That's one reason you can see through a window. But when light moves through an optical fiber, it is reflected within the fiber. It doesn't pass through the outside surface. For this reason, there is little loss of light from one end to the other—an important condition for transmitting messages!

A pair of optical fibers, the thickness of a human hair, can carry 625,000 phone calls at one time. One quarter pound of glass fiber can replace over two tons of copper wire. This difference is a big advantage when installing long lines like those that carry messages under the ocean. Because optical fibers are so efficient, they are being used to replace most copper telephone and cable television lines. Another benefit of glass fiber is its stability. Since the glass does not corrode as metals do, the lines are easier to maintain.

Section 3 Review

1. What property of ceramics makes them useful as the walls for ovens or as insulating materials?

2. In what ways can the properties of glass be changed?

3. How is a message transmitted through a glass fiber?

4. **Thinking Critically** **Applying Concepts**
   Before ceramics were invented, people stored food in containers such as baskets, leather bags, and wooden bowls. What properties of ceramics made them better containers for food?

Check Your Progress

CHAPTER PROJECT

Devise a plan to test some chemical and physical properties of the polymers you have collected. Tests might include hardness, fiber strength, flexibility, color, density, solubility in water, or reaction to corrosive chemicals. Construct a data table on which you can record results of your tests.

④ Radioactive Elements

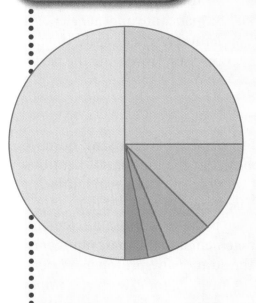

How Much Goes Away?

1. Make a circle about 8–10 centimeters in diameter on a piece of paper. You can do this by tracing the rim of a round container.

2. Use a straightedge to draw a line dividing the circle in half. Then divide one half into quarters, then into eighths, and so on, as shown in the diagram.

3. ✂ With scissors, cut out your circle. Now cut away the undivided half circle. Next, cut away the undivided quarter circle. Continue until you are left with one segment.

4. Place the segments on your desktop in the order you cut them.

Think It Over

Making Models How is the piece of paper changing each time? Suppose the original circle was a model for a sample of radioactive material, and the paper you cut away is material that became nonradioactive. What would eventually happen?

More than a thousand years ago, some people came up with what they thought was a great idea. Take some dull, cheap lead metal and turn it into valuable gold! They heated the lead, cooled it, added acid to it. They ground it into a powder and mixed it with everything they could think of. Of course, nothing worked. There is no chemical reaction that converts one element into another.

Even so, elements do sometimes change into other elements. A uranium atom can become a thorium atom. Atoms of carbon can become atoms of nitrogen. (But lead never changes into gold, unfortunately!) How is it possible for these changes to happen?

GUIDE FOR READING

◆ What happens during radioactive decay?

◆ How is half-life a useful property of radioactive isotopes?

◆ In what ways are radioactive isotopes useful?

Reading Tip As you read, use the headings to make an outline about the properties and uses of radioactive isotopes.

Figure 17 This painting from 1570 shows people trying to change lead into gold. No such chemical reaction was ever accomplished.

Carbon-12

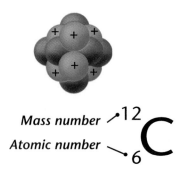

Mass number ⟋12 C
Atomic number ⟍6

Carbon-14

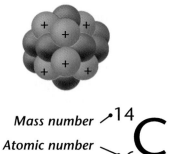

Mass number ⟋14 C
Atomic number ⟍6

Figure 18 All carbon atoms have 6 protons in each nucleus, but the isotope carbon-12 has 6 neutrons and the isotope carbon-14 has 8 neutrons.

Figure 19 Radioactive elements give off mass and energy during radioactive decay.
Interpreting Diagrams Which type of decay does not result in a different element?

Nuclear Reactions

You have already learned that an atom consists of a nucleus of protons and neutrons, surrounded by a cloud of electrons. A chemical change always involves the electrons but doesn't affect the nucleus. Since the number of protons determines the identity of the atom, one element can't be made into another element by a chemical reaction. Such a change happens only during **nuclear reactions** (NOO klee ur)—reactions involving the particles in the nucleus of an atom.

Isotopes

Remember that all the atoms of an element have the same number of protons (same atomic number), but the number of neutrons can vary. Atoms with the same number of protons and different numbers of neutrons are called **isotopes** (EYE suh tohps).

To show the difference between isotopes of the same element, you write both the name of the element and the mass number of the isotope. **Mass number** is the sum of the protons and neutrons in the nucleus of an atom. Consider, for example, isotopes of carbon. Most carbon atoms are carbon-12, having six protons and six neutrons (and six electrons). About one out of every trillion carbon atoms, however, has eight neutrons. That isotope is carbon-14. Figure 18 shows you how to write the symbol for the two isotopes. Note that the atomic number is included, too.

☑ *Checkpoint* *Why do mass numbers for isotopes differ?*

Radioactive Decay

Some isotopes are unstable. The nucleus of an unstable atom does not hold together well. Unstable isotopes undergo nuclear reactions, often forming atoms with different atomic numbers or atomic masses. In a process called **radioactive decay,** the atomic nuclei of unstable isotopes release fast-moving particles and energy. There are three types of radioactive decay, each determined by the type of radiation released by the unstable

Alpha Decay

Radioactive nucleus → 2 protons and 2 neutrons lost

Alpha particle

Beta Decay

Radioactive nucleus → One less neutron, one more proton

Beta particle

Gamma Decay

Radioactive nucleus → No gain or loss of particles

Gamma rays

nucleus. **Radioactive decay can produce alpha particles, beta particles, and gamma rays.** (Alpha, beta, and gamma are the first three letters of the Greek alphabet.) The particles and energy produced during radioactive decay are forms of **nuclear radiation.**

Alpha Decay An **alpha particle** consists of two protons and two neutrons. It is the same as a helium nucleus. Release of an alpha particle by an atom decreases the atomic number by 2 and the mass number by 4. Although alpha particles move very fast, they are stopped by collisions with atoms. Alpha radiation can cause an injury much like a bad burn. But a sheet of paper or thin piece of metal foil will act as a shield.

Beta Decay When a neutron inside the nucleus of an unstable atom breaks apart, it forms a beta particle and a proton. A **beta particle** is an electron given off by a nucleus during radioactive decay. The new proton remains inside the nucleus. That means that the nucleus now has one less neutron and one more proton. Its mass number remains the same, but its atomic number increases by 1.

Beta particles travel much faster than alpha particles. They can pass through an aluminum sheet 3 millimeters thick. They can also travel into the human body and damage its cells.

Gamma Decay Alpha and beta decay are almost always accompanied by gamma radiation. **Gamma radiation** is high-energy waves, similar to X-rays. Gamma radiation (also called gamma rays) does not cause a change in either the atomic mass or the atomic number of the atom formed. But the energy released is the most penetrating type of radiation. You would need a piece of lead several centimeters thick or a concrete wall about a meter thick to stop gamma rays. They can pass right through a human body, causing severe damage to cells.

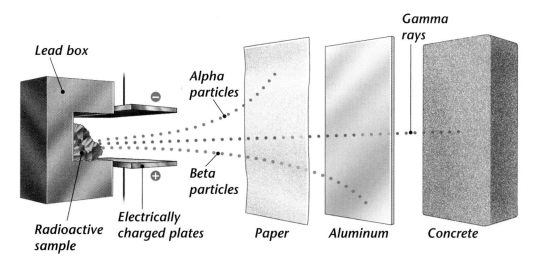

Lead box

Alpha particles

Gamma rays

Beta particles

Radioactive sample

Electrically charged plates

Paper

Aluminum

Concrete

Figure 20 The three types of nuclear radiation can be separated according to charge and penetrating power. *Inferring Which type of radiation is the most penetrating?*

Figure 24 The radioactive isotope technetium-99 is used in medical studies of the heart, lungs, liver, and bones. **A.** In these healthy lungs, the red areas show greater absorption of the isotope than the yellow or green areas. **B.** In the hand, the bones are colored orange.

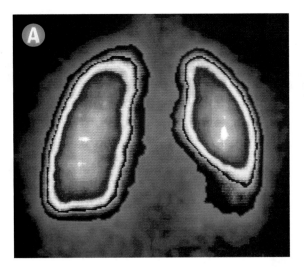
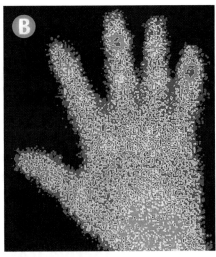

Social Studies CONNECTION

Using radioactive materials can provide benefits such as electricity or advanced medical care. But what happens to the unavoidable radioactive waste? People aren't so comfortable having that around!

NIMBY is short for the phrase "not in my backyard." It stands for the idea that people don't want unpleasant or possible hazardous conditions near where they live. They would prefer to see radioactive wastes go elsewhere.

In Your Journal

Your local government has invited citizens to a meeting to discuss possible options for storing radioactive wastes from nearby medical or industrial uses. Write a one- or two-paragraph speech to the public meeting, expressing your opinion.

gamma-ray images, structural engineers can detect small cracks in the metal of bridges and building frames. Without these images, a problem might not be discovered until a disaster occurs.

Uses in Medicine Doctors use radioactive isotopes to detect medical problems and to treat some diseases.

INTEGRATING HEALTH Tracers injected into the body travel to organs and other structures where that chemical is normally used. Using equipment that detects radiation, technicians make images of the bone, blood vessel, or organ affected. For example, tracers made with technetium-99 are frequently used to diagnose problems in the bones, liver, kidneys, and digestive system. Other isotopes, such as thallium-201 in the heart and xenon-133 in the lungs, help doctors diagnose disease in these organs.

In a process called **radiation therapy,** radioactive elements are used to destroy unhealthy cells. Iodine-131, for example, is given to patients with tumors of the thyroid gland, a gland in the neck that controls the rate at which nutrients are used. Because the thyroid gland uses iodine, the radioactive iodine-131 collects in the gland. Radiation from this isotope destroys unwanted cells in the gland without serious effects on other parts of the body.

Cancer tumors of different kinds often are treated from outside the body with high-energy gamma rays. Many hospitals use cobalt-60 for this purpose. When gamma radiation is focused on a cancer tumor, it causes changes that kill the cancer cells.

Nuclear Power Nuclear reactions release enormous quantities of energy compared to chemical reactions. For this reason, some power plants use radioactive isotopes as fuel. Carefully controlled reactions, most often using uranium-235, provide electric power in many parts of the world.

✓ *Checkpoint* What is a tracer?

Safe Use of Radioactive Materials

Despite the positive uses of radioactive materials, they also are dangerous. Radiation penetrates living tissue, knocking electrons from atoms. This process produces ions that then can interfere with chemical reactions in living cells. Illness, disease, and even death may result from overexposure to radiation.

The dangers of radioactive materials mean that their use must be carefully managed. People who work with these materials must wear protective clothing and use insulating shields. Radioactive wastes can't just be thrown away. After radiation therapy, for example, contaminated equipment and clothing can still be hazardous. These items must be disposed of properly. Materials with low levels of radiation may be buried in landfills. Such landfills are carefully monitored to prevent contamination of the environment. Isotopes with long half-lives, however, will remain hazardous for hundreds or even thousand of years. Plans are under way to dispose of these kinds of materials in specially designed containers that will be buried in very dry underground tunnels. In that way the radioactive wastes can be isolated for many generations.

Figure 25 Waste Isolation Pilot Plant (WIPP) is a site in New Mexico where the United States government is developing safe storage for radioactive wastes. Large underground rooms (left), will house the wastes in secure barrels (right).

Section 4 Review

1. Describe the three types of radiation given off during radioactive decay.
2. How are radioactive isotopes helpful for studying rocks and fossils?
3. Give two examples of how tracers are used. Tell why radioactive isotopes work as tracers.
4. **Thinking Critically Making Judgments** If there were a proposal in your state to ban the use of radioactive materials because of the hazards of radioactive waste, would you support the idea? Why or why not?

Check Your Progress

CHAPTER PROJECT

After your teacher approves your plan, perform your tests. Record all results in your data table. If there is time, perform your tests more than once to obtain multiple sets of data. Try to organize your samples into groups based on the results of your tests. Identify similarities and differences among the groups.

Turning Down the Volume on
SONIC BOOMS

Dr. Christine Mann Darden (center) grew up in Monroe, North Carolina. She received her Ph.D. in Mechanical Engineering at George Washington University in Washington, D.C. A national expert on sonic booms, she now works at NASA's Langley Research Center in Hampton, Virginia. She manages a group of scientists who are developing supersonic airplanes. Dr. Darden is shown here with other members of the Sonic Boom Group, Kathy Needleman (left) and Robert Mack (right).

*I*t happens every time a space shuttle returns to Earth. The spacecraft drops down from orbit and streaks toward its landing site in Florida or California. A few seconds after it passes overhead—BOOM! A window-rattling sound like a giant cannon shot is heard. Most scientists at the space center are monitoring the shuttle itself when it comes down from a mission. But Dr. Christine Darden is more interested in that big boom.

Dr. Darden is a research engineer at the National Aeronautics and Space Administration (NASA). She is in charge of the space agency's Sonic Boom Group. Her team of scientists is investigating the distinctive "sound print" made by aircraft that travel faster than the speed of sound. Dr. Darden and her co-workers are looking for ways to soften sonic booms. They hope to make supersonic travel—travel at speeds faster than the speed of sound—more common in the future.

Talking with Dr. Christine Darden

Breaking the Sound Barrier

The sound barrier was first broken in 1947. Since then, people have complained about sonic booms so much that the government has passed regulations. It's now against the law to fly most aircraft at supersonic speeds over the United States.

"If it is loud enough, a sonic boom can actually break windows and do damage to buildings," says Dr. Darden. "People find it very disturbing. Right now, the boom is one of the biggest obstacles to commercial supersonic air service."

Today supersonic aircraft such as the Concorde fly mainly over the ocean. But what if scientists can find ways to lower the volume of sonic booms? Then someday supersonic commercial jets may be allowed to fly across the country.

What Is a Sonic Boom?

You have probably heard the sound that is made when an airplane breaks the sound barrier. A sonic boom sounds like a clap of thunder or a sharp explosion high in the sky. Just what are you hearing?

"A sonic boom is a compression or pressure wave," Dr. Darden explains. "An airplane pushes a wave of air molecules ahead of it as it travels forward, just as a ship's bow pushes out a wave as it moves through the water. Those compressions travel outward from the plane as a shock wave of high pressure. When that shock wave reaches our ears, we hear it as a boom."

Both the SR-71 Blackbird (above) and F-16 (opposite page) are military supersonic planes.

"Think of blowing up a balloon," Dr. Darden says. "With the balloon inflated, the air on the inside is much more compressed than the air on the outside. When the balloon pops, the compression immediately flies outward in the form of a shock wave."

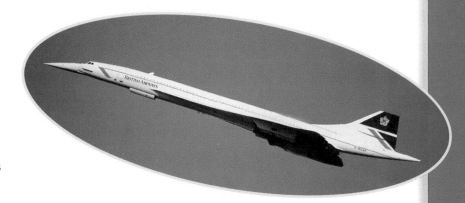

Scheduled flights (to the United States) of the Concorde, a supersonic commercial plane, are made only between New York and London or Paris.

How Do You Research What You Can't See?

"Part of our work is coming up with new ways to observe and measure the phenomenon we're studying," says Dr. Darden. "For example, we know that all waves have similar properties. So we look at how waves behave in water to tell us something about how they behave in the air."

Choosing Engineering

Dr. Darden's study of waves in water and air is a long way from her first career as a math teacher. In the late 1960s, she was teaching in a school in Hampton, Virginia. At that time, the NASA labs nearby were working on a program to send astronauts to the moon. Dr. Darden went to work for NASA as a mathematician.

She quickly became fascinated with the work of the NASA research engineers. "They were the ones who were working with the really tough challenges of the program," she says. "They were doing the interesting, hands-on work." As a result of her experience, she decided to get a graduate degree in engineering.

How Do You Test Supersonic Aircraft?

Working hands-on is one way that Dr. Darden and her team study how airplanes create sonic booms. They

1 A sonic boom results when an airplane moves at supersonic speed. Air is compressed at the front of the plane, creating shock waves.

2 The shock waves move out behind the plane in a cone shape.

3 When the shock waves reach the ground, people hear them as a sonic boom.

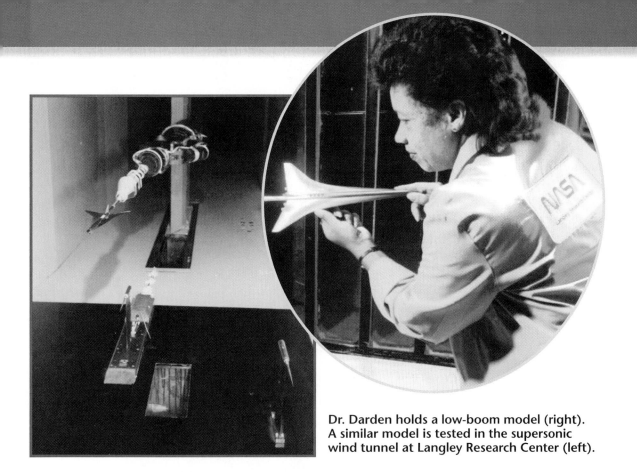

Dr. Darden holds a low-boom model (right). A similar model is tested in the supersonic wind tunnel at Langley Research Center (left).

"fly" model aircraft in a high-speed wind tunnel. The scientists place the steel models in the tunnel and watch how they behave in winds moving at up to three times the speed of sound. (The speed of sound varies with altitude and air pressure. At sea level on a 16°C day, the speed of sound is about 1,207 kilometers per hour.)

Instruments on the sides of the tunnel allow Dr. Darden to "hear" the sonic boom created by the model. By adding very fine smoke, she can even watch how the air moves over the plane. "We can actually see the shock wave," she says.

Can the Sonic Boom Effect Be Reduced?

Dr. Darden and her group at NASA have found that the shape of an aircraft determines the size of the boom it creates. They have performed tests with computer programs, on actual supersonic

jets, and in wind tunnels. Their experiments have shown that angling the wings back sharply reduces the size of the shock wave and the loudness of the sonic boom. But the same features that make planes quieter also make them harder to fly.

"You could put a needle up there supersonically and you wouldn't get a sonic boom," explains Dr. Darden. "But you wouldn't have much of an airplane, either."

In Your Journal

In her research, Dr. Darden made predictions about how the angle of an airplane wing might affect a sonic boom. Then her team set up a series of experiments to test these predictions.

Now think of different-shaped boats moving through water: a kayak, a tugboat, and a rowboat. Predict the type of wave that each boat will make. How could you use models to test your predictions?

CHAPTER 9 Motion

www.phschool.com

SECTION 1 **Describing and Measuring Motion**

Discover How Fast and How Far?
Try This Sunrise, Sunset
Skills Lab Inclined to Roll

Integrating Earth Science

SECTION 2 **Slow Motion on Planet Earth**

Discover How Slow Can It Flow?
Sharpen Your Skills Predicting
Science at Home Fingernail Growth
Real-World Lab Stopping on a Dime

SECTION 3 **Acceleration**

Discover Will You Hurry Up?

Speeds à la Carte

Imagine that you have traveled thousands of miles to visit the tropics of South America. Suddenly, vivid reds and blues brighten the green of the rain forest as a group of macaws swoop down and perch above you in a nut tree. They squawk at each other as they crack nuts with their powerful jaws and eat the meat. In a few minutes they spread their wings to take off, and vanish from sight. The macaws cracking nuts, flapping their wings, and flying through the forest are all examples of motion. Your plane flight to South America is another.

In this chapter, you will learn how to describe and measure motion. You will find examples of motion and describe how fast different objects move. You will measure the speeds of various common moving things.

Your Goal To identify several examples of motion and measure how fast each one moves. You will arrange your results from slowest to fastest.

Your project must
- include careful distance and time measurements
- use your data to calculate the speed of each example
- provide display cards that show data, diagrams, and calculations
- follow the safety guidelines in Appendix A

Get Started Brainstorm with a group of your classmates several examples of motion. For example, you might consider a feather falling, the water level rising in a bathtub, or the minute hand moving on a clock. Which examples will be easy to measure? Which will be more challenging?

Check Your Progress You'll be working on this project as you study this chapter. To keep your project on track, look for Check Your Progress boxes at the following points.

Section 1 Review, page 293: Create a data table.
Section 3 Review, page 306: Repeat measurements and make calculations.

Present Your Project At the end of the chapter (page 309), you will compare the speeds recorded by the class.

These red-and-green macaws live in the Amazon River basin in Peru.

SECTION 1 Describing and Measuring Motion

DISCOVER

ACTIVITY

How Fast and How Far?

1. Find out how long it takes you to walk 5 meters at a normal pace. Record your time.

2. Now find out how far you can walk in 5 seconds if you walk at a normal pace. Record your distance.

3. Repeat Steps 1 and 2, walking slower than your normal pace. Then repeat Steps 1 and 2, walking faster than your normal pace.

Think It Over

Inferring What is the relationship between the distance you walk, the time it takes you to walk, and your walking speed?

GUIDE FOR READING

◆ When is an object in motion?

◆ How can you find the speed and velocity of an object?

Reading Tip Before you read, rewrite the headings in the section as questions. As you read, look for answers.

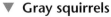

▼ **Gray squirrels**

It's three o'clock and school is over! You hurry out of class to enjoy the bright afternoon. A light breeze is blowing. A few clouds are lazily drifting across the sky, and colorful leaves float down from the trees. Two birds fly playfully over your head. A bunch of frisky squirrels chase one another up a tree. You spend a few minutes with some friends who are kicking a ball around. Then you head home.

Does anything strike you about this afternoon scene? It is filled with all kinds of motion: blowing, drifting, fluttering, flying, and chasing. There are simple motions and complicated motions, motions

282

Figure 1 Whether or not an object is in motion depends on the reference point you choose. *Comparing and Contrasting Which people are moving if you compare them to the escalator? Which people are moving if you compare them to Earth?*

that are over in a moment, and motions that continue all afternoon. How else can you describe all of these examples of motion? There is actually a great deal to understand about how and why all these things move as they do. In this section, you will learn how scientists describe and measure motion.

Recognizing Motion

Deciding if an object is in motion isn't as easy as it sounds. For example, you are probably sitting as you read this paragraph. Are you moving? Other than your eyes blinking and your chest moving up and down, you would probably say that you (and this book) are not moving. An object is in **motion** when its distance from another object is changing. Since the distance between you and the walls of your room is not changing, you conclude that neither you nor the book is moving.

At the same time that you think you are sitting still, you are actually moving about 30 kilometers every second. At that speed, you could travel from New York City to Los Angeles in about 2 minutes! You are moving because you are on planet Earth, which is orbiting the sun. Earth moves about 30 kilometers every second, so you and everything else on Earth are moving at that speed as well.

Whether an object is moving or not depends on your point of view. If you compare the books on a desk to the floor beneath them, they are not moving.

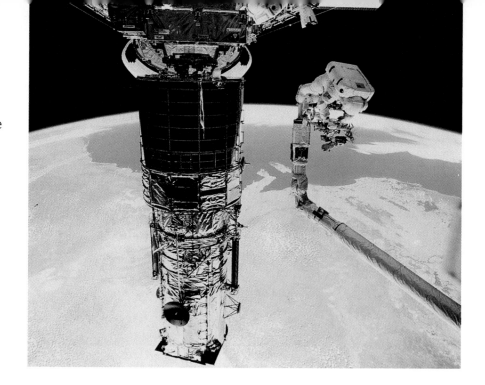

Figure 2 Both the Hubble Space Telescope and the astronaut are actually moving rapidly through space. But compared to the Hubble Space Telescope, the astronaut is not moving and can therefore complete necessary repairs.

Sunrise, Sunset

Earth rotates as it moves around the sun. But to you, the sun appears to move.

1. Choose a spot from which you can observe the sky throughout one day.

2. From the same spot, observe the sun at 6 to 8 different times during the day. **CAUTION:** *Be careful not to look directly at the sun.* Describe its position by comparing it with things around you, such as trees and buildings.

3. Draw a diagram of the sun throughout the day.

Observing What reference point(s) did you use to study the sun? Did the sun appear to move when compared with those reference points? Did it really move?

But if you compare them to the sun, the books are moving quite rapidly. Earth and the sun are different reference points. A **reference point** is a place or object used for comparison to determine if something is in motion. **An object is in motion if it changes position relative to a reference point.** You assume that the reference point is stationary, or not moving.

If you have ever been on a slow-moving train, you know that you may not be able to tell the train is moving unless you look out the window. A nearby building is a good reference point, and a glance at it will tell you if you and the train are moving. But it is important to choose your reference point carefully. Have you ever been in a school bus stopped right next to another school bus? Suddenly, you think your bus is moving backward. When you look out the window on the other side, you find that your bus isn't moving at all. Actually, the other bus is moving forward! Your bus seemed to be moving backward because you used the other bus as a reference point. You assumed your reference point was stationary. But in fact, your reference point—the other bus—was really moving.

Describing Distance

INTEGRATING MATHEMATICS To describe motion further, you need to use units of measurement. Whether you realize it or not, you use units, or standard quantities, all the time. You might, for example, measure 2 cups of milk for a recipe, swim 100 yards after school, or buy 3 pounds of fruit at the store. Cups, yards, and pounds are all units.

Scientists all over the world use the same system of units so that they can communicate information clearly. This system of measurement is called the International System of Units, or in French, Système International (SI). SI is a system based on the number ten. This makes calculations with the system relatively easy.

The basic SI unit of length is the **meter** (m). A meter is a little longer than a yard. The Eiffel Tower in Figure 3 is measured in meters. To measure the length of an object smaller than a meter, scientists use the metric unit called the centimeter (cm). The prefix *centi-* means "one hundredth." A centimeter is one hundredth of a meter, so there are 100 centimeters in a meter. The beautiful butterfly in Figure 3 is measured in centimeters. For even smaller lengths, the millimeter (mm) is used. The prefix *milli-* means "one thousandth," so there are 1,000 millimeters in a meter. In the International System, long distances are measured in kilometers (km). The prefix *kilo-* means "one thousand." There are 1,000 meters in a kilometer.

SI units are also used to describe quantities other than length. You can find more information about SI units in the Skills Handbook on page 752 of this textbook.

☑ *Checkpoint* *What unit would you use to describe the width of your thumb?*

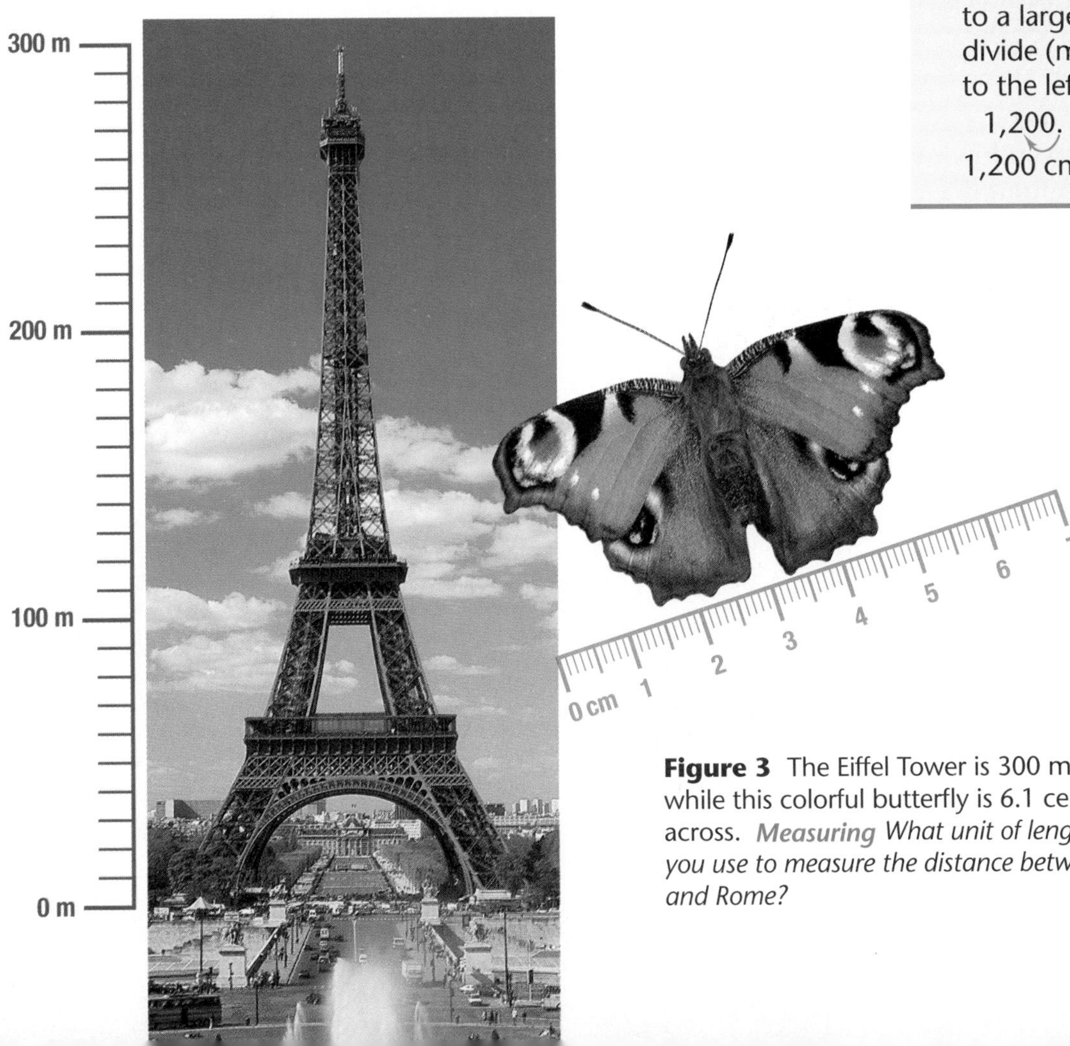

Figure 3 The Eiffel Tower is 300 meters tall, while this colorful butterfly is 6.1 centimeters across. *Measuring What unit of length would you use to measure the distance between Paris and Rome?*

Math TOOLBOX

Converting Units

When you convert one metric unit to another, you must move the decimal point.

1. How many millimeters are in 14.5 meters? You are converting from a larger unit to a smaller one, so you multiply. There are 1,000 millimeters in a meter. To multiply by 1,000, move the decimal to the right three places.
14.500 m = 14,500. mm
There are 14,500 mm in 14.5 m.

2. Convert 1,200 centimeters to meters. You are converting from a smaller unit to a larger one, so you divide (move the decimal to the left).
1,200. cm = 12.00 m
1,200 cm equals 12 m.

Speed affects the shape of cities. Because people want to travel quickly, they live close to major transportation routes—highways and railroads. Thus a city often looks like a hub with spokes coming out of it along the transportation routes.

In Your Journal

People prefer not to travel more than one hour from home to work. The table shows a city's travel routes.

Route	Average Speed
Highway 1	75 km/h
Highway 2	55 km/h
Blue Rail	60 km/h
Red Rail	75 km/h
Main Street	35 km/h

Along which two routes would you expect to find people living farther from the center of the city? Explain why. Draw a map of what you think this city might look like.

Calculating Speed

Scientists use SI units to describe the distance an object travels. A car, for example, might travel 90 kilometers. An ant might travel 2 centimeters. If you know the distance an object travels in a certain amount of time, you know the speed of the object. To be more exact, the **speed** of an object is the distance the object travels in one unit of time. Speed is a type of rate. A rate tells you the amount of something that occurs or changes in one unit of time.

To calculate the speed of an object, divide the distance the object travels by the amount of time it takes to travel that distance. This relationship can be written as follows.

$$\text{Speed} = \frac{\text{Distance}}{\text{Time}}$$

Speed measurements consist of a unit of distance divided by a unit of time. If you measure distance in meters and time in seconds, you express speed in meters per second (m/s). (The slash is read as "per.") If you measure distance in kilometers and time in hours, you express speed in kilometers per hour (km/h).

If a car travels 90 kilometers in one hour, the car is traveling at a speed of 90 km/h. An ant that moves 2 centimeters in one second is moving at a speed of 2 centimeters per second, or 2 cm/s. The ant is much slower than the car.

Constant Speed A ship traveling across the ocean may move at the same speed for several hours. Or a horse cantering across a field may keep a steady pace for several minutes. If so, the ship and the horse travel at constant speeds. If the speed of an object does not change, the object is traveling at a constant speed. When an object travels at a constant speed, you know that its speed is the same at all times during its motion.

Figure 4 This horse is cantering at a constant speed. *Problem Solving* What information do you need to calculate the horse's speed?

Figure 5 The cyclists do not travel at a constant speed throughout this cross-country race. *Comparing and Contrasting How does average speed differ from constant speed?*

If you know the distance an object travels in a given amount of time, you can use the formula for speed to calculate the object's constant speed. Suppose, for example, that the horse in Figure 4 is moving at a constant speed. Find the horse's speed if it canters 21 meters in 3 seconds. Divide the distance traveled, 21 meters, by the time, 3 seconds, to find the horse's speed.

$$Speed = \frac{21\ m}{3\ s} = 7\ m/s$$

The horse's speed is 7 meters per second, or 7 m/s.

Average Speed Most objects do not move at constant speeds for very long. The cyclists in Figure 5, for example, change their speeds many times during the race. They might glide along on level ground, move more slowly as they climb steep inclines, and dash down hills. Occasionally, they stop to fix a tire.

Unlike the horse described earlier, you cannot use any one speed to describe the motion of the cyclists at every point during the race. You can, however, find the average speed of a cyclist throughout the entire race. To find the average speed, divide the total distance traveled by the total time.

Suppose a cyclist travels 32 kilometers during the first two hours of riding, and 13 kilometers during the next hour. The average speed of the cyclist during the trip is the total distance divided by the total time.

$$Total\ distance = 32\ km + 13\ km$$

$$Total\ time = 2\ h + 1\ h$$

$$Average\ speed = \frac{45\ km}{3\ h} = 15\ km/h$$

The average speed of the cyclist is 15 kilometers per hour.

Checkpoint *How do you calculate average speed?*

EXPLORING *Motion Graphs*

Motion graphs provide an opportunity to analyze changes in distance and time.

FIRST DAY
Start with Enthusiasm.
The jogger travels at a constant speed of 170 m/min. The graph of constant speed is a slanted straight line. Notice that the speed is the same at every point on the graph. You can use the graph to analyze the jogger's motion. How far does the jogger run in 10 minutes? (1,700 m) How long does she run to travel 680 meters? (4 min)

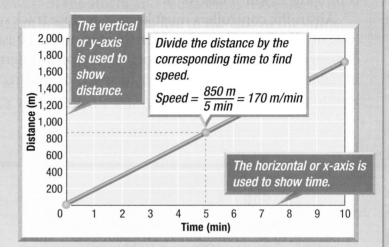

The vertical or y-axis is used to show distance.

Divide the distance by the corresponding time to find speed.

$$Speed = \frac{850\ m}{5\ min} = 170\ m/min$$

The horizontal or x-axis is used to show time.

SECOND DAY
Take a Break.
The jogger again runs at a constant speed of 170 m/min, but she takes a break after running 850 m. The horizontal line shows that distance did not change during the break—thus there is no motion. What is the jogger's average speed if she ran a total distance of 1190 m? (119 m/min)

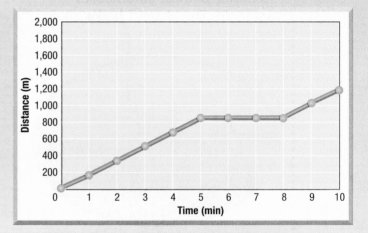

THIRD DAY
Slow Down.
As on the first day, the jogger runs at a constant speed, but this time she runs at a slower speed— 100 m/min. Notice that the slant, or slope, of the graph is smaller than it was on the first day. The slope is related to the speed. The faster the speed, the greater the slope. How far does the jogger run in 10 minutes on this day? (1,000 m)

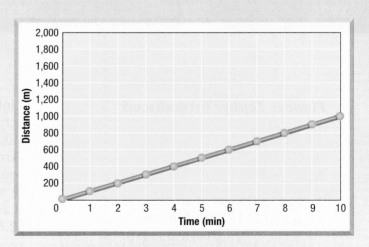

Figure 6 During a complicated maneuver an airplane's direction changes continuously, along with its speed.

Stunt pilots make spectacular use of their control over the velocity of their aircraft. To avoid colliding with other aircraft, these skilled pilots must have precise control of both speed and direction. Stunt pilots use this control to stay in close formation while flying graceful maneuvers.

Graphing Motion

INTEGRATING MATHEMATICS   You can show the motion of an object on a line graph in which you plot distance against time. Time is shown on the horizontal, or *x*-axis. It is represented by the first coordinate of the point—*x*. Distance is shown on the vertical, or *y*-axis. It is represented by the second coordinate of the point—*y*. A point (*x*, *y*) on the graph represents the location of an object at a particular time. To see examples of how graphs represent motion, read about the jogger in *Exploring Motion Graphs* on page 290.

Slope of a Line The steepness, or slant, of a line on a graph is called its **slope.** The slope tells you how fast one variable changes in relation to the other variable. In other words, slope tells you the rate of change. Since speed is the rate of change of distance in relation to time, the slope of a distance-time graph represents speed. The faster the motion, the steeper the slope, because the object moves a greater distance in a given amount of time. A distance-time graph with a constant slope represents motion at a constant speed.

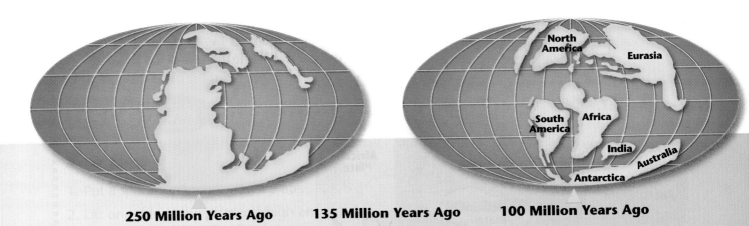

| 250 Million Years Ago | 135 Million Years Ago | 100 Million Years Ago |

Figure 10 The shapes and positions of Earth's continents have changed greatly over time and will continue to change in the future.
Interpreting Maps Locate Australia on the map. How does its position change over time?

to multiply the speed of the plate by the time during which the plate travels at that speed.

$$Distance = \frac{5\ cm}{1\ yr} \times 1{,}000\ yr = 5{,}000\ cm$$

The plate moves 5,000 centimeters in 1,000 years. Since 5,000 is a large number, try expressing this distance in meters. Recall that there are 100 centimeters in 1 meter, so you can divide by 100 by moving the decimal to the left two places.

$$5{,}000.\ cm = 50.00\ m$$

So in 1,000 years, which is well over ten average lifetimes, this plate moves only 50 meters. Walking at a brisk pace, you can probably travel the same distance in about 30 seconds!

Converting Units Suppose you want to know the speed of the plate in centimeters per day rather than centimeters per year. You can convert from one unit of measurement to another by using a conversion factor, a fraction in which the numerator and denominator are equal. In this example, 1 year is equal to 365 days. So you choose a conversion factor from these two possibilities.

$$\frac{1\ yr}{365\ d} = 1 \quad or \quad \frac{365\ d}{1\ yr} = 1$$

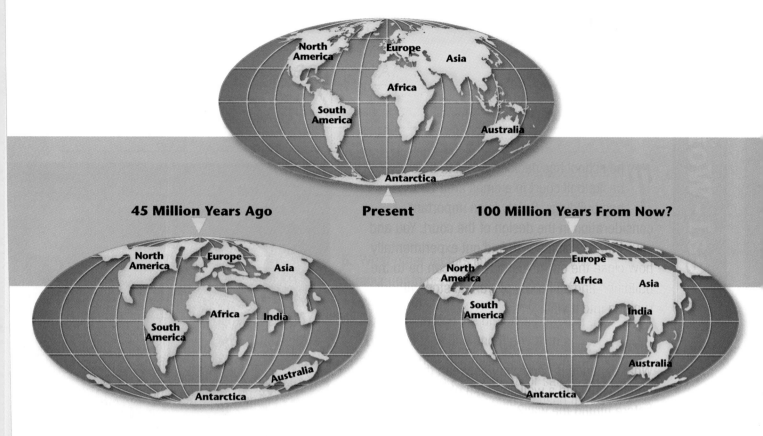

45 Million Years Ago   **Present**   **100 Million Years From Now?**

The conversion factor you need is the one that will allow you to cancel the years units. This factor is the one that has years in the numerator.

$$\frac{5\ cm}{1\ yr} \times \frac{1\ yr}{365\ d} = 0.0137\ cm/d$$

So you can describe the speed of this plate as 5 centimeters per year or as 0.0137 centimeters per day.

Section 2 Review

1. What is the theory that explains the slow movement of continents on Earth's surface?
2. Give two reasons why you don't notice the land moving beneath you. (*Hint*: Remember reference points.)
3. Suppose you are studying the motion of one of Earth's plates. What units would you probably use to describe its speed? Explain why.
4. **Thinking Critically Problem Solving** A certain plate moves 5 mm in 100 days. What is its speed in mm/d? What is its speed in mm/yr?

Science at Home

Fingernail Growth Have each member of your family measure the length of the white part at the end of one fingernail. Write down the results (and which finger you used) and mark your calendar for a date in exactly three weeks. On that day, measure the new length of the white part of the same fingernail. Then calculate the speed, in millimeters per day, at which your fingernail grew. Discuss with your family how your results compare with the typical speed with which continents move.

ACTIVITY

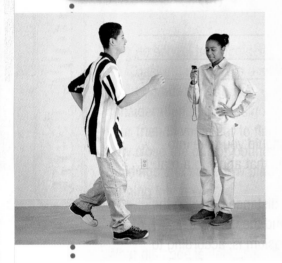

Will You Hurry Up?

1. Measure 10 meters in an area in which you can walk freely. Mark the distance with a piece of masking tape.

2. Walk the 10 meters in such way that you keep moving faster throughout the entire distance. Have a partner time you.

3. Repeat Step 2, but try to walk the 10 meters in less time than you did before. Try it again, but this time walk it in twice the amount of time as the first. Remember that you must keep speeding up throughout the entire 10 meters.

Think It Over
Inferring How is the change in your speed related to the time during which you walk the 10-meter course?

GUIDE FOR READING

◆ What happens to the motion of an object as it accelerates?

◆ How is acceleration calculated?

Reading Tip As you read, list the three different types of acceleration. Then give several examples of each.

Figure 11 The batter accelerates the softball as she hits it.
Relating Cause and Effect How does the motion of the ball change?

T he pitcher winds up. She throws. The ball speeds to the batter and, *crack*—off the bat it goes. It's going, it's going, it's gone—a home run!

Before falling beyond the fence, the softball went through several changes in its motion. It started moving in the pitcher's hand, sped up, stopped moving at the bat, changed direction, and eventually slowed down. Most examples of motion involve similar changes. In fact, it is rare for any motion to stay the same for very long. You can describe changes in motion in much the same way as you did when you learned how to describe motion in terms of speed and velocity.

Acceleration in Science

Consider a car stopped at a red light. When the light changes to green, the driver of the car gently steps on the accelerator. As a result, the car speeds up, or accelerates. In everyday language, *acceleration* means "speeding up."

Acceleration has a more precise definition in science. **Acceleration** is the rate at which velocity changes. Recall that velocity has two components (speed and direction). Acceleration involves a change in either of these components. **In science, acceleration refers to increasing speed, decreasing speed, or changing direction.**

Increasing Speed Any time the speed of an object increases, the object experiences acceleration. Can you think of examples of acceleration? A softball accelerates when the pitcher throws it, and again when a bat hits it. A car that begins to move from a stopped position or speeds up to pass another car is accelerating.

People can experience acceleration as well. The runners in Figure 12 increase their speed to sprint down the track. A figure skater will accelerate as he speeds up before jumping into the air. Similarly, a gymnast might accelerate as she runs into a tumbling routine. You accelerate as you speed up to catch the bus for school.

Decreasing Speed Just as objects can speed up, they can also slow down. Motion in which speed decreases is also considered acceleration in science. This change in speed is sometimes called deceleration, or negative acceleration.

Can you think of examples of deceleration? A softball decelerates as it rolls to a stop. A car decelerates when it comes to a stop at a red light. A jet decelerates as it lands on an aircraft carrier. The diver in Figure 12 decelerates as she travels through the water.

Changing Direction A car on a highway may be traveling at constant speed. Thus you may be tempted to conclude that it is not accelerating. Recall, however, that velocity involves *both* speed and direction. Therefore, an object can be accelerating even if its speed is constant. The car, for example, will be accelerating if it follows a gentle curve in the road or changes lanes. The skaters in Figure 12 accelerate as they round the turns on the track.

Figure 12 The diver, the skaters, and the runners are all accelerating. *Classifying Can you identify the change in motion in each example?*

Figure 13 The Ferris wheel is accelerating, because it is changing direction. *Making Generalizations What path does the Ferris wheel follow?*

Many objects continuously change direction without changing speed. The simplest example of this type of motion is circular motion, or motion along a circular path. The seats on the Ferris wheel accelerate because they move in a circle.

INTEGRATING SPACE SCIENCE In a similar way, the moon accelerates because it is continuously changing direction. Just as Earth revolves around the sun, the moon revolves around Earth. Another object that continuously accelerates is an artificial satellite orbiting Earth.

☑ *Checkpoint How is it possible for a car to be accelerating if its speed is a steady 65 km/h?*

Calculating Acceleration

Acceleration describes the rate at which velocity changes. **To determine the acceleration of an object, you must calculate the change in velocity during each unit of time.** This is summarized by the following formula.

$$\text{Acceleration} = \frac{\text{Final velocity} - \text{Initial velocity}}{\text{Time}}$$

If velocity is measured in meters/second and time is measured in seconds, the unit of acceleration is meters per second per second. This unit is written as m/s^2. This unit may sound peculiar at first. But acceleration is the change in velocity per unit of time and velocity is the change in distance per unit of time. Therefore, acceleration has two units of time. Suppose velocity is measured in kilometers/hour and time is measured in hours. Then the unit of acceleration becomes kilometers per hour per hour, or km/h^2.

If the object's speed changes by the same amount during each unit of time, the acceleration at any time during its motion is the same. If, however, the acceleration varies, you can describe only the average acceleration.

For an object moving without changing direction, the acceleration of the object is the change in its speed during one unit of time. Consider, for example, a small airplane moving on a runway. The speed of the airplane at the end of each of the first 5 seconds of its motion is shown in Figure 14.

To calculate the acceleration of the airplane, you must first subtract the initial speed (0 m/s) from the final speed (40 m/s). This gives the change in speed, 40 m/s. Then divide the change in speed by the time, 5 seconds. The acceleration is 40 m/s divided by 5 seconds, which is 8 m/s^2.

The acceleration tells you how the speed of the airplane in Figure 14 changes during each second. Notice that after each interval of one second, the speed of the airplane is 8 m/s greater

Change in Speed Over Time	
Time (s)	Speed (m/s)
0	0
1	8
2	16
3	24
4	32
5	40

Figure 14 The speed of the airplane increases by the same amount each second.

Sample Problem

A roller coaster car rapidly picks up speed as it rolls down a slope. As it starts down the slope, its speed is 4 m/s. But 3 seconds later, at the bottom of the slope, its speed is 22 m/s. What is its average acceleration?

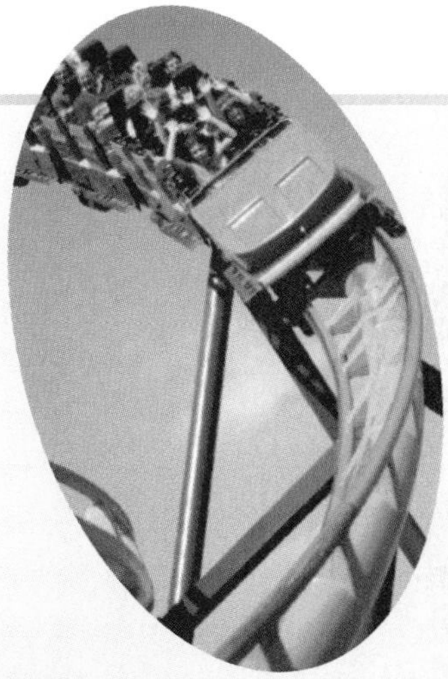

Analyze. You know the initial velocity and final velocity of the car, and the length of time during which its velocity changed. You are looking for its acceleration.

Write the formula.

$$Acceleration = \frac{Final\ velocity - Initial\ velocity}{Time}$$

Substitute and solve.

$$Acceleration = \frac{22\ m/s - 4\ m/s}{3\ s}$$

$$Acceleration = \frac{18\ m/s}{3\ s}$$

$$Acceleration = 6\ m/s^2$$

Think about it. The answer is reasonable. If the car's velocity increases by 6 m/s each second, its velocity will be 10 m/s after one second, 16 m/s after two seconds, and 22 m/s after three seconds.

Practice Problem

1. A car advertisement states that a certain car can accelerate from rest to 90 km/h in 9 seconds. Find the car's average acceleration.
2. An eagle accelerates from 15 m/s to 22 m/s in 4 seconds. What is the eagle's average acceleration?

Changes in Speed and Distance Over Time		
Time (s)	Speed (m/s)	Distance (m)
0	0	0
1	10	5
2	20	20
3	30	45
4	40	80
5	50	125

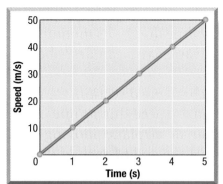 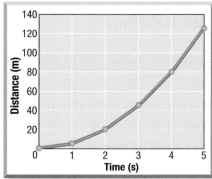

Figure 15 These graphs plot the motion of an accelerating object. *Predicting* How would the slope of the speed and time graph change if the object were accelerating more rapidly? More slowly? What do you think the graph of a decelerating object would look like?

than during the previous interval. So after one second, its speed is 8 m/s. After two seconds, its speed is 8 m/s + 8 m/s, or 16 m/s, and so on. Since the acceleration of the airplane does not change during the 5 seconds, you can use this formula for any time interval during the five seconds. Try it.

Graphing Acceleration

You can use a graph to analyze the motion of an object that is accelerating. Figure 15 shows the data for an object that is accelerating at 10 m/s². The graph showing speed versus time is a slanted straight line. The straight line shows that acceleration is constant. For every increase of one second, the speed increases by 10 m/s. Thus the graphed line rises the same amount each second and shows a **linear** relationship. If the object accelerated by a different amount each second, the graph would not be a straight line.

The graph of distance versus time is a curved line and shows a **nonlinear** relationship. This tells you that the distance traveled by the accelerating object varies each second. As the speed increases, the graph curves upward.

Section 3 Review

1. What three kinds of change in motion are called acceleration? Give an example of each.
2. What formula is used to calculate acceleration?
3. A horse trots around a large circular track, maintaining a constant speed of 5 m/s. Is the horse accelerating? Explain.
4. **Thinking Critically** **Problem Solving** A car is creeping down a deserted highway at 1 m/s. Sometime later, its speed is 25 m/s. This could have happened if the car accelerated at 3 m/s² for 8 seconds. Is this the only way the increase in speed could have happened? Explain.

Check Your Progress

CHAPTER PROJECT

You can improve the accuracy of your speed estimations by repeating measurements and by using averaged data. Make all your calculations in an organized, step-by-step manner. Prepare display cards that show how you calculated each speed.

SECTION 1 — Describing and Measuring Motion

Key Ideas

◆ The motion of an object is determined by its change of position relative to a reference point.

◆ Speed is the distance an object travels in one unit of time. If an object moves at constant speed, its speed can be determined by dividing the distance it travels by the time taken. If an object's speed varies, then dividing distance by time gives you the object's average speed.

◆ When you state both the speed of an object and the direction in which it is moving, you are describing the object's velocity.

◆ The steepness, or slant, of a line on a graph is called its slope. The slope of a distance-time graph represents speed.

Key Terms

motion
reference point
meter
speed
velocity
slope

SECTION 2 — Slow Motion on Planet Earth

INTEGRATING EARTH SCIENCE

Key Idea

◆ The plates that make up Earth's outer layer move very slowly, only centimeters per year, in various directions.

Key Term

plate

SECTION 3 — Acceleration

Key Ideas

◆ Acceleration is the rate at which velocity changes. It involves increasing speed, decreasing speed, or changing direction.

◆ Acceleration can be calculated by dividing the change in velocity by the amount of time it took that change to occur.

Key Terms

acceleration   linear   nonlinear

Organizing Information

Concept Map   Copy the concept map about motion onto a separate sheet of paper. Then complete it and add a title. (For more on concept maps, see the Skills Handbook.)

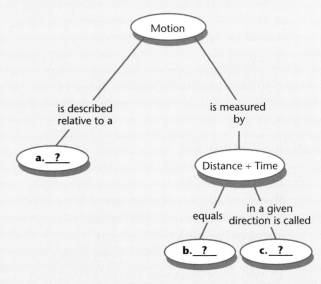

Reviewing Content

 For more review of key concepts, see the Interactive Student Tutorial CD-ROM.

Multiple Choice

Choose the letter of the best answer.

1. A change in position with respect to a reference point is
   a. acceleration.
   b. velocity.
   c. direction.
   d. motion.

2. To find the average speed of an object,
   a. add together its different speeds and divide by the number of speeds.
   b. divide the distance it travels by the time taken to travel that distance.
   c. divide the time it takes to travel a distance by the distance traveled.
   d. multiply the acceleration by the time.

3. If you know a car travels 30 km in 20 minutes, you can find its
   a. acceleration.
   b. average speed.
   c. direction.
   d. graph

4. A child on a merry-go-round is accelerating because the child
   a. is moving relative to the ground.
   b. does not change speed.
   c. is moving relative to the sun.
   d. is always changing direction.

5. If you divide the increase in an object's speed by the time taken for that increase, you are determining the object's
   a. acceleration.
   b. constant speed.
   c. average speed.
   d. velocity.

True or False

If the statement is true, write true. If it is false, change the underlined word or words to make the statement true.

6. In a moving elevator, you are not moving from the reference point of the <u>elevator</u>.

7. The graph of distance versus time for an object moving at constant speed is a <u>curve</u>.

8. The upper layer of Earth is made of pieces called <u>reference points</u>.

9. Acceleration is a change in speed or <u>direction</u>.

10. The distance an object travels in one unit of time is called <u>acceleration</u>.

Checking Concepts

11. Suppose you walk toward the rear of a moving train. Describe your motion as seen from a reference point on the train. Then describe it from a reference point on the ground.

12. Which has a greater speed, a hawk that travels 600 meters in 60 seconds or a tiny warbler that travels 60 meters in 5 seconds? Explain.

13. You have a motion graph for an object that shows distance and time. How does the slope of the graph relate to the object's speed?

14. How can you tell if an object is moving if its motion is too slow to see?

15. An insect is on a compact disc that is put into a compact disc player. The disc spins around and the insect hangs on for dear life. Is the insect accelerating? Explain why or why not.

16. **Writing to Learn** Suppose that one day some of the things that usually move very slowly start to go faster, while some things that usually move quickly slow to a snail's pace. Write a description of some of the strange events that might occur during this weird day. Include a few actual speeds as part of your description.

Thinking Critically

17. **Making Generalizations** Suppose you make two measurements. One is the time that a car takes to travel a city block. The other is the time the car takes to travel the next city block. From these measurements, explain how you decide if the car is moving at a steady speed or if it is accelerating.

18. **Problem Solving** Two drivers start at the same time to make a 100-km trip. Driver 1 takes 2 hours to complete the trip. Driver 2 takes 3 hours, but stops for an hour at the halfway point. Which driver had a greater average speed for the whole trip? Explain.

19. **Applying Concepts** A family takes a car trip. They travel for an hour at 80 km/h and then for 2 hours at 40 km/h. Find the average speed. (*Hint:* Remember to consider the total distance and the total amount of time.)

Applying Skills

Use the illustration of the motion of a ladybug to answer Questions 20–22.

A — Start   B   C — Finish

20. **Measuring** Measure the distance from the starting line to line B, and from line B to the finish line. Measure to the nearest tenth of a centimeter.

21. **Calculating** Starting at rest, the ladybug accelerated to line B and then moved at constant speed until she reached the finish line. If she took 2.5 seconds to move from line B to the finish line, calculate her constant speed during that time.

22. **Interpreting Data** The speed you calculated in Question 21 is also the speed the ladybug had at line B (at the end of her acceleration). If she took 2 seconds to accelerate from the start line to line B, what is her acceleration during that time?

CHAPTER PROJECT
Performance ▽ Assessment

Present Your Project Organize your display cards so that they are easy to follow. Remember to put a title on each card stating the speed that was being measured. Place them in order from the slowest speed to the fastest. Then display your cards to your class. Compare your results with those of other students.

Reflect and Record When you measured the same speed more than once, were the data always the same? Explain. What factors make measuring a speed difficult?

Test Preparation

Use these questions to prepare for standardized tests.

Study the graph. Then answer Questions 23–27.

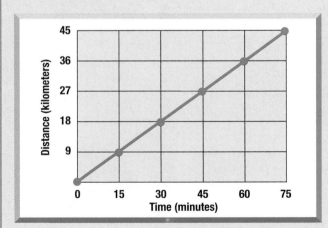

23. What would be the best title for this graph?
    a. Train at Rest
    b. Train Moving at Constant Acceleration
    c. Train Moving at Constant Speed
    d. Train Slowing to a Stop

24. During each 15-minute interval, the train travels a distance of
    a. 9 kilometers.   b. 18 kilometers.
    c. 36 kilometers.   d. 45 kilometers.

25. According to the graph, how long does it take for the train to travel 27 kilometers?
    a. 15 minutes   b. 30 minutes
    c. 45 minutes   d. 1 hour

26. What is the train's speed?
    a. 9 km/h   b. 18 km/h
    c. 36 km/h   d. 72 km/h

27. After 75 minutes, the train stops for 5 minutes to pick up passengers. How would the graph look during this period?
    a. The line would slant downward.
    b. The line would be horizontal.
    c. The line would be broken.
    d. The line would stop at a point and continue from the same point once the train begins to move again.

WEB ACTIVITY
www.phschool.com

SECTION
1 The Nature of Force

Discover **What Changes Motion?**
Try This **Around and Around**
Science at Home **Coin Inertia**
Skills Lab **Forced to Accelerate**

SECTION
2 Force, Mass, and Acceleration

Discover **How Do the Rocks Roll?**

SECTION
3 Friction and Gravity

Discover **Which Lands First?**
Try This **Spinning Plates**
Sharpen Your Skills **Calculating**
Real-World Lab **Sticky Sneakers**

Newton Scooters

A strong kick sends the soccer ball soaring toward the goal. The goalie does his best to stop the ball. Both the kicker and the goalie exert forces on the ball to change its motion. In this chapter you will learn how forces change all kinds of motion. You will find that there are forces acting on the ball even when it is soaring through the air.

In this chapter, you will learn how Newton's three basic laws of motion govern the relationship of forces and motion. You will use Newton's third law to build a scooter. Unlike the soccer ball, the scooter must move without being kicked!

Your Goal To design and build a vehicle that is powered only through Newton's third law of motion.

Your vehicle must

◆ move forward by pushing back on something
◆ not be powered by any form of electricity or use gravity in order to move
◆ travel a minimum distance of 1.5 meters
◆ be built following the safety guidelines in Appendix A

Get Started Brainstorm possible designs for your vehicle, but be careful not to lock yourself into a single idea. Remember that a car with wheels is only one type of vehicle. Try to think of ways to recycle household materials to build your vehicle.

Check Your Progress You'll be working on this project as you study this chapter. To keep your project on track, look for Check Your Progress boxes at the following points.

Section 2 Review, page 322: Determine factors that will affect the acceleration of your vehicle.

Section 3 Review, page 329: Draw a diagram of your proposed design.

Section 4 Review, page 337: Construct your vehicle and identify the force that propels it.

Present Your Project At the end of the chapter (page 343), demonstrate how your vehicle moves.

Both the kicker and the goalie use forces to control the motion of the soccer ball.

SECTION 4 Action and Reaction

Discover How Pushy Is a Straw?
Try This Colliding Cars

SECTION 5 Orbiting Satellites
Integrating Space Science

Discover What Makes an Object Move in a Circle?
Science at Home Swing the Bucket

ACTIVITY

What Changes Motion?

1. Stack several metal washers on top of a toy car.

2. Place a heavy book on the floor near the car.

3. Predict what will happen to both the car and the washers if you roll the car into the book. Test your prediction.

Think It Over

Observing What happened to the car when it hit the book? What happened to the washers? What might be the reason for any difference between the motions of the car and the washers?

GUIDE FOR READING

◆ How are balanced and unbalanced forces related to motion?

◆ What is Newton's first law of motion?

Reading Tip As you read, use your own words to define each boldfaced word.

An arrow soars through the air to its distant target. A long jumper comes to a sudden stop in a cloud of sand. You kick a soccer ball around your opponent. There is some type of motion involved in each of these activities. But why does each object move as it does? What causes an object to start moving, stop moving, or change direction? The answer is a force. In each of these activities, a force is exerted on, or applied to, an object.

What Is a Force?

In science the word *force* has a simple and specific meaning. A **force** is a push or a pull. When one object pushes or pulls another object, you say that the first object is exerting a force on the second object. You exert a force on a pen when you write, on a book when you lift it, on a zipper when you pull it, and on a

ball when you throw it. You exert a force on a pebble when you skim it across a pond, on a wagon when you pull it, and on a nail when you hammer it into a piece of wood.

Like velocity and acceleration, forces are described not only by how strong they are, but also by the *direction* in which they act. If you push on a door, you exert a force in a different direction than if you pull on the door.

Unbalanced Forces

Suppose you need to push a heavy box across a floor. When you push on the box, you exert a force on it. If a friend helps you, the total force exerted on the box is the sum of your force plus your friend's force. When two forces act in the same direction, they add together.

Figure 1 uses arrows to show the addition of forces. The head of each arrow points in the direction of a force. The width of each arrow tells you the strength of a force. A wider arrow shows a greater force. (When forces are shown in this book, the strength of a force will usually be shown by the width of an arrow.)

When forces act in opposite directions, they also add together. However, you must pay attention to the direction of each force. Adding a force acting in one direction to a force acting in the opposite direction is the same as adding a positive number and a negative number. So when two forces act in opposite directions, they combine by subtraction. If one force is greater than the other force, the overall force is in the direction of the greater force. You can see

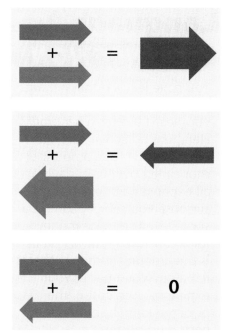

Figure 1 Two forces can combine so that they add together (top), or subtract from each other (center). They may also cancel each other (bottom).

Figure 2 The arrow, the jumper, and the soccer ball are all in motion. *Making Generalizations What makes an arrow fly through the air to its target, a long jumper thud to a stop, and a soccer ball change direction?*

what happens when the students in the center of the next page exert unequal forces in opposite directions.

In any situation, the overall force on an object after all the forces are added together is called the **net force.** When there is a net force acting on an object, the forces are said to be unbalanced. **Unbalanced forces** can cause an object to start moving, stop moving, or change direction. **Unbalanced forces acting on an object will change the object's motion.** In other words, an unbalanced force will cause an object to accelerate. For example, if two unequal forces acting in opposite directions are applied to a box, the box will accelerate in the direction of the greater force.

Balanced Forces

Forces exerted on an object do not always change the object's motion. Consider the forces involved when the dogs in Figure 3 pull on a stocking in opposite directions. Even though there are forces acting on it, the motion of the stocking does not change. While one dog exerts a force on the stocking in one direction, the other dogs exert an equal force on the stocking in the opposite direction.

Equal forces acting on one object in opposite directions are called **balanced forces.** One force is exactly balanced by the other force. **Balanced forces acting on an object will not change the object's motion.** When you add equal forces exerted in opposite directions, the net force is zero. You can also see how balanced forces cancel in the example at the bottom of the next page. The box does not move at all.

✓ *Checkpoint* Which cause change in motion—balanced forces or unbalanced forces?

Figure 3 These dogs are exerting a great deal of force, but they aren't moving. *Applying Concepts What would happen if one of the dogs pulled harder? Explain why.*

EXPLORING Combined Forces

What happens when two friends push on the same object? The forces they exert combine in different ways, depending on the directions in which they push.

UNBALANCED FORCES IN THE SAME DIRECTION

When two forces act in the same direction, the net force is the sum of the two individual forces. The box moves to the left.

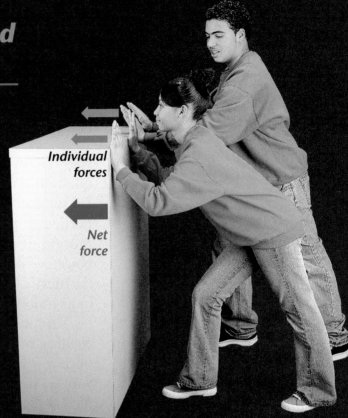

Individual forces

Net force

Individual forces

Net force

UNBALANCED FORCES IN OPPOSITE DIRECTIONS

When forces act in opposite directions, the net force is the difference between the two forces. The box moves to the right.

Individual forces

Net force = 0

BALANCED FORCES IN OPPOSITE DIRECTIONS

When two equal forces act in opposite directions, they cancel each other out. The box doesn't move.

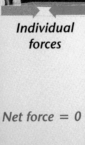

315

TRY THIS

Around and Around

An object moving in a circle has inertia.

ACTIVITY

1. Tape one end of a length of thread (about 1 m) to a table tennis ball.

2. Suspend the ball in front of you and swing it in a horizontal circle. Keep the ball about 2 or 3 cm above the floor.

3. Let go of the thread and observe the direction in which the ball rolls.

4. Repeat this several times, letting go of the thread at different points.

Inferring At what point do you need to let go of the thread if you want the ball to roll directly away from you? Toward you? Draw a diagram as part of your answer.

Newton's First Law of Motion

The ancient Greeks observed that objects have natural resting places. Objects move toward those places. A rock falls to the ground. A puff of smoke rises into the air. Once an object is in its natural resting place, it cannot move by itself. They also thought that for an object to stay in motion, a force has to act on it.

Inertia In the early 1600s, the Italian astronomer Galileo Galilei questioned the idea that a force is needed to keep an object moving. He suggested that once an object is in motion, no push or pull is needed to keep it moving. Force is needed only to change the motion of an object. But whether it is moving or at rest, every object resists any change to its motion. This resistance is called inertia. **Inertia** (in UR shuh) is the tendency of an object to resist change in its motion.

You may have observed this yourself. A puck that rides on a cushion of air in an "air-hockey" game glides along quite freely once you push it. Similarly, a tennis ball flies through the air once you hit it with a racket. In both cases, the object continues to move even after you remove the force.

Galileo's ideas paved the way for the English mathematican Sir Isaac Newton. Newton discovered the three basic laws of motion in the late 1600s. The first of Newton's three laws of motion restates Galileo's idea. **Newton's first law of motion states that an object at rest will remain at rest and an object that is moving at constant velocity will continue moving at constant velocity unless acted upon by an unbalanced force.** Newton's first law of motion is also called the law of inertia.

Figure 4 These crash-test dummies weren't wearing safety belts. *Relating Cause and Effect What caused them to move forward even after the car stopped?*

Inertia explains many common events. For example, if you are in a car that stops suddenly, inertia causes you to continue moving forward. The crash test dummies in Figure 4 don't stop when the car does. Passengers in a moving car have inertia. Therefore a force is required to change their motion. That force is exerted by the safety belt. If the safety belt is not worn, that force may be exerted by the windshield instead!

Mass Which is more difficult to move, a jar of pennies or a jar of plastic foam "peanuts"? Obviously, the jar of pennies is harder to move. What is the difference between the jar of pennies and the jar of plastic peanuts? After all, you can see in Figure 5 that both jars occupy the same amount of space, and so have the same volume. The difference is the amount of mass each one has. Mass is the amount of matter in an object. The jar of pennies has more mass than the jar of plastic peanuts.

The SI unit of mass is the kilogram (kg). A small car might have a mass of 1,000 kilograms. A bicycle without a rider might have a mass of about 10 kilograms, and a student might have a mass of 45 kilograms. You describe the mass of smaller objects in terms of grams (1 kilogram = 1,000 grams). The mass of a nickel is about 5 grams.

The amount of inertia an object has depends on its mass. The greater the mass of an object, the greater its inertia. Mass, then, can also be defined as a measure of the inertia of an object.

Figure 5 The two jars have the same volume, but very different masses.

Section 1 Review

1. What are the differences in how balanced and unbalanced forces affect motion?
2. What is inertia? How is it involved in Newton's first law of motion?
3. Two children who are fighting over a toy pull on it from opposite sides. The result is a stand-off. Explain this in terms of the net force.
4. **Thinking Critically** **Applying Concepts** Draw a diagram in which two forces acting on an object are unbalanced and a diagram in which two balanced forces act on an object. Use arrows to show the forces.

Science at Home

Coin Inertia Fill a paper cup with water. Cover the cup with an index card and place a coin or paper clip in the center of the index card. Challenge your family members to move the coin from the card to the cup without touching the coin or holding on to the card. If they cannot think how to do it, show them how. Hold the cup and use your finger to flick the card with a sharp sideways force. The force doesn't have to be very strong, but it must be sharp. Explain what happens to the coin in terms of inertia.

Forced to Accelerate

In this lab, you will practice the skill of interpreting data as you explore the relationship between force and acceleration.

Problem

How is the acceleration of a skateboard related to the force that is pulling it?

Materials

skateboard meter stick spring scale, 5 N
string masking tape stopwatch
several bricks or other large mass(es)

Procedure

1. Attach a loop of string to a skateboard. Place the bricks on the skateboard.
2. Using masking tape, mark off a one-meter distance on a level floor. Label one end "Start" and the other "Finish."
3. Attach a spring scale to the loop of string. Pull it so that you maintain a force of 2.0 N. Be sure to pull with the scale straight out in front. Practice applying a steady force to the skateboard as it moves.
4. Make a data table in your notebook like the one below.

5. Find the smallest force needed to pull the skateboard at a slow, constant speed. Do not accelerate the skateboard. Record this force on the first line of the table.
6. Add 0.5 N to the force in Step 5. This will be enough to accelerate the skateboard. Record this force on the second line of the table.
7. Have one of your partners hold the front edge of the skateboard at the starting line. Then pull on the spring scale with the force you found in Step 6.
8. When your partner says "Go" and releases the skateboard, maintain a constant force until the skateboard reaches the finish line.
9. A third partner should time how long it takes the skateboard to go from start to finish. Record the time in the column labeled Trial 1.
10. Repeat Steps 7, 8, and 9 twice more. Record your results in the columns labeled Trial 2 and Trial 3.
11. Repeat Steps 7, 8, 9, and 10, using a force that is 1.0 N greater than the force you found in Step 5.
12. Repeat Steps 7, 8, 9 and 10 twice more. Use forces that are 1.5 N and 2.0 N greater than the force you found in Step 5.

DATA TABLE

Force (N)	Trial 1 Time (s)	Trial 2 Time (s)	Trial 3 Time (s)	Avg Time (s)	Avg Speed (m/s)	Final Speed (m/s)	Acceleration (m/s^2)

Analyze and Conclude

1. For each force you used, find the average of the three times that you measured. Record the average in your data table.

2. Find the average speed of the skateboard for each force. Use this formula:

   Average speed = 1 m ÷ Average time
   Record this value for each force.

3. To obtain the final speed of the skateboard, multiply each average speed by 2. Record the result in your data table.

4. To obtain the acceleration, divide each final speed you found by the average time. Record the acceleration in your data table.

5. Make a line graph. Show the acceleration on the *y*-axis and the force on the *x*-axis. The *y*-axis scale should go from zero to about 1 m/s^2. The *x*-axis should go from zero to 3.0 newtons.

6. If your data points seem to form a straight line, draw a line through them.

7. Your first data point is the force required for an acceleration of zero. How do you know the force for an acceleration of zero?

8. According to your graph, how is the acceleration of the skateboard related to the pulling force?

9. **Think About It** Which variable is the manipulated variable? Which is the responding variable?

Design an Experiment

Design an experiment to test how the acceleration of the loaded skateboard depends on its mass. Think about how you would vary the mass of the skateboard. What quantity would you need to measure that you did not measure in this experiment? Do you have the equipment to make that measurement? If not, what other equipment would you need?

Changes in Force and Mass

How can you increase the acceleration of the wagon? Look again at the equation for acceleration: Acceleration = Force ÷ Mass. One way to increase acceleration is by changing the force. According to the equation, acceleration and force change in the same way. An increase in force causes an increase in acceleration. So to increase the acceleration of the wagon, you can increase the force you use to pull it. You can pull harder.

Another way to increase acceleration is to change the mass. According to the equation, acceleration and mass change in opposite ways. This means that an increase in mass causes a decrease in acceleration. It also means that a decrease in mass causes an increase in acceleration. So to increase the acceleration of the wagon, you can decrease its mass. Instead of you, the boys should ride in the wagon.

Figure 6 The acceleration of an object depends on the force acting on it and the object's mass.

Section 2 Review

1. What three quantities are related in Newton's second law of motion? What is the relationship among them?
2. When the net force on an object increases, how does the object's acceleration change?
3. Suppose you know the acceleration of a shopping cart as it rolls down a supermarket aisle. You want to find the net force with which it was pushed. What other information do you need in order to find the force?
4. **Thinking Critically** **Problem Solving** Suppose you doubled the force acting on an object. In what way could you change its mass to keep its acceleration unchanged?

CHAPTER PROJECT

Check Your Progress

The vehicle for your project will need to accelerate from a resting position. From Newton's second law of motion, you know that Acceleration = Force ÷ Mass. This means you have two ways of increasing acceleration: increasing force or decreasing mass. How can you either increase the force acting on your vehicle or decrease its mass?

SECTION
3 Friction and Gravity

DISCOVER ••• ACTIVITY

Which Lands First?

Do you think a quarter will fall more quickly than a dime? More quickly than a nickel? Record your predictions and find out!

1. Place a dime, a nickel, and a quarter along the edge of a desk.

2. Put a ruler behind the coins. Line it up with the edge of the desk.

3. Keeping the ruler parallel to the edge of the desk, push all three coins over the edge at the same time. Observe any time difference when the coins land.

Think It Over

Predicting Did you see a pattern in the time the coins took to fall? Use your observations about the coins to predict whether a soccer ball will fall more quickly than a marble. Will a pencil fall more quickly than a book? How can you test your predictions?

What happens if you push a book slowly across your desk and then stop pushing? Will it keep moving? Without actually pushing a book, you can predict that it will come to a stop. Now think about lifting a book above your desk and letting it go. Again, without actually dropping the book, you can predict that it will fall. In both of these situations, you first exert a force to change the motion of a book, and then you remove the force.

According to Newton's first law of motion, the book's motion changes only if an unbalanced force acts on it. A force should not be necessary to keep the book moving at a constant speed. So why does the book stop sliding after you push it? And why does the book fall back to the ground once you stop exerting a force to hold it up?

From Newton's first law of motion, we know that in each case an unbalanced force must be acting on the book. Two other forces do indeed act on the book. When the book slides, the force of friction causes it to slow to a stop. When the book falls, the force of the gravity causes it to accelerate downward. In this section you will learn that these two forces affect nearly all motion.

GUIDE FOR READING

◆ What factors determine the friction force between two surfaces?

◆ How does mass differ from weight?

◆ What is the law of universal gravitation?

Reading Tip As you read, compare and contrast friction and gravity.

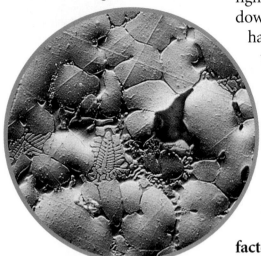

Figure 7 If you look at a polished metal surface under a special microscope, you'll find that it is actually quite rough. *Predicting What would a rough surface look like?*

Friction

When you push a book across a table, the surface of the book rubs against the surface of the table. In the same way, the skin of a firefighter's hands rubs against the polished metal pole as she slides down. Although surfaces may seem quite smooth, they actually have many irregularities. When two surfaces rub, the irregularities of one surface get caught on those of the other surface. The force that one surface exerts on another when the two rub against each other is called **friction.**

The Nature of Friction Friction acts in a direction opposite to the object's direction of motion. Without friction, the object would continue to move at constant speed forever. Friction, however, opposes motion. Eventually friction will cause an object to come to a stop.

The strength of the force of friction depends on two factors: the types of surfaces involved and how hard the surfaces push together. Rough surfaces produce greater friction than smooth surfaces. The skiers in Figure 8 get a fast ride because there is very little friction between their skis and the snow. The reindeer would not be able to pull them easily over a rough surface such as sand. The force of friction also increases if the surfaces push harder against each other. If you rub your hands together forcefully, there is more friction than if you rub your hands together lightly.

Figure 8 These reindeer can't fly. But they can give an exciting ride to the two Finlanders on skis.

Friction force

Friction force

Force exerted on skiers

Figure 9 Friction enables these students to draw on the pavement. Friction also enables the metalworker to smooth a metal surface. *Inferring How can you tell that the grinder is producing heat?*

Is Friction Useful or Not? Is friction necessarily a bad thing? No—whether or not friction is useful depends on the situation. You are able to walk, for example, because friction acts between the soles of your shoes and the floor. Without friction your shoes would only slide across the floor, and you would never move forward. An automobile moves because of friction between its tires and the road. Thanks to friction you can light a match and you can walk on a sidewalk.

Friction is so useful that at times people want to increase it. If you are walking down a snow-covered hill, you might wear rubber boots or spread sand to increase the friction and slow you down. Ballet dancers spread a sticky powder on the soles of their shoes so that they do not slip on the dance floor.

Controlling Friction There are different kinds of friction. When solid surfaces slide over each other, the kind of friction that occurs is called **sliding friction.** When an object rolls over a surface, the kind of friction that occurs is **rolling friction.** The force needed to overcome rolling friction is much less than the force needed to overcome sliding friction.

Ball bearings are one way of reducing friction between two surfaces. Ball bearings are small, smooth steel balls. The balls roll between rotating metal parts. The wheels of in-line skates, skateboards, and bicycles all have ball bearings. Many automobile parts have ball bearings as well.

The friction that occurs when an object moves through a fluid is called **fluid friction.** The force needed to overcome fluid friction is usually less than that needed to overcome sliding friction. The fluid keeps surfaces from making direct contact and thus reduces friction. The moving parts of machines are bathed in oil so that they can slide past each other with less friction.

☑ *Checkpoint* *What are two ways to reduce friction?*

Spinning Plates

Find out if the force of rolling friction is really less than the force of sliding friction.

1. Stack two identical pie plates together. Try to spin the top plate.
2. Now separate the plates and fill the bottom of one pie plate loosely with marbles.
3. Place the second plate in the plate with marbles.
4. Try to spin the top plate again. Observe the results.

Drawing Conclusions What applications are there for the rolling friction modeled in this activity?

Figure 10 As soon as they jump from their airplane, skydivers begin accelerating. *Predicting Will a skydiver with greater mass accelerate more quickly than a skydiver with less mass?*

Gravity

Friction explains why a book comes to a stop when it is pushed. But why does the same book fall to the ground if you lift it and let it go? Newton realized that a force acts to pull objects straight down toward the center of Earth. He called this force gravity. **Gravity** is the force that pulls objects toward Earth.

Free Fall When the only force acting on a falling object is gravity, the object is said to be in **free fall.** An object in free fall accelerates as it falls. Do you know why? In free fall the force of gravity is an unbalanced force, and unbalanced forces cause an object to accelerate.

How much do objects accelerate as they fall? Near the surface of Earth, the acceleration due to the force of gravity is 9.8 m/s^2. This means that for every second an object is falling, its velocity increases by 9.8 m/s. Suppose that an object is dropped from the top of a building. Its starting velocity is 0 m/s. At the end of the first second of falling, its velocity is 9.8 m/s. After two seconds, its velocity is 19.6 m/s (9.8 m/s + 9.8 m/s). After 3 seconds the velocity is 29.4 m/s. The velocity tends to increase as long as the object falls.

While it may seem hard to believe at first, all objects in free fall accelerate at the same rate regardless of mass. If you do not believe that the rates are the same, look at the two balls in Figure 11A.

Figure 11 A. Two balls with different masses are dropped to the ground. In a vacuum they would fall at exactly the same rate, regardless of their masses. B. A special device is used to drop one ball vertically and throw another ball horizontally at the same time.

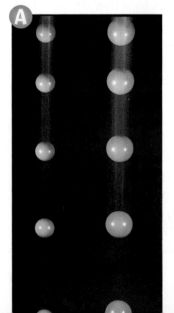

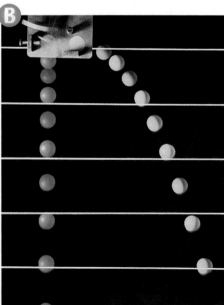

Projectile Motion Rather than dropping a ball straight down, what happens if you throw it horizontally? An object that is thrown is called a **projectile** (pruh JEK tul). Will a projectile land on the ground at the same time as an object dropped straight down?

An object that is simply dropped and one that is thrown horizontally are both in free fall. The horizontal motion of the thrown object does

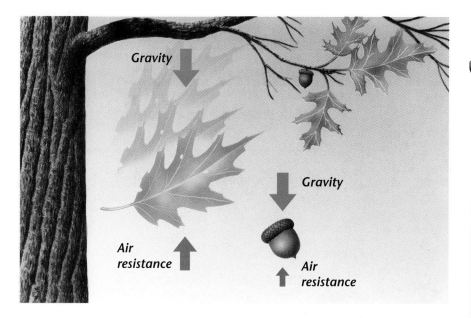

Figure 12 When air is present, air resistance exerts an upward force on objects. *Inferring The oak leaf and the acorn fall at the same rate in the vacuum tube on the right. Is there any air resistance?*

not interfere with its free fall. Both objects will hit the ground at exactly the same time.

Air Resistance Despite the fact that all objects are *supposed* to fall at the same rate, you know that this is not always the case. For example, an oak leaf flutters slowly to the ground, while an acorn drops straight down. Objects falling through air experience a type of fluid friction called **air resistance.** Remember that friction is in the direction opposite to motion, so air resistance is an upward force. Air resistance is not the same for all objects. The greater the surface area of an object, the greater the air resistance. That is why a leaf falls more slowly than an acorn. In a vacuum, where there is no air, all objects fall with exactly the same rate of acceleration.

Air resistance increases with velocity. So as a falling object speeds up, the air resistance against it increases. Eventually, the air resistance equals the force of gravity. Remember that when forces are balanced, there is no acceleration. So although the object continues to fall, its velocity no longer increases. This velocity, the greatest velocity the object reaches, is called **terminal velocity.**

✓ *Checkpoint* *At what rate does an object in free fall accelerate?*

Weight The force of gravity on a person or object at the surface of a planet is known as weight. When you step on a bathroom scale, you are determining the force with which Earth is pulling you. Do not confuse weight with mass! **Weight is a measure of the force of gravity on an object, and mass is a measure of the amount of matter in that object.**

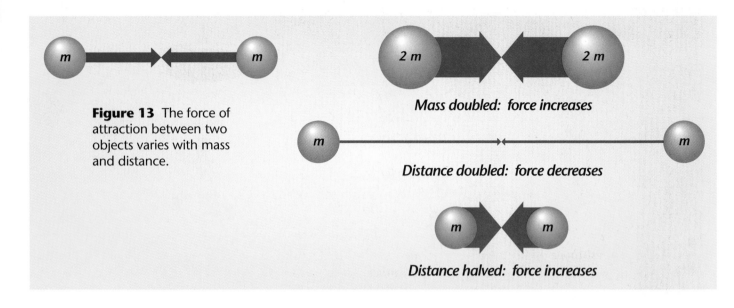

Figure 13 The force of attraction between two objects varies with mass and distance.

Mass doubled: force increases

Distance doubled: force decreases

Distance halved: force increases

Since weight is a force, you can rewrite Newton's second law of motion, Force = Mass × Acceleration, to find weight.

Weight = Mass × Acceleration due to gravity

Weight is usually measured in newtons, mass in kilograms, and acceleration due to gravity in m/s^2. So a 50-kilogram person weighs 50 kg × 9.8 m/s^2 = 490 newtons on Earth's surface.

Universal Gravitation

Newton realized that Earth is not the only object that exerts a gravitational force. Instead, gravity acts everywhere in the universe. Gravity is the force that makes an apple fall to the ground. It is the force that keeps the moon orbiting around Earth. It is also the force that keeps all the planets orbiting around the sun.

What Newton discovered is now called the law of universal gravitation. **The law of universal gravitation states that the force of gravity acts between all objects in the universe.** Any two objects in the universe, without exception, attract each other. This means that you are not only attracted to Earth, but you are also attracted to all the other objects around you! Earth and the objects around you are attracted to you as well.

Why don't you notice that the objects around you are pulling on you? After all, this book exerts a gravitational force on you. The reason is that the strength of the force depends on the masses of the objects involved. The force of gravity is much greater between you and Earth than between you and your book.

 INTEGRATING SPACE SCIENCE Although your mass would remain the same on another planet or moon, your weight would be different. For example, the force of gravity on Earth's moon is about one sixth that on Earth. Your weight on

Figure 14 This astronaut jumps
easily on the moon.
*Comparing and Contrasting How
do his mass and weight on the
moon compare to his mass and
weight on Earth?*

the moon, then, would be about a sixth of what it is on Earth. That is why the astronaut in Figure 14 can leap so easily.

If the gravitational force depends on mass, you might then expect to notice a force of attraction from a massive object, such as the moon or the sun. But you do not. The reason is that the gravitational force also depends on the distance between the objects. The farther apart the objects are, the weaker the force.

Astronauts travel great distances from Earth. As they travel from Earth toward the moon, Earth's gravitational pull becomes weaker. At the same time, the moon's gravitational pull becomes stronger. At the surface of the moon an astronaut feels the pull of the moon's gravity, but no longer notices the pull of Earth's gravity.

Section 3 Review

1. What factors determine the strength of the friction force when two surfaces slide against each other?
2. What is the difference between weight and mass?
3. State the law of universal gravitation in your own words.
4. **Thinking Critically Problem Solving** A squirrel drops a nut over a cliff. What is the velocity of the nut after 3 seconds? After 5 seconds? After 10 seconds? (Ignore air resistance. Remember that the acceleration due to gravity is 9.8 m/s^2.)

CHAPTER
PROJECT

*Check Your
Progress*
Draw a diagram of your vehicle. Use labeled arrows to show each place that a force is acting on it. Be sure to include friction forces in your diagram. Brainstorm ways to reduce forces that slow down your vehicle.

Sticky Sneakers

The appropriate sneaker for an activity should have a specific type of tread to grip the floor or the ground. In this lab you will test different sneakers by measuring the amount of friction between the sneakers and a table.

Problem

How does the amount of friction between a sneaker and a surface compare for different types of sneakers?

Skills Focus

forming operational definitions, measuring, controlling variables

Materials

three or more different types of sneakers
spring scale, 20 N   mass set(s)   tape
spring scale, 5 N   large paper clip   balance

Procedure

1. Sneakers are designed to deal with various friction forces, including these:
   ◆ starting friction, which is involved when you start from a stopped position
   ◆ forward-stopping friction, which is involved when you come to a forward stop
   ◆ sideways-stopping friction, which is involved when you come to a sideways stop

2. Prepare a data table in which you can record each type of friction for each sneaker.
3. Find the mass of each sneaker. Then put masses in each sneaker so that the total mass of the sneaker plus the masses is 1,000 g. Spread the masses out evenly inside the sneaker.
4. You will need to tape the paper clip to each sneaker and then attach a spring clip to the paper clip. To measure
   ◆ starting friction, attach the paper clip to the back of the sneaker
   ◆ forward-stopping friction, attach the paper clip to the front of the sneaker
   ◆ sideways-stopping friction, attach the paper clip to the side of the sneaker

DATA TABLE			
Sneaker	Starting friction (N)	Sideways-stopping friction (N)	Forward-stopping friction (N)
A			
B			

5. To measure starting friction, pull the sneaker backward until it starts to move. Use the 20-N spring scale first. If the reading is less than 5 N, use a 5-N scale. The force necessary to make the sneaker start moving is equal to the friction force. Record the starting friction force in your data table.

6. To measure either type of stopping friction, use the spring scale to pull each sneaker at a slow, constant speed. Record the stopping friction force in your data table.

7. Repeat Steps 3 and 4 for the remaining sneakers.

Analyze and Conclude

1. What are the manipulated and responding variables in this experiment? Explain. (See the Skills Handbook for a discussion of experimental variables.)

2. Why is the reading on the spring scale equal to the friction force in each case?

3. Do you think that using a sneaker with a small amount of mass in it is a fair test of the friction of the sneakers? (Consider the fact that sneakers are used with people's feet inside them.) Explain your answer.

4. Draw a diagram that shows the forces acting on the sneaker for each type of motion.

5. Why did you pull the sneaker at a slow speed to test for stopping friction? For starting friction, why did you pull a sneaker that wasn't moving?

6. Which sneaker had the most starting friction? Which had the most forward stopping friction? Which had the most sideways stopping friction?

7. Can you identify a relationship between the type of sneaker and the type of friction you observed? What do you observe about the sneakers that would cause one to have better traction than another?

8. **Apply** Wear a pair of your own sneakers. Start running and notice how you press against the floor with your sneaker. How do you think this affects the friction between the sneaker and the floor? How can you test for this variable?

Getting Involved

Go to a store that sells sneakers. If possible take a spring scale and, with the clerk's permission, do a quick friction test on sneakers designed for different activities. Also, note the materials they are made of, the support they provide for your feet, and other features. Then decide whether it is necessary to buy specific sneakers for different activities.

④ Action and Reaction

DISCOVER •••ACTIVITY•••

How Pushy Is a Straw?

1. Stretch a rubber band around the middle of the front cover of a small or medium-sized hardcover book.

2. Place four marbles in a small square on a table. Carefully place the book on the marbles so that the cover with the rubber band is on top.

3. Hold the book steady by placing one index finger on the center of the binding. Then, as shown in the illustration, push a straw against the rubber band with your other index finger.

4. Push the straw so that the rubber band stretches about ten centimeters. Then let go of both the book and the straw at the same time.

Think It Over

Developing Hypotheses What did you observe about the motion of the book and the straw? Write a hypothesis to explain what happened in terms of the forces on the book and the straw.

GUIDE FOR READING

◆ What is Newton's third law of motion?

◆ What is the law of conservation of momentum?

Reading Tip Before you read, preview the illustrations and predict what *action* and *reaction* mean.

Imagine that you are an astronaut making a space walk outside your space station. In your excitement about your walk, you lose track of time and use up all the fuel in your jet pack. How do you get back to the station? Your jet pack is empty, but it can still get you back to the station if you throw it away. To understand how, you need to know Newton's third law of motion.

Newton's Third Law of Motion

Newton realized that forces are not "one-sided." Whenever one object exerts a force on a second object, the second object exerts a force back on the first object. The force exerted by the second object is equal in strength and opposite in direction to the first force. Newton called one force the "action" and the other force the "reaction." **Newton's third law of motion states that if one object exerts a force on another object, then the second object exerts a force of equal strength in the opposite direction on the first object.**

Figure 15 A hammer exerts a force on a nail, pushing it into a piece of wood. At the same time, the nail exerts a force back on the hammer, causing its motion to come to a sudden stop.

Equal but Opposite You may already be familiar with examples of Newton's third law of motion. Perhaps you have watched figure skaters and have seen one skater push on the other. As a result, both skaters move—not only the skater who was pushed. The skater who pushed is pushed back with an equal force, but in the opposite direction.

The speeds with which the two skaters move depend on their masses. If they have the same mass, they will move at the same speed. But if one skater has a greater mass than the other, she will move backward more slowly. Although the action and reaction forces will be equal and opposite, the same force acting on a greater mass results in a smaller acceleration. Recall that this is Newton's second law of motion.

Now can you figure out how to return from your space walk? In order to get a push back to the space station, you need to push on some object. You can remove your empty jet pack and push it away from you. In return, the jet pack will exert an equal force on you, sending you back to the safety of the space station.

Figure 16 One skater pushes gently on the other. The result is that the other skater pushes back with an equal force—even if she isn't trying. *Applying Concepts Which of Newton's laws describes this phenomenon?*

Action-Reaction in Action Newton's third law is in action all around you. When you walk, you push the ground with your feet. The ground pushes back on your feet with an equal and opposite force. You go forward when you walk because the ground is pushing you! A bird flies forward by exerting a force on the air with its wings. The air pushes back on those wings with an equal force that propels the bird forward.

INTEGRATING LIFE SCIENCE A squid applies Newton's third law of motion to move itself through the water. The squid exerts a force on the water that it expels from its body cavity. At the same time, the water exerts an equal and opposite force on the squid, causing it to move.

Figure 17 When a squid pushes water out, the expelled water pushes back and forces the squid to move ahead (to the right). The force the squid exerts on the water is the action force.

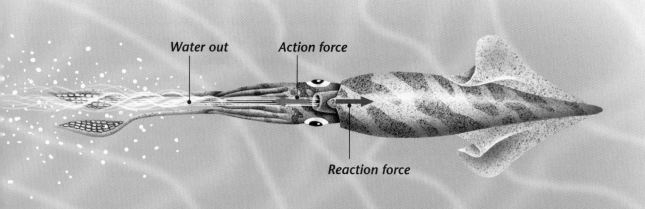

Water out   Action force

Reaction force

Force on
wrists

Force on
ball

Forces on hands

Force
on ball

Force
on ball

Figure 18 In these photographs, red arrows show action forces and blue arrows show reaction forces. **A.** The player's wrists exert the action force. **B.** As two players jump for the ball, the ball exerts reaction forces on both of them.

Do Action-Reaction Forces Cancel? In Section 1 you learned that balanced forces, which are equal and opposite, add up to zero. In other words, balanced forces cancel out. They produce no change in motion. Why then don't the action and reaction forces in Newton's third law of motion cancel out as well? After all, they are equal and opposite.

To answer this question, you have to consider the object on which the forces are acting. Look, for example, at the two volleyball players in Figure 18B. When they hit the ball from opposite directions, each of their hands exerts a force on the ball. If the forces are equal in strength, but opposite in direction, the forces cancel out. The ball does not move either to the left or to the right.

Newton's third law, however, refers to forces on two different objects. If only one player hits the ball, as shown in Figure 18A, the player exerts an upward action force on the ball. In return, the ball exerts an equal but opposite downward reaction force back on her wrists. One force is on the ball, and the other is on the player. The action and reaction forces cannot be added together because they are acting on different objects. Forces can be added together only if they are acting on the same object.

✓ *Checkpoint* *Why don't action and reaction forces cancel each other?*

Momentum

When Newton presented his three laws of motion, he used two different words to describe moving objects. He used the word velocity, but he also wrote about something that he called the "quantity of motion." What is this quantity of motion? Today we call it momentum. The **momentum** (moh MEN tum) of an object is the product of its mass and its velocity.

$$Momentum = Mass \times Velocity$$

What is the unit of measurement for momentum? Since mass is measured in kilograms and velocity is measured in meters per second, the unit for momentum is kilogram-meters per second (kg·m/s). Like velocity and acceleration, momentum is described by its direction as well as its quantity. The momentum of an object is in the same direction as its velocity.

The more momentum an object has, the harder it is to stop. You can catch a baseball moving at 20 m/s, for example, but you cannot stop a car moving at the same speed. Why does the car have more momentum than the ball? The car has more momentum because it has a greater mass.

A high velocity also can produce a large momentum, even when mass is small. A bullet shot from a rifle, for example, has a large momentum. Even though it has a small mass, it travels at a high speed.

Sample Problem

Which has more momentum: a 3-kg sledgehammer swung at 1.5 m/s or an 4-kg sledgehammer swung at 0.9 m/s?

Analyze. You know the mass and velocity of two different objects. You need to determine the momentum of each.

Write the formula. Momentum = Mass × Velocity

Substitute and solve. (a) 3 kg × 1.5 m/s = 4.5 kg·m/s

(b) 4 kg × 0.9 m/s = 3.6 kg·m/s

Think about it. The lighter hammer has more momentum than the heavier one, because it is swung at a greater velocity—almost twice as fast.

Practice Problems
1. A golf ball travels at 16 m/s, while a baseball moves at 7 m/s. The mass of the golf ball is 0.045 kg and the mass of the baseball is 0.14 kg. Which has greater momentum?
2. What is the momentum of a bird with a mass of 0.018 kg flying at 15 m/s?

Figure 19 In the absence of friction, momentum is conserved when two train cars collide. This is true regardless of whether the train cars bounce off each other or couple together during the collision. *Interpreting Diagrams In which diagram is all of the momentum transferred from car X to car Y?*

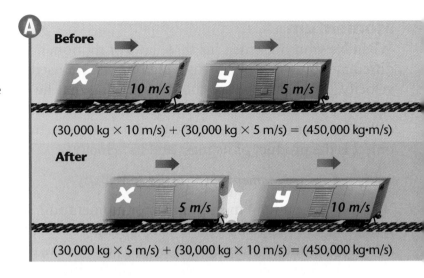

A

Before

X 10 m/s   Y 5 m/s

(30,000 kg × 10 m/s) + (30,000 kg × 5 m/s) = (450,000 kg·m/s)

After

X 5 m/s   Y 10 m/s

(30,000 kg × 5 m/s) + (30,000 kg × 10 m/s) = (450,000 kg·m/s)

Conservation of Momentum

You know that if someone bumps into you from behind, you gain momentum in the forward direction. Momentum is useful for understanding what happens when an object collides with another object. When two objects collide in the absence of friction, momentum is not lost. This fact is called the law of conservation of momentum. The **law of conservation of momentum** states that the total momentum of the objects that interact does not change. The quantity of momentum is the same before and after they interact. **The total momentum of any group of objects remains the same unless outside forces act on the objects.** Friction is an example of an outside force.

Before you hear the details of this law, you should know that the word *conservation* means something different in physical science than in everyday usage. In everyday usage, conservation means saving resources. You might conserve water or fossil fuels, for example. In physical science, the word conservation refers to conditions before and after some event. A quantity that is conserved is the same after an event as it was before the event.

Two Moving Objects Look at the two train cars traveling in the same direction on a track shown in Figure 19A. Car X is traveling at 10 m/s and car Y is traveling at 5 m/s. Eventually, car X will catch up with car Y and bump into it. During this collision, the speed of each car changes. Car X slows down to 5 m/s, and car Y speeds up to 10 m/s. Momentum is conserved— the momentum of one train car decreases while the momentum of the other increases.

One Moving Object Suppose that car X moves down the track at 10 m/s and hits car Y, which is not moving. Figure 19B shows that after the collision, car X is no longer moving, but car Y is

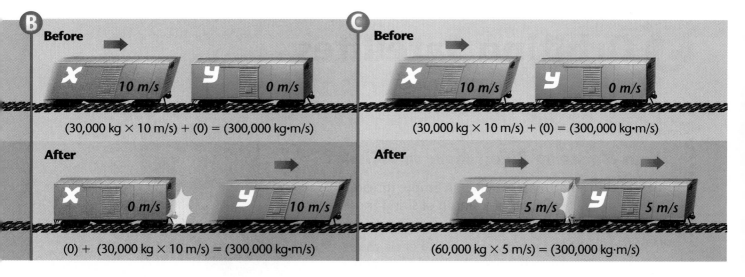

B

Before

X 10 m/s   y 0 m/s

(30,000 kg × 10 m/s) + (0) = (300,000 kg·m/s)

After

X 0 m/s   y 10 m/s

(0) + (30,000 kg × 10 m/s) = (300,000 kg·m/s)

C

Before

X 10 m/s   y 0 m/s

(30,000 kg × 10 m/s) + (0) = (300,000 kg·m/s)

After

X 5 m/s   y 5 m/s

(60,000 kg × 5 m/s) = (300,000 kg·m/s)

moving. Even though the situation has changed, momentum is still conserved. The total momentum is the same before and after the collision. This time, all of the momentum has been transferred from car X to car Y.

Two Connected Objects Now suppose that, instead of bouncing off each other, the two train cars couple together when they hit. Is momentum still conserved? The answer is yes. You can see in Figure 19C that the total momentum before the collision is again 300,000 kg·m/s. But after the collision, the coupled train cars make one object with a total mass of 60,000 kilograms (30,000 kilograms + 30,000 kilograms). The velocity of the coupled trains is 5 m/s—half the velocity of car X before the collision. Since the mass is doubled, the velocity must be divided in half in order for momentum to be conserved.

Section 4 Review

1. According to Newton's third law of motion, how are action and reaction forces related?
2. What is meant by "conservation of momentum"?
3. Suppose you and a friend, who has exactly twice your mass, are on skates. You push away from your friend. How does the force with which you push your friend compare to the force with which your friend pushes you? How do your accelerations compare?
4. **Thinking Critically** Comparing and Contrasting Which has more momentum, a 250-kg dolphin swimming at 6 m/s, or a 450-kg manatee swimming at 2 m/s?

CHAPTER PROJECT

Check Your Progress
Construct your vehicle. Is your vehicle powered according to Newton's third law of motion? Add to your diagram so that it shows the force exerted by your vehicle and the force exerted on your vehicle to make it move. What exerts the force that moves your vehicle? Be ready to explain the diagram to other students.

SECTION 5 Orbiting Satellites

DISCOVER •••••••••••••••••••••••••••••••••••••••ACTIVITY•••

What Makes an Object Move in a Circle?

1. Tie a small mass, such as an empty thread spool, to the end of a length of string (no more than one meter long).

2. Swing the object rapidly around in a circle that is perpendicular to the floor. Make sure no one is near the swinging object, and don't let it go!

3. Predict what will happen if you decrease the speed of the object. Test your prediction.

4. Predict how the length of the string affects the motion of the object. Test your prediction.

Think It Over
Forming Operational Definitions Describe the motion of the object. How do you know that the string exerts a force?

GUIDE FOR READING

◆ How does a rocket lift off the ground?

◆ What keeps a satellite in orbit?

Reading Tip As you read, make a list of main ideas and supporting details about rockets and satellites.

What would it be like to be at Cape Canaveral in Florida for a space shuttle launch? The countdown is broadcast over a loudspeaker—ten—nine—eight—seven—six—five—four. White steam comes out of the base of the rocket—three—two—one. The rocket rises into space and begins to turn slightly and roll. The noise hits you, and the ground shakes. With an astonishingly loud rumble, the rocket rises in the distance. Everyone cheers. You watch the rocket until it is too far away to see.

How Do Rockets Lift Off?

The awesome achievement of lifting a rocket into space against the force of gravity can be explained using Newton's third law of motion. As a rocket burns fuel, it expels exhaust gases. When the gases are forced out of the rocket, they exert an equal and opposite force back on

Figure 20 The action force pushes the rocket's exhaust gases downward. The reaction force sends the rocket into space.

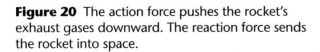

the rocket. **A rocket can rise into the air because the gases it expels with a downward force exert an equal but opposite force on the rocket.** As long as this upward pushing force, called thrust, is greater than the downward pull of gravity, there is a net force in the upward direction. As a result, the rocket accelerates upward.

Figure 21 As this rocket moves higher, its path tilts more and more. Eventually its path is parallel to Earth's surface. *Predicting How will the direction of the accelerating force change?*

☑ *Checkpoint* *When a rocket is launched, what is the direction of the reaction force?*

What Is a Satellite?

Rockets are often used to carry satellites into space. A **satellite** is any object that travels around another object in space. An artificial satellite is a device that is launched into orbit around Earth. Artificial satellites are designed for many purposes. They are used in space research, communications, military intelligence, weather analysis, and geographical surveys.

Circular Motion Artificial satellites travel around Earth in an almost circular path. Recall that an object traveling in a circle is accelerating because it is constantly changing direction. If an object is accelerating, there must be a force acting on it to change its motion. Any force that causes an object to move in a circle is called a **centripetal force** (sen TRIP ih tul). The word *centripetal* means "center-seeking." For a satellite, the centripetal force is the gravitational force that pulls the satellite toward the center of Earth.

Satellite Motion If gravity pulls satellites toward Earth, why doesn't a satellite fall, as a ball thrown into the air would? The answer is that satellites do not travel straight up into the air. Instead, they move around Earth. If you throw a ball horizontally, for example, it will move out in front of you at the same time that it is pulled to the ground. If you throw the ball faster, it will land even farther in front of you. The faster you throw a projectile, the farther it travels before it lands.

Figure 22 The faster a projectile like this ball is thrown, the farther it travels before it hits the ground.

Figure 23 A projectile with enough velocity will move in a circular orbit around Earth. *Interpreting Diagrams The force of gravity is always toward the center of Earth. How does the direction of gravity compare to the direction of the projectile's motion at any point?*

Isaac Newton wondered what would happen if you were on a high mountain and were able to throw a stone as fast as you wanted. The faster you threw it, the farther away it would land. At a certain speed, the path of the object would match the curve of Earth. Although the stone would keep falling due to gravity, Earth's surface would curve away from the stone at the same rate. Thus the object would circle Earth, as in Figure 23.

Satellites in orbit around Earth continually fall toward Earth, but because Earth is curved they travel around it. In other words, a satellite is a projectile that falls around Earth rather than into it. A satellite does not need fuel because it continues to move ahead due to its inertia. At the same time, gravity continuously changes the satellite's direction. The speed with which an object must be thrown in order to orbit Earth turns out to be about 7,900 m/s! This speed is almost 200 times as fast as a pitcher can throw a baseball.

Satellite Location Some satellites, such as the space shuttle, are put into low orbits. The time to complete a trip around Earth in a low orbit is about 90 minutes. Other satellites are sent into higher orbits. At these distances, the satellite travels more slowly and takes longer to circle Earth. For example, communications satellites travel about 36,000 kilometers above the surface. At this height they circle Earth once every 24 hours. Since Earth rotates once every 24 hours, a satellite above the equator always stays above the same point on Earth as it orbits.

Section 5 Review

1. Use action-reaction forces to explain why a rocket can lift off the ground.
2. Why doesn't an orbiting satellite fall back to Earth?
3. Is it correct to say that satellites stay in orbit rather than falling to Earth because they are beyond the pull of Earth's gravity? Explain.
4. **Thinking Critically Applying Concepts** When a rocket travels higher, air resistance decreases as the air becomes less dense. The force of gravity also decreases because the rocket is farther from Earth, and the rocket's mass decreases as its fuel is used up. Explain how acceleration is affected.

Science at Home

Swing the Bucket Fill a small plastic bucket halfway with water and take it outdoors. Challenge a family member to swing the bucket in a vertical circle. Explain that the water won't fall out at the top if the bucket is moving fast enough. Tell your family member that if the bucket falls as fast as the water, the water will stay in the bucket. Relate this activity to a satellite that also falls due to gravity, yet remains in orbit.

The Nature of Force

Key Ideas
◆ The sum of all the forces acting on an object is the net force.
◆ Unbalanced forces change the motion of an object, whereas balanced forces do not.
◆ According to Newton's first law of motion, an object at rest will remain at rest and an object in motion will continue in motion at constant speed unless the object is acted upon by an unbalanced force.

Key Terms
force   balanced forces
net force   inertia
unbalanced forces

 Force, Mass, and Acceleration

Key Idea
◆ Newton's second law of motion states that the net force on an object is the product of its acceleration and its mass.

Key Term
newton

 Friction and Gravity

Key Ideas
◆ Friction is a force that one surface exerts on another when they rub against each other.
◆ Weight is a measure of the force of gravity on an object, and mass is a measure of the amount of matter that an object contains.
◆ The force of gravity acts between all objects in the universe.

Key Terms
friction   free fall
sliding friction   projectile
rolling friction   air resistance
fluid friction   terminal velocity
gravity

 Action and Reaction

Key Ideas
◆ Newton's third law of motion states that every time there is an action force on an object, the object will exert an equal and opposite reaction force.
◆ The momentum of an object is the product of its mass and its velocity.
◆ The law of conservation of momentum states that the total momentum is the same before and after an event, as long as there are no outside forces.

Key Terms
momentum
law of conservation of momentum

Orbiting Satellites

INTEGRATING SPACE SCIENCE

Key Ideas
◆ A rocket burns fuel and produces gases. The rocket pushes these gases downward. At the same time, the gases apply an equal force to the rocket, pushing it upward.
◆ Even though a satellite is pulled downward by gravity, it stays in orbit because it is moving so quickly. Earth's surface curves away from the satellite as the satellite falls.

Key Terms
satellite   centripetal force

Organizing Information

Compare/Contrast Table Copy the compare/contrast table below on a separate sheet of paper. Complete the table to compare and contrast friction and gravity. (For more information on compare/ contrast tables see the Skills Handbook.)

Force	Direction of Force	Force Depends Upon
Friction	a. ?	b. ?
Gravity	c. ?	d. ?

Reviewing Content

 For more review of key concepts, see the Interactive Student Tutorial CD-ROM.

Multiple Choice
Choose the letter of the best answer.

1. When an unbalanced force acts on an object, the force
   a. changes the motion of the object.
   b. is canceled by another force.
   c. does not change the motion of the object.
   d. is equal to the weight of the object.

2. When two equal forces act in opposite directions on an object, they are called
   a. friction forces. b. balanced forces.
   c. centripetal forces. d. gravitational forces.

3. The resistance of an object to any change in its motion is called
   a. inertia. b. friction.
   c. gravity. d. weight.

4. According to Newton's second law of motion, force is equal to mass times
   a. inertia. b. weight.
   c. direction. d. acceleration.

5. The product of an object's mass and its velocity is called the object's
   a. net force. b. weight.
   c. momentum. d. gravitation.

True or False
If the statement is true, write true. If it is false, change the underlined word or words to make the statement true.

6. According to Newton's third law of motion, whenever you exert a force on an object, the object exerts a force back on you that is <u>greater than</u> your force.

7. Mass is a measure of the amount of <u>force</u> that an object has.

8. <u>Weight</u> is the measure of the force of gravity exerted on an object.

9. <u>Conservation</u> in science refers to the amount of some quantity staying the same before and after an event.

10. The force that causes a satellite to orbit Earth is <u>gravity</u>.

Checking Concepts

11. Explain how force, mass, and acceleration are related.

12. Why do slippery fluids such as oil reduce sliding friction?

13. One student tosses a chalkboard eraser horizontally so that the eraser hits the ground 5 meters away. At exactly the same time, another student drops an eraser. Which eraser hits the ground first? Explain.

14. Explain why a flat sheet of paper dropped from a height of 2 meters will not accelerate at the same rate as a sheet of paper crumpled into a ball.

15. Why do athletes' shoes often have cleats?

16. Compare your mass and weight on Earth with your mass and weight on an asteroid, which is much smaller than Earth.

17. When you drop a golf ball to the pavement, it bounces up. Is a force needed to make it bounce up? If so, what exerts the force?

18. Draw a diagram showing the motion of a satellite around Earth. Is the satellite accelerating?

19. **Writing to Learn** You are a reporter for a local television station, and you like to give your stories a physical-science twist. Write a story for the evening news in which you describe an event in terms of the forces involved. Use a catchy title.

Thinking Critically

20. **Comparing and Contrasting** If you stand up in a rowboat and take a step toward the dock, you may fall in the water. Explain what happens in this situation. How is it similar to what happens when you take a step on land? How is it different?

21. **Problem Solving** If a toy train has a mass of 1.5 kg and accelerates at a rate of 20 m/s², calculate the force acting on it.

22. **Applying Concepts** You are riding fast on a skateboard when your wheel suddenly gets stuck in a crack on the sidewalk. Using the term *inertia*, explain what happens.

Applying Skills

Use the illustration showing a collision between two balls to answer Questions 23–25.

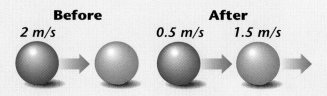

Before **After**
2 m/s   0.5 m/s   1.5 m/s

23. **Calculating** Use the formula for momentum to find the momentum of each ball before and after the collision. Assume the mass of each ball is 0.4 kg.
24. **Inferring** Find the total momentum before and after collision. Is the law of conservation of momentum satisfied in this collision? Explain.
25. **Designing Experiments** Design an experiment in which you could show that momentum is not conserved between the balls when friction is strong.

Performance CHAPTER PROJECT **Assessment**

Present Your Project Test your vehicle to make sure it will work on the type of floor in your classroom. Will the vehicle stay within the bounds set by your teacher? Identify all the forces acting on the vehicle. List at least three features you included in the design of the vehicle that led to an improvement in its performance. For example, did you give it a smooth shape for low air resistance?

Reflect and Record What was the most significant source of friction for your vehicle? What was the most successful way to overcome the friction? In your journal, describe the features of your vehicle that led to its success or that kept it from succeeding.

Test Preparation

Use these questions to prepare for standardized tests.

Read the passage. Then answer Questions 26–30.

Hannah needs to move a bag of volleyball equipment 15 m across the gymnasium floor. The mass of the bag is 30 kg. Hannah pulls with a force of 60 N. Her friend helps and pulls with a force of 45 N. The friction force between the bag and the floor is 15 N.

26. What is the net force on the bag?
    a. 90 N
    b. 105 N
    c. 120 N
    d. 15 N
27. What law can you use to calculate the acceleration of the bag?
    a. Newton's First Law of Motion
    b. Newton's Second Law of Motion
    c. Newton's Third Law of Motion
    d. the Law of Universal Gravitation

28. What is the acceleration of the bag?
    a. 3.0 m/s
    b. 3.0 m/s^2
    c. 3.5 m/s^2
    d. 4.0 m/s
29. How could the girls make the bag accelerate more?
    a. They could move it a shorter distance.
    b. They could add mass to it.
    c. They could exert a smaller force.
    d. They could exert a greater force.
30. What would happen to the motion if a third student pulled the bag in the opposite direction with a force of 40 N?
    a. The bag will move in the opposite direction.
    b. The bag will stop moving.
    c. The bag will continue to move in the same direction, but it will accelerate more slowly.
    d. The bag will continue to move in the same direction, but it will accelerate more quickly.

SECTION 1 Pressure

Discover **Can You Blow Up a Balloon in a Bottle?**
Sharpen Your Skills **Developing Hypotheses**
Science at Home **Under Pressure**
Real-World Lab **Spinning Sprinklers**

SECTION 2 Transmitting Pressure in a Fluid

Discover **How Does Pressure Change?**

SECTION 3 Floating and Sinking

Discover **What Can You Measure With a Straw?**
Sharpen Your Skills **Measuring**
Skills Lab **Sink and Spill**
Try This **Dive!**

Staying Afloat

With its powerful hind legs, a frog can jump several times its own length—if it is on land. This frog isn't exerting itself. Instead, it's swimming slowly and letting the water carry its weight. Whether an object sinks or floats depends on more than just its weight. In this chapter, you will learn about forces that act in water and other fluids. You will find out how these forces make an object sink or float. You will also learn how these forces make common devices work.

Your Goal To construct a boat that can carry a cargo and float in water. You should compare different materials and designs in order to build the most efficient boat you can.

Your boat should
◆ be made of metal only
◆ support a cargo of 50 pennies without allowing any water to enter for at least 10 seconds
◆ be built following the safety guidelines in Appendix A

Get Started Begin by thinking about the shape of real ships. Then look for common objects made from metal that you can form into a boat. You might want to look ahead at Section 3 to learn more about what makes an object float.

Check Your Progress You'll be working on this project as you study this chapter. To keep your project on track, look for Check Your Progress boxes at the following points.
Section 2 Review, page 357: Experiment with materials and shapes.
Section 3 Review, page 364: Measure the weight of your boat, and modify your design.

Present Your Project At the end of the chapter (page 371), launch your boat to see if it will float and to show that it can carry its cargo of pennies.

A frog barely shows its head above the water as it waits for its breakfast to fly by.

Integrating Technology

SECTION 4 Applying Bernoulli's Principle

Discover Does Water Push or Pull?
Science at Home Atomizer

1 Pressure

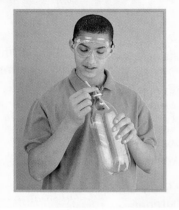

ACTIVITY

Can You Blow Up a Balloon in a Bottle?

1. Holding the neck, insert a balloon into an empty bottle. Try to blow up the balloon.

2. Now insert a straw into the bottle, next to the balloon. Keep one end of the straw sticking out of the container as shown in the photo. Try again to blow up the balloon.

Think It Over
Developing Hypotheses Did holding the straw next to the balloon make a difference? If it did, develop a hypothesis to explain why.

GUIDE FOR READING

◆ What causes pressure in fluids?

◆ How does pressure change with altitude and depth?

Reading Tip Before you read, write down what you know about pressure. Then check how your understanding of pressure changes as you read.

Think of the last time you heard a friend say "I'm under a lot of pressure!" Maybe she was talking about having two tests on the same day. That sort of pressure is over in a day or two. But everyone is under another kind of pressure that never lets up. This pressure, as you will learn, is due to the air that surrounds you!

What Is Pressure?

The word *pressure* is related to the word *press.* It refers to a force pushing on a surface. For example, when you lean against a wall, you push against the wall and so exert pressure on it. When you stand on the ground, the force of gravity pulls you downward. So the soles of your shoes push down on the ground and exert pressure on it.

Figure 1 Snowshoes make it easier to travel in deep snow. The woman on the right wishes she had a pair.

Force and Pressure Suppose you try to walk on top of deep snow. Most likely you will sink into the snow, much as the woman on the right in Figure 1. But if you walk with snowshoes, you will be able to walk without sinking. The downward force you exert on the snow—your weight—doesn't change. Your weight is the same whether you wear boots or snowshoes. So what's the difference?

The difference is the size of the area over which your weight is distributed. When your weight is distributed over the smaller area of the soles of your boots, you sink. When your weight is distributed over the much larger area of the snowshoes, you don't sink. The larger area results in less downward pressure on the snow. So force and pressure are closely related, but they are not the same thing.

Calculating Pressure The relationship of force, area, and pressure is summarized by this formula.

$$Pressure = \frac{Force}{Area}$$

Pressure is equal to the force exerted on a surface divided by the total area over which the force is exerted. Force is measured in newtons (N). When area is measured in square meters (m²), the SI unit of pressure is the newton per square meter (N/m²). This unit of pressure is also called the **pascal** (Pa): 1 N/m² = 1 Pa.

A smaller unit of measure for area is often more practical to use, such as a square centimeter instead of a square meter. When square centimeters are used, the unit of pressure is N/cm².

Area

Area is a measure of a surface. The area of a rectangle is found by multiplying the length by the width. The area of the rectangle below is 2 cm × 3 cm, or 6 cm².

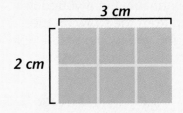

Notice that area is written as cm². This is read as "square centimeter."

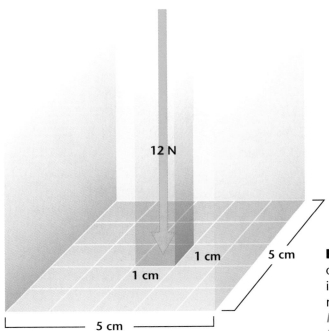

Figure 2 The force a fluid exerts on each square centimeter in the illustration is 12 N. So the resulting pressure is 12 N/cm². *Problem Solving What is the total force on the entire bottom surface?*

If you took a sip from the straw on the left, you would be able to drink the lemonade. But if you took a sip from the straw on the right, you would not be able to quench your thirst.

What is the difference between the two illustrations? What can you conclude about how you drink through a straw? Write a hypothesis that explains why you can drink through one straw and not the other.

You can produce a lower pressure by increasing the area a force acts on. Or you can work the other way around. You can produce a much higher pressure by decreasing the area a force acts on. For instance, the blades of ice skates have a very small surface area. They exert a much higher pressure on the ice than ordinary shoes would.

Fluid Pressure

In this chapter, you will learn about the pressure exerted by fluids. A **fluid** is a substance that can easily flow. As a result, a fluid is able to change shape. Both liquids and gases have this property. Air, helium, water, and oil are all fluids.

Fluids exert pressure against the surfaces they touch. To understand how fluids exert forces on surfaces, you must think about the particles that make up the fluid. Fluids, like all matter, are made up of molecules. These molecules are tiny particles that are much too small to be seen using your eyes or even a good microscope. One liter of water contains about 33 trillion trillion molecules (that's 33 followed by 24 zeros)!

In fluids, molecules are constantly moving in all directions. In air, for example, molecules are moving around at high speeds. They are constantly colliding with each other and with any surface that they meet.

As each molecule collides with a surface, it exerts a force on the surface. **All of the forces exerted by the individual molecules in a fluid add together to make up the pressure exerted by the fluid.** The number of particles is so large that you can consider the fluid as if it were not made up of individual particles. Thus fluid pressure is the total force exerted by the fluid divided by the area over which the force is exerted.

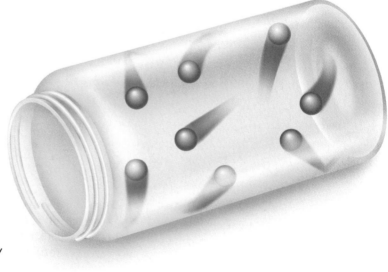

Figure 3 In a gas, molecules move at different speeds in all directions. As they hit surfaces, the molecules exert forces on those surfaces. The total force divided by the area of the surface gives the pressure of the gas. *Inferring Do you think that the pressure inside the jar is the same as the pressure outside the jar? How can you tell?*

Fluid Pressure All Around

Hold your hand out in front of you, palm up. You are holding up a weight equivalent to that of a washing machine. How can this be? You are surrounded by a fluid that presses down on you all the time. This fluid is the mixture of gases that makes up Earth's atmosphere. The pressure exerted by the air is usually referred to as air pressure, or atmospheric pressure.

Air exerts pressure because it has mass. You may forget that air has mass, but each cubic meter of air around you has a mass of about 1 kilogram. The force of gravity on this mass produces air pressure. The pressure from the weight of air in the atmosphere is great because the atmosphere is over 100 kilometers high.

Average air pressure at sea level is about 10.13 N/cm^2. Think about a square measuring one centimeter by one centimeter on the palm of your hand. Air is pushing against that small square with a force of 10.13 newtons. The total surface area of your hand is probably about 100 square centimeters. So the total force due to the air pressure on your hand is about 1,000 newtons.

☑ *Checkpoint* *Why does the atmosphere exert pressure on you?*

Balanced Pressures

How could your hand possibly support the weight of the atmosphere when you don't feel a thing? In a fluid that is not moving, pressure at a given point is exerted equally in all directions. Air is pushing down on the palm of your hand with 10.13 N/cm^2 of pressure. It is also pushing up on the back of your hand with the same 10.13 N/cm^2 of pressure. These two pressures balance each other exactly.

INTEGRATING LIFE SCIENCE So why aren't you crushed even though the air pressure outside your body is so great? The reason again has to do with a balance of pressures. Pressure inside your body balances the air pressure outside your body. But where does the pressure inside your body come from? It comes from fluids within your body. Some parts of your body, such as your lungs, sinus cavities, and your inner ear, contain air. Other parts of your body, such as your cells and your blood, contain liquids.

Figure 4 The pressure within a fluid is the same at any given level and is exerted in all directions. So the pressure pushing down on your hand is the same as the pressure pushing up. That's why you don't feel any pressure at all.

Figure 5 A vacuum pump removes the air from a metal can. The pump produces dramatic results in a few moments.
Inferring Can you think of a way to crush the can without pumping out the air inside it? Explain why your idea works.

Are you still having trouble believing that the air pressure around you is so high? Take a look at the metal container in Figure 5. When the can is filled with air, the air pressure pushing out from within the can balances the air pressure pushing in on the can. But when the air is removed from the can, there is no longer the same pressure pushing from within the can. The greater air pressure outside the can crushes it.

☑ *Checkpoint* *What is the effect of balanced pressures acting on an object?*

Variations in Fluid Pressure

The pressure of a fluid is the same at any given level in the fluid. But what happens to pressure as you move up to a higher elevation or down to a deeper depth within a fluid?

Pressure and Elevation Have your ears ever "popped" as you rode up in an elevator? **Air pressure decreases as elevation increases.** Remember that air pressure at a given point results from the weight of air above that point. At higher elevations, there is less air above and therefore less weight of air to support.

The fact that air pressure decreases as you move up in elevation explains why your ears pop. When the air pressure outside your body changes, the air pressure inside will adjust too, but more slowly. For a moment, the air pressure behind your eardrums is greater than it is outside. Your body releases this pressure with a "pop" so that the pressures are once again balanced.

Pressure and Depth Fluid pressure depends on depth. The pressure at one meter below the surface of a swimming pool is the same as the pressure one meter below the surface of a lake. But if you dive deeper into the water in either case, pressure becomes greater as you descend. The deeper you swim, the greater the pressure you feel. **Water pressure increases as depth increases.**

As with air, you can think of water pressure being due to the weight of the water above a particular point. At greater depths, there is more water above and therefore more weight to support. In addition, air in the atmosphere pushes down on the water. Therefore, the total pressure at a given point beneath the water results from the weight of the water plus the weight of the air above it. In the deepest parts of the ocean, the pressure is more than 1,000 times the air pressure you experience every day.

Figure 6 The strength of the stream of water coming out of the holes in the jug depends on the water pressure at each level. *Interpreting Photos At which hole is the pressure greatest?*

Section 1 Review

1. Explain how fluids exert pressure.
2. How does air pressure change as you move farther away from the surface of Earth? Explain why it changes.
3. Why aren't deep-sea fish crushed by the tremendous pressure of the water above them?
4. **Thinking Critically Applying Concepts** Why do you think an astronaut must wear a pressurized suit in space?
5. **Thinking Critically Comparing and Contrasting** Suppose a woman wearing high-heeled shoes has a mass of 50 kg and an elephant has a mass of 5,000 kg. Explain how the woman can exert pressure on a floor about three times the pressure exerted by the elephant.

Science at Home

Under Pressure Fill a small plastic container—a bottle or a cup—to the brim with water. Place an index card over the entire opening of the container. Ask your family to predict what would happen if the container were turned upside down. Test the predictions by slowly turning the container upside down while holding the cardboard in place. Let go of the cardboard and see what happens. Without touching the cardboard, turn the container on its side. Use air pressure to explain why the cardboard stays in place and why the water stays in the container.

Spinning Sprinklers

There's nothing like running through a lawn sprinkler on a hot summer day. One type of sprinkler uses the pressure of the escaping water to cause it to spin. Its operation is similar to an ancient device known as Hero's engine. Hero's engine used the pressure of escaping steam to cause a sphere to spin.

Problem

What factors affect the speed of rotation of a lawn sprinkler?

Skills Focus

making models, designing experiments, controlling variables

Materials

6 empty soda cans with tabs attached
fishing line, 30 cm
waterproof marker
wide-mouth jar or beaker
stopwatch or clock with second hand
small nail
medium nail
large nail
large basin to catch water

Procedure

1. Fill the jar with enough water to completely cover a can. Place it in the basin.
2. Bend up the tab of a can and tie the end of a length of fishing line to it. **CAUTION:** *Be careful not to cut yourself on the edge of the can opening.*
3. Place a mark on the can to help you keep track of how many times the can spins.
4. Using the small nail, make a hole in the side of the can about 1 cm up from the bottom. Poke the nail straight in. Then twist the nail until it makes a right angle with the radius of the can. See the diagram below. **CAUTION:** *Nails are sharp and should be used only to puncture the cans.*

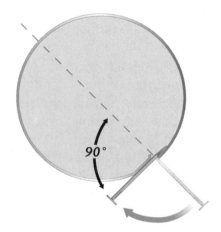

90°

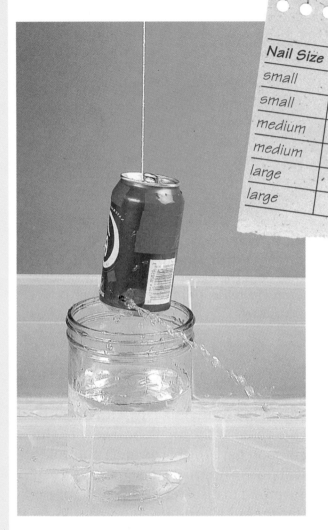

Nail Size	# of Holes	# of spins in 15 seconds
small	1	
small	2	
medium	1	
medium	2	
large	1	
large	2	

DATA TABLE

5. Submerge the can in the jar and fill the can to the top with water.

6. Quickly lift the can with the fishing line so that it is 1–2 cm above the water level in the jar. Count how many spins the can completes in 15 seconds. Record the result.

7. Design a way to investigate how the size of the hole affects the number of spins made by the can. Propose a hypothesis and then test the relationship. Record your results.

8. Design a way to investigate how the number of holes affects the number of spins made by the can. Propose a hypothesis and then test the relationship. Record your results.

Analyze and Conclude

1. How does the size of the hole affect the rate of spin of the can?

2. How does the number of holes affect the rate of spin of the can?

3. Explain the motion of the can in terms of water pressure.

4. Explain the motion of the can in terms of Newton's third law of motion (Chapter 10).

5. How could you make the can spin in the opposite direction?

6. What will cause the can to stop spinning?

7. You made a hole in the can at about 1 cm above the bottom of the can. Predict what would happen if you made the hole at a higher point on the can. How could you test your prediction?

8. **Apply** Use your observations to explain why a spinning lawn sprinkler spins.

Getting Involved

Many sprinkler systems use water pressure to spin the sprinklers. Examine one of these sprinklers to see the size, direction, and number of holes. What would happen if you could put a second sprinkler in line with the first?

② Transmitting Pressure in a Fluid

DISCOVER · ACTIVITY · · ·

How Does Pressure Change?

1. Fill an empty two-liter plastic bottle to the top with water. Then screw on the cap tightly. There should be no bubbles in the bottle (or only very small bubbles).

2. Lay the bottle on its side. Pick a spot on the bottle, and push in with your left thumb.

3. With your right thumb, push in fairly hard on a spot at the other end of the bottle, as shown in the diagram. What does your left thumb feel?

4. Pick another spot on the bottle for your left thumb and repeat Step 3.

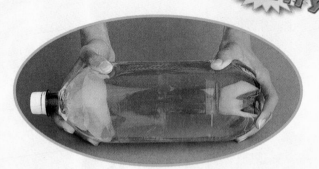

Think It Over

Observing When you push in with your right thumb, does the water pressure in the bottle increase, decrease, or remain the same? How do you know?

GUIDE FOR READING

◆ What does Pascal's principle say about an increase in fluid pressure?

◆ How does a hydraulic device work?

Reading Tip As you read, make a list of devices that apply Pascal's principle. Write one sentence describing each device.

Piercing sirens shatter the morning quiet. Dark smoke rolls into the air. Bright flames shoot from a burning building. Firefighters arrive on the scene. Quickly, with the push of a button, a huge ladder is raised to the top floor. The firefighters climb up the ladder and soon have the blaze under control.

Thanks to equipment on the firetruck, this story has a happy ending. You might be surprised to discover that the truck is capable of using fluids to lift the ladder and its equipment to great heights. As you read on, you'll find out how.

Figure 7 A fire truck uses fluids under high pressure both to lift its ladder and to put out a fire.

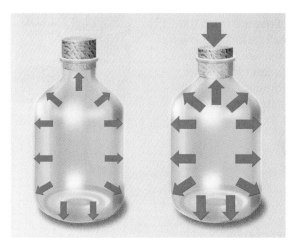

Figure 8 A liquid completely filling a bottle exerts pressure in all directions. When the stopper is pushed farther into the bottle, the pressure increases. *Predicting Suppose you poked a hole in the side of the bottle. What would happen when you pushed down on the stopper? Explain why.*

Pascal's Principle

As you learned in the last section, a fluid exerts pressure on any surface in contact with it. For example, the water in each bottle in Figure 8 exerts pressure on the entire inside surface of the bottle—up, down, and sideways.

What happens if you push the stopper down even farther? The water has nowhere to go, so it presses harder on the inside surface of the bottle. The pressure in the water increases everywhere in the bottle. This is shown by the increased width of the arrows on the right in Figure 8.

Pressure increases by the same amount throughout an enclosed, or confined, fluid. This fact was discovered in the 1600s by a French mathematician named Blaise Pascal. (Pascal's name is used for the unit of pressure.) **When force is applied to a confined fluid, an increase in pressure is transmitted equally to all parts of the fluid.** This relationship is known as **Pascal's principle.**

Force Pumps

What would happen if you increased the pressure at one end of a fluid in a container with a hole at the other end? If you have ever used a squeeze bottle or a tube of toothpaste, you already know what happens. Because it is not confined by the container, the fluid is pushed out of the opening. This simple example shows you how a force pump works. A force pump causes a fluid to move from one place to another by increasing the pressure in the fluid.

Your heart consists of two force pumps. One of them pumps blood to the lungs, where it can pick up oxygen from the air you breathe. This blood, now carrying oxygen, returns to your heart. It is then pumped to the rest of the body by the second pump.

☑ *Checkpoint* **What is the effect on fluid pressure if you press down on the stopper of a bottle full of water?**

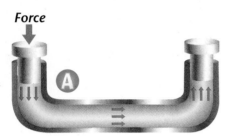

Figure 9 **A.** In a hydraulic device, a force applied to one piston increases the pressure in the fluid.

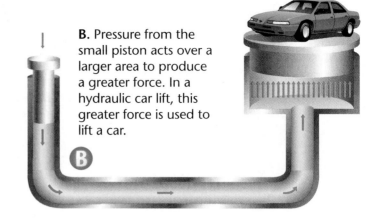

B. Pressure from the small piston acts over a larger area to produce a greater force. In a hydraulic car lift, this greater force is used to lift a car.

Using Pascal's Principle

Suppose you fill the small U-shaped tube shown in Figure 9A with water and push down on the piston on the left side. (A piston is similar to a stopper that can slide up and down inside the tube.) The increase in pressure will be transmitted to the piston on the right.

What can you determine about the force exerted on the right piston? According to Pascal's principle, both pistons will experience the same fluid pressure. If both pistons have the same area, then they will also experience the same force.

Now suppose that the right piston has a greater area than the left piston. For example, the small piston in the U-shaped tube in Figure 9B has an area of 1 square meter. The large piston has an area of 20 square meters. If you push down on the left piston with a force of 500 newtons, the increase in pressure on the fluid is 500 N/m^2. A pressure increase of 500 N/m^2 means that the force on every square meter of the piston's surface increases by 500 newtons. Since the surface area of the right piston is 20 square meters, the total increase in force on the right piston is 10,000 newtons. The push exerted on the left piston is multiplied twenty times on the right piston! Depending on the size of the pistons, you can multiply force by any amount.

Hydraulic Systems **Hydraulic systems** are designed to take advantage of Pascal's principle. **A hydraulic system multiplies a force by applying the force to a small surface area. The increase in pressure is then transmitted to another part of a confined fluid, which pushes on a larger surface area.** In this way, the force is multiplied. A common hydraulic system is used to lift the heavy ladder on a fire truck.

You also rely on Pascal's principle every time you ride in a car. The brake system of a car is a hydraulic system. A brake system with disc brakes is shown in simplified form in Figure 10. When a driver pushes down on

Figure 10 The hydraulic brake system of a car multiplies the force exerted on the brake pedal.

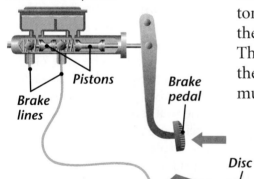

Pistons

Brake lines

Brake pedal

Disc

Brake fluid

Pistons

Brake pad

Fluid

Tube foot

Figure 11 A sea star exerts pressure on fluids in its cavities in order to move around. *Classifying* Why are the tube feet considered part of a hydraulic device?

the brake pedal, he or she pushes a piston. The piston exerts pressure on the brake fluid. The increased pressure is transmitted through the brake lines to pistons within the wheels of the car. Each of these pistons pushes on a brake pad. The brake pad then rubs against the brake disc, and the wheel's motion is slowed down by the force of friction. Because the brake system multiplies force, a person can stop a very large car with only a light push on the brake pedal.

Pascal's Principle in Nature The sea stars shown in Figure 11

 INTEGRATING LIFE SCIENCE use a natural hydraulic system called the water vascular system in order to move. Sea stars have rows of small suckers at the ends of their hollow tube feet. Each tube foot is filled with fluid. A valve is located at each foot. When the valve closes, the foot becomes a hydraulic container. As the sea star contracts different muscles, it changes the pressure in the fluid. The change in pressure causes the tube foot to push down on the sucker. By the coordinated action of all of its tube feet, a sea star is able to move—even to climb straight up rock surfaces!

Section 2 Review

1. Explain Pascal's principle in your own words.
2. How does a hydraulic device multiply force?
3. What fluid is pumped by your heart?
4. **Thinking Critically Applying Concepts** How can you increase the force a hydraulic device produces without increasing the size of the force you apply to the small piston?
5. **Thinking Critically Comparing and Contrasting** How is the braking system of a car similar to the water vascular system of a sea star?

Check Your Progress ····· CHAPTER PROJECT

Experiment with various metal items in your home to see how they work as boats. Keep in mind that your designs don't have to look like real boats. Experiment with various shapes. Determine how the material and the shape relate to whether or not the boat floats or sinks. What works better: a wide but shallow boat or a narrow but deep boat? Keep a log that describes the material, the shape, and your results.

SECTION 3 Floating and Sinking

DISCOVER · ACTIVITY · · · ·

What Can You Measure With a Straw?

1. Cut a plastic straw to a 10-centimeter length.

2. Use a waterproof marker to make marks on the straw that are 1 centimeter apart.

3. Roll a ball of modeling clay about 1.5 centimeters in diameter. Stick one end of the straw in the clay. You have constructed a hydrometer.

4. Place the hydrometer in a glass of water. If it sinks, remove some clay. About half of the straw should remain above water. Make sure no water gets into the straw.

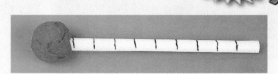

5. Dissolve 10 spoonfuls of sugar in a glass of water. Try out your hydrometer in this liquid.

Think It Over

Predicting Compare your observations in Steps 4 and 5. Then predict what will happen if you use 20 spoonfuls of sugar in a glass of water. Test your prediction.

GUIDE FOR READING

◆ **What is the efffect of the buoyant force?**

◆ **What is Archimedes' principle?**

◆ **How does the density of an object determine whether it floats or sinks?**

Reading Tip As you read, write a paragraph explaining how buoyancy and Archimedes' principle are related.

I n April of 1912, the *Titanic* departed from England on its first and only voyage. It was as long as three football fields and as tall as a twelve-story building. It was the largest ship that had been built until that time, and its furnishings were the finest and most luxurious. The *Titanic* was also the most technologically advanced ship afloat. Its hull was divided into compartments, and it was considered to be unsinkable.

Yet a few days into the voyage, the *Titanic* struck an iceberg. Two hours and forty minutes later, the bow of the great ship slipped underwater. As the stern rose high into the air, the ship broke in two. Both pieces sank to the bottom of the Atlantic Ocean. More than a thousand people died.

Figure 12 This painting shows the bow section of the *Titanic* resting on the sea floor.

How is it possible that a huge ship can float easily in water under certain conditions? Yet in a few hours the same ship can become a sunken wreck. And why does most of an iceberg lie hidden beneath the surface of the water? To answer these questions, you need to find out what makes an object float and what makes an object sink.

Buoyancy

If you have ever picked up an object under water, you know that it seems lighter in water than in air. Water exerts a force called the **buoyant force** that acts on a submerged object. **The buoyant force acts in the upward direction, against the force of gravity, so it makes an object feel lighter.**

As you can see in Figure 13, a fluid exerts pressure on all surfaces of a submerged object. Since the pressure in a fluid increases with depth, the upward pressure on the bottom of the object is greater than the downward pressure on the top. The result is a net force acting upward on the submerged object. This is the buoyant force.

A submerged object displaces, or takes the place of, a volume of fluid equal to its own volume. You can see this by looking at Figure 14. An object that floats on the surface of a fluid, however, displaces a smaller volume. It displaces a volume of fluid equal to the portion of the object that is submerged.

Archimedes' principle relates the amount of fluid a submerged object displaces to the buoyant force on the object. This relationship is named for its discoverer, the ancient Greek mathematician Archimedes. **Archimedes' principle states that the buoyant force on an object is equal to the weight of the fluid displaced by the object.**

✓ *Checkpoint* *Compare the direction of the buoyant force to the direction of the force of gravity.*

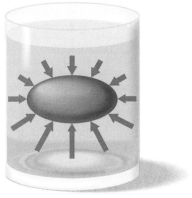

Figure 13 The pressure at the bottom of a submerged object is greater than the pressure at the top. The result is a net force in the upward direction. *Applying Concepts What is this upward force called?*

Figure 14 The volume of water displaced by an object is equal to the volume of the object. If the object floats, the volume of displaced water is equal to the volume of the portion of the object that is under water.

Sharpen your Skills

Measuring **ACTIVITY**

How can you measure an object's volume?
Measure in centimeters (cm) the length, width, and height of a wooden block. Then multiply length times width times height. The product is the volume. Volume has units of cubic centimeters (cm^3).

Sink and Spill

In this lab, you will use data on floating objects to practice the skill of drawing conclusions.

Problem

How is the buoyant force on a floating object related to the weight of the water it displaces?

Materials

paper towels
beaker, 250 mL
triple-beam balance
beaker, 600 mL
table salt
jar with watertight lid, about 30 mL

Procedure

1. Preview the procedure and copy the data table into your notebook.
2. Find the mass, in grams, of a dry paper towel and the 250-mL beaker together. Multiply the mass by 0.01. This gives you the weight in newtons. Record it in your data table.
3. Carefully fill the 600-mL beaker to the very top with water. Put the 250-mL beaker, with the dry paper towel under it, next to the spout of the 600-mL beaker.
4. Place a small amount of salt in the jar. (The jar and salt must be able to float in water.) Then find the mass of the dry jar (with its cover on) in grams. Multiply the mass by 0.01. Record this weight in your data table.
5. Gently lower the jar into the 600-mL beaker. (If the jar sinks, take it out and remove some salt. Repeat Steps 2, 3, and 4.) Estimate the fraction of the jar that is underwater, and record it.
6. Once all of the displaced water has been spilled, find the total mass of the paper towel and 250-mL beaker containing the water. Multiply the mass by 0.01 and record the result in your data table.
7. Empty the 250-mL beaker. Dry off the beaker and the jar.
8. Repeat Steps 2 through 7 several more times. Each time fill the jar with a different amount of salt, but make sure the jar still floats.

DATA TABLE						
Jar	Weight of Empty 250-mL Beaker and Dry Paper Towel (N)	Weight of Jar, Salt, and Cover (N)	Weight of 250-mL Beaker with Displaced Water and Paper Towel (N)	Fraction of Jar Submerged in Water	Buoyant Force (N)	Weight of Displaced Water (N)
1						
2						
3						

9. Calculate the buoyant force for each trial and record it in your data table. (*Hint:* When an object floats, the buoyant force is equal to the weight of the object.)

10. Calculate the weight of the displaced water in each case. Record it in your data table.

Analyze and Conclude

1. In each trial, the jar had a different weight. How did this affect the way that the jar floated?

2. The jar had the same volume in every trial. Why did the volume of displaced water vary?

3. What can you conclude about the relationship between the buoyant force and the weight of the displaced water?

4. Can you suggest places where errors may have been introduced?

5. **Think About It** If you put too much salt in the jar, it will sink. What can you conclude about the buoyant force in this case? How can you determine the buoyant force for an object that sinks?

Design an Experiment

How do you think your results would change if you used a different liquid that is more dense or less dense than water? Design an experiment to test your hypothesis. What liquid or liquids will you use? Will you need equipment other than what you have used for this experiment? If so, what will you need? If you carry out your new experiment, be sure to have your teacher check your design before you begin.

Figure 15 The illustration shows the forces on three different cubes. All three cubes have the same volume. *Comparing and Contrasting* Why don't all three cubes float?

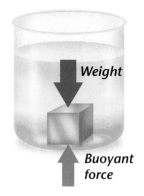

Weight

Buoyant force

Weight

Buoyant force

Weight

Buoyant force

Dive!

In this activity you will construct a device called a Cartesian diver.

1. Bend a plastic straw into a U shape and cut the ends so that each side is about 4 cm long. Attach the ends with a paper clip.

2. Attach additional paper clips to the first paper clip. The straw should float with its top about half a centimeter above the surface. This is the diver.

3. Fill a plastic jar or bottle almost completely with water. Drop the diver in, paper clips first. Then put the lid on the jar.

4. Slowly squeeze and release the jar several times.

Drawing Conclusions Explain the behavior of the diver.

Floating and Sinking

Remember that there is always a downward force on a submerged object. That force is the weight of the object. If the weight of the object is greater than the buoyant force, the net force on a submerged object will be downward. The object will sink. If the weight of the object is less than the buoyant force, the object will begin to sink. It will only sink deep enough to displace a volume of fluid with a weight equal to its own. At that level, it will stop sinking deeper, and will float. If the weight of the object is exactly equal to the buoyant force, the two forces are balanced.

Density

Exactly why do some objects float and others sink? By comparing the density of an object to the density of a fluid, you can decide if it will float. But what is density?

The density of a substance is its mass per unit volume.

$$Density = \frac{Mass}{Volume}$$

For example, one cubic centimeter (cm³) of lead has a mass of 11.3 grams, so its density is 11.3 g/cm³.

$$Density\ of\ lead = \frac{11.3\ g}{1\ cm^3} = 11.3\ g/cm^3$$

In contrast, one cubic centimeter of cork has a mass of only about 0.25 gram. So its density is about 0.25 g/cm³. You would say that lead is more dense than cork. The density of water is 1.0 g/cm³, so it is less dense than lead but more dense than cork.

By comparing densities, you can explain the behavior of the objects shown in Figure 15. **An object that is more dense than the fluid in which it is immersed sinks. An object that is less dense than the fluid in which it is immersed floats to the surface.** And if the density of an object is equal to the density of the fluid in which it is immersed, the object neither rises nor sinks in the fluid. Instead it floats at a constant level.

Now you know why lead sinks: It is several times denser than water. Cork, which is less dense than water, floats. An ice cube floats in water because the density of ice is less than the density of water. But it's just a little less! So most of a floating ice cube is below the surface. Since an iceberg is really a very large ice cube, the part that you see above water is only a small fraction of the entire iceberg. This is one reason why icebergs are so dangerous to ships.

☑ *Checkpoint* **To calculate the density of a substance, what two properties of the substance do you need to know?**

Densities of Substances Figure 16 shows several substances and their densities. Notice that liquids can float on top of other liquids. (You may have seen that salad oil floats on top of vinegar.) Notice also that the substances with the greatest densities are near the bottom of the cylinder.

Don't forget that air is also a fluid. Objects float in air if their densities are less than the density of air. A helium balloon rises because helium is less dense than air. An ordinary balloon filled with air, however, is more dense than the surrounding air because it is under pressure. So the balloon falls to the ground once you let go of it.

Changing the density of an object can make it float or sink in a given fluid. The density of a submarine, for example, is decreased when water is pumped out of its flotation tanks. The overall mass of the submarine decreases. Since its volume remains the same, its density decreases when its mass decreases. So the submarine will float to the surface. To dive, the submarine takes in water. In this way, it increases its mass (and thus its density), and sinks.

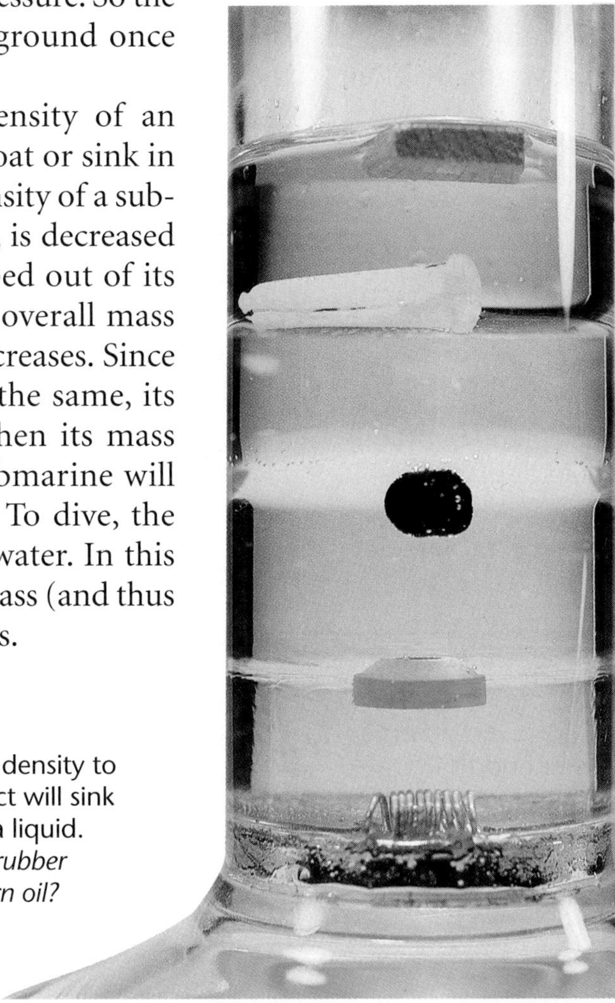

Figure 16 You can use density to predict whether an object will sink or float when placed in a liquid. *Interpreting Data Will a rubber washer sink or float in corn oil?*

Substance	Density (g/cm³)
Wood	0.7
Corn oil	0.925
Plastic	0.93
Water	1.00
Tar ball	1.02
Glycerin	1.26
Rubber washer	1.34
Corn syrup	1.38
Copper wire	8.8
Mercury	13.6

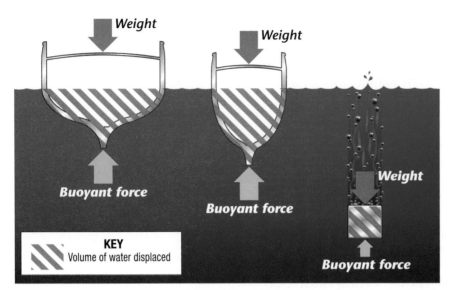

Figure 17 A solid cube of steel sinks when placed in water. A steel ship with the same weight floats.

KEY
Volume of water displaced

Buoyancy and Density Another way of changing density is to change volume. In Figure 17, the amount of steel present in the three objects is the same. Yet two of the figures float, and one sinks. Solid steel sinks rapidly in water, and so will the hull of a ship that is full of water. Usually, however, the hull of a ship contains a large volume of air. This air reduces the ship's overall density, and so allows it to float.

You can explain why a ship floats not just in terms of density, but also by means of the force of buoyancy. Since the buoyant force is equal to the weight of the displaced fluid, the buoyant force will increase if more fluid is displaced. The amount of fluid displaced depends on the volume of a submerged object. A large object displaces more fluid than a small object. Therefore, the object with greater volume has a greater buoyant force acting on it—even if the objects have the same weight.

The shape of a ship causes it to displace a greater volume of water than a solid piece of steel of the same mass. The greater the volume of water displaced, the greater the buoyant force. A ship stays afloat as long as the buoyant force is greater than its weight.

Section 3 Review

1. How does the buoyant force affect a submerged object?
2. How does Archimedes' principle relate the buoyant force acting on an object to the fluid displaced by the object?
3. How can you use the density of an object to predict whether it will float or sink in water?
4. An object that weighs 340 N is floating on a lake. What is the buoyant force on it? What is the weight of the displaced water?
5. **Thinking Critically Applying Concepts** Some canoes have compartments on either end that are hollow and watertight. These canoes won't sink, even when they capsize. Explain why.

Check Your Progress

CHAPTER PROJECT

Don't be content with the first design that floats. Try several more, considering the characteristics that make your boat useful. How much space does your boat have for cargo? How does the weight of your boat affect the amount of cargo it can carry? (*Hint:* To measure the weight of each boat, see how many pennies will balance it on a double-pan balance.) Select your best boat and determine the number of pennies it can carry as it floats.

SECTION 4 Applying Bernoulli's Principle

DISCOVER · ACTIVITY

Does Water Push or Pull?

1. Hold a plastic spoon loosely by the edges of its handle so it is swinging freely between your fingers.

2. Turn on a faucet to produce a steady stream of water. Predict what will happen if you bring the curved back of the spoon into contact with the stream of water.

3. Test your prediction. Repeat the test several times.

4. Predict how your observations might change if you were to use a plastic fork instead of a spoon.

5. Test your prediction.

Think It Over

Inferring On what side of the spoon is the pressure lower? How do you know? Does the fork behave any differently from the spoon? If so, develop a hypothesis to explain why.

In December of 1903, Wilbur and Orville Wright brought an odd-looking vehicle to a deserted beach in Kitty Hawk, North Carolina. People had flown in balloons for more than a hundred years, but the Wright brothers' goal was something no one had ever done before. They flew a plane that was heavier (denser) than air! They had spent years experimenting with different wing shapes and surfaces, and they had carefully studied the flight of birds. Their first flight at Kitty Hawk lasted just 12 seconds. The plane flew 36 meters and made history.

What did the Wright brothers know about flying that allowed them to construct the first airplane? And how can the principles they used explain how a jumbo jet can fly across the country? The answer has to do with fluid pressure and what happens when a fluid moves.

Bernoulli's Principle

So far in this chapter you have learned about fluids that are not moving. But what happens when a fluid, such as air or water, moves? Consider what happens if you hold a plastic spoon in a stream of running water. You might predict that the spoon would be pushed away by the water. But it is not. Surprisingly, the spoon is pushed toward the stream of water.

GUIDE FOR READING

◆ How is fluid pressure related to the motion of a fluid?

Reading Tip Before you read, preview *Exploring Wings* and predict how you can explain flight in terms of fluid pressure.

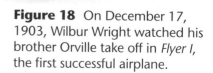

Figure 18 On December 17, 1903, Wilbur Wright watched his brother Orville take off in *Flyer I*, the first successful airplane.

The behavior of the spoon demonstrates **Bernoulli's principle.** The Swiss scientist Daniel Bernoulli (bur NOO lee) found that the faster a fluid moves, the less pressure the fluid exerts. **Bernoulli's principle states that the pressure exerted by a moving stream of fluid is less than the pressure of the surrounding fluid.** The water running along the spoon is moving but the air on the other side of the spoon is not. The moving water exerts less pressure than still air. The result is that the greater pressure of the still air on one side of the spoon pushes the spoon into the stream of water.

Similarly, if you blow above a sheet of tissue paper, the paper will rise. Moving air blown over the tissue paper exerts less pressure than the still air below the paper. The greater pressure below the paper pushes it upward.

✓ Checkpoint How is the pressure exerted by a fluid related to how fast the fluid moves?

Objects in Flight

Bernoulli's principle is a factor in flight—from a small bird to a huge airplane. Objects can be designed so that their shapes cause air to move at different speeds above and below them. If the air moves faster above the object, pressure pushes the object upward. But if the air moves faster below the object, pressure pushes it downward. The shape of the sail of a ship is somewhat like an airplane wing. The difference in the pressure on the two sides of the sail moves the ship forward. Look through *Exploring Wings* to see how Bernoulli's principle can be applied to airplanes, birds, and race cars.

Bernoulli's Principle at Home

Bernoulli's principle can help you understand many common occurences. For example, you can sit next to a fireplace enjoying a cozy fire thanks to Bernoulli's principle. Smoke rises up the chimney partly because hot air rises, and partly because it is pushed. Wind blowing across the top of a chimney lowers the air pressure there. The higher pressure at the bottom then pushes air and smoke up the chimney.

Figure 19 Thanks to Bernoulli's principle, you can enjoy an evening by a warm fireplace without having the room fill up with smoke.
Making Generalizations Why does the smoke rise up the chimney?

EXPLORING Wings

Bernoulli's principle helps explain how air moving around a wing produces a force.

Airplane Wings

The top of this airplane wing is curved. Air that moves over the top of the wing must travel farther than air that moves along the bottom of the wing. Also, the air moving over the top moves faster and exerts less pressure than the air on the bottom. This difference in pressure creates an upward force on the wing, called lift.

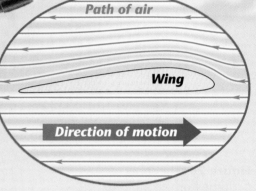

Path of air

Wing

Direction of motion

Bird Wings

Like the airplane wing above, a bird's wing is curved on the top. A bird's wing is flexible, allowing it to propel the bird as well as producing lift.

Direction of motion

Spoiler

Path of air

Spoilers

The spoiler on the back of a racing car is curved on the lower side, so a spoiler is an upside-down version of the wing above. The greater pressure pushing downward on a spoiler gives the car better traction from its rear wheels.

Figure 20 The spray of perfume from an atomizer is an application of Bernoulli's principle. *Applying Concepts Why is the perfume pushed up and out of the flask?*

Bernoulli's principle can help you understand the operation of other familiar devices. In the atomizer shown in Figure 20, you squeeze a rubber bulb. Squeezing the bulb causes air to move quickly past the top of the tube. The bottom of the tube is in the liquid in the flask. The moving air lowers the pressure at the top of the tube. The greater pressure in the flask pushes the liquid up into the tube. When the liquid reaches the air stream, the action of the air stream breaks it into small drops. The liquid comes out as a fine mist.

Section 4 Review

1. What does Bernoulli's principle say about the pressure exerted by a moving fluid?
2. Why does the air pressure above an airplane wing differ from the pressure below it? How is this pressure difference involved in flight?
3. **Thinking Critically** **Relating Cause and Effect** A roof is lifted off a building during a severe windstorm. Explain this in terms of Bernoulli's principle.
4. **Thinking Critically** **Applying Concepts** You are riding in a car on a highway when a large truck speeds by you. Explain why your car is forced toward the truck.

Science at Home

Atomizer You can make your own atomizer using a straw. Cut a plastic straw partway through. Hold one end of the straw in a glass of water and bend the other half of the straw at a right angle at the cut, as shown. Blow hard through the straw, making sure that no one is in the way! Show your device to your family. See if they know what it is and why it works. Explain the device to them in terms of Bernoulli's principle.

SECTION 1 Pressure

Key Ideas

◆ Pressure is the force per unit area on a surface.

◆ Fluid pressure results from the motion of the atoms or molecules that make up the fluid.

◆ Pressure at a given level in a fluid is the same in all directions. Pressure decreases with altitude and increases with depth.

Key Terms

pressure
pascal
fluid

SECTION 2 Transmitting Pressure in a Fluid

Key Ideas

◆ According to Pascal's principle, an increase in pressure on a confined fluid is transmitted equally to all parts of the fluid.

◆ A hydraulic device works by transmitting an increase in pressure from one part of a confined fluid to the other. A small force exerted over a small area at one place results in a large force exerted by a larger area at another place.

Key Terms

Pascal's principle   hydraulic system

SECTION 3 Floating and Sinking

Key Ideas

◆ The upward force on an object submerged in a fluid is called the buoyant force.

◆ The buoyant force on an object is equal to the weight of the fluid displaced by the object. This is Archimedes' principle.

◆ An object will sink, rise to the surface, or stay where it is in a fluid depending on whether its density is less than, greater than, or equal to the density of the fluid.

Key Terms

buoyant force
Archimedes' principle

SECTION 4 Applying Bernoulli's Principle

INTEGRATING TECHNOLOGY

Key Idea

◆ The pressure in a fluid decreases as the speed of the fluid increases. This is Bernoulli's principle.

Key Term

Bernoulli's principle

Organizing Information

Flowchart Create a flowchart that shows how a hydraulic device multiplies force. (For more on flowcharts, see the Skills Handbook.)

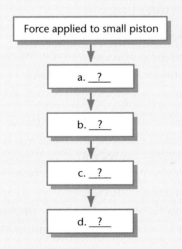

Force applied to small piston

↓

a. _?_

↓

b. _?_

↓

c. _?_

↓

d. _?_

Reviewing Content

 For more review of key concepts, see the Interactive Student Tutorial CD-ROM.

Multiple Choice

Choose the letter of the answer that best completes each statement.

1. Pressure can be measured in units of
   a. N.
   b. N/cm^2.
   c. N/cm.
   d. N/cm^3.
2. The operation of a hydraulic device can be explained in terms of
   a. Pascal's principle.
   b. Bernoulli's principle.
   c. Archimedes' principle.
   d. Newton's third law.
3. If the buoyant force on an object in water is greater than the object's weight, the object will
   a. sink.
   b. hover beneath the surface of the water.
   c. rise to the surface and float.
   d. be crushed by the water pressure.
4. A stone will sink in water because
   a. it is very heavy.
   b. its density is less than that of water.
   c. it has a small buoyant force on it.
   d. its density is greater than that of water.
5. Much of the lift that enables an airplane to fly can be explained using
   a. Pascal's principle.
   b. Bernoulli's principle.
   c. Archimedes' principle.
   d. Newton's first law.

True or False

If the statement is true, write true. If it is false, change the underlined word or words to make the statement true.

6. Pressure is force per unit of <u>mass</u>.
7. As you rise higher into the atmosphere, the air pressure <u>increases</u>.
8. The braking system of a car is an example of a <u>hydraulic device</u>.
9. You can determine the buoyant force on an object if you know the weight of the <u>object</u>.
10. The pressure exerted by a moving stream of fluid is <u>less than</u> the pressure exerted by the same fluid when it is not moving.

Checking Concepts

11. How does the amount of pressure you exert on the floor when you are lying down compare with the amount of pressure you exert when you are standing up?
12. You have a closed bottle of soda. The force on the bottle cap due to the carbonation of the soda is 14 N. If the area of the bottle cap is 7 cm^2, what is the pressure on the cap?
13. Name two hydraulic devices that an auto mechanic is familiar with.
14. Why do you seem to weigh more in air than you do in water?
15. Explain how Bernoulli's principle can keep a bird in the air.
16. **Writing to Learn** You have a job greeting vacationers who are learning to scuba dive. Prepare a brochure or handout explaining the pressure changes they should expect to experience as they dive. Be sure to describe the reasons for the changes.

Thinking Critically

17. **Developing Hypotheses** A sphere made of steel is put in water and, surprisingly, it floats. Develop a hypothesis to explain this observation.
18. **Applying Concepts** One method of raising a sunken ship to the surface is to inflate large bags or balloons inside its hull. Explain why this procedure could work.
19. **Designing Experiments** You have two fluids of unknown density. Suggest an experiment to determine which is denser without mixing the two fluids.
20. **Relating Cause and Effect** Your kite rises into the air as you run quickly on a windy day. Is the air pressure greater above the kite or below it? Explain your answer.

Applying Skills

Use the illustration to answer Questions 21–24. It shows an object being supported by a spring scale in and out of water.

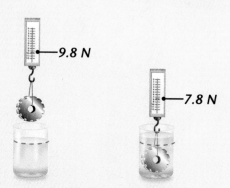

9.8 N

7.8 N

21. **Applying Concepts** Why is there a difference between the weight of the object in air and its weight in water?
22. **Calculating** What is the buoyant force on the object?
23. **Drawing Conclusions** What can you conclude about the water above the dotted line?

24. **Predicting** If the spring scale were removed, would the object float or sink? How do you know?

CHAPTER PROJECT

Performance Assessment

Present Your Project Test your boat to make sure it does not leak. Then display it for the class and demonstrate how it floats. Be sure to include the diagrams you drew of the different designs you tried. Display the observations and data you recorded for each design. Point out to your classmates the features you incorporated into your final design.

Reflect and Record Suppose you had no limitations on what materials you could use for your boat. Also suppose you could form your material into any shape you choose. In your journal, sketch and describe the boat you would design.

Test Preparation

Use these questions to prepare for standardized tests.

Read the passage. Then answer Questions 25–28.

Luis has a small stone. He fills a large beaker to the top with water and places a small beaker below the spout of the large beaker. Luis drops the stone into the large beaker and it sinks to the bottom. He then notes the volume of water that spills into the small beaker.

25. What does Luis learn about the stone?
    a. its mass   b. its volume
    c. its density   d. its composition
26. Luis can find the buoyant force on the stone by finding the
    a. weight of the displaced water.
    b. weight of the small beaker and the displaced water.
    c. weight of the large beaker with the water and stone in it.
    d. increase in the weight of the large beaker after the stone is dropped into it.

27. What conclusion can Luis draw about the density of the stone?
    a. It is less than the density of the water.
    b. It is equal to the density of the water.
    c. It is greater than the density of the water.
    d. It depends on the initial volume of water in the large beaker.
28. Luis chips a piece off the stone and repeats his experiment. What does he notice?
    a. The density of the stone decreases.
    b. The volume of displaced water decreases.
    c. The density of the stone increases.
    d. The volume of displaced water increases.

www.phschool.com

SECTION
1 What Is Work?

Discover What Happens When You Pull at an Angle?
Sharpen Your Skills Inferring

SECTION
2 Mechanical Advantage and Efficiency

Discover Is It a Machine?
Try This Going Up
Science at Home Household Machines
Skills Lab Seesaw Science

SECTION
3 Simple Machines

Discover How Can You Increase Your Force?
Try This Modeling a Screw
Sharpen Your Skills Classifying
Real-World Lab Angling for Access

CHAPTER 12 PROJECT

The Nifty Lifting Machine

For thousands of years, machines have helped people do work. Whether a person is using a diesel-powered crane to unload a lumber truck, or a shovel to dig in the garden, any task is made easier by using machines. Even complex machines such as automobiles accomplish a given task by combining the action of many simple machines.

In this chapter, you will learn about the different types of machines and how you use them in your daily life. As you work through this chapter, you will build your own lifting machine and demonstrate it at work.

Your Goal To use a combination of at least two simple machines to build a machine that can lift a 600-gram soup can 5 centimeters.

Your machine must
◆ consist of at least two simple machines working in combination
◆ use another soup can gradually filled with sand as the input force
◆ be built following the safety guidelines in Appendix A

Get Started Brainstorm with your classmates ideas for different designs of machines. Discuss possible materials that might be useful for constructing each machine.

Check Your Progress You'll be working on the project as you study this chapter. To keep your project on track, look for Check Your Progress boxes at the following points.
  Section 1 Review, page 377: Determine the amount of work your machine must do.
  Section 3 Review, page 396: Analyze factors affecting efficiency and mechanical advantage, and construct your machine.

Present Your Project At the end of the chapter (page 405), demonstrate your machine.

Horses or oxen would once have done the work of this machine.

SECTION
4

Integrating Life Science
Machines in the Human Body

Discover **Are You an Eating Machine?**
Science at Home **Finger Forces**

SECTION ① What Is Work?

After a heavy snowstorm, a neighbor's car gets stuck in a snowdrift. You shovel some snow away from the car, and then try to push it backward. The spinning tires whine as the driver attempts to move. Although you try as hard as you can, the car just won't budge. After 10 minutes of strenuous pushing, you are nearly exhausted. Unfortunately, the car is still lodged in the snow. That was sure hard work, wasn't it? You exerted a lot of force. You did some work shoveling the snow. But you might be surprised to discover that in scientific terms you didn't do any work at all on the car!

The Meaning of Work

In science you do **work** on an object when you exert a force on the object that causes the object to move some distance. If you push a child on a swing, for example, you are doing work on the child. If you pull your books out of your

Force   Motion

Force
Motion

Figure 1 Lifting a bin full of newspapers is work, but carrying the bin is not. *Interpreting Photos Why does the girl do no work when she carries the bin?*

374

book bag, you do work on the books. If you lift a bag of groceries out of a shopping cart, you do work on the bag of groceries.

No Work Without Motion So why didn't you do work when trying to push the car out of the snow? The car didn't move. **In order for you to do work on an object, the object must move some distance as a result of your force.** If the object does not move, no work is done no matter how much force is exerted.

Figure 2 You may be making a great effort, but if the car doesn't move, you do no work.

There are many situations in which you exert a force but don't do any work. Suppose, for example, you are asked to hold a piece of wood while you are helping on a construction project. You definitely exert a force to hold the wood in place, so it might seem as if you do work. But because the force you exert does not make the wood move, you are not doing any work on it.

Only Force in the Same Direction How much work do you do when you carry your heavy books to school? You may think you do a lot of work, but actually you don't. **In order to do work on an object, the force you exert must be in the same direction as the object's motion.** When you carry an object at constant velocity, you exert an upward force to hold the object so that it doesn't fall to the ground. The motion of the object, however, is in the horizontal direction. Since the force is vertical and the motion is horizontal, you don't do any work on the object as you carry it.

How much work do you do when you pull a sled? When you pull a sled, you pull on the rope at an angle to the ground. Therefore your force has both a horizontal part (to the right) and a vertical part (upward). When you pull this way, only part of your force does work—the part in the same direction as the motion of the sled. The rest of your force does not help pull.

Figure 3 When you pull a sled with a rope, not all of your force does work to move the sled.

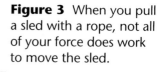

Part of total force that does not do work

Total force

Part of total force that pulls sled

Sharpen your Skills

If you did the Discover activity, you know that your effort will be more effective when you reduce the angle at which you push or pull an object. That is, exert as much of your force as possible in the direction of the object's motion. Keep this in mind the next time you rake a pile of leaves or vacuum a floor.

☑ *Checkpoint* *How can you determine if work is done on an object?*

Calculating Work

Which do you think involves more work: exerting a force of 100 N to lift a potted tree a meter off the ground or exerting a force of 200 N to lift a heavier tree to the same height? Is it more work to lift a tree from the ground to a wheelbarrow or from the ground to the top story of a building? Your common sense may suggest that lifting a heavier object, which demands a greater force, requires more work than lifting a lighter object. Also, moving an object a greater distance requires more work than moving the object a shorter distance. Both of these are true.

The amount of work you do depends on both the amount of force you exert and the distance the object moves:

$$\text{Work} = \text{Force} \times \text{Distance}$$

The amount of work done on an object can be determined by multiplying force times distance.

Sample Problem

To help rearrange the furniture in your classroom, you exert a force of 20 N to push a desk 10 m. How much work do you do?

Analyze. You know the force exerted on the desk and the distance the desk moved. You want to find the amount of work done. Draw a diagram similar to the one shown to help you.

Write the formula. Work = Force × Distance

Force = 20 N

Substitute and solve. Work = 20 N × 10 m

Work = 200 N·m, which is 200 J

Think about it. The answer tells you that the work you do on the desk is 200 J.

Distance = 10 m

Practice Problems

1. A hydraulic lift exerts a force of 12,000 N to lift a car 2 m. How much work is done on the car?
2. You exert a force of 0.2 N to lift a pencil off the floor. How much work do you do if you lift it 1.5 m?

When force is measured in newtons and distance is measured in meters, the SI unit of work is the newton × meter (N·m). This unit is also called a joule (JOOL) in honor of James Prescott Joule, a physicist who studied work in the middle 1800s. One **joule** (J) is the amount of work you do when you exert a force of 1 newton to move an object a distance of 1 meter.

With the work formula, you can compare the amount of work you do to lift the trees. When you lift an object at constant speed, the upward force you exert must be equal to the object's weight. To lift the first tree, you would have to exert a force of 100 newtons. If you were to raise it 1 meter, you would do 100 newtons × 1 meter, or 100 joules of work. To lift the heavier tree, you would have to exert a force of 200 newtons. So the amount of work you do would be 200 newtons × 1 meter, or 200 joules. Thus you do more work to move the heavier object.

Now think about lifting the tree higher. You did 100 joules of work lifting it 1 meter. Suppose an elevator lifted the same tree to the top floor of a building 40 meters tall. The elevator would exert the same force on the tree for a greater distance. The work done would be 100 newtons × 40 meters, or 4,000 joules. The elevator would do 40 times as much work as you did.

Figure 4 These students are doing work as they transplant a tree. *Inferring How much work would they do if the tree weighed twice as much? If they had to lift it four times as far?*

Section 1 Review

1. If you exert a force, do you always do work? Explain your answer.
2. What is the formula for calculating work?
3. Compare the amount of work done when a force of 2 N moves an object 3 meters with the work done when a force of 3 N moves an object 2 meters.
4. **Thinking Critically Applying Concepts** You need to move five large cans of paint from the basement to the second floor of a house. Will you do more work on the cans of paint if you take them up all at once (if possible) or if you take them up individually? Explain.

CHAPTER PROJECT

Check Your Progress

Determine the amount of work that your machine must do to lift a 600-g soup can 5 cm. Draw a diagram showing the forces involved and the direction of those forces. Jot down some suggestions for accomplishing this work. Brainstorm with classmates about what materials you could use to build your machine.

SECTION 2 Mechanical Advantage and Efficiency

DISCOVER ·ACTIVITY· · ·

Is It a Machine?

1. Your teacher will give you an assortment of objects. Examine each object closely.

2. Sort the objects into those that you think are machines and those you think are not machines.

3. Determine how each object that you have identified as a machine functions. Explain each object to another student.

Think It Over

Forming Operational Definitions Why did you decide certain objects were machines while other objects were not?

GUIDE FOR READING

◆ **How do machines make work easier?**

◆ **What is the difference between actual and ideal mechanical advantage?**

◆ **How can you calculate the efficiency of a machine?**

Reading Tip As you read, use the headings to make an outline showing what machines do.

A truckload of mulch for your new garden has just arrived. The only problem is that the pile of mulch has been dumped 10 meters from where it belongs. What can you do? You could move the mulch by handfuls, but that would take a very long time. You could use a shovel and a wheelbarrow, which would make the job much easier. Or you could have a bulldozer move it. That would make the job easier still.

What Is a Machine?

Shovels and bulldozers are examples of machines. A **machine** is a device with which you can do work in a way that is easier or more effective. You may be used to thinking of machines as complex gadgets that run on electricity, but a machine can be as simple as a shovel or even a ramp.

Perhaps you think that a machine decreases the amount of work that is done. But it doesn't. Moving the pile of mulch, for example, will involve the same amount of work no matter how you do it. Similarly, you have to do the same amount of work to lift a piano whether you lift it by hand or push it up a ramp.

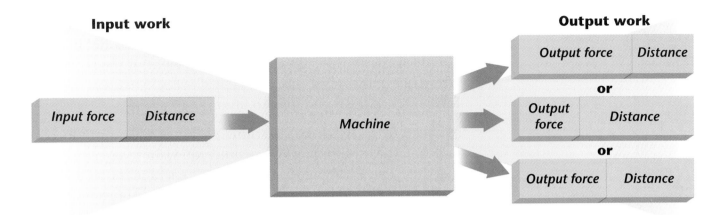

Input work

Output work

| Input force | Distance |

| Output force | Distance |

or

| Output force | Distance |

or

| Output force | Distance |

Machine

What the shovel and the ramp do is to change the way in which you do the work. **A machine makes work easier by changing the amount of force you exert, the distance over which you exert your force, or the direction in which you exert your force.** You might say that a machine makes work easier by multiplying either force or distance, or by changing direction.

When you do work with a machine, you exert a force over some distance. For example, you exert a force on the handle when you use a shovel to lift mulch. The force you exert on the machine is called the **input force,** or sometimes the effort force. The machine then does work, by exerting a force over some distance. The shovel, in this case, exerts a force to lift the mulch. The force exerted by the machine is called the **output force.** Sometimes the term resistance force is used instead, because the machine must overcome some resistance.

Multiplying Force In some machines, the output force is greater than the input force. How can you exert a smaller force than is necessary for a job if the amount of work is the same? Remember the formula for work: Work = Force × Distance. If the amount of work stays the same, a decrease in force must mean an increase in distance. So if a machine allows you to use less force to do some amount of work, you must apply the input force over a greater distance. In the end, you do as much work with the machine as you would without the machine, but the work is easier to do.

What kind of device might allow you to exert a smaller force over a longer distance? Think about a ramp. Suppose you have to lift a piano onto the stage in your school auditorium. You could try to lift it vertically, or you could push it up a ramp. If you use

Figure 5 A machine can make a task easier in one of three ways. *Interpreting Diagrams How does the output force compare to the input force in each type of machine?*

Figure 6 The input force exerted on the shovel is greater than the output force exerted by the shovel.

the ramp, the distance over which you must exert your force is greater than if you lift the piano directly. This is because the length of the ramp is greater than the height of the stage. The advantage of the ramp, then, is that it allows you to exert a smaller force to push the piano than to lift it.

Multiplying Distance In some machines, the output force is less than the input force. Why would you want to use a machine like this? The advantage of this kind of machine is that it allows you to exert your input force over a shorter distance than you would without the machine. For you to apply a force over a shorter distance, you need to apply a greater force.

When do you use this kind of machine? Think about taking a shot with a hockey stick. You move your hands a short distance, but the other end of the stick moves a greater distance to hit the puck. The hockey puck moves much faster than your hands. What happens when you fold up a sheet of paper and wave it back and forth to fan yourself? You move your hand a short distance, but the other end of the paper moves a longer distance to cool you off on a warm day. And when you ride a bicycle in high gear, you apply a large force to the pedals over a short distance. The bicycle, meanwhile, moves a much longer distance.

Changing Direction Some machines don't multiply either force or distance. What could be the advantage of these machines? Well, think about raising the sail in Figure 7. You could raise the sail by climbing the mast of the boat and pulling up on the sail with a rope. But it is much easier to stand on the deck and pull down than to lift up. By running a rope through the top of the mast as shown, you can raise the sail by pulling down on the rope. This rope system is a machine that makes your job easier by changing the direction in which you exert your force.

☑ *Checkpoint* *What are three ways in which a machine can make work easier?*

Figure 7 One, two, three, pull! Up goes the sail. This sailor pulls down on the rope in order to hoist the sail into position. *Applying Concepts Why is the rope system considered a machine?*

Figure 8 Chop, chop, chop. A knife is a machine that makes your work easier when you prepare a tasty meal.

Mechanical Advantage

If you compare the input force to the output force, you can determine the advantage of using a machine. **A machine's mechanical advantage is the number of times a force exerted on a machine is multiplied by the machine.** Finding the ratio of output force to input force gives you the **mechanical advantage** of a machine.

$$Mechanical\ advantage = \frac{Output\ force}{Input\ force}$$

Mechanical Advantage of Multiplying Force For a machine that multiplies force, the mechanical advantage is greater than 1. That is because the output force is greater than the input force. For example, consider a manual can opener. If you exert a force of 20 newtons on the opener, and the opener exerts a force of 60 newtons on a can, the mechanical advantage of the can opener is 60 newtons ÷ 20 newtons, or 3. The can opener tripled your force! Or suppose you would have to exert 3,200 newtons to lift a piano. If you use a ramp, you might only need to exert 1,600 newtons. The mechanical advantage of this ramp is 3,200 newtons ÷ 1,600 newtons, or 2. The ramp doubles the force that you exert.

Mechanical Advantage of Multiplying Distance For a machine that multiplies distance, the output force is less than the input force. So in this case, the mechanical advantage is less than 1. If, for example, you exert an input force of 20 newtons and the machine produces an output force of 10 newtons, the mechanical advantage is 10 newtons ÷ 20 newtons, or 0.5. The output force of the machine is half your input force, but the machine exerts that force over a longer distance.

Mechanical Advantage of Changing Direction What can you predict about the mechanical advantage of a machine that changes the direction of the force? If only the direction changes, the input force will be the same as the output force. The mechanical advantage will be 1.

Going Up ACTIVITY

Does a rope simply turn your force upside down? Find out!

1. Tie a piece of string about 50 cm long to an object, such as an empty cooking pot. Make a small loop on the other end of the string.

2. Using a spring scale, slowly lift the pot 20 cm. Note the reading on the scale.

3. Now loop the string over a pencil and pull down on the spring scale to lift the pot 20 cm. Predict the reading on the scale. Were you correct?

Developing Hypotheses How did the readings on the spring scale compare? If the readings were different, suggest a reason why. What might be an advantage to using this system?

Figure 15 This Calder mobile, entitled "Lobster Trap and Fish Tail," is in the Museum of Modern Art in New York City.

To understand how levers work, think about opening a paint can with a spoon. The spoon acts as a lever. The spoon rests against the edge of the can, which acts as the fulcrum. The tip of the spoon is under the lid of the can. When you push down on the handle, you exert an input force and the spoon pivots about the fulcrum. As a result, the tip of the spoon pushes up, thereby exerting an output force on the lid.

The lever helps you in two ways. First, it increases the effect of your input force. Second, the lever changes the direction of your input force. You push down and the lid is pried up.

Different Types of Levers When a spoon is used as a lever, the fulcrum is located between the input and output forces. But this is not always the case. There are three different types of levers, classified according to the location of the fulcrum relative to the input and output forces. Examples are described in *Exploring the Three Classes of Levers.*

Advantage of a Lever When you opened the paint can, you had to push the spoon handle for a long distance in order to move the lid a short distance. However, you were able to apply a smaller force than you would have without the spoon.

You can calculate the ideal mechanical advantage of a lever using the distances between the forces and the fulcrum.

$$\text{Ideal mechanical advantage} = \frac{\text{Distance from fulcrum to input force}}{\text{Distance from fulcrum to output force}}$$

Remember the case of the paint can opener. The distance from the fulcrum to the input force was greater than the distance from the fulcrum to the output force. This means that the ideal mechanical advantage was greater than 1. A typical ideal mechanical advantage for a paint can opener is 16 centimeters ÷ 0.8 centimeter = 20. That's a big advantage!

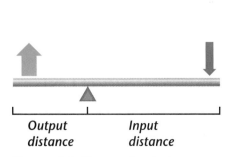

Output distance   *Input distance*

Figure 16 The mechanical advantage of this lever is greater than 1.

✓ *Checkpoint* *What point on a lever does not move?*

EXPLORING *the Three Classes of Levers*

The three classes of levers differ in the positions of the fulcrum, input force, and output force. Note the locations of the labels in each example.

FIRST-CLASS LEVERS

If the distance from the fulcrum to the input force is greater than the distance from the fulcrum to the output force, these levers multiply force. Otherwise, they multiply distance. Note that this kind of lever also changes the direction of the input force. Other examples include scissors, pliers, and seesaws.

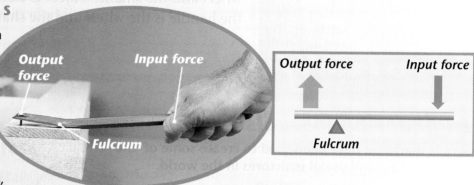

SECOND-CLASS LEVERS

These levers always multiply force. They do not, however, change the direction of the input force. Other examples include doors, nutcrackers, and bottle openers.

THIRD-CLASS LEVERS

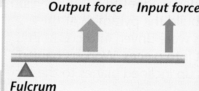

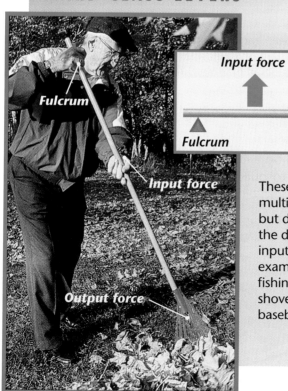

These levers multiply distance, but do not change the direction of the input force. Other examples include fishing poles, shovels, and baseball bats.

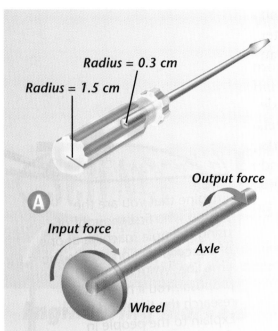

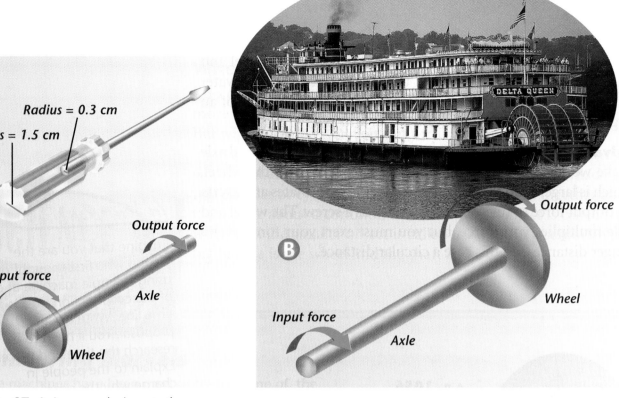

Radius = 0.3 cm

Radius = 1.5 cm

A

Output force

Input force

Axle

Wheel

B

Output force

Input force

Axle

Wheel

Figure 17 **A.** In some devices, such as a screwdriver, the wheel turns an axle. **B.** In the case of the riverboat paddle wheel, the axle turns the wheel. *Interpreting Photos How is work made easier by the wheel and axle on the riverboat?*

You can calculate the ideal mechanical advantage of a **wheel and axle using the radius of the wheel and the radius of the axle.** (Each radius is the distance from the outside to the common center of the wheel and axle.)

$$Ideal\ mechanical\ advantage = \frac{Radius\ of\ wheel}{Radius\ of\ axle}$$

For a screwdriver, a typical ideal mechanical advantage would be 1.5 centimeters ÷ 0.3 centimeter, or 5.

A Variation on the Wheel and Axle What would happen if the input force were applied to the axle rather than the wheel? For the riverboat in Figure 17, the force of the engine is applied to the axle of the large paddle wheel. The large paddle wheel in turn pushes against the water. In this case, the input force is exerted over a short distance while the output force is exerted over a long distance. So when the input force is applied to the axle, a wheel and axle multiplies distance. This means that the ideal mechanical advantage of the paddle wheel is less than 1.

☑ *Checkpoint* *How does a doorknob work?*

Pulley

When you raise or lower a flag on a flagpole or open and close window blinds, you are using a simple machine known as a pulley. A **pulley** is a grooved wheel with a rope (or a chain, or even a steel cable) wrapped around it. You use a pulley by pulling on the rope. As a result, you can change the amount and direction of your input force.

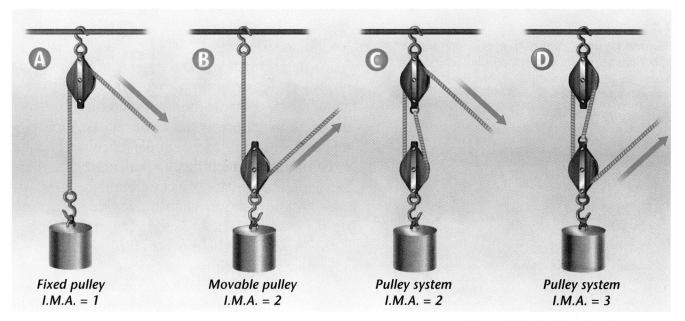

A Fixed pulley
I.M.A. = 1

B Movable pulley
I.M.A. = 2

C Pulley system
I.M.A. = 2

D Pulley system
I.M.A. = 3

Figure 18 **A.** A fixed pulley changes the direction of your force. **B.** A movable pulley multiplies your force. **C, D.** You can combine fixed and movable pulleys to increase the mechanical advantage.

Fixed Pulleys A pulley that you attach to a structure is called a fixed pulley. A single fixed pulley, as shown in Figure 18A, does not change the amount of force you apply. Instead it changes the direction of the input force. The ideal mechanical advantage of a single fixed pulley is 1. A single fixed pulley can be used to raise a sail, as you read in the previous section.

Movable Pulleys If you attach a pulley to the object you wish to move, then you are using a movable pulley. As you see in Figure 18B, the object is then supported by each side of the rope that is looped around the pulley. As a result, the ideal mechanical advantage of a movable pulley is 2. The output force on the object is twice the input force that you exert on the rope. You can also see that you must exert your force over a greater distance. For every meter you lift the object with a movable pulley, you need to pull the rope two meters.

Notice that with the movable pulley, your input force is in the same direction as the output force. A movable pulley is especially useful when you are lifting an object from above. Large construction cranes often work with a movable pulley. A hook fastened to the pulley carries the building materials.

Pulley Systems If you combine fixed and movable pulleys, you can make a pulley system. Such a pulley system is also called a "block and tackle." The pulley system pictured in Figure 18C has an ideal mechanical advantage of 2. The pulley system in Figure 18D has an ideal mechanical advantage of 3. **The ideal mechanical advantage of a pulley system is equal to the number of sections of the rope that support the object.** (Don't include the rope on which you pull downward, because it does not support the object.)

Classifying
Even though levers and pulleys may seem very different, pulleys can be classified as levers.

When you pull down on a fixed pulley, the object rises. In other words, the pulley changes the direction of your input force. This is what happens with a first-class lever. Instead of a bar, you apply your force to a rope. The center of the pulley acts like the fulcrum of the lever.

Draw a diagram showing how a single fixed pulley is like a first-class lever. Why is the mechanical advantage 1?

Figure 19 Both a pencil sharpener and a clock are examples of compound machines that use gears. *Applying Concepts What is a compound machine?*

Compound Machines

Many devices that you can observe around you do not resemble the six simple machines you just read about. That is because more complex machines consist of combinations of simple machines. A machine that utilizes two or more simple machines is called a **compound machine.** To calculate the ideal mechanical advantage of a compound machine, you need to know the mechanical advantage of each simple machine. The overall mechanical advantage is the product of the individual ideal mechanical advantages of the simple machines.

A mechanical pencil sharpener is a good example of a compound machine. When you turn the handle, you are using a wheel and axle to turn the mechanism inside the sharpener. The two cutting wheels inside are screws that whittle away at the end of the pencil until it is sharp.

Inside the pencil sharpener in Figure 19 is an axle that turns **gears.** The gears then turn the cutting wheels. A system of gears is a device with toothed wheels that fit into one another. Turning one wheel causes another to turn. Gears form a compound machine with one wheel and axle linked to another wheel and axle. Sometimes this link is direct, as in the gears shown in Figure 19. In other devices, such as a bicycle, this link is through a chain.

Section 3 Review

1. List and give an example of each of the six kinds of simple machines.
2. Explain how to find the ideal mechanical advantage of four types of simple machines.
3. What kind of lever is the flip-top opener on a soda can? Explain your answer with the help of a diagram.
4. **Thinking Critically Making Generalizations** Some machines give a mechanical advantage less than 1. Explain why you might want to use such a machine.

CHAPTER PROJECT

Check Your Progress

Think about whether force or distance is multiplied by each simple machine in your design. Consider how making levers longer, adding pulleys, or changing the angle of your inclined planes will affect the mechanical advantage. What measurements will you need to know to calculate the ideal mechanical advantage of your lifting machine? Finalize your design, and build your machine. As you build, consider how you can use lubrication or polishing to improve its efficiency.

Automation in the Workplace—Lost Jobs or New Jobs?

Workers 150 years ago spent long days stitching clothes by hand. In a modern American factory, a worker makes a shirt with a sewing machine and much less effort. Since ancient times, people have invented machines to help with work. Today, factories can use automated machines to perform jobs that are difficult, dangerous, or even just boring. Like science-fiction robots, these machines can do a whole series of different tasks.

But if a machine does work instead of a person, then someone loses a job. How can society use machines to make work easier and more productive without having some people lose their chance to work?

The Issues

What Are the Effects of Automation?
New machines replace some jobs, but they also can create jobs. Suppose an automobile factory starts using machines instead of people to paint cars. At first, some workers may lose their jobs. But the factory may be able to produce more cars. Then it may need to hire more workers—to handle old tasks as well as some new ones. New jobs are created for people who are educated and skilled in operating and taking care of the new machines.

Still, some workers whose skills are no longer needed lose their jobs. Some are forced to work in different jobs for less money. Others may be unable to find new jobs. The challenge to society is to provide workers who have lost jobs with the skills needed for good new jobs.

What Can People Do?
Education programs can train young people for new jobs and give older workers new skills. Those who learn how to use computers and other new machines can take on new jobs. Learning how to sell or design a product can also prepare workers for new jobs. Workers who have lost jobs can train for very different types of work—work that cannot be done by machines. A machine, for example, cannot replace human skill in day care or medical care.

Who Should Pay?
Teaching young people how to work in new kinds of jobs costs money. So do training programs for adult workers who have lost jobs. What is the fairest way to pay these costs? Businesses might share some of the costs. Some businesses give workers full pay until they are retrained or find new work. The government might provide unemployment pay or training for the unemployed. Then all taxpayers would share the costs.

You Decide

1. **Identify the Problem**
   Describe in your own words the benefits and drawbacks of workplace automation.

2. **Analyze the Options**
   List ways society could deal with the effects of automation. For each plan, give the benefits and drawbacks and tell how it would be paid for.

3. **Find a Solution**
   The owner of the pizza shop in your neighborhood has bought an automated pizza-making system. Make a plan for the shop to use the system without having to fire workers.

ANGLING FOR ACCESS

You and your friends have volunteered to help build a wheelchair-access ramp for the local public library. The design of the ramp has not been decided upon yet, so you need to build a model inclined plane. The model will help you determine what the steepness of the ramp should be.

Problem

How does the steepness of a wheelchair-access ramp affect its usefulness?

Skills Focus

making models, measuring, calculating

Materials

board, at least 10 cm wide and 50 cm long
wooden block with eye-hook
spring scale, 0–5 N   metric ruler
4 books, about 2 cm thick   marker

Procedure

1. Preview the following steps that describe how you can construct and use a ramp. Then copy the data table into your notebook.

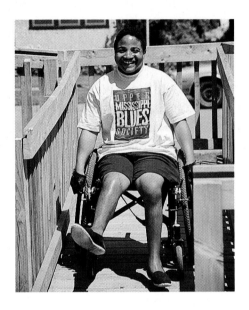

2. The output force with an inclined plane is equal to the weight of the object. Lift the block with the spring scale to measure its weight. Record this value in the data table.

3. Make a mark on the side of the board about 3 cm from one end. Measure the length from the other end of the board to the mark and record it in the data table.

4. Place one end of the board on top of a book. The mark you made on the board should be even with the edge of the book.

DATA TABLE

Number of Books	Output Force (N)	Length of Incline (cm)	Height of Incline (cm)	Input Force (N)	Ideal Mechanical Advantage	Actual Mechanical Advantage
1						
2						
3						
4						

5. Measure the vertical distance in centimeters from the top of the table to where the underside of the incline touches the book. Record this value in the data table as "Height of Incline."

6. Lay the block on its largest side and use the spring scale to pull the block straight up the incline at a slow, steady speed. Be sure to hold the spring scale parallel to the incline, as shown in the photograph. Measure the force needed and record it in the data table.

7. Predict how your results will change if you repeat the investigation using two, three, and four books. Test your predictions.

8. For each trial, calculate the ideal mechanical advantage and the actual mechanical advantage. Record the calculations in your data table.

Analyze and Conclude

1. How did the ideal mechanical advantage and the actual mechanical advantage compare each time you repeated the experiment? Explain your answer.

2. Why do you write ideal and actual mechanical advantage without units?

3. What happens to the mechanical advantage as the inclined plane gets steeper? On the basis of this fact alone, which of the four inclined planes models the best steepness for a wheelchair-access ramp?

4. What other factors, besides mechanical advantage, should you consider when deciding on the steepness of the ramp?

5. **Apply** Suppose the door of the local public library is 2 m above the ground and the distance from the door to the parking lot is 15 m. How would these conditions affect your decision about how steep to make the ramp?

Getting Involved

Find actual ramps that provide access for people with disabilities. Measure the heights and lengths of these ramps and calculate their ideal mechanical advantages. Find out what the requirements are for access ramps in your area. Should your ramp be made of a particular material? Should it level off before it reaches the door? How wide should it be? How does it provide water drainage?

SECTION 4 Machines in the Human Body

DISCOVER
·····················ACTIVITY·····

Are You an Eating Machine?

1. Using your front teeth, bite off a piece of a cracker. As you bite, observe how your teeth are breaking the cracker. Also think about the shape of your front teeth.

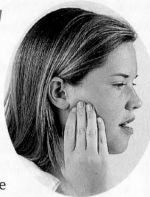

2. Now chew the cracker. Pay attention to how your lower jaw moves. Touch your jaw below your ear, as shown in the photo. As you chew, push in slightly there so that you can feel how your jaw moves. If the structure is still not clear, try opening your mouth wide while you feel the back of the jaw.

Think It Over

Observing When you bite and chew, your teeth and jaws serve as two kinds of machines. What are they?

GUIDE FOR READING

◆ How does the body use levers and wedges?

Reading Tip Before you read, preview the illustrations and predict how simple machines are related to the human body.

I t's Saturday night, and you and your friends are taking a well-deserved break from your school work. You're watching a great movie, happily eating popcorn from a big bowl. Are you doing any work? Surprisingly, you are!

Every time you reach for the popcorn, your muscles exert a force that causes your arm to move. And when you chew on the popcorn, breaking it into bits that you can easily swallow, you are again doing work.

How are you able to do all this work without even noticing? The answer is machines! You probably don't think of the human body as being made of machines. But believe it or not, machines are involved in much of the work that your body does.

Living Levers

Most of the machines in your body are levers that consist of bones and muscles. Every time you move, you use a muscle. Your muscles are attached to your bones by tough connective tissue called **tendons.** Tendons and muscles pull on bones, making them work as levers. The joint, near where the tendon is attached to the bone, acts as the fulcrum of the lever. The muscles produce the input force. The output force is used for everything from lifting your hand to swinging a hammer.

A muscle by itself cannot push; it can only pull. When a muscle contracts, or becomes shorter, it pulls the bone to which it is attached. So how can you bend your arm as shown in *Exploring Levers in the Body?* The answer is that most muscles work in pairs. For example, when your biceps muscle (on the front of the upper arm) contracts, it exerts a force on the bone in your forearm. The result is that you arm bends at the elbow joint, which in this case is the fulcrum of the lever. When the triceps muscle (on the back of the upper arm) contracts, it opens the elbow joint.

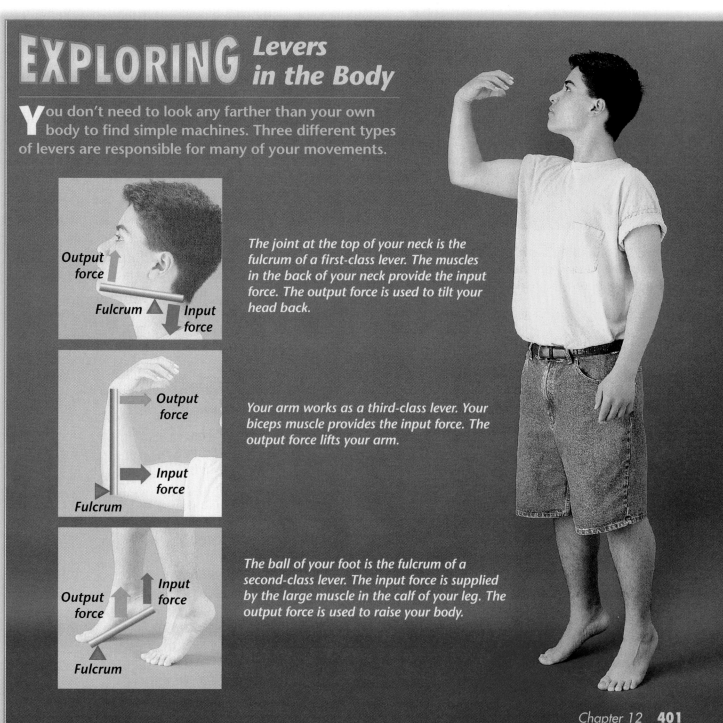

EXPLORING *Levers in the Body*

You don't need to look any farther than your own body to find simple machines. Three different types of levers are responsible for many of your movements.

Output force

Fulcrum   Input force

The joint at the top of your neck is the fulcrum of a first-class lever. The muscles in the back of your neck provide the input force. The output force is used to tilt your head back.

Output force

Input force

Fulcrum

Your arm works as a third-class lever. Your biceps muscle provides the input force. The output force lifts your arm.

Input force

Output force

Fulcrum

The ball of your foot is the fulcrum of a second-class lever. The input force is supplied by the large muscle in the calf of your leg. The output force is used to raise your body.

Figure 20 Your front teeth are shaped like wedges. These wedges allow you to cut through food, such as an apple.

Look again at the different levers in *Exploring Levers in the Body*. You will see that you can find a lever in your neck and another lever in your leg and foot. Just as you found with shovels, wheelbarrows, and fishing poles, the type of lever you find in the human body depends on the locations of the fulcrum, input force, and output force.

Working Wedges

Have you ever paid attention to the shape of your teeth? Some of your teeth are wedge-shaped, others are pointed, and still others are relatively flat. This is because they have different uses.

When you bite into an apple, you use your sharp front teeth, called incisors. These teeth are shaped to enable you to bite off pieces of food. What simple machine do these teeth resemble? **Your incisors are shaped like wedges.** When you bite down on something, the wedge shape of your front teeth produces enough force to break it in half, just as an ax is used to split a log. Your rear teeth, or molars, are more flat. These teeth are used to grind your food into pieces that are small enough to be swallowed and digested.

There's a lot more to chewing than you may have realized. The next time you take a bite of a crunchy apple, think about the machines in your mouth!

 Section 4 Review

1. In what way do your bones and muscles operate as levers?
2. Where in your body can you identify wedges? What role do they play in your daily life?
3. Point your left index finger (your pointing finger) in front of you. Then move it to the right. Where is the fulcrum? Where is the input force? What kind of lever is your finger?
4. **Thinking Critically Inferring** Make a motion as if you were going to throw a ball. What muscle do you think you use to straighten out your arm when you throw? What kind of lever are you using?

Science at Home

Finger Forces Have a family member place a wooden toothpick between the ends of his or her fingers as shown in the upper photograph. Ask that person to try to break the toothpick by pressing down with the first and third fingers. Now repeat the procedure, but this time have the person hold the toothpick as shown in the lower photograph. Explain to your family why the toothpick was easier to break on the second try. How were the positions of the forces and fulcrum different in each case?

SECTION 1 — What Is Work?

Key Ideas

◆ Work is done on an object when a force causes that object to move some distance.

◆ The amount of work done on an object is equal to the force on the object in the direction of its motion multiplied by the distance the object moves.

$$Work = Force \times Distance$$

Key Terms

work   joule

SECTION 2 — Mechanical Advantage and Efficiency

Key Ideas

◆ A machine makes work easier by changing the direction or amount of force needed to accomplish a task.

◆ The efficiency of a machine is the percentage of the input work that is changed to output work.

$$Efficiency = \frac{Output\ work}{Input\ work} \times 100\%$$

◆ The mechanical advantage of a machine is obtained by dividing the output force by the input force.

$$Mechanical\ advantage = \frac{Output\ force}{Input\ force}$$

◆ The ideal mechanical advantage of a machine is the mechanical advantage that it would have if there were no friction.

Key Terms

machine
input force
output force
mechanical advantage
efficiency
actual mechanical advantage
ideal mechanical advantage

SECTION 3 — Simple Machines

Key Ideas

◆ There are six basic kinds of simple machines: the inclined plane, the wedge, the screw, the lever, the wheel and axle, and the pulley.

◆ A compound machine is a machine that is made from two or more simple machines.

Key Terms

inclined plane	wheel and axle
wedge	pulley
screw	compound machine
lever	gears
fulcrum	

SECTION 4 — Machines in the Human Body

INTEGRATING LIFE SCIENCE

Key Ideas

◆ Most of the machines in your body are levers that consist of bones with muscles attached to them.

◆ When you bite into something, your front teeth use the principle of the wedge.

Key Term

tendon

Organizing Information

Compare/Contrast Table Complete a compare/contrast table similar to the one shown below. For each of three other basic types of simple machines, you should show how to calculate the ideal mechanical advantage and give an example. (For more on compare/contrast tables, see the Skills Handbook.)

Simple Machine	Mechanical Advantage	Example
Inclined Plane	Length of incline ÷ Height of incline	Ramp

Reviewing Content

 For more review of key concepts, see the Interactive Student Tutorial CD-ROM.

Multiple Choice

Choose the letter of the answer that best completes each statement.

1. The amount of work done on an object is obtained by multiplying
   a. input force and output force.
   b. force and distance.
   c. time and force.
   d. efficiency and work.

2. One way a machine can make work easier for you is by
   a. decreasing the amount of work you do.
   b. changing the direction of your force.
   c. increasing the amount of work required for a task.
   d. decreasing the friction you encounter.

3. The output force is greater than the input force for a
   a. nutcracker.
   b. fishing pole.
   c. single fixed pulley.
   d. rake.

4. An example of a second-class lever is a
   a. seesaw.   b. shovel.
   c. paddle.   d. wheelbarrow.

5. An example of a compound machine is a
   a. screwdriver.   b. crowbar.
   c. bicycle.   d. ramp.

True or False

If the statement is true, write true. If it is false, change the underlined word or words to make the statement true.

6. If none of the force on an object is in the direction of the object's <u>motion</u>, no work is done.

7. <u>Friction</u> reduces the efficiency of a machine.

8. The comparison between output work and input work is <u>ideal mechanical advantage</u>.

9. A <u>pulley</u> can be thought of as an inclined plane wrapped around a central cylinder.

10. Your front teeth act as a <u>fulcrum</u> when you bite into something.

Checking Concepts

11. The mythical god Atlas was supposed to hold the stationary Earth on his shoulders. Was Atlas performing any work? Explain your answer.

12. Suppose that you do 1,000 joules of work when you operate an old can opener. However, the can opener does only 500 joules of work in opening the can. What is the efficiency of the can opener?

13. The actual mechanical advantage of a machine is 3. If you exert an input force of 5 N, what output force is exerted by the machine?

14. Which has a greater ideal mechanical advantage, a ramp that is 12 m long and 2 m high or a ramp that is 6 m long and 2 m high? Explain your answer.

15. When you let water into a bathtub, what kind of machine helps you open the tap?

16. Describe a lever in your body. Locate the input force, output force and fulcrum.

17. **Writing to Learn** You are a brilliant inventor. Recently you completed your most outstanding project—an odd-looking, but very important machine. Write an explanation describing your machine, how you built it, what it is made of, and what it does. You may wish to illustrate your explanation.

Thinking Critically

18. **Applying Concepts** To open a door, you push on the part farthest from the hinges. Why would it be harder to open the door if you pushed on the center?

19. **Classifying** What type of simple machine would be used to lower an empty bucket into a well and then lift the bucket full of water?

20. **Relating Cause and Effect** Describe the relationship between friction and the efficiency of a machine.

21. **Inferring** Why would sharpening a knife or ax blade improve its mechanical advantage?

Applying Skills

Use the illustration to answer Questions 22–25.

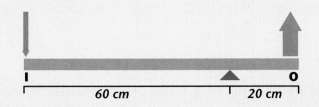

60 cm   20 cm

22. **Calculating** The figure shows the distance from the fulcrum to the input force (point I) and from the fulcrum to the output force (point O). Use the distance to calculate the ideal mechanical advantage of the lever.

23. **Predicting** What would the ideal mechanical advantage be if the distance from the fulcrum to the input force were 20 cm, 40 cm, or 80 cm?

24. **Graphing** Use your answers to Questions 22 and 23 to graph the distance from the fulcrum to the input force on the *x*-axis and the ideal mechanical advantage of the lever on the *y*-axis.

25. **Interpreting Data** What does your graph show you about the relationship between the ideal mechanical advantage of a first-class lever and the distance between the fulcrum and the input force.

Performance ▽ CHAPTER PROJECT Assessment

Present Your Project Ask a classmate to review your project with you. Does your machine lift the loaded can 5 cm? Is it made up of two or more simple machines? Check all measurements and calculations. When you demonstrate your nifty lifting machine to the class, explain why you built it as you did. Describe any other designs that you considered along the way.

Reflect and Record If you were just beginning this project, you could use the knowledge you've gained to build an even better machine. Draw diagrams and write a short paragraph in your journal to explain how you would improve the machine you built.

Test Preparation

Use these questions to prepare for standardized tests.

Use the diagram to answer Questions 26–28.

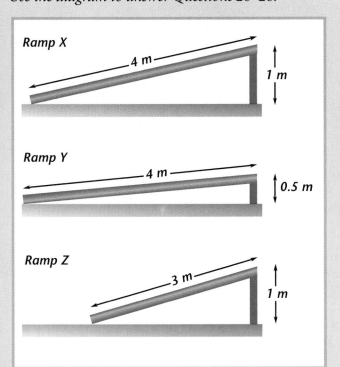

Ramp X — 4 m — 1 m

Ramp Y — 4 m — 0.5 m

Ramp Z — 3 m — 1 m

26. Which ramp has the greatest ideal mechanical advantage?
    a. X
    b. Y
    c. Z
    d. X and Y are the same.

27. To increase the ideal mechanical advantage of a ramp, you can
    a. increase the length and the height by the same amount.
    b. increase the length or decrease the height.
    c. decrease the length or increase the height.
    d. decrease the length and the height by the same amount.

28. What would the ideal mechanical advantage of Ramp Z become if the height were changed to 0.5 m and the length remained the same?
    a. 1.5   b. 3.5
    c. 6   d. 15

CHAPTER

13 Energy and Power

WEB ACTIVITY
www.phschool.com

SECTION
1 The Nature of Energy

Discover How High Does a Ball Bounce?
Skills Lab Soaring Straws

SECTION
2 Energy Conversion and Conservation

Discover What Would Make a Card Jump?
Try This Pendulum Swing
Science at Home Hot Wire

SECTION
3 Energy Conversions and Fossil Fuels

Discover What Is a Fuel?
Sharpen Your Skills Graphing

406

Roller Coaster!

Slowly, but steadily, you climb the mighty hill. Up, up, up, and then whoosh—you plunge swiftly down the other side. You curve left, then right, and then up again. This thrilling roller coaster ride is brought to you courtesy of energy. In this chapter you will learn about energy, the forms it takes, and how it is transformed and conserved. You will use what you learn to design and construct your own roller coaster.

Your Goal To design and construct a roller coaster that uses kinetic and potential energy to move.

Your project must

- be no wider than 2 meters and be easily disassembled and reassembled
- have a first hill with a height of 1 meter and have at least two additional hills
- have a car that moves along the entire track without stopping
- follow the safety guidelines in Appendix A

Get Started If you or any of your classmates have ridden a roller coaster, share your experiences. Brainstorm the characteristics of a good roller coaster. Consider how fast the roller coaster moves and how its speed changes throughout the ride.

Check Your Progress You'll be working on this project as you study this chapter. To keep your project on track, look for Check Your Progress boxes at the following points.

Section 1 Review, page 413: Experiment with different hill heights and inclines.

Section 3 Review, page 425: Describe how your vehicle moves along its tracks in terms of potential and kinetic energy.

Section 4 Review, page 430: Add turns and loops to determine their effect.

Present Your Project At the end of the chapter (page 433), you will show how your roller coaster car can move up and down at least three hills once you release it.

The cars on a roller coaster like this one may reach speeds of more than 100 kilometers per hour.

SECTION 4
Integrating Mathematics
Power

Discover Is Work Always the Same?
Real-World Lab Can You Feel the Power?

DISCOVER • **ACTIVITY** • • •

How High Does a Ball Bounce?

1. Hold a meter stick vertically, with the zero end on the ground.

2. Drop a tennis ball from the 50-centimeter mark and record the height to which it bounces.

3. Drop the tennis ball from the 100-centimeter mark and record the height to which it bounces.

4. Predict how high the ball will bounce if dropped from the 75-centimeter mark. Test your prediction.

Think It Over
Observing How does the height from which you drop the ball relate to the height to which the ball bounces?

GUIDE FOR READING

◆ How are work and energy related?

◆ What are the two basic kinds of energy?

◆ What are some of the different forms of energy?

Reading Tip Before you read, list several familiar examples of energy. Add to your list as you read the section.

Brilliant streaks of lightning flash across the night sky. The howl of the wind and the crashing of thunder drown out the sound of falling rain. Then a sound like a railroad locomotive approaches. As the sound grows louder, a small town experiences the power and fury of a tornado. Whirling winds of more than 250 kilometers per hour blow through the town. Roofs are lifted off of buildings. Cars are thrown about like toys. Then, in minutes, the tornado is gone.

The next morning, as rescuers survey the damage, a light breeze delicately carries falling leaves past the debris. How strange it is that the wind is violent enough to destroy buildings one night and barely strong enough to carry a leaf the next morning. Wind is just moving air, but it possesses energy. As you read on, you'll find out what energy is.

What Is Energy?

When wind moves a leaf, or even a house, it causes a change. In this case, the change is in the position of the object. Recall that work is done when a force moves an object through a distance. The ability to do work or cause change is called **energy.** So the wind has energy.

Figure 1 The energy of a tornado can devastate a town in minutes.

Figure 2 A bowling ball can do work because it is moving. *Applying Concepts What is the ability to do work called?*

When an object or organism does work on another object, some of its energy is transferred to that object. **You can think of work, then, as the transfer of energy.** When energy is transferred, the object upon which the work is done gains energy. Energy is measured in joules—the same units as work.

Kinetic Energy

There are two general kinds of energy. **The two kinds of energy are kinetic energy and potential energy.** Whether energy is kinetic or potential depends on whether an object is moving or not.

The examples you have read about so far have involved things that were moving. A moving object can collide with another object and move it some distance. In that way, the moving object does work. For example, a bowling ball knocks over a bowling pin.

Because the moving object can do work, it must have energy. The energy of motion is called **kinetic energy.** The word kinetic comes from the Greek word *kinetos*, which means "moving."

Mass and Velocity The kinetic energy of an object depends on both its mass and its velocity. Think about rolling a golf ball and a bowling ball so that they travel at the same velocity. Which ball would you have to roll more forcefully? You would have to exert a greater force on the bowling ball because it has more mass than the golf ball.

Since energy is transferred during work, the more work you do, the more energy you give to the ball. So a bowling ball has more kinetic energy than a golf ball traveling at the same velocity. Kinetic energy increases as mass increases.

What would you have to do to make the bowling ball move faster? You would have to throw it harder, or use a greater force.

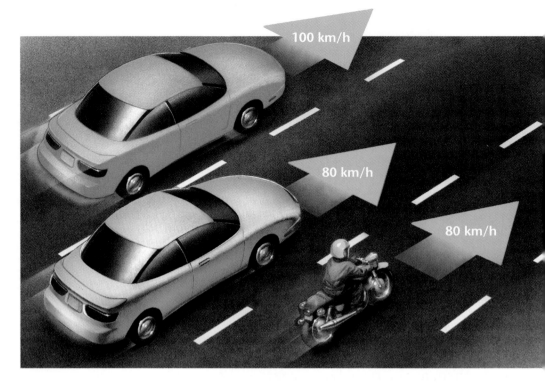

Figure 3 Kinetic energy increases as mass and velocity increase.
Interpreting Diagrams List the three vehicles in order of increasing kinetic energy.

100 km/h

80 km/h

80 km/h

In other words, you have to do more work on the bowling ball to give it a greater velocity. Kinetic energy increases when velocity increases.

Calculating Kinetic Energy Kinetic energy depends on both mass and velocity. The mathematical relationship between kinetic energy, mass, and velocity is written as follows.

$$\text{Kinetic energy} = \frac{\text{Mass} \times \text{Velocity}^2}{2}$$

Do changes in velocity and mass have the same effect on kinetic energy? No—changing the velocity of an object will have a greater effect on its kinetic energy than changing its mass. This is because velocity is squared in the energy equation. For instance, doubling the mass of an object will double its kinetic energy. But doubling its velocity will quadruple its kinetic energy.

☑ *Checkpoint* *What is kinetic energy?*

Potential Energy

Sometimes when you transfer energy to an object, you change its position or shape. For example, you lift a book up to your desk or you compress a spring to wind a toy. Unlike kinetic energy, which is the energy of motion, potential energy is stored. It might be used later on when the book falls to the floor or the spring unwinds. Energy that is stored and held in readiness is called **potential energy.** This type of energy has the *potential* to do work.

Math TOOLBOX

Squared Numbers

A squared number is written with an exponent of 2. For example, you can write 2^2, 3^2, or 4^2. To find the value of a squared number, multiply the number by itself.

$$2^2 = 2 \times 2 = 4$$
$$3^2 = 3 \times 3 = 9$$
$$4^2 = 4 \times 4 = 16$$

Notice how fast the squared numbers increase. For example, although the numbers 2 and 3 only differ by one, their squares differ by five.

An archer gives potential energy to a bow by pulling it back. The stored energy can send an arrow whistling to its target. The potential energy associated with objects that can be stretched or compressed is called **elastic potential energy.**

You give a different type of potential energy to an object when you lift it. Potential energy that depends on height is **gravitational potential energy.**

The gravitational potential energy an object has is equal to the work done to lift it. Remember that Work = Force × Distance. The force is the force you use to lift the object, or its weight. The distance is the distance the object moves, or its height. This gives you the following formula.

Gravitational potential energy = Weight × Height

When weight is measured in newtons and height is measured in meters, the unit of energy is the newton-meter. This unit is also known as the joule (J). Recall from Chapter 12 that a joule is the amount of work you do when you exert a force of 1 newton to move an object a distance of 1 meter. Work and energy share the same unit because energy and work are so closely related.

Once you know weight and height, you can calculate gravitational potential energy. Suppose that a hiker climbs 40 meters up a hill and that he weighs 680 newtons. The hiker has gained 27,200 joules (680 newtons × 40 meters) of gravitational potential energy at the top of the climb.

The greater the weight of an object or the greater the height it is lifted, the greater its gravitational potential energy. The hiker would gain more gravitational potential energy by climbing to a greater height or by increasing weight, maybe by wearing a backpack.

What if you know the mass of an object instead of its weight? Then you multiply the mass of the object (in kilograms) by the acceleration of gravity (9.8 m/s^2) to find its weight in newtons. Now you can write a second formula for gravitational potential energy.

Gravitational potential energy =
Mass × Gravitational acceleration × Height

Again, the unit of measure is the joule.

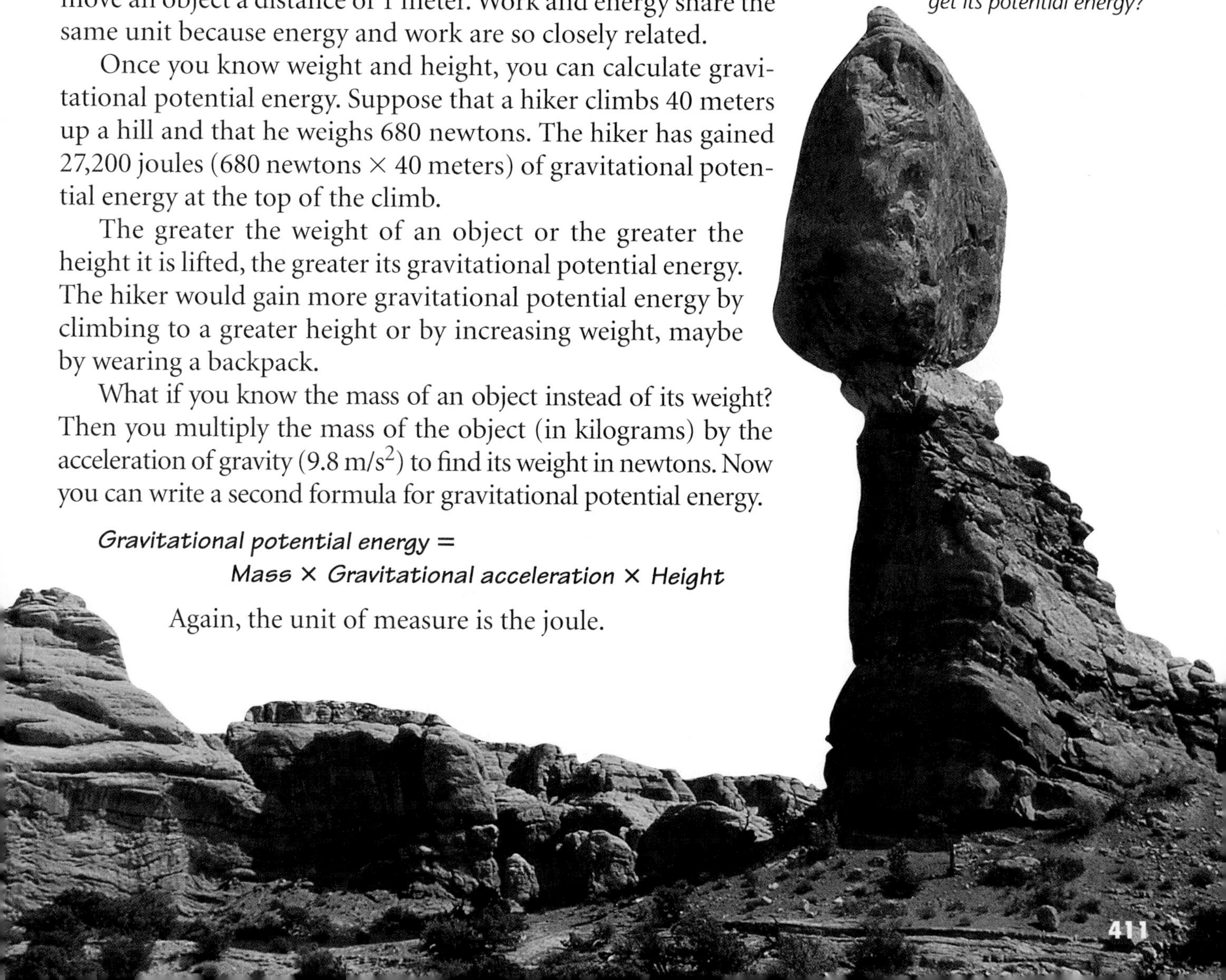

Figure 4 A rock poised for a fall has potential energy. *Inferring How did the rock get its potential energy?*

Different Forms of Energy

The examples of energy you have read about so far involve objects being moved or physically changed. But both kinetic energy and potential energy have a variety of different forms. **Some of the major forms of energy are mechanical energy, thermal energy, chemical energy, electrical energy, electromagnetic energy, and nuclear energy.**

Mechanical Energy The school bus you ride in, a frog leaping through the air, and even the sounds you hear all have mechanical energy. **Mechanical energy** is the energy associated with the motion or position of an object. Mechanical energy can occur as kinetic energy or potential energy.

Thermal Energy All matter is made up of small particles, called atoms and molecules. These particles have both potential energy and kinetic energy due to their arrangement and motion. Thermal energy is the total energy of the particles in an object. When the thermal energy of an object increases, its particles move faster, making it feel warm to the touch. Ice cream melts when its thermal energy increases.

Chemical Energy Chemical compounds, such as chocolate, wood, and wax, store **chemical energy.** Chemical energy is potential energy stored in chemical bonds that hold chemical compounds together. Chemical energy is stored in the foods you eat and in a match that is used to light a candle. Chemical energy is even stored in the cells of your body.

Figure 5 Energy is all around you in many different forms. The leaping frog is an example of mechanical energy, and the melting ice is an example of thermal energy.
Observing Which forms of energy are shown in the photographs of the sparkler, the sun, and the lightning?

Electrical Energy When you receive a shock from a metal door-knob, you experience electrical energy. Moving electric charges produce electricity and the energy they carry is called **electrical energy.** You rely on electrical energy from batteries or power lines to run electrical devices such as radios, lights, and computers.

Electromagnetic Energy The light that you see each day is a form of **electromagnetic energy.** Electromagnetic energy travels in waves. These waves have some electrical properties and some magnetic properties. In addition to visible light, ultraviolet radiation, microwaves, and infrared radiation are all examples of electromagnetic energy.

Nuclear Energy Another type of potential energy, called **nuclear energy,** is stored in the nucleus of an atom and is released during nuclear reactions. One kind of nuclear reaction occurs when a nucleus splits (nuclear fission). Another kind occurs when nuclei fuse, or join together (nuclear fusion). These reactions release tremendous amounts of energy. Nuclear power plants use fission reactions to produce electricity. Nuclear fusion occurs in the sun and other stars.

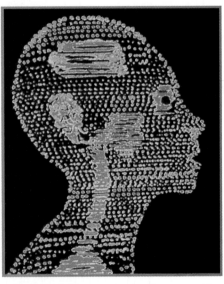

Figure 6 Electromagnetic energy is used to take a CT scan.

Section 1 Review

1. Are energy and work the same thing? Explain.
2. How are kinetic and potential energy different?
3. List the forms of energy and give an example of each.
4. **Thinking Critically Problem Solving** A boulder that weighs 200 N is poised at the edge of a 100-meter cliff. What is its gravitational potential energy? Draw a diagram showing how its potential energy changes as it falls to 50 m, 20 m, and 10 m.

SOARING STRAWS

In this lab you will use the skill of controlling variables. You will investigate the relationship between the height reached by a rocket and the amount of stretch in a rubber band.

Problem

How does the gravitational potential energy of a straw rocket depend on the elastic potential energy of the rubber band launcher?

Materials

scissors
3 plastic straws
marker
balance
empty toilet paper tube

rubber band
meter stick
metric ruler
masking tape

Procedure

1. Construct the rocket and launcher following the instructions below. Use a balance to find the mass of the rocket in grams. Record the mass.

2. Hold the launcher in one hand with your fingers over the ends of the rubber band. Load the launcher by placing the straw rocket on the rubber band and pulling down from the other end as shown in the photograph. Let go and launch the rocket straight up. **CAUTION:** *Be sure to aim the straw rocket into the air, not at classmates.*

3. Have your partner hold a meter stick, or tape it to the wall, so that its zero end is even with the top of the rocket launcher. Measure the height, in meters, to which the rocket rises. If the rocket goes higher than a single meter stick, use two meter sticks.

4. In your notebook, make a data table similar to the one on the next page.

5. You can measure the amount of stretch of the rubber band by noting where the markings on the rocket line up with the bottom of the launching cylinder. Launch the rocket using five different amounts of stretch. Record your measurements.

MAKING A ROCKET AND LAUNCHER

A. Cut a rubber band and tape it across the open end of a hollow cylinder, such as a toilet paper tube. The rubber band should be taut, but only stretched a tiny amount. This is the launcher.

B. Cut about 3 cm off a plastic straw.

C. Lay 2 full-length straws side by side on a flat surface with the 3-cm piece of straw between them. Arrange the straws so that their ends are even.

D. Tape the straws together side by side.

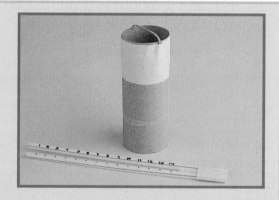

E. Starting from the untaped end, make marks every centimeter on one of the long straws. This is the rocket.

DATA TABLE

Amount of Stretch (cm)	Height (Trial 1) (m)	Height (Trial 2) (m)	Height (Trial 3) (m)	Average Height (m)	Gravitational Potential Energy (mJ)

6. For each amount of stretch, find the average height to which the rocket rises. Record the height in your data table.

7. Find the gravitational potential energy for each amount of stretch:

Gravitational potential energy =
 Mass × Gravitational acceleration × Height

You have measured the mass in grams. So the unit of energy is the millijoule (mJ), which is one thousandth of a joule. Record the results in your data table.

Analyze and Conclude

1. Which variable in your data table is the manipulated variable? The responding variable? How do you know?

2. Graph your results. Show gravitational potential energy on the vertical axis and amount of stretch on the horizontal axis.

3. What measurement is related to the elastic potential energy in this experiment?

4. Look at the shape of the graph. What conclusions can you reach about the relationship between the gravitational potential energy of the rocket and the elastic potential energy of the rubber band?

5. How do you think the amount of energy before the rocket was released compares to the amount of energy after the rocket was released? Account for any losses.

6. Think About It Besides the amount of stretch, what other variables might affect the height to which the straw rocket rises? Have you been able to control these variables in your experiment? Explain why or why not.

More to Explore

Use your launcher to investigate launches at angles other than straight up. Instead of manipulating the amount of stretch, hold that variable constant and manipulate the angle of launch. Measure both the heights and distances of the rocket. **CAUTION:** *Be careful not to aim the rocket near any of your classmates.*

② Energy Conversion and Conservation

What Would Make a Card Jump?

1. Fold an index card in half as shown.

2. In the edge opposite the fold, cut two slits that are about 2 cm long and 2 cm apart.

3. Open the card a little, and loop a rubber band through all four slits. Keeping the fold upward, flatten the card and hold it flat as shown.

4. Predict what will happen to the card if you let go. Then test your prediction.

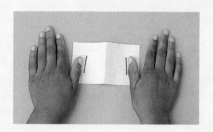

Think It Over

Forming Operational Definitions Describe what happened to the card. Define potential and kinetic energy in terms of the card and the rubber band.

GUIDE FOR READING

◆ How are different forms of energy related?

◆ What is the law of conservation of energy?

Reading Tip As you read, draw a flowchart to show each example of energy conversions.

The spray of water bounces off your raincoat as you look up at the millions of liters of water plunging toward you. The roar of water is deafening. You hold on to the rail as you are rocked back and forth by the rough waves. Are you doomed? Fortunately not—you are on a sightseeing boat at the foot of the mighty Niagara Falls, located on the border between the United States and Canada. The waterfall carries the huge amount of water that drains from the upper Great Lakes. It is an awesome sight that has attracted visitors from all over the world for hundreds of years.

What many visitors don't know, however, is that Niagara Falls serves as much more than just a spectacular view. The waterfall is the center of a network of electrical power lines. The falling water is used to generate electricity for much of the neighboring region.

Figure 7 Niagara Falls is more than 50 meters high.

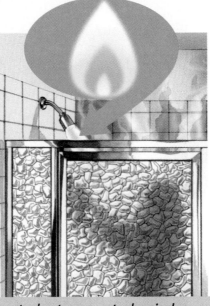

The lamp and clock convert electrical energy to electromagnetic energy.

A water heater converts chemical energy in natural gas to thermal energy.

The student's body converts chemical energy in food to mechanical energy.

Conversions Between Forms of Energy

What does water have to do with electricity? You may already know that the mechanical energy of moving water can be converted, or transformed, into electrical energy. A change from one form of energy to another is called an **energy conversion,** or an energy transformation. **Most forms of energy can be converted into any other form.**

You encounter energy conversions frequently. A toaster, for example, converts electrical energy to thermal energy. In an electric motor, electrical energy is converted to mechanical energy that can be used to run a machine.

Your body converts the chemical energy in the food you eat to the mechanical energy you need to move your muscles. Chemical energy in food is also converted to the thermal energy your body uses to maintain its temperature. Chemical energy is even converted to the electrical energy your brain uses to think.

Often a series of energy conversions is needed to do a task. Strike a match, for example, and the mechanical energy used to move the match is converted to thermal energy. The thermal energy causes the match to release stored chemical energy, which is converted to thermal energy and to the energy you see as light.

In a car engine another series of conversions occurs. Electrical energy produces a hot spark. The thermal energy of the spark releases chemical energy in the fuel. When the fuel burns, this chemical energy in turn becomes thermal energy. Thermal energy is converted to mechanical energy used to move the car, and to electrical energy that produces more sparks.

Figure 8 In just the first few minutes of the morning, this student experiences numerous energy conversions. Imagine how many more can be identified throughout the course of a single day!

☑ *Checkpoint* *Give an example of an energy conversion.*

Figure 9 Energy conversions enable this athlete to vault more than six meters into the air. *Predicting What energy conversions will occur after the vaulter falls over the bar?*

Figure 10 When an object is tossed into the air, energy conversions take place.

Maximum potential energy

50% kinetic energy
50% potential energy

Maximum kinetic energy

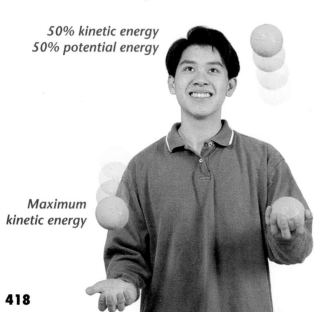

Kinetic and Potential Energy

One of the most common conversions is the conversion of potential energy to kinetic energy. When you stretch a rubber band, you give it elastic potential energy. If you let it go, the rubber band flies across the room. When the rubber band is moving, it has kinetic energy. The potential energy of the stretched rubber band is converted to the kinetic energy of the moving rubber band.

Energy Conversion in Juggling Any object that rises or falls experiences a change in its kinetic and gravitational potential energy. Look at the orange in Figure 10. When it moves, the orange possesses kinetic energy. As it rises, it slows down. Its kinetic energy decreases. But because its height increases, its potential energy increases. At the highest point in its path, it stops moving. At this point, it no longer possesses kinetic energy, but it possesses potential energy. As the orange falls, the entire energy conversion is reversed—kinetic energy increases while potential energy decreases.

Energy Conversion in a Waterfall There is a conversion between potential and kinetic energy on a large scale at Niagara Falls, which you read about earlier. The water at the top of the falls has gravitational potential energy because it is higher than the bottom of the falls. But as the water falls, its height decreases and so it loses potential energy. At the same time, its kinetic energy increases because its velocity increases. Thus potential energy is converted into kinetic energy.

Energy Conversion in a Pole Vault As a pole vaulter runs, he has kinetic energy because he is moving. When he plants his pole to jump, the pole bends. His kinetic energy is converted to elastic potential energy in the pole. As the pole straightens out, the vaulter is lifted high into the air. The elastic potential energy of the pole is converted to the gravitational potential energy of the pole vaulter. Once over the bar, the vaulter's gravitational potential energy is converted into kinetic energy as he falls to the safety cushion below.

Energy Conversion in a Pendulum A continuous conversion between kinetic energy and potential energy takes place in a pendulum. At the highest point in its swing, the pendulum in Figure 11 has only gravitational potential energy. As the pendulum starts to swing downward, it speeds up and its gravitational potential energy changes to kinetic energy. At the bottom of its swing, all its energy is kinetic energy. Then, as it swings to the other side and slows down, it regains gravitational potential energy, and at the same time loses kinetic energy. At the top of its swing on the other side it again has only gravitational potential energy. And so the pattern of energy conversion continues.

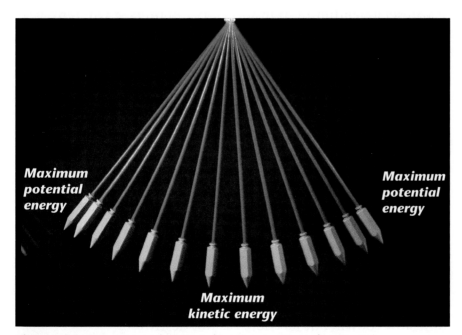

Maximum potential energy

Maximum potential energy

Maximum kinetic energy

Figure 11 Conversions between kinetic energy and potential energy take place in a pendulum. *Interpreting Diagrams At what two points is potential energy greatest?*

Pendulum Swing

1. Set up a pendulum using washers or a rubber stopper, string, a ring stand, and a clamp.

2. Pull the pendulum back so that it makes a 45° angle with the vertical. Measure the height of the stopper. Then set it in motion and observe the height to which it swings.

3. Use a second clamp to reduce the length of the pendulum as shown. The pendulum will run into the second clamp at the bottom of its swing.

4. Pull the pendulum back to the same height as you did the first time. Predict the height to which the pendulum will swing. Then set it in motion and observe it.

Observing How high did the pendulum swing in each case? Explain your observations.

Figure 12 M. C. Escher's print "Waterfall" was done in 1961.

Conservation of Energy

If you set a pendulum in motion, do you think it will remain in motion forever? No, it will not. Does that mean that energy is destroyed over time? The answer is no. The **law of conservation of energy** states that when one form of energy is converted to another, no energy is destroyed in the process. **According to the law of conservation of energy, energy cannot be created or destroyed.** So the total amount of energy is the same before and after any process. All energy can be accounted for.

Energy and Friction So what happens to the kinetic energy of the pendulum? As the pendulum moves, it encounters friction at the pivot of the string and from the air through which it moves. When an object experiences friction, the motion (and thus the kinetic energy) of the atoms or molecules increases. This means its thermal energy increases. So the mechanical energy of the moving pendulum is converted to thermal energy. The pendulum slows down, but its energy is not destroyed.

The fact that friction converts mechanical energy to thermal energy should not surprise you. After all, you take advantage of such thermal energy when you rub your cold hands together to warm them up. The fact that energy is converted to thermal energy because of friction explains why no machine is 100 percent efficient. Recall from Chapter 12 that the work output of a machine is always less than the work input. Now you know that energy is converted to thermal energy in a machine.

Energy and Matter You might have heard of Albert Einstein's theory of relativity. Einstein's theory included a small change to the law of conservation of energy. He explained that energy can sometimes be created—by destroying matter! This process is not important for most of the energy conversions described in this chapter. But it is important in nuclear reactions, where huge amounts of energy are produced by destroying tiny amounts of matter. This discovery means that in some situations energy alone is not conserved. But scientists say that matter and energy together are always conserved. Just as different forms of energy can be converted to one another, matter and energy can be converted back and forth.

Conserving Energy

Figure 13 Albert Einstein published his theory of special relativity in 1905.

![Integrating Environmental Science icon] *INTEGRATING ENVIRONMENTAL SCIENCE* When you hear or read about conserving energy, don't get confused with the law of conservation of energy. Conserving energy means saving energy, or not wasting it. In other words, conserving energy means we should not waste fuels, such as gasoline, or our resources will be used up quickly. The law of conservation of energy in physical science, however, refers to a quantity that remains constant. In science, energy is always conserved because its total quantity does not change.

Section 2 Review

1. What is an energy conversion?
2. State the law of conservation of energy in your own words.
3. Describe the energy conversions that occur when a ball is dropped and bounces back up. Why do you think the ball bounces a little lower each time?
4. **Thinking Critically Applying Concepts** A roller coaster car with a mass of 500 kg is at the top of a hill that is 30 m high. Without friction, what would its kinetic energy be as it reached the bottom of the hill?

Science at Home

Hot Wire Straighten a wire hanger. Have your family members feel the wire and observe whether it feels cool or warm. Then hold the ends of the wire and bend it several times. **CAUTION:** *If the wire breaks, it can be sharp.* Do not bend it more than a few times. After bending the wire, have your family members feel it again. Ask them to explain how energy conversions can produce a change in temperature.

SECTION 3 Energy Conversions and Fossil Fuels

DISCOVER •• ACTIVITY ••••

What Is a Fuel?

1. Put on your goggles. Attach a flask to a ring stand with a clamp. Then place a thermometer in the flask.

2. Add enough water to the flask to cover the thermometer bulb. Record the temperature of the water, and remove the thermometer.

3. Fold a wooden coffee stirrer in three places to look like a W.

4. Stand the bent coffee stirrer in a small aluminum pan so that the W is upright. Position the pan 4–5 cm directly below the flask.

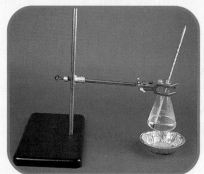

5. Ignite the coffee stirrer at the center. **CAUTION:** *Be careful when using matches.*

6. When the coffee stirrer has stopped burning, find the temperature of the water again. Wait until the flask has cooled before cleaning up.

Think It Over

Forming Operational Definitions Gasoline in a car, kerosene in a lantern, and a piece of wood are all fuels. Based on your observations, what is a fuel?

GUIDE FOR READING

◆ What is the source of the energy stored in fossil fuels?

◆ How is energy converted when fossil fuels are used?

Reading Tip Before you read, preview *Exploring Energy Conversions* on page 424. Write down any questions that you may have. Then look for answers as you read.

Envision a lush, green, swampy forest. Ferns as tall as trees block the view as they rise up to 30 meters. Enormous dragonflies buzz through the warm, moist air. And huge cockroaches, some longer than your finger, crawl across the ground. Where is it? Actually, the question should be, When is it? The time is over 400 million years ago. That's even before the dinosaurs lived! What does this ancient forest have to do with you? You might be surprised to find out just how important this forest is to you.

Figure 14 The plants and animals in this painting of an ancient forest have become the fossil fuels you use today. *Applying Concepts What are fossil fuels?*

422

Figure 15 Fossil fuels such as coal store chemical potential energy. *Predicting How do you think the stored energy is utilized?*

Formation of Fossil Fuels

The plants of vast forests that once covered Earth provide you with energy you use today. This energy is stored in fuels. A fuel is a material that stores chemical potential energy. The gasoline used in your school bus, the propane used in a gas barbecue grill, and the chemicals used to launch a space shuttle are examples of fuels. Some of the fuels used today were formed hundreds of millions of years ago by geological processes. These fuels, which include coal, petroleum, and natural gas, are known as **fossil fuels.**

As you'll discover in *Exploring Energy Conversions* on page 424, coal was formed from the ancient forests you just read about. When ancient plants and animals died, they formed thick layers in swamps and marshes. Clay and sand sediments covered the plant and animal remains. Over time, more and more sediment piled up. The resulting pressure along with high temperatures turned the animal and plant remains into coal.

Energy is conserved. That means that fuels do not create energy. So if fossil fuels store energy, they must have gotten energy from somewhere else. But where did it come from? **Fossil fuels contain energy that came from the sun.** In fact, the sun is the major source of energy for most of Earth's processes. Within the dense core of the sun, hydrogen atoms are moving at such high velocities that when they collide they join, or fuse, together to form helium atoms. During this process of nuclear fusion, nuclear energy is converted to electromagnetic energy. A portion of this energy reaches Earth.

When the sun's energy reaches Earth, plants, algae, and certain bacteria convert some of the light energy to chemical potential energy. This process is known as photosynthesis because the plants or bacteria synthesize, or make, complex chemicals. Some of this chemical energy is used for the plant's daily needs, and the rest is stored. Animals that eat plants convert some of the

Graphing ACTIVITY

The following list shows what percent of power used in a recent year in the United States came from each power source: coal, 23%; nuclear, 8%; oil, 39%; natural gas, 24%; water, 3%; and biofuels, 3%. Prepare a circle graph that presents these data. (See the Skills Handbook for more on circle graphs.)

What fuel source does the United States rely on most? What percent of total energy needs is met by coal, oil, and natural gas combined?

EXPLORING Energy Conversions

The energy you use to toast your bread may have had a very long history—hundreds of millions of years worth.

1 The sun converts nuclear energy to electromagnetic energy.

2 Ancient plants and animals convert electromagnetic energy from the sun to stored chemical energy.

3 Remains of plants and animals become coal over millions of years.

4 Stored chemical energy in coal is converted to thermal energy when the coal is burned to make steam.

5 Thermal energy is converted to mechanical energy as turbines are turned by steam.

6 Mechanical energy is converted to electrical energy as turbines turn electric generators.

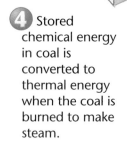

7 Electrical energy is converted to thermal energy in your toaster.

stored chemical energy to chemical energy that is stored in their own cells. The rest is converted to other forms of energy, such as mechanical energy used in movement or thermal energy used to maintain body temperature.

When ancient animals and plants died, the chemical potential energy they had stored was trapped within them. This is the chemical potential energy that is found in coal.

☑ *Checkpoint* *What is the process that produces the sun's energy?*

Use of Fossil Fuels

Fossil fuels can be burned to release the potential chemical energy stored millions of years ago. The process of burning fuels is known as combustion. During combustion, the fuel's chemical potential energy is converted to thermal energy. This thermal energy can be used to heat water until the water boils and produces steam.

In modern coal-fired power plants, the steam is raised to a very high temperature in a boiler. When it leaves the boiler it has enough pressure to turn a turbine. A turbine is like a fan, with blades attached to a shaft. The pressure of the steam on the blades causes the turbine to spin very fast. In this process, the thermal energy of the steam is converted to the mechanical energy of the moving turbine. Turbines are in turn connected to generators. Generators are just electric motors made to run backward. When they are spun by turbines, they produce electricity. In other words, in a power plant mechanical energy is converted to electrical energy. This energy is then used to light your home and run other electrical devices, such as a toaster.

Section 3 Review

1. How is the chemical energy in fossil fuels related to the sun's energy?
2. How is the energy of coal released?
3. Describe the energy conversions involved in the formation of coal.
4. **Thinking Critically** **Making Judgments** What general statement can you make about the supply of fossil fuels, given what you know about their formation?

Check Your Progress

CHAPTER PROJECT

Experiment with different design ideas for your roller coaster vehicle. What variables affect how fast your vehicle moves? How do potential and kinetic energy change as you make modifications to your design? At what point does the vehicle have the greatest kinetic energy? The greatest potential energy? How does friction affect the performance of your roller coaster? How can you relate the law of conservation of energy to your design?

SECTION
4 Power

DISCOVER

Is Work Always the Same?

1. Obtain a pinwheel and a hair dryer with at least two different power settings.

2. Set the dryer on its lowest setting. Use it to blow the pinwheel. Observe the pinwheel's motion.

3. Set the dryer on its highest setting. Again, use it to blow the pinwheel. Observe the pinwheel's motion.

Think It Over

Inferring Explain why work is done in spinning the pinwheel. What differences can you identify between the two situations? Is the amount of work greater for the high or low speed?

GUIDE FOR READING

◆ How do you calculate power?

◆ What is the difference between power and energy?

Reading Tip As you read, use your own words to describe the relationship among work, power, and energy.

The ad for a sleek new sports car catches your eye as you read a magazine. Its manufacturer boasts that the car can go from 0 to 100 km/h in 5 seconds because it has a 320-horsepower engine. But what does a car have to do with horses? You may find more than you think.

What Is Power?

A car does work to accelerate from rest. Some car engines do this work rapidly, while others do it more slowly. The faster an engine can do an amount of work, the more power the engine has. **Power** is the rate at which work is done or the amount of work done in a unit of time.

When you carry an object up some stairs, you do the same amount of work whether you walk or run up the stairs. (Work is the weight of the object times the height of the stairs.) But you exert more power when you run because you are doing the work faster.

You can think of power in another way. A device that is twice as powerful as another can do the same amount of work in half the time. Or it can do twice the work in the same time.

Calculating Power Whenever you know how fast work is done, you can calculate power. **Power is calculated by dividing the amount of work done by the amount of time taken to do the work.** This can be written as the following formula.

$$Power = \frac{Work}{Time}$$

Since work is equal to force times distance, you can rewrite the equation for power as follows.

$$Power = \frac{Force \times Distance}{Time}$$

When work is measured in joules and time in seconds, the unit of power is the joule per second (J/s). This unit is also known as the watt (W), in honor of James Watt, who made great improvements to the steam engine. One watt of power is produced when one joule of work is done in one second. In other words, 1 watt = 1 J/s.

A watt is a relatively small unit of power. For example, you produce about one watt of power if you raise a glass of water to your mouth in one second. Because a watt is so small, power is often measured in larger units. One kilowatt (kW) equals 1,000 watts. A washing machine uses about one kilowatt when it is running. An electric power plant produces millions of kilowatts.

☑ *Checkpoint* **What is power?**

A crane lifts an 8,000-N beam 75 m to the top of a building in 30 s. How much power does the crane use?

Analyze.	The force needed to lift the beam will be equal to its weight, 8,000 N. The distance and time are given, so the formula for power can be used.
Write the formula.	$Power = \dfrac{Force \times Distance}{Time}$
Substitute and solve.	$Power = \dfrac{8,000\ N \times 75\ m}{30\ s}$
	$Power = \dfrac{600,000\ N \cdot m}{30\ s}$ or $\dfrac{600,000\ J}{30\ s}$
	$Power = 20,000\ J/s = 20,000\ W$ or $20\ kW$
Think about it.	The answer tells you that the crane used 20,000 W to lift the beam. That equals 20 kW.

Practice Problems

1. A motor exerts a force of 10,000 N to lift an elevator 6 m in 5 s. What is the power produced by the motor?
2. A tow truck exerts a force of 9,000 N to pull a car out of a ditch. It moves the car a distance of 6 m in 25 s. What is the power of the tow truck?

Reviewing Content

 For more review of key concepts, see the Interactive Student Tutorial CD-ROM.

Multiple Choice

Choose the letter of the answer that best completes each statement.

1. Energy of motion is called
   a. elastic potential energy.
   b. kinetic energy.
   c. gravitational potential energy.
   d. chemical energy.
2. When you stretch a slingshot you give it
   a. kinetic energy.
   b. elastic potential energy.
   c. gravitational potential energy.
   d. power.
3. Whenever energy is transformed, some energy is converted to
   a. nuclear energy.
   b. electrical energy.
   c. thermal energy.
   d. mechanical energy.
4. Coal stores energy from the sun as
   a. chemical energy.
   b. electromagnetic energy.
   c. mechanical energy.
   d. electrical energy.
5. The rate at which work is done is called
   a. energy.   b. efficiency.
   c. power.   d. conservation.

True or False

If the statement is true, write true. If it is false, change the underlined word or words to make the statement true.

6. Kinetic energy is due to the <u>position</u> of an object.
7. Gravitational potential energy depends on <u>weight</u> and height.
8. Green plants convert the electromagnetic energy of the sun into <u>mechanical</u> energy.
9. The SI unit of <u>power</u> is the joule.
10. A device that has three times the <u>power</u> of another can do the same amount of work in one third the time.

Checking Concepts

11. Describe the difference between kinetic energy and potential energy.
12. For each of the following, decide which forms of energy are present: a leaf falls from a tree; a candle burns; a rubber band is wrapped around a newspaper.
13. An eagle flies from its perch in a tree to the ground to capture its prey. Describe its energy transformations as it descends.
14. When you walk upstairs, how are you obeying the law of conservation of energy?
15. One chef places a pie in the oven at a low setting so that it is baked in one hour. Another chef places a pie in the oven at a high setting so that the pie bakes in half an hour. Is the amount of transformed energy the same in each case? Is the power the same?
16. **Writing to Learn** As you saw in the figures on pages 412 and 413, you can find different forms of energy all around you. Imagine you are writing your own biography. Pick three major events in your life. Write a paragraph about the form of energy that was most important in each event.

Thinking Critically

17. **Calculating** A 1300-kg car travels at 11 m/s. What is its kinetic energy?
18. **Problem Solving** A 500-N girl walks down a flight of stairs so that she is 3 m below her starting level. What is the change in the girl's gravitational potential energy?
19. **Applying Concepts** You turn on an electric fan to cool off. Describe the energy conversions involved.
20. **Relating Cause and Effect** A motorcycle, an automobile, and a bus are all traveling at the same speed. Which has the least kinetic energy? The greatest kinetic energy? Explain your answer.

Applying Skills

Use the illustration of a golfer taking a swing to answer the Questions 21–23. The golf club starts at point A and ends at point E.

21. Inferring At which point(s) does the golf club have the greatest potential energy? At which point(s) does it have the greatest kinetic energy?

22. Communication Describe the energy conversions from point *A* to point *E*.

23. Drawing Conclusions The kinetic energy of the club at point *C* is more than the potential energy of the club at point *B*. Does this mean that the law of conservation of energy is violated?

CHAPTER PROJECT

Performance ▽ **Assessment**

Present Your Project Present your roller coaster to the class. Explain how you selected your materials, as well as the effect of hill height, incline, turns, and loops on the motion of the roller coaster. You should also explain how energy is converted as the roller coaster moves along the tracks. Point out an interesting feature of your roller coaster.

Reflect and Record In your journal, explain how you might improve your roller coaster. Think about what you knew about kinetic and potential energy before the project began, and what you know now. Which features would you change? Which would you keep the same?

Test Preparation

Use these questions to prepare for standardized tests.

Read the passage. Then answer Questions 24–26. It's the day of the big archery competition. Suki is the first contestant. She steps up to the line, raises her bow and pulls her arrow back. The bow bends and she lets go of the arrow. The bow returns to its original shape as the arrow flies through the air toward the target. However, her arrow falls to the ground before it reaches the target.

24. What type of energy did the arrow have as it moved through the air?
  a. potential energy
  b. kinetic energy
  c. electromagnetic energy
  d. chemical energy

25. Where did the energy of the arrow come from?
  a. It always had the energy.
  b. It gained energy from the air as it moved.
  c. Energy was stored in the arrow when the bow was pulled back.
  d. Energy transferred to the bow as it was pulled back was transferred to the arrow.

26. What might have caused the arrow to fall short of the target?
  a. It did not have enough energy because Suki did not pull the bow back far enough.
  b. It had too much energy because Suki pulled the bow back too far.
  c. Its kinetic energy was converted to gravitational potential energy as it moved.
  d. Its kinetic energy was converted to potential energy as it moved.

Bright colors in this thermogram show areas that radiate the most heat.

www.phschool.com

SECTION
1 **Temperature and Thermal Energy**

Discover How Cold Is the Water?
Science at Home Room Temperature

SECTION
2 **The Nature of Heat**

Discover What Does It Mean to Heat Up?
Sharpen Your Skills Inferring
Try This Feel the Warmth
Skills Lab Just Add Water

SECTION
3 Integrating Chemistry
Thermal Energy and States of Matter

Discover What Happens to Heated Metal?
Sharpen Your Skills Observing
Science at Home Freezing Air

In Hot Water

This unusual image is not from a cartoon or horror movie. It's a thermogram of a house. A thermogram is an image formed by heat given off by an object. You might be very interested in a thermogram of your own house, because it can help you find expensive heat losses.

In this chapter, you will find out what heat is and how it relates to thermal energy and temperature. As you read the chapter, you will use what you learn to construct a device that will insulate a container of hot water.

Your Goal To build a container for a 355-mL (12-oz) aluminum can that keeps water hot.

Your project must

- reduce the loss of thermal energy from the container
- be constructed from available raw materials rather than be a ready-made insulating container
- have insulation no thicker than 3 cm
- not use electricity or heating chemicals
- follow the safety guidelines in Appendix A

Get Started With a group of classmates, brainstorm different materials that prevent heat loss. Consider such questions as the following: What properties do the materials seem to have in common? Which materials are easy to get? How can you find out which materials best prevent heat loss?

Check Your Progress You'll be working on this project as you study this chapter. To keep your project on track, look for Check Your Project boxes at the following points.

Section 2 Review, page 445: Perform experiments to determine the best insulating materials and keep a log of your results.
Section 4 Review, page 458: Build and test the device.

Present Your Project At the end of the chapter (page 461), you will test the performance of your insulating device.

SECTION

4 **Uses of Heat**

Discover **What Happens at the Pump?**
Try This **Shake It Up**

Temperature and Thermal Energy

How Cold Is the Water?

1. Fill a plastic bowl with cold water, another with warm water, and a third with water at room temperature. Label each bowl.

2. Line up the three bowls. Place your right hand in the cold water and your left hand in the warm water.

3. After about a minute, place both your hands in the third bowl at the same time.

Think It Over

Observing How did the water in the third bowl feel when you touched it? Did it feel the same on each hand? If not, can you explain why?

GUIDE FOR READING

◆ What are the three common temperature scales?

◆ How does temperature differ from thermal energy?

Reading Tip As you read, use the headings to make an outline about temperature and thermal energy. Leave space to add definitions as you read.

The radio weather report says that today's high temperature will be 25 degrees. What should you wear? Do you need a coat and a scarf to keep warm, or only shorts and a T-shirt? What you decide depends on the temperature scale. On one scale, 25 degrees is below freezing, while on another scale 25 degrees is quite comfortable.

Temperature

You don't need a science book to tell you that the word *hot* means higher temperatures or the word *cold* means lower temperatures. You wear different clothes on a hot day than on a cold day. When scientists think about temperature, however, they are considering the particles that make up matter.

Matter is made up of tiny particles called atoms and molecules. These particles are always in motion even if the object they make up isn't moving at all. As you recall, the energy of motion is called kinetic energy, so all particles of matter have kinetic energy. The faster particles move, the more kinetic energy they have. Temperature is a measure of the average kinetic energy of the individual particles in an object.

Figure 1 The particles of hot cocoa move faster than those of cold chocolate milk. *Applying Concepts Which drink has particles with greater average kinetic energy?*

436

Look at the mug of hot cocoa and the glass of cold chocolate milk in Figure 1. The hot cocoa has a higher temperature than the cold chocolate. Its particles are moving faster, so they have greater average kinetic energy. If the chocolate milk is heated, its particles will move faster, so their kinetic energy will increase. This means that the temperature of the milk will rise.

Temperature Scales

If you did the Discover activity, you know that whether something feels hot or cold depends on what you compare it to. Walking into an air-conditioned building on a hot day can give you a chill. You need a few minutes to get comfortable with the indoor temperature. Since you can't rely on your sense of touch, you need a scale to measure temperature accurately. **The three common scales for measuring temperature are the Fahrenheit, Celsius, and Kelvin scales.**

Fahrenheit Scale In the United States, the most common temperature scale is called the **Fahrenheit scale.** On this scale, the number 32 is assigned to the temperature at which water freezes. The number 212 is assigned to the temperature at which water boils. The interval between these two temperatures is divided into 180 equal intervals called degrees Fahrenheit (°F).

Celsius Scale The temperature scale used in most of the world is the **Celsius scale.** On this scale, the number 0 is assigned to the temperature at which water freezes. The number 100 is assigned to the temperature at which water boils. The interval between freezing and boiling is divided into 100 equal parts, called degrees Celsius (°C).

Kelvin Scale The temperature scale commonly used in physical science is the **Kelvin scale.** Units on the Kelvin scale are the same size as those on the Celsius scale, and are called kelvins (K). Any

Figure 2 This illustration compares the three temperature scales.
Comparing and Contrasting How do the three temperature scales differ from one another?

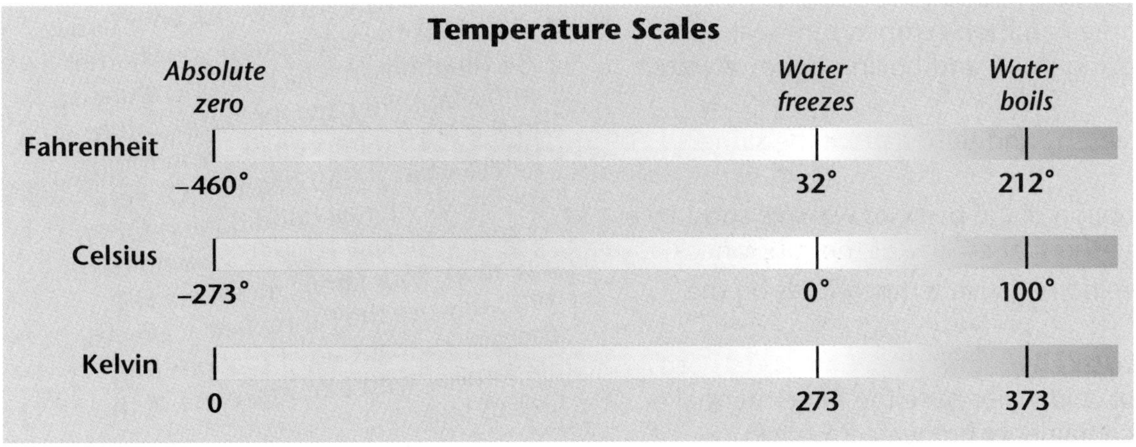

Temperature Scales

	Absolute zero	Water freezes	Water boils
Fahrenheit	−460°	32°	212°
Celsius	−273°	0°	100°
Kelvin	0	273	373

Figure 3 A large pot of hot cocoa can have the same temperature as a small cup of cocoa.
Comparing and Contrasting Do both containers have the same thermal energy?

temperature on the Kelvin scale can be changed to Celsius degrees by subtracting 273 from it. So the freezing point of water on the Kelvin scale is 273 K and the boiling point is 373 K.

Why is the number 273 so special? Experiments have led scientists to conclude that –273°C is the lowest temperature possible. At this temperature, called **absolute zero,** no more energy can be removed from matter. The Kelvin scale is defined so that zero on the Kelvin scale is absolute zero.

☑ *Checkpoint* *What three points define the common temperature scales?*

Thermal Energy

The total energy of all of the particles in a substance is called thermal energy, or sometimes internal energy. Even if two samples of matter are at the same temperature, they do not necessarily have the same total energy.

The more particles a substance has at a given temperature, the more thermal energy it has. For example, 2 liters of hot cocoa at 75°C has more thermal energy than 0.15 liter at 75°C. **So temperature is a measure of the average kinetic energy of the individual particles. Thermal energy is the total energy of all of the particles.**

Thermal energy does not depend on just temperature and the number of particles in a substance. It also depends on how the particles are arranged. In Section 3 you will learn about how thermal energies differ for solids, liquids, and gases.

Section 1 Review

1. Name the three common temperature scales. Give the freezing point and boiling point of water for each.
2. Are thermal energy and temperature the same? Explain.
3. How is the motion of the particles within a substance related to the thermal energy of the substance?
4. Why are there no negative temperatures on the Kelvin scale?
5. **Thinking Critically** **Applying Concepts** Can a container of cold water have the same thermal energy as a container of hot water? Explain.

② The Nature of Heat

What Does It Mean to Heat Up?

1. Obtain several utensils made of different materials, such as silver, stainless steel, plastic, and wood.

2. Press a small gob of frozen butter on the handle of each utensil. Make sure that when the utensils stand on end, the butter is at the same height on each.

3. 🖐 Stand the utensils in a beaker so that they do not touch each other.

4. Pour hot water into the beaker until it is about 6 cm below the butter. Watch the utensils for the next several minutes. What do you see happening?

5. The utensils will be greasy. Wipe them off and wash them in soapy water.

Think It Over

Observing What happened to the butter? Did the same thing happen on every utensil? How can you account for your observations?

Blacksmithing is hot work. A piece of iron held in the forge becomes warmer and begins to glow as thermal energy from the fire travels along it. At the same time, the blacksmith feels hot air rising from the forge. He also feels the glow of the fire directly on his face and arms. Each of these movements of energy is a form of heat. **Heat** is the movement of thermal energy from a substance at a higher temperature to another at a lower temperature.

GUIDE FOR READING

◆ How is heat related to thermal energy?

◆ What are the three forms of heat transfer?

◆ How is specific heat related to thermal energy?

Reading Tip Before you read, define heat in your own words. Make any necessary corrections to your definition as you read the section.

Figure 4 This blacksmith uses heat to soften a piece of iron before he hammers it into shape.

Inferring

ACTIVITY

You pull some clothes out of the dryer as soon as they are dry. You grab your shirt without a problem, but when you pull out your jeans, you quickly drop them. The metal zipper is too hot to touch! What can you infer about which material in your jeans conducts thermal energy better? Explain.

Notice that the scientific definition of heat is different from its everyday use. In a conversation, you might hear someone say that an object contains heat. Matter, however, contains not heat but thermal energy. Only when thermal energy is transferred is it called heat. **Heat is thermal energy moving from a warmer object to a cooler object.** Recall from Chapter 13 that work also involves the transfer of mechanical energy. So work and heat are both energy transfers, and they are both measured with the same unit—joules.

How Is Heat Transferred?

There are three ways that heat can move. **Heat is transferred by conduction, convection, and radiation.** The blacksmith experienced all three.

Conduction In the process of **conduction,** heat is transferred from one particle of matter to another without the movement of matter itself. Think of a metal spoon in a pot of water being heated on an electric stove. The fast-moving particles of the hot electric coil collide with the slow-moving particles of the cool pot. Heat is transferred, causing the slower particles to move faster. Then the particles of the pot collide with the particles of the water, which in turn collide with the particles at one end of the spoon. As the particles move faster, the metal spoon becomes hotter. This process of conduction is repeated all along the metal until the entire spoon becomes hot.

In Figure 5, the horseshoes in a blacksmith's forge glow red as heat is transferred to the metal from the forge. This transfer of heat throughout the horseshoes is due to conduction.

Figure 5 The entire horseshoe becomes hot even though only its underside touches the hot forge. *Inferring By what method is heat transferred through the metal?*

440

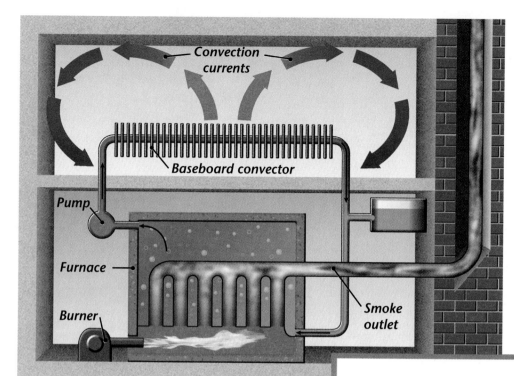

Convection currents

Baseboard convector

Pump

Furnace

Burner

Smoke outlet

Figure 6 Just as convection currents move heat throughout the liquid in a pot, convection currents move heat from the baseboard throughout the room.

Convection If you watch a pot of hot water on a stove, you will see the water moving. **Convection** is the movement that transfers heat within the water. In convection, heat is transferred by the movement of currents within a fluid (a liquid or gas).

When the water at the bottom of the pot is heated, its particles move faster, and they also move farther apart. As a result, the heated water becomes less dense. Recall from Chapter 11 that a less dense fluid will float on top of a more dense one. So the heated water rises. The surrounding cooler water flows into its place. This flow creates a circular motion known as a **convection current,** as shown in Figure 6.

Convection currents are used to transfer heated air throughout a building. As the air near the baseboard heater in Figure 6 is heated, it becomes less dense and rises. When the warm air rises, the surrounding cool air flows into its place.

INTEGRATING EARTH SCIENCE Convection currents occur in the environment as well. A soaring bird, such as a hawk, takes advantage of this fact and rides updrafts where warm air rises. In fact, convection currents transfer air heated by the sun throughout Earth's atmosphere. They produce the global winds that form Earth's weather.

☑ *Checkpoint* *How does convection transfer heat?*

Figure 7 Radiation from the heat lamps above keeps food warm in a cafeteria.

Feel the Warmth

How is heat transferred from a light bulb?

ACTIVITY

1. Turn on a lamp without the shade. Wait about a minute.

2. Hold the palm of your hand about 10 cm from the side of the bulb for about 15 seconds. Remove it sooner if it gets too warm.

3. Now hold the palm of your hand about 10 centimeters above the top of the bulb for about 15 seconds.

Drawing Conclusions In which location did your hand feel warmer? Explain your observations in terms of heat transfer.

Radiation **Radiation** is the transfer of energy by electromagnetic waves. You can feel radiation from a bonfire or a heat lamp across a distance of several meters. And of course a blacksmith feels the glow of radiation from his forge. There is an important difference between radiation and the processes of conduction and convection. Radiation does not require matter to transfer thermal energy. All of the sun's energy that reaches Earth travels through millions of kilometers of empty space.

Heat Moves One Way

If two substances have different temperatures, heat will flow from the warmer object to the colder one. When heat flows into a substance, the thermal energy of the substance increases. As the thermal energy increases, its temperature increases. At the same time, the temperature of the substance giving off heat decreases. Heat will flow from one substance to the other until the two substances have the same temperature. A bowl of hot oatmeal cools to room temperature if you don't eat it quickly.

What happens when you make something cold, like ice cream? The ingredients used, such as milk and sugar, are not nearly as cold as the finished ice cream. In an ice cream maker, the ingredients are put into a metal can that is packed in ice. You might think that the ice transfers cold to the ingredients in the can. But this is not the case. There is no such thing as "coldness." Instead, the ingredients grow colder as thermal energy flows from them to the ice. Heat transfer occurs in only one direction.

✓ *Checkpoint* *In what direction does heat move?*

Conductors and Insulators

Have you ever stepped from a rug to a tile floor on a cold morning? The tile floor feels colder than the rug. Yet if you measured their temperatures, they would be the same—room temperature. The difference between them has to do with how materials conduct heat.

A material that conducts heat well is called a conductor. Metals such as silver and stainless steel are good conductors. A metal spoon conducts heat faster than a wooden or plastic spoon. A material that does not conduct heat well is called an **insulator.** Wood, wool, straw, paper, and cork are good insulators. Gases, such as air, are also good insulators.

A good conductor, such as a tile floor, will feel cool to the touch because it transfers heat away from your skin easily. An insulator such as a rug, on the other hand, slows the transfer of heat from your skin, so it feels warmer.

Clothes and blankets are insulators that slow the transfer of heat out of your body. Mammals and birds have natural insulation. Birds have feathers that trap air under them, and mammals such as walruses have a layer of fat called blubber.

A well-insulated building is comfortable inside whether the weather is hot or cold outdoors. Insulation prevents heat from entering the building in hot weather and prevents heat from escaping in cold weather. Fiberglass is a common insulating material in buildings. It is made of a tangle of thin glass fibers that trap air. Air is a poor conductor of heat, and trapped air cannot transfer heat by convection. So fiberglass slows the transfer of heat through the walls or roof.

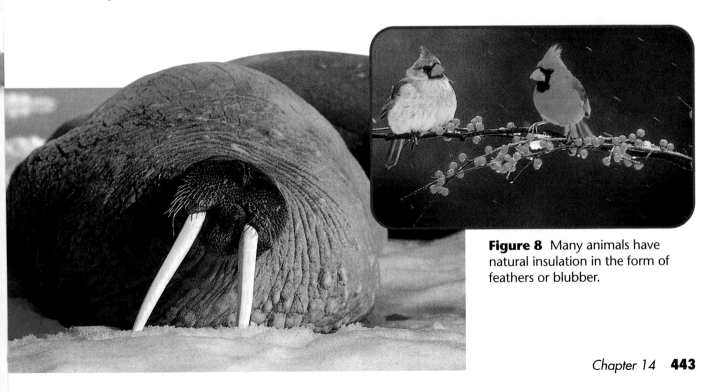

Figure 8 Many animals have natural insulation in the form of feathers or blubber.

Just Add Water

I f you add hot water to cold water, what will happen? In this lab, you'll make a device that measures changes in thermal energy. It is called a calorimeter. You will use the skill of interpreting data to calculate the thermal energy transferred.

Problem

When hot and cold water are mixed, how much thermal energy is transferred from the hot water to the cold water?

Materials

4 plastic foam cups   2 thermometers
hot tap water   balance
scissors   pencil
beaker of water kept in an ice bath

Procedure

1. Predict how the amount of thermal energy lost by hot water will be related to the amount of thermal energy gained by cold water.
2. Copy the data table into your notebook.
3. Follow the instructions in the box to make two calorimeters. Find the mass of each empty calorimeter (including the cover) on a balance and record each mass in your data table.

MAKING A CALORIMETER

A. Label a plastic foam cup with the letter C ("C" stands for cold water).
B. Cut 2 to 3 cm from the top of a second plastic foam cup. Invert the second cup inside the first. Label the cover with a C also. The cup and cover are your cold-water calorimeter.
C. Using a pencil, poke a hole in the cover large enough for a thermometer to fit snugly.
D. Repeat Steps A, B, and C with two other plastic foam cups. This time, label both cup and cover with an H. This is your hot-water calorimeter.

4. From a beaker of water that has been sitting in an ice bath, add water (no ice cubes) to the cold-water calorimeter. Fill it about one-third full. Put the cover on, find the total mass, and record the mass in your data table.
5. Add hot tap water to the hot-water calorimeter. Fill it about one-third full.
   CAUTION: *Hot tap water can cause burns.* Put the cover on, find the total mass, and record the mass in your data table.

DATA TABLE

	Mass of Empty Cup (g)	Mass of Cup and Water (g)	Mass of Water (g)	Starting Temp. (°C)	Final Temp. (°C)	Change in Temp. (°C)
Cold Water Calorimeter						
Hot Water Calorimeter						

6. Calculate the mass of the water in each calorimeter. Record the results in your data table.
7. Put thermometers through the holes in the covers of both calorimeters. Wait a minute or two and then record the temperatures.
8. Remove both thermometers and covers. Pour the water from the cold-water calorimeter into the hot-water calorimeter. Put the cover back on the hot-water calorimeter, and insert a thermometer. Record the final temperature as the final temperature for both calorimeters.

Analyze and Conclude

1. What is the temperature change of the cold water? Record your answer in the data table.
2. What is the temperature change of the hot water? Record your answer in the data table.
3. Calculate the amount of thermal energy that enters the cold water by using the formula for the transfer of thermal energy. The specific heat of water is 4.18 J/(g·K), so you use the following formula.

Thermal energy transferred =
4.18 J/(g·K) × Mass of cold water × Temperature change of cold water
Remember that a change of 1°C is equal to a change of 1 K.

4. Now use the formula to calculate the thermal energy leaving the hot water.
5. What unit should you use for your results for Questions 3 and 4?
6. Was your prediction from Step 1 confirmed? How do you know?
7. **Think About It** What sources of error might have affected your results? How could the lab be redesigned in order to reduce the errors?

Design an Experiment

How would your results be affected if you started with much more hot water than cold? If you used more cold water than hot? Make a prediction. Then design a procedure to test your prediction. Get your teacher's approval, and try your new procedure.

Insulation — And a Breath of Clean Air

People want to save money. They also want to conserve the fossil fuels—oil, coal, and natural gas—used to heat and cool buildings. So, since the 1970s, new homes, offices, and schools have been built to be energy-efficient. Builders have constructed large, square buildings with thick insulation, less outside wall space, and smaller, airtight windows. These features slow the transfer of thermal energy into and out of buildings.

Limiting the transfer of thermal energy, however, often means limiting the transfer of air. As a result, viruses, bacteria, and pollutants are not carried away by fresh outdoor air. People who live and work in these buildings sometimes develop illnesses. These illnesses cost billions of dollars a year in medical expenses and lost work.

The Issues

How Can Indoor Air Be Made Cleaner?
Limiting indoor pollutants—or getting rid of them altogether—is a major way of reducing building-related illness. Toward this end, builders can construct buildings with materials and insulation that do not pollute the air. They can use natural wood, for instance, instead of plastics and particle board, which give off irritating chemicals. Indoor air can be filtered. Walls, floors, and carpets can be cleaned frequently. Machines that give off irritating chemicals, such as copiers, can be placed in specially ventilated rooms. In this way, pollution can be kept out of the air that most people in the building breathe.

How Can Ventilation Be Improved?
Good ventilation requires at least 10 liters per second of fresh air for each person. If less fresh air comes in, some people may get illnesses or eye, nose, and throat irritations. There are several ways to increase ventilation. In some buildings, machines such as fans and blowers are used to move air in and out. People in those buildings must be careful not to block air vents with furniture or equipment. Special attention must be paid to ventilation during times of increased pollution, such as when a room is being painted.

Increasing air flow into buildings means using more energy for heating and air conditioning. So the energy savings from efficient buildings are reduced. To make up for this loss, people can wear heavier clothing in winter. They can set their thermostats lower and use less energy for heating. They can also wear lighter clothes in summer, and use less energy for air conditioning.

Another way to obtain clean air while conserving energy is called energy recovery ventilation. Heat is transferred from stale, but warm, indoor air to fresh, but cold, outdoor air. The air goes out but the energy stays inside.

You Decide

1. Identify the Problem
In your own words, describe the problem caused by thick layers of insulation.

2. Analyze the Options
List five different options for reducing building-related illnesses. How would each option affect the amount of fuel needed for heating?

3. Find a Solution
You're building a new school. Make a checklist of steps to take to prevent illness but still keep heating costs down.

SECTION 3 Thermal Energy and States of Matter

DISCOVER • **ACTIVITY**

What Happens to Heated Metal?

1. Wrap one end of a one-meter-long metal wire around a clamp on a ring stand.

2. Tie the other end through several washers. Adjust the clamp so that the washers swing freely, but nearly touch the floor.

3. 🔥 Light a candle. Hold the candle with an oven mitt, and heat the wire. **CAUTION:** *Be careful near the flame, and avoid dripping hot wax on yourself.* Predict how heat from the candle will affect the wire.

4. With your hand in the oven mitt, swing the wire. Observe any changes in the motion of the washers.

5. Blow out the candle and allow the wire to cool. After several minutes, swing the wire again and observe its motion.

Think It Over

Inferring Based on your observations, what can you conclude about the effect of heating a solid?

Throughout the day, temperatures at an orange grove drop steadily. The anxious farmer awaits the updated weather forecast. The news is not good. The temperature is expected to fall even further during the night. Low temperatures could wipe out the entire crop. He considers picking the crop early, but the oranges are not yet ripe.

Instead, the farmer tells his workers to haul in long water hoses. He has them spray the orange trees with water. As the temperature drops, the water turns to ice. The ice keeps the oranges warm!

How can ice possibly keep anything warm? The answer has to do with how thermal energy is transferred as water becomes ice.

GUIDE FOR READING

◆ What causes matter to change state?

◆ Why does matter expand when it is heated?

Reading Tip As you read, take notes on how each illustration helps to explain the text.

Figure 12 Imagine using ice to keep something warm! These oranges were sprayed with water because freezing temperatures threatened them.

Figure 13 Matter exists in three states—solid, liquid, and gas. *Comparing and Contrasting* How does the motion of the particles relate to the state of matter?

Gas

Solid

Liquid

Three States of Matter

What happens when you hold an ice cube in your hand? It melts. The solid and the liquid are both the same substance—water. Water can exist in three different forms. In fact, all matter exists in three **states**—solid, liquid, and gas. Although the chemical composition of a substance remains the same, the arrangement of the particles that make up the matter differ from one state to another.

Solids An ice cube, a coin, a book, and the crystal of fluorite shown above are all solids. The particles that make up a solid are packed together in relatively fixed positions. Particles of a solid cannot move out of their positions. They can only vibrate back and forth. This is why solids retain a fixed shape and volume.

Liquids Water, orange juice, and the molten steel shown at the left are all liquids. The particles that make up a liquid are close together, but they are not held together as tightly as those of a solid. Because liquid particles can move around, liquids don't have a definite shape. But liquids do have a definite volume.

Gases Air, helium, and the neon used in colored signs are all gases. In a gas, the particles are moving so fast that they don't even stay close together. Gases expand to fill all the space available. They do not have a fixed shape or volume.

Changes of State

The physical change from one state of matter to another is called a **change of state.** A change of state most often occurs between the solid and liquid states, and between the liquid and gas states.

The state of a substance depends on the amount of thermal energy it possesses. The more thermal energy a substance has, the faster its particles move. Since a gas has more thermal energy than a liquid, the particles of a gas move faster than the particles of the same substance in the liquid or solid state. Particles in a liquid are freer to move around than particles in the solid state.

Matter will change from one state to another if thermal energy is absorbed or released. Figure 14 is a graph of changes of state. Thermal energy is shown on the horizontal axis and temperature is shown on the vertical axis. You can see that as thermal energy increases, a substance changes from a solid to a liquid and then to a gas. A substance changes from a gas to a liquid and then to a solid as thermal energy is removed from it.

The flat regions of the graph show conditions under which thermal energy is changing but temperature remains the same. Under these conditions matter is changing from one state to another. During a change of state, the addition or loss of thermal energy changes the arrangement of the particles. However, the average kinetic energy of those particles does not change. Since temperature is a measure of average kinetic energy, the temperature does not change as a substance changes state.

Solid–Liquid Changes of State

On the lower left portion of the graph in Figure 14, matter goes through changes between the solid and liquid states of matter. These changes are known as melting and freezing.

Melting The change of state from a solid to a liquid is called melting. Melting occurs when a solid absorbs thermal energy. As the thermal energy of the solid increases, the rigid structure of its particles begins to break down. The particles become freer to move around. The temperature at which a solid changes to a liquid is called the melting point.

Checkpoint What is a change of state?

Language Arts
CONNECTION

All around you, you can observe substances in different states of matter. You can also observe matter changing from one state to another.

In Your Journal

Write a one-page description of a scene in which the state of matter changes. Here are some ideas: a glass of lemonade with ice cubes, a pond freezing in winter, a puddle of water on a hot pavement, water boiling on a stove, or rain falling on a desert. Write about how the scene would affect your senses of sight, smell, touch, taste, and hearing.

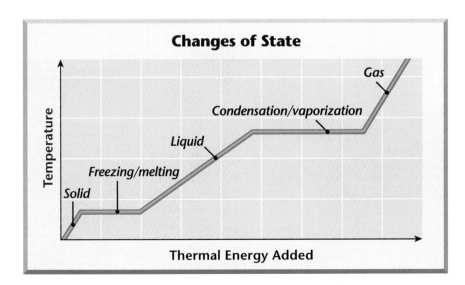

Changes of State

Gas

Condensation/vaporization

Liquid

Freezing/melting

Solid

Temperature

Thermal Energy Added

Figure 14 This graph shows how thermal energy and temperature change as a pure substance changes from one state to another.

Freezing The change of state from a liquid to a solid is called freezing. Freezing occurs when a substance loses thermal energy. The temperature at which a substance changes from a liquid to a solid is called its **freezing point.** For a given substance, the freezing point and the melting point are the same. The only difference between the two is whether the substance is gaining or releasing thermal energy.

The fact that freezing involves a release of energy explains why the farmer had his workers spray the orange trees with water. The liquid water released thermal energy as it froze. Some of this thermal energy was transferred to the oranges, and kept them from freezing.

Liquid–Gas Changes of State

The upper right portion of Figure 14 shows changes between the liquid and gas states of matter. These changes are known as vaporization and condensation.

Vaporization The process by which matter changes from the liquid to the gas state is called vaporization. During this process, particles in a liquid absorb thermal energy. This causes the particles to move faster. Eventually they move fast enough to escape the liquid, as gas particles.

If vaporization takes place at the surface of a liquid, it is called evaporation. At higher temperatures, vaporization can occur below the surface of a liquid as well. This process is called boiling. When a liquid boils, gas bubbles formed within the liquid rise to the surface. The temperature at which a liquid boils is called its boiling point.

Condensation You have seen that beads of water appear on the outside of a cold drinking glass or on the bathroom mirror after you take a shower. This occurs because water vapor that is

Figure 15 Water vapor in the air begins to condense soon after sunset. *Applying Concepts As it condenses, does water absorb or release thermal energy?*

Figure 16 Joints on bridges and spaces in sidewalks allow for the expansion and contraction of matter. *Applying Concepts What happens to the spaces in the expansion joint as the bridge gets warmer?*

present in the air loses thermal energy when it comes in contact with the cold glass. When a gas loses a sufficient amount of thermal energy, it will change into a liquid. A change from the gas state to the liquid state is called condensation.

☑ *Checkpoint* *What is the difference between boiling and evaporation of a liquid?*

Thermal Expansion

Have you ever loosened a tight jar lid by holding it under a stream of hot water? This works because the metal lid expands a little. Do you know why? **As the thermal energy of a substance increases, its particles spread out and the substance expands.** This is true even when the substance is not changing state. The expanding of matter when it is heated is known as **thermal expansion.**

When a substance is cooled, thermal energy is released. This means that the motion of the particles slows down and the particles move closer together. So as a substance is cooled, it contracts, or decreases in size.

Thermometers You are already familiar with one application of thermal expansion—a thermometer. In a common thermometer, a liquid such as mercury or alcohol is sealed within a glass tube. As the liquid is heated, it expands and climbs up the tube. As the liquid is cooled, it contracts and flows down in the tube.

Expanding Teeth Your teeth also expand and contract with

INTEGRATING HEALTH changes in temperature. If you have a filling, the material used for the filling must expand and contract with your tooth. If it didn't, the filling could cause the tooth to crack, or the filling could loosen. So dentists use fillings that have the same expansion properties as teeth.

Figure 17 A bimetallic strip is an important part of many thermostats. When the temperature drops, the strip uncoils and closes a switch that starts a heating system. *Relating Cause and Effect* *What causes the bimetallic strip to coil and uncoil?*

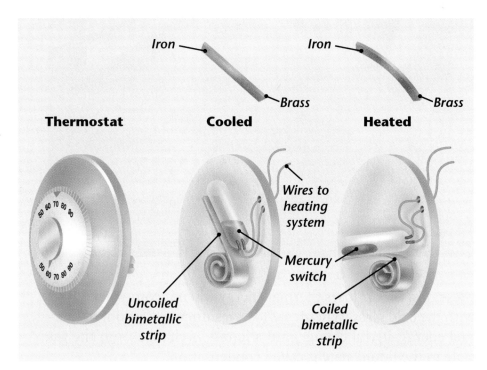

Iron
Brass
Thermostat

Iron
Brass
Cooled

Heated

Wires to heating system

Mercury switch

Uncoiled bimetallic strip

Coiled bimetallic strip

Thermostats Thermal expansion is used in **thermostats,** or heat-regulating devices. Many thermostats contain **bimetallic strips,** which are strips of two different metals joined together. Different metals expand at different rates. When the bimetallic strip is heated, one side expands more than the other. This causes the strip to bend into a curve.

The movement of the strip operates a switch. If the switch is connected to a furnace or other heating system, the thermostat will turn the heating system on and off. In addition to home heating systems, thermostats are used on such devices as air conditioners, ovens, toasters, and electric blankets.

Section 3 Review

1. How does thermal energy produce a change from one state of matter to another?
2. What is thermal expansion?
3. What happens to the temperature of a substance during a change of state? What happens to thermal energy during a change of state?
4. How does a thermostat make use of thermal expansion?
5. **Thinking Critically** **Applying Concepts** Why do cookbooks recommend that you poke holes in a potato before baking it?

Science at Home

Freezing Air Blow up two medium-sized balloons so that they are the same size. Have a family member use a measuring tape to measure the circumference of the balloons. Then ask them to place one of the balloons in the freezer for fifteen to twenty minutes. Remove the balloon from the freezer and measure both balloons again. Explain how changes in thermal energy cause the change in circumference.

SECTION
4 Uses of Heat

DISCOVER • ACTIVITY

What Happens at the Pump?

1. Obtain a bicycle pump and a deflated basketball or soccer ball.

2. Feel the pump with your hand. Note if it feels cool or warm.

3. Use the pump to inflate the ball to the recommended pressure.

4. As soon as you stop pumping, feel the pump again. Observe any changes in temperature.

Think It Over

Developing Hypotheses Propose an explanation for any changes that you observed.

For more than 100 years, the steam locomotive was a symbol of power and speed. It first came into use in the 1830s, and was soon hauling hundreds of tons of freight faster than a horse could gallop. Yet today, trains are pulled by diesel locomotives that are far more efficient. You will probably only see a coal-burning locomotive as a tourist attraction.

Heat Engines

To power a steam locomotive, a fireman shovels coal into a roaring fire. Heat is then transferred from the fire to water in the boiler. But how can heat move a train?

The thermal energy of the coal fire must be converted to the mechanical energy, or energy of motion, of the moving train. You already know about the reverse process, the conversion of mechanical energy to thermal energy. It happens when you rub your hands together to make them warm.

The conversion of thermal energy to mechanical energy requires a device called a **heat engine.** Heat engines usually make use of combustion. Combustion is the process of burning a fuel, such as coal or gasoline. During combustion, chemical energy that is stored in fuel is converted to thermal energy. **Heat engines convert thermal energy to mechanical energy.** Heat engines are classified according to whether combustion takes place outside the engine or inside the engine.

GUIDE FOR READING

◆ How is thermal energy related to heat engines and refrigerators?

Reading Tip Before you read, preview the illustrations showing how engines work. Write down any questions you have, and answer them as you read.

Shake It Up

How does work relate to temperature?

1. Place a handful of dry sand in a metal container that has a cover.

2. Measure the temperature of the sand with a thermometer.

3. Cover the can and shake it vigorously for a minute or two.

4. Predict any change in the temperature of the sand. Was your prediction correct?

Classifying Identify any energy conversions and use them to explain your observations.

External Combustion Engines In an **external combustion engine,** the fuel is burned outside the engine. A steam engine is an example of an external combustion engine. The combustion of wood, coal, or oil heats water in a boiler outside the engine. As its thermal energy increases, the water turns to water vapor, or steam. The steam is then passed through a valve into the engine where it pushes against a metal plunger called a piston. The piston moves back and forth in a tube called a cylinder.

Figure 18 shows how steam can do work, such as moving the wheels of a locomotive. Steam enters at the right end of the cylinder, pushing the piston to the left. Steam then enters at the left end of the cylinder and pushes the piston back. This type of external combustion engine can also move the propellers of a steamship. Modern steam engines are more efficient than old-fashioned piston steam engines. But in both types of engine, thermal energy is converted to mechanical energy.

Internal Combustion Engines In an **internal combustion engine,** the fuel is burned in cylinders inside the engine. Diesel and gasoline engines, which power most automobiles, are both examples of internal combustion engines. A piston inside a cylinder moves up and down, turning a crankshaft. The motion of the crankshaft is transferred to the wheels of the car.

Each up or down movement by a piston is called a stroke. Most diesel and gasoline engines are four-stroke engines, as shown in *Exploring a Four-Stroke Engine.* Automobile engines usually have four, six, or eight cylinders. The four-stroke process occurs in each cylinder, and is repeated many times each second.

☑ *Checkpoint* What happens during the process of combustion?

Figure 18 This cutaway illustration shows a steam-powered external-combustion engine. The sliding valve reverses at the end of each piston stroke.

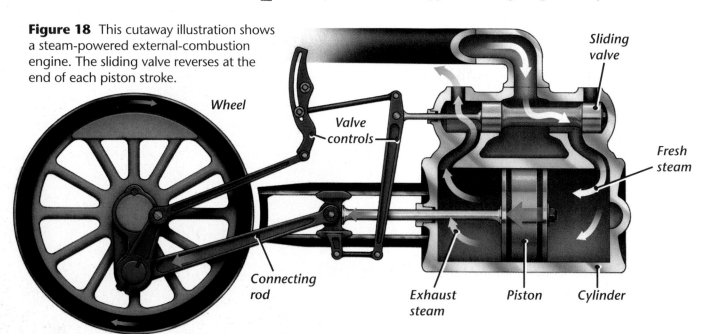

Wheel

Valve controls

Sliding valve

Fresh steam

Connecting rod

Exhaust steam

Piston

Cylinder

EXPLORING *a Four-Stroke Engine*

Most automobiles use four-stroke heat engines. These four strokes occur repeatedly in each cylinder in the engine.

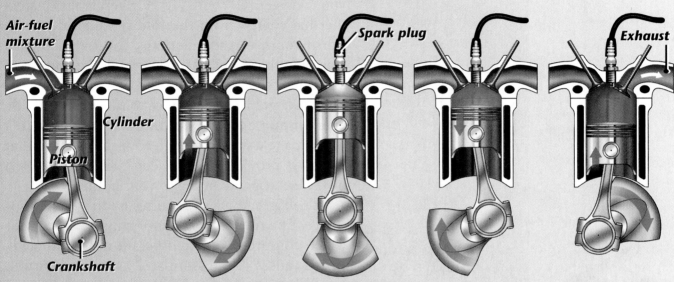

Air-fuel mixture

Spark plug

Exhaust

Cylinder

Piston

Crankshaft

Intake Stroke
A mixture of fuel and air is drawn into the cylinder as the piston moves down.

Compression Stroke
The mixture is squeezed, or compressed, into a smaller space as the piston moves back up.

Ignition
When the piston is almost at the top of the cylinder, a spark plug ignites the mixture. Stored chemical energy is converted to thermal energy, which heats the gas.

Power Stroke
As the heated gas expands, it pushes the piston down. The piston, in turn, moves the crankshaft. Thus thermal energy is converted to mechanical energy.

Exhaust Stroke
The piston moves back up, pushing the heated gas out. This makes room for new fuel and air, so that the cycle can be repeated.

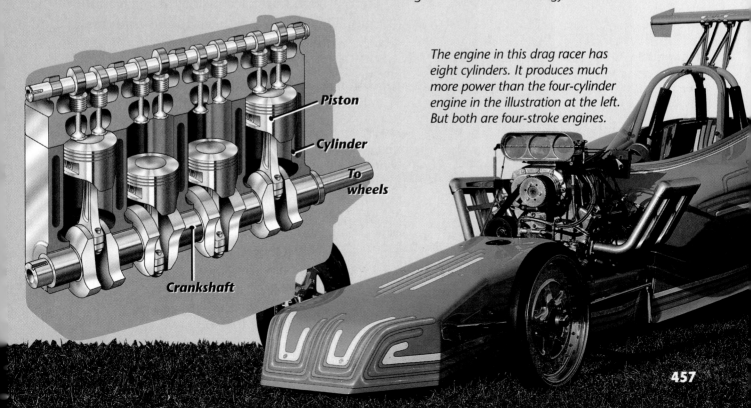

Piston

Cylinder

To wheels

Crankshaft

The engine in this drag racer has eight cylinders. It produces much more power than the four-cylinder engine in the illustration at the left. But both are four-stroke engines.

457

Heat

MILK

Heat into room

Refrigerant

Compressor

Figure 19 This diagram shows the basic parts of a refrigerator. *Interpreting Diagrams How are changes of state used to cool food?*

Refrigerators

Energy conversion can also be used to keep food cool. Does that seem surprising? After all, heat naturally flows from a warm body to a cold body—not the other way around. So how can you refrigerate food? A refrigerator transfers thermal energy from the cold space inside to the warm room outside. Perhaps you have felt this energy in the warm air blown out at the bottom of a refrigerator.

A refrigerator is a device that uses an outside energy source to transfer thermal energy from a cool area to a warm area. In your refrigerator, that energy is provided by an electric motor, powered by the electricity coming to your home.

A refrigerator also requires a refrigerant substance. The refrigerator motor runs a compressor which compresses the refrigerant in the gas state, which causes its pressure and its temperature to rise. When this happens, the gas gives off thermal energy. This heat is transferred to the outside air. As the gas loses thermal energy, it changes from a gas to a liquid. The liquid is then allowed to evaporate. As it evaporates, it cools. The cold gas is then pumped through tubes inside the walls of the refrigerator. There the gas absorbs heat from inside the refrigerator. And so thermal energy is transferred from the space inside the refrigerator to the gas. The gas then returns to the compressor, and the whole cycle begins again.

An air conditioner operates in the same way. But it cools the area inside a building and transfers thermal energy to the air outdoors.

Section 4 Review

1. What is a heat engine?
2. Describe the process that occurs in a refrigerator.
3. What are the parts of the four-stroke cycle?
4. **Thinking Critically Comparing and Contrasting** What are the two types of heat engines? How are they alike? How are they different?

Check Your Progress

CHAPTER PROJECT

Build and test your container. Remember that you need to be able to get to the aluminum can at the beginning of the test so that hot water can be poured into it. You must also be able to measure the temperature of the water at the end of the test.

SECTION 1 Temperature and Thermal Energy

Key Ideas

◆ Temperature is a measure of the average kinetic energy of each particle within an object.
◆ Three temperature scales are Fahrenheit, Celsius, and Kelvin.
◆ Thermal energy is the total energy of the particles that make up an object.

Key Terms

Fahrenheit scale   Kelvin scale
Celsius scale   absolute zero

SECTION 2 The Nature of Heat

Key Ideas

◆ Heat is a transfer of thermal energy from an object at a higher temperature to an object at a lower temperature.
◆ Heat is transferred by conduction, convection, and radiation.
◆ A conductor transfers heat well, whereas an insulator does not.
◆ The amount of heat necessary to raise a unit of mass of a substance by a specific unit of temperature is called the specific heat.

Key Terms

heat   radiation
conduction   insulator
convection   specific heat
convection current

SECTION 3 Thermal Energy and States of Matter

INTEGRATING **CHEMISTRY**

Key Ideas

◆ Matter can undergo a change of state when thermal energy is added or removed.
◆ In general, matter expands when it is heated and contracts when it is cooled.

Key Terms

state   thermal expansion
change of state   thermostat
freezing point   bimetallic strip

SECTION 4 Uses of Heat

Key Ideas

◆ A heat engine converts thermal energy to mechanical energy that can do work.
◆ A refrigerator transfers thermal energy from a cool region to a warm region.

Key Terms

heat engine   internal combustion engine
external combustion engine

Organizing Information

Concept Map Copy the thermal energy concept map onto a separate sheet of paper. Then complete it and add a title. (For more on concept maps, see the Skills Handbook.)

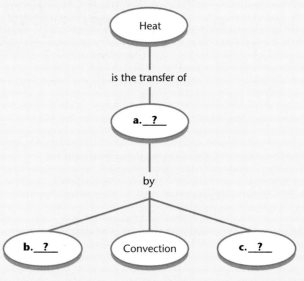

Reviewing Content

 For more review of key concepts, see the Interactive Student Tutorial CD-ROM.

Multiple Choice

Choose the letter of the answer that best completes each statement.

1. The average kinetic energy of the particles of an object is its
   a. heat content.
   b. temperature.
   c. specific heat.
   d. thermal energy.

2. The process by which heat moves from one end of a solid to the other is called
   a. convection.
   b. conduction.
   c. radiation.
   d. insulation.

3. If you want to know the amount of heat needed to raise the temperature of 2 kg of steel by 10°C, you need to know steel's
   a. temperature.
   b. thermal energy.
   c. heat content.
   d. specific heat.

4. The change of state that occurs when a gas becomes a liquid is called
   a. evaporation.
   b. boiling.
   c. freezing.
   d. condensation.

5. Heat engines convert thermal energy to
   a. chemical energy.
   b. electrical energy.
   c. mechanical energy.
   d. radiant energy.

True or False

If the statement is true, write true. If it is false, change the underlined word or words to make the statement true.

6. The temperature reading of zero on the <u>Celsius</u> scale is equal to absolute zero.

7. Heat transfer by <u>radiation</u> can occur in a vacuum.

8. In order to decrease the amount of thermal energy that moves from one place to another, you would use a <u>conductor</u>.

9. When a substance melts, the temperature of the substance <u>increases</u>.

10. In an <u>external</u> combustion engine, the fuel is burned inside the cylinder.

Checking Concepts

11. What happens to the particles of a solid as the thermal energy of the solid increases?

12. When you heat a pot of water on the stove, a convection current is formed. Explain how this happens.

13. When night falls on a summer day, the air temperature drops by 10°C. Will the temperature of the water in a nearby lake change by the same amount? Explain why or why not.

14. How can you add thermal energy to a substance without increasing its temperature?

15. When molten steel becomes solid, is energy absorbed or released by the steel?

16. Describe how a thermostat controls the temperature in a building.

17. **Writing to Learn** Haiku is a form of poetry that began in Japan. A haiku has three lines. The first and third lines have five syllables each. The second line has seven syllables. Write a haiku describing how you might feel on a frosty winter morning or a sweltering summer afternoon.

Thinking Critically

18. **Problem Solving** Suppose a mercury thermometer contains 2 grams of mercury. If the thermometer's reading changes from 25°C to 40°C, how much heat was needed? The specific heat of mercury is 140 J/(kg·K).

19. **Relating Cause and Effect** Why is the air pressure in a car's tires different before and after the car has been driven for an hour?

20. **Applying Concepts** Telephone lines are allowed to sag when they are hung. Can you think of a reason why?

21. **Relating Cause and Effect** A refrigerator is running in a small room. The refrigerator door is open, but the room does not grow any cooler. Use the law of conservation of energy to explain why the temperature does not drop.

Applying Skills

Use the drawing of three containers of water to answer Questions 22–24.

30°C   30°C   60°C

100 g   200 g   200 g

22. **Interpreting Data** Compare the average motion of the molecules in the three containers. Explain your answer.
23. **Drawing Conclusions** Compare the total amount of thermal energy in the three containers. Explain your answer.

24. **Calculating** Determine how much heat you would need to raise the temperature of each container by 1°C. (See Figure 10 on page 444.) Show your work.

Performance CHAPTER PROJECT **Assessment**

Present Your Project Talk with your classmates about their designs. When you've had a chance to look them over, predict the final water temperature for each device. Record the starting temperature for each one, including your own. Record the final temperatures at the end of the demonstrations.

Reflect and Record In your journal, answer the following questions: Which insulating materials seemed to work the best? Which design worked best?

Test Preparation
Use these questions to prepare for standardized tests.

Read the passage. Then answer Questions 25–27.
Water has quite a high specific heat. This property of water affects the climate in many places. Because of the high specific heat of water, the temperature of ocean water does not vary much from summer to winter. In winter, the water is warmer than the air and so the water warms the air that moves over it. In summer, the water is cooler than the air so the water cools the air that moves over it.

During the winter on the west coast, warm air over the Pacific Ocean blows onto land. In the summer, cooler air over the ocean blows onto land. As a result, the city of Portland, Oregon, is warmer in winter and cooler in the summer than the city of Minneapolis, Minnesota, which is at about the same latitude as Portland. Because Minneapolis is farther from the ocean than Portland, it is less affected by the temperature of the water.

25. What is this passage mostly about?
    a. how latitude affects temperature
    b. why the southern states are warmer than the northern states
    c. how the oceans affect the coastal climates
    d. how the specific heat of water compares to other materials
26. Since the specific heat of water is higher than that of land
    a. the temperature of land rises less than that of water given the same amount of energy.
    b. the temperature of water rises less than that of land given the same amount of energy.
    c. land absorbs more energy than water for the same temperature change.
    d. water is always warmer than land.
27. Why is Portland, Oregon, cooler than Minneapolis, Minnesota, in the summer?
    a. Winds carry warm air to Minneapolis.
    b. Winds carry cool air to Portland.
    c. Minneapolis is lower in latitude.
    d. Portland is lower in latitude.

B·R·I·D·G·E·S

FROM VINES TO STEEL

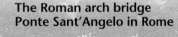

HAVE YOU EVER . . .

balanced on a branch or log to cross a brook?

jumped from rock to rock in a streambed?

swung on a vine or rope over a river?

Then you have used the same ways that early people used to get over obstacles. Fallen trees, twisted vines, and natural stones formed the first bridges.

Bridges are easy ways of getting over difficult obstacles. For thousands of years, bridges have also served as forts for defense, scenes of great battles, and homes for shops and churches. They have also been sites of mystery, love, and intrigue. They span history—linking cities, nations, and empires and encouraging trade and travel.

But bridges have not always been as elaborate as they are today. The earliest ones were made of materials that were free and plentiful. In deep forests, people used beams made from small trees. In tropical regions where vegetation was thick, people wove together vines and grasses, then hung them to make walkways over rivers and gorges.

No matter what the structures or materials, bridges reflect the people that built them. Each of the ancient civilizations of China, Egypt, Greece, and Rome designed strong, graceful bridges to connect and control its empire.

**The Roman arch bridge
Ponte Sant'Angelo in Rome**

The Balance of Forces

What keeps a bridge from falling down? How does it support its own weight and the weight of people and traffic on it? Builders found the answers by considering the various forces that act on a bridge.

The weight of the bridge and the traffic on it are called the *load*. When a heavy truck crosses a beam bridge, the weight of the load forces the beam to curve downward. This creates a tension force that stretches the bottom of the beam. At the same time, the load also creates a compression force at the top of the beam.

Since the bridge doesn't collapse under the load, there must be upward forces to balance the downward forces. In simple beam bridges, builders attached the beam to the ground or to end supports called abutments. To cross longer spans or distances, they construct piers under the middle span. Piers and abutments are structures that act as upward forces—reaction forces.

Another type of bridge, the arch bridge, is strong in compression. A heavy load on a stone arch bridge squeezes or pushes the stones together, creating compression throughout the structure. Weight on the arch bridge pushes down to the ends of the arch. The side walls and abutments act as reaction forces.

Early engineers discovered that arch bridges made of stone could span wider distances than simple beam bridges. Arch bridges were also stronger and more durable. Although the Romans were not the first to build arch bridges, they perfected the form in their massive, elegant structures. Early Roman arch bridges were built without mortar or "glue." The arch held together because the stones were skillfully shaped to work in compression. After nearly 2,000 years, some of these Roman arch bridges are still standing.

Bikers ride across a beam bridge in Scotland.

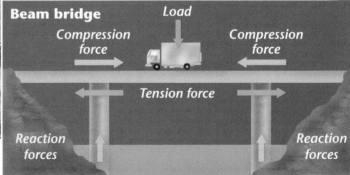

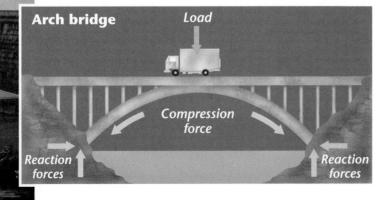

The Golden Age of Bridges

In the 1800s in the United States, the invention of the steam locomotive and the expansion of railroads increased the demand for bridges. Trains pulling heavy freight needed strong, flat bridges. Builders began to use cast iron instead of stone and wood. By the late 1800s, they were using steel, which was strong and relatively lightweight.

The use of new building materials was not the only change. Engineers began designing different types of bridges as well. They found that they could build longer, larger bridges by using a suspension structure.

Suspension bridges are modern versions of long, narrow woven bridges found in tropical regions. These simple, woven suspension bridges can span long distances. Crossing one of these natural structures is like walking a tightrope. The weight of people and animals traveling over the bridge pushes down on the ropes, stretching them and creating tension forces.

Modern suspension bridges follow the same principles of tension as do woven bridges. A suspension bridge is strong in tension. In suspension bridges, parallel cables are stretched the entire length of the bridge—over giant towers. The cables are anchored at each end of the bridge. The roadway hangs from the cables, attached by wire suspenders. The weight of the bridge and the load on it act to pull apart or stretch the cables. This pulling apart creates tension force.

The towers act as supports for the bridge cables. The abutments that anchor the cables exert reaction forces as well. So forces in balance keep a suspension bridge from collapsing.

Brooklyn Bridge today

Suspension bridge

Tension force

Load

Reaction forces

Reaction forces

Each of the smaller cables that hang from the four main cables of the Brooklyn Bridge is made up of seven bundles of seven steel wires.

A Great Engineering Feat

When it opened in 1883, the Brooklyn Bridge was the longest suspension bridge in the world—one half span longer than any other. It connected Brooklyn and Manhattan. Yet when the idea was first proposed, people said it couldn't be done.

In the mid-1800s, many people from Brooklyn had jobs across the East River in Manhattan. But the only way to get there was by ferry. Fierce ocean tides, stormy weather, and ice chunks in winter could make the journey risky. In 1868 John Augustus Roebling, a German immigrant engineer, was hired to build a bridge.

An engineering genius, Roebling designed a suspension bridge using four cables stretched over two giant granite towers. Roebling was the first engineer to design bridge cables of strong, flexible steel instead of cast iron.

Each cable, about 16 inches in diameter, would contain nearly 5,300 wires. After the cables were in place, 1,500 smaller suspension cables would be attached to the main cables to support the roadway. It's not surprising that people didn't believe that it could be done.

It was impossible to lift heavy cables over the towers. So for each cable, builders had to reel wire back and forth across the East River—3,515 miles of wire for each cable! To "spin the cables" John Roebling invented a traveling wheel that could carry the wire in a continuous loop, from one side of the river over the towers to the other side and back. It's an invention that is still used today.

Science Activity

Work in groups to make a suspension bridge, using 2 chairs, a wooden plank, rope, and some books.

◆ Place 2 chairs back to back and stretch 2 ropes over the backs of the chairs. Hold the ropes at both ends.

◆ Tie 3 pieces of rope to the longer ropes. Place the plank through the loops.

◆ Have students hold the ropes tightly at each end. Load books on top of the plank to see how much it will hold.

Why is it important to anchor the ropes tightly at each end?

Against All Odds

When John Roebling was hired in 1868 to build the Brooklyn Bridge, he was already an experienced suspension bridge engineer. He had plans for the bridge that he'd been working on since 1855.

But before bridge construction even began in 1869, John Roebling died in a bridge-related accident. Fortunately, he had worked out his bridge design to the last detail. His son, Colonel Washington Roebling, who was also a skilled engineer, dedicated himself to carrying out his father's plans.

The construction dragged on for 14 years and cost nearly 30 lives. Colonel Roebling himself became so disabled that he was forced to direct construction from his home. Using a telescope, Colonel Roebling followed every detail. His remarkable, energetic wife, Emily Warren Roebling, learned enough engineering principles to deliver and explain his orders to the workers.

The dedication of the Roebling family—John (left), Washington (center), and Emily (right)—ensured the success of the Brooklyn Bridge.

As soon as the giant towers were up, workers unrolled the steel wire back and forth across the towers to weave the cables. The next step was to twist the wires together. But the workmen were terrified of hanging so high on the bridge and refused to work. Finally, Frank Farrington, the chief mechanic, crossed the river on a small chair dangling from a wheel that ran across an overhead line. Farrington completed his journey to the roar of the crowd. This feat was billed as the greatest trapeze act of all time. Somewhat reassured, the builders returned to work. But it took two more years to string the cables. The bridge was one of the greatest engineering achievements of its time.

In the end, the Brooklyn Bridge project succeeded only because of the determination and sacrifices of the Roebling family. It became the model for hundreds of other suspension bridges.

Workers building the Brooklyn Bridge

Social Studies Activity

How do you think the Brooklyn Bridge changed the lives of New Yorkers? In groups, research the history of another famous bridge. Present your findings to your class along with drawings and photos. Find out
- when and why the bridge was built
- the type of bridge
- how peoples' lives changed after it was built—include effects on trade, travel, and population
- how landforms affected the bridge building
- events connected to the bridge

The New York Times   *May 25, 1883*

Two Great Cities United

The Brooklyn bridge was successfully opened yesterday. The pleasant weather brought visitors by the thousands from all around. Spectators were packed in masses through which it was almost impossible to pass, and those who had tickets to attend the ceremonies had hard work to reach the bridge. Every available house-top and window was filled, and an adventurous party occupied a tall telegraph pole. It required the utmost efforts of the police to keep clear the necessary space.

After the exercises at the bridge were completed the Brooklyn procession was immediately re-formed and the march was taken up to Col. Roebling's residence. From the back study on the second floor of his house Col. Roebling had watched through his telescope the procession as it proceeded along from the New-York side until the Brooklyn tower was reached. Mrs. Roebling received at her husband's side and accepted her share of the honors of the bridge.

For blocks and blocks on either side of the bridge there was scarcely a foot of room to spare. Many persons crossed and re-crossed the river on the ferry boats, and in that way watched the display. Almost every ship along the river front was converted into a grand stand.

The final ceremonies of the opening of the great bridge began at eight o'clock, when the first rocket was sent from the center of the great structure, and ended at 9 o'clock, when a flight of 500 rockets illuminated the sky. The river-front was one blaze of light, and on the yachts and smaller vessels blue fires were burning and illuminating dark waters around them.

THE GRAND DISPLAY OF FIREWORKS AND ILLUMINATIONS

This historic painting shows fireworks at the opening of the Brooklyn Bridge in 1883.

▲ Story adapted from *The New York Times*, May 25, 1883

Language Arts Activity

A reporter's goal is to inform and entertain the reader. Using a catchy opening line draws interest. Then the reader wants to know the facts—what, who, where, when, why, and how (5 Ws and H).

You are a school reporter. Write about the opening of a bridge in your area. It could be a highway overpass or a bridge over water, a valley, or railroad tracks.

◆ Include some of the 5 Ws and H.

◆ Add interesting details and descriptions.

Mathematics

Bridge Geometry

As railroad traffic increased in the late 1800s, truss bridges became popular. Designed with thin vertical and diagonal supports to add strength, truss bridges were really reinforced beam bridge structures. Many of the early wood truss bridges couldn't support the trains that rumbled over them. Cast iron and steel trusses soon replaced wood trusses.

Using basic triangular structures, engineers went to work on more scientific truss bridge designs. The accuracy of the design is crucial to handling the stress from heavy train loads and constant vibrations. As in all bridge structures, each steel piece has to be measured and fitted accurately—including widths, lengths, angles, and points of intersection and attachment.

Forces Acting on Geometric Shapes

 A basic triangle in a truss bridge is strong because its shape cannot be distorted.

 A triangle in a truss bridge can support a heavy load with its relatively small weight.

 A square or rectangle is not as strong as a triangle.

 It can collapse into a parallelogram under a heavy load.

Look closely at the truss patterns. In drawing bridge plans, engineers use geometric shapes.

parallel lines

right angle

obtuse angle

acute angle

intersecting lines

Truss bridge over Rio Grande Gorge in New Mexico

Math Activity

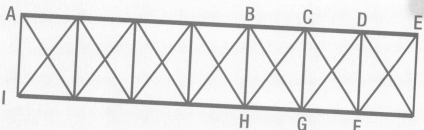

The chief building engineer has asked you to draw up exact plans for a new truss bridge. How well will you do as an assistant? You will soon find out by answering these questions:

1. Which lines are parallel?
2. Which lines intersect?
3. What kind of figure is formed by ABHI?
4. What kind of figure is formed by HCF?
5. What kind of angle is BGF—obtuse or right?
6. What kind of angle is CHG?
7. What kind of triangle is BHG? What makes it this kind of triangle?
8. Why is a triangle stronger than a square?

Tie It Together

Bridge the Gap

Work in small groups to build a model of a bridge out of a box of spaghetti and a roll of masking tape. Meet as a group to choose the type of bridge you will build. Each bridge should be strong enough to hold a brick. You can build—

◆ a beam bridge
◆ a truss bridge
◆ an arch bridge
◆ a suspension bridge (This one is challenging.)

After drawing a sketch of the bridge design, assign jobs for each team member. Then

◆ decide how long the bridge span will be
◆ measure and cut the materials
◆ build the roadway first for beam, truss, and suspension bridges
◆ build the arch first in an arch bridge

When your bridge is complete, display it in the classroom. Test the strength of each bridge by placing a brick on the roadway. Discuss the difference in bridge structures. Determine which bridge design is the strongest.

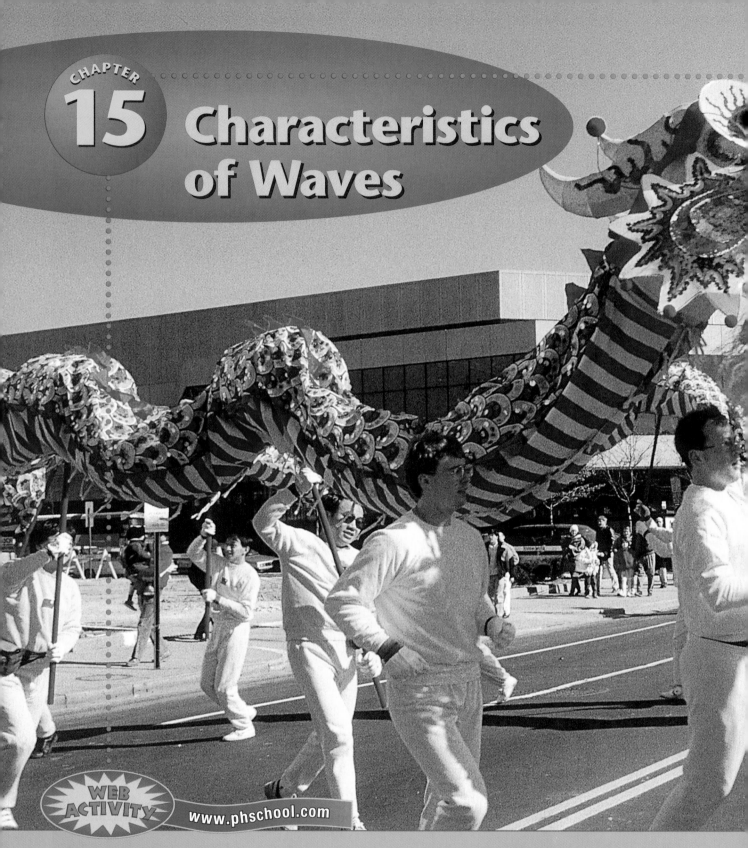

CHAPTER

15 Characteristics of Waves

WEB ACTIVITY

www.phschool.com

SECTION

1 What Are Waves?

Discover How Do Waves Travel?

SECTION

2 Properties of Waves

Discover How Can You Change a Wave?
Skills Lab Wavy Motions

SECTION

3 Interactions of Waves

Discover How Does a Ball Bounce?
Sharpen Your Skills Observing
Try This Standing Waves
Science at Home Waves in a Sink
Skills Lab Making Waves

Passers-by watch as the Chinese dragon moves to the music.

CHAPTER 15 PROJECT

Over and Over and Over Again

It's time to celebrate the Chinese New Year! The parade passes through the streets to the delight of the people watching. The dragon dancers use poles to move the dragon up and down. The dragon moves just like a wave.

In this chapter, you will discover how waves travel. Some waves involve repeating patterns, or cycles. Any motion that repeats itself at regular intervals is called periodic motion. The hands on a clock, a child on a swing, a ride on a Ferris wheel, and the beating of your heart are just a few examples of periodic motion. As you work through the project, you will investigate the properties of periodic motion.

Your Goal To find and describe examples of periodic motion.

To complete this project you will
- identify several examples of periodic motion or other events that have periodic characteristics
- collect and organize data on the frequency and duration of each event
- present your findings as a poster, display, or demonstration

Get Started Brainstorm examples of repeating patterns you have observed. Think about objects or events that go back and forth or alternate from high to low, dark to light, loud to quiet, or crowded to uncrowded.

Check Your Progress You'll be working on this project as you study this chapter. To keep your project on track, look for Check Your Progress boxes at the following points.
Section 1 Review, page 475: List examples of periodic motion you'd like to study.
Section 2 Review, page 481: Record your observations of the frequency, length, and amplitude of the periodic events.

Present Your Project At the end of the project (page 495), you will present your findings to your class.

Integrating Earth Science

SECTION 4 **Seismic Waves**

Discover Can You Find the Sand?
Science at Home Sounds Solid

SECTION 4 Seismic Waves

DISCOVER ·····················ACTIVITY···

Can You Find the Sand?

1. Fill a plastic film canister with sand and replace the lid tightly.

2. Place the canister on a table with four other identical but empty canisters. Mix them around so that a classmate does not know which can is which.

3. With your fist, pound on the table a few times. Have your classmate try to figure out which canister contains the sand.

4. Stick each canister to the table with some modeling clay. Pound on the table again. Now can your classmate figure out which canister contains the sand?

Think It Over

Inferring Pounding on a table makes waves. Why might the canister containing the sand respond differently from the empty canisters?

GUIDE FOR READING

◆ What happens when rock beneath Earth's surface moves?

◆ What are the different types of seismic waves?

◆ How does a seismograph work?

Reading Tip As you read, make a table comparing primary, secondary, and surface waves.

Some of the most dramatic waves originate deep inside Earth. On August 27, 1883, the eruption of Krakatau volcano in Indonesia caused a series of earthquakes. Vibrations from the earthquakes formed waves that traveled from the island through the surrounding water. On the open ocean, the waves were only about 1 meter high. As they entered shallower water, near land, the waves traveled more slowly. This caused the waves at the back to catch up to the waves at the front and to pile on top. The first wave grew into a wall of water over 35 meters high. People on ships far out at sea could not even tell when the waves went by. But on the islands of Java and Sumatra thousands of people were killed as the enormous waves crashed onto the land.

Figure 14 This illustration shows a giant wave reaching the coast of Java. The wave was caused by earthquakes related to the eruption of Krakatau volcano 40 kilometers away.

Types of Seismic Waves

An earthquake occurs when rock beneath Earth's surface moves. The movement of Earth's plates creates stress in the rock. **When the stress in the rock builds up enough, the rock breaks or changes shape, releasing energy in the form of waves or vibrations.** The waves produced by earthquakes are known as **seismic waves.** (The word *seismic* comes from the Greek word *seismos,* meaning "earthquake.")

Seismic waves ripple out in all directions from the point where the earthquake occurred. As the waves move, they carry the energy through Earth. The waves can travel from one side of Earth to the other. **Seismic waves include primary waves, secondary waves, and surface waves.**

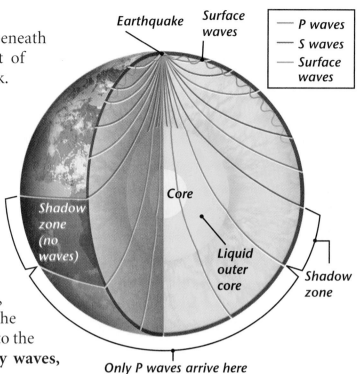

Only P waves arrive here

Figure 15 P waves travel through all parts of Earth. S waves do not travel through Earth's core. Surface waves travel only along Earth's surface. The shadow zone is where there are no seismic waves.
Applying Concepts Why don't S waves travel through Earth's core?

Primary Waves Some seismic waves are longitudinal waves. Longitudinal seismic waves are known as **primary waves,** or P waves. They are called primary waves because they move faster than other seismic waves and so arrive at distant points before other seismic waves. Primary waves are made up of compressions and rarefactions of rock inside Earth.

Secondary Waves Other seismic waves are transverse waves with crests and troughs. Transverse seismic waves are known as **secondary waves,** or S waves. Secondary waves cannot travel through liquids. Since part of Earth's core is liquid, S waves do not travel directly through Earth and cannot be detected on the side of Earth opposite an earthquake. Because of this, scientists on the side of Earth opposite the earthquake detect mainly P waves.

Surface Waves When P waves and S waves reach Earth's surface, some of them are transformed into surface waves similar to waves on the surface of water. Recall that surface waves are a combination of longitudinal and transverse waves. Even though surface waves travel more slowly than either P or S waves, they produce the most severe ground movements.

Earthquakes that occur underwater can cause huge surface waves on the ocean called **tsunamis** (tsoo NAH meez). Tsunamis can cause great damage when they reach land.

☑ *Checkpoint* *How are P waves different from S waves?*

Reviewing Content

For more review of key concepts, see the Interactive Student Tutorial CD-ROM.

Multiple Choice

Choose the letter of the best answer.

1. A wave carries
   a. energy.   b. matter.
   c. water.   d. air.
2. The distance between one crest and the next crest is the wave's
   a. amplitude.   b. wavelength.
   c. frequency.   d. speed.
3. In a given medium, if the frequency of a wave increases, its
   a. wavelength increases.
   b. speed increases.
   c. amplitude decreases.
   d. wavelength decreases.
4. The bending of a wave due to a change in its speed is
   a. interference.
   b. diffraction.
   c. reflection.
   d. refraction.
5. Seismic waves that do *not* travel through liquids are
   a. P waves.
   b. S waves.
   c. surface waves.
   d. tsunamis.

True or False

If the statement is true, write true. If it is false, change the underlined word or words to make the statement true.

6. <u>Transverse</u> waves have compressions and rarefactions.
7. When the particles of a medium move a great distance as the wave passes, the wave has a large <u>amplitude</u>.
8. When a wave changes speed as it enters a new medium at an angle, it undergoes <u>diffraction</u>.
9. Nodes and antinodes occur in <u>longitudinal</u> waves.
10. <u>Secondary</u> waves arrive at distant points before other seismic waves.

Checking Concepts

11. Explain the difference between transverse and longitudinal waves. Use diagrams to illustrate your explanation.
12. How can you find the amplitude of a longitudinal wave?
13. How are a wave's speed, wavelength, and frequency related?
14. Describe the difference between constructive and destructive interference.
15. Explain how seismographs work.
16. **Writing to Learn** Suppose you are a sportswriter with a background in science. While at a baseball game, you notice that at various times, entire sections of people stand up and sit down again. This "wave" travels around the stadium. Write a short newspaper article that describes what the crowd is doing. Be sure to use terms such as amplitude, frequency, wavelength, and speed in your description. Give your article a title.

Thinking Critically

17. **Comparing and Contrasting** One wave has half the amplitude of a second wave. The two waves interfere constructively. Draw a diagram and describe the resulting wave. Describe the resulting wave if two waves of equal amplitude interfere destructively.
18. **Calculating** A wave travels at 10 m/s and has a wavelength of 2 m. What is the frequency of the wave? If the speed of the wave doubles but the wavelength remains the same, what is the new frequency? Show your work.
19. **Making Models** Describe a way to model refraction of a wave as it enters a new medium.
20. **Applying Concepts** Suppose a wave moves from one side of a lake to the other. Does the water move across the lake? Explain.

Applying Skills

The wave in the illustration is a giant ocean wave produced by an underwater earthquake. Use the illustration to answer Questions 21–24.

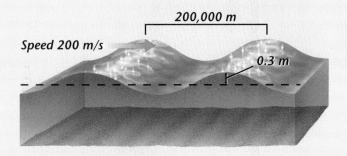

200,000 m

Speed 200 m/s

0.3 m

21. Classifying What kind of wave is shown in the above diagram?

22. Interpreting Diagrams What is the amplitude of the wave shown? What is its speed? Find the frequency of the wave. Show your work.

23. Predicting What could happen if this wave hits a coastal city? What property of a wave determines how much damage it could do?

24. Calculating How long would it take this wave to travel 5,000 km?

Performance CHAPTER PROJECT Assessment

Present Your Project Share your examples of periodic events and patterns with your classmates. On your display, highlight the repeating patterns and the frequency of each example. Which periodic events involve the transmission of waves through the vibrations of a medium?

Reflect and Record In your journal, describe the common or unusual events in your life that repeat periodically. Did you and your classmates observe the same things, or did your classmates surprise you with the examples they found?

Test Preparation

Use these questions to prepare for standardized tests.

Read the passage. Then answer Questions 25–29.
During a visit to a nearby lake, you throw a stone into the water. As you sit back, you watch the ripple of waves created by the rock. Not far from where you threw the stone, you see a leaf bobbing up and down on the water.

25. What type of waves did you create by throwing the stone?
  a. transverse
  b. longitudinal
  c. surface
  d. seismic

26. What is the medium for the waves?
  a. stone
  b. water
  c. leaf
  d. air

27. What was transferred by the waves?
  a. water
  b. energy
  c. objects floating on the water
  d. air

28. When the leaf was raised to its highest position by the wave, it was at the wave's
  a. trough.
  b. compression.
  c. crest.
  d. rarefaction.

29. What two factors do you need to know to determine the wave's speed?
  a. amplitude and frequency
  b. amplitude and wavelength
  c. angle of incidence and angle of reflection
  d. wavelength and frequency

WEB ACTIVITY
www.phschool.com

SECTION 1 The Nature of Sound

Discover What Is Sound?
Sharpen Your Skills Graphing
Science at Home Ear to the Sound
Skills Lab The Speed of Sound

SECTION 2 Properties of Sound

Discover How Does Amplitude Affect Loudness?
Try This The Short Straw
Try This Pipe Sounds

SECTION 3 Combining Sound Waves

Discover How Can You Produce Patterns of Sound?
Try This Plucking Rubber Bands
Real-World Lab Musical Notes

Music to Your Ears

Music, one of the oldest arts, forms an important part of many occasions. Early Chinese, Egyptian, and Babylonian people made stringed instruments from animal hair, whistles from bones, and trumpets from animal horns. Today, musical instruments are made of wood, brass, silver, and nylon.

In this chapter you will investigate the properties of sound. You will learn how sound is produced by different objects, including musical instruments. As you work through the chapter, you will gather enough knowledge to help you to complete the project.

Your Goal To design, build, and play a simple musical instrument.

To complete this project you must
◆ design a simple musical instrument
◆ construct and modify your instrument
◆ play a simple tune on your instrument

Get Started Begin now by discussing different kinds of instruments with your classmates. What kind of music do you enjoy? What instruments are common in your favorite type of music? Do you or any of your classmates already play an instrument? Which type of instrument would you like to build?

Check Your Progress You'll be working on this project as you study this chapter. To keep your project on track, look for Check Your Progress boxes at the following points.
Section 2 Review, page 509: Make a list of materials you could use to build your instrument.
Section 3 Review, page 517: Design and construct your instrument.
Section 5 Review, page 528: Test your instrument. Modify and test it again.

Present Your Project At the end of the chapter (page 531), you will demonstrate how you can vary the loudness and pitch of the sound of your instrument and play a simple tune.

These musical instruments play a part in African ceremonial life.

 Integrating Life Science

SECTION 4 How You Hear Sound

Discover Where Is the Sound Coming From?
Try This Listen to Sounds
Science at Home Sound Survey

SECTION 5 Applications of Sound

Discover How Can You Use Time to Measure Distance?
Sharpen Your Skills Designing Experiments

SECTION 1 The Nature of Sound

What Is Sound?

1. Fill a bowl with water.

2. Tap a tuning fork against the sole of your shoe. Place the tip of one of the prongs in the water. What do you see?

3. Tap the tuning fork again. Predict what will happen when you hold it near your ear. What do you hear?

Think It Over

Observing How do you think your observations are related to the sound you hear? What might change if you use a tuning fork of a different size? What would change in the sound you hear?

GUIDE FOR READING

◆ What is sound?

◆ What factors affect the speed of sound?

Reading Tip Before you read, preview the headings in the section. Record the headings in outline form, leaving room to add notes.

Here is an old riddle: If a tree falls in a forest and no one is there to hear it, does the tree make a sound? To answer the question, you must decide how to define the word "sound." If sound is something that a person must hear with his or her ears, then you might say that the tree makes no sound.

When a tree crashes down, the energy with which it strikes the forest floor is transmitted through the ground and the surrounding air. This energy causes the ground and the air to vibrate. If sound is a disturbance that travels through the ground or the air, then sound is created even if no one is around. So the tree does make a sound.

Sound and Longitudinal Waves

Just like the waves you studied in Chapter 15, sound begins with a vibration. When a tree crashes to the ground, the surrounding air particles are disturbed. This disturbance causes other vibrations in nearby particles.

How Sound Travels Like all waves, **sound** waves carry energy through a medium without the particles of the medium traveling along. A common medium for sound is air. Each molecule in the air moves back and forth as the disturbance goes by. **Sound is a disturbance that travels through a medium as a longitudinal wave.** When the disturbance reaches the air near your ears, you hear the sound.

How Sounds Are Made A drum also makes sounds by creating vibrations. When you beat a drum, the surface of the drum begins to vibrate so quickly that you cannot see it move. Air is

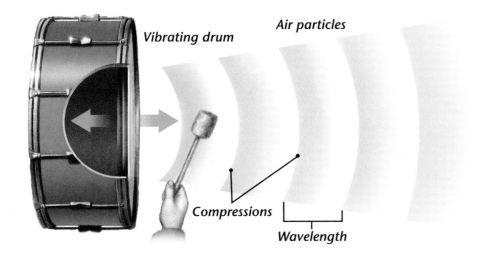

Vibrating drum

Air particles

Compressions

Wavelength

Figure 1 As the drum vibrates back and forth, it creates compressions and rarefactions in the air. *Classifying What type of wave does a drum make?*

mostly made up of tiny particles, or molecules, of gases. Figure 1 shows how the vibration of a drum creates a disturbance in the molecules in the air near it. When the drumhead moves to the right, it pushes the molecules together, creating a compression. When the drumhead moves to the left, the molecules move farther apart, creating a rarefaction.

When you pluck a guitar string, it vibrates back and forth, creating compressions and rarefactions. These compressions and rarefactions travel through the air as longitudinal waves similar to the longitudinal waves that you saw travel along a spring.

INTEGRATING LIFE SCIENCE Your vocal cords act like vibrating guitar strings. Whenever you speak or sing, you force air from your lungs up through your voice box, or **larynx.** Your larynx consists of two folds of tissue called vocal cords, shown in Figure 2. The forced air rushes by your vocal cords, making them vibrate. As your vocal cords move toward each other, the air between them is compressed. As they move apart, the air spreads out, or is rarefied. Like vibrating guitar strings, your vocal cords produce compressions and rarefactions in the air. The air carries these longitudinal waves to other people's ears as well as to your own.

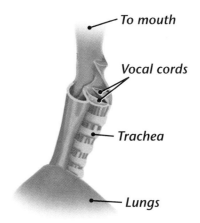

To mouth

Vocal cords

Trachea

Lungs

Figure 2 When a person speaks or sings, the vocal cords vibrate. The vibrations produce longitudinal sound waves in the air.

Sound in Solids and Liquids
Sound can also travel through solids and liquids. When you knock on a door, the particles of the door vibrate. The vibration creates sound waves that travel through the door. When the sound waves reach the other side of the door, they make sound waves in the air on the far side. In old western movies, you may see someone put an ear to a railway track to tell if

499

Figure 3 When sound waves enter a room through an open door, they spread out. This is called diffraction.

Figure 4 The speed of sound depends upon the medium through which it is traveling. *Making Generalizations In general, does sound travel faster in solids, liquids, or gases?*

Speed of Sound	
Medium	**Speed (m/s)**
Gases	
Air (0°C)	330
Air (20°C)	342
Liquids	
Fresh water	1,490
Salt water	1,530
Solids (25°C)	
Lead	1,210
Plastic	1,800
Silver	2,680
Copper	3,100
Gold	3,240
Brick	3,650
Hard wood	4,000
Glass	4,540
Iron	5,000
Steel	5,200

a train is on the way. The sound of the train travels easily through the steel tracks. If you put your ear to the ground, you might hear distant traffic. Sound waves from the traffic are traveling through the ground as well as through the air.

Sound can travel only if there is a medium to transmit the compressions and rarefactions. In outer space, there are no molecules to compress or rarefy. The energy of the original vibrations has nothing through which to travel. So sound does not travel through outer space.

How Sound Bends When sound waves hit a barrier with a small hole in it, some of the waves pass through the hole. Just as diffraction causes water waves to spread out in a harbor, the sound waves spread out, or diffract, as they go through the hole. When sound waves go through a doorway, they spread out. Even if you are off to the side of the room, you may still hear sound from outside. If you are outside the room and not too far from the doorway, you can hear sound coming from inside the room.

Because of diffraction, you can also hear sounds from around corners. Waves passing a corner spread out as they pass.

The Speed of Sound

If you have ever seen a live band perform, you've noticed that the sounds produced by the different instruments and singers all reach your ears at the same time. If they did not travel at the same speed, the sounds that were played together would reach you at different times and would not sound very pleasant.

The speed of sound depends on the properties of the medium it travels through. At room temperature, about 20°C, sound travels at about 342 m/s. This is much faster than most jet airplanes travel through the air. Figure 4 shows the speed of sound through some common materials.

As the properties of a medium change, so too does the speed of the sound that travels through it. **The speed of sound depends on the elasticity, density, and temperature of the medium.**

Elasticity Since sound is a transfer of energy, its speed depends on how well the particles in the medium bounce back after being disturbed. If you stretch a rubber band and then let it go, it returns to its original shape. However, when you stretch modeling clay and then let it go, it stays stretched. Rubber bands are more elastic than modeling clay. **Elasticity** is the ability of a material to bounce back after being disturbed. If a medium is very elastic, its particles easily go back to their original positions. Sound travels more quickly in mediums that have a high degree of elasticity because when the particles are compressed, they quickly spread out again.

Figure 5 Some substances are more elastic than others. Sponges and rubber bands are more elastic than modeling clay. *Predicting Is sound likely to travel faster through a sponge, a rubber band, or a piece of modeling clay?*

Solid materials are usually more elastic than liquids or gases, so compressions and rarefactions travel very well in solids. The particles of a solid do not move very far, so they bounce back and forth quickly as the compressions and rarefactions of the sound waves go by. Most liquids are not very elastic. Sound is not transmitted as well in liquids as it is in solids. Gases are generally very inelastic and are the poorest transmitters of sound.

Density The speed of sound also depends on how close together the particles of the substance are. The density of a medium is how much matter, or mass, there is in a given amount of space, or volume.

In materials in the same state of matter—solid, liquid, or gas—sound travels more slowly in denser mediums. The denser the medium, the more mass it has in a given volume. The particles of a dense material do not move as quickly as those of a less-dense material. Sound travels more slowly in dense metals, such as lead or silver, than in iron or steel.

Temperature In a given medium, sound travels more slowly at lower temperatures and faster at higher temperatures. At a low temperature, the particles of a medium are more sluggish. They are more difficult to move and return to their original positions more slowly.

At 20°C, the speed of sound in air is about 340 m/s. At 0°C, the speed is about 330 m/s. At higher altitudes the air is colder, so sound travels more slowly at higher altitudes.

☑ *Checkpoint* How does elasticity affect the speed of sound?

Graphing **ACTIVITY**

Graph the following data, to show how the speed of sound through air changes with temperature. Show temperature from –20°C to 30°C on the horizontal axis. (*Note:* Negative numbers are less than zero.) Plot speed from 300 m/s to 400 m/s on the vertical axis.

Air Temperature (°C)	Speed (m/s)
–20	318
–10	324
0	330
10	336
20	342
30	348

How does air temperature affect the speed of sound?

Figure 6 On October 14, 1947, Captain Chuck Yeager became the first person to fly a plane faster than the speed of sound (top). On October 15, 1997, Andy Green officially became the first person to drive a land vehicle faster than the speed of sound (bottom).

Moving Faster Than Sound

The supersonic age began with a bang on October 14, 1947. Far above the California desert, Captain Chuck Yeager of the United States Air Force had just "broken the sound barrier." Captain Yeager was at an altitude of 12,000 meters and just about out of fuel. He had used much of his fuel to get higher rather than faster because the speed of sound is less higher up. Wide open throttles accelerated his plane to over 293 meters per second, the speed of sound at that altitude. Thus, when he hit 294 meters per second, he exceeded the speed of sound at that altitude. At a lower altitude, the speed of sound is much higher and he would not have had the power or speed to exceed it. Yeager's team chose to go high in part because the temperature there is lower and the speed of sound is less. Each pilot today who "goes supersonic" owes Chuck Yeager a debt of gratitude.

Fifty years later, Andy Green stood poised on Nevada's Black Rock desert. He had traveled all the way from Great Britain to go supersonic—on the ground! He chose the desert because it is flat, wide open, and cold in the morning. All of these factors were important to the attempt. On October 15, 1997, at the coolest time of the day, Green blasted off in his jet-powered car, *Thrust*. A short time later he traveled a measured distance at an average speed of 339 meters per second—7 meters per second faster than the speed of sound at that altitude. Andy Green was the first person to break the sound barrier on the ground.

Section 1 Review

1. How does sound travel through a medium?
2. How do elasticity, density, and temperature affect the speed of sound through a medium?
3. Explain why sound cannot travel through outer space.
4. **Thinking Critically** **Applying Concepts** Sound travels faster through glass than through gold. Based on this information, which material would you say is more dense? Explain.

Science at Home

Ear to the Sound Find a long metal railing or water pipe. **CAUTION:** *Beware of sharp edges and rust.* Put one ear to the pipe while a family member taps on the pipe some distance away. Do you hear the sound first with the ear touching the pipe or with your other ear? Compare the sound you hear through the metal with the sound coming through the air. What accounts for the difference?

The Speed of Sound

Sound travels at different speeds through different materials. In this lab, you will measure the speed of sound in air.

Problem

How fast does sound travel in air?

Materials (per group of 3)

metric tape measure
drum and drumstick (or empty   digital stopwatch
   coffee can and metal spoon)   thermometer

Procedure

1. With the approval of your teacher, select an outdoor area such as a football field.
2. Record the outdoor air temperature in °C.
3. Measure a distance of 100 meters in a straight line. How long do you think it should take for a sound to travel the 100 m?
4. Stand at one end of this measured distance with the drum. Have two teammates go to the other end with a stopwatch. One teammate, the "watcher," should watch you and the drum. The other, the "listener," should face away from the drum and listen for the sound.
5. Create a short but loud noise by striking the drum.
6. As you strike the drum, the watcher should start the stopwatch. When the listener hears the sound, he or she should immediately say "stop." Then the watcher stops the watch. Record the time to one tenth of a second.
7. Repeat Steps 1–6 five times. How consistent are your times? What accounts for any differences?
8. Now switch roles. Repeat Steps 1–6 with different students beating the drum, watching, and listening.

Analyze and Conclude

1. How far did the sound travel? How long did it take? (Calculate the average of the five measured times.)
2. To calculate the speed of sound in air, use this formula:

$$Speed = \frac{Distance}{Time}$$

3. How well does your result compare with the prediction you made in Step 3? Make a list of reasons for any differences. What could you do to improve the accuracy of your measurements?
4. **Think About It** Another way to measure the speed of sound would be to stand near a tall building, shout, and wait to hear the echo. To use the echo method, what adjustments would you have to make to the procedure in this lab?

Design an Experiment

How could you find out the effect of changing air temperature on the speed of sound? Write a set of procedures you could use to conduct such an experiment.

503

Properties of Sound

DISCOVER

How Does Amplitude Affect Loudness?

1. 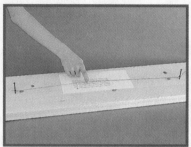 Your teacher will give you a wooden board with two nails in it. Fasten a guitar string to the board by wrapping each end tightly around a nail.

2. Hold the string near the middle. Pull it about 1 cm to one side. This distance is the amplitude of vibration. Let it go. How far does the string move to the other side? Describe the sound you hear.

3. Repeat Step 2 four more times. Each time, pull the string back a greater distance. Describe how the sound changes each time.

Think It Over

Forming Operational Definitions How would you define the amplitude of the vibration? How did you change the amplitude each time? What effect did changing the amplitude have on the sound?

GUIDE FOR READING

◆ How are sound intensity and loudness related?

◆ How are frequency and pitch related?

◆ What causes the Doppler effect?

Reading Tip As you read, use your own words to write a phrase or sentence describing each boldfaced word.

Suppose you and a friend are standing next to each other. You are talking in your normal speaking voice. After you say good-bye and your friend has walked away, you realize you have forgotten to tell your friend something important. How do you get your friend's attention? You will need to shout to be heard. When you shout, you take a deep breath and exhale very fast, and your voice sounds louder.

Intensity and Loudness

Compare the sound of a whisper to that of a hearty shout. The sounds are different because the amount of energy carried by the sound waves is different. The sound waves caused by a shout carry much more energy than those of a whisper.

Intensity You have seen how you can change the amplitude of a wave along a rope. If you move the rope a greater distance, you give it more energy as you shake it. When a sound wave carries a large amount of energy, the molecules of the medium move a greater distance as the waves pass by, and the sound wave has a greater amplitude. The **intensity** of a sound wave is the amount of energy the wave carries per second through a unit area. Intensity is measured in watts per square meter (W/m^2).

Loudness If you did the Discover activity with the guitar string, you noticed how pulling the string back different distances affected the loudness of the sound you heard. You changed the amplitude of vibration of the string. Sound waves of higher amplitude have a greater intensity because they carry more energy per second through a given area. Though intensity and loudness are not exactly the same, the greater the intensity of a sound wave, the louder it is. **Loudness** describes what you actually hear. **A sound wave of greater intensity generally sounds louder.**

To increase the loudness of the music coming from a CD player, you adjust the volume control. Loudspeakers or headphones give off sound by vibrating a cone of material. Figure 7 shows how the vibrations make compressions and rarefactions in the air, just like a vibrating drumhead. As you turn up the volume, the cone vibrates with a greater amplitude and the sound you hear is louder.

Loudness, or sound level, is measured in **decibels (dB).** Figure 8 shows the loudness of some familiar sounds. The loudness of a sound you can barely hear is about 0 dB. Each 10 dB increase in sound level represents a tenfold increase in intensity. For example, a sound at 30 dB is ten times more intense than a sound at 20 dB. Sounds louder than 100 dB can cause damage to your ears, especially if you listen to those sounds for long periods of time. Sounds louder than 120 dB can cause pain and sometimes permanent hearing loss.

Figure 7 A loudspeaker gives out sound by vibrating cones of material. The greater the amplitude of vibration, the greater the volume, or loudness, of the sound.

✓ *Checkpoint* *How does amplitude affect the loudness of a sound?*

Loudness of Sounds

Sound	Loudness (dB)	Hearing Damage
Threshold of human hearing	0	None
Rustling leaves	10	
Whisper	20	
Very soft music	30	
Classroom	35	
Average home	40–50	
Loud conversation	60–70	
Heavy street traffic	70	
Loud music	90–100	After long exposure
Subway train	100	
Rock concert	115–120	Progressive
Jackhammer	120	Threshold of pain
Jet engine	120–170	
Space shuttle engine	200	Immediate and irreversible

Figure 8 Some sounds are so soft, you can barely hear them. Others are so loud that they can damage your ears. *Applying Concepts How is the sound of a space shuttle engine different from that of a whisper?*

The Short Straw

Try this activity to see how the 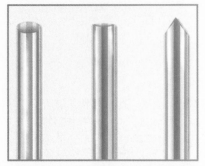 length of a straw affects the sound it makes when you blow through it.

1. Flatten one end of a drinking straw and cut the end to form a point.
2. Blow through the straw. Describe what you hear.

Predicting What changes would you hear if you shortened the straw by cutting off some of the straight end? Test your prediction.

Frequency and Pitch

A barbershop quartet consists of four singers with very different voices. When all four people sing together, the different voices combine to make a pleasing sound.

Frequency When a person sings, muscles in the throat stretch and relax the vocal cords. This changes the frequency of the sounds. When the vocal cords are stretched, they vibrate more often as the air rushes past them. This creates higher-frequency sound waves. When the vocal cords are relaxed, they vibrate less often and produce lower-frequency sound waves. The frequency of a sound wave is the number of vibrations that occur per second. A frequency of 50 Hz means fifty vibrations per second. A bass singer can produce a range of frequencies from about 80 Hz to about 260 Hz. A trained soprano voice can produce frequencies over 1,000 Hz.

Most people can hear sounds with frequencies between 20 Hz and 20,000 Hz. Sound waves with frequencies above the normal human range of hearing are called **ultrasound**. The prefix *ultra-* means "above." Sounds with frequencies below the normal human range of hearing are called **infrasound**. The prefix *infra-* means "below."

Pitch Before a barbershop quartet begins to sing, one member plays a note on a pitch pipe. This gives the lead singer the correct starting note. The **pitch** of a sound is a description of how high or low the sound seems to a person. **The pitch of a sound that you hear depends on the frequency of the sound wave.** Sound waves of high frequency have a high pitch, while sound waves of low frequency have a low pitch.

Figure 9 A barbershop quartet consists of four singers, whose voices sound good together. *Comparing and Contrasting In what way are the four voices different?*

Figure 10 The key farthest to the left on a piano is attached to the longest string. This key plays the note with the lowest pitch. *Developing Hypotheses Why do longer strings generally produce lower notes than shorter ones?*

When a string vibrates, the pitch of the sound depends on the material used, the length and thickness of the string, and on how tightly it is stretched. You can change the pitch of a sound by changing the properties of the string that produces it. For example, violinists and guitarists tune their instruments by turning knobs that stretch the strings. A tighter string produces a higher frequency. You hear the higher frequency as a sound with higher pitch.

Different lengths of string produce different frequencies, too. In general, a short string produces a higher pitch than a long string under the same tension. Consider the range of notes you can play on a piano. The key farthest to the left on a piano keyboard produces the note with the lowest pitch. It is attached to the longest string, which vibrates at a frequency of about 27 Hz. The key farthest to the right on a piano keyboard produces the note with the highest pitch. It is attached to the shortest string, which vibrates at a frequency of 4,186 Hz.

✓ *Checkpoint* *How are frequency and pitch related?*

Figure 11 Some musical instruments can produce notes with vibrations that match the natural frequency of a crystal glass. If the note is sustained, the amplitude of vibration can cause the glass to shatter.

Resonance Have you ever heard of an opera singer who could shatter a glass with a sustained high note? How can that happen? All objects vibrate naturally. The vibrations are so frequent that you usually cannot see them. The frequency of the vibrations depends on the type and shape of the object. If the frequency of sound waves exactly matches the natural frequency of an object, the sound waves can add to the object's vibrations. Resonance occurs when the frequency of the sound waves and the natural frequency of the object are the same.

Suppose a note has the same frequency as the natural vibration of a crystal glass. If the note is played steadily, the sound waves can add to the amplitude of vibration of the glass. If the note is played loudly enough and for long enough, the amplitude of vibration can increase so much that the glass shatters.

The Doppler Effect

Even though a sound may have a constant frequency, it does not always sound that way to a listener. Have you ever heard a police car speed by with its siren on? If you listen carefully you will notice something surprising. As the car moves toward you, the pitch of the siren is higher. As the car goes by and moves away, the pitch drops. But the frequency of the siren is not really changing. If you were riding in the police car, you would hear the same pitch all the time. The apparent change in frequency as a wave source moves in relation to the listener is called the **Doppler effect.** If the waves are sound waves, the change in frequency is heard as a change in pitch.

The Doppler Demonstration The Doppler effect was named after Christian Doppler, an Austrian scientist who described it about 150 years ago. To demonstrate the effect, Doppler put a musical band on an open flatcar of a train. He stood on the ground nearby. As the train approached him, the notes the musicians played seemed to be a higher pitch. As the train passed, the notes seemed to drop in pitch. Doppler repeated the experiment, but this time he stood on the train and had the musicians play while they were seated on the ground. Doppler heard the same changes in pitch as the train he rode approached and passed the band. The effect was the same regardless of who was moving, the band or Doppler.

Changing Pitch To understand what causes this apparent change in pitch, imagine you are standing still and throwing tennis balls at a wall about 5 meters in front of you. If you throw one ball each second, the balls hit the wall at a rate of one per second. The frequency is 1 per second, or 1 Hz. Now suppose you walk toward the wall, still throwing one ball per second.

Figure 12 As the police car speeds by, the pitch of the siren seems to change. Ahead of the car, the sound waves are piling up, so the pitch is higher. Behind the car the waves spread out, so the pitch is lower.

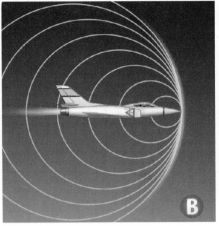
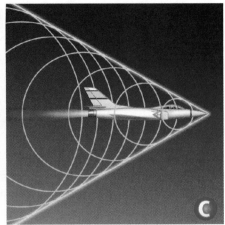

Figure 13 A, B. When a plane approaches the speed of sound, its sound waves pile up in front of it. C. When the plane exceeds the speed of sound, it flies through these waves, causing a shock wave we hear as a sonic boom.

Because each ball has a shorter distance to travel than the one before, it takes less time to get there. The balls hit the wall more often than one per second, or with a higher frequency than before. Similarly, if you throw balls at the wall as you back away, the balls will hit the wall with lower frequency. Each ball has farther to travel before it hits the wall, so it takes longer to get there.

Figure 12 shows how sound waves from a moving source behave. **As a sound source moves toward the listener, the waves reach the listener with a higher frequency. The pitch appears to increase because of the Doppler effect.**

This piling up of sound waves has a spectacular effect in the air. Figures 13A and B show how as a plane travels almost as fast as the speed of sound, the sound waves pile up in front of the plane. This pile-up is the "sound barrier." When the plane flies faster than the speed of sound, it breaks through the barrier. When the sound barrier is broken, as in Figure 13C, a huge amount of energy is released in the form of a shock wave. People on the ground nearby hear a loud noise called a sonic boom.

Section 2 Review

1. What makes some sounds louder than others?
2. Explain the relationship between frequency and pitch.
3. How can you change the pitch produced by a vibrating string?
4. Explain how resonance can cause a crystal glass to shatter.
5. What is the Doppler effect?
6. **Thinking Critically** Relating Cause and Effect If you are riding in a fire truck with the siren blaring, you do not hear the Doppler effect. Explain.

CHAPTER PROJECT

Check Your Progress
Think about the design of your instrument and how it will produce sounds. Consider how you will vary the sound produced by your instrument. Make a list of the materials you could use to build your instrument. Begin to collect your materials.

Combining Sound Waves

How Can You Produce Patterns of Sound?

1. Obtain an empty coffee can.

2. Stretch the palm area of a latex glove over the open end. Glue a small mirror tile in the center of the glove.

3. Shine a flashlight so that the light reflects off the mirror and onto a wall.

4. Ask a classmate to continuously tap a spoon on the closed end of the can. Make sure you keep the light shining on the mirror. Observe the light patterns that are reflected on the wall. What do the patterns look like? Draw and label what you observe.

5. Have your classmate change the frequency of the tapping. Draw what you observe.

Think It Over

Inferring What causes the moving patterns on the wall? What happens when you change the frequency of the tapping? Explain.

◆ What is sound quality?

◆ How are music and noise different?

◆ What happens when two or more sound waves interact?

Reading Tip Before you read, list as many musical instruments as you can. Write a short description of how you think each one works. Revise your list as you read.

Imagine you are waiting for a train at a busy station. In the middle of all the hustle and bustle, you notice lots of different sounds. A baby wails while a teenager listens to a favorite radio station. Then the train rolls in. Why are some sounds pleasing to hear while others make you want to cover your ears? The answer is in the way sound waves combine.

Busy train station ▶

Sound Quality

Think of all the different sounds you hear on a given day. Some sounds are pleasant, such as your favorite kind of music, a babbling brook, or a baby cooing. Other sounds are unpleasant, such as loud power tools, fingernails scratching on a chalkboard, or a constant drip of water from a tap. Your ears hear all kinds of sounds—some that you like and some that you don't.

To understand the quality of sound, consider the example of a violin string. As the string vibrates, waves travel along the string and then reflect back, setting up a standing wave. Figure 14 shows how a string vibrates with different frequencies. The frequency at which a standing wave occurs is the string's resonant frequency. Every object, including musical instruments, has its own resonant frequency.

The resonant frequency produces a pitch called the fundamental tone. However, most of the sounds you hear are not pure tones. Although a tuning fork or pitch pipe produces a single tone, more complex instruments produce several tones at once. For example, a string can vibrate at several frequencies at the same time. The higher frequencies produce sounds heard as having higher pitch. The higher pitches, or overtones, have frequencies of two, three, or four times the frequency of the fundamental tone.

Timbre (TAM bur) describes the quality of the sound you hear. Overtones can be weak, strong, or missing. The timbre of a sound depends on which overtones are present. **The blending of the fundamental tone and the overtones makes up the characteristic sound quality, or timbre, of a particular sound.**

Sounds produced by different instruments have different timbres. The sound of a note played on a trumpet has a different timbre from the same note played on a violin or flute. The trumpet, the violin, and the flute produce different overtones. The size, shape, and materials used also affect the timbre of an instrument.

✓ *Checkpoint* What factors affect the quality of a sound?

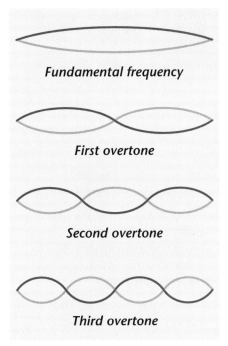

Figure 14 When half a wave takes up the whole string, a fundamental tone is produced (top). Waves half, one third, one fourth, and so on, as long as the fundamental wave produce overtones. *Inferring How does the pitch of each overtone compare with the pitch of the fundamental tone?*

Fundamental frequency

First overtone

Second overtone

Third overtone

Making Music

If the combination of the fundamental tone and the overtones results in a sound with a pleasing timbre and a clear pitch, the sound is considered **music.** Most music contains only a few fundamental tones and their overtones. **Music is a set of tones combined in ways that are pleasing to the ear.** The design of a musical instrument affects the overtones it produces when a note is played. All musical instruments produce vibrations when played. The material that vibrates varies. The major groups of instruments are strings, brass, woodwinds, and percussion.

Strings Stringed instruments have strings that vibrate when plucked, struck, or rubbed with a bow. A short string vibrates at a higher frequency and so produces a higher-pitched sound than a long string. As they play, musicians place their fingers on different places along the string to vary the pitch. The material, thickness, and tightness of a string also affects the pitch it produces. Instruments such as guitars, violins, and cellos also have a box, or sounding board. The box improves the quality of the sound produced by the strings. Larger stringed instruments, such as the cello and the double bass, produce lower pitches.

Brass and Woodwinds Brass instruments, such as trumpets and trombones, produce sound when the player's lips vibrate against the mouthpiece. This vibration causes the air column inside the instrument to vibrate. The musician adjusts the length of the air column by pressing valves or moving slides.

Figure 15 Violins are stringed instruments, flutes and clarinets are woodwinds, and trumpets are brass instruments.
Making Generalizations What do all these musical instruments have in common?

Many woodwind instruments, such as clarinets and oboes, have a thin, flexible strip of material called a reed. When the player blows into the mouthpiece, the reed vibrates along with the column of air. The longer the column of air, the lower the pitch. Larger woodwind and brass instruments, such as the bassoon and the tuba, produce lower pitches.

Percussion Percussion instruments, such as drums, bells, cymbals, and xylophones, vibrate when struck. The sound they produce depends on the material from which they are made. It also depends on the size of the instrument, and the part of the instrument that is played. For example, larger drums produce lower pitches.

Figure 16 Percussion instruments vibrate when struck. *Predicting Describe the sound produced by a large drum compared with that of a small drum of the same material.*

☑ *Checkpoint* *What are the main groups of musical instruments?*

Noise

You are sitting comfortably in your classroom chair, watching a classmate write on the board. Suddenly, you hear the accidental scratch of fingernails as the chalk flies from your friend's grasp. The sound makes you wince.

Why is the squeak of fingernails on a chalkboard so unpleasant? One answer is that the squeak is noise. **Noise** is a mixture of sound waves that do not sound pleasing together. **Noise has no pleasing timbre and no identifiable pitch.** Consider the noise of chalk squeaking on a chalkboard or the noise of a jackhammer working in the street. The vibrations that produce these sounds are random. Even if an engine produces a hum that has a fundamental tone and overtones, the lack of rhythm in the sound makes us call it noise instead of music.

Sounds that are music to some people are noise to others. Some rock bands and orchestras play compositions with tones that seem to have no musical relationship. The sound produced when these notes are played together is called **dissonance.** Dissonance is music to the ears of people who enjoy the sound.

Music
CONNECTION

One of the most widely known compositions of Sergei Prokofiev, a Russian composer who lived from 1891 to 1953, is *Peter and the Wolf.* In this work, each instrument, or group of instruments, represents a character in the story.

In Your Journal

Listen to a recording of *Peter and the Wolf.* Write a review of this work. Do you agree with how Prokofiev matched instruments with characters? Which instrument would you have chosen to represent each character?

EXPLORING *Making Music*

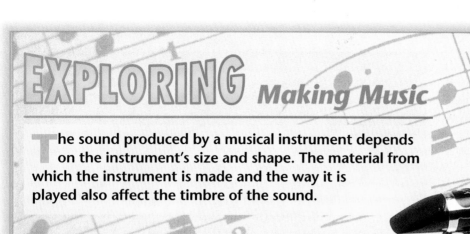

The sound produced by a musical instrument depends on the instrument's size and shape. The material from which the instrument is made and the way it is played also affect the timbre of the sound.

Violin
The violin is a carefully crafted wooden box with strings. The strings are attached to tuning pegs, which can be turned to adjust the tension. When the strings are rubbed with a bow, they vibrate. The violinist controls the pitch by placing the fingers at different positions along the string.

Harp
The harp consists of a row of strings, each one a different length. The harpist gracefully plucks the strings with the fingers to produce music. The short strings produce higher pitches than the long strings do.

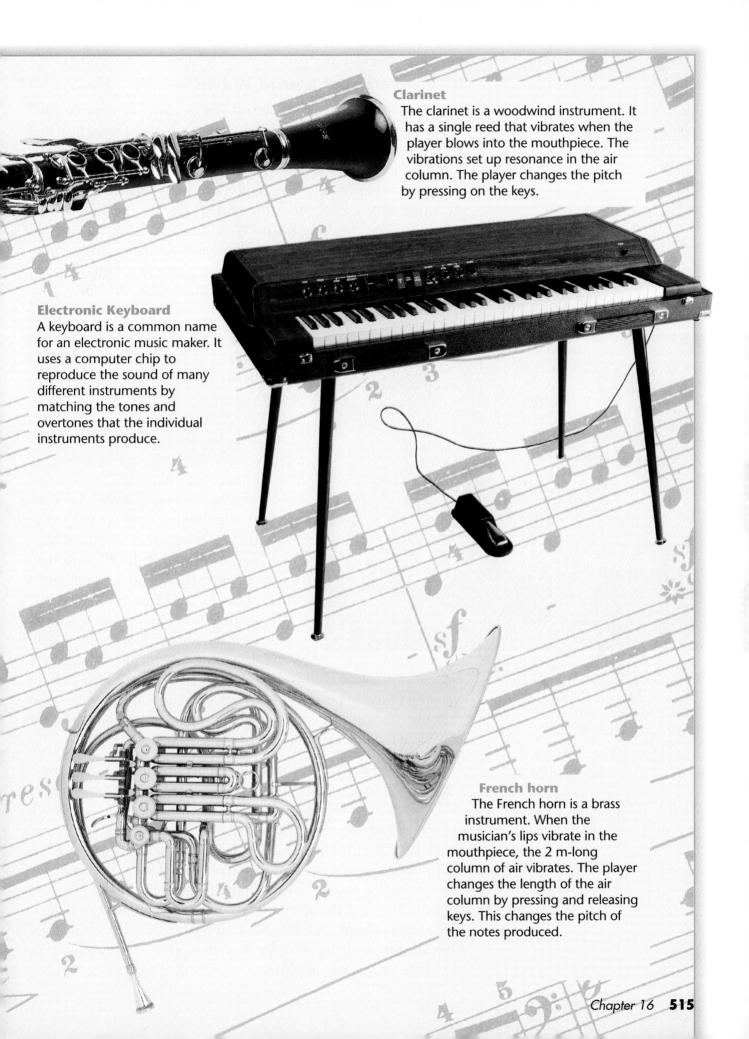

Clarinet

The clarinet is a woodwind instrument. It has a single reed that vibrates when the player blows into the mouthpiece. The vibrations set up resonance in the air column. The player changes the pitch by pressing on the keys.

Electronic Keyboard

A keyboard is a common name for an electronic music maker. It uses a computer chip to reproduce the sound of many different instruments by matching the tones and overtones that the individual instruments produce.

French horn

The French horn is a brass instrument. When the musician's lips vibrate in the mouthpiece, the 2 m-long column of air vibrates. The player changes the length of the air column by pressing and releasing keys. This changes the pitch of the notes produced.

Interference of Sound Waves

You have probably heard sound waves interfering with each other, though you may not have known what you were hearing. **Interference occurs when two or more sound waves interact.** The amplitudes of the two waves combine, causing the loudness of the sound to change. When interference is constructive, compressions of waves occur at the same place, and the amplitudes combine. The resulting sound is louder than either of the two original sounds. When the interference is destructive, compressions of one wave occur at the same place as rarefactions of another wave and the amplitudes cancel each other out. The resulting wave is softer or completely concealed.

Figure 17 A concert hall must be designed to provide the highest sound quality possible. The design should eliminate echoes and destructive interference.

Acoustics The way in which sound waves interact is very important in concert halls. In a concert hall, sound waves of different frequencies reach each listener from many directions at the same time. These sound waves may come directly from the orchestra or they may first bounce off the walls or ceiling. People sitting in various seats may hear different sounds because of the particular interactions of sound waves at their locations. In a poorly designed hall, seats may be located where destructive interference occurs. The sound will seem distorted.

Acoustics describe how well sounds can be heard in a particular room or hall. When designing auditoriums, acoustical engineers must carefully consider the shape of the room and the materials used to cover walls, floors, ceilings, and seats. Because they absorb sound instead of reflecting it, some materials can eliminate the reflected waves that cause interference.

Canceling Sounds Sometimes destructive interference is welcome. *INTEGRATING TECHNOLOGY* Airplane passengers use earphones to listen to music, but the throbbing of the plane's engines can drown out much of the sound. Some airline earphones use destructive interference to cancel out the steady engine noise. The earphones produce sound waves that interfere destructively with the engine sound. The passenger's ears receive both the engine sound waves and the sound waves produced by the earphones. These waves cancel each other out, so the passenger hears neither. Only the music is left. This type of technology also allows factories to reduce noise levels to protect the hearing of workers.

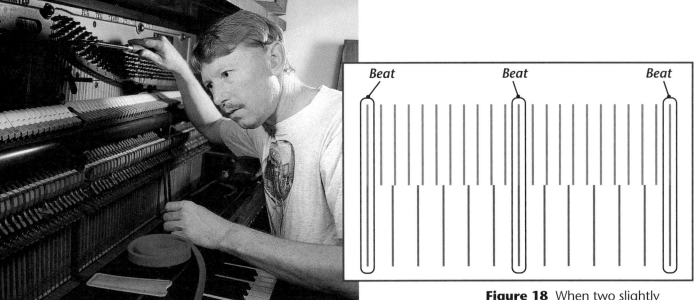

Figure 18 When two slightly different frequencies are combined, they interfere constructively at regular intervals (above right). A piano tuner listens to the sound of a note and a tuning fork together (above left). *Inferring How does the piano tuner know when a key is perfectly tuned?*

Beats If two sound waves are close in frequency, they can combine so that they interfere both constructively and destructively at regular intervals. Figure 18 shows how two frequencies can combine at certain times. The resulting sound gets louder and softer at regular intervals. The intervals depend on the difference between the two frequencies. The repeated changes in loudness are called **beats.**

Piano tuners use beats to tune pianos. A piano tuner strikes a tuning fork of a particular frequency and hits the corresponding key on a piano at the same time. If the tuner hears beats, that means that the frequency of vibration of the piano string does not exactly match that of the tuning fork. The tuner then adjusts the piano string until no beat can be heard. Then the piano key is perfectly tuned.

 Section 3 Review

1. What factors determine the quality of a sound?
2. What is the difference between music and noise?
3. How can sounds cancel each other out?
4. How can the interference of two sound waves produce a louder sound?
5. What are beats?
6. **Thinking Critically Applying Concepts** Explain why a sound in an empty room will sound different from the same sound in a room with a carpet, curtains, and furniture.

Check Your Progress

CHAPTER PROJECT

Begin building the instrument you have designed. As you build your instrument, experiment with different materials to find the most appealing sound. How do different kinds of materials affect the sounds? Explore and experiment with the sounds your instrument makes. How does adding or removing certain parts or materials affect the loudness of the sound? How can you vary the pitch of your instrument?

Musical Notes

Musical instruments produce sound by setting up standing waves. Those waves can be on a string or in a column of air. In this lab, you will see how you can use bottles to produce different musical notes, maybe enough to play a simple tune.

Problem

How can you produce different notes with bottles of water?

Skills Focus

predicting, observing, inferring

Materials

3 identical glass bottles
water
masking tape
marking pen
pencil

Procedure

1. Label the bottles A, B, and C.
2. Put water in each bottle so that bottle A is one-fourth full, bottle B is half full, and bottle C is three-fourths full.
3. Copy the data table into your lab notebook. Measure the distance from the top of each bottle to the surface of the water. Then measure the height of the water in each bottle. Record your measurements.
4. Predict the difference in pitch you will hear if you blow across the top of each bottle in turn. Give reasons for your prediction.
5. Test your prediction by blowing over the top of each bottle. Listen to the sound you produce. Describe each sound in terms of its pitch— low, medium, or high. Record the pitch of each sound.

DATA TABLE

Bottle	Length of Column of Air (cm)	Height of Water (cm)	Pitch Produced by Blowing Across Top of Bottle	Pitch Produced by Tapping Pencil on Side of Bottle
A				
B				
C				

6. When you gently tap the side of a bottle with a pencil, you produce another sound. Do you think the sound will be similar to or different from the sound produced by blowing across the top of the bottle? Explain.

7. Test your prediction by tapping on the side of each bottle with a pencil. Record the pitch of each sound.

Analyze and Conclude

1. Describe how the sound is produced in Step 5. Which bottle produced the highest pitch? Which bottle produced the lowest pitch?

2. What caused the change in pitch from bottle to bottle?

3. Describe how the sound is produced in Step 7. Which bottle produced the highest pitch? Which bottle produced the lowest pitch?

4. What caused the change in pitch from bottle to bottle? What change in pitch can you produce by tapping on a different part of the bottle?

5. Compare the sounds you produced by blowing across the bottles with those produced by tapping on the bottles. What was the difference in pitch for each bottle? Explain your observations.

6. Look at your data table. How does the length of the column of air affect the pitch? How does the height of the water affect the pitch?

7. **Think About It** Based on your observations in this lab, what statements can you make about the relationship between the sounds produced and the medium through which the sound travels?

More to Explore

To play simple tunes, you will need eight notes. Set up a row of eight bottles, each with a different amount of water. Adjust the water level in each bottle until you can play a simple scale. Practice playing a simple tune on your bottles.

SECTION 4 How You Hear Sound

DISCOVER

ACTIVITY

Where Is the Sound Coming From?

1. Ask your partner to sit on a chair, with eyes closed.

2. Clap your hands near your partner's left ear. Ask your partner to tell you the direction the sound came from.

3. Now clap near your partner's right ear. Again, ask your partner to tell you the direction the sound came from. Continue clapping above your partner's head, in front of the face, and below the chin in random order. How well can your partner detect the direction the sound is coming from?

4. Switch places with your partner and repeat Steps 1–3.

Think It Over

Observing As you clap, record the answers given by your partner. Which locations are easily identified? Which locations were impossible to identify? Is there a pattern? If so, can you think of a possible explanation for this pattern?

GUIDE FOR READING

◆ How do you hear sound?

◆ What causes hearing loss?

Reading Tip As you read, draw a flowchart to show how you hear sound.

The house is quiet. You are sound asleep. All of a sudden, your alarm clock goes off. Startled, you jump up out of bed. Your ears detected the sound waves produced by the alarm clock. But how exactly did your brain receive the information?

How You Hear Sound

Once the sound waves enter your ear, how does your brain receive the information? Your ear has three main sections: the outer ear, the middle ear, and the inner ear. Each has a different function. **The outer ear funnels sound waves, the middle ear transmits the waves inward, and the inner ear converts the sound waves into a form that your brain can understand.**

Outer Ear As the alarm clock rings, the sound waves reach your ears. The curved surface of the outermost part of your ear looks and acts like a funnel. It collects sound waves and directs them into a narrower region known as the **ear canal.** Your ear

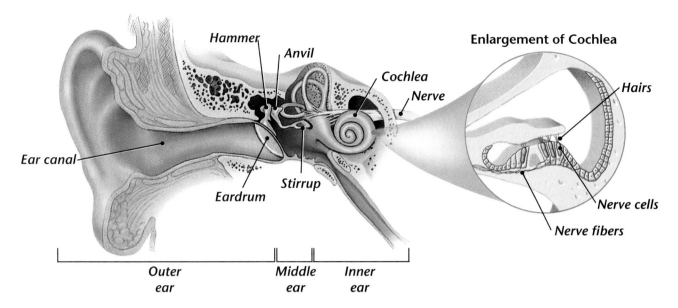

Figure 19 The illustrations show the structure of the human ear and the inside of the cochlea. *Interpreting Diagrams How is sound transmitted through the middle ear?*

canal is a few centimeters long and ends at the eardrum. The **eardrum** is a small, tightly stretched, drumlike membrane. The sound waves make your eardrum vibrate, just as a drum vibrates when you beat it with a drumstick.

Middle Ear Behind the eardrum is an area called the middle ear. The **middle ear** contains the three smallest bones in the human body—the hammer, the anvil, and the stirrup. If you look at them in Figure 19, you'll see how they got their names. The hammer is attached to the eardrum, so when the eardrum vibrates, the hammer does too. The hammer then hits the anvil, which then shakes the stirrup.

Inner Ear The inner ear is separated from the middle ear by another membrane. Behind this membrane is a cavity filled with liquid. This cavity, the **cochlea** (KAHK lee uh), is shaped like a snail shell. Inside, it is lined with more than 10,000 tiny hairs. When the stirrup vibrates against the membrane, the vibrations pass into the liquid in the cochlea. As the liquid moves, the hairs sway back and forth. The hairs are attached to nerve cells that detect this movement. Nerve fibers send messages to the brain. The brain processes these messages and tells you that you've heard sound.

✓ *Checkpoint* **What are the three main areas of the ear?**

Listen to Sounds

How does sound travel to your ears?

1. Tie two strings to the handle of a metal spoon. Each string should be about 40 cm long.
2. Hold one end of each string in each hand. Bump the bowl of the spoon against a desk or other hard solid object. Listen to the sound.
3. Now wrap the ends of the string around your fingers.
4. Put your index fingers up against your ears and bump the spoon against the object again.

Inferring How does the first sound compare with the sound you heard with your fingers up against your ears? What can you conclude about how sound travels to your ears?

Figure 20 Hearing aids can make sounds louder as the sounds enter the ear.

Hearing Loss

The human ear can normally detect sounds as soft as breathing (about 2–10 dB). The normal range of frequencies a person can hear is 20–20,000 Hz. However, when hearing loss occurs, a person may have difficulty hearing very soft sounds or high pitches. **Many people suffer hearing loss as a result of injury, infection, or aging.**

Hearing Loss Due to Injury or Infection A head injury can cause the tiny hammer, anvil, and stirrup to disconnect from each other. When this happens, sound cannot be transmitted through the middle ear. Surgery can usually correct this type of hearing loss.

If your eardrum becomes damaged or punctured, you may experience hearing loss. (Imagine trying to play a torn drum!) For this reason, it is dangerous to put objects into your ear, even to clean it. Viral or bacterial infections can also damage the delicate inner ear, causing permanent hearing loss.

Hearing Loss Due to Aging The most common type of hearing loss occurs gradually as people age. As a person gets older, the tiny hair cells in the cochlea become less effective at detecting the signals. Many older people cannot hear higher-frequency sounds.

Extended exposure to loud sounds can kill the nerve cells attached to the hairs. If the hairs are damaged by loud sounds, they can no longer transmit signals to the brain. You can prevent this type of hearing loss by wearing ear plugs or other hearing protection when you know you are going to be exposed to loud noises.

Some types of hearing loss can be helped using hearing aids. Hearing aids are amplifiers. Some are so tiny that they can fit invisibly in the ear. Others are made specifically for a person and amplify mainly the frequencies that person has lost the ability to hear.

Section 4 Review

1. How do your ears detect sound waves?
2. How can sound damage your hearing?
3. Describe how the eardrum works.
4. What happens once sound waves enter the ear?
5. **Thinking Critically Classifying** Make a chart that lists some common sounds you might hear in a day. Estimate the loudness of each sound and state whether each one could produce hearing loss. (*Hint:* Refer to Figure 8 on page 505.)

Science at Home

Sound Survey Invite family members to make a survey of the kinds of sounds they hear throughout one day. Have each member rate the sounds as quiet, normal, loud, or painful. Then rate each sound as pleasant, neutral, or annoying. State the source of each sound, the location, the time of day, and the approximate length of time that they are exposed to the sound. How are the ratings alike and different?

SCIENCE AND SOCIETY

Keeping It Quiet...

A construction worker operates a jackhammer; a woman waits in a noisy subway station; a factory worker uses loud machinery. All three are victims of noise pollution. In the United States, 80 million people say they are "continually" bothered by noise, and 40 million face danger to their health.

One burst of sound from a passing truck can be enough to raise blood pressure. People start to feel pain at about 120 decibels. Exposure to even 85 decibels (the noise level of a kitchen blender or a loudly crying baby) can eventually damage the hairs of the cochlea. Noise that "doesn't hurt" can still damage your hearing. As many as 16 million Americans may have permanent hearing loss caused by noise. What can we do to keep it quiet?

The Issues

What Can Individual People Do? Some work conditions are noisier than others. Construction workers, factory employees, and people who drive large vehicles are often at risk. All workers in noisy environments can benefit from ear protectors, such as plugs or headphone-like mufflers. Ear protectors can reduce noise levels by 35 decibels.

A listener at a rock concert, a hunter firing a rifle, or someone using an electric drill can also prevent damage with ear protectors. In addition, people should, if possible, avoid extreme noise. They can buy quieter machines and respect neighbors by not using noisy machines, such as lawn mowers and snow blowers, at quiet times of day or night. Simply turning down the volume on headphones, radios, CD players, and tape players can prevent one of the most frequent causes of permanent hearing loss in young people.

What Can Communities Do?

Transportation—planes, trains, trucks, and cars—is the largest source of noise pollution. Fifteen million Americans live near airports or under airport flight paths. Careful planning to locate highways and airports away from homes and buildings can reduce noise. Cities and towns can also prohibit flights late at night.

Many communities have laws against noise of more than a fixed decibel level, but these laws are not always enforced. In some cities "noise police" can fine the owners of noisy equipment.

What Can Government Do? A national Office of Noise Abatement and Control was set up in the 1970s. It required labels on power tools and lawnmowers telling how much noise they make. In 1982, this office was closed down. Some lawmakers want to bring the office back and have nationwide limits to many types of noise. However, critics say that national laws have little effect in controlling noise. The federal government could also encourage—and pay for—research into making quieter vehicles and machines.

You Decide

1. **Identify the Problem**
   In your own words, describe the problem of noise pollution.

2. **Analyze the Options**
   List as many methods as you can for dealing with noise. How would each method work to reduce noise or to protect people from noise? Who would be affected by each method?

3. **Find a Solution**
   Propose one method for reducing noise in your community. Make a poster that encourages people to carry out your proposal.

How Can You Use Time to Measure Distance?

1. Measure a distance 3 meters from a wall and mark the spot with a piece of masking tape.

2. Roll a soft ball in a straight line from that spot toward the wall. What happens to the ball?

3. Roll the ball again. Try to roll the ball at the same speed each time. Have a classmate use a stopwatch to record the time it takes for the ball to leave your hand, reflect off the wall, and then return to you.

4. Now move 6 meters away from the wall. Mark the spot with tape. Repeat Steps 2 and 3.

5. Compare the time for both distances.

Think It Over

Inferring What does the difference in time tell you about the distance the ball has traveled?

GUIDE FOR READING

◆ How is sonar used to tell distances?

◆ How do animals use sound?

◆ How is ultrasound used in medicine?

Reading Tip As you read, write a sentence or two that describes each application of sound waves.

You and your friend are in a long, dark cave. Every sound you make seems to come right back to you. For fun, both of you shout and scream and then listen as the echoes bounce around the cave.

Reflection of Sound Waves

When a sound wave hits a surface through which it cannot pass, it bounces back, or reflects. A reflected sound wave is called an echo.

Sometimes an echo is much fainter than the original sound. This is usually because some of the energy of the wave is absorbed along the way. Some materials reflect sound very well, while others absorb most of the sound that strikes them. Most of the practical applications of sound are based on the fact that sound reflects off some surfaces.

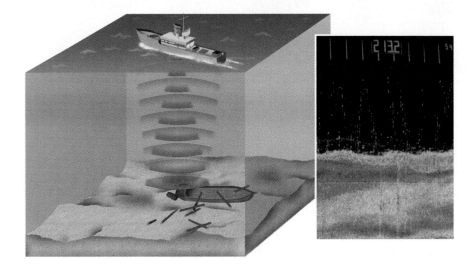

Figure 21 Sonar is used to determine distances and to locate objects under water. *Applying Concepts What two quantities must be known to calculate how far a sound wave has traveled?*

Sonar

Reflected sound waves have many uses. They can be used to determine the depth of water, to locate a sunken shipwreck or cargo, to find schools of fish, or to locate boats out on the ocean.

Sonar is a system of detecting reflected sound waves. The word *sonar* comes from the initial letters of **so**und **n**avigation **a**nd **r**anging. "Navigation" means finding your way around on the ocean (or in the air), and "ranging" means finding the distance between objects. Submarines and ships use sonar to detect other submarines and ships by sending sound waves through the water close to the surface. When the waves hit another boat near the surface of the water, they reflect back and are picked up by the sonar device.

How Sonar Works A sonar machine, or depth finder, produces a burst of high-frequency ultrasonic sound waves that travels through the water. When the waves hit an object or the ocean floor, they reflect. The reflected waves are detected by the sonar machine. **The sonar device measures the time it takes to detect the reflected sound waves.** It uses the data to calculate the distance that the sound has traveled. The intensity of the reflected waves tells the size and shape of the object that reflected the waves.

Calculating Distances The farther a sound wave travels before bouncing off a barrier, the longer it takes to come back. To calculate the depth of water, the sonar machine must calculate the distance traveled by the sound waves. It measures the time taken for the waves to come back. The sonar device then multiplies the speed of sound in water by the time taken. The total distance traveled by the sound is twice the depth of the water. Because the waves traveled to the bottom and then back, the sonar machine divides the total distance by two to find the actual depth.

☑ *Checkpoint* *What are three uses for sonar?*

Sharpen your **Skills**

Designing Experiments

1. Stand a square piece ACTIVITY of cardboard on a table. Prop it up with a book.

2. Put two empty paper towel or aluminum foil tubes on the table. The tubes should be at an angle to each other and almost touching at the end near the cardboard. Leave a gap of about 6 cm between the cardboard and the ends of the tubes.

3. Put your ear near the other end of one of the tubes. Cover one ear with your hand so that the only sounds you hear are coming through the tube.

4. Place a ticking watch in the second tube and cover the open end with your hand. What do you hear?

5. Design an experiment to determine how sound reflects off different materials, such as a variety of fabrics.

Figure 22 Elephants communicate using low-frequency, or infrasonic, sound waves.

Uses of Ultrasound and Infrasound

The dog trainer stands quietly, watching the dog a short distance away. To get the dog's attention, the trainer blows into a small whistle. You don't hear a thing. But the dog stops, cocks an ear, and then comes running toward the trainer. What did the dog hear that you didn't? Dogs can hear ultrasonic frequencies of over 20,000 Hz, well above the upper limit for humans.

Some animals communicate using sounds with frequencies that humans cannot hear. When elephants get upset, they stomp on the ground. The stomping produces low-frequency, or infrasonic, sound waves—too low for humans to hear. The waves travel through the ground for distances of up to 50 kilometers and can be detected by other elephants.

Ultrasound in the Ocean Dolphins and whales emit pings of sound at frequencies that are high, but not too high for you to hear. **Echolocation** (ek oh loh KAY shun) is the use of sound waves to determine distances or to locate objects. Dolphins and whales use echolocation to find their way in the ocean, and to find their prey.

INTEGRATING
LIFE SCIENCE

It was once thought that fish couldn't hear the high frequencies that dolphins and whales emit. But scientists have discovered that shad, herring, and some other fish can hear sounds as high as 180,000 Hz, nine times as high as the highest frequency you can hear. The fish may use this ability to avoid being eaten by dolphins and whales.

Because sound waves travel so well in water, ultrasound has many uses in the sea. Some fisherman attach ultrasonic beepers to their nets. The ultrasound annoys the dolphins, who then swim away from the nets and do not get caught. Other devices can protect divers from sharks by surrounding the divers with ultrasonic waves that keep sharks away.

Figure 23 Dolphins emit high-frequency sounds to communicate with each other, to navigate, and to find food.

Echolocation in Bats Imagine walking around in a totally dark room. You would bump into the walls and furniture quite often. Bats, however, can fly around dark areas and not bump into anything. **Bats use echolocation to navigate and to find food.**

As bats fly, they send out pulses of sound at frequencies of about 100,000 Hz. Then they listen to how long the sound takes to return. By picking up the reflections, or echoes, a bat can tell if it is about to bump into something. Though bats are not blind, they tend to rely more on their hearing than on their vision to "see" where they are going. Echolocation also tells the bat where its prey is. Bats can use echolocation to hunt. Most bats hunt insects, but some hunt small animals such as mice, rats, frogs, or birds.

Ultrasound in Medicine Ultrasound allows doctors to get a

INTEGRATING HEALTH picture, called a **sonogram,** of the inside of the human body. **Doctors use ultrasound to look inside the human body and to diagnose and treat medical conditions.**

To examine a pregnant woman, the doctor holds a small probe on the woman's abdomen. The probe generates very high-frequency sound waves (about 4 million Hz). The ultrasound device detects and measures the ultrasonic waves that bounce back. By analysing the intensity and frequency of the reflected waves, the device builds up a picture. The sonogram can show the position of the developing baby. Sonograms can also show if more than one baby is to be born. In addition to a still picture, an ultrasound can produce a video of a developing baby in motion.

Because of their high frequency, carefully focused ultrasound waves can also painlessly destroy unwanted tissues. In many cases ultrasound can eliminate the need for surgery.

Figure 24 Bats use echolocation to locate food and to avoid bumping into objects. Their large ears are used for collecting sound waves.

Figure 25 A doctor examines a pregnant woman with an ultrasound machine. A picture of the developing baby is displayed on a screen.

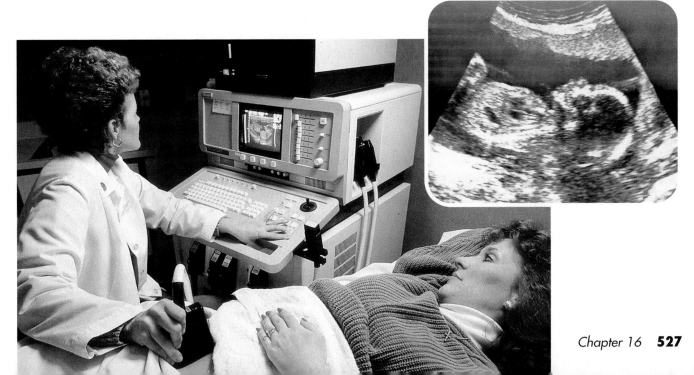

Figure 26 Some examples of common household objects that use ultrasound include an automatic focus camera, an ultrasonic toothbrush, and an ultrasonic jewelry cleaner.

Ultrasound at Home As technology progresses, more and more everyday objects use ultrasonic waves. Imagine cleaning your teeth with sound! If you have used one of the newer electric toothbrushes, you have done just that. The toothbrush sends out high-frequency sound waves that can reach into places that the bristles of the brush cannot.

Ultrasonic jewelry cleaners can clean delicate pieces of jewelry that might be damaged by brushes or harsh detergents. The tub is filled with water and a mild detergent. When the cleaner is switched on, the sound waves move through the water. When they reach the jewelry, the vibrations shake the dirt away, without causing scratches or other damage.

Some cameras use ultrasound to focus automatically. You look through the viewfinder at the object to be photographed. As you push the button to take a picture, the camera sends out ultrasonic waves that reflect off the object and travel back to the camera. The camera measures the time taken for the waves to come back, just like a sonar machine. The camera then calculates the distance to the object and adjusts the lens accordingly.

Section 5 Review

1. What is sonar?
2. How do animals use ultrasound and infrasound?
3. How is ultrasound used in medicine?
4. What household devices use sound waves? What is the function of sound in each device?
5. **Thinking Critically** **Calculating** The speed of sound in ocean water is about 1,530 m/s. If it takes 3 seconds for a sound wave to travel from the bottom of the ocean back to a ship, what is the depth of the water?

CHAPTER PROJECT

Check Your Progress
Test your musical instrument. Is it pleasing to the ear? Can you play a wide range of notes? Can you vary the loudness? Make further adjustments to your instrument. From what you have learned about pitch and frequency, what changes can you make to produce different notes? You may want to try tuning your instrument with a piano or pitch pipe. Try to play a musical scale or a simple song. Or make up your own song.

SECTION 1 — The Nature of Sound

Key Ideas
◆ Sound is a disturbance that travels through a medium as a longitudinal wave.
◆ The speed of sound depends on the elasticity, density, and temperature of the medium.

Key Terms
larynx   elasticity

SECTION 2 — Properties of Sound

Key Ideas
◆ A sound wave of greater intensity sounds louder. Loudness is measured in decibels.
◆ The pitch of a sound that you hear depends on the frequency of the sound wave.
◆ As a sound source moves toward the listener, the waves reach the listener with a higher frequency. The pitch appears to increase because of the Doppler effect.

Key Terms
intensity   infrasound
loudness   pitch
decibels (dB)   Doppler effect
ultrasound

SECTION 3 — Combining Sound Waves

Key Ideas
◆ The blending of the fundamental tone and the overtones makes up the characteristic sound quality, or timbre, of a particular sound.
◆ Music is a set of tones that combine in ways that are pleasing to the ear.
◆ Noise has no pleasing timbre or identifiable pitch.
◆ Interference occurs when two or more sound waves interact.

Key Terms
timbre   noise   acoustics
music   dissonance   beats

SECTION 4 — How You Hear Sound

INTEGRATING LIFE SCIENCE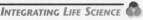

Key Ideas
◆ The outer ear funnels sound waves, the middle ear transmits the sound inward, and the inner ear converts the sound into a form your brain can understand.

Key Terms
ear canal   eardrum   middle ear   cochlea

SECTION 5 — Applications of Sound

Key Ideas
◆ A sonar device measures the time it takes to detect reflected sound waves.
◆ Animals use sound waves to communicate, to navigate, and to find food.

Key Terms
sonar   echolocation   sonogram

Organizing Information

Concept Map Copy the concept map about sound onto a separate sheet of paper. Then complete it and add a title. (For more on concept maps, see the Skills Handbook.)

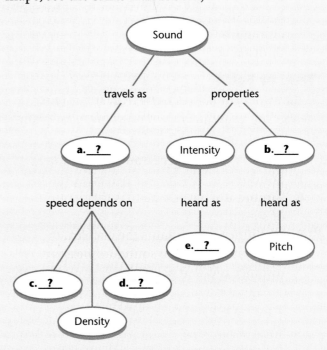

Reviewing Content

 For more review of key concepts, see the Interactive Student Tutorial CD-ROM.

Multiple Choice

Choose the letter of the best answer.

1. Sound does *not* travel through
   a. water.
   b. steel rails.
   c. wooden doors.
   d. outer space.
2. The Doppler effect causes an apparent change in
   a. loudness.
   b. intensity.
   c. pitch.
   d. resonance.
3. Beats result from
   a. reflection.
   b. refraction.
   c. diffraction.
   d. interference.
4. The hammer, anvil, and stirrup are in the
   a. outer ear.
   b. middle ear.
   c. inner ear.
   d. cochlea.
5. Sonar is used to find
   a. time.
   b. speed.
   c. angle of reflection.
   d. distance.

True or False

If the statement is true, write true. If it is false, change the underlined word or words to make the statement true.

6. Sound travels <u>faster</u> in air than in water.
7. Loudness is how the ear perceives <u>pitch</u>.
8. <u>Timbre</u> is what you hear as the quality of sound.
9. The <u>inner</u> ear contains the cochlea.
10. The system of using sound to measure distance is called <u>acoustics</u>.

Checking Concepts

11. When a drum vibrates, the air molecules that begin vibrating next to it do not reach your ear, yet you hear the sound of the drum. Explain.
12. What are the factors that affect the sound of a vibrating guitar string?
13. As a car drives past you, the driver keeps a hand on the horn. Describe what you hear as the car approaches you then passes by.
14. How can loud noises damage your hearing?
15. Why is ultrasound useful in medicine?
16. **Writing to Learn** You have been hired to produce an informational brochure about sound. This brochure will be presented to soon-to-arrive visitors from outer space. They have no concept of sound, and everything they learn will come from your brochure. Write a brief description of sound for the visitors.

Thinking Critically

17. **Comparing and Contrasting** How do sound waves behave like the waves in spring toys? How are they different?
18. **Controlling Variables** If you are measuring the speed of sound, what variable(s) should you try to keep constant?
19. **Calculating** At 0°C, sound travels through air at a speed of 330 m/s. At this speed, how long would it take sound to travel a distance of 1000 m? (*Hint:* Speed = Distance/Time)
20. **Applying Concepts** If one musician plays a note on an instrument and another plays a slightly higher note on a similar instrument, what will you hear?
21. **Inferring** Thunder and lightning happen at the same time. Why do you think you usually see the lightning before you hear the thunder?

Applying Skills

The table below shows the range of frequencies produced and heard by various animals and birds. Use the data to answer Questions 22–23.

Animal	Highest Frequency Heard (Hz)	Highest Frequency Produced (Hz)
Human	20,000	1,100
Dog	50,000	1,800
Cat	65,000	1,500
Bat	120,000	120,000
Porpoise	150,000	120,000
Frog	10,000	8,000
Robin	21,000	13,000

22. **Graphing** Draw a bar graph to compare the highest frequencies heard by each animal and the highest frequencies produced by each animal.

23. **Calculating** If the speed of sound in air is 330 m/s, calculate the wavelength of the highest-frequency sound heard by humans. Use the following formula:

$$\text{Wavelength} = \frac{\text{Speed}}{\text{Frequency}}$$

CHAPTER PROJECT

Performance Assessment

Present the Project Describe your instrument and explain how it was built. Discuss how you solved any design problems. Using your instrument, demonstrate how you can play different sounds. Show how you change the pitch or loudness of your instrument.

Reflect and Record In your journal write an evaluation of your project. How would you improve on the design of the instrument? How is your instrument like or different from the instruments your classmates built?

Test Preparation
Use these questions to prepare for standardized tests.

Study the chart. Then answer Questions 24–26.

Substance	Speed of Sound (m/s)
Rubber	60
Air at 0°C	330
Air at 25°C	346
Lead	1,210
Water at 25°C	1,498
Silver	2,680
Wood (Oak)	3,850
Glass	4,540
Aluminum	5,000
Iron	5,100
Steel	5,200

24. What information does this table provide?
    a. the speed of sound in different states of the same matter
    b. the speed of sound over different distances
    c. the speed of sound at several different temperatures
    d. the speed of sound in different substances

25. In which substance does sound travel most slowly?
    a. water   b. air
    c. steel   d. rubber

26. Sound travels faster through air at 25°C than it does at 0°C. This shows that sound travels
    a. faster at lower temperatures.
    b. more slowly at lower temperatures.
    c. more slowly at higher temperatures.
    d. only at temperatures above 0°C.

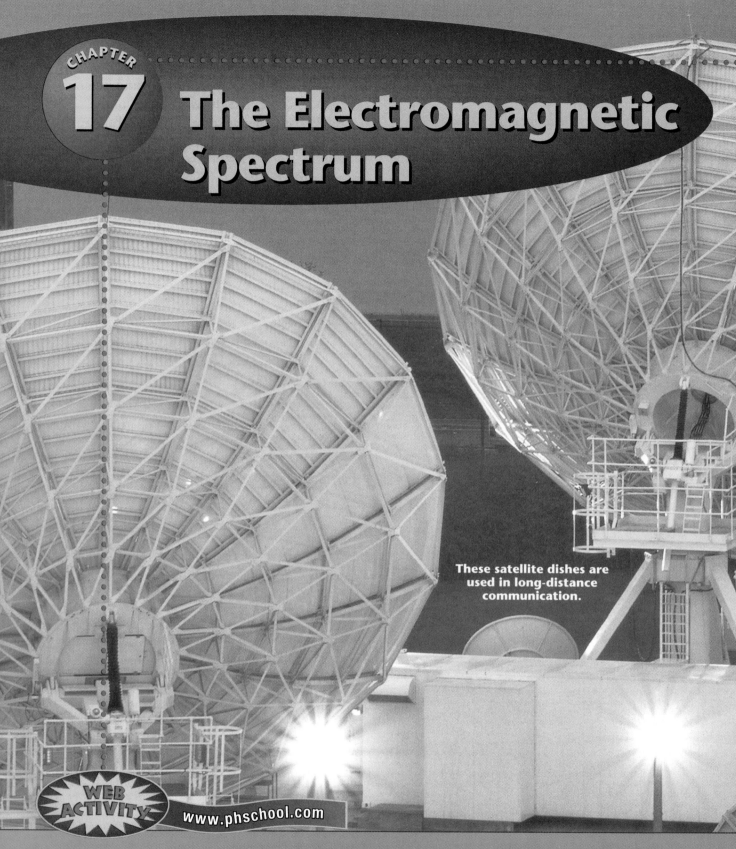

These satellite dishes are used in long-distance communication.

WEB ACTIVITY
www.phschool.com

SECTION
1 The Nature of Electro-magnetic Waves

Discover How Does a Beam of Light Travel?
Try This How Do Light Beams Behave?
Science at Home Sunglasses

SECTION
2 Waves of the Electro-magnetic Spectrum

Discover What Is White Light?
Try This What Does a Bee See?

SECTION
3 Producing Visible Light

Discover How Do Light Bulbs Differ?
Sharpen Your Skills Observing
Science at Home Buying Bulbs
Real-World Lab Comparing Light Bulbs

You're on the Air

Communication technology is developing at a rapid rate. Technology now makes it possible to store and process huge amounts of information. Communication technology will continue to improve as scientific advances are made. Look around you! How do people communicate? Radios, televisions, cellular phones, and electronic pagers are part of everyday life. Wireless communication has made it convenient for people to communicate anytime and anywhere.

In this chapter you will study and research the use of several wireless communication devices.

Your Goal To collect data about when, where, and why people use radios, televisions, cellular telephones, and other kinds of communication devices.

To complete this project you must
◆ design a survey sheet about the use of communication devices
◆ distribute your survey sheet to students in your school and to adults in your community
◆ compile and analyze your data
◆ create graphs to show your results

Get Started To get started, brainstorm what kinds of questions you will ask. Think about the format and content of your survey sheet. How might you involve students in other classes so you can gather more data?

Check Your Progress You will be working on this project as you study this chapter. To keep your project on track, look for Check Your Progress boxes at the following points.
Section 2 Review, page 547: Design and distribute your survey.
Section 4 Review, page 561: Compile, analyze, and graph your results.

Present Your Project At the end of the chapter (page 567), you will present the results of your survey to the class.

SECTION 4

Integrating Technology
Wireless Communication

Discover How Can Radio Waves Change?
Try This Produce Electromagnetic Interference
Real-World Lab Build a Crystal Radio

SECTION
① The Nature of Electromagnetic Waves

DISCOVER •• ACTIVITY •••

How Does a Beam of Light Travel?

1. Punch a small hole (about 0.5 cm in diameter) in each of four large index cards.

2. Stand each card upright so that the long side of the index card is on the tabletop. Use binder clips or modeling clay to hold the cards upright.

3. Space the cards about 10 cm apart. To make sure the holes in the cards are in a straight line, run a piece of string through the four holes and pull it tight.

4. Place the flashlight in front of the card nearest you. Shut off all the lights, so that the only light you see comes from the flashlight. What do you see on the wall?

5. Move one of the cards sideways about 3 cm and repeat Step 4. Now what do you see on the wall?

Think It Over

Inferring Explain what happened in Step 5. What does this activity tell you about the path of light?

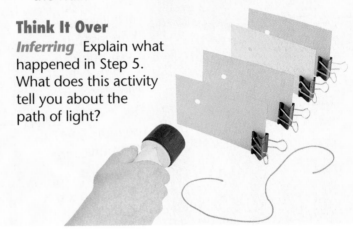

GUIDE FOR READING

◆ What is an electromagnetic wave?

◆ What is light?

Reading Tip As you read, keep a list of the words that are used to describe the nature of electromagnetic waves.

Close your eyes for a moment and imagine you are in a shower of rain. Are you getting wet? Do you feel anything? Believe it or not, you are being "showered." Not by rain but by waves, most of which you cannot feel or hear. As you read this, you are surrounded by radio waves, infrared waves, visible light, ultraviolet waves, and maybe even tiny amounts of X-rays and gamma rays. If you have ever tuned a radio, spoken on a cordless or cellular phone, felt warmth on your skin, turned on a light, or had an X-ray taken, you have experienced electromagnetic waves.

Figure 1 Even though you cannot feel them, you are being showered by electromagnetic waves.

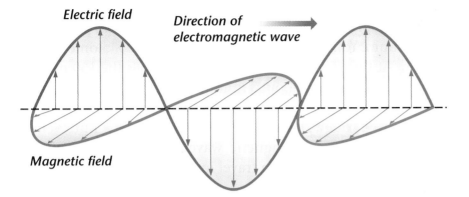

Electric field

Direction of
electromagnetic wave

Magnetic field

Figure 2 An electromagnetic wave occurs when electric and magnetic fields vibrate at right angles to each other.

Electromagnetic Waves

You have seen waves travel through water and move along ropes and springs. You have also heard sound waves travel through air, metal, and water. All these waves have two things in common— they transfer energy from one place to another, and they require a medium through which to travel.

But a group of waves called electromagnetic waves can transfer energy without a medium. **Electromagnetic waves** are transverse waves that have some electrical properties and some magnetic properties. **An electromagnetic wave consists of changing electric and magnetic fields.**

Electric and Magnetic Fields Electromagnetic waves travel as vibrations in electric and magnetic fields. An electric field is a region in which charged particles can be pushed or pulled. Wherever there is an electric charge, there is an electric field associated with it. A moving electric charge is part of an electric current.

An electric current is surrounded by a magnetic field. A magnetic field is a region in which magnetic forces are present. If you place a paper clip near a magnet, the paper clip moves toward the magnet because of the magnetic field surrounding the magnet.

When the electric field changes, so does the magnetic field. The changing magnetic field causes the electric field to change. When one field vibrates, so does the other. In this way, the two fields constantly cause each other to change. The result is an electromagnetic wave, as shown in Figure 2.

Electromagnetic Radiation The energy that is transferred by electromagnetic waves is called **electromagnetic radiation.** Because electromagnetic radiation does not need a medium, it can travel through the vacuum of outer space. If it could not, light from the sun and stars could not travel through space to Earth. NASA officials could not make contact with space shuttles in orbit.

SECTION 2 Waves of the Electromagnetic Spectrum

DISCOVER · ACTIVITY· · ·

What Is White Light?

1. Line the inside of a cardboard box with white paper. Hold a small triangular prism up to direct sunlight. **CAUTION:** *Do not look directly at the sun.*

2. Rotate the prism until the light coming out of the prism appears on the inside of the box. What colors do you see? What is the order of the colors? Describe how the colors progress from one to the next.

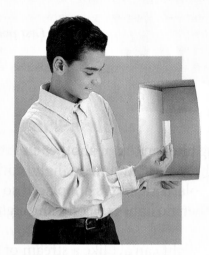

3. Using colored pencils, draw a picture of what you see inside the box.

Think It Over
Forming Operational Definitions The term *spectrum* describes a range. How do you think this term is related to what you just observed?

GUIDE FOR READING

◆ How do electromagnetic waves differ from each other?

◆ What are the waves of the electromagnetic spectrum?

Reading Tip Before you read, use the headings to make an outline about the different electromagnetic waves. As you read, make notes about each type of wave.

Can you imagine trying to keep food warm with a flashlight? How about trying to tune in a radio station on your television? Light and radio waves are both electromagnetic. But each has properties that make it useful for some purposes and useless for others. What makes radio waves different from light or ultraviolet rays?

Characteristics of Electromagnetic Waves

All electromagnetic waves travel at the same speed, but they have different wavelengths and different frequencies. Radiation in the wavelengths that your eyes can see is called visible light. Only a small portion of electromagnetic radiation is visible light. The rest of the wavelengths are invisible. Your radio detects wavelengths that are much longer and have a lower frequency than visible light.

Recall how speed, wavelength, and frequency are related:

$$Speed = Wavelength \times Frequency$$

Since the speed of all electromagnetic waves is the same, as the wavelength decreases, the frequency increases. Waves with the longest wavelengths have the lowest frequencies. Waves with the shortest wavelengths have the highest frequencies. The amount of energy carried by an electromagnetic wave increases with frequency. The higher the frequency of a wave, the higher its energy.

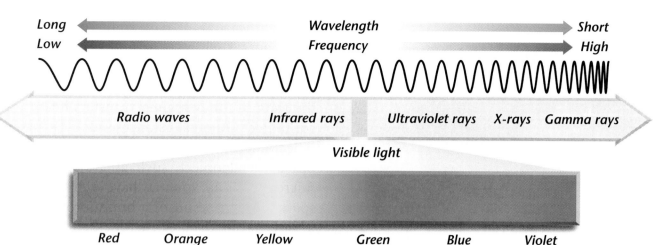

Figure 5 The electromagnetic spectrum shows the different electromagnetic waves in order of increasing frequency and decreasing wavelength.
Interpreting Diagrams Which electromagnetic waves have the highest frequencies?

The **electromagnetic spectrum** is the name for the range of electromagnetic waves when they are placed in order of increasing frequency. Figure 5 shows the electromagnetic spectrum. **The electromagnetic spectrum is made up of radio waves, infrared rays, visible light, ultraviolet rays, X-rays, and gamma rays.**

☑ *Checkpoint* *How are the frequency and wavelength of electromagnetic waves related?*

Radio Waves

Radio waves are the electromagnetic waves with the longest wavelengths and lowest frequencies. Like all electromagnetic waves, radio waves can travel through a vacuum. Most of the radio waves we receive, though, have traveled through air. Antennas pick up radio waves from the air and send them through wires to your radio. The radio converts the electromagnetic waves into the sound that comes out of the radio speakers.

Each radio station in an area broadcasts at a different frequency. To change the station on your radio, you adjust the tuning dial or press a button. This allows the tuner to pick up waves of a different frequency. The numbers on your radio tell you the frequency of the station you are listening to.

Microwaves The radio waves with the shortest wavelengths and the highest frequencies are **microwaves.** One of their most common uses is in microwave ovens. When you switch on a microwave oven, it gives off electromagnetic waves that bounce around inside the oven, penetrating the food. Water molecules in the food absorb the energy from the microwaves, causing the food to get hot.

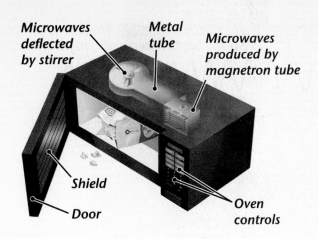

Microwaves deflected by stirrer

Metal tube

Microwaves produced by magnetron tube

Shield

Door

Oven controls

Figure 6 Microwaves produced in a microwave oven are absorbed by water molecules in foods. The energy raises the temperature of the food faster than an ordinary oven, so the food takes less time to cook. *Applying Concepts Why are metal containers not suitable for use in a microwave oven?*

Microwaves can pass right through some substances, such as glass and plastic. For this reason, microwaves do not heat glass and plastic containers. If the container gets hot, it is because the food in the container transfers heat to the container. Other substances, such as metals, reflect microwaves. If you have ever accidentally put a metal object, such as a spoon, into a microwave oven, you may have seen sparks. The sparks are the result of a buildup of electrical energy in the metal caused by the microwaves. Metal containers and utensils should never be used in microwave ovens.

Microwaves are not easily blocked by structures such as trees, buildings, and mountains. For this reason, microwaves are used to transmit cellular telephone calls. You will read more about cellular phones in Section 4.

Radar Short-wavelength microwaves are used in radar. **Radar,** which stands for **ra**dio **d**etection **a**nd **r**anging, can be used to locate objects. A radar device sends out short pulses of radio waves. These waves are reflected by objects that they strike. A receiver detects the reflected waves and measures the time it takes for them to come back. From the time and the known speed of the waves, the receiver calculates the distance to the object. Radar is used to monitor airplanes landing and taking off at airports, as Figure 7 shows. Radar is also used to locate ships at sea and to track weather systems.

In Chapter 16, you learned how the frequency of a sound wave seems to change when the source of the sound moves toward you or away from you. The Doppler effect occurs with electromagnetic waves too, and has some very useful applications. Police use radio waves and the Doppler effect to find the speeds of vehicles.

Figure 7 Radar is used to monitor airplanes taking off and landing at airports.

Figure 8 Radio waves and the Doppler effect are used to find the speeds of moving vehicles (left) and of moving balls at sporting events such as tennis matches (right).

A radar gun sends blips of radio waves toward a moving car. The waves are then reflected. Because the car is moving, the frequency at which the reflected blips arrive is different from the frequency at which the waves were sent out. The radar device uses the difference in frequency to calculate the speed of the car. If the car is going faster than the speed limit, the police often give a speeding ticket.

Radar is also used at some sports events to measure the speed of a moving ball. The radio waves bounce off a moving ball. The speed at which the ball is hit or thrown can then be displayed on a board like the one in Figure 8.

Figure 9 Magnetic resonance imaging (MRI) uses radio waves to create pictures of human tissue. It is used to examine the brain, spinal cord, and other organs.

Magnetic Resonance Imaging (MRI) Radio waves are also

INTEGRATING HEALTH used in medicine to produce pictures of tissues in the human body. This process is called **magnetic resonance imaging,** or MRI. In MRI, a person is placed in a machine that gives out short bursts of radio waves. The radio waves, combined with strong magnetic fields, cause atoms within the body to line up in the same direction. The atoms return to their original directions at different rates. By analyzing the responses, the MRI machine can create pictures of internal organs, including the brain. The pictures show clear images of muscles and other soft tissues that do not show up on X-rays. MRI is particularly useful in detecting brain and spine disorders.

☑ *Checkpoint* *What are three uses of radio waves?*

Infrared Rays

If you switch on an electric stove, you can feel infrared rays even before the element turns red. As the element gets warmer, it gives out energy that you feel as heat. This energy is infrared radiation, or infrared rays. **Infrared rays** have shorter wavelengths and higher

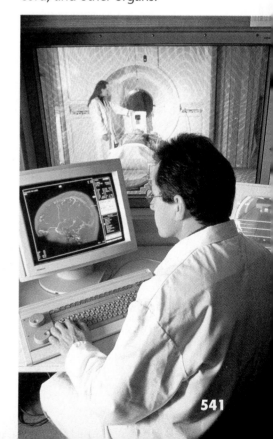

frequencies than radio waves. *Infra-* is a Latin prefix that means "below." So *infrared* means "below red." The next waves in the spectrum are red light.

Infrared rays range in wavelength from a little shorter than radio waves to just longer than visible light. Because you can feel the longest infrared rays as warmth, these rays are often called heat rays. Heat lamps have bulbs that give off more infrared rays and less visible light waves than regular bulbs. Some people have heat lamps in their bathrooms. You may also have seen heat lamps keeping food warm at cafeteria counters.

Most objects give off some infrared rays. Warmer objects give off infrared waves with more energy and higher frequencies than cooler objects. An infrared camera takes pictures using infrared

EXPLORING *the Electromagnetic Spectrum*

Electromagnetic waves are all around you—in your home, around your neighborhood and town, at the beach or pool, and in hospitals.

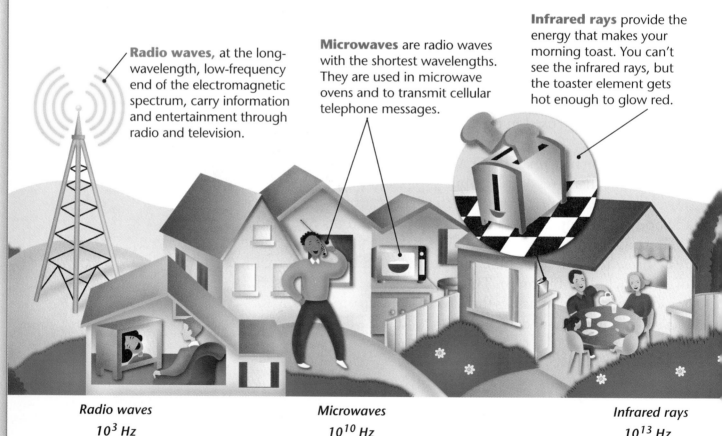

Radio waves, at the long-wavelength, low-frequency end of the electromagnetic spectrum, carry information and entertainment through radio and television.

Microwaves are radio waves with the shortest wavelengths. They are used in microwave ovens and to transmit cellular telephone messages.

Infrared rays provide the energy that makes your morning toast. You can't see the infrared rays, but the toaster element gets hot enough to glow red.

Radio waves	Microwaves	Infrared rays
10^3 Hz	10^{10} Hz	10^{13} Hz

rays instead of light. These pictures are called thermograms. A **thermogram** shows regions of different temperatures in different colors. Figure 10 shows a thermogram of a person. Thermograms identify the warm and cool parts of an object by analyzing infrared rays. Thermograms are especially useful for checking structures, such as houses, for energy leaks.

Even though your eyes cannot see the wavelengths of infrared rays, you can use an infrared camera or binoculars to detect people or animals in the dark. Satellites in space use infrared cameras to study the growth of plants and to observe the motions of clouds to help determine weather patterns.

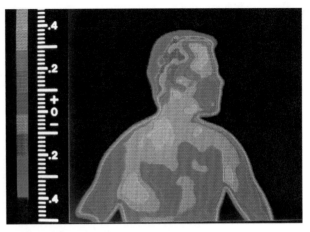

Figure 10 Infrared rays can be used to produce a thermogram. On a thermogram, regions of different temperatures appear in different colors.

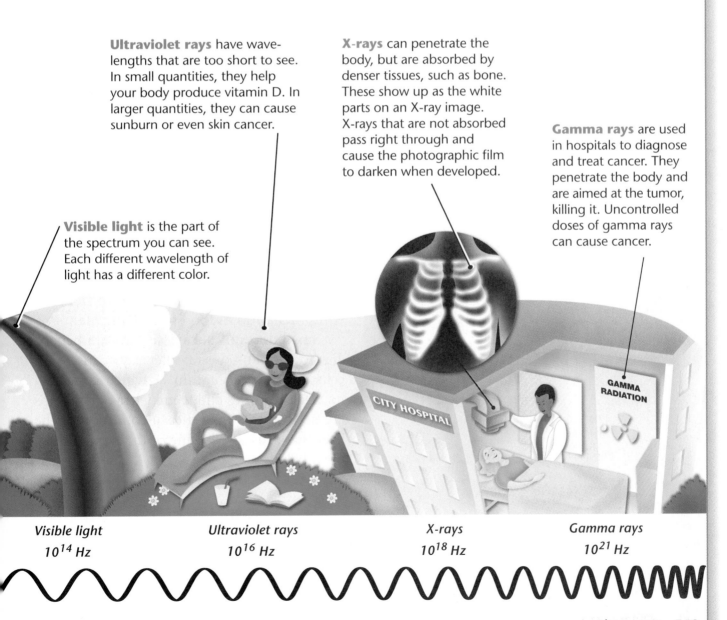

Ultraviolet rays have wavelengths that are too short to see. In small quantities, they help your body produce vitamin D. In larger quantities, they can cause sunburn or even skin cancer.

X-rays can penetrate the body, but are absorbed by denser tissues, such as bone. These show up as the white parts on an X-ray image. X-rays that are not absorbed pass right through and cause the photographic film to darken when developed.

Gamma rays are used in hospitals to diagnose and treat cancer. They penetrate the body and are aimed at the tumor, killing it. Uncontrolled doses of gamma rays can cause cancer.

Visible light is the part of the spectrum you can see. Each different wavelength of light has a different color.

GAMMA RADIATION

CITY HOSPITAL

| Visible light | Ultraviolet rays | X-rays | Gamma rays |
| 10^{14} Hz | 10^{16} Hz | 10^{18} Hz | 10^{21} Hz |

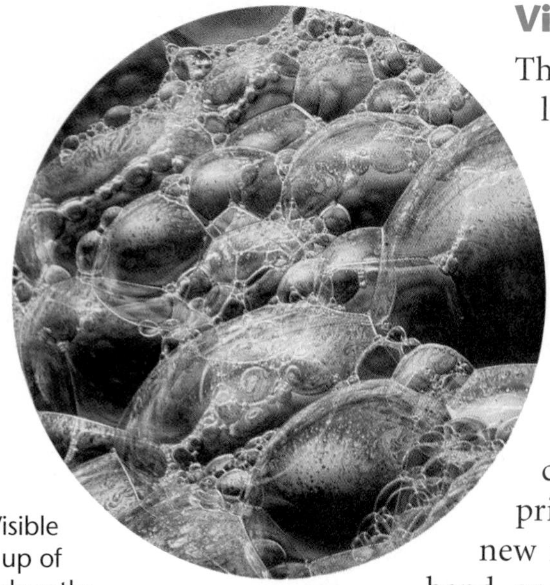

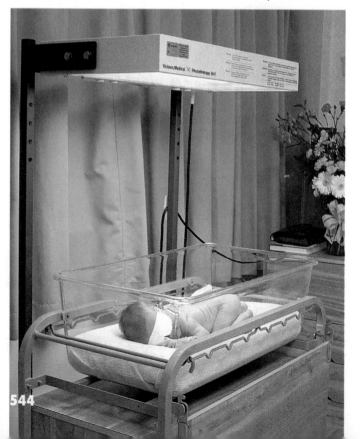

Figure 11 Visible light is made up of different wavelengths. Each wavelength has its own color. When light bounces off a bubble, interference produces some of the colors of the visible spectrum.

Visible Light

The electromagnetic waves that you can see are light. They make up only a small part of the electromagnetic spectrum. **Visible light** has shorter wavelengths and higher frequencies than infrared waves. The longest wavelengths of visible light are red. As the wavelengths decrease and the frequencies increase, you can see other colors of light. The shortest wavelengths are purple, or violet.

Have you ever seen a rainbow in the sky, colors on a bubble, or light passing through a prism? Recall what happens when waves enter a new medium, such as water or glass. The waves bend, or refract. Different wavelengths of light refract by different amounts, so the waves separate into the various colors. The colors in the visible spectrum are red, orange, yellow, green, blue, and violet, in order of increasing frequencies. Most visible light is made up of a mixture of these colors.

Checkpoint *What are the colors of the visible spectrum?*

Ultraviolet Rays

Electromagnetic waves with wavelengths just shorter than those of visible light are called **ultraviolet rays,** or UV. *Ultra-* is a Latin prefix that means "beyond." So *ultraviolet* means "beyond violet." UV waves have higher frequencies than visible light, so they carry more energy. Because the energy of ultraviolet rays is great enough to damage or kill living cells, ultraviolet lamps are often used to kill bacteria on hospital equipment and in food processing plants.

Small doses of ultraviolet rays are beneficial to humans. Ultraviolet rays cause skin cells to produce vitamin D, which is needed for healthy bones and teeth. Ultraviolet lamps are used to treat jaundice, a condition of the liver that causes yellowing of the skin, in newborn babies.

Figure 12 Ultraviolet light is used to treat jaundice in newborn babies. The baby's eyes are protected because too much ultraviolet light could damage them.

The ultraviolet rays present in sunlight can burn your skin. Too much exposure can cause skin cancer and damage your eyes. If you apply sunblock lotion and wear sunglasses, you can limit the damage to your body caused by UV rays.

INTEGRATING LIFE SCIENCE Although ultraviolet light is invisible to humans, many insects can see it. For example, bees have good color vision, but they do not see the same range of wavelengths that humans do. Bees see less of the lower frequency red waves and more of the higher frequency ultraviolet waves. Flowers that appear to be one color to a human appear very different to a honeybee. To the bee, the part of a flower that contains nectar looks different from the rest of the flower. The bee can head straight for the nectar!

X-Rays

X-rays are electromagnetic waves with very short wavelengths. Their frequencies are just a little higher than ultraviolet rays. Because of their high frequencies, X-rays carry more energy than ultraviolet rays and can penetrate most matter. Dense matter, such as bone or lead, absorbs X-rays and does not allow them to pass through. For this reason, X-rays are used to make images of bones inside the body. X-rays pass right through skin and soft tissues and cause the photographic film in the X-ray machine to darken when it is developed. The bones, which absorb X-rays, appear as the lighter areas on the film, as shown in Figure 13.

Too much exposure to X-rays can cause cancer. If you've ever had a dental X-ray, you'll remember how the dentist gave you a lead apron to wear during the procedure. The lead absorbs X-rays and prevents them from entering the body.

X-rays are sometimes used in industry and engineering. For example, to find out if a steel or concrete structure has tiny cracks, engineers can take an X-ray image of the structure. X-rays will pass through tiny cracks that are invisible to the human eye. Dark areas on the X-ray film show the cracks. This technology is often used to check the quality of joints in oil and gas pipelines.

What Does a Bee See?

Load a roll of UV-sensitive film into a camera. Take photos of a variety of flowers. Include white flowers and flowers that you see bees near. Have the film developed and look at the prints.

Observing What can bees see that you cannot? How is this useful to the bees?

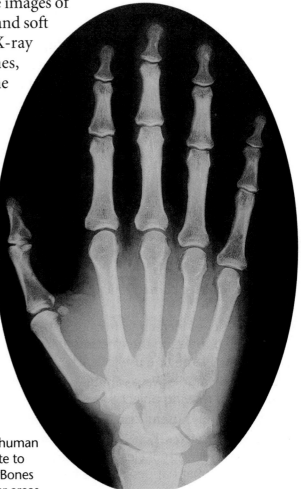

Figure 13 X-rays pass through softer human tissues and cause the photographic plate to darken behind them when developed. Bones absorb X-rays so they show up as lighter areas.

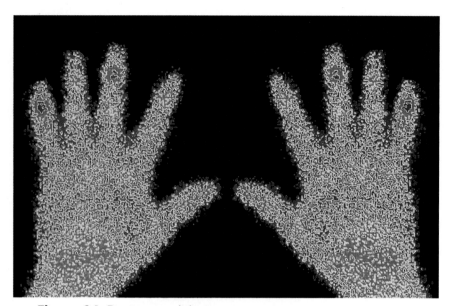

Figure 14 Doctors can inject radioactive liquids into the body and use gamma ray detectors to trace them. The detectors build images that doctors can use to examine the inside of the body.

Gamma Rays

Gamma rays have the shortest wavelengths and highest frequencies of the electromagnetic spectrum. Because they have the greatest amount of energy, they are the most penetrating of all the electromagnetic waves.

Some radioactive substances and certain nuclear reactions produce gamma rays. Because of their great penetrating ability, gamma rays can cause serious illness. However, when used in controlled conditions, gamma rays have some medical uses. For example, gamma rays can be used to kill cancer cells in radiation therapy. Gamma rays can also be used to examine the body's internal structures. A patient can be injected with a fluid that emits gamma rays. Then a gamma ray detector can form an image of the inside of the body.

INTEGRATING SPACE SCIENCE Some objects far out in space give off bursts of gamma rays. The gamma rays travel for billions of years before they reach Earth. Earth's atmosphere blocks these gamma rays, so gamma-ray telescopes that detect them must orbit above Earth's atmosphere. Astronomers think that collisions of dying stars in distant galaxies could produce these gamma rays. Some gamma-ray telescopes also detect the stronger gamma rays given off in the atmosphere as a result of nuclear weapons tests on Earth.

Section 2 Review

1. How are all electromagnetic waves alike? How are they different?
2. List in order of increasing frequency the kinds of waves that make up the electromagnetic spectrum. Name one use for each.
3. Explain how radio waves are used to find the speed of a moving object.
4. How are X-rays useful? How are they dangerous?
5. **Thinking Critically** Applying Concepts
   As the wavelength of electromagnetic waves decreases, what happens to the frequency? To the energy?

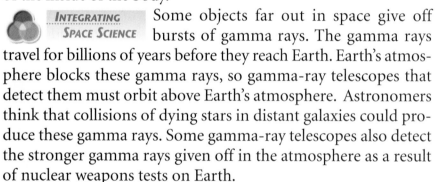

Check Your Progress
Write the questions for your survey. Some categories you might want to include are types of communication devices, how often they are used, when and where they are used, and the purposes for which they are used. Do people use these devices for personal reasons or for business? (*Hint:* To make your survey easy to complete, ask questions that require short answers.) Give the survey sheet to your classmates and other students in the school for their families and neighbors to complete.

Food Irradiation

Food sometimes travels a long way to reach your plate. Potatoes from Maine and strawberries from Florida or Mexico must stay fresh until you eat them. But every so often, food makes people ill. Millions of Americans get sick every year from contaminated or spoiled food.

One way to prevent such illness is food irradiation. In the most common method, gamma rays are sent through fresh or frozen food. The radiation slows decay and kills organisms that could make people sick. It makes food safer to eat and also helps the food stay fresh longer. Five minutes of irradiation will allow strawberries to stay fresh for an extra nine or ten days.

Some people worry about the possible dangers of eating irradiated food. More than 40 countries, including the United States, permit food irradiation. Others forbid it. Is food irradiation safe?

TREATED BY
IRRADIATION

The Issues

Does Irradiation Destroy Nutrients in Food? Radiation kills living cells. But it can also make chemical changes in the food itself. It may destroy useful nutrients, such as vitamins A, B-1, E, and K. Up to ten percent of these vitamins can be lost when food is irradiated. Of course, other methods of protecting and preserving food— such as refrigeration or canning fruits and vegetables—also lead to small losses in nutrition. Even cooking food makes it lose some vitamins.

Does Irradiation Change the Food Itself? Irradiating food doesn't make the food radioactive. But irradiation may change the molecular structure of some foods, creating chemicals such as benzene and formaldehyde. In small doses, these substances have little effect. But large amounts can be harmful to people. Supporters say that these same substances are found naturally in food. Some critics say irradiation should not be used until

there is further research. Researchers want to determine whether people who eat irradiated food for a long time are more likely to develop cancer or other diseases. Other experts say that the short-term research already done shows that irradiation is safe. Some alternatives to irradiation, such as spraying with pesticides, are clearly more harmful.

Will Irradiating Food Make People Less Careful About Handling Food? In the United States, all irradiated food must be labeled. But if people are not careful about washing their hands before preparing food, irradiated food can still become contaminated. Also, the amounts of radiation allowed won't kill all harmful organisms. It's still necessary to cook food properly before eating it, especially meat and eggs. Some food experts worry that irradiation will make people feel falsely safe and become careless about preparing food.

You Decide

1. Identify the Problem

In your own words, explain the problem of food irradiation.

2. Analyze the Options

List reasons for and against: (a) requiring all food to be irradiated; (b) permitting, but not requiring, food irradiation; and (c) banning food irradiation.

3. Find a Solution

You see two containers of a food at the supermarket. One is irradiated; one is not. The price is the same. Which would you buy? Explain why.

SECTION
3 Producing Visible Light

DISCOVER ● ACTIVITY ● ● ● ●

How Do Light Bulbs Differ?

1. Your teacher will give you one incandescent and one fluorescent light bulb.

2. Examine each bulb closely. What is the shape and size of each? Describe the differences between the bulbs. Draw each type of bulb and record your observations.

3. How do you think each bulb produces light?

Think It Over
Posing Questions Make a list of five questions you could ask to help you understand how each bulb works.

GUIDE FOR READING

◆ **What are the different types of light bulbs?**

◆ **What colors of light are produced by an incandescent bulb?**

Reading Tip As you read, compare and contrast the different ways in which light can be produced.

Figure 15 An incandescent light bulb glows when electricity passes through the tungsten filament. *Inferring Why do incandescent bulbs get so hot?*

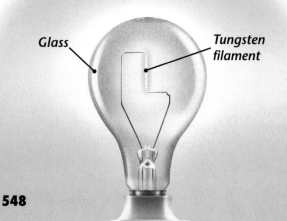

Glass

Tungsten filament

---

ook around the room. Most of the objects you see are visible because they reflect light. If no light source were present, you could not see the objects. An object that can be seen because it reflects light is an **illuminated** object. Light illuminates the page you are reading and your desk. An object that gives off its own light is a **luminous** object. A light bulb, a burning match, and the sun are examples of luminous objects.

There are many different types of lighting. **Common types of lighting include incandescent, fluorescent, neon, sodium vapor, and tungsten-halogen light bulbs.** Some light bulbs produce a continuous spectrum of wavelengths. Others produce only a few wavelengths of light. You can use an instrument called a **spectroscope** to view the different colors of light produced by each type of bulb.

Incandescent Lights

Have you heard the phrase "red hot"? When some objects get hot enough, they glow, giving off a faint red light. If they get even hotter, the glow turns into white light. The objects are said to be "white hot." **Incandescent lights** (in kun DES unt) glow when a filament inside them gets hot.

Look closely at a clear, unlit incandescent bulb. You'll notice that inside is a thin wire coil called a filament. It is made of a metal called tungsten. When an electric current passes through this filament, it heats up. When the filament gets hot enough, it gives off red light, which has low frequencies. As it gets hotter, the filament begins to give off light waves with higher frequencies. Once the filament gets hot enough to give off enough violet light, all the frequencies of light combine to produce white light. **Incandescent lights give off all the colors of visible light: red, orange, yellow, green, blue, and violet.**

The American inventor Thomas Edison is credited with developing a long-lasting incandescent light bulb in 1879. Edison knew that if he passed an electric current through a wire, it would get hot and glow. By experimenting with different types of filaments, Edison developed a light bulb that would glow for a long time.

Incandescent bulbs are not very efficient in giving off light. Less than ten percent of the energy is actually given out as light. Most of the energy produced by an incandescent bulb is given off as infrared rays. Incandescent bulbs can get quite hot when they have been left on for a while.

Fluorescent Lights

Have you ever noticed the long, narrow light bulbs in stores and offices? They are **fluorescent lights** (floo RES uhnt). Maybe you have some in your school. Each glass tube contains a gas and is coated on the inside with a powder.

When an electric current passes through a fluorescent bulb, it causes the gas to emit ultraviolet waves. When the ultraviolet waves hit the powder coating inside the tube, the coating emits visible light. This process is called fluorescing.

Unlike incandescent lights, fluorescent lights give off most of their energy as light. They usually last longer than incandescent bulbs and use less electricity, which makes them less expensive to run.

✓ *Checkpoint* *Why are fluorescent bulbs more economical than incandescent bulbs?*

Sharpen your Skills

Observing **ACTIVITY**

Use a spectroscope to observe light from different sources. **CAUTION:** *Do not look at the sun with the spectroscope.*

1. Look through the spectroscope at an incandescent light. Using colored pencils, draw and label the band of colors as they appear in the spectroscope.

2. Now, look at a fluorescent light through the spectroscope. Again, draw and label what you see.

How are the two bands of color the same? How are they different? Can you explain the differences?

Figure 16 Fluorescent lights are commonly used in offices, stores, and schools. They are efficient and inexpensive.

Figure 17 Neon lights are used in advertising signs and decoration. *Applying Concepts* Why are neon lights so colorful?

Neon Lights

Some gases can be made to produce light by passing an electric current through them. For example, a **neon light** consists of a sealed glass tube filled with neon. When an electric current passes through the neon, particles of the gas absorb energy. However, the gas particles cannot hold the energy for very long. The energy is released in the form of light. This process is called electric discharge through gases.

Pure neon gives out red light. Often, what is called a neon light has a different gas, or a mixture of gases, in the tube. Different gases produce different colors of light. For example, both argon gas and mercury vapor produce greenish blue light. Helium gives a pale pink light. Krypton gives a pale violet light. Sometimes the gases are put into colored glass tubes to produce other colors. Neon lights are commonly used for bright, flashy signs.

Sodium Vapor Lights

Sodium vapor lights contain a small amount of solid sodium as well as some neon and argon gas. When the neon and argon gas are heated, they begin to glow. This glow heats up the sodium, causing it to change from a solid into a gas. The particles of sodium vapor give off energy in the form of yellow light.

Sodium vapor lights are commonly used for street lighting. They require very little electricity to give off a great deal of light, so they are quite economical.

Figure 18 Sodium vapor light bulbs give off a yellow light. They are commonly used to illuminate streets and parking lots.

Tungsten-Halogen Lights

Tungsten-halogen lights work partly like incandescent bulbs. They have tungsten filaments and contain a gas. The gas is one of a group of gases called the halogens. When electricity passes through the filament, the filament gets hot and glows. The halogen makes the filament give off a bright white light.

Tungsten-halogen lights have become very popular because they provide bright light from small bulbs, but use relatively little electricity. They are used in overhead projectors and also in floor lamps. Because halogen bulbs become very hot, they must be kept away from flammable materials, such as paper and curtains.

Figure 19 Tungsten-halogen light bulbs contain a tungsten filament and a halogen gas. Even small bulbs can produce very bright light.

Bioluminescence

INTEGRATING LIFE SCIENCE Have you ever seen a firefly? On a warm summer evening, they flash their lights in patterns to attract mates. Fireflies are examples of organisms that produce their own light in a process called bioluminescence. **Bioluminescence** (by oh loo muh NES uns) occurs as a result of a chemical reaction among proteins and oxygen in an organism. The reaction produces energy that is given off in the form of light. Unlike a light bulb, which gives off most of its energy as infrared rays, the reaction that produces bioluminescence gives off almost all of its energy as light.

There are also bioluminescent organisms in the oceans. Some types of jellyfish give off light when they are disturbed. Deep in the ocean, where sunlight cannot reach, bioluminescence is the only source of light. Some deep-sea fish use bioluminescence to search for food or to attract mates.

Figure 20 This jellyfish produces its own light by bioluminescence.

Section 3 Review

1. What are five common types of lighting?
2. How does an incandescent light bulb work?
3. Compare luminous objects with illuminated objects. Give two examples of each.
4. Why are fluorescent lights commonly used in businesses and schools?
5. **Thinking Critically** **Making Judgments** Make a list of the different rooms in your home. Which type of light do you think is best for each room? Give reasons for each choice.

Science at Home

Buying Bulbs Invite family members to visit a hardware store that sells light bulbs. Ask the salesperson to describe the different kinds of bulbs available. Read the information about each bulb on the side panel of each package. Ask the salesperson to explain any terms you don't understand. Look for the cost and expected life of the bulbs, too. How does this information help you and your family purchase the most economical bulbs?

SECTION 4 Wireless Communication

DISCOVER • ACTIVITY

How Can Radio Waves Change?

1. Trace the wave diagram onto a piece of tracing paper. Then transfer the wave diagram onto a flat piece of latex from a balloon or latex glove.

2. Stretch the latex horizontally. How is the stretched wave different from the wave on the tracing paper?

3. Now stretch the latex vertically. How is this wave different from the wave on the tracing paper? How is it different from the wave in Step 2?

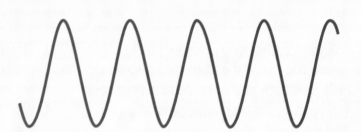

Think It Over

Making Models Which stretch changes the amplitude of the wave? Which stretch changes the frequency of the wave?

GUIDE FOR READING

◆ **How are radio waves used to transmit information?**

◆ **How do cellular phones and pagers use electromagnetic waves?**

◆ **How are satellites used to relay information?**

Reading Tip Before you read, preview the diagrams and captions in the section. List any terms you are not familiar with. As you read, write the definition of each term on your list.

Recent advances in technology have turned our world into a global village. Today it is possible to communicate with people on the other side of the world in just seconds. You can watch a television broadcast of a soccer game from Europe or a news report from the Middle East. Once scientists discovered that messages could be carried on electromagnetic waves, they realized that communication signals could travel at the speed of light.

Radio and Television

How does your favorite radio station or television program travel to you? Both radio and television programs are carried, or transmitted, by radio waves. Radio transmissions are produced when charged particles move back and forth in transmission antennas. These transmissions are broadcast, or sent out in all directions. Radio waves carry information from the antenna of a broadcasting station to the receiving antenna of your radio or television. Don't confuse the sound that comes from your radio with radio waves. Your radio converts the radio transmission into sound waves.

There are many different radio and television stations, all sending out signals. So how can each individual program or song come through clearly? As you move your radio tuner up and down the dial, you can hear different radio stations. Look at the radio dial in Figure 21. Each number on the dial represents a dif-

ferent frequency measured either in kilohertz (kHz) or megahertz (MHz).

Recall that a hertz is one cycle per second. If something vibrates 1,000 times a second, it has a frequency of 1,000 Hz, or 1 kilohertz (kHz). (The prefix *kilo-* means "one thousand.") If something vibrates 1,000,000 times a second, it has a frequency of 1,000,000 Hz, or 1 megahertz (MHz). (The prefix *mega-* means "one million" and is represented by a capital M.)

In the United States, the Federal Communications Commission, or FCC, assigns different frequencies of radio waves for different uses. Radio stations are allowed to use one part of the spectrum, and television stations use other parts. Taxi and police radios are also each assigned a set of frequencies. In this way, the entire spectrum of radio waves is divided into bands that are used for different purposes.

Each radio or television station is assigned a basic broadcast frequency, known as a carrier frequency. Each station is identified by the frequency at which it broadcasts. Radio stations broadcast in one of two main frequency bands—AM and FM.

AM Radio   AM stands for **amplitude modulation.** On AM broadcasts, the frequency of the wave remains constant. The information that will become sound, such as speech and music, is coded in changes, or modulations, in the amplitude of the wave. **At the broadcasting station, music and speech are converted from sound into electronic signals. The electronic signals for AM broadcasts are then converted into a pattern of changes in the amplitude of a radio wave.**

Figure 22 Sound signals are carried by varying either the amplitude (AM) or the frequency (FM) of radio waves.
Interpreting Diagrams What remains constant in the AM wave? In the FM wave?

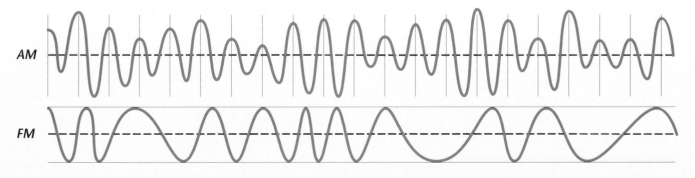

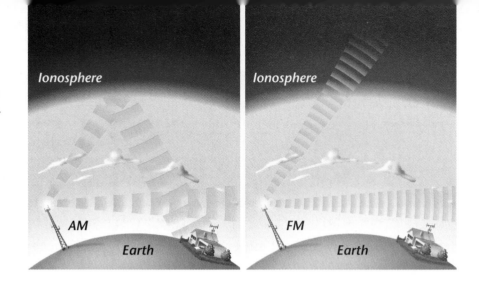

Figure 23 AM radio waves are reflected by the ionosphere. FM radio waves pass through the ionosphere. *Applying Concepts Which type of broadcast has a longer range on Earth?*

Your radio picks up the wave and converts the coded information back into an electronic signal. This signal travels to your radio's speaker and comes out as sound waves.

The AM frequencies used for radio broadcasts range from 535 kHz to 1,605 kHz. These radio waves vibrate at frequencies ranging from 535 to 1,605 thousand times per second.

AM waves have relatively long wavelengths and are easily reflected by Earth's ionosphere. The ionosphere is an electrically charged layer high in the atmosphere. Figure 23 shows how this reflection allows the AM waves to bounce back to Earth's surface. This is why AM radio stations can broadcast over long distances, especially at night when the absorption of radio waves by the ionosphere is reduced. However, the reception of AM waves is sometimes not very clear. For this reason, AM radio stations usually broadcast more talk shows than music.

FM Radio FM stands for **frequency modulation.** On FM broadcasts, the amplitude of the wave remains constant. **FM signals travel as changes, or modulations, in the frequency of the wave.**

If you look at an FM dial on a radio, you will see that the stations broadcast at frequencies from 88 MHz to 108 MHz. FM radio waves vibrate from 88 million to 108 million times each second. The frequencies of FM stations are much higher than the frequencies of AM radio stations, which vibrate only thousands of times per second.

Because FM waves have higher frequencies and more energy than AM waves, they penetrate the atmosphere instead of being reflected back to Earth. For this reason, FM waves do not travel as far as AM waves. If you've ever gone on a long car trip with the radio on, you have probably lost reception of radio stations and had to tune in new ones as you traveled. FM waves are usually received clearly and produce a better sound quality than AM waves. They are generally used to broadcast music.

dial the telephone number o[...] a telephone or another pager [...] then enter your telephone n[...] Some pagers even allow the u[...] **When you leave a messag[...] first sent to a receiving stati[...] electromagnetic waves to the [...]** or vibrates, letting the owner l[...] pagers are two-way pagers. Th[...] electromagnetic signals to the [...] to the person who sent the ori[...]

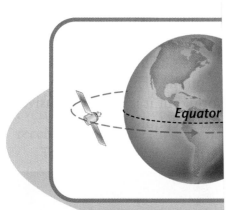

Equator

1940

195[...]

Sputni[...]

On October [...] the Soviet Uni[...] became the first country [...] successfully launch a[...] artificial satellite into orb[...] This development led to [...] new era in communication[...] Since then, more tha[...] 5,000 artificial satellites hav[...] been placed in orbi[...]

Television Television broadcasts are similar to radio broadcasts, except that the electromagnetic waves carry picture signals as well as sound. There are two main bands of television wave frequencies: Very High Frequency (VHF) and Ultra High Frequency (UHF). VHF television channels range from frequencies of 54 MHz to 216 MHz, and correspond to Channels 2 through 13 on your television set. This band of frequencies includes some FM radio frequencies, so television stations are restricted from using the frequencies that are reserved for radio stations. UHF channels range from frequencies of 470 MHz to 806 MHz, and correspond to Channels 14 through 69.

Weather can affect the reception of television signals. For better reception, cable companies now pick up the signals, improve them, and send them through cables into homes. Cable television reception is usually clearer than reception with an antenna. About half of American homes that have television now have cable reception.

✓ *Checkpoint* **What do the terms VHF and UHF mean?**

Cellular Telephones

Cellular phones have become very common. **Cellular telephones transmit and receive signals using high-frequency radio waves, or microwaves.** The cellular system works over regions divided up into many small cells. Each cell has its own transmitter and receiver. Cells that are next to each other are assigned different frequencies, but cells that are not next to each other can be assigned the same frequency. Cellular telephone signals are strong enough to reach only a few nearby cells. They cannot travel great distances. This allows many phones in different areas to use the same frequency at the same time, without interfering with each other.

As cellular phone users travel from one cell to another, the signals are transferred from one cell to another with very little interruption. If you travel outside one cellular phone company's area, another company becomes responsible for transmitting the signals.

Most cellular phones are more expensive to use than wired phones. But they are becoming more and more affordable. Cellular phones allow users to make and receive calls almost anywhere without having to use someone else's phone or look for a pay phone.

Figure 24 Cellular telephones transmit and receive radio waves that travel short distances.

SCIENCE & History

Wireless Commu...

Since the late 1800s, many d...
have turned our world into a...

1895

First Wir...
Transmiss...

Italian engi...
Guglielmo ...
used radio ...
coded wirel...
distance of ...

190...

1888

Electromagnetic Waves

German scientist
Heinrich Hertz proved
James Clerk Maxwell's
prediction that radio
waves exist. Hertz
demonstrated that the
waves could be
reflected, refracted,
diffracted, and
polarized just
like light
waves.

558

How It Works

Build a Crystal Radio

The first radio, called a crystal set, was invented in the early 1900s. At first, people built their own crystal sets to receive broadcast transmissions from local radio stations. In this lab, you will build your own crystal radio and learn how it works.

Problem

How can you build a device that can collect and convert radio signals?

Skill Focus

measuring, observing, problem solving, drawing conclusions

Materials (per group)

cardboard tube (paper towel roll)
3 pieces of enameled or insulated wire, 1 about 30 m long, and 2 about 30 cm long
wirestrippers or sandpaper
2 alligator clips
scissors
aluminum foil
2 pieces of cardboard (sizes can range from 12.5 cm × 20 cm to 30 cm × 48 cm)
masking tape
crystal diode
earphone
2 pieces of insulated copper antenna wire, 1 about 30 m long, and 1 about 0.5 m long

Procedure

Part 1 Wind the Radio Coil

(*Hint:* All ends of the insulated wires need to be stripped to bare metal. If the wire is enameled, you need to sandpaper the ends.)

1. Carefully punch two holes approximately 2.5 cm apart in each end of a cardboard tube. The holes should be just large enough to thread the insulated wire through.
2. Feed one end of the 30-m piece of insulated wire through one set of holes. Leave a 50-cm lead at that end. Attach alligator clip #1 to this lead. See Figure 1.
3. Wind the wire tightly around the cardboard tube. Make sure the coils are close together but do not overlap one another.
4. Wrap the wire until you come to the end of the tube. Feed the end of the wire through the other set of holes, leaving a 50-cm lead as before. Attach alligator clip #2 to this lead. See Figure 2.

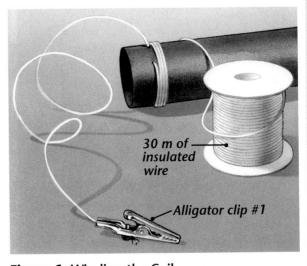

30 m of insulated wire

Alligator clip #1

Figure 1 Winding the Coil

562

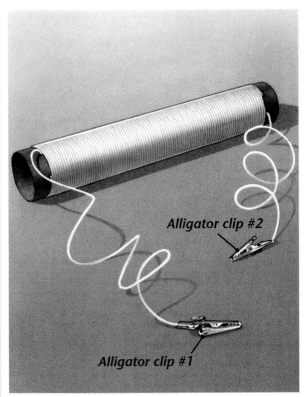

Figure 2 The Finished Coil

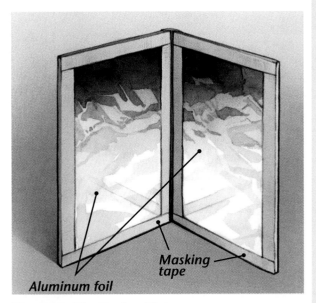

Figure 3 The Tuning Plates

Part 2 Make the Tuning Plates

5. Without wrinkling the aluminum foil, cover one side of each piece of cardboard with the foil. Trim off any excess foil and tape the foil in place.

6. Hold the pieces of cardboard together with the foil facing inward. Tape along one edge to make a hinge. It is important for the foil pieces to be close together but not touching. See Figure 3.

7. Make a small hole through the cardboard and foil near a corner of one side. Feed one of the short pieces of insulated wire through the hole and tape it onto the foil as shown. Tape the other short piece of insulated wire to the corner of the other side. See Figure 4.

8. Connect one end of the wire from the foil to alligator clip #1. Connect the other wire from the foil to alligator clip #2.

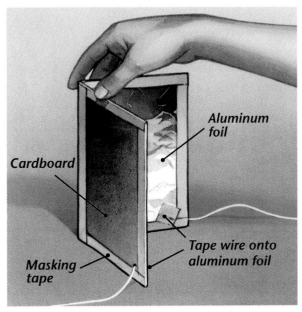

Figure 4 Connecting the Tuning Plates

Part 3 Prepare the Earphone

9. Handle the diode carefully. Connect one wire from the diode to alligator clip #1. The arrow on the diode should point to the earphone. Tape the other end of the diode wire to one of the earphone wires.

10. Connect the other wire from the earphone to alligator clip #2. See Figure 5.

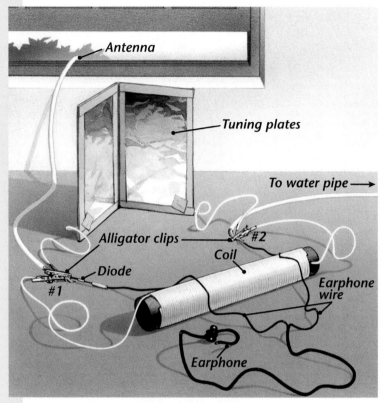

Antenna

Tuning plates

To water pipe →

Alligator clips

Coil

#2

Diode

#1

Earphone wire

Earphone

Figure 5 The Completed Radio

Part 4 Hook Up the Antenna

11. String the long piece of antenna wire along the floor to an outside window. Connect the other end of the wire to alligator clip #1.

12. Connect one end of the shorter piece of antenna wire to a cold-water pipe or faucet. Connect the other end to alligator clip #2. See Figure 5.

13. Put on the earphone and try to locate a station by squeezing the tuning plates slowly until you hear a signal. Some stations will come in when the plates are close together. Other stations will come in when the plates are opened far apart.

Analyze and Conclude

1. How many stations can you pick up? Where are the stations located geographically? Which station has the strongest signal? Keep a log of the different stations you receive.

2. How does adjusting the tuning plates affect the radio signals?

3. A crystal radio is not a powerful receiver. You can improve reception by having a good antenna. How can you improve your antenna?

4. **Apply** What are the similarities and differences between a modern radio and a crystal radio? How is one more efficient?

Design an Experiment

Use your crystal radio or any radio to test signal reception at various times of the day. Do you receive more stations at night or in the morning? Why do you think certain times of the day are better for receiving radio waves?

SECTION 1 The Nature of Electromagnetic Waves

Key Ideas
- An electromagnetic wave transfers energy by means of changing electric and magnetic fields.
- Sometimes light acts as though it is a set of waves. Sometimes light acts as though it is a stream of particles.

Key Terms
electromagnetic wave
electromagnetic radiation
polarized light
photoelectric effect
photon

SECTION 2 Waves of the Electromagnetic Spectrum

Key Ideas
- All electromagnetic waves travel at the same speed, but they have different wavelengths and different frequencies.
- The electromagnetic spectrum is made up of radio waves, infrared rays, visible light, ultraviolet rays, X-rays, and gamma rays.
- Radio waves and the Doppler effect can be used to tell the speeds of moving objects.

Key Terms
electromagnetic spectrum
radio wave
microwave
radar
magnetic resonance imaging
infrared ray
thermogram
visible light
ultraviolet ray
X-ray
gamma ray

SECTION 3 Producing Visible Light

Key Ideas
- Light bulbs can be incandescent, fluorescent, neon, sodium vapor, or tungsten-halogen.

Key Terms
illuminated
luminous
spectroscope
incandescent light
fluorescent light
neon light
sodium vapor light
tungsten-halogen light
bioluminescence

SECTION 4 Wireless Communication

INTEGRATING TECHNOLOGY

Key Ideas
- At broadcasting stations, music and speech are converted from sound into an electrical signal and then into a pattern of changes in a radio wave.
- AM broadcasts transmit information by modifying the amplitude of the signal. FM broadcasts change the frequency of the signal.
- Cellular telephones transmit and receive signals using high-frequency radio waves.
- When you leave a message for a pager, the information is first sent to a receiving station. There it is coded and directed to the correct pager.
- Radio, television, and telephone signals are sent from Earth up to communications satellites, which then relay the signals to receivers around the world.

Key Terms
amplitude modulation (AM)
frequency modulation (FM)

Organizing Information

Concept Map Copy the concept map about electromagnetic waves onto a sheet of paper. Then complete it and add a title. (For more on concept maps, see the Skills Handbook.)

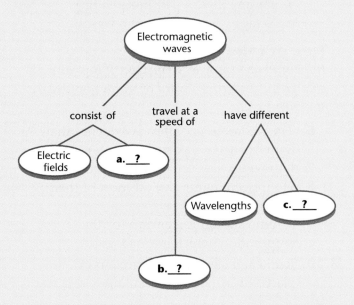

Reviewing Content

 For more review of key concepts, see the Interactive Student Tutorial CD-ROM.

Multiple Choice

Choose the letter of the best answer.

1. All electromagnetic waves have the same
   a. frequency.
   b. speed.
   c. wavelength.
   d. energy.
2. The electromagnetic waves with the longest wavelengths are
   a. radio waves.
   b. infrared rays.
   c. X-rays.
   d. gamma rays.
3. Which of the following does *not* belong in the electromagnetic spectrum?
   a. X-ray
   b. sound
   c. infrared ray
   d. radio wave
4. Light bulbs that glow when a filament inside them gets hot are called
   a. bioluminescent lights.
   b. fluorescent lights.
   c. incandescent lights.
   d. neon lights.
5. Television signals are transmitted by
   a. gamma rays.   b. infrared rays.
   c. X-rays.   d. radio waves.

True or False

If the statement is true, write true. If it is false, change the underlined word or words to make the statement true.

6. The photoelectric effect is evidence that light can act as a <u>particle</u>.
7. <u>Ultraviolet</u> rays can be felt as heat.
8. Fluorescent lights give off most of their energy as <u>infrared rays</u>.
9. A radio station is identified by the <u>amplitude</u> at which it broadcasts.
10. Radio and television transmitters can be placed on <u>satellites</u> and sent into orbit.

Checking Concepts

11. How do you know that electromagnetic waves can travel through a vacuum?
12. How does polarization show that light can act as a wave?
13. How is the Doppler effect used to find the speeds of moving objects?
14. Explain the difference between cellular telephones and cordless telephones.
15. A person lost in the woods at night may signal for help by turning a flashlight on and off according to a code known as Morse code. This is actually a modulated signal. Is it AM or FM? Explain your answer.
16. **Writing to Learn** Develop an advertising campaign to sell fluorescent lights. Your ad should describe two advantages of fluorescent lights over incandescent lights. Be sure to include a catchy slogan.

Thinking Critically

17. **Applying Concepts** What important information can be gathered from a thermogram of a house? How could this information be used to help save energy?
18. **Relating Cause and Effect** The waves of the electromagnetic spectrum that have the greatest frequency are also the most penetrating and can cause the most harm. Explain.
19. **Classifying** List five examples of luminous objects and five examples of illuminated objects.
20. **Problem Solving** Suppose you are building an incubator for young chicks and need a source of heat. What type of light bulbs would you use? Explain.
21. **Comparing and Contrasting** Make a table to compare the different types of wireless communication. Include headings such as: type of information transmitted; distance over which signal can be transmitted; one-way or two-way communication.

Applying Skills

The table below gives information about four radio stations. Use the table to answer Questions 22–24.

Call letters	Frequency
KLIZ	580 kHz
KMOM	103.7 MHz
WDAD	1030 kHz
WJFO	89.7 MHz

22. Interpreting Data Which radio station broadcasts at the longest wavelength? The shortest wavelength?

23. Classifying Which radio stations are AM? Which are FM?

24. Predicting You are going on a car trip across the United States. Which station would you expect to receive for the greater distance: KLIZ or KMOM?

Performance CHAPTER PROJECT **Assessment**

Present Your Project Now you are ready to present your findings to your classmates. You could mount your graphs on posterboard. Alternatively, you could put your graphs on transparencies and use an overhead projector to show the results of your survey. You could also use a computer to create a slide show.

Reflect and Record What in your results was most surprising? How could you have done a better job of collecting your data? Has this project given you a better understanding of the usage of the various devices? Think about the world 25 years from now. Predict the types of devices that will be used in the future.

Test Preparation

Use these questions to prepare for standardized tests.

Use the diagram to answer Questions 25–28.

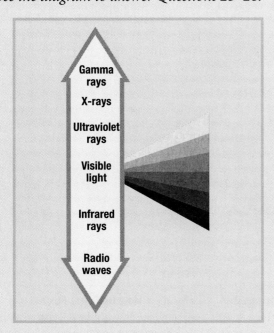

25. What would be the best title for this diagram?
   a. Colors of the Spectrum
   b. The Electromagnetic Spectrum
   c. Visible Light
   d. The Speed of Electromagnetic Waves

26. Which waves have the lowest frequency?
   a. radio waves   b. infrared rays
   c. visible light   d. gamma rays

27. Which waves have the shortest wavelength?
   a. radio waves   b. infrared rays
   c. visible light   d. gamma rays

28. What color would be at the "top" of the visible light spectrum?
   a. violet   b. green
   c. yellow   d. red

CHAPTER
18 Light

This kaleidoscope image is formed by two mirrors at right angles. Colored objects between the mirrors are reflected to form a repeated pattern.

WEB ACTIVITY www.phschool.com

SECTION 1 Reflection and Mirrors

Discover **How Does Your Reflection Wink?**
Sharpen Your Skills **Classifying**

SECTION 2 Refraction and Lenses

Discover **How Can You Make an Image Appear on a Sheet of Paper?**
Try This **Disappearing Glass**
Science at Home **Pencil Bending**
Skills Lab **Looking at Images**

SECTION 3 Color

Discover **How Do Colors Mix?**
Sharpen Your Skills **Developing Hypotheses**
Real-World Lab **Changing Colors**

What a Sight!

Look inside a kaleidoscope. Small beads or pieces of colored glass are reflected by mirrors, forming colorful, ever-changing patterns. Kaleidoscopes are optical instruments, devices that use arrangements of mirrors or lenses to produce images. In this chapter, you will study how mirrors and lenses reflect and refract light. You will learn what causes the different colors of the objects all around you. You will use these ideas to create your own optical instrument.

Your Goal To construct an optical instrument that serves a specific purpose. It can be a kaleidoscope, a telescope, a periscope, a microscope, or something of your own creation.

To complete this project successfully you must
- design and build an optical instrument that includes at least one mirror or one lens
- demonstrate how your instrument works
- prepare a manual that explains the purpose of each part of your instrument

Get Started Begin to think about what you would like your optical instrument to do. Which would you like to see better—tiny objects or distant objects? Would you like to see around corners? Maybe you would prefer your instrument to produce striking images!

Check Your Progress You'll be working on this project as you study this chapter. To keep your project on track, look for Check Your Progress boxes at the following points.
Section 1 Review, page 574: Draw your optical instrument.
Section 3 Review, page 585: Build your optical instrument.
Section 5 Review, page 600: Test and modify your instrument. Prepare a manual explaining how your instrument works.

Present Your Project At the end of the chapter (page 603), you will demonstrate how your instrument works. You will also present your manual, showing the design and use of the instrument.

Integrating Life Science

SECTION 4 Seeing Light

Discover Can You See Everything With One Eye?
Try This True Colors
Science at Home Optical Illusion

SECTION 5 Using Light

Discover How Does a Pinhole Viewer Work?
Try This What a View!

SECTION 1 Reflection and Mirrors

DISCOVER · ACTIVITY

How Does Your Reflection Wink?

1. Look at your face in a mirror. Wink your right eye. Which eye does your reflection wink?

2. Tape two mirrors together so that they open and close like a book. Open them so they form a 90° angle with each other. **CAUTION:** *Be careful of any sharp edges.*

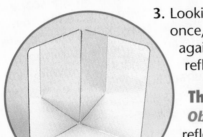

3. Looking into both mirrors at once, wink at your reflection again. Which eye does your reflection wink now?

Think It Over

Observing How does your reflection wink at you? How does the second reflection compare with the first reflection?

GUIDE FOR READING

◆ What happens when light strikes an object?

◆ What are the two kinds of reflection?

◆ What types of images are produced by plane, concave, and convex mirrors?

Reading Tip Before you read, preview the section and write down any new terms. As you read, find the meaning of each term.

◀ Glare on a window

Have you ever looked at a store window on a bright, sunny day? In order to see inside, you may have used your hands to block the glare. The glare is actually reflected light. The glare from the store window shows that glass can reflect light. But if you look at a clear glass window with no glare, you can see right through it.

When Light Strikes an Object

When light strikes an object, the light can be reflected, absorbed, or transmitted. Most objects reflect or absorb light. A material that reflects or absorbs all of the light that strikes it is **opaque** (oh PAYK). Most objects are opaque. You cannot see through opaque objects because light cannot pass through them. Examples of opaque materials include wood, metal, and cotton and wool fabrics.

A **transparent** material transmits light. When light strikes a transparent object, it passes right through, allowing you to see what is on the other side. Clear glass, water, and air are examples of transparent materials.

Other materials allow some light to pass through. This type of material is translucent. **Translucent** (trans LOO sunt) materials scatter light as it passes through. You can usually tell that there is something behind a translucent object, but you cannot see details clearly. Frosted glass and wax paper are translucent. Figure 1 shows opaque, transparent, and translucent objects.

Figure 1 The spools of thread are opaque. They reflect light of various colors. The pitcher and glass are transparent. They transmit light, allowing you to see the milk inside. The leaf is translucent. The frog's shadow can be seen through the leaf.

Kinds of Reflection

When you look at some objects, such as a shiny metal fixture or a mirror, you can see yourself. But when you look at other objects, such as a book, a wooden table, or your pencil, you see only the object itself. **You can see most objects because light reflects, or bounces, off them.** What you see when you look at an object depends on how its surface reflects light.

Regular Reflection To show how light travels and reflects, you can represent light waves as straight lines called **rays.** Light rays reflect from a surface according to the law of reflection: the angle of reflection equals the angle of incidence.

Regular reflection occurs when parallel rays of light hit a smooth surface. All the rays are reflected at the same angle. For example, if you look at a sheet of shiny metal, you can see your own reflection. The light rays coming from you strike the smooth surface and are reflected regularly.

Diffuse Reflection When parallel rays of light hit a bumpy, or uneven, surface, **diffuse reflection** occurs. Each ray obeys the law of reflection. But since each ray hits the surface at a different angle, the rays are reflected at different angles. Because the reflected rays travel in all directions, diffuse reflection allows you to see an object from any position.

Most objects reflect light diffusely. This is because most objects do not have smooth surfaces. Even surfaces that appear to be smooth, such as a freshly painted wall, have small bumps that scatter light. If you look at a wall through a magnifying glass, you will see that the surface is not really smooth.

Regular reflection

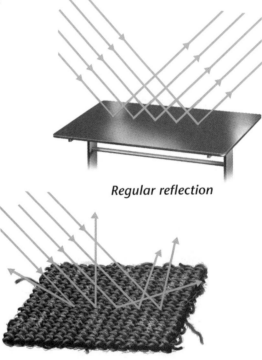

Diffuse reflection

Figure 2 When light strikes a surface at an angle, it is reflected at the same angle. If the surface is smooth, the reflection is regular (top). If the surface is uneven, the reflection is diffuse (bottom).

Mirrors

Did you look in a mirror this morning? Maybe you combed your hair or brushed your teeth in front of a mirror. A mirror is a sheet of glass that has a smooth, silver-colored coating on one side. When light passes through the glass, the coating on the back reflects the light regularly, allowing you to see an image. An **image** is a copy of an object formed by reflected or refracted rays of light.

Mirrors can be flat or curved. The shape of the surface determines how the image will look. Depending on the shape of the mirror, the image can be the same size as the object, or it can be larger or smaller.

Plane Mirrors Look into a flat mirror, or **plane mirror.** You will see an image that is the same size as you are. Your image will seem to be the same distance behind the mirror as you are in front of it. **A plane mirror produces an image that is right-side up and the same size as the object being reflected.**

The image you see when you look in a plane mirror is a virtual image. **Virtual images** are right-side up, or upright. "Virtual" describes something that you can see, but does not really exist. You can't reach behind a mirror and touch your image.

Why do you see a virtual image? Figure 3 shows how the image of the dancer is formed by a plane mirror. Light rays reflected from the dancer travel out in all directions. They strike the mirror and are reflected toward the eye. The human brain assumes that light travels in a straight line. Even though the rays are reflected, the brain treats them as if they had come from behind the mirror. It is easiest to consider just the rays from the top and the bottom of the dancer. The dashed lines show the points from which the light rays appear to come. Since the dashed lines appear to come from behind the mirror, this is where the dancer's image appears to be located.

✓ *Checkpoint* *What is a virtual image?*

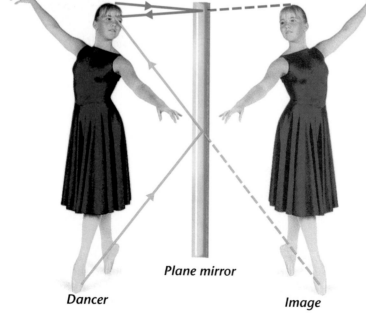

Dancer   *Plane mirror*   *Image*

Figure 3 A plane mirror forms a virtual image. When the dancer looks in the mirror, the rays of light from her body are reflected toward her. The rays appear to come from behind the mirror, where the image is formed.

Concave Mirrors A mirror with a surface that curves inward like the inside of a bowl is a **concave mirror.** Figure 4 shows how a concave mirror can reflect parallel rays of light so that they meet at a point. The point at which the rays meet is called the **focal point.**

Concave mirrors can form either virtual images or real images. The type of image formed by a concave mirror depends on the position of the object in relation to the focal point. Figure 5 shows how concave mirrors form images. If the object is farther away from the mirror than the focal point, the reflected rays form a real image. A **real image** is formed when rays actually meet at a point. Real images are upside down, or inverted. A real image may be larger or smaller than the object. If the object is between the focal point and the mirror, the image appears to be behind the mirror and is right-side up. Then it is a virtual image.

Some concave mirrors are used to project rays of light. For example, a car headlight has a bulb at the focal point of a concave mirror. When the light from the bulb spreads out and hits the mirror, the rays are reflected parallel to each other. This projects the light on the road ahead. Concave mirrors are also used to produce magnified images, as in makeup mirrors.

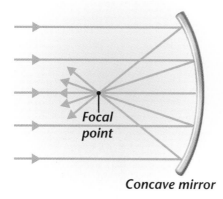

Figure 4 This concave mirror reflects parallel rays of light back through the focal point.

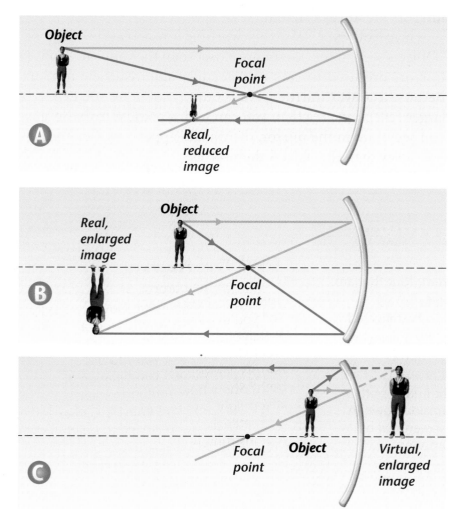

Figure 5 The type of image formed by a concave mirror depends on the position of the object in relation to the focal point. **A,B.** If the object is farther from the mirror than the focal point, the image is real and inverted. **C.** If the object is between the mirror and the focal point, the image is virtual and upright. *Interpreting Diagrams How can you tell that the images in A and B are real?*

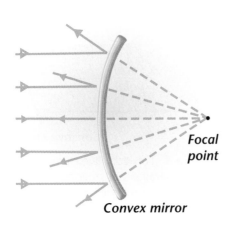

Focal point

Convex mirror

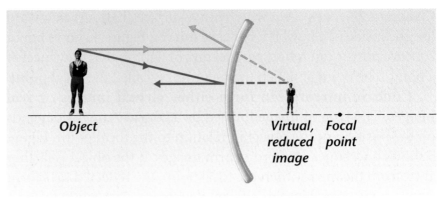

Object

Virtual, reduced image

Focal point

Figure 6 A convex mirror reflects parallel rays of light as though they came from the focal point behind the mirror. The image formed by a convex mirror is always virtual. *Applying Concepts What is a convex mirror?*

Convex Mirrors A mirror with a surface that curves outward is called a **convex mirror.** Figure 6 shows how some convex mirrors reflect parallel rays of light. The rays spread out but appear to come from a focal point behind the mirror. The focal point of a convex mirror is the point from which the rays appear to come. **Since the rays do not actually meet, images formed by convex mirrors are always virtual.**

Have you ever seen this warning on a rearview mirror? "Objects seen in the mirror are closer than they appear." Convex mirrors are used in cars as passenger-side rearview mirrors. Because a convex mirror spreads out rays of light, you can see a larger reflection area than you can with a plane mirror. Because you see more in the mirror, the images appear smaller and farther away than the objects themselves.

Section 1 Review

1. List four materials that are transparent, four that are translucent, and four that are opaque.
2. Describe two ways in which light can be reflected.
3. What types of images are produced by a plane mirror? A concave mirror? A convex mirror?
4. **Thinking Critically** **Applying Concepts** A slide projector projects an upright image onto a screen. The slides must be placed upside down in the projector. Is the image on the screen real or virtual? Give two reasons for your answer.

② Refraction and Lenses

DISCOVER •••ACTIVITY•••

How Can You Make an Image Appear on a Sheet of Paper?

1. Hold a hand lens about 2 meters from a window. Look through the lens. What do you see? **CAUTION:** *Do not look at the sun.*

2. Move the lens farther away from your eye. What changes do you notice?

3. Now hold the lens between the window and a sheet of paper, but closer to the paper. Slowly move the lens away from the paper and toward the window. Keep watching the paper. What do you see? What happens as you move the lens?

Think It Over

Observing How do you think an image is formed on a sheet of paper? Describe the image. Is it real or virtual? How do you know?

A fish tank can play tricks on your eyes. If you look through the side, the fish seems closer than if you look over the top. If you look through the corner, you may see the same fish twice. You see one image of the fish through the front of the tank and another image through the side of the tank. The two images appear in different places!

Refraction of Light

As you look into a fish tank, you are seeing the light bend as it passes through three different mediums. The mediums are the water, the glass of the tank, and the air. As the light passes from one medium to the next, it refracts. **When light rays enter a new medium at an angle, the change in speed causes them to bend, or change direction.**

Refraction can cause you to see something that may not actually be there. For example, refraction can form a mirage. It can also cause a beautiful sight, a rainbow.

GUIDE FOR READING

◆ What happens when light rays enter a medium at an angle?

◆ How do convex and concave lenses form images?

Reading Tip As you read, draw diagrams to show how each type of lens refracts light.

Figure 7 There is only one fish in this tank, but the refraction of light makes it look as though there are two.

Disappearing Glass

Try this activity to see how different liquids refract light.

1. Place a small drinking glass inside a larger drinking glass. Can you see the small glass inside the larger one?

2. Fill both glasses with water. Look at the glasses from the side. Can you still see the smaller glass?

3. Empty and dry the glasses and refill them with vegetable oil. Describe what you see.

Inferring Why does the vegetable oil create a different effect from the water's effect?

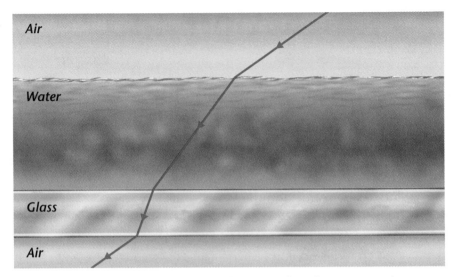

Figure 8 As light passes from a less dense medium into a more dense medium, it slows down and is refracted. *Inferring Why does the light leaving the glass and entering air travel in its original direction?*

Index of Refraction Some mediums cause light to bend more than others. Figure 8 shows how light passes from air into water, from water into glass, and from glass into air again. When light passes from air into water, the light slows down. Light slows down even more when it passes from water into glass. Light travels fastest in air, a little slower in water, and slower still in glass. When light passes from glass back into air, the light speeds up. Notice that the ray that leaves the glass is traveling in the same direction as it was before it entered the water.

Glass causes light to bend more than either air or water because glass refracts light more. Another way to say this is that glass has a higher index of refraction than either air or water. A material's **index of refraction** is a measure of how much a ray of light bends when it enters that material. The higher the index of refraction of a medium, the more it bends light. The index of refraction of a vacuum is 1. The index of refraction of diamond is 2.42.

Prisms Figure 9 shows that a beam of white light can be separated to show all the colors of the visible spectrum. Remember that white light is actually a mixture of many wavelengths of light, each with its own color. When white light enters a prism, each wavelength is refracted by a different amount. The longer the wavelength, the less the wave will be bent by a prism.

Figure 9 Passing white light through a prism causes the light to separate into its component colors. *Applying Concepts What determines the order in which the colors appear?*

Rainbows When white light from the sun shines through tiny drops of water, a rainbow may appear. **INTEGRATING EARTH SCIENCE** Raindrops act like tiny prisms, refracting and reflecting the light and separating the colors. The colors of the rainbow always appear in the same order because raindrops refract the shorter wavelengths the most. Red, with the longest wavelength, is refracted the least. Violet, with the shortest wavelength, is refracted the most. The result is that white light is separated into the colors of the visible spectrum: red, orange, yellow, green, blue, and violet.

Mirages Imagine that you are in a car moving down a road on a hot, sunny day. The road ahead looks wet. Yet when you get there, the road is perfectly dry. Did the puddles disappear just before you got there? No, they were never there at all! What you saw was a mirage. A **mirage** (mih RAHJ) is an image of a distant object caused by refraction of light.

Figure 11 shows how a mirage forms. The air higher up is cooler than the air near the road. Light travels faster when it reaches the warmer air. As a result, the rays bend as they travel downward. Near the ground, the rays are traveling almost parallel to the ground but continue to bend until they begin to travel upward. As they travel upward they bend in the other direction. Your brain assumes that the rays have traveled in a straight line. They look just like rays reflected off a smooth surface, such as water. The observer sees a mirage.

✓ *Checkpoint* *What causes a mirage?*

Figure 10 A rainbow forms when sunlight is refracted and reflected by tiny water droplets.

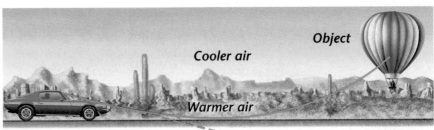

Figure 11 Light travels faster through hot air than through cool air. This causes light from the sky to curve as it approaches the ground. You see a mirage when refracted light appears to come from the ground.

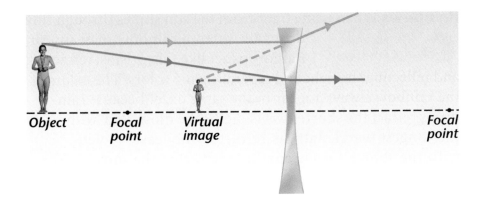

Figure 12 The ray that travels horizontally from the top of the object is refracted as though it is coming from the focal point on the same side of the lens as the object. The ray that travels toward the other focal point is refracted so it travels horizontally.
Interpreting Diagrams Why do the rays from a concave lens never meet?

Object   Focal point   Virtual image   Focal point

Lenses

Have you ever looked through binoculars, used a microscope or a camera, or worn eyeglasses? If so, you have used a lens to bend light. A **lens** is a curved piece of glass or other transparent material that is used to refract light. A lens forms an image by refracting light rays that pass through it. Like mirrors, lenses can have different shapes. The type of image formed by a lens depends on the shape of the lens.

Concave lens

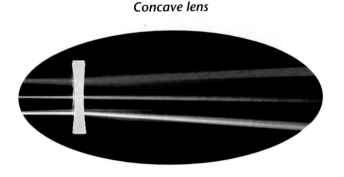

Convex lens

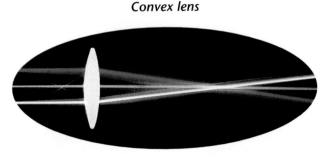

Figure 13 A concave lens refracts parallel rays of light so that they appear to come from one of the focal points. A convex lens refracts parallel rays of light so that they meet at the focal point.

Concave Lenses A **concave lens** is thinner in the center than at the edges. As parallel rays of light pass through a concave lens, they are bent away from the center of the lens. Figure 12 shows how the rays spread out, but appear to come from the focal point on the opposite side of the lens. **Because the light rays never meet, a concave lens can produce only a virtual image.**

Convex Lenses A **convex lens** is thicker in the center than at the edges. As parallel light rays pass through a convex lens, they are bent toward the center of the lens. The rays meet at the focal point of the lens and then continue on. The more curved the lens, the more it refracts light.

A convex lens acts somewhat like a concave mirror, because it focuses rays of light. **The type of image formed by a convex lens depends on the position of the object in relation to the focal point.** Figure 14 shows three examples. If the object is farther away than the focal point, the refracted rays form a real image on the other side of the lens. If the object is between the lens and the focal point, a virtual image forms on the same side of the lens as the object.

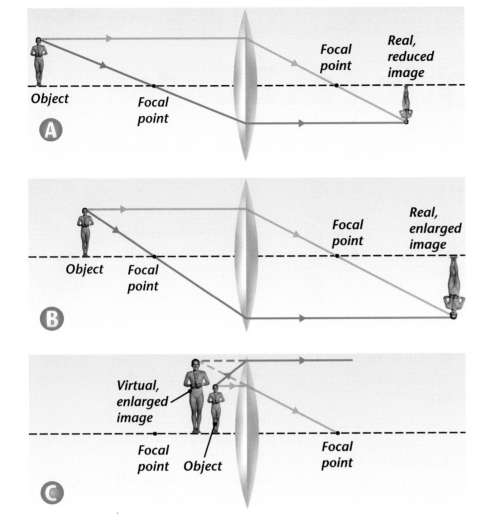

Figure 14 The type and size of image formed by a convex lens depend on the position of the object. **A, B.** If the object is farther from the focal point than the lens, the image is real and inverted. **C.** If the object is between the focal point and the lens, the image is virtual.

Section 2 Review

1. What happens to light rays as they pass from one medium into another medium?
2. What determines the type of image that is formed by a convex lens?
3. Why is it impossible for a concave lens to form a real image?
4. Explain why you sometimes see a rainbow during a rain shower or shortly afterward.
5. **Thinking Critically Problem Solving** Suppose you wanted to closely examine the leaf of a plant. Which type of lens would you use? Explain.

Science at Home

Pencil Bending Here's how you can bend a pencil without touching it. Put a pencil in a glass of water, as shown in the photograph. Have your family members look at the pencil from the side. Using the idea of refraction, explain to your family why the pencil appears as it does.

Looking at Images

In this lab, you will control variables as you explore how images are formed by a convex lens.

Problem

How does the distance between an object and a convex lens affect the image formed?

Materials (per group)

tape
cardboard stand
light bulb and socket
battery and wires

convex lens
blank sheet of paper
clay, for holding the lens
meterstick

Procedure

1. Tape the paper onto the cardboard stand.
2. Place a lit bulb more than 2 m from the paper. Use the lens to focus light from the bulb onto the paper. Measure the distance from the lens to the paper. This is the approximate focal length of the lens you are using.
3. Copy the data table into your notebook.
4. Now place the bulb more than twice the focal length away from the lens. Record the position and size of the focused image on the paper. Measure the height of the bulb.
5. Now, move the bulb so that it is just over one focal length away from the lens. Record the position and size of the image.

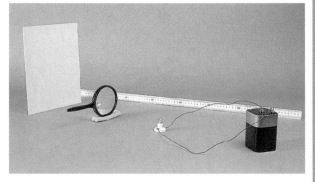

Analyze and Conclude

1. Is the image formed by a convex lens always upside down? If not, under what conditions is the image upright?
2. What happens to the size of the image as the bulb moves toward the lens? What happens to the position of the image?
3. What happens if the bulb is within one focal length of the lens? Explain.
4. **Think About It** Make a list of the variables in this experiment. Which variables did you keep constant? Which was the manipulated variable? Which was the responding variable?

Design an Experiment

With your teacher's approval and supervision, design an experiment to study images formed by convex lenses of various focal lengths. How does the focal length of the lens affect the position and size of the images produced?

DATA TABLE

Focal Length of Lens: _____ cm   Height of Bulb: _____ cm

Distance from Bulb to Lens (cm)	Image Position (upright or upside down)	Image Size (height in cm)

SECTION
3 Color

DISCOVER

•• **ACTIVITY** ••••

How Do Colors Mix?

1. ✂ Carefully cut a disk with a diameter of about 10 cm out of a piece of sturdy white cardboard. Divide the disk into three equal-size segments. Use colored pencils to color one segment red, the next green, and the third blue.

2. Carefully punch two holes, about 2 cm apart, on opposite sides of the center of the disk.

3. Thread a string about 1 m long through the holes. Tie the ends of the string together so that the string forms a loop that passes through both holes.

4. With equal lengths of string on each side of the disk, turn the disk so that you are winding up the string. Predict what color(s) you will see if the disk spins fast.

5. Spin the disk by pulling and relaxing the string.

Think It Over

Observing What color do you see as the wheel spins fast? Was your prediction correct?

A s the morning sun slowly rises over the flower garden, the sunlight begins to reveal bright pink and orange poppies, purple pansies, and a striking display of many other colors. Each flower is beautiful, yet different. The light from the sun allows you to see each color clearly. But sunlight is white light. What makes each flower appear to be a different color?

The Color of Objects

The color of a flower depends on how it reflects light. Each flower absorbs some wavelengths of light and reflects other wavelengths. **The color of an object is the color of the light it reflects.**

GUIDE FOR READING

◆ What determines the color of an object?

◆ What are the primary colors of light?

◆ How is mixing pigments different from mixing light?

Reading Tip Before you read, use the section headings to make an outline about color. Leave space to take notes as you read.

Objects in White Light Flowers and other objects reflect different colors of light. For example, when white light strikes the orange petals of a lily, the petals reflect mostly orange wavelengths. The petals absorb the other wavelengths. You see the petals as orange because orange wavelengths of light bounce off them and enter your eyes. On the other hand, the stem and leaves appear green. They reflect mostly green wavelengths and absorb the other colors.

What happens with black and white objects? A skunk looks black and white because some parts of it reflect all wavelengths of light while other parts do not reflect any light. When white light strikes the skunk's stripe, all the colors are reflected. The colors combine, so you see white light. When white light strikes the black parts of the skunk, all the light is absorbed and none is reflected. Your eyes see black.

Even colored and white objects can appear black if there is no light to reflect off them. Imagine being in a dark room. If there is no light present, then no light can reflect off the things in the room. No light enters your eyes, so you see nothing. If there is a small amount of light in the room, you may be able to make out the shapes of objects. However, you will not be able to tell their colors.

Objects in Colored Light Objects can look a different color depending on the color of light in which they are seen. Figure 17 shows two photographs of a desktop, each taken under different light. The first picture was taken under ordinary white light. In it, the keyboard is blue and the folder is red. The second picture was taken under green light. When green light shines on an object,

Figure 15 The petals of this lily appear orange because they reflect orange light. The stems and leaves appear green because they reflect green light.

Figure 16 The white part of this skunk reflects all colors of light. *Applying Concepts Why do the skunk's legs look black?*

582

Figure 17 In white light, objects appear in many different colors (left). If viewed under green light, the same objects appear in shades of green or black (right).
Predicting How would these objects look under blue light?

the object either reflects or absorbs the green light. Since red and blue objects reflect only red and blue light, they absorb all of the green light. The binder looks black.

Objects Seen Through Filters Some transparent materials allow only certain colors of light to pass through them. They reflect or absorb the other colors. Such materials are called color filters. For example, a red filter is a piece of glass or plastic that allows only red light to pass through. Spotlights on theater stages often use color filters to produce different color effects. Photographic slides are color filters, too. A slide projector shines white light through a combination of color filters. The image you see on the screen shows the colors that each part of the slide allows through.

☑ *Checkpoint* *What is a color filter?*

Combining Colors

An understanding of color is very useful in photography, art, theater lighting, and printing. People who work with color must know how to produce a wide range of colors from just a few basic colors. It is possible to produce any color by mixing colors of the spectrum in varying amounts. Three colors that can be used to make any other color are called **primary colors.** Any two primary colors combined in equal amounts produce a **secondary color.**

Mixing Colors of Light **The primary colors of light are red, green, and blue. When combined in equal amounts, the primary colors produce white light.** But if they are combined in varying amounts, they can produce any other color. For example, red and green combine to form yellow light. Yellow is a secondary color of light because it is produced from two primary colors.

Developing Hypotheses

1. Carefully make a color wheel with eight segments. Use colored pencils to color alternate blue and yellow segments.

2. Predict what color you will see if you spin the wheel. Write a hypothesis of what you think the outcome will be. Be sure to write your hypothesis as an *"If . . . then . . ."* statement.

3. Spin the wheel. What do you see? Does it confirm your hypothesis?

4. Repeat the activity with color wheels that have different pairs of colors.

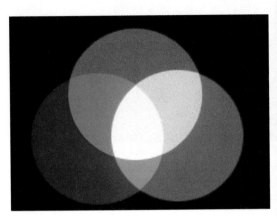

Primary colors of light

Figure 18 The primary colors of light are red, green, and blue. When combined in equal amounts, the primary colors of light form white light. A color television produces all colors of light by combining red, green, and blue light in varying amounts. *Interpreting Photographs How does a television show black?*

Visual Arts
CONNECTION

Ever since the first cave artists painted about 20,000 years ago, pigments made from natural materials have been used to create pictures. In the 1400s, Renaissance painters such as Leonardo da Vinci and Raphael used many more colorful pigments to create their vivid paintings. Pigments were derived from minerals, plants, and animals.

In Your Journal

Look at the color names for markers, paints, or crayons. Do you see vermilion (red), azure (blue) or ochre (brown)? These colors were all originally made from minerals. Now these colors are made from chemicals. Can you find the names of other colors that may have originally come from minerals?

The secondary colors of light are yellow (red + green), cyan (green + blue), and magenta (red + blue). Figure 18 shows the primary colors of light.

A primary color and a secondary color can combine to make white. Any two colors that combine to form white light are called **complementary colors.** Yellow and blue are complementary colors, as are cyan and red, and magenta and green.

INTEGRATING TECHNOLOGY A color television screen produces only three colors of light. Figure 18 shows a magnified portion of a color television screen. Notice that the picture on the screen is made up of little groups of red, green, and blue lights. By varying the brightness of each colored light, the television produces pictures of many different colors.

Mixing Pigments How do artists produce the many shades of colors you see in paintings? Paints and dyes have different colors because of the pigments they contain. **Pigments** are substances that are used to color other materials. Color pigments are opaque substances that reflect particular colors. The color you see is the color that particular pigment reflects.

Mixing colors of pigments is different from mixing colors of light. **As pigments are added together, fewer colors of light are reflected and more are absorbed.** The more pigments that are combined, the darker the mixture looks.

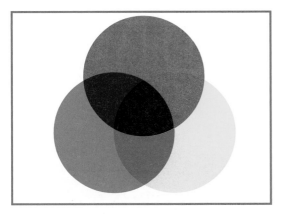

Primary colors of pigments

Figure 19 The primary colors of pigments are cyan, yellow, and magenta (left). The photograph shows a printed image and the round inset shows an enlargement of it. Four-color printing uses the three primary colors of pigment, plus black.

The primary colors of pigments are cyan, yellow, and magenta. If you combine all three primary colors of pigments in equal amounts, you get black. If you combine two primary colors of pigments in equal amounts, you get a secondary color. The secondary colors of pigments are red (magenta + yellow), green (cyan + yellow), and blue (magenta + cyan). By combining pigments in varying amounts, you can produce any other color. Figure 19 shows the primary colors of pigments.

If you use a magnifying glass to look at color pictures in this book, you will see that the pictures are made up of tiny dots of different colors of ink. The colors used are cyan, yellow, and magenta. Black ink is also used to make pictures darker. Because of the four colors of ink used, the process that produced this book is called four-color printing.

Section 3 Review

1. Why do objects have different colors?
2. What are the primary colors of light? What happens when the primary colors of light are mixed in equal amounts?
3. What happens when the primary colors of pigments are mixed in equal amounts?
4. What colors are used in the four-color printing process?
5. **Thinking Critically Comparing and Contrasting** Make a table that compares and contrasts the primary and secondary colors of light and those of pigments.

Check Your Progress

CHAPTER PROJECT

Build your optical instrument according to the sketch you prepared. How does your instrument use reflection or refraction to produce and clarify images? Do you need to be able to change the focus of the image? Does your instrument have moving parts? How will you combine the different parts of the instrument?

Changing Colors

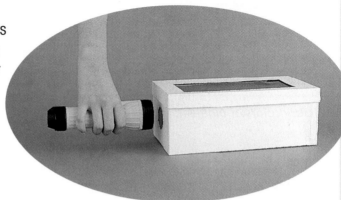

Stage lighting in theaters uses color filters to control the colors of light on stage. In this lab you will study the effect of color filters on white light.

Skills Focus

observing, predicting, inferring

Materials (per group)

shoe box
flashlight
scissors
removable tape
red object (such as a ripe tomato)
yellow object (such as a ripe lemon)
blue object (such as blue construction paper)
red, green, and blue cellophane, enough to cover
  the top of the shoe box

Procedure

1. Carefully cut a large rectangular hole in the lid of the shoe box. The hole should be just a little smaller than the lid of the box.
2. Carefully cut a small, round hole in the center of one of the ends of the shoe box.
3. Tape the red cellophane under the lid of the shoe box, covering the hole in the lid.
4. Place the objects in the box and put the lid on.
5. In a darkened room, shine the flashlight into the shoe box through the side hole. Note the apparent color of each object in the box.
6. Repeat Steps 3–5 using the other colors of cellophane.

Analyze and Conclude

1. What did you see when you looked through the red cellophane? Explain why each object appeared as it did.
2. What did you see when you looked through the blue cellophane? Explain.
3. What color of light does each piece of cellophane allow through?
4. Predict what you would see under each piece of cellophane if you put a white object in the box. Test your prediction.
5. Use diagrams to show how each color of cellophane affects the white light from the flashlight.
6. **Think About It** Do color filters work more like pigments or like colors of light? What would happen if you shined a flashlight through both a red and a green filter? Explain.

Getting Involved

Visit a local theater or talk to a lighting designer to find out how color filters are used to produce different stage effects.

SECTION 4 Seeing Light

Can You See Everything With One Eye?

1. Write an X and an O on a sheet of paper. They should be about 5 cm apart.
2. Hold the sheet of paper at arm's length.
3. Close or cover your left eye. Stare at the X with your right eye.
4. Slowly move the paper toward your face while staring at the X. What do you notice?

5. Repeat the activity, keeping both eyes open. What difference do you notice?

Think It Over

Posing Questions Write two questions about vision that you could investigate using the X and the O.

The excitement mounts as the pitcher goes into his windup. As he goes through his motion, he keeps his eye on the strike zone. The batter watches the pitcher release the ball, then swings. Crack! The batter strikes the ball, drops the bat, and sprints toward first base. From your seat behind home plate, you watch the ball travel toward the outfield. Will it be a base hit? The left fielder watches the ball leave the bat and travel toward him. It goes over his head—a two-base hit!

Everyone involved has been following the first rule of baseball: Keep your eye on the ball. As the ball moves, the eyes must adjust continuously to keep it in focus. Fortunately, this change in focus happens automatically.

GUIDE FOR READING

◆ How do your eyes allow you to see?

◆ What kind of lenses are used to correct vision problems?

Reading Tip As you read, make a flowchart that shows how light travels through the eye and how the brain interprets the image.

Figure 20 As the ball moves through the air, your eyes must continuously adjust their focus to see the ball.

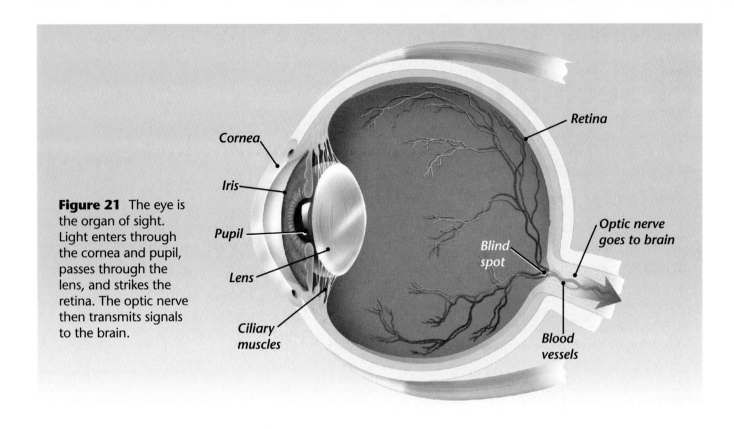

Figure 21 The eye is the organ of sight. Light enters through the cornea and pupil, passes through the lens, and strikes the retina. The optic nerve then transmits signals to the brain.

Cornea

Iris

Pupil

Lens

Ciliary muscles

Retina

Optic nerve goes to brain

Blind spot

Blood vessels

The Human Eye

Your eyes are complicated organs, with each part playing its own role in helping you see. **You see objects because of a series of steps that involve the structures of the eye and the brain.**

The Cornea Light enters the eye through the transparent front surface called the **cornea.** The cornea protects the eye. It also acts as a lens, bending rays of light as they enter the eye. Each time you blink, your eyelids act like little windshield wipers, cleansing and moistening the cornea.

The Iris The **iris** is a ring of muscle that contracts and expands to change the amount of light that enters the eye. The iris gives the eye its color. In most people the iris is brown; in others it is blue or green.

The Pupil The **pupil** is the part of the eye that looks black. It is actually a hole, covered by the clear cornea. The pupil looks black because it is an opening into the dark inside of the eye. Figure 22 shows how the size of the pupil depends on whether the iris is contracted or expanded. In dim light, the pupil becomes larger, allowing more light in. In very bright light, the pupil becomes smaller, reducing the amount of light that enters the eye.

Figure 22 In dim light, the iris contracts. The pupil gets bigger and allows more light into the eye. *Relating Cause and Effect What happens in bright light?*

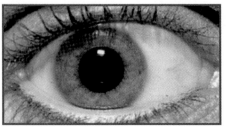

The Lens Just behind the pupil is the lens. The lens of your eye is a convex lens. The lens refracts light, forming an image on the lining of your eyeball. Figure 23 shows how the lens changes its focus. When you focus on a distant object, the ciliary muscles holding the lens relax, making the lens longer and thinner. When you focus on a nearby object, the muscles contract and the lens becomes shorter and fatter.

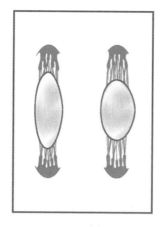

Figure 23 The ciliary muscles holding the lens in place relax (left) or contract (right) to change the shape of the lens.

The Retina The layer of cells lining the inside of the eyeball is the **retina.** As the cornea and the lens refract light, an upside-down image is formed on the retina. The retina is made up of millions of tiny, light-sensitive cells called rods and cones. The rods and cones generate small nerve signals when they are hit by light.

The **rods** contain a pigment that reacts to small amounts of light. The rods distinguish among black, white, and shades of gray. They allow you to see in dim light, so they are important for night vision.

The **cones** respond to colors. There are three types of cones: those that detect red light, those that detect green light, and those that detect blue light. The cone cells function only in bright light. This is why it is difficult to distinguish colors in dim light.

The Optic Nerve and the Brain The signals generated by the rods and cones travel to your brain along a short, thick nerve called the **optic nerve.** When the signals reach your brain, it automatically turns the image right-side up. Your brain also combines the two images, one from each eye, into a single three-dimensional image.

There is one spot on the retina that does not have any rods or cones. This blind spot is the part of the retina where the optic nerve begins. You cannot see light that falls on the blind spot. However, an object whose light falls on the blind spot of one eye can usually be seen with the other eye. If you keep both eyes open, you do not notice the effect of the blind spots.

✓ *Checkpoint* *Where in the eye is the image formed?*

Correcting Vision

In some people, the eyeball is slightly too long or too short, so the image on the retina is slightly out of focus. Fortunately, wearing glasses or contact lenses can usually correct this type of vision problem. **Some lenses in eyeglasses are convex and some are concave. The type of lens used depends on whether the eyeball is too long or too short.**

True Colors ACTIVITY
When you stare too long at a color, the cones in your eyes get tired.

1. Stare at the bottom right star of the flag for at least 60 seconds. Do not move your eyes or blink during that time.

2. Now stare at a sheet of blank white paper.

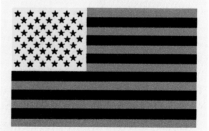

Observing What do you see when you look at the white paper? How are the colors you see related to the colors in the original art?

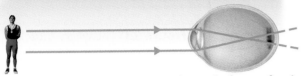

Nearsightedness (eyeball too long)

Image forms in front of retina

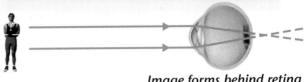

Farsightedness (eyeball too short)

Image forms behind retina

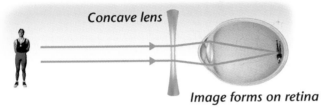

Correction

Concave lens

Image forms on retina

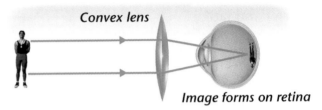

Correction

Convex lens

Image forms on retina

Figure 24 Nearsightedness and farsightedness are caused when the eyeball is a little too long or too short. Both can be corrected by wearing lenses.

Nearsightedness A **nearsighted** person can see nearby things clearly, but objects at a distance appear blurry. This happens because the eyeball is a little too long. The lens focuses the image in front of the retina. A nearsighted person can wear eyeglasses with concave lenses to see more clearly. A concave lens spreads out the rays a little before they enter the lens of the eye. This causes the image to form a little farther back, on the retina.

Farsightedness A **farsighted** person can see distant objects clearly, but nearby objects appear blurry. This happens when the eyeball is a little too short. The lens focuses the rays of light so that they would meet behind the retina. The image that falls on the retina is out of focus. A farsighted person can wear glasses with convex lenses. A convex lens makes the rays bend toward each other a little before they enter the eye. A clear image is then formed on the retina.

Section 4 Review

1. Describe briefly the function of each of these structures in allowing a person to see: the cornea, pupil, lens, retina, optic nerve, brain.
2. How and why does the pupil change size?
3. What causes nearsightedness? Farsightedness? How can each be corrected?
4. **Thinking Critically Comparing and Contrasting** Compare and contrast the functions of the rods and the cones.

Science at Home

Optical Illusion Roll a sheet of paper into a tube and hold one end up to your right eye. Hold your left hand against the left side of the far end of the tube with your palm facing toward you. Keeping both eyes open, look at a distant object. Draw and label a diagram of what you see. What do you think causes this optical illusion?

SECTION 5 Using Light

DISCOVER ···········ACTIVITY····

How Does a Pinhole Viewer Work?

1. ✂ Carefully use a pin to make a tiny hole in the center of the bottom of a paper cup.

2. Place a piece of wax paper over the open end of the cup. Hold the paper in place with a rubber band.

3. Turn off the room lights. Point the end of the cup with the hole in it at a bright window. **CAUTION:** *Do not look directly at the sun.*

4. Look at the image formed on the wax paper.

Think It Over

Classifying Describe the image you see. Is it upside down or right-side up? Is it smaller or larger than the actual object? What type of image is it?

Have you ever seen photos of the moons of Jupiter? Have you ever thought it would be exciting to fly close to the rings of Saturn? Of course you know that traveling in space has been done for only a few decades. But you might be surprised to know that the moons of Jupiter and the rings of Saturn had not been seen by anyone before the year 1600. It was only about 1609 that a new invention, the telescope, made those objects visible to people on Earth.

Since the 1600s, astronomers have built more powerful telescopes that allow them to see objects in space that are very far from Earth. The Trifid Nebula, for example, is a cloud of gas and dust in space 28,000 trillion kilometers from Earth. It took about 3,000 years for light from this nebula to travel to Earth.

In this section you will learn how simple a device the telescope is. You may wonder why no one invented it sooner!

GUIDE FOR READING

◆ How do telescopes and microscopes work?

◆ How does a camera work?

◆ How is laser light different from ordinary light?

Reading Tip Before you read, preview the section to identify devices that use light. As you read, make notes about how each device is commonly used.

The Trifid Nebula ▶

591

Uses of Lasers

Lasers have many practical applications. Lasers are widely used by surveyors and engineers. A laser beam is so straight that it can be used to make sure that surfaces are level and that bridges and tunnels are properly aligned. For example, a laser beam was used to guide the tunnel diggers who dug the Channel Tunnel between England and France. Some very powerful lasers can even cut through steel. Many stores and supermarkets use lasers. A laser scans the universal product code, or bar code. The store's computer then displays the price of the object.

Compact Discs Lasers can be used to store and read information. A compact disc is produced by converting data into electrical signals. The electrical signals are converted to a laser beam, which cuts a pattern of pits on a blank disc. When you play a compact disc or read one with a computer, a laser beam shines on the surface and is reflected. The reflection patterns vary because

SCIENCE & History

Optical Instruments

The development of optical instruments has changed the way we look at the world and beyond. It has allowed major scientific discoveries.

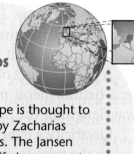

1595 THE NETHERLANDS
Microscopes

The first useful microscope is thought to have been constructed by Zacharias Jansen or his father, Hans. The Jansen microscope could magnify images up to nine times the size of the object. By the mid-1600s, microscopes looked like the one shown.

| 1300 | 1400 | 1500 | 1600 |

1350 ITALY
Spectacles

Craftsmen made small disks of glass that could be framed and worn in front of the eyes. Early spectacles consisted of convex lenses. They were used as reading glasses.

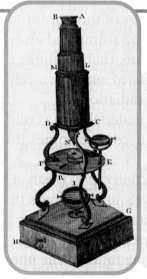

1607 THE NETHERLANDS
Telescopes

The first telescope was made of two convex lenses. It was from this simple invention that the Italian scientist Galileo developed his more powerful telescopes shown here.

of the pits. The compact disc player or disc drive changes these patterns into electrical signals. The signals are sent to speakers and you hear sound.

Surgery Doctors can use lasers instead of scalpels to make incisions. The beam of light can be powerful enough to cut through flesh. As the laser makes the incision, it seals the cut blood vessels. This reduces the amount of blood a patient loses. Laser incisions usually heal faster than scalpel cuts, so the patient's recovery time is reduced.

INTEGRATING HEALTH

Eye doctors use lasers to repair detached retinas. If the retina falls away from the inside of the eye, the rods and cones can no longer send signals to the brain. This can lead to total or partial blindness. The doctor can use a laser to "weld" or burn the retina back onto the eyeball. Lasers can also be used to destroy or remove skin blemishes and cancerous growths.

In Your Journal

Find out more about early photography and people's reactions to it. Then imagine you are an early photographer explaining photography to someone who has never seen a photo. Create a two-page dialog in which you answer that person's questions on the process and possible uses of photography.

1990 UNITED STATES

Hubble Space Telescope

This large reflecting telescope was launched by the crew of the space shuttle *Discovery.* It can detect infrared, visible, and ultraviolet rays in space and send pictures back to Earth.

| 1700 | 1800 | 1900 | 2000 |

1826 FRANCE

Cameras

The earliest camera, the pinhole camera, was adapted to form and record permanent images by Joseph Nicéphore Niepce and Louis-Jacques-Mandé Daguerre of France. This is one of Nicéphore Niepce's earliest photographic images.

1960 UNITED STATES

Lasers

The first laser, built by American Theodore Maiman, used a rod of ruby to produce light. Since then, lasers have been used in numerous ways, including engineering, medicine, and communications.

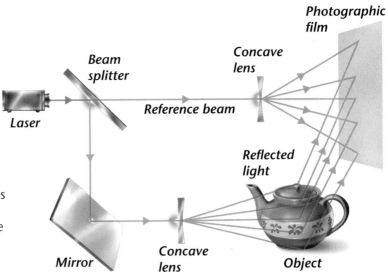

Figure 30 To form a hologram, the light from a laser is split into two beams. When the two beams strike the photographic film, an interference pattern produces the image, or hologram.

Holography Check out your local video store or newsstand. Some videos and magazines have pictures that appear to move as you walk by. A **hologram** is a three-dimensional photograph created by using the light from a laser. The process is called holography.

Figure 30 shows how a hologram is produced. A laser beam is split into two beams. One beam passes through a concave lens, behind which is a piece of photographic film. The concave lens spreads out the rays of light before they hit the film. The second beam is sent to a mirror and reflected toward another concave lens, behind which is the object being photographed. Again, the rays are spread out by the lens before they hit the object. The object then reflects these rays toward the film, where they interfere with rays from the first beam. The interference pattern recorded on the film produces a three-dimensional image when viewed in laser light.

☑ *Checkpoint* *What are four uses of lasers?*

Optical Fibers

Lasers are also used in communications. A laser beam is electromagnetic radiation of a single wavelength. It is similar to radio waves and so can carry signals by modulation. Unlike radio waves, laser beams are not usually sent through the air. Instead, they are sent through optical fibers. **Optical fibers** are long, thin strands of glass or plastic that can carry light for long distances without allowing the light to fade out. You may have seen optical fibers in lamps or in the small hand-held lights that are sometimes sold at circuses and other shows.

Figure 31 Optical fibers are thin strands of glass or plastic that carry light.

EXPLORING Uses of Lasers

The invention of the laser has led to many developments in technology and communication.

A laser beam reads information from tiny pits on a compact disc. ▲

▲ Civil engineers use laser beams to ensure that buildings are straight.

▼ Optical fibers carry beams of laser light great distances. One tiny fiber can carry thousands more phone conversations than the traditional copper wire cable.

▲ A supermarket scanner reflects a laser off a set of lines known as a universal product code, or UPC. Each product has a unique code. This code represents a number that is programmed into the store's computer. The computer then displays the name of the object and the price on a screen near the cash register.

Small, hand-held lasers are commonly used as pointers in lectures and presentations.

◀ Banks now commonly put small holograms on credit cards for security reasons. The hologram makes credit cards difficult to copy.

▶ Laser surgery can correct vision by reshaping the cornea of the eye.

THE MAGIC OF THE MOVIES

LIGHTS! CAMERA! ACTION!

- A dinosaur, 12 feet tall, roars from the forest.
- An alien spaceship lands in Washington, D.C.
- A pig calls out orders to a herd of sheep.

When you go to the movies, you expect to be entertained. You want a movie to make you laugh or cry or shiver. A movie is simply a series of pictures shown at tremendous speed on a flat screen. Even so, millions of people go to the movies every week.

Movies have been around for about 100 years. Until 1927, movies were silent and filmed in black and white. Then in the late 1920s and 1930s, the movie industry changed. Moviemakers added sound to make the first "talking pictures." Not long after that, they added color.

What makes movies so special? Much of the magic of the movies comes from the different ways in which directors use light, color, special effects, camera angles, editing, and computer wizardry. These techniques help to make a movie scene scary or exciting or romantic.

Picking a Point of View

A screenwriter writes the script or story for a movie from a certain point of view. For example, when a movie tells a story from the point of view of one main character, the audience shares that character's thoughts and feelings. The person may tell parts of the story as a "voice-over." If you were the main character telling the story, you might say, "As my wagon reached the top of the hill, I saw the beautiful sunrise." In contrast, the voice-over sometimes is given by a narrator who you don't see in the movie. The narrator tells the same story, but from a different point of view. For example, the narrator might describe the scene with the wagon saying, "As the wagon reached the top of the hill, the light of the rising sun revealed a tired horse and an even more tired driver."

The movie *Babe* begins with a narrator's voice describing what happens to pigs when they leave the farm. Then the camera zooms in on Babe, a pig who has the ability to carry on conversations with his animal friends. The movie alternates between Babe's point of view and the narrator's.

Often, the point of view shifts from character to character as the camera moves. In a hospital scene, for instance, the camera may look up from the patient's point of view. Then the camera may look down at the patient, representing the point of view of doctors, nurses, or family members.

Editing is key to the movemaking process. The film editors, as well as the director, decide what the audience will see in each shot. They also plan actions and conversations that make people like or admire certain characters and dislike others.

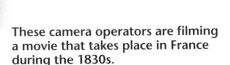

These camera operators are filming a movie that takes place in France during the 1830s.

Language Arts Activity

Think of a story or book you have read that you would like to see as a movie. In one or two paragraphs, write a summary of the plot of the movie. Then explain what point of view you would use to tell the story as a movie. Why would you choose that point of view?

How Pictures Seem to Move

The movie opens. The film rolls, and the action begins. What is happening? A movie is a fast-moving series of small photographs projected onto a screen. The pictures appear so fast—at about 24 pictures per second—that your eyes blend them together in continuous motion. But your eyes are tricking you. You are seeing an optical illusion.

When you watch a movie, your eyes see each picture for just a fraction of a second. Then the picture is replaced by the next one. The pictures move so fast that even when one image is gone, your brain continues to see it. Seeing this after-image is called "persistence of vision." It creates the illusion of motion.

Many discoveries and inventions in the 1800s combined to make the first motion picture. For example, in 1834, a toy called a zoetrope was invented. The zoetrope contained pictures inside a drumlike device with slits. People could spin the drum while looking through the slits. The motion of the zoetrope made the pictures appear to move.

By the late 1800s, American inventor Thomas Edison was working on a movie camera. It used a plastic called celluloid to coat film. Edison made the film 35 millimeters wide, a width still used today. Edison punched holes along the edge of the film so it would wind on a spool. If you've loaded film into a camera, you may have seen these holes. In the late 1920s, moviemakers added another strip to the film that gave sound to movies.

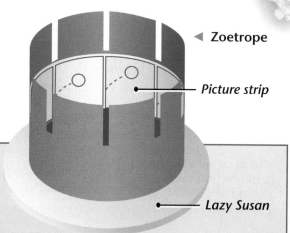

◀ **Zoetrope**

Picture strip

Lazy Susan

Science Activity

Make your own moving picture by building a zoetrope.

◆ Cut a strip of white paper 45.5 cm by 7.5 cm. Mark the strip to make 8 equal picture frames.

◆ Near the center of the first frame, draw a picture. Your picture should be a simple outline of an object such as an animal or person.

◆ Draw your object again in the second frame, but change its position slightly. Repeat the step until you have drawn the object in every frame. Remember to change its position a bit each time, as shown in the illustration below.

◆ Cut a piece of black construction paper to measure 45.5 cm by 15 cm.

◆ Mark 8 vertical slits on the top half of the black paper, each 5.5 cm apart. Cut the slits, making each 4 mm wide and 7.5 cm deep.

◆ Tape the black paper into a circle with the slits on top.

◆ Tape the picture strip into a circle with the pictures on the inside. Slide the strip inside the black circle to create your zoetrope.

◆ Place your zoetrope on a record player or Lazy Susan. Center it. Look through the slits as you spin the zoetrope. What do you see?

Model makers built a number of small-scale ship models to use in the movie *TITANIC*®.

Making Models

A sinking luxury liner, a fiery train crash, a city devastated by an earthquake—these scenes look real on the screen. But moviemakers don't sink ships or destroy cities. They use models.

Often a movie uses several models in different sizes. The makers of the movie *TITANIC*, for example, built a nearly full-size model of one side of the huge ship. It floated in a tank big enough to hold 65 million liters of water. Another large tank held full-size models of different rooms and decks on the ship. These models were used for scenes with actors.

The movie also used smaller *Titanic* models that were built to scale. Scale is a ratio that compares the measurements of a model to the actual size of the object. One *Titanic* model was built to a scale of 1 : 20 (1 meter in the model to 20 meters in actual size). Even so, it was still almost 14 meters long. Interior curtains and furniture were added to make the model look real. After scenes were filmed with this model, computer-generated images added water, smoke curling from smokestacks, and passengers.

Models must be to scale. For example, if a car is 3.5 meters (350 centimeters) long, a model at a scale of 1 : 16 would be almost 22 centimeters long. A larger model of the car, at 1 : 4, would be about 87.5 centimeters long.

Camera tricks make models look more real. Because miniatures weigh less than actual objects, they move differently. Instead of crashing through a wall, a model car might bounce off it. To solve this problem, directors often photograph miniatures moving slowly. This makes the models appear to move like larger, heavier objects. Other camera tricks can make a tiny model look larger and farther away.

Math Activity

Sketch a simple scene, such as a room interior or a city scene. Pick four objects in the scene and estimate or measure the actual size of each. The objects could include a chair, a person, a car, or a skyscraper. (*Note:* One story in a modern building equals about 4 meters.) Decide on a scale for your model, such as 1 : 4, 1 : 12, or 1 : 16. After determining the actual sizes of the objects, calculate the size of each scale model.

A Trip to the Moon, 1902
This early French movie represents an astronomer's dream. In the dream, men travel to the moon inside a capsule shot from a giant cannon.

Them!, 1954
In this 1954 movie, nuclear tests in the American southwest create mutant giant ants.

Reflecting the Times

When moviemakers look for an idea for a new movie, they think first about what people are interested in seeing. Moviemakers want to know what's important to people. Advances in science and technology and recent events in history all influence people. Movies often reflect changes in people's lives.

In the early 1900s, people were just beginning to fly airplanes. Early science fiction movies of the 1920s and 1930s were pure fantasy.

By the 1950s, space flight technology was developing. In 1957, the Soviet Union sent the first satellite, *Sputnik,* into orbit. Soon after, the United States and the Soviet Union were competing in space exploration. Both nations also were making powerful nuclear weapons. The idea of nuclear war frightened people. Many movies of the 1950s and 1960s reflected these fears. Giant insects and other monsters appeared on movie screens. Science fiction movies featured alien invasions.

The "space race" continued in the 1960s. American astronauts and Russian cosmonauts orbited Earth. In July 1969, three American astronauts became the first people to reach the moon. Later, space probes sent back pictures of other planets. These space flights made people dream about space travel. About the same time, people began using computers. Some people were afraid the new machines would control them. In the 1968 movie *2001: A Space Odyssey,* the computer HAL did just that.

Interest in space kept science fiction movies popular in the 1980s and 1990s. By that time, computers were part of everyday life. They were

E. T., 1982
E. T. is an alien stranded on Earth. He is found by a 10-year-old boy, and they become friends.

not instruments to be feared. Tension between the United States and Russia was relaxing. Movies seemed more optimistic about the future than in the 1950s. In popular movies such as *E.T.* and *Close Encounters of the Third Kind*, the human characters showed more curiosity than fear about aliens—even those that visited Earth. The movie *Men in Black* featured aliens who were more often humorous than threatening.

Social Studies Activity

Think of some recent movies that you and others may have seen. With your classmates, organize a panel discussion on the links between movies and current events. Think about the changes that have occurred in the world around you. How have space probes, planet explorations, computers, video games, the Internet, and political events influenced these movies?

Tie It Together

Making a Movie

Put your movie ideas into action. With your classmates, plan a short (10–15 minute) movie. If possible, use a video camera to make your movie. Use what you've learned about point of view, the use of scale models, and editing.

◆ Think of a subject or event for your movie. As a class, outline the script for the movie.

◆ Work in small groups to make storyboards—drawings showing key scenes in the movie.

◆ Choose a director, actors, a camera operator, and a film editor.

◆ Assign groups to plan lights, sound effects, model-building, props, background painting, and photography.

◆ After shooting and editing your movie, present it for other students in your school.

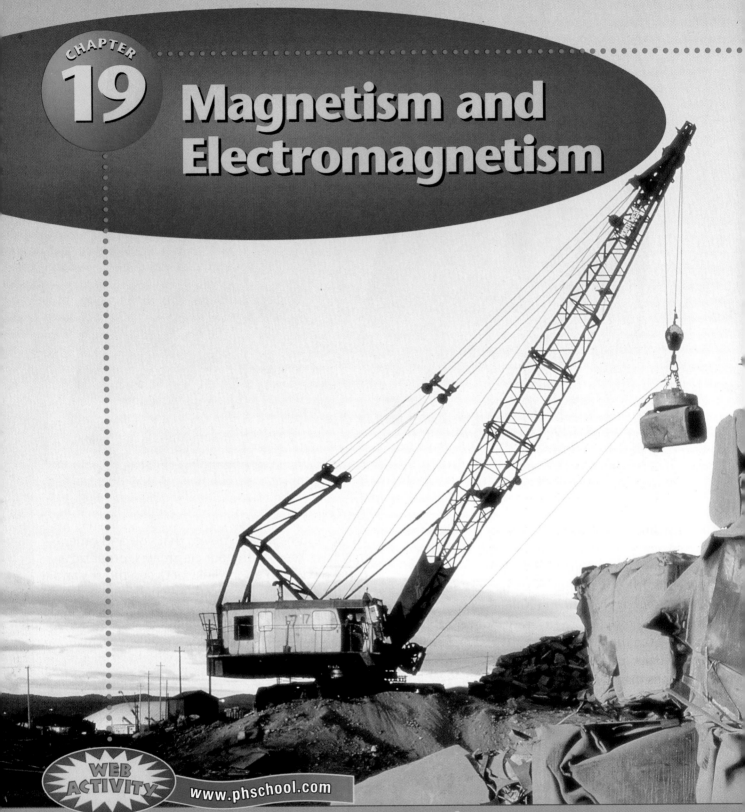

19 Magnetism and Electromagnetism

WEB ACTIVITY
www.phschool.com

SECTION 1 The Nature of Magnetism

Discover **What Do All Magnets Have in Common?**
Sharpen Your Skills **Observing**
Try This **How Attractive!**
Real-World Lab **Detecting Fake Coins**

Integrating Earth Science

SECTION 2 Magnetic Earth

Discover **Can You Use a Needle to Make a Compass?**
Sharpen Your Skills **Measuring**
Try This **Spinning in Circles**
Science at Home **House Magnets**

SECTION 3 Electric Current and Magnetic Fields

Discover **Are Magnetic Fields Limited to Magnets?**
Sharpen Your Skills **Classifying**
Real-World Lab **Build a Flashlight**

610

Electromagnetic Fishing Derby

If you went fishing for cars, what kind of hook would you use—a ship's anchor? Though they resemble giant fishing rods, the cranes used in junkyards to move scrap cars don't use hooks—they use electromagnets.

In this chapter, you will learn what magnets are and how they are used. You will learn about electric current. And you will find out how electric current can be used to produce strong magnets, called electromagnets, that can be turned on and off. As you read the chapter, you will use what you learn to construct an electromagnetic fishing rod. Now go fish!

Your Goal To build an electromagnetic fishing rod that can lift paper clips from one container and drop them into another.

To complete your project you must
- ◆ make a model of a fishing rod that has a magnet as its hook
- ◆ design an on-off switch for an electromagnet suspended by string from the end of the rod and powered by a single D cell
- ◆ modify variables so you can move as many paper clips as possible from one container to another in one minute
- ◆ follow the safety guidelines in Appendix A

Get Started Think about fishing rods. Discuss some of their features. Then think about how you could catch and let go of a paper clip with a similar fishing device. Brainstorm ideas for using a magnet as a "hook."

Check Your Progress You'll be working on this project as you study this chapter. To keep your project on track, look for Check Your Progress boxes at the following points.
Section 1 Review, page 619: Make an initial model with a permanent magnet.
Section 3 Review, page 633: Design a switch.
Section 4 Review, page 638: Construct and improve your electromagnet by experimenting with variables.

Present Your Project At the end of the chapter (page 641), you will use your rod to fish alongside classmates in an electromagnetic fishing derby.

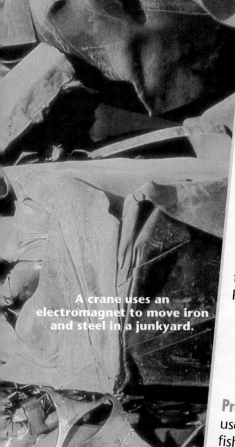

A crane uses an electromagnet to move iron and steel in a junkyard.

SECTION
4 Electromagnets

Discover How Do You Turn a Magnet On and Off?

The Nature of Magnetism

What Do All Magnets Have in Common?

1. Obtain a bar magnet and a horseshoe magnet.
2. See how many paper clips you can make stick to different parts of each magnet.
3. Draw a diagram showing the number and location of paper clips on each magnet.

Think It Over

Observing Where does each magnet hold the greatest number of paper clips? What similarities do you observe between the two magnets?

GUIDE FOR READING

◆ How do magnetic poles interact?

◆ What is the shape of magnetic lines of force?

◆ How are the domains of a magnet arranged?

Reading Tip As you read, use the headings to make an outline of the main ideas and supporting details about magnetism and electricity.

Imagine zooming along in a train that glides without even touching the ground. You feel no vibration and hear no noise from solid steel tracks. You can just sit back and relax as you speed toward your destination at nearly 400 kilometers per hour.

Are you dreaming? No, you are not. Although you have probably not ridden on such a train, trains capable of floating a few centimeters in air do exist. What makes them float? Believe it or not, magnets make them float.

Figure 1 This Japanese high-speed train is moved by strong magnets instead of wheels. It is called a magnetically levitating train, or maglev train.

Magnets

When you think of magnets, you might think about the magnets that hold notes on your refrigerator. But magnets can also be found in many familiar devices, such as doorbells, televisions, and computers.

Magnets have many modern uses, but they are not new. More than 2000 years ago, people living in a region known as Magnesia discovered an unusual rock. (Magnesia is in Greece.) The rock attracted materials that contained iron. It contained a mineral that we call magnetite. Both the word *magnetite* and the word *magnet* come from the name "Magnesia." **Magnetism** is the attraction of a magnet for another object.

About a thousand years ago, people in other parts of the world discovered another interesting property of magnets. If they allowed the magnetic rock to swing freely from a string, one part of the rock would always point in the same direction. That direction was toward a certain northern star, called the leading star, or lodestar. For this reason, magnetic rocks also became known as lodestones.

Figure 2 Magnetic rocks contain the mineral magnetite.

Magnetic Poles

The magnets with which you are familiar are not found in nature, but they are made to have the same properties as lodestone. Any magnet, no matter what its shape, has two ends, each one called a **magnetic pole.** A pole is the area of a magnet where the magnetic effect is strongest. Just as one end of a piece of magnetite always points toward the north star, one pole of a magnet will also point north and is labeled the north pole. The other pole is labeled the south pole. Two north poles or two south poles are a pair of like poles. A north pole and a south pole are a pair of unlike, or opposite poles.

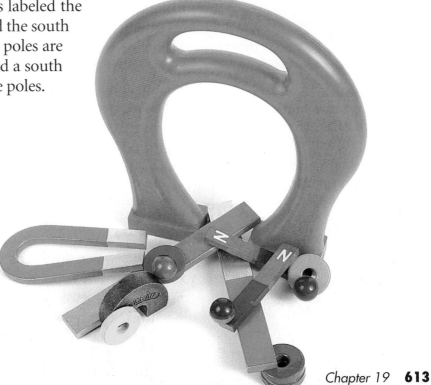

Figure 3 Modern magnets come in a variety of shapes and sizes. *Classifying How many different shapes of magnets can you identify in the photograph?*

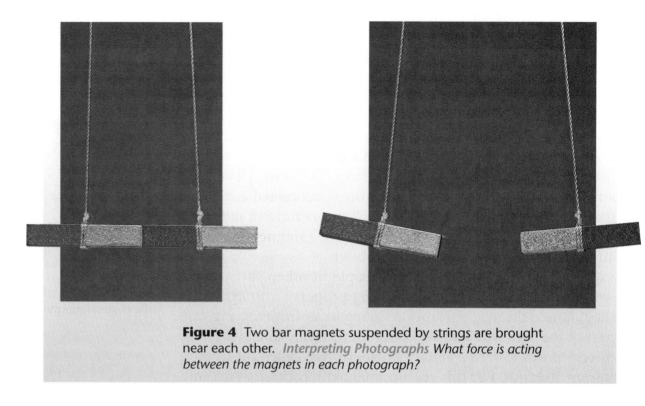

Figure 4 Two bar magnets suspended by strings are brought near each other. *Interpreting Photographs What force is acting between the magnets in each photograph?*

Interactions Between Magnetic Poles What happens if you bring two magnets together? The answer depends on how you hold the poles of the magnets. If you bring two north poles together, the magnets push away from each other. The same is true if two south poles are brought together. However, if you bring the north pole of one magnet near the south pole of another, the two magnets attract one another. **Magnetic poles that are alike repel each other and magnetic poles that are unlike attract each other.** Figure 4 shows how two bar magnets interact.

The force of attraction or repulsion between magnetic poles is magnetism. Any material that exerts magnetic forces is considered a magnet.

The maglev train you read about earlier depends on magnetism. Magnets in the bottom of the train and in the guideway on the ground have like poles. Since like poles repel, the two magnets push each other away. The result is that the train car is lifted up, or levitated. Other magnets push and pull the train forward.

Paired Poles What do you think happens if you break a magnet in two? Will you have a north pole in one hand and a south pole in the other? The answer is no. Rather than two separate poles, you will have two separate magnets. Each smaller magnet will be complete with its own north pole and south pole. And if you break those two halves again, you will then have four magnets.

✓ *Checkpoint* *What is a magnetic pole?*

Observing

ACTIVITY

1. Use a pencil to poke a hole in the bottom of a foam cup. Turn the cup upside-down and stand the pencil in the hole.

2. Place two circular magnets on the pencil, so that their like sides are together.

3. Remove the top magnet. Flip it over and replace it on the pencil.

What happens to the magnets in each case? Explain your observations.

Magnetic Fields

The magnetic force is strongest at the poles of a magnet, but it is not limited to the poles. Magnetic forces are exerted all around a magnet. The region of magnetic force around a magnet is known as its **magnetic field.** Magnetic fields allow magnets to interact without touching.

Figure 5A shows the magnetic field of a bar magnet. The lines, called **magnetic field lines,** map out the magnetic field around a magnet. **Magnetic field lines spread out from one pole, curve around a magnet, and return to the other pole.** The lines form complete loops from pole to pole and never cross.

Although you can't actually see a magnetic field, you can see its effects, as shown in Figure 5B. This photograph shows iron filings sprinkled on a sheet of plastic over a magnet. The magnetic forces act on the iron filings so that they point toward the poles of the magnet. The result is that the iron filings form a pattern similar to the magnetic field lines in Figure 5A.

The iron filings and the diagram are both on flat surfaces. But a magnetic field exists in three dimensions. You can see in Figure 5C that the magnetic field completely surrounds the magnet.

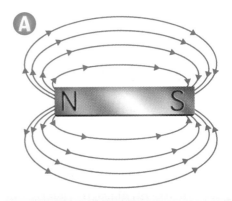

Figure 5 A magnetic field surrounds a magnet. **A.** In this diagram, magnetic field lines are shown in red. **B.** You can see the same magnetic field mapped out by iron filings. **C.** Iron filings also show that a magnetic field has three dimensions.

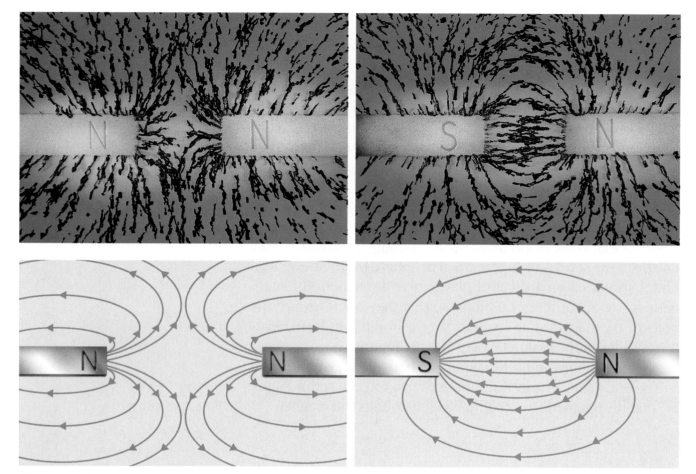

Figure 6 The magnetic field of each bar magnet is altered when two bar magnets are brought together.
Applying Concepts What do these photos and diagrams show about the interaction between magnetic poles?

When the magnetic fields of two or more magnets overlap, the result is a combined field. Figure 6 shows the magnetic fields produced when the poles of two bar magnets are brought near each other.

Inside a Magnet

What happens if you bring a piece of wood, glass, or plastic near a pile of paper clips? Nothing happens. These materials have no effect on the paper clips. But if you bring a bar magnet near the same pile, the paper clips will cling to the magnet. Why do some materials have strong magnetic fields while others do not?

Electron Spin The magnetic properties of a material depend on the structure of its atoms. All matter is made up of atoms. An atom is the smallest particle of an element that has the properties of that element. An element is one of about 100 basic materials that make up all matter.

The center of every atom is called a nucleus. The nucleus contains particles within it. Protons are nuclear particles that carry a positive charge. Orbiting the nucleus are other tiny particles called electrons, which carry a negative charge. Each of the electrons in an atom acts as if it is spinning as it orbits the nucleus. A moving electron produces a magnetic field. The spinning and orbiting motion of the electrons make each atom a tiny magnet.

Magnetic Domains In most materials the magnetic fields of the atoms point in random directions. The result is that the magnetic fields cancel one another almost entirely. The magnetism of most materials is so weak that you cannot usually detect it.

In certain materials, the magnetic fields of the spinning electrons of many atoms are aligned with one another. A cluster of billions of atoms that all have magnetic fields that are lined up in the same way is known as a **magnetic domain.** The entire domain acts like a bar magnet with a north pole and a south pole.

In a material that is not magnetized, the domains point in random directions as shown in Figure 7. The magnetic fields exerted by some of the domains cancel the magnetic fields exerted by other domains. The result is that the material is not a magnet. **In a magnetized material all or most of the domains are arranged in the same direction.** In other words, the domains are aligned.

Magnetic Materials A material can be a strong magnet if it forms magnetic domains. A material that shows strong magnetic effects is said to be a **ferromagnetic material.** The word *ferromagnetic* comes from the Latin *ferrum*, which means "iron." Iron, nickel, and cobalt are the common ferromagnetic materials. Others include the rare elements samarium and neodymium, which can be made into magnets that are extremely powerful. Some very strong magnets are also made from mixtures, or alloys, of several metals.

☑ *Checkpoint* *How is magnetism related to domains?*

Figure 7 The arrows represent the domains of a material. The arrows point toward the north pole of each domain. *Comparing and Contrasting How does the arrangement of domains differ between magnetized iron and unmagnetized iron?*

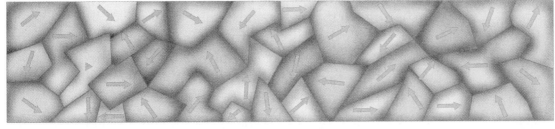

Unmagnetized Iron

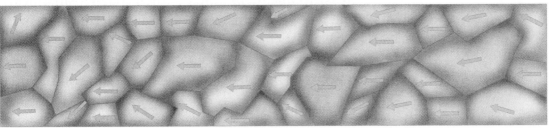

Magnetized Iron

Figure 8 The magnet attracts the metal paper clips. *Applying Concepts How can a paper clip be attracted to a magnet?*

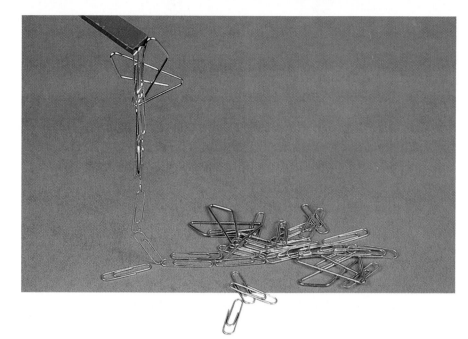

Making Magnets

You know that magnetite exists in nature. The magnets you use everyday, however, are made by people. A magnet can be made from a ferromagnetic material. This is done by placing the unmagnetized material in a strong magnetic field or by rubbing it with one pole of a strong magnet.

If the magnetic field is strong enough, two processes take place. First, the domains that point in the direction of the magnetic field become larger by lining up the fields of neighboring domains. Second, domains that are not pointing in the same direction as the magnetic field rotate toward the magnetic field. The result is that the majority of domains line up in the same direction. With its domains aligned, the material is a magnet.

The ability to make a magnet explains why an unmagnetized object, such as a paper clip, can be attracted to a magnet. Paper clips are made of steel, which is mostly iron. The magnet's field causes domains in the paper clip to line up slightly so that the clip becomes a magnet. Its north pole faces the south pole of the magnet. The paper clip can attract other paper clips for the same reason. After the magnet is removed, however, the domains of the paper clips return to their random arrangements. Thus the paper clips are no longer magnetic.

Some metals, such as the ordinary steel that paper clips are made of, are easy to magnetize but lose their magnetism quickly. Magnets made from these materials are called temporary magnets. Harder metals, such as other types of steel, are more difficult to magnetize but tend to stay magnetized. A magnet made of a material that keeps its magnetism is called a **permanent magnet.**

☑ *Checkpoint How does a magnet attract another object?*

TRY THIS

How Attractive!

You can use iron filings to find out how materials become magnetic.

ACTIVITY

1. Fill a clear plastic tube about two-thirds full with iron filings. Seal the tube.
2. Observe the arrangement of the filings.
3. Rub the tube lengthwise about 30 times in the same direction with one end of a strong magnet.
4. Again observe the arrangement of the filings.

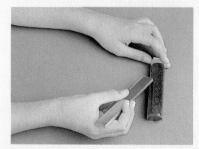

Making Models How do the iron filings in the tube model magnetic domains?

618

Destroying Magnets

Just as paper clips lose their magnetism when their domains become randomly arranged, a permanent magnet can also become unmagnetized. One way is to drop it or strike it hard. If a magnet is hit hard, its domains can be knocked out of alignment. Heating a magnet will also destroy its magnetism. When an object is heated, its particles vibrate faster and more randomly. This makes it more difficult for all the domains to stay lined up. In fact, above a certain temperature a material loses the property of ferromagnetism. The temperature depends on the material.

Breaking Magnets

Now that you know about domains, you can understand why breaking a magnet in half does not result in two pieces that are individual poles. Within the original bar magnet shown in Figure 9, there are many north and south poles facing each other. These poles balance each other.

At the ends of the magnet, there are many poles that are not facing an opposite pole. This produces strong magnetic effects at the north and south poles. If the magnet is cut in half, the domains will still be lined up in the same way. So the shorter pieces will still have strong ends made up of many north or south poles. Figure 9 shows the results of dividing a magnet into four pieces.

Figure 9 No matter how many times a magnet is cut in half, each piece retains its magnetic properties.

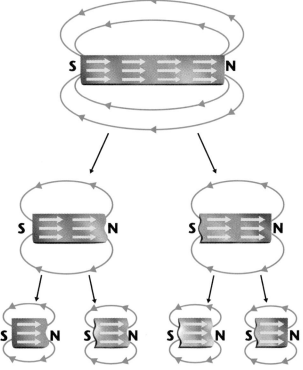

Section 1 Review

1. What happens if you bring together two like poles? Two unlike poles?
2. How are magnetic domains arranged in a magnet? How are they arranged in an unmagnetized object?
3. What parts of an atom produce magnetism?
4. How is a magnet made?
5. **Thinking Critically Applying Concepts** Iron filings align with the magnetic field of a bar magnet. What must be happening to the domains in the iron filings in the magnetic field?

Check Your Progress

CHAPTER PROJECT

Gather materials for the different parts of your fishing rod. Consider such items as a broom handle, dowel, or meter stick for the rod. You'll also need a string. Draw a basic design for your fishing rod. Make a model of the rod with a permanent magnet. Test how easily you can maneuver your model.

SECTION 2 Magnetic Earth

DISCOVER

Can You Use a Needle to Make a Compass?

1. Magnetize a large needle by rubbing it several times in the same direction with one end of a strong bar magnet. Push the needle through a ball of foam or tape it to a small piece of cork.

2. Place a drop of dishwashing soap in a dish of water. Then float the foam or cork in the water. Adjust the needle until it floats horizontally.

3. Allow the needle to stop moving. Which way does it point?

4. Use a local map to determine the direction in which it points.

Think It Over

Observing In what direction did the needle point? Will it always point in the same direction? What does this tell you about Earth?

GUIDE FOR READING

◆ What are the magnetic properties of Earth?

◆ What are the effects of Earth's magnetic field?

Reading Tip As you read, make a table that compares the magnetic fields of Earth and a bar magnet.

When Christopher Columbus sighted land in 1492, he didn't really know what he had found. He was trying to find a shortcut from Europe to India. Where he landed, however, was on an island in the Caribbean Sea just south of the present-day United States. He had no idea that such an island even existed.

In spite of his error, Columbus had successfully followed a course west to the Americas without the help of an accurate map. Instead, Columbus used a compass for navigation. A **compass** is a device that has a magnetized needle that can spin freely. The compass needle usually points north, and as you read you'll find out why.

Figure 10 In 1492, Columbus set sail across the Atlantic Ocean. He and his crews navigated using compasses like these.

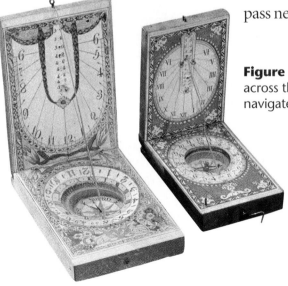
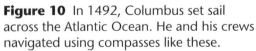

Figure 11 William Gilbert demonstrates his research to Queen Elizabeth I.

Earth As a Magnet

In the late 1500s, the English physician Sir William Gilbert became interested in compasses. He spoke with several navigators and experimented with his own compass. Gilbert confirmed that a compass always points in the same direction, no matter where you are. But no one knew why.

Gilbert suggested that a compass behaves as it does because Earth acts as a giant magnet. Although many educated people of his time laughed at this idea, Gilbert turned out to be correct. **Earth has an immense magnetic field surrounding it, just as there is a magnetic field around a bar magnet.**

Gilbert believed that the center of Earth contains magnetic rock. Scientists now believe that this is not the case, since Earth's core is too hot for the rock to be solid. Earth's magnetism is still not completely understood. Scientists do know that it is due to the circulation of molten metal (iron and nickel) within Earth's core.

The fact that Earth has a magnetic field explains why a compass works as it does. The poles of the magnetized needle on the compass align themselves with Earth's magnetic field.

✓ Checkpoint *What was Gilbert's new idea about Earth?*

Magnetic Declination

Earth's magnetic poles are not the same as the geographic poles. For example, the magnetic north pole (in northern Canada) is about 1,250 kilometers from the geographic north pole. The geographic north pole is sometimes called true north. The magnetic south pole is located near the coast of Antarctica.

Sharpen your Skills

Measuring *ACTIVITY*

1. Use a local map to locate geographic north relative to your school. Mark the direction on the floor with tape or chalk.

2. Use a compass to find magnetic north. Again mark the direction.

3. Use a protractor to measure the number of degrees between the two marks.

Compare the directions of magnetic and geographic north. Is magnetic north to the east or west of geographic north?

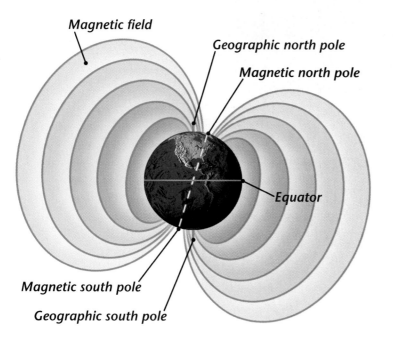

Magnetic field

Geographic north pole

Magnetic north pole

Equator

Magnetic south pole

Geographic south pole

Figure 12 The magnetic poles are not located exactly at the geographic poles.

You can see the difference between the magnetic and geographic poles more clearly by imagining lines that connect each set of poles together. Figure 12 shows that the line connecting Earth's magnetic poles is tipped slightly from Earth's axis—the imaginary line around which Earth rotates.

If you use a compass you have to account for the fact that the geographic and magnetic poles are different. Suppose you could draw a line between you and the geographic north pole. The direction of this line is geographic north. Then imagine a second line between you and the magnetic pole. The angle between these two lines is the angle between geographic north and the north to which a compass needle points. This angle is known as **magnetic declination.**

Magnetic declination differs depending on where you are. Figure 13 shows magnetic declination in various locations in the United States. In North Carolina, for example, a hiker must head about 8 degrees east of the compass reading to get to a place that

Figure 13 Magnetic declination varies with location.
Interpreting Maps *What is the magnetic declination where you live?*

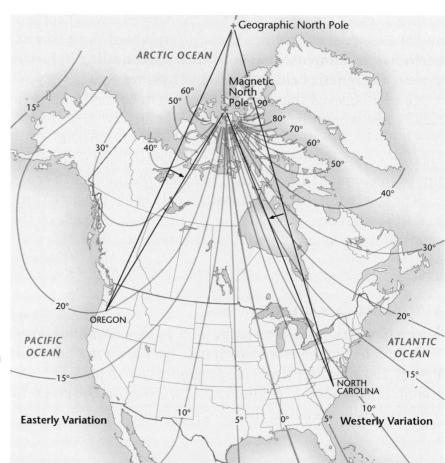

Geographic North Pole

ARCTIC OCEAN

Magnetic North Pole

15°

60°
50°

90°

80°
70°
60°

30°

40°

50°

40°

20°

30°

OREGON

PACIFIC OCEAN

ATLANTIC OCEAN

20°

15°

15°

NORTH CAROLINA

Easterly Variation

10°

5°

0°

10°

5°

Westerly Variation

624

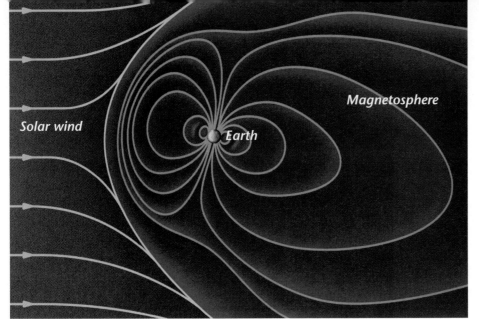

Figure 14 Earth's magnetic field differs from that of a bar magnet due to the solar wind. The solar wind causes the magnetic field to stretch out on the side of Earth experiencing night.

is directly north on a map. A hiker in Oregon would have to head about 20 degrees west of the compass reading.

Magnetic declination changes over time because the magnetic poles move slowly. Between 1580 and 1820, for example, the direction of magnetic north in London changed by 35 degrees.

☑ *Checkpoint* *What is magnetic declination?*

The Magnetosphere

Earth's magnetic field extends into space, which contains electrically charged particles. **Earth's magnetic field affects the movements of electrically charged particles in space. Charged particles also affect Earth's magnetic field.**

Between 1,000 and 25,000 kilometers above Earth's surface are two doughnut-shaped regions called the **Van Allen belts.** They are named after their discoverer, J. A. Van Allen. These regions contain electrons and protons traveling at very high speeds. At one time it was feared the particles would be dangerous for spacecraft passing through them, but this has not been the case.

Other electrically charged particles in space come from the sun. Earth and the other planets experience a solar wind. The **solar wind** is a stream of electrically charged particles flowing at high speeds from the sun. The solar wind pushes against Earth's magnetic field, and surrounds the field, as shown in Figure 14. The region of Earth's magnetic field shaped by the solar wind is called the **magnetosphere.** The solar wind constantly reshapes the magnetosphere as Earth rotates on its axis.

Although most particles in the solar wind cannot penetrate Earth's magnetic field, some particles do. They follow the lines of Earth's magnetic field to the magnetic poles. At the poles the magnetic field lines dip down to Earth's surface.

Spinning in Circles

Which way will a compass point? **ACTIVITY**

1. Place a bar magnet in the center of a sheet of paper.
2. Place a compass about 2 cm beyond the north pole of the magnet. Draw a small arrow showing the direction of the compass needle.
3. Repeat Step 2 at 20 to 30 different positions around the magnet.
4. Remove the magnet and observe the pattern of arrows you drew.

Drawing Conclusions What does your pattern of arrows represent? Do compasses respond only to Earth's magnetic field?

Figure 15 A band of colors called an aurora appears in the sky near the magnetic poles. *Relating Cause and Effect What causes an aurora?*

Language Arts
CONNECTION

From ancient times, people have sought to explain what they observe in nature. Imagine trying to explain the auroras without knowing that Earth is magnetic.

The Fox people in Wisconsin feared that the aurora was made up of the ghosts of their dead enemies.

A common belief among Eskimos in the Hudson Bay area of North America is that the aurora can be attracted by whistling to it. A hand clap will cause it to move away.

In Your Journal

Imagine that the aurora could really be attracted by whistling to it. Write a story about what might happen. Before you write the story, plan who the characters will be and what events will happen.

When charged particles get close to Earth's surface, they interact with atoms in the atmosphere. This causes the atoms to give off light. The result is one of Earth's most spectacular displays—a curtain of shimmering bright light in the atmosphere. A glowing region caused by charged particles from the sun is called an **aurora.** In the northern hemisphere, an aurora is called the Northern Lights, or aurora borealis. In the southern hemisphere, it is called the Southern Lights, or aurora australis.

Effects of Earth's Magnetic Field

You learned that a material such as iron can be made into a magnet by a strong magnetic field. **Since Earth produces a strong magnetic field, Earth itself can make magnets.**

Earth as a Magnet Maker Suppose you leave an iron bar lying in a north-south direction for many years. Earth's magnetic field can attract the domains strongly enough to cause them to line up in the same direction. (Recall that a strong magnetic field can cause the magnetic domains of a ferromagnetic material to increase in size or to line up in the same direction.) To speed the process, you could gently tap on the bar with a hammer. This vibrates the domains and they can then be aligned by the magnetic field.

What objects might be lying in Earth's magnetic field for many years? Consider metal objects or appliances that are left in the same position for many years, such as filing cabinets in your school. Even though no one has tried to make them into magnets, Earth might have done so anyway.

Earth Leaves a Record Earth's magnetic field also acts on rocks that contain magnetic material, such as rock on the ocean floor. The ocean floor is produced from molten material that seeps up through a long crack in the ocean floor, known as the mid-ocean ridge. When the rock is molten, the iron it contains lines up in the direction of Earth's magnetic field. As the rock cools and hardens, the iron is locked in place. This creates a permanent record of the magnetic field.

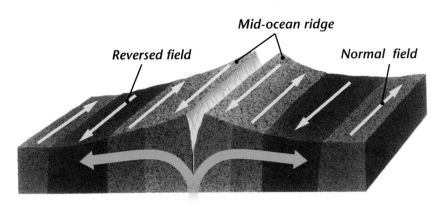

Figure 16 When volcanic lava on the ocean floor hardens into rock, the direction of Earth's magnetic field at that time is permanently recorded.

As scientists studied such rock, they discovered that the direction and strength of Earth's magnetic field has changed over time. Earth's magnetic field completely reversed itself 750,000 years ago.

The yellow arrows in Figure 16 indicate the direction of Earth's magnetic field. Notice that the patterns of bands on either side of the ridge are mirror images. This is because the sea floor spreads apart from the mid-ocean ridge. So rocks farther from the ridge are older than rocks near the ridge. The magnetic record in the rock depends on when the rock was formed.

You might be wondering why Earth's magnetic field changes direction. If so, you're not alone. Scientists have asked the same question. Earth's magnetic field arises from the motion of molten metal in Earth's core. Changes in the flow of that metal result in changes in Earth's magnetic field. But the details of this theory have not been worked out, and so scientists cannot explain why the flow changes. Maybe someday you will be able to shed light on this area.

Section 2 Review

1. How is Earth like a magnet?
2. Compare Earth's geographic poles with its magnetic poles.
3. How does a compass work?
4. What evidence of changes in Earth's magnetic field is found in rocks?
5. **Thinking Critically** **Developing Hypotheses** Some insects and birds have tiny particles of iron in parts of their body that are connected by nerves to their brain. What could be the function of the iron particles?

Science at Home

House Magnets Explore your home with a compass. Use the compass to discover objects that are magnetized. For example, test the top and bottom of the stove, refrigerator, or a metal filing cabinet. Try metal objects that have been in the same position over a long period of time. Explain why these objects attract or repel a compass needle.

Electric Current and Magnetic Fields

Are Magnetic Fields Limited to Magnets?

1. Obtain two wires with the insulation removed from both ends. Each wire should be 20 to 30 cm long.

2. Connect one end of each wire to a socket containing a small light bulb.

3. Connect the other end of one of those wires to a D cell.

4. Place 3 compasses near the wire at any 3 positions. Note the direction in which the compasses are pointing.

5. Center the wire over the compasses. Make sure the compass needles are free to turn.

6. Touch the free end of the remaining wire to the battery. Observe the compasses as current flows through the wire. Move the wire away from the battery, and then touch it to the battery again. Watch the compasses.

Think It Over

Inferring What happened to the compasses? What can you infer about electricity and magnetism?

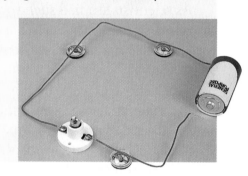

GUIDE FOR READING

◆ How is an electric current related to a magnetic field?

◆ How are conductors different from insulators?

◆ What are the characteristics of an electric circuit?

Reading Tip As you read, use the headings to make an outline.

I n 1820, the Danish scientist Hans Christian Oersted (ur sted) was teaching a class at the University of Copenhagen. During his lecture, he allowed electricity to flow through a wire, just as electricity flows through wires to your electrical appliances. When electricity flowed, he noticed that the needle of a compass near the wire changed direction.

Oersted's observations surprised him. He could have assumed that something was wrong with his equipment. Instead, he investigated further. He set up several compasses around a wire. Oersted discovered that whenever he turned on the electricity, the compass needles lined up in a circle around the wire.

Oersted's discovery showed that magnetism and electricity are related. But just how are they related? To find out, you must learn about electric current.

Electric Current

You learned in Section 1 that all matter contains particles called electrons and protons. Electrons and protons have a property called **electric charge.** Electrons are negatively charged, and protons are positively charged.

◀ Oersted's demonstration

B. Compass needles align themselves with the magnetic field of a current moving upward (blue arrow).

C. Compass needles reverse their directions to align with the magnetic field of a current moving downward.

Figure 17 Current in a wire affects a compass needle.
A. With no current flowing, the compass needles all point to magnetic north.

When electric charges flow through a wire or similar material, they create an electric current. **Electric current** is the flow of charge through a material. The amount of charge that passes through the wire in a unit of time is the rate at which electric current flows. The unit of current is the ampere (amp or A), named for André-Marie Ampère. You will often see the name of the unit shortened to "amp." The number of amps tells the amount of charge flowing past a given point each second.

What does all of this have to do with magnetism? **An electric current produces a magnetic field.** The lines of the magnetic field produced by a current in a straight wire are in the shape of circles with the wire at their center. You can see in Figure 17 that compasses placed around a wire line up with the magnetic field. The iron filings in Figure 18 map out the same field. The direction of the current determines the direction of the magnetic field. If the current is reversed, the magnetic field reverses as well. You can see this from the compasses in Figure 17C.

Moving Charge and Magnetism

Ampère carried out many experiments with electricity and magnetism. He hypothesized that all magnetism is a result of circulating charges. Atoms, for example, can become magnets because of the motion of the electrons. Based on modern knowledge of magnetism, Ampère's hypothesis is correct. All magnetism is caused by the movement of charges.

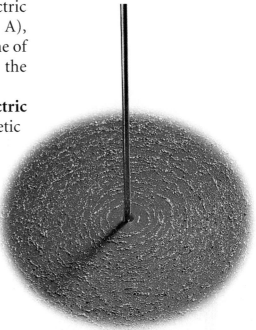

Figure 18 Iron filings show the field lines around a wire that carries a current.
Observing What is the shape of the field lines?

✓ *Checkpoint* *What particles have electric charge?*

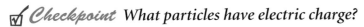

Electric Circuits

An electric current will not flow automatically through every wire. Current flows only through electric circuits. An **electric circuit** is a complete path through which electric charges can flow. All electrical devices, from toasters to radios to electric guitars and televisions, contain electric circuits.

All circuits have the same basic features. **First, a circuit has a source of electrical energy.** Energy is the ability to do work. **Second, circuits have devices that are run by electrical energy.** A radio, a computer, a light bulb, and a refrigerator are all devices that convert electrical energy into another form of energy. A light bulb, for example, converts electrical energy to electromagnetic energy (it gives off light) and thermal energy (it gives off heat).

Third, electric circuits are connected by conducting wires and a switch. In order to describe a circuit, you can draw a circuit diagram. *Exploring Electric Circuits* on the next page shows a circuit diagram along with the symbols that represent the parts of the circuit. As you read, identify the parts of a circuit and their symbols.

Conductors and Insulators

Electric current flows through metal wires. Will it also flow through plastic or paper? The answer is no. Electric current does not flow through every material.

Electric currents move freely through materials called conductors. Metals, such as copper, silver, iron, and aluminum, are good conductors. **In a conductor, some of the electrons are only loosely bound to their atoms.** These electrons, called conduction electrons, are able to move throughout the conductor. As these electrons flow through a conductor, they form an electric current.

Did you ever wonder why a light goes on the instant you flip the switch? How do the electrons get to your lamp from the electric company so fast? The answer is that electrons are not created and sent to you when you flip a switch. They are present all along in the conductors that make up the circuit. When you flip the switch, conduction electrons at one end of the wire are pulled while those at the other end are pushed. The result is a continuous flow of electrons as soon as the circuit is completed.

Insulators are a different kind of material in which charges are not able to move freely. **The electrons in an insulator are bound tightly to their atoms and do not flow easily.** Examples of insulators are rubber, glass, sand, plastic, and wood.

☑ *Checkpoint* *What moves freely in a conductor?*

Figure 19 Charges behave like the chairs on a ski lift. Charges in all parts of a conducting wire begin to flow at the same time.

EXPLORING *Electric Circuits*

Electric circuits are all around you. They are so common that you probably don't think about them. An electric circuit has several basic features.

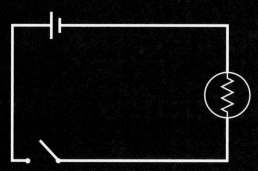

This circuit diagram represents the circuit shown in the photograph. Special symbols are used for the parts of the circuit.

Circuit Symbols

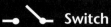 Switch

 Energy source

 Resistor

Battery
A source of electrical energy makes charges move around a circuit.

Resistor
A device such as a light bulb, appliance, or computer converts electrical energy to another form. Such a device is called a resistor.

Switch
A switch is used to open and close the circuit. When the switch is closed, the electric circuit is complete. When the switch is open, the circuit is broken. Charges cannot flow through a broken path.

Real-World Lab

BUILD A FLASHLIGHT

Imagine that you are camping in a forest. You hear noises outside your tent; something is rustling and bumping around nearby. At this moment, there is one device you might *really* appreciate having— a flashlight. Have you ever examined one to determine how it works?

Problem

How can you build a flashlight that works?

Skills Focus

making models, observing, inferring

Materials

one cardboard tube	one D cell
flashlight bulb	aluminum foil
paper cup	duct tape
scissors	

2 lengths of wire, about 10 cm, with the insulation stripped off about 2 cm at each end

1 length of wire, 15–20 cm, with the insulation stripped off each end

Procedure

1. Check that the D cell fits inside the cardboard tube. Make two holes in the side of the tube about 2–3 cm apart. The holes should be near the middle of the tube.

2. Use duct tape to connect a 10-cm wire to each terminal of the battery. Touch the other ends of the wires to a flashlight bulb in order to find where to connect them. (*Hint:* Most bulbs have a bottom contact and a side contact. If there is no obvious side contact, try touching the metal on the side of the base.)

3. Line a paper cup with aluminum foil. Use a pencil to poke a hole in the bottom of the paper cup. The hole should be slightly smaller than the bulb, but large enough to allow the base of the bulb through.

4. Insert the base of the light bulb through the hole. Be sure the bulb fits securely.

5. Pass the long wire through one of the holes in the tube. Tape it to the inside of the tube, leaving about 2 cm outside the tube. The other end should reach the end of the tube.

6. Place the battery in the tube. Pass the wire attached to the bottom of the battery through the other hole in the tube. (Make sure the two wires outside the tube can touch.)

7. Make a sling from duct tape to hold the battery inside the tube.

CHAPTE

The Nature of Magnetis

Key Ideas

◆ Unlike magnetic poles attract; like ma
poles repel.

◆ A magnetic field is a region around a
which magnetic attraction acts.

◆ Magnetic domains are regions in whic
magnetic fields of atoms are aligned.

◆ In a magnetized material, most of its
are lined up in the same direction.

Key Terms

magnetism
magnetic pole
magnetic field
magnetic field lines

magnetic domai
ferromagnetic m
permanent magr

Magnetic Earth

INTEGRATING EARTH

Key Ideas

◆ Earth has a north magnetic pole and a
magnetic pole.

◆ A compass can be used to find direction
its needle lines up with Earth's magnet

◆ Earth's magnetic poles are not at exactl
same locations as the geographic poles.

◆ The magnetosphere is the magnetic fiel
Earth as shaped by the solar wind.

Key Terms

compass
magnetic declination
Van Allen belts

solar wind
magnetosphere
aurora

8. Attach the wires from the end of the tube to the contact points on the bulb.

9. Tape the cup on top of the tube, keeping all connections tight.

10. Touch the two free ends of the wires together to see if the bulb lights. If it doesn't, check to be sure all connections are taped together securely.

Analyze and Conclude

1. What is the purpose of lining the cup with aluminum foil?

2. Does it matter which way the battery is placed in the tube? Explain.

3. Why does the bulb have to be connected at two points in order for it to light?

4. How could you make your flashlight brighter? How could you make it more rugged?

5. Compare your flashlight to a manufactured one. Explain the differences.

6. **Apply** Design a more convenient switch for your flashlight. You may want to use materials such as paper clips, brass fasteners, or aluminum foil. Have your teacher approve your switch design and then build and test the switch.

Getting Involved

People use different types of flashlights for different purposes. Some are narrow and flexible while others are wide and sturdy. Compare several different flashlights. Describe the flashlights. Note the type and number of batteries required, the type of switch used, and any other features that you observe. Suggest useful applications for each flashlight. Then design a new flashlight based on a need that you observe.

Figure 25 A magnified photograph shows a pattern of magnetic domains on a cassette tape.

Audiotape

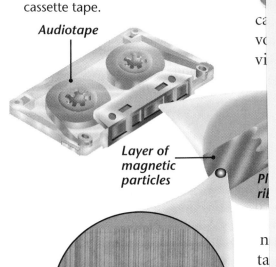

Layer of magnetic particles

Magnified photograph of tape

Section 4 Rev

1. Describe an electromagnet in your own words.
2. How is an electromagnet different from permanent magnet?
3. What are some uses for electromagne
4. **Thinking Critically Predicting** W bringing a strong magnet near a comp disk or videotape cause damage to th recorded information? Explain.

638

Reviewing Content

For more review of key concepts, see the Interactive Student Tutorial CD-ROM.

Multiple Choice
Choose the letter of the answer that best completes each statement.

1. The region in which magnetic forces act is called a
   a. line of force.   b. pole.
   c. magnetic field.   d. field of attraction.
2. An example of a ferromagnetic material is
   a. plastic.   b. wood.
   c. copper.   d. iron.
3. The person who first suggested that Earth behaves as a magnet was
   a. Ampère.
   b. Oersted.
   c. Gilbert.
   d. Columbus.
4. The region in which Earth's magnetic field is found is called the
   a. atmosphere.
   b. stratosphere.
   c. aurora.
   d. magnetosphere.
5. A coil of current-carrying wire with an iron core is called a(an)
   a. ferromagnet.
   b. electromagnet.
   c. compass.
   d. maglev.

True or False
If the statement is true, write true. If it is false, change the underlined word or words to make the statement true.

6. Like poles of magnets <u>repel</u> each other.
7. The type of magnetic mineral found in nature is called <u>platinum</u>.
8. A compass needle points in the direction of Earth's <u>geographic</u> north pole.
9. An electric circuit is a complete path through which <u>domains</u> can flow.
10. You can <u>increase</u> the strength of an electromagnet by adding more turns of a wire to it.

Checking Concepts

11. Explain why you are not left with one north pole and one south pole if you break a magnet in half. Draw a diagram to support your answer.
12. How does a material become a magnet?
13. How does Earth act like a magnet?
14. What is an aurora? How is it produced?
15. Why does a compass needle change direction when it is placed near a current-carrying wire?
16. Draw a simple electric circuit. Label and define the basic parts.
17. How is a conductor different from an insulator? Give two examples of each.
18. **Writing to Learn** Did you ever think of a chore that would be much easier if you only had some futuristic device? Here's your chance. Describe a task that you would like to make easier. Then think about how you could use an electromagnet to carry out the task. Be creative in describing your design.

Thinking Critically

19. **Problem Solving** Cassia borrowed her brother's magnet. When she returned it, it was barely magnetic. What might Cassia have done to the magnet?
20. **Comparing and Contrasting** What is the difference between a magnetized iron bar and an unmagnetized one?
21. **Drawing Conclusions** Why might an inexperienced explorer get lost using a compass?
22. **Inferring** A compass points north until a bar magnet is brought next to it. The compass needle is then attracted or repelled by the magnet. What inference can you make about the strengths of the magnetic fields of Earth and the bar magnet?
23. **Relating Cause and Effect** Why does opening a switch in an electric circuit stop the flow of current?
24. **Applying Concepts** How are the uses of an electromagnet different from those of a permanent bar magnet?

640

Applying Skills

Use the illustration of four electromagnets to answer Questions 25–27.

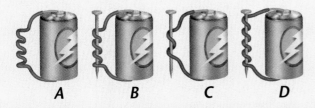

A   B   C   D

25. **Predicting** Will device A or B produce a stronger magnetic field? Will device B or C produce a stronger magnetic field? Explain your choices.

26. **Controling Variables** Can you tell which electromagnet is the strongest of the four? Explain why or why not.

27. **Designing Experiments** Without changing the number of turns of wire, how could you change the strength of each electromagnet?

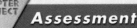

Performance · Assessment

Present Your Project Test your final electromagnet. Cut the tops off two empty plastic milk containers. Practice moving paper clips from one container to the other until you are ready for a "fishing" competition. After your teacher gives you a one-minute opportunity to fish, compare the most successful designs in the class.

Reflect and Record In your journal, describe the features of other students' designs that worked well. Which switch designs were easiest to operate? What contributed to making the strongest magnets?

Test Preparation

Use these questions to prepare for standardized tests.

Read the passage. Then answer Questions 28–30.

Substances can be classified according to their ability to conduct electric charges. Those that conduct charges well are conductors, and those that do not are insulators.

Whether a substance is classified as a conductor or an insulator depends on how tightly the electrons are bound to the atoms of the substance. Outer electrons of the atoms in a metal, for example, are not anchored to the nuclei of particular atoms. Instead, they are free to roam in the material. This makes metals good conductors. The electrons in other materials, such as rubber, plastic, and glass, are tightly bound and remain with particular atoms. These materials are insulators.

28. What is this passage mostly about?
    a. how electric current flows through materials
    b. the characteristics of conductors and insulators
    c. the difference between atoms and electrons
    d. how atoms move in different materials

29. Conductors are different from insulators in that they
    a. have electrons that are free to move within the material.
    b. contain more electrons.
    c. contain more atoms.
    d. are missing some electrons.

30. Based on the passage, which substance do you think might be used to cover electrical wires in a building?
    a. steel   b. copper
    c. plastic   d. aluminum

WEB ACTIVITY www.phschool.com

SECTION 1 Electric Charge and Static Electricity

Discover **Can You Make a Can Move Without Touching It?**
Sharpen Your Skills **Drawing Conclusions**
Try This **Sparks Are Flying**
Science at Home **Standing on End**
Skills Lab **The Versorium**

SECTION 2 Circuit Measurements

Discover **How Can Current Be Measured?**
Try This **Down the Tubes**
Sharpen Your Skills **Calculating**
Real-World Lab **Constructing a Dimmer Switch**

SECTION 3 Series and Parallel Circuits

Discover **Do the Lights Keep Shining?**
Sharpen Your Skills **Predicting**

Cause for Alarm

Airplane pilots rely on instruments to tell them about all parts of an airplane. The instruments are connected to the rest of the airplane by electric circuits. In this chapter, you will learn about electric charges and how they are involved in static electricity and current electricity. You will also learn about types of current and types of circuits, and how to use electricity safely.

As you work on this chapter project, you will choose an event, such as the opening or closing of a door or window, and design a circuit that alerts you when the event happens.

Your Goal To construct an alarm circuit that will light a bulb in response to some event.

Your circuit must
◆ be powered by one or two D cells
◆ have a switch that detects your chosen event
◆ turn on a light when the switch is closed
◆ follow the safety guidelines in Appendix A

Get Started How can you design a switch that detects some event? Brainstorm with your classmates about ways to make two pieces of a conductor come in contact. Make a list of the different ideas your group comes up with.

Check Your Progress You'll be working on this project as you study this chapter. To keep your project on track, look for Check Your Progress boxes at the following points.
Section 2 Review, page 659: Design a detector switch to complete your circuit when the event happens.
Section 3 Review, page 665: Build an alarm circuit completed by your dectector switch.

Present Your Project At the end of this chapter (page 673), you'll demonstrate your alarm circuit.

Electric current lights the instruments in an airplane and also the runway ahead.

Integrating Health 🌐

SECTION 4

Electrical Safety

Discover **How Can You Blow a Fuse?**
Science at Home **Circuit Diagrams**

Electric Charge and Static Electricity

Can You Move a Can Without Touching It?

1. Place an empty aluminum can on its side on the floor.
2. Blow up a balloon. Then rub the balloon back and forth on your hair several times.
3. Hold the balloon about 3 to 4 centimeters away from the can.
4. Slowly move the balloon farther away from the can. Observe what happens.
5. Move the balloon to the other side of the can and observe what happens.

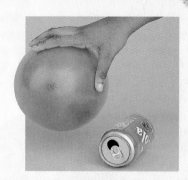

Think It Over

Inferring What happens to the can? What can you infer from your observation?

GUIDE FOR READING

◆ How do electric charges interact?
◆ How does static electricity differ from electric current?
◆ How are electrons transferred in static discharge?

Reading Tip Before you read, preview the headings and record them in outline form. Fill in details as you read.

You're in a hurry to get dressed for school, but you can't find one of your socks. You quickly head for the pile of clean laundry. You've gone through everything, but where's the sock? The dryer couldn't have really destroyed it, could it? Oh no, there it is. Your sister has found the sock stuck to one of her shirts. What makes clothes stick together? The explanation has to do with tiny electric charges.

Types of Electric Charge

The charged parts of atoms are electrons and protons. As you have learned, protons and electrons are charged particles. When two protons come close, they push one another apart. In other words, they repel each other. But if a proton and an electron come close, they attract one another.

Why do protons repel protons but attract electrons? The reason is that they have different types of charge. Protons and electrons have opposite charges. The charge on the proton is

Figure 1 The interaction of electric charges is making this girl's hair stand on end.

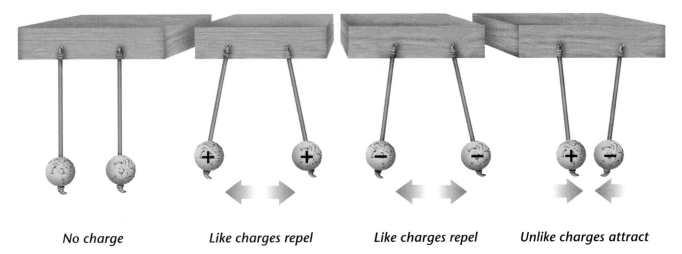

No charge   Like charges repel   Like charges repel   Unlike charges attract

Figure 2 Charged objects exert forces on each other. They can either attract or repel.
Interpreting Diagrams What is the rule for the interaction of electric charges?

called positive (+), and the charge on the electron is called negative (−). The names positive and negative were given to charges by Benjamin Franklin in the 1700s. They have been used by scientists ever since.

Interactions Between Charges

The two types of charge interact in specific ways. **Charges that are the same repel each other. Charges that are different attract each other.**

Does this sound familiar to you? This rule is the same as the rule for interactions between magnetic poles. Recall that magnetic poles that are alike repel each other and magnetic poles that are different attract each other.

There is one important thing about electric charges that is different from magnetic poles. Recall that magnetic poles do not exist alone. Whenever there is a south pole, there is always a north pole. Electric charges can exist alone. In other words, a negative charge can exist without a positive charge.

✓ *Checkpoint* How are the interactions between electric charges similar to the interactions between magnetic poles?

Electric Fields

Just as magnetic poles exert their forces over a distance, so do electric charges. An electric charge exerts a force through the **electric field** that surrounds the charge. An electric field extends outward from every charged particle.

When a charged particle is placed in the electric field of another charged particle, it is either pushed or pulled. It is pushed away if the two charges are the same. It is pulled toward the other charge if the two charges are different.

Drawing Conclusions

ACTIVITY

1. Tear tissue paper into small pieces, or cut circles out of it with a hole punch.

2. Run a plastic comb through your hair several times.

3. Place the comb close to, but not touching, the tissue paper pieces. What do you observe?

What can you conclude about the electric charges on the comb and the tissue paper?

Electric Fields Around Single Charges You will recall using magnetic field lines to picture a magnetic field in an earlier chapter. In a similar way, you can use electric field lines to visualize the electric field. Electric field lines are drawn with arrows to show the direction of the force on a positive charge.

The electric fields in Figure 3A are strongest where the lines are closest together. You can see that the strength of the electric field is greatest near the charged particle. The field decreases as you move away from the charge.

Electric Fields Around Multiple Charges When there are two or more charges, the resulting electric field is altered. The electric fields due to the individual charges combine. Figure 3B shows the electric fields from two sets of charges.

☑ *Checkpoint* *Where is an electric field strongest?*

Static Charge

If matter consists of charged particles that produce electric fields, why aren't you attracted to or repelled by every object around you—your book, your desk, or your pen? The reason is that each atom has an equal number of protons and electrons. And the size, or magnitude, of the charge on an electron is the same as the size of the charge on a proton. So each positive charge is balanced by a negative charge. The charges cancel out and the object as a whole is neutral. As a result there is no overall electrical force.

Figure 3 Electric charges can attract or repel one another. **A.** The arrows show that a positive charge repels another positive charge. A negative charge attracts a positive charge. **B.** When two charged particles come near each other, the electric fields of both particles are altered.

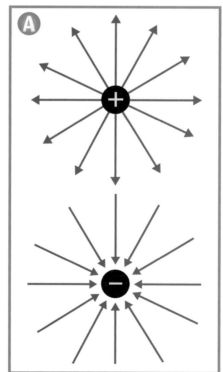

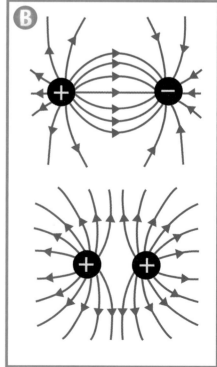

646

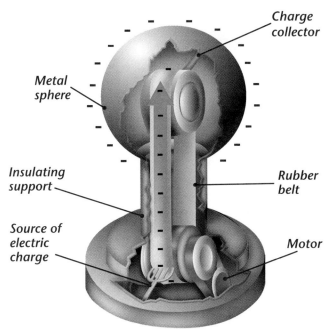

Charge collector

Metal sphere

Insulating support

Source of electric charge

Rubber belt

Motor

Figure 4 A Van de Graaff generator produces static electricity. Electrons are carried up a rubber belt and are transferred to the metal sphere. The charge built up on the sphere is enough to send a spark several meters through the air.

Charged Objects Protons are bound tightly in the center of an atom, but electrons can sometimes leave their atoms. Whether or not an electron will move depends on the material. Atoms in insulators, such as wood, rubber, plastic, and glass, hold their electrons tightly. Atoms in conductors, such as gold, silver, copper, and aluminum, hold some of their electrons loosely. These electrons move freely from atom to atom within the material.

A neutral object can become charged by gaining or losing electrons. If an object loses electrons, it is left with more protons (positive charge) than electrons (negative charge). Thus the object is positively charged overall. If, instead, an object gains electrons, it has more electrons than protons. Thus it has an overall negative charge.

The buildup of charges on an object is called **static electricity.** Static electricity behaves quite differently from electric currents. In an electric current, charges move continuously. **In static electricity, charges build up, but they do not flow.**

Transferring Charge Exactly how do charges build up? Charges must be transferred from one object to another. There are three methods by which charges are transferred: friction, conduction, and induction. Friction is the transfer of electrons from one object to another by rubbing. **Conduction** is the transfer of electrons from a charged object to another object by direct contact.

Sparks Are Flying

You can make your own lightning.

1. Cut a strip 3 cm wide from the middle of a foam plate. Fold the strip to form a T. Tape it to the center of an aluminum pie plate as a handle.

2. Rub a second foam plate on your hair. Put it upside down on a table.

3. Use the handle to pick up the pie plate. Hold the pie plate about 30 cm over the foam plate and drop it.

4. Now, very slowly, touch the tip of your finger to the pie plate. Be careful not to touch the foam plate. Then take your finger away.

5. Use the handle to pick up the pie plate again. Slowly touch the pie plate again.

Inferring What did you observe each time you touched the pie plate? How can you explain your observations?

Induction is the movement of electrons to one part of an object caused by the electric field of another object. The three methods of transferring charge are illustrated in *Exploring Static Electricity.*

Keep in mind that charges are not created or destroyed. If an object gives up electrons, another object gains those electrons. Electrons are only transferred from one location to another. This is known as the law of **conservation of charge.**

Static Cling Static electricity explains why clothes stick together in the clothes dryer. In a dryer, different fabrics rub together. Electrons from one fabric rub off onto another. In this way, the clothes become charged. A positively charged sock might then be attracted to a negatively charged shirt—the clothes stick together.

Your clothes are less likely to stick together if you use a fabric softener sheet. These sheets add a thin coating to your clothes as they bounce around in the dryer. The coating prevents electrons from rubbing off the clothing, so the clothes don't become charged.

Can you think of situations in which you might want to increase static electricity? Think about wrapping leftover food in plastic wrap. Plastic wrap picks up a charge when you unroll it. Since plastic is an insulator, the charge cannot easily move off it. So the wrap keeps its charge. When you place the plastic wrap on a container, it charges the edges of the container by induction. The force between the opposite charges on the wrap and the container causes the wrap to cling.

Static electricity allows you to make copies quickly. In a photocopier, a drum is given a negative static charge that is the image of the page to be copied. This charged image picks up positively charged particles of a very fine black powder. The drum then rolls against a negatively charged piece of paper, and the powder is transferred to the paper. Finally, the paper is heated to melt the powder, and the powder sticks to the paper.

☑ *Checkpoint* *What is the law of conservation of charge?*

Static Discharge

An object that gains a static charge doesn't hold the charge forever. Electrons tend to move, returning the object to its neutral condition. **When a negatively charged object and a positively charged object are brought together, electrons move until both objects have the same charge.** The loss of static electricity as electric charges move off an object is called **static discharge.**

Humidity If you rub a balloon on your clothing and then hold it next to a wall, it should stick. But the balloon may not always stick. Why is that? The answer could have to do with the weather.

EXPLORING *Static Electricity*

Static electricity involves the transfer of electrons from one object to another. Electrons are transferred by friction, conduction, or induction.

CHARGING BY FRICTION

When you rub two objects together, electrons move from one object to the other. This is known as charging by friction.

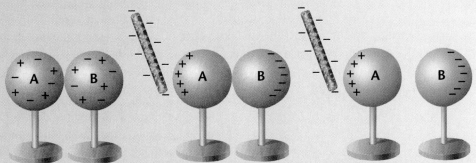

CHARGING BY CONDUCTION

When the charged rod or cloth touches the sphere, electrons are transferred by direct contact. This is known as conduction.

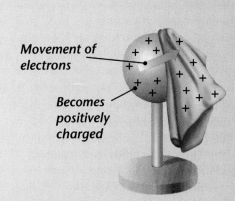

Movement of electrons

Becomes negatively charged

Movement of electrons

Becomes positively charged

CHARGING BY INDUCTION

During induction, charges within the spheres are rearranged without direct contact with the charged rod.

Neutral charge

Negative charges in the rod repel negative charges in the spheres.

When the spheres are separated, each one is charged.

Removing the charged rod leaves two charged spheres.

On a humid day, the air is filled with water molecules. Extra electrons on an object are carried off by molecules of water in the air. Thus the charges do not have a chance to build up on objects such as the balloon.

Sparks and Lightning Have you ever felt a shock from touching a doorknob after walking across a carpet? That shock is the result of static discharge. For example, as you walk across the carpet, electrons may rub off the soles of your shoes. This gives you a slight positive charge. When you touch the doorknob, electrons jump from the doorknob to your finger, making you neutral again.

Lightning is a dramatic example of static discharge. Lightning is basically a huge spark. During thunderstorms, air swirls violently. Water droplets within the clouds become electrically charged. Notice in Figure 5 that electrons collect in the lower parts of the cloud. To restore a neutral condition, electrons move from areas of negative charge to areas of positive charge. As electrons jump, they produce an intense spark. You see that spark as lightning.

Much of the lightning in a storm occurs between different regions of a cloud or between different clouds. But some lightning reaches Earth. This is because the cloud causes the surface of Earth to become charged by induction, as shown in Figure 5. Negative charges on the bottom of a cloud repel electrons, leaving the surface of Earth with a positive charge. If the charge buildup is sufficient, a huge spark of lightning is produced. The spark jumps between the cloud and Earth's surface or tall objects on the surface, such as trees or buildings.

✓ *Checkpoint* *How can you get a shock from a doorknob?*

Figure 5 Lightning is a spectacular discharge of static electricity. Lightning can occur within a cloud, between two clouds, or between a cloud and Earth.

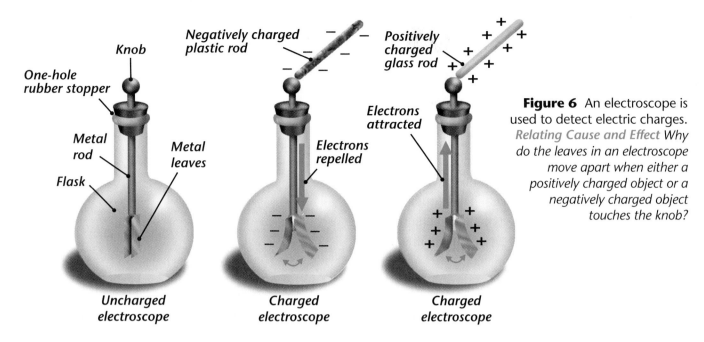

Knob

One-hole
rubber stopper

Metal
rod

Flask

Metal
leaves

*Uncharged
electroscope*

Negatively charged
plastic rod

Electrons
repelled

*Charged
electroscope*

Positively
charged
glass rod

Electrons
attracted

*Charged
electroscope*

Figure 6 An electroscope is
used to detect electric charges.
*Relating Cause and Effect Why
do the leaves in an electroscope
move apart when either a
positively charged object or a
negatively charged object
touches the knob?*

Detecting Charge

Electric charge is invisible, but it can be detected by a special
instrument called an **electroscope.** A typical electroscope consists of a metal rod with a knob at the top. At the bottom of the
rod are two sheets, or leaves, of very thin metal (aluminum,
silver, or gold). When the electroscope is uncharged, the leaves
hang straight down.

When a charged object touches the metal knob, electric
charge travels along the rod and into or out of the leaves. The
leaves then have a net charge. Since the charge on both leaves is
the same, the leaves repel each other and spread apart.

The leaves of an electroscope move apart in response to
either negative charge or positive charge, so you cannot use an
electroscope to determine the type of charge. You can use an
electroscope only to detect the presence of charge.

Section 1 Review

1. How do particles with the same charge interact?
   How do particles with opposite charges interact?
2. What is static electricity?
3. What are the three ways by which static charge
   is produced?
4. How is static electricity discharged?
5. How does an electroscope detect charge?
6. **Thinking Critically Comparing and
   Contrasting** How are electric charges similar
   to magnetic poles? How are they different?

Science at Home

Standing on End Rub a balloon against
your hair and bring the balloon near one
of your arms. Then bring your other arm
near the front of a television screen that is
turned on. Ask a family member to explain
why the hairs on your arms are attracted to
the balloon and to the screen. Explain that
this is evidence that there is a static charge
on both the balloon and the screen.

THE VERSORIUM

You are going to build a device that was first described in 1600 by Sir William Gilbert. He called this device a *versorium,* which is a Latin word meaning "turnabout." As you construct a versorium, you will use the skill of developing hypotheses.

Problem

Why does a versorium turn?

Materials

foam cup	plastic foam plate	pencil
aluminum foil	wool fabric	paper
scissors		

Procedure

1. Cut a piece of aluminum foil approximately 3 cm by 10 cm.
2. Make a tent out of the foil strip by gently folding it in half in both directions.
3. Push a pencil up through the bottom of an inverted cup. **CAUTION:** *Avoid pushing the sharpened pencil against your skin.* Balance the center point of the foil tent on the point of the pencil as shown.
4. Make a copy of the data table.

5. What will happen if you bring a foam plate near the foil tent? Record your prediction in the data table.
6. What will happen if you rub the foam plate with a piece of wool fabric and then bring it near the foil tent? Record your prediction.
7. What will happen if you bring the rubbed wool near the foil tent? Again record your prediction.
8. Test your predictions and record your observations in the data table.
9. Develop a hypothesis to explain your observations. Be sure to use an "If . . . then . . ." statement.

DATA TABLE

	Unrubbed Foam Plate	Rubbed Foam Plate	Rubbed Wool Fabric
Aluminum tent: Prediction			
Aluminum tent: Observation			
Paper tent: Prediction			
Paper tent: Observation			

652

10. Use your hypothesis to predict how your observations would change if you used a piece of paper instead of the aluminum foil.

11. Design an experiment to test your hypothesis about the paper versorium. Record your predictions and observations.

Analyze and Conclude

1. At the beginning of the lab, is the foil negatively charged, positively charged, or neutral? Explain your answer.

2. What was the effect of rubbing the foam plate with the wool fabric?

3. Explain the behavior of the aluminum foil as the foam plate is brought near it. Explain the behavior as the wool fabric is brought near it.

4. After you bring the materials near it, is the foil negatively charged, positively charged, or neutral? Explain your answer.

5. How is the paper tent charged before and after you bring the objects near it? How do you know?

6. Explain the behavior of the paper versorium as the foam plate is brought near it, and as the wool fabric is brought near it.

7. Modify your hypothesis to account for the difference, if any, between the results for the foil versorium and the paper versorium.

8. Can you use a versorium to determine whether an object is positively or negatively charged? Explain.

9. Why should you avoid touching the foam plate or the wool fabric to your clothing or any other object while you are using it to test a versorium?

10. **Think About It** How useful was your hypothesis? Did your hypothesis lead to predictions of what you actually observed?

Design an Experiment

What other materials besides foam or wool might have an effect on the versorium? Think of other materials you could use to make the versorium tent. Make predictions, and test the materials to see if they respond in a fashion similar to the aluminum foil and paper tents.

DISCOVER ••••••••••••••••••••••••••••••••••••• **ACTIVITY**••••

How Can Current Be Measured?

1. Obtain four pieces of wire with the insulation removed from both ends. Each piece should be about 25 cm long.

2. Wrap one of the wires four times around the compass as shown. You may use tape to keep the wire in place.

3. Build a circuit using the remaining wire, wrapped compass, two bulbs, and a D cell as shown. Adjust the compass so that the wire is directly over the compass needle.

4. Make sure the compass is level. If it is not, place it on a lump of modeling clay, so that the needle swings freely.

5. Observe the compass needle as you complete the circuit. Record the number of degrees the needle turns.

6. Repeat the activity using only one bulb, and again with no bulb. Record the number of degrees the needle turns.

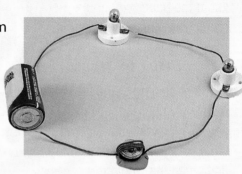

Think It Over

Inferring Based on your observations of the compass, when did the most current flow in your circuit? How can you explain your observations?

GUIDE FOR READING

◆ What causes electric current to flow?

◆ How does increasing voltage affect current?

◆ How does increasing resistance affect current?

Reading Tip Before you read, preview the boldfaced vocabulary terms. Write them down, leaving spaces between them for notes.

You're on a visit to a botanical garden. After a walk through the plush greenery, you rest by an artificial waterfall constructed in the middle of the garden. The continuous flow of water over the falls is soothing. You might be wondering what a waterfall could possibly have to do with electricity. Although there is an electric pump that keeps the water flowing, it is not the kind of pump that matters. The falling water itself, or any flowing liquid, is similar in some ways to the current in an electric circuit.

Electrical Potential

When water gets to the top of a waterfall it starts to fall down. When you lift something, you give it energy by doing work against the force of gravity. The type of energy that depends on position is called potential energy.

An object will move from a place of high potential energy to a place of low potential energy. The potential energy of the water is greater at the top of the waterfall than at the bottom. So water flows from the top to the bottom.

In a similar way, electrons in a circuit have potential energy. This potential energy, however, is related not to height but rather to the force exerted by electric fields. The potential energy per unit of electric charge is called **electrical potential.**

Voltage

Just as water flows downhill, electrons flow from places of higher potential to places of lower potential. The difference in electrical potential between two places is called the **potential difference.** It provides the force that pushes charge through a circuit. The unit of measure of potential difference is the volt (V). For this reason, potential difference is also called **voltage.** Electrons will flow as long as there is a potential difference, or voltage between two parts of a circuit.

Recall that the flow of electrons through a material is called electric current. Now you know what causes current to flow. **Voltage causes current to flow through an electric circuit.**

Figure 7 The diagram shows how a hidden pump feeds the waterfall in the photo. The movement of the water is similar to the current in an electric circuit.

Figure 8 As the difference in height between the two ends of the pipe increases, the flow of water increases. *Making Models How is the water pipe a model for voltage and current?*

Voltage Sources

What happens to the water when it gets to the bottom of the waterfall in the botanical garden? If nothing brings the water back to the top, the water flow will quickly stop. But this waterfall has a pump that pushes the water back up to the top. Once the water returns to the top, it can flow back down again. Another way to describe this process is to say that the pump maintains the potential difference between the top and bottom of the falls. As long as this difference exists, the water can continue to flow.

An electric circuit also requires a device to maintain a potential difference, or voltage. A **voltage source** creates a potential difference in an electric circuit. Batteries and generators are examples of voltage sources.

You will learn more about voltage sources in the next chapter. For now, all you need to know is that a voltage source has two terminals. The potential difference, or voltage, between the terminals causes charges to move around the circuit.

Some voltage sources are stronger than others. You can compare voltage to the downward slant of the pipe near the top of the waterfall. If a pipe is nearly level, the water just trickles out as shown in Figure 8. But if one end is much higher than the other, the rate of water flow is greater. The greater the difference in height, the greater the flow of water. **Just as an increase in the difference in height causes a greater flow of water, an increase in voltage causes a greater flow of electric current.**

Resistance

The amount of water that flows through a pipe in the waterfall depends on more than just the angle of the pipe. It also depends on the pipe through which the water travels. A long pipe will resist

Figure 9 Water flows more easily through a short, wide pipe than through a long, narrow pipe. Similarly, electrons flow more easily through wires that are short and thick.

the flow of water more than a short pipe. And a thin pipe will resist the flow of water more than a wide pipe. In addition, a clogged pipe will offer more resistance than a clean pipe.

Current Depends on Resistance In a similar way, the amount of current that flows in a circuit depends on more than just the voltage. Current also depends on the resistance offered by the material through which it travels. Recall that electrical resistance is the opposition to the flow of charge. **The greater the resistance, the less current there is for a given voltage.**

The resistance of a wire depends on the thickness and length of the wire. Long wires have more resistance than short wires. Thin wires have more resistance than thick wires. Resistance also depends on how well the material conducts current. Electrons are slowed down by interactions with atoms of the wire. Electrons flow freely through conductors, but not through insulators.

One more factor, temperature, affects electrical resistance. In Chapter 19 you learned that electrical resistance can decrease as temperature decreases. You can also say that as the temperature of most conductors increases, resistance increases as well.

Path of Least Resistance Perhaps you have heard it said that someone is taking the "path of least resistance." This means that the person is doing something the easiest way. In a similar way, if an electric current can travel through either of two paths, more current will travel through the one with the lower resistance.

Have you ever seen a flock of birds perched comfortably on high-voltage power lines? The reason the birds don't get hurt is that current flows through the path of least resistance. Since a bird's body offers more resistance than the wire, current continues to flow directly through the wire without harming the bird.

☑ *Checkpoint* *What two factors affect the flow of a current?*

Down the Tubes

Use water to make a model of an electric current.

1. Set up a funnel, tubing, beaker, and ring stand as shown.

2. Have a partner start a stopwatch as you pour 200 mL of water into the funnel. Be careful not to let it overflow.

3. Stop the stopwatch when all of the water has flowed into the beaker.

Making Models How did your model represent electric current, voltage, and resistance?

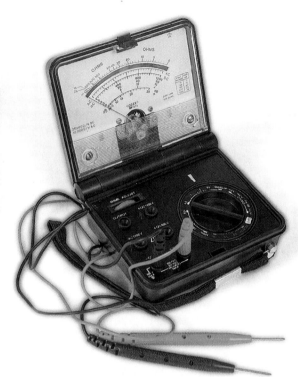

Figure 10 This multimeter can measure resistance, voltage, and small currents.

Ohm's Law

In the 1820s, the German physicist Georg Ohm experimented with many substances to study electrical resistance. He analyzed various types of wire in order to determine the characteristics that affect a wire's resistance. As a result of Ohm's valuable experiments, the unit of resistance is named the ohm (Ω).

How can you measure the resistance of a wire? In order to measure resistance, Ohm set up a voltage between two points on a conductor. He then measured the current produced. Potential difference, or voltage, is measured with a device called a **voltmeter.** Current, which has units of amps, is measured with a device called an **ammeter.** Voltmeters and ammeters are often combined into a single device like the one in Figure 10.

Ohm found that the resistance for most conductors does not depend on the voltage across them. A conductor or any other device that has a constant resistance regardless of the voltage is said to obey **Ohm's law.** Most of the conductors that you will learn about do obey Ohm's law.

Ohm's law states that the resistance is equal to the voltage divided by the current.

$$Resistance = \frac{Voltage}{Current} \quad or \quad Ohms = \frac{Volts}{Amps}$$

The letter R can be used to represent resistance, I to represent current, and V to represent voltage. This formula is shorter.

$$R = \frac{V}{I}$$

You can rearrange the resistance formula as follows.

$$I = \frac{V}{R} \quad or \quad V = IR$$

If any two of the values in these formulas are known, you can solve for the third value.

You can use the formulas to see how changes in resistance, voltage, and current are related. For example, what happens to current if voltage is doubled without changing the resistance? For a constant resistance, if voltage is doubled, current is doubled as well. Thus the greater the voltage, the greater the current.

What happens if, instead, you double the resistance without changing the voltage? If resistance is doubled, the current will be cut in half. So for a greater resistance, the current is less.

It is sometimes important to increase the resistance in a circuit in order to prevent too much current from flowing. Specially constructed resistors, some no larger than a grain of rice, are

An automobile headlight is connected to a 12-volt battery. If the resulting current is 0.40 amps, what is the resistance of the headlight?

Analyze.   You know the voltage and the current. You are looking for the resistance.

Write the formula. $R = \dfrac{V}{I}$

Substitute and solve. $R = \dfrac{12\ V}{0.40\ A} = 30\ \Omega$

Think about it.   The answer makes sense because you are dividing the voltage by a decimal number. The answer should be greater than either number in the fraction, which it is.

Practice Problems

1. In a circuit, 0.5 A is flowing through the bulb. The voltage across the bulb is 4.0 V. What is the bulb's resistance?
2. In order for a waffle iron to operate efficiently, a current of 12 A must flow through its coils. If the resistance is 10 Ω, what must the voltage be?

added to circuits. Televisions, radios, and other similar devices contain dozens of such resistors.

Some resistors do not obey Ohm's law. For instance, the resistance of a light bulb increases when the bulb is turned on and the filament heats up. A filament has the lowest resistance before it heats up, and so a cold filament conducts the most current. That is one reason a bulb might burn out the instant you switch it on.

Section 2 Review

1. What is voltage?
2. How is voltage related to electric current?
3. How is resistance related to electric current?
4. **Thinking Critically** **Calculating** You light a light bulb with a 1.5-volt battery. If the bulb has a resistance of 10 ohms, how much current is flowing?
5. **Thinking Critically** **Relating Cause and Effect** In order to increase the amount of current flowing in a circuit, should you increase the voltage or the resistance? Explain.

Check Your Progress

CHAPTER PROJECT

Pick the event that will close your switch, for example, the closing of a door. To make your switch, you might tape one of the free wires to a door and the other wire to the frame of the door. The wires will touch when the door closes. Here are some other ideas to explore: an object falling, a slight vibration or breeze, or a container filling with salt water. Draw a circuit diagram that includes a battery, a switch, and a light bulb.

Constructing a
Dimmer Switch

Most light switches turn a light bulb on and off. There doesn't seem to be any setting in between. Suppose you wanted to find a way to dim lights slowly. Think about how you would design a switch that controls the brightness of a bulb.

Skills Focus

observing, predicting, designing experiments

Problem

What materials can be used to make a dimmer switch?

▲ Engineer at a sound mixing board

Materials

flashlight bulb in a socket
D cell
thick lead from mechanical pencil
uninsulated copper wire, the same length as the pencil lead
rubber tubing, the same length as the pencil lead
1 wire 10–15 cm long
2 wires 20–30 cm long, with alligator clip attached to one end

Procedure

1. Construct the circuit shown in the photo. To begin, attach wires to the ends of the D cell.
2. Connect the other end of one of the wires to the bulb in a socket. Attach a wire with an alligator clip to the other side of the bulb.
3. Attach an alligator clip to the other wire.
4. The pencil lead will serve as a resistor that can be varied—a variable resistor. Attach one alligator clip firmly to the tip of the pencil lead. Be sure the clip makes good contact with the lead. (*Note:* Pencil "lead" is actually graphite, a form of the element carbon.)
5. Will the brightness of the bulb increase or decrease if you slide the other alligator clip back and forth along the lead? Test your prediction.
6. What will happen to the brightness of the bulb if you replace the lead with a piece of uninsulated copper wire? Adapt your pencil-lead investigation to test the copper wire.

7. Predict what will happen to the brightness of the bulb if you replace the pencil lead with a piece of rubber tubing. Adapt your pencil-lead investigation to test the rubber tubing.

Analyze and Conclude

1. What variable did you manipulate by sliding the alligator clip along the pencil lead in Step 5?
2. What happened to the brightness of the bulb when you slid the alligator clip along the pencil lead?
3. Explain your reasoning in making predictions about the brightness of the bulb in Steps 6 and 7. Were your predictions supported by your observations?
4. Do you think that pencil lead has more or less resistance than copper? Do you think it has more or less resistance than rubber? Use your observations to explain your answers.

5. Which material tested in this lab would make the best dimmer switch? Explain your answer.
6. **Apply** If you wanted to sell your dimmer switch to the owner of a movie theater, how would you describe your device and explain how it works?

More to Explore

The volume controls on some car radios and television sets also contain variable resistors, called rheostats. The sliding volume controls on a sound mixing board are rheostats, as well. Homes and theaters may use rheostats to adjust lighting. Where else in your house would variable resistors be useful? (*Hint:* Look for applications where the output is graduated rather than all or nothing.)

SECTION 3 Series and Parallel Circuits

DISCOVER .... ACTIVITY

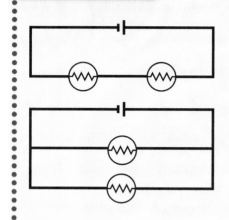

Do the Lights Keep Shining?

1. Construct both of the circuits shown using a battery, several insulated wires, and two light bulbs for each circuit.

2. Connect all wires and observe the light bulbs.

3. Now unscrew one bulb in each circuit. Observe the remaining bulbs.

Think It Over

Observing What happened to the remaining light bulbs when you unscrewed the first bulb? How can you account for your observations?

GUIDE FOR READING

◆ How many paths can current take in a series circuit?

◆ How does a parallel circuit differ from a series circuit?

Reading Tip As you read, create a table comparing series and parallel circuits.

It's a cool, clear night as you stroll by the harbor with your family. The night is dark, but the waterfront is bright thanks to the thousands of twinkling white lights that outline the tall ships. They make a striking view.

As you walk, you notice that a few of the lights are burned out. The rest of the lights, however, burn brightly. If one bulb is burned out, how can the rest of the lights continue to shine? The answer depends on how the electric circuit is designed. The parts of a circuit can be arranged in series or in parallel.

Figure 11 The lights that line the rigging of this ship are parts of a parallel circuit. If one goes out, the rest keep shining.

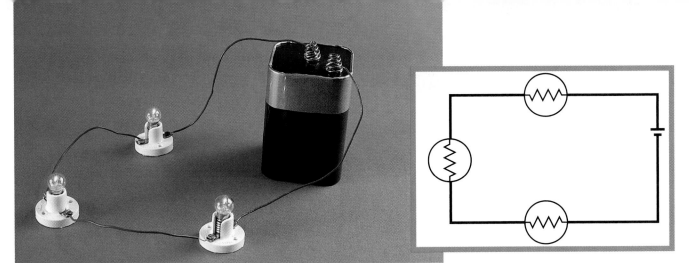

Figure 12 A series circuit provides only one path for the flow of electrons. *Applying Concepts* What will happen to the other bulbs if one bulb burns out?

Series Circuits

If all the parts of an electric circuit are connected one after another, the circuit is a **series circuit.** Figure 12 illustrates a series circuit. **In a series circuit, there is only one path for the current to take.** For example, a switch and the device it controls are connected in series with each other.

One Path A series circuit is very simple to design and build, but it has some disadvantages. What happens if a bulb in a series circuit burns out? A burned-out bulb is a break in the circuit, and there is no other path for the charges to take. So if one light goes out, all the lights go out.

Added Resistors Another disadvantage of a series circuit is that the light bulbs in the circuit become dimmer as more bulbs are added. Why does that happen? Think about what happens to the overall resistance of a series circuit as you add more bulbs. The resistance increases. Remember that if resistance increases, current decreases. So as light bulbs are added to a series circuit, the current decreases. The result is that the bulbs burn less brightly.

Ammeters Different meters are wired into circuits in different ways. Recall from the previous section that an ammeter is used to measure current. If you want to measure the current through some device in a circuit, the ammeter should be connected in series with the device.

✓ *Checkpoint* How does resistance change as you add bulbs to a series circuit?

Parallel Circuits

Could the lights on the ships have been connected in series? No—if the lights were part of a series circuit, all of the lights would have gone off when one burned out. What you saw, however, was that a few lights were burned out and the rest were brightly lit.

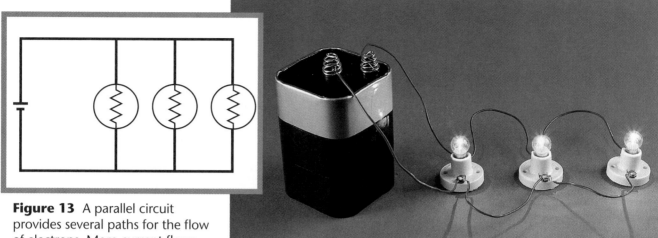

Figure 13 A parallel circuit provides several paths for the flow of electrons. More current flows, and the bulbs are brighter than in the series circuit.

The ships' lights were connected in parallel circuits. In a **parallel circuit,** the different parts of the circuit are on separate branches. Figure 13 shows a parallel circuit. **In a parallel circuit, there are several paths for current to take.** Notice that each bulb has its own path from one terminal of the battery to the other.

Several Paths What happens if a light burns out in a parallel circuit? If there is a break in one branch, current can still move through the other branches. So if one bulb goes out, the others remain lit. Switches can be placed along each branch so that individual bulbs can be turned on and off without affecting the others.

Added Branches What happens to the resistance of a parallel circuit when you add a branch? Although you might think that the overall resistance increases, it actually decreases. To understand this, consider the flow of water once again. Suppose water is being released from a reservoir held by a dam. If the water is allowed to flow through one pipe, a certain amount of water comes out. But if two pipes are used instead of one, twice as much water flows. The water will flow more easily because it has two paths to take. The same is true for a parallel circuit. As new paths, or branches, are added, the electric current has more paths to follow, and so total resistance decreases.

What does this tell you about current? If resistance decreases, the current must increase. The increased current travels along the new branch without affecting the original branches. So as you add branches to a parallel circuit, the brightness of the light bulbs does not change.

Voltmeters Recall from Section 2 that a voltmeter is used to measure voltage. When you measure the voltage across some device, the voltmeter and the device should be wired as parallel circuits.

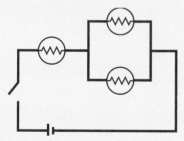

Figure 14 Parallel circuits are used in your home.
Interpreting Diagrams How many circuits does this house have?

Household Circuits

Would you want the circuits in your home to be series circuits? Of course you would not. With a series circuit, all the electrical devices in your home would go off every time a light bulb burned out or a switch was turned off. Instead, the circuits in your home are parallel circuits.

Electricity is fed into a home by heavy wires called lines. These lines have very low resistance. You can see in Figure 14 that parallel branches extend out from the lines to wall sockets, appliances, and lights in each room. The voltage in these household circuits is 120 volts. Switches are located in places where they can be used to control one branch of the circuit at a time.

Section 3 Review

1. What are the two types of electric circuits? You can draw a diagram of each to explain your answer.
2. What happens to the bulbs in a series circuit if one of the bulbs burns out? Explain.
3. What happens to the bulbs in a parallel circuit if one of the bulbs burns out? Explain.
4. **Thinking Critically Comparing and Contrasting** You are building a string of lights using several bulbs. How is the brightness of the lights related to whether you connect the bulbs in series or in parallel?

CHAPTER PROJECT

Check Your Progress
Construct a circuit, either series or parallel, that lights a bulb when the switch is closed. Use the detector switch you designed earlier to close the circuit. Test the circuit to make sure that the switch closes when the event you are detecting occurs. Then make sure that the bulb lights when the switch is closed.

SECTION 4 Electrical Safety

DISCOVER

How Can You Blow a Fuse?

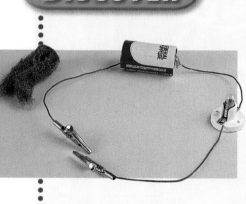

1. Begin by constructing the circuit shown using a D cell, a light bulb, and two alligator clips.
2. Pull a steel fiber out of a piece of steel wool. Wrap the ends of the steel fiber around the alligator clips.
3. Complete the circuit and observe the steel fiber and the bulb.

Think It Over

Developing Hypotheses Write a hypothesis to explain your observations.

GUIDE FOR READING

◆ How does a lightning rod protect a building?

◆ What safety devices are used in electric circuits?

◆ How is injury from an electric shock on the human body related to current?

Reading Tip As you read, make a list of ways that you can protect yourself from an electric shock.

The ice storm has ended, but it has left a great deal of destruction in its wake. Trees have been stripped of their branches, and a thick coating of ice covers the countryside. Perhaps the greatest danger is from the downed high-voltage lines left sparking in the streets. Residents are being warned to stay far away from them. What makes these power lines so dangerous?

Becoming Part of a Circuit

The sparks from those power lines should give you a clue as to what the danger is. One of the two parts of an electric company's circuit is a "live" wire carrying energy from the generating plant. The other part is a return or "ground" from the customer back to the generating plant. If a power line is damaged, the ground connection may be made through Earth itself. A person who touches a downed power line could create a short circuit to Earth through his or her body. A **short circuit** is a connection that allows current to take an unintended path. Rather than flowing through the return, or ground wire, the current would flow through the person.

The unintended path in a short circuit may offer less resistance than the intended path. So the current through a short circuit can be high. The result is a potentially fatal electric shock.

Exposed Wires Fallen high-voltage power lines are not the only potential source of electric shocks. Many people are hurt or killed by shocks from common household circuits. If you touch your hand to a 120-volt circuit, a potential difference, or voltage, is created between your hand and Earth. Since current flows when there is voltage, current will flow through your body.

Figure 15 Power must be shut off while work crews repair damaged lines.

The wires to the electrical devices in your home are protected by insulation. Sometimes that insulation wears off, leaving the wire exposed. If you touch such a wire, you become part of the circuit. You will get a painful, possibly harmful shock.

In some cases, the exposed wire is inside an electrical device such as a toaster. If the wire comes in contact with the outside metal case of the toaster, the entire toaster will conduct electricity. Then you could receive a shock from simply touching the toaster.

Resisting Current Is there any way to protect yourself if you become part of a circuit? The soles of your shoes will normally provide a large resistance between your feet and the surface of Earth. As a result, the current would not be enough to cause serious injury. But what happens if you're barefoot, or are standing in the bathtub when you touch the circuit? In either case, your resistance will be smaller. Ordinary tap water is not a very good conductor of electricity, but it does decrease your resistance. This means that the voltage can still produce enough current to seriously injure you.

Grounding

Additional grounding wires protect people from shocks. If a short circuit occurs in a device, current will go directly into Earth through a low-resistance grounding wire. In this way a person who touches the device will be protected.

Third Prong Have you ever noticed that some plugs have a third prong on them, as shown in Figure 16? The two flat prongs connect the appliance to the household circuit. This **third prong,** which is round, connects the metal shell of an appliance to the ground wire of a building.

In order to protect people from shocks, electrical systems are grounded. A circuit is electrically **grounded** when charges are able to flow directly from the circuit into the ground connection in the event of a short circuit.

Figure 16 The rounded prong on this plug is a safety device. *Relating Cause and Effect How does the third prong protect you if the appliance is faulty?*

because the fluid in human cells contains ions, which are charged particles that conduct electricity.

Another factor is whether your skin is wet or dry. If your skin is very dry, your resistance might be very high. When your skin is wet, however, your resistance might be hundreds of times lower. So you are more likely to suffer a serious electric shock if you are wet than if you are exposed to the same voltage when you are dry.

Electrical Safety Tips

As you have learned, electricity is one of the most useful energy resources. But it can also be quite dangerous if not used carefully. Here are some important rules to remember when using electricity.

◆ Never handle electrical appliances when you or your hands are wet, or if you are standing in water.
◆ Never stick your fingers or any object other than a plug into an electrical outlet.
◆ Always unplug an electrical appliance before attempting to open or repair it.
◆ Never overload a circuit by attaching too many appliances to it.
◆ Never touch wires on power poles or wires that have fallen.
◆ Never use broken or frayed wires.

DANGER
HIGH VOLTAGE
AUTHORIZED PERSONNEL ONLY
PELIGRO
ALTO VOLTAJE

Section 4 Review

1. Describe how a bolt of lightning passes through a lightning rod to the ground.
2. How are fuses and circuit breakers alike? How are they different?
3. Are all electrical shocks to the body equally dangerous? Explain.
4. **Thinking Critically** **Applying Concepts** Why do you think the Empire State Building in New York City is often hit by lightning?

Science at Home

Circuit Diagrams Along with members of your family, find out if the circuits in your home are protected by fuses or circuit breakers. **CAUTION:** Be careful not to touch the wiring as you inspect it. How many circuits are there in your home? Make a diagram showing the outlets and appliances on each circuit. Explain the role of fuses and circuit breakers. Ask your family members if they are aware of these devices in other circuits, such as in a car.

SECTION 1
Electric Charge and Static Electricity

Key Ideas

◆ Like charges repel each other and unlike charges attract each other.

◆ An electric field is produced in the region around an electric charge. The field can be represented by electric field lines.

◆ Static electricity results when electrons move from one object to another, or from one location to another within an object.

◆ During an electric discharge, charges leave a charged object, making the object neutral.

Key Terms

electric field
static electricity
conduction
induction

conservation of charge
static discharge
electroscope

 SECTION 2
Circuit Measurements

Key Ideas

◆ Electric current flows when voltage is applied to a circuit.

◆ Voltage, which is measured in volts, is the potential difference between two places in a circuit.

◆ Resistance, which is measured in ohms, is the opposition to the flow of charge.

◆ If resistance is held constant, an increase in voltage produces an increase in current.

◆ If voltage is held constant, an increase in resistance produces a decrease in current.

Key Terms

electrical potential
potential difference
voltage
voltage source
voltmeter
ammeter
Ohm's law

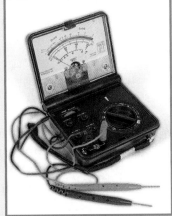

 SECTION 3
Series and Parallel Circuits

Key Ideas

◆ A series circuit is a circuit in which charges have only one path to flow through.

◆ A parallel circuit is a circuit that contains different branches through which charges can flow. Household circuits are parallel circuits.

Key Terms

series circuit   parallel circuit

SECTION 4
Electrical Safety

INTEGRATING HEALTH

Key Ideas

◆ Fuses, circuit breakers, and grounded plugs are all important safety devices found in electric circuits.

◆ A lightning rod provides a conducting path to Earth, so that electric charges from lightning can travel directly into Earth without damaging a structure.

◆ The human body can be seriously injured by shocks, even those of less than one ampere.

Key Terms

short circuit   grounded   fuse
third prong   lightning rod   circuit breaker

Organizing Information

Venn Diagram Copy the Venn diagram comparing series and parallel circuits. Then complete it and add a title. (For more information on Venn Diagrams, see the Skills Handbook.)

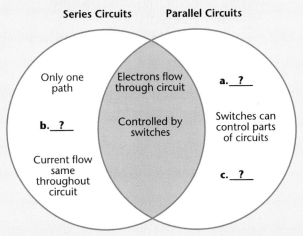

Series Circuits   Parallel Circuits

Only one path

Electrons flow through circuit

a. ?

b. ?

Controlled by switches

Switches can control parts of circuits

Current flow same throughout circuit

c. ?

Reviewing Content

 For more review of key concepts, see the Interactive Student Tutorial CD-ROM.

Multiple Choice

Choose the letter of the answer that best completes each statement.

1. A particle that carries a negative electric charge is called a(n)
   a. neutron.　　b. atom.
   c. proton.　　d. electron.

2. When you charge an electroscope by touching it with a charged balloon, the process is called
   a. friction.　　b. conduction.
   c. induction.　　d. grounding.

3. The potential difference that causes charges to move in a circuit is
   a. voltage.
   b. resistance.
   c. current.
   d. electric discharge.

4. An example of a voltage source is a
   a. voltmeter.　　b. battery.
   c. resistance.　　d. switch.

5. A circuit that is connected to Earth is said to be
   a. series.　　b. parallel.
   c. grounded.　　d. discharged.

True or False

If the statement is true, write true. If it is false, change the underlined word or words to make the statement true.

6. Your hair might be attracted to your comb as your hair and the comb become <u>oppositely</u> charged.

7. A neutral object becomes negatively charged when it <u>loses</u> electrons.

8. <u>Conduction</u> is the process of charging an object without touching it.

9. Electrical resistance is low in a good <u>conductor</u>.

10. A <u>circuit breaker</u> contains a thin strip of metal that melts if too much current passes through it.

Checking Concepts

11. Describe the electric field surrounding a charge.

12. What is static electricity?

13. What does it mean to say that an object is charged? Describe the three ways in which an object can become charged.

14. How is lightning related to static electricity?

15. State and describe Ohm's Law.

16. What units are used to measure voltage, current, and resistance?

17. What type of meter is used to measure current? To measure voltage? How should each meter be connected in a circuit?

18. Discuss three safety rules to follow while using electricity.

19. How do fuses and circuit breakers act as safety devices in a circuit?

20. **Writing to Learn** You are an electrician about to design the electrical wiring system for a new house. Your plans call for parallel circuits, but the owners insist that a series circuit will be simpler and cheaper. Write a letter, with diagrams, to the owners explaining why you need to use parallel circuits.

Thinking Critically

21. **Problem Solving** A toaster is plugged into a 120-volt socket. If it has a resistance of 20 ohms, how much current will flow through the toaster coils? Show your work.

22. **Classifying** Identify each of the following statements as characteristic of series circuits, parallel circuits, or both:
    a. $I = V \div R$
    b. Total resistance increases as more light bulbs are added.
    c. Total resistance decreases as more branches are added.
    d. Current in each part of the circuit is the same.
    e. A break in any part of the circuit will cause current to stop.

23. **Applying Concepts** Explain why the third prong of a grounded plug should not be removed.

Applying Skills

Use the illustration of an electric circuit to answer Questions 24–27.

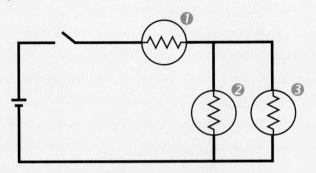

24. **Classifying** Is the circuit in the illustration series or parallel? Explain.
25. **Controlling Variables** Would the other bulbs continue to shine if you removed Bulb 1? Would they shine if you removed Bulb 2 instead? Explain your reasoning.
26. **Predicting** Will any of the bulbs be lit if you open the switch? Explain.

27. **Making Models** Redraw the circuit diagram to include a switch that controls only Bulb 3.

Performance CHAPTER PROJECT **Assessment**

Present Your Project Prepare a description and circuit diagram for your display. If any parts of your alarm circuit are not visible, you should draw a second diagram showing how all the parts are assembled. Then present your alarm to your class and explain how it could be used.

Reflect and Record Describe the reliability of your switch. Does it work most of the time? All of the time? If your alarm circuit were to be used for a full year, would it still work? Draw sketches in your journal of parts of your alarm that would need to be redesigned so that it would last longer.

Test Preparation

Use these questions to prepare for standardized tests.

Use the diagram to answer Questions 28–30.

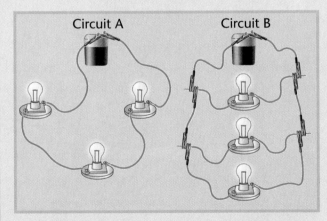

Circuit A   Circuit B

28. What will happen to the remaining bulbs in Circuit A if one of the bulbs burns out?
    a. They will continue to light, but they will be brighter.
    b. They will continue to light, but they will be dimmer.
    c. They will all go out.
    d. They will stay on until the current in the wire is used up and then go out.

29. Which of the following will happen if you add a fourth light to Circuit A?
    a. All of the lights will become brighter.
    b. The brightness of the lights will not change.
    c. The brightness of the lights located after the new light will become dimmer.
    d. All of the lights will become dimmer.

30. What will happen to the remaining bulbs in Circuit B if one of the bulbs burns out?
    a. They will remain lit with the same brightness.
    b. They will go out as well.
    c. They will continue to light, but they will be brighter.
    d. They will continue to light, but they will be dimmer.

CHAPTER
21

Electricity and Magnetism at Work

www.phschool.com

SECTION 1
Electricity, Magnetism, and Motion

Discover How Does a Magnet Move a Wire?
Real-World Lab Building an Electric Motor

SECTION 2
Generating Electric Current

Discover Can You Produce Electric Current Without a Battery?
Try This Keeping Current
Sharpen Your Skills Classifying

SECTION 3
Using Electric Power

Discover How Can You Make a Bulb Burn More Brightly?
Sharpen Your Skills Observing

Electrical Energy Audit

Have you ever heard someone complain about high electric bills? Electricity can be expensive, but there are good reasons why. Generating electricity and delivering it to customers is a complicated business.

In this chapter, you will discover how electricity is generated and used. As you work through the chapter, you will study electrical energy consumption in your home.

High-voltage transmission lines glisten in the sunlight.

Your Goal To analyze the ways you use electricity at home and to determine how much electricity you and your family use.

To complete the project you will
- prepare a list of appliances in your home, including lights, that use electricity
- record the length of time each appliance is used during an average week
- calculate how much electrical energy is used to operate each appliance
- follow the safety guidelines in Appendix A

Get Started Begin by preparing a data table you can use to keep track of your observations. You should include columns for the name of the appliance, whether it is plugged in or battery operated, the primary use of the appliance, and the number of hours it is used each day.

Check Your Progress You'll be working on this project as you study this chapter. To keep your project on track, look for Check Your Progress boxes at the following points.

Section 1 Review, page 679: List all of the electric appliances in your home.

Section 2 Review, page 689: Calculate the amount of time each appliance is used during a week.

Section 3 Review, page 696: Calculate the amount of energy consumed by each appliance.

Present Your Project At the end of the chapter (page 707), you will calculate the total amount of electrical energy consumed and determine which appliance in your home uses the most electrical energy.

Integrating Chemistry

SECTION 4 Batteries

Discover Can You Make Electricity With Spare Change?
Science at Home Recharge Your Batteries
Skills Lab Electricity Grows on Trees

① Electricity, Magnetism, and Motion

How Does a Magnet Move a Wire?

1. Make an electromagnet by winding insulated copper wire around a steel nail.

2. Make a pile of books, and place a ruler between the top two books.

3. Hang the electromagnet over the ruler so that it hangs free.

4. Complete the circuit by connecting the electromagnet to a switch and a battery.

5. Set a horseshoe magnet near the electromagnet. Then close the switch briefly and observe what happens to the electromagnet.

6. Reverse the wires connected to the battery and repeat Step 5.

Think It Over

Inferring What happened to the electromagnet when you closed the switch? Was anything different when you reversed the wires? How can you use electricity to produce motion?

◆ **How can electrical energy be converted into mechanical energy?**

◆ **What do galvanometers and electric motors do?**

Reading Tip Preview the figures and captions. Then read to find out how magnetic forces and electric current are related to motion.

What comes to mind when you think about electricity? You may think of the bright lights of a big city, or the music from the radio in your bedroom. If you are familar with electric motors like the one in a movie projector, then you already know about a very important application of electricity. Electricity can produce motion.

Electrical and Mechanical Energy

As you have learned, magnets can produce motion. They can move together or move apart, depending on how their poles are arranged. You have also learned that an electric current in a wire produces a magnetic field similar to that of a magnet. So you can understand that a magnet can move a wire, as it would move another magnet.

The wire at the top of Figure 1 is placed in a magnetic field. When current flows through the wire, the magnetic force pushes the wire down. If the current is reversed, the magnetic force pulls the wire up. The direction in which the wire moves depends on the direction of the current.

676

The interaction between electricity and magnetism can cause something to move—in this case, a wire. The ability to move an object some distance is called energy. The energy associated with electric currents is called electrical energy. And the energy an object has due to its movement or position is called mechanical energy.

Energy can be changed from one form into another. **When a current-carrying wire is placed in a magnetic field, electrical energy is converted into mechanical energy.** This happens because the magnetic field of the current makes the wire move.

☑ *Checkpoint* *What is energy?*

Galvanometers

The upper part of the wire in Figure 1 moves up or down in the magnetic field. What will happen if you place a loop in a magnetic field? Look at the rectangular loop of wire in Figure 2. The current in the wire travels up one side of the loop and down the other. In other words, current travels in opposite directions on the two sides of the loop.

Since the direction the wire moves depends on the direction of the current, the two sides move in opposite directions. Once each side has moved as far up or down as it can go, it will stop moving. The result is that the loop rotates half a turn.

The rotation of a loop of wire in a magnetic field is the basis of a device called a **galvanometer,** which is used to measure small currents. In a galvanometer several loops of wire are suspended between the poles of a magnet. The loops of wire are also attached to a pointer and to a spring, as in Figure 2. When current flows through the wire, the current produces a magnetic field. This field interacts with the field of the magnet, causing the loops of wire and the pointer to rotate. **Electric current is used to turn the pointer of a galvanometer.** The force of the

Force is down

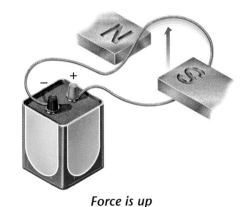

Force is up

Figure 1 The magnetic field of the permanent magnet interacts with the magnetic field produced by the current in the wire. *Interpreting Diagrams How does the direction of the current affect the force on the wire?*

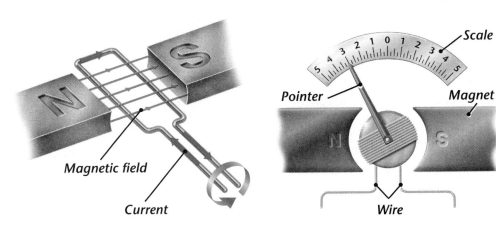

Magnetic field

Current

Scale

Pointer

Magnet

Wire

Figure 2 Since current travels in a different direction in each half of the wire loop (left), one side is pushed down while the other is pulled up. A galvanometer (right) uses loops of wire to move a pointer.

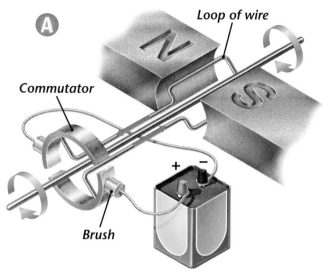

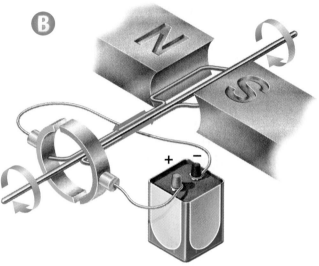

A

Loop of wire

Commutator

Brush

Figure 3 A loop of wire in a motor spins continuously. **A.** The magnetic field of the loop makes it rotate to a vertical position. **B.** As the loop of wire passes the vertical position, each half of the commutator makes contact with the opposite brush. The direction of current flow changes, and so does the direction of the magnetic force on the loop. The loop continues to spin the same direction.

B

Social Studies
CONNECTION

The sewing machine was invented before electricity came into general use. Find out about the sewing machine, the refrigerator, or some other household device that was originally operated without an electric motor.

In Your Journal

Sketch an advertising poster that could have been used to introduce the new, electrically operated version of the device. Be sure to show how electricity has improved the machine and the lives of its users.

interaction of the fields acts against the spring. So the amount of rotation of the loops of wire and the pointer depends on the amount of current in the wire. A galvanometer has a scale that is marked to show how much the pointer turns for a known current. An unknown current can then be measured with a galvanometer.

✓ *Checkpoint* **How does a galvanometer work?**

Electric Motors

The wire in the magnetic field of a galvanometer cannot rotate more than half a turn. Suppose you could make a loop of wire rotate continuously. Instead of moving a pointer, the wire could turn a rod, or axle. The axle could then turn something else, such as the blades of a fan or blender. Such a device would be an electric motor. An **electric motor** is a device that uses an electric current to turn an axle.

An electric motor converts electrical energy into mechanical energy. An electric motor is different from a galvanometer because in a motor, a loop of current-carrying wire spins continuously.

How a Motor Works How can you make a loop of wire continue to spin? The direction of the force on the wire depends on the current and the magnetic field surrounding the coil. In a motor, current is reversed just as the loop gets to the vertical position.

This reverses the force on each side of the loop. The side of the loop that was pushed up on the left is now pushed down on the right. The side of the loop that was pushed down on the right is now pushed up on the left. The current reverses after each half turn so that the loop spins continuously in the same direction.

Parts of a Motor A **commutator** is a device that reverses the flow of current through an electric motor. You can see in Figure 3 that a commutator consists of two parts of a ring. Each half of the commutator is attached to one end of the loop of wire. When the loop of wire rotates, the commutator rotates as well. As it moves, the commutator slides past two contact points called **brushes**. Each half of the commutator is connected to the current source by one of the brushes.

As the loop of wire gets to the vertical position, each half of the commutator makes contact with the other brush. Since the current runs through the brushes, changing brushes reverses the direction of the current in the loop. Changing the direction of the current causes the loop of wire to spin continuously.

Instead of a single loop of wire, practical electric motors have dozens or hundreds of loops of wire wrapped around an iron core. This arrangement of wires and iron core is called an **armature**. Using many loops increases the strength of the motor and allows it to rotate more smoothly. Large electric motors also use electromagnets in place of permanent magnets.

Figure 4 This armature contains hundreds of coils of wire. *Interpreting Photos Where is the axle of the motor?*

Section 1 Review

1. How can electricity be used to produce motion?
2. What energy conversion takes place in an electric motor and a galvanometer?
3. What measurement can be made with a galvanometer?
4. Describe how the commutator and brushes of an electric motor operate.
5. **Thinking Critically** Relating Cause and Effect Why is it important to change the direction of the current in a motor?

EXPLORING Energy Resources

Electric power can be produced in several ways. Each kind of generating plant converts a particular kind of energy into electrical energy.

Solar Energy
The sun's rays can be focused on a tower by large mirrors to boil water. The resulting steam then turns a turbine. One type of solar cell can also collect the sun's energy and convert it directly into electrical energy.

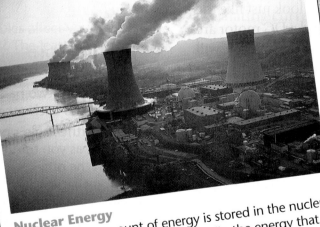

Nuclear Energy
A tremendous amount of energy is stored in the nucleus of an atom. When the nucleus is split, the energy that is released is used to heat water. The water turns into steam, which expands and turns a turbine.

Energy From Falling Water
Hydroelectric plants near the bases of dams or waterfalls use water to turn turbines.

Geothermal Energy
In a few locations on Earth, underground water heated by molten rock turns to steam. This steam, which can be obtained through steam vents or drilling, is then used to turn a turbine.

Energy From Fossil Fuels
Coal, natural gas, and oil can be burned in generating plants to produce steam. The steam pushes against the blades of a turbine, causing it to turn.

Tidal Energy
As tides move in and out in a basin behind a dam, the moving water can be used to turn a turbine.

Energy From Wind
A windmill is essentially a turbine. As the wind blows, it turns the blades of the windmill, which then turn a generator.

ELECTRICITY GROWS ON TREES

An electrochemical cell changes chemical energy into electrical energy. In this lab, you will practice the skill of drawing conclusions as you make a simple electrochemical cell starting with an apple.

Problem

How can you make a simple wet cell out of common household materials?

Materials

2 galvanized (zinc coated) nails
    about 10 cm long
2 pieces of copper about the same
    size as the nails
3 30-cm pieces of insulated wire with about
    2 cm of insulation removed from each end
2 marble-sized lumps of clay
4 clothes pins (the "pinch" type with springs)
2 apples
calculator powered by one 1.5-volt dry cell

Procedure ✂

Part 1 Single Apple Power

1. Use the calculator to do some calculations to be sure it works.
2. Remove the dry cell from the calculator.
3. Stick a galvanized nail into an apple so that about three or four centimeters of the nail are showing. Stick a piece of stiff copper wire into the apple as well. **CAUTION:** *Take care handling sharp nails.*

4. Connect a piece of wire to the free end of the nail. Connect another piece of wire to the free end of the copper wire. Use clothespins to keep the connections tight.
5. Connect the free ends of the two wires to the open terminals of the calculator. Secure the connections with clothespins or pieces of clay.
6. Try using the calculator. If it doesn't work, be sure the connections are tight.
7. Reverse the connections. Again, be sure the connections are tight.

8. If you get the calculator to work, try using it to do some calculations. If not, continue on.

Part 2 Double Apple Power

9. Make another apple cell by repeating Steps 3 and 4 with a second apple, nail, piece of copper, and two pieces of wire.

10. Experiment with different ways of connecting the second cell until the calculator works.

11. Do you think the apple cell will work if you use two galvanized nails in each apple instead of using copper? Design an experiment to find out.

Analyze and Conclude

1. Draw circuit diagrams for the arrangements from Parts I and II.

2. Relate the parts of the apple cell to a typical electrochemical cell.

3. How does the calculator perform when powered by one apple? By two apples? How can you account for any differences?

4. Does the calculator work as well with the apple as it does with a dry cell?

5. Did the apple cell work with two nails? Explain why or why not.

6. What parts of the apple battery correspond to the positive end and the negative end of a dry cell? How do you know?

7. **Think About It** What was the result of reversing the connections? Why do you think this happened?

More to Explore

Are apples the only fruit that can be used to make enough electricity to power a calculator? Try oranges, lemons, tomatoes, or other fruits. Are there other instruments or appliances that can be powered with apple wet cells? Try small toys, electronic games, or electronic clocks. (*Hint:* The apple cells generate a low voltage.)

Disposing of Batteries—Safely

Americans use more than 2 billion batteries each year, for everything from flashlights and toys to cameras and computers. When batteries wear out, people throw most of them into the trash. The dead batteries end up buried in landfills or burned in incinerators.

The trouble with throwing away batteries is that they contain poisonous metals, such as mercury and cadmium. Mercury harms the nervous system, and cadmium can cause cancer. As batteries break down in landfills, they can release these metals into the soil. Eventually the metals can enter the water supply. Burning batteries in incinerators isn't any better, because the metals are released into the air as the batteries are burned. So what's the safest way to dispose of batteries?

The Issues

What Type of Battery Is Best? Alkaline batteries are used in toys, flashlights, radios, and watches. These batteries contain mercury. Even though there are some rechargeable alkaline batteries, most are thrown away once they are dead.

Nickel-cadmium (Ni-Cad) batteries are often used in hand-held video games and cordless telephones. These batteries contain cadmium. Ni-Cad batteries are rechargeable. One Ni-Cad battery can last as long as 12 single-use alkaline batteries. Yet they still don't last forever. Eventually they wear out and must be disposed of.

Where Should People Dispose of Batteries? Health experts say that batteries should be collected separately from ordinary trash and disposed of in secure, hazardous-waste landfills. These sites have clay or other materials underneath the waste to stop poisons from leaking into soil and water.

Some cities collect batteries at collection centers. Some stores also provide for special disposal or recycling. However, even when battery collection is offered, many people throw batteries into the trash simply because it's easier.

What Can People Do? Some government officials want laws that require manufacturers to reduce the amount of poisonous metals in batteries. At present, most states do not have such a law. In the last 20 years, manufacturers have lowered the amount of mercury used in alkaline batteries by 70 percent.

Local governments could fine people who don't follow the rules for disposal of batteries. But enforcing battery disposal rules would be expensive. It also would involve checking everyone's trash—a violation of people's privacy. A few states do require battery manufacturers to collect and recycle batteries. But this process is costly for companies and results in higher prices for batteries.

While people search for solutions, batteries continue to pile up.

You Decide

1. **Identify the Problem**
   In your own words, explain the problem of safe battery disposal.

2. **Analyze the Options**
   Examine the pros and cons of changing disposal regulations and changing the materials used to make batteries. In each case, who would the change affect?

3. **Find a Solution**
   Your community is debating the problem of battery disposal. Take a position and write a speech supporting your opinion.

SECTION 1

Electricity, Magnetism, and Motion

Key Ideas

◆ A magnetic field exerts a force on a wire carrying current, causing the wire to move.

◆ A galvanometer uses the magnetic force on a current-carrying wire to turn a pointer on a scale. The scale can then be used to measure current.

◆ An electric motor converts electrical energy into mechanical energy.

Key Terms

galvanometer
electric motor
commutator

brushes
armature

 SECTION 2

Generating Electric Current

Key Ideas

◆ A current is induced in a wire in a moving or changing magnetic field.

◆ Current that moves in one direction only is called direct current. Current that reverses direction is called alternating current.

◆ A generator converts mechanical energy into electric energy.

◆ Mechanical energy is required to move a turbine. That energy can be supplied by falling water, the burning of fossil fuels, the wind, the sun, the tides, or steam from within Earth.

Key Terms

electromagnetic
  induction
alternating current
direct current
electric generator

slip rings
turbine
renewable resource
nonrenewable
  resource

 SECTION 3

Using Electric Power

Key Ideas

◆ Power is the rate at which energy is converted.

◆ A transformer increases or decreases voltage.

◆ The voltage of alternating current can be stepped up and stepped down.

Key Terms

power
transformer

step-up transformer
step-down transformer

SECTION 4

Batteries

INTEGRATING **CHEMISTRY**

Key Ideas

◆ An electrochemical cell consists of two different metals, called electrodes, and a substance through which charges can flow, called an electrolyte.

◆ In a battery, two or more electrochemical cells are connected in series to increase the voltage.

Key Terms

electrochemical cell
electrolyte
terminal

battery
wet cell
dry cell

rechargeable
battery

Organizing Information

Concept Map Copy the concept map about electromagnetism onto a separate sheet of paper. Then complete the concept map and add a title. (For more about concept maps, see the Skills Handbook.)

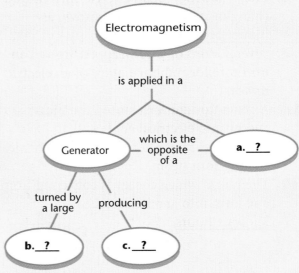

Reviewing Content

 For more review of key concepts, see the Interactive Student Tutorial CD-ROM.

Multiple Choice

Choose the letter of the answer that best completes each statement.

1. Electrical energy is converted into mechanical energy in a
   a. motor.
   b. generator.
   c. transformer.
   d. battery.

2. Mechanical energy is converted into electrical energy in a
   a. motor.
   b. galvanometer.
   c. generator.
   d. commutator.

3. Power is equal to
   a. energy × time.
   b. voltage × current.
   c. energy × current.
   d. current ÷ voltage.

4. A device that changes the voltage of alternating current is a
   a. transformer.
   b. motor.
   c. generator.
   d. galvanometer.

5. The metal plates in an electrochemical cell are called
   a. electrolytes.
   b. electrodes.
   c. armatures.
   d. brushes.

True or False

If the statement is true, write true. If it is false, change the underlined word or words to make the statement true.

6. The production of an electric current by a changing magnetic field is known as <u>induction</u>.

7. Several loops of wire wrapped around an iron core form the <u>armature</u> of an electric motor.

8. A <u>generator</u> converts stored chemical energy into electrical energy.

9. Large generators often get their mechanical energy from <u>steam</u>.

10. The rate at which energy is converted from one form into another is called <u>kilowatt-hours</u>.

Checking Concepts

11. How is a galvanometer similar to a motor? How is it different?

12. What is the role of the commutator and brushes in an electric motor?

13. Describe the operation of an AC generator.

14. Compare and contrast alternating and direct current.

15. What is the purpose of a turbine in generating electricity?

16. What are the pros and cons of coal, wind power, and nuclear power?

17. Explain how transformers are used to carry electricity from the utility company to your home.

18. What is a chemical reaction? How are chemical reactions related to batteries?

19. **Writing to Learn** Sometimes you may think that everything that could possibly be invented already exists. Many people thought the same thing during the 1800s. Write an article for a modern newspaper describing new uses for generators and motors.

Thinking Critically

20. **Problem Solving** The voltage of a car battery is 12 volts. When the car is started, the battery produces a 40-amp current. How much power does it take to start the car?

21. **Comparing and Contrasting** Compare the cost of using the following two bulbs. Assume that each one is used for 5 hours a day for 360 days per year. The cost of electricity is 8 cents/kWh.
    a. A 100-watt light bulb that costs $1.00
    b. A fluorescent bulb that costs $9 but provides equal brightness with only 20 watts

22. **Applying Concepts** How could you modify a battery to produce a higher voltage?

23. **Making Diagrams** Make a diagram of a wire loop in a magnetic field. Show how the direction of a current in the wire is related to the direction of rotation of the loop.

Applying Skills

Use the illustration to answer Questions 24–26.

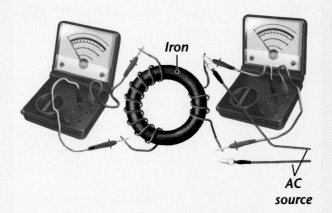

Iron

AC source

24. Classifying What type of transformer is shown in the illustration? How do you know?

25. Inferring Which coil is the primary coil and which is the secondary coil?

26. Predicting What will the two voltmeters show when the circuit on the right side of the diagram is completed?

Performance Assessment
CHAPTER PROJECT

Present Your Project Present the results of your energy audit to the class in a visual format. You might make a bar, circle, or line graph showing the appliances and the energy they used. What appliance uses the most electrical energy in a week? Compare the appliances that are rated at 800 watts and higher. What do they have in common? How might this conclusion be helpful to a consumer who is interested in paying the least for electricity?

Record and Reflect In your journal, write about how you calculated energy use. What problems did you have? What information couldn't you collect?

Test Preparation

Use these questions to prepare for standardized tests.

Study the table. Then answer Questions 27–30.

Appliance	Power (W)
Stove	6,000
Clothes dryer	5,400
Water heater	4,500
Washing machine	1,200
Hair dryer	1,200
Iron	1,100
Coffee maker	1,000
Food processor	500

27. If all of these appliances were used for one hour, which would use the greatest amount of energy?
  a. food processor   b. hair dryer
  c. clothes dryer   d. stove

28. Which device uses energy at the same rate as ten 100-watt light bulbs?
  a. food processor
  b. coffee maker
  c. washing machine
  d. stove

29. If standard household voltage is 120 volts, what is the current through the stove?
  a. 0.05 amp
  b. 20 amps
  c. 50 amps
  d. 750 amps

30. An electric company charges $0.25 for every kilowatt-hour of energy. How much does it cost to run a water heater for 2 hours?
  a. $0.50   b. $1.13
  c. $2.25   d. $4.50

CHAPTER
22 Electronics

www.phschool.com

SECTION 1 Electronic Signals and Semiconductors

Discover **Can You Send Information With a Flashlight?**
Sharpen Your Skills **Communicating**
Real-World Lab **Design a Battery Sensor**

SECTION 2 Electronic Communication

Discover **Are You Seeing Spots?**
Science at Home **Remote Controls**

SECTION 3 Computers

Discover **How Fast Are You?**
Sharpen Your Skills **Calculating**
Skills Lab **The Penny Computer**

This red wolf wears a collar that sends radio tracking signals to naturalists.

Bits and Bytes

Red wolves are very intelligent animals, but their survival is threatened. They may benefit from the work of scientists who track their movements with electronic equipment. In a similar way, you benefit from electronics every day. Both a comfortable air-conditioned building and an airmail letter from thousands of miles away are made possible by electronics. In this chapter you will learn about the devices that make computers possible, how computers work, and how they are used. As you complete the chapter, you will identify a new computer use, or application.

Your Goal To study an existing computer application and then propose and detail a new application.

Your project must

◆ show what the existing computer application does and explain its benefits

◆ explain how data are received and transformed by the computer

◆ describe each step that occurs as your new application runs

Get Started Brainstorm with your classmates about existing computer applications. Make a list of devices that use programmed information, such as clock radios, automated bank teller machines, and grocery store bar-code scanners.

Check Your Progress You'll be working on this project as you study this chapter. To keep your project on track, look for Check Your Progress boxes at the following points.
Section 1 Review, page 716: Research a computer application.
Section 3 Review, page 733: Develop a new computer application.

Present Your Project At the end of this chapter (page 743), you will present both the existing application and your new one to the class.

SECTION
4
Integrating Technology
The Information Superhighway

Discover How Important Are Computers?
Try This What a Web You Weave
Science at Home Computer Age

SECTION 1 Electronic Signals and Semiconductors

DISCOVER

Can You Send Information With a Flashlight?

1. Write a short sentence on a sheet of paper.

2. Morse code is a language that uses dots and dashes to convey information. Convert your sentence to dots and dashes using the International Morse Code chart at the right.

3. Turn a flashlight on and off quickly to represent dots. Leave the flashlight on a little longer to represent dashes. Practice using the flashlight for several different letters.

4. Use the flashlight to transmit your sentence to a partner. Ask your partner to translate your message and write down your sentence.

International Morse Code	A ·—	B —···	C —·—·	D —··	E ·
	F ··—·	G ——·	H ····	I ··	J ·———
				K —·—	L ·—··
	M ——	N —·	O ———	P ·——·	Q ——·—
				R ·—·	S ···
	T —	U ··—	V ···—	W ·——	X —··—
				Y —·——	Z ——··

Think It Over

Inferring Were you able to transmit information using light? How does your light message differ from the same message read aloud?

GUIDE FOR READING

◆ How is electronics related to electricity?

◆ What are analog and digital signals?

◆ How are semiconductors used in solid-state devices?

Reading Tip As you read, write a phrase describing each boldfaced term in your own words.

No matter where you live, you can't go far without seeing an electronic device. Your radio and television are electronic, and so are video cameras and telephones. Making popcorn in a microwave oven requires electronics. Even an automobile engine won't run without electronics.

Most of these devices are plugged into a source of electric current. You might wonder, then, why they aren't just called electrical devices. The difference between electrical and electronic devices is in the way that they use electric current.

Electricity Versus Electronics

So far in this book, you have been learning about electricity. In electrical devices, a continuous flow of electric current is required. A light bulb is an example of an electrical device because it relies on a continuous supply of electric current.

Electronics is the use of electricity to control, communicate, and process information. **Electronics treats electric currents as a means of carrying information.** If you did the Discover activity, you turned a beam of light on and off to send a message. You controlled the current by turning a flashlight on and off. You used the flashlight as an electronic device.

710

Figure 1 Electronic controls can be found in many electrical appliances.

Electronic Signals

Electronics is based on electronic signals. An **electronic signal** is a varying electric current that represents information. Anything that can be measured or numbered, whether it is electrical or not, can be converted to a signal.

There are two basic kinds of electronic signals: analog signals and digital signals. Thermometers are a good example to show the difference between digital and analog.

Analog and Digital Devices You may have noticed that there are two different kinds of thermometers. One kind shows temperature as the height of a liquid in a tube. The height of the liquid rises and falls smoothly with the temperature. This is an analog thermometer. The other kind of thermometer is the kind you might see in front of a bank. It is called a digital thermometer. It shows a number that represents the temperature.

The number on this type of outdoor digital thermometer is constant for a few minutes, or perhaps several hours. Then the number changes suddenly by a whole degree. You probably know that the temperature doesn't really change so suddenly. But the thermometer can only show the temperature to the nearest degree, and so the temperature seems to jump.

Analog and Digital Signals The terms analog and digital are usually applied to the transmission of information using electric current. Just as there are two ways of representing temperature, there are two kinds of electronic signals. In **analog signals,** a current is varied smoothly to represent information. **An analog signal is created when a current is smoothly changed or varied.**

Figure 2 These two thermometers are examples of analog and digital devices. *Applying Concepts What do digital and analog clocks look like?*

In **digital signals,** pulses of current are used to represent information. **A digital signal consists of a current that changes in steps.** Rather than changing smoothly to represent information, a digital signal carries information in pulses. If you did the Discover activity, you used pulses of light to represent letters.

Sound Recordings The photos in Figure 3 show an analog sound recording. When you play an old plastic record, a needle runs along a spiral groove. As the needle moves back and forth in the groove, it creates a small electric current. This current matches the wavy pattern of the groove in the record.

The current produced by the needle forms an analog signal. The signal continuously changes as it copies the information on the record. The analog signal is fed into an amplifier and then into a speaker, which changes the signal back into sound.

As you can see in Figure 4, a CD, or compact disc, is very different. It contains microscopic holes, called pits. The level areas between the pits are called flats. These pits and flats are arranged in a spiral, like the groove on a record. Although you can't tell from the photograph, the spiral on a compact disc is divided into pieces of equal length. The arrangement of pits and flats within each piece of the spiral is a code. Each piece of this code represents the volume of sound at one instant.

Figure 3 The magnified photo shows the needle of a record player moving along the groove of a record. *Interpreting Photos Why does the smooth shape of the groove represent an analog signal?*

MOZART
CLARINET CONCERTO IN A MAJOR (K. 622)
Allegro
Adagio
Rondo

STPL 511.110   Side 1
                      Rec. in Stuttgart
                      29:46 min.

Jost MICHAELS, clarinet
Westphalia Symphony Orchestra
HUBERT REICHERT, conductor
STPL 511.110 A

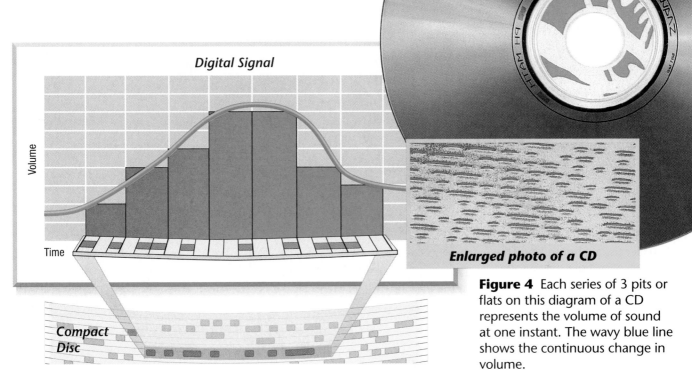

Digital Signal

Volume

Time

Compact
Disc

Enlarged photo of a CD

Figure 4 Each series of 3 pits or flats on this diagram of a CD represents the volume of sound at one instant. The wavy blue line shows the continuous change in volume.

When the CD is played, it spins around, and a beam of light scans the pits and flats. Like the bar code scanner used in a supermarket, this beam produces tiny flashes of light. The light flashes are then converted to pulses of electric current, or a digital signal. The digital signal is fed into an amplifier and then a speaker, where it is changed back into sound.

☑ *Checkpoint* *What are the two types of electronic signals?*

Semiconductors

How can you control a voltage in order to transmit analog or digital signals? After all, you have learned that current flows continuously through a conductor, but does not flow at all through an insulator. Yet to transmit an electronic signal you need to be able to vary the current through a circuit. When you vary current, you use a semiconductor.

A semiconductor is a material that conducts current better than insulators but not as well as conductors. A semiconductor conducts electricity only under certain conditions.

How can a material conduct electricity only under certain conditions? Silicon and other semiconductors are elements that have extremely high resistance in their pure forms. However, if atoms of other elements are added to semiconductors, they conduct current much more easily. By controlling the number and type of atoms added, scientists produce two types of semiconductors. They combine these two types of semiconductors in layers. This structure allows the delicate control of current needed for electronic devices. Such control is impossible with true conductors.

Figure 5 The electrical resistance of pure silicon, shown here, is reduced by adding atoms of other elements to it.

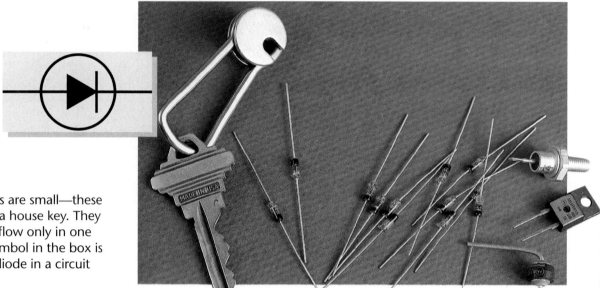

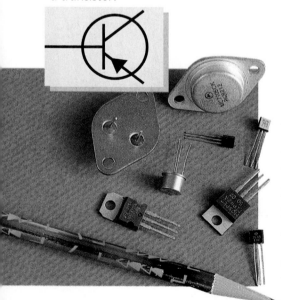

Figure 6 Diodes are small—these are smaller than a house key. They allow current to flow only in one direction. The symbol in the box is used to show a diode in a circuit diagram.

Figure 7 Transistors come in a variety of shapes and sizes. The symbol for a transistor is shown in the box. *Applying Concepts What is a transistor?*

Solid-State Components

A **solid-state component** is part of a circuit in which a signal is controlled by a solid material, such as a semiconductor. **The two types of semiconductors can be combined in different ways to produce different solid-state components. These components include diodes and transistors.** Since the 1950s, solid-state components have become dominant in electronic devices.

Diodes A solid-state component that consists of layers of the two types of semiconductors joined together is a **diode.** A diode allows current to flow in one direction only. If you connect a diode in a circuit in one direction, current will flow. But if you turn the diode around, current will not flow.

Recall that there are two types of current: alternating current and direct current. Your home uses alternating current. A battery-operated game uses direct current. Electronic devices are designed to run on only one type of current. However, you can plug some direct-current devices into an alternating-current outlet if you have a converter. A converter does not change the way the device operates. Instead, a converter changes, or converts, the current.

An alternating current reverses direction over and over again. When a diode is placed in a circuit with alternating current, the diode allows current to flow only when it is moving in one direction. So a converter allows only part of the alternating current to flow—the part flowing in one direction. Alternating current goes into the converter, but direct current comes out.

Transistors When a layer of either type of semiconductor is sandwiched between two layers of the other type of semiconductor, a transistor is formed. A **transistor** carries out one of two functions: it either amplifies an electronic signal or switches current on and off.

When electronic signals are sent, they gradually grow weak. When they are received, signals must be amplified, or made stronger, so that we can use them. Transistors revolutionized the electronics industry by making amplifiers much cheaper and more reliable.

When a transistor acts as a switch, it either lets current through or cuts it off. Millions of transistors that act as switches are what make computers work.

Integrated Circuits Single transistors have low cost and long lives. These advantages were multiplied by the invention of the integrated circuit. An **integrated circuit** is a circuit that has been manufactured on a tiny slice of semiconductor known as a chip. A chip smaller than 0.5 centimeters on each side can contain hundreds of thousands of components, such as diodes, transistors, and resistors. Electronic signals flow through integrated circuits at tremendous speeds because the various components are so close together. On some chips, the space between two components can be one-fiftieth as thick as a human hair. The high speed of signals and small size of integrated circuits make possible devices from video games to spacecraft.

✓ *Checkpoint* *What is a solid-state component?*

Sharpen your Skills

Communicating

ACTIVITY

How do you make someone understand how tiny a chip is or how fast an electronic signal travels? An analogy can help communicate what a measurement means. An analogy uses a similarity between two things that are otherwise unlike each other. For example, "a chip is as small as a baby's fingernail" is an analogy. So is "an electronic signal moves as fast as a bolt of lightning." Write your own analogies to describe how many diodes there are in one integrated circuit chip.

Figure 8 An integrated circuit chip is smaller than a fingernail. Yet the integrated circuit contains hundreds of thousands of diodes, transistors, and resistors.

Past and Future Electronics

Electronic devices were not always small and convenient. In the 1940s, for example, some radios were as large as a chest of drawers, and a computer filled an entire room. Before solid-state devices were developed, electronics relied on bulky vacuum tubes to control electric current.

A **vacuum tube** is a sealed glass tube from which most of the air has been removed. A metal filament and plate are located inside the vacuum tube. When the filament is heated under certain conditions, electrons flow from the filament to the plate. Since the electrons can only flow in one direction, a vacuum tube acts as a diode. Adding a third piece between the filament and the plate produces a triode vacuum tube. This kind of tube is able to amplify a signal. Triode tubes were first used before 1910.

Once solid-state components became available, most vacuum tubes were quickly replaced. Solid-state components are much smaller and lighter than vacuum tubes. They give off less heat, use less electrical energy, are more dependable, and last longer. They are also less expensive.

In the years since the invention of the transistor, electronic devices have shrunk rapidly. The change is equivalent to shrinking a ship the size of the *Titanic* down to the size of a mouse.

Even solid-state components might someday be replaced in devices requiring extreme speed. Researchers are developing new electronic components based on superconducting materials and other new types of materials. Recall that when certain materials are cooled to very low temperatures, their resistance to the flow of electrons disappears entirely. This makes them superconductors. Superconducting components are faster and smaller than the smallest semiconductors.

Figure 9 Although they made the first electronic devices possible, vacuum tubes like this one were large and heavy, and burned out frequently.

Section 1 Review

1. What is electronics? How are electronic signals different from ordinary electricity?
2. How is an analog signal different from a digital signal?
3. What solid-state devices can be made from semiconductors?
4. What do diodes and transistors do in electronic devices?
5. **Thinking Critically** **Applying Concepts** How are integrated circuits related to the reduction in size of electronic devices?

Check Your Progress
CHAPTER PROJECT

Select an existing computer application that interests you. List what you know about it. Then find out how it was developed, how it works, and who uses it. Why is it useful? What signal is put into the computer? What signal comes out? In addition to doing research at the library, see if you can locate someone in your community who uses this application.

Design a Battery Sensor

In this lab, you will work in the role of an electrical engineer. First you will discover the properties of an electronic component called a light-emitting diode (LED). Then you will design a way to use the LED.

Problem

How can an LED be used to tell if a battery is installed correctly?

Skills Focus

making models, designing experiments

Materials

2 D cells
LED
bicolor LED (optional)
flashlight using 2 D cells
flashlight bulb and socket
two insulated wires with alligator clips

Procedure

Part 1
LED Properties

1. Attach one wire to each terminal of the LED.
2. Tape the two cells together, positive terminal to negative terminal, to make a 3-volt battery.
3. Attach the other ends of the wires to the terminals of the battery and observe the LED.
4. Switch the wires connected to the battery terminals and observe the LED again.
5. Repeat Steps 1–4, but substitute a flashlight bulb in its socket for the LED.

Part 2 Sensor Design

6. Many electrical devices that run on batteries will not run if the batteries are installed backwards (positive where negative should be). Design a device that uses an LED to indicate if batteries are installed backwards.
7. Draw your design. Show how the LED, the device, and the battery are connected. (*Hint:* The LED can be connected either in series or in parallel with the battery and the device.)
8. Make a model of your sensor to see if it works with a flashlight.

Analyze and Conclude

1. What did you observe in Part 1 when you connected the LED to the battery the first time? The second time?
2. Based on your observations, is the LED a diode? That is, does it allow current to flow in only one direction? How do you know?
3. Compare and contrast your results with the LED and with the flashlight bulb.
4. **Apply** Did you have any trouble designing and building your sensor in Part 2? If so, how did you revise your design? Describe how you could use your sensor with other electronic devices.

More to Explore

A bicolor LED contains two LEDs. The LED glows red when current travels through it in one direction. It glows green when current travels in the other direction. How do you think the LEDs within a bicolor LED are arranged? Think of at least one application for this component.

② Electronic Communication

DISCOVER •••••••••••••••••••••••••••••••••••••ACTIVITY••••

Are You Seeing Spots?

1. Turn on a color television. Hold a hand lens at arm's length up to the television screen.

2. Move the lens closer to and farther from the screen until you can see a clear image through it. What do you see within the image?

Think It Over

Classifying What three colors make up the images on the television screen? How do you think these colors make up the wide range of colors you see on television?

GUIDE FOR READING

◆ How is sound transmitted by a telephone?

◆ How are electromagnetic waves involved in the transmission of information?

◆ How do radio and television stations transmit signals?

Reading Tip Before you read, rewrite the headings in the section as *how*, *why*, or *what* questions. As you read, look for answers to these questions.

Have you ever thought about the amazing technology that enables you to see and hear an event as it happens half way around the globe? Since the first telegraph message was sent in 1844, people have become accustomed to long distance communication by telephone, radio, and television. Each improvement in the speed, clarity, and reliability of communication has come from advancements in the field of electronics.

Telephones

In a telephone, an electronic signal is transmitted at one end and received at the other. The first telephone was invented by Alexander Graham Bell in 1876. Even though the modern telephone hardly resembles Bell's version, the basic operation has not changed much over the decades. A telephone has three main parts: a transmitter, a receiver, and a dialing mechanism.

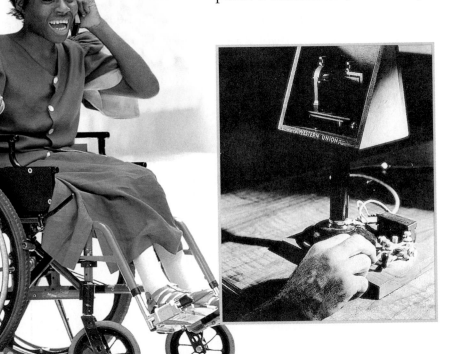

Figure 10 The clicking of a telegraph key (right) was an early form of electronic communication. Now we are accustomed to hearing the voices of people in other cities, or even on other continents.

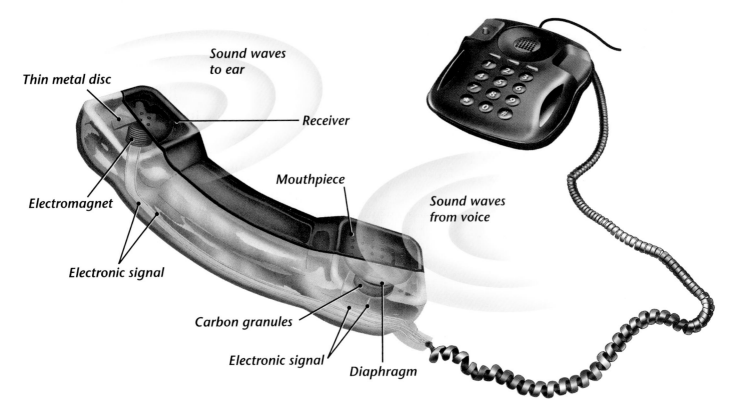

Thin metal disc

Sound waves to ear

Receiver

Electromagnet

Mouthpiece

Sound waves from voice

Electronic signal

Carbon granules

Electronic signal

Diaphragm

Figure 11 In telephone transmission, sounds are converted into electronic signals in the transmitter. *Interpreting Diagrams* Where are the signals converted back into sounds?

Transmitter **Sound is converted into an electronic signal in the transmitter of a telephone.** Converting sound into an electronic signal is possible because sound travels as waves of vibrating matter. For example, when you speak, your vocal cords vibrate back and forth. As they move, they cause the air particles around them to vibrate as well. By passing along the vibration, sound is able to travel through matter.

The transmitter of a telephone is located in the mouthpiece. When you speak into the mouthpiece, the sound waves of your voice cause a thin metal disk to vibrate. In early telephones, the disk pushed against a small chamber of carbon granules, or grains. When the disk vibrated in one direction, it pushed the grains together. When the disk vibrated in the opposite direction, it pulled the grains apart.

A current was passed through the carbon grains. The grains conduct current better when they are close together than when they are apart. So the strength of the current depended on the vibration of the disk, which matched the vibration of the voice.

In most of today's telephones, carbon grains have been replaced by semiconductors, and transistors are used to amplify the signal. Modern telephone equipment can also convert the electronic signals to a pattern of light that travels through optical fibers. In either case, the electronic signal is then sent through a series of switches and wires to the receiving telephone.

Figure 12 A fax machine uses some of the principles of a telephone to transmit images as electronic signals.

Receiver **The telephone receiver, located in the earpiece, contains a small speaker. The speaker changes the electric current back into sound.** The receiver contains an electromagnet that attracts another thin metal disk. Since the amount of electric current changes according to the signal, the strength of the magnetic field around the electromagnet changes as well. This causes the disk to vibrate in a pattern that matches the electronic signal. The vibrating disk creates sound waves, which you hear when you listen to the telephone. Many modern receivers now use semiconductors instead of electromagnets.

Dialing Mechanism The third part of the telephone is the dial or push-button device. When you dial a telephone number, you are telling the switching system where you want the call to go. A dial telephone sends a series of pulses or clicks to the switching network. A push-button device sends different tones. These act as signals that can be interpreted by electronic circuits in the switching network.

Fax Machines A fax machine can send pictures or printed text by means of an electronic signal. To convert a page to a signal, a beam of light scans a page in very narrow strips. The pattern of dark and light in each strip is converted to a signal, and the signal is transmitted through a telephone line.

When another fax machine receives the signal, it prints out the strips, one after another. If you have ever looked closely at a faxed page, you can see that some of the edges of the image are irregular. This shows where the page has been printed in strips.

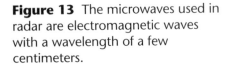 *Checkpoint* *What does a telephone transmitter do?*

Electromagnetic Waves

You learned in the last section that electronic signals are transmitted through solid-state components within electronic

Figure 13 The microwaves used in radar are electromagnetic waves with a wavelength of a few centimeters.

devices. But, in the case of radio and television, the electronic signal first has to travel over a long distance from a radio or television station. **Electronic signals can be carried over long distances by electromagnetic waves.**

Electric and Magnetic Fields You are already familiar with some types of waves, such as water waves or sound waves. Electromagnetic waves share some characteristics with these waves. However, as you learned in Chapter 17, electromagnetic waves do not need to travel through matter. An electromagnetic wave is a wave that consists of changing electric and magnetic fields.

A wave made out of electric and magnetic fields may sound a little strange at first. But you have already learned that electricity and magnetism are related. You know that a changing magnetic field produces an electric field. The reverse is also true—a changing electric field produces a magnetic field.

If a magnetic field is changing, like the up-and-down movements of a water wave, a changing electric field will form. The changing electric field that is formed then produces a changing magnetic field. The electric and magnetic fields will keep producing each other over and over again. The result is an electromagnetic wave.

You are already more familiar with electromagnetic waves than you may realize. The light that you see, the microwaves that heat food in a microwave oven, and the X-rays that a dentist or doctor uses are all types of electromagnetic waves.

Figure 14 Light from a rainbow consists of electromagnetic waves with wavelengths that are a tiny fraction of a centimeter. Wavelengths of X-rays are shorter still.

Figure 15 Amplitude or frequency of a carrier wave can be modulated.

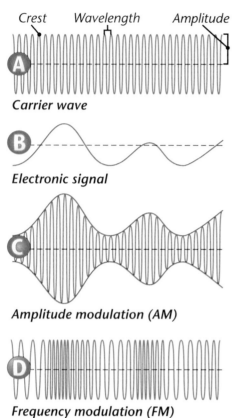

Crest   Wavelength   Amplitude

A

Carrier wave

B

Electronic signal

C

Amplitude modulation (AM)

D

Frequency modulation (FM)

Amplitude and Frequency Modulation All waves have certain basic characteristics. Figure 15A shows a simple wave moving from left to right. The high points are called crests and the low points are called troughs. Waves are described in terms of two quantities, amplitude and frequency. The amplitude is the height from the center line to a crest or trough. The frequency of a wave is the number of waves passing a given point each second.

The amplitude and frequency of an electromagnetic wave can be changed, or modulated, to carry an electronic signal. The wave that is modulated, shown in Figure 15A, is called the carrier wave. Figure 15B shows an electronic signal. In this case, the signal is an analog signal in which the strength, or amplitude, of an electric current changes.

The carrier wave can be modulated to match the electronic signal in two different ways, as shown in Figures 15C and 15D. One way is to change the amplitude of the carrier wave to match that of the signal. This process is known as amplitude modulation (AM). The other way is to change the frequency of the carrier wave to match the amplitude of the signal. Then the space between the waves varies with the strength of the signal. This process is known as frequency modulation (FM).

Figure 16 In radio transmission, sounds are converted to electronic signals that are carried by electromagnetic waves.

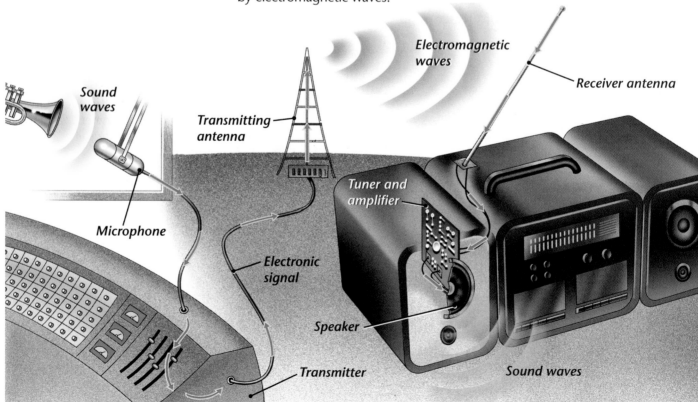

Electromagnetic waves

Receiver antenna

Sound waves

Transmitting antenna

Tuner and amplifier

Microphone

Electronic signal

Speaker

Transmitter

Sound waves

Radio

Voices or music on an AM or FM radio station are electronic signals carried by an electromagnetic wave. But where do the sounds you hear come from?

Transmission The process begins at a radio station, where sounds are converted into an electronic signal. If a musician plays into a microphone at a radio station, the sound waves produce a varying electric current. This current is an analog signal that represents the sound waves. It is sometimes called an audio signal.

The electronic audio signal is then sent to a transmitter. The transmitter amplifies the signal and combines it with an electronic carrier signal. The signal is then sent to an antenna, which sends out electromagnetic waves in all directions.

Reception Your radio has its own antenna that receives the electromagnetic waves from the radio station. The carrier wave has a specific frequency. You tune in to the wave by selecting that frequency on your radio. Your radio amplifies the signal and separates it from the carrier wave. The signal is then sent to the radio's speaker, which is the reverse of a microphone. The speaker converts the electronic signal back into sound.

☑ *Checkpoint* *What is an audio signal?*

Television

Electromagnetic waves can be used to carry images as well as sound. The transmission of the images and sounds on television is very similar to that of radio sounds.

Transmission Television signals are usually sent from transmitting antennas on the ground. Sometimes, however, the signal is blocked by the landscape of an area or by nearby buildings. Or sometimes a transmitter cannot reach homes that are too far away. To solve these problems, local cable television networks have been developed. These networks distribute television signals through cables from a central receiver to individual homes.

Communications satellites are also used to relay television signals. A communications satellite orbits Earth, always staying above the same point on the ground. These satellites receive signals from one part of the planet and transmit them to another almost instantly. This enables you to watch events from around the world as they occur.

Figure 17 A communications satellite orbits Earth at the same rate at which Earth spins. Therefore it stays above the same point on Earth.
Applying Concepts How are communications satellites involved in the transmission of video signals?

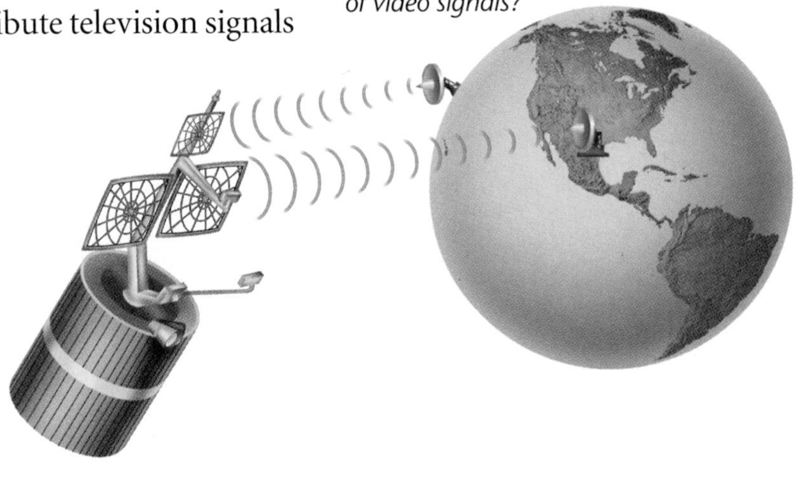

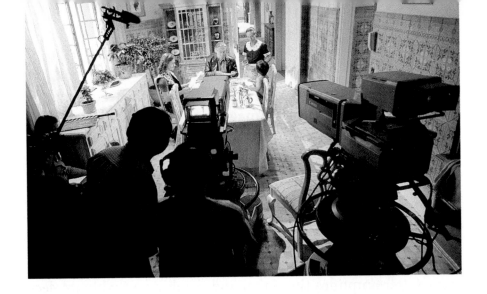

Figure 18 To create a video signal, a television camera scans an image line by line. The camera works like a fax machine, but much faster.

At a television station, cameras turn the light and sound of live action into picture, or video, and audio electronic signals. Both signals are carried by electromagnetic waves.

Reception No matter how video and audio signals are sent, they are accepted by a receiver at your home. As in the case of radio, the carrier wave for each television station is at a specific frequency, which you tune in by selecting a channel on your television. Your television amplifies the signal and separates it from the carrier wave. The audio signal is converted back into sound by the television's speakers.

Cathode-Ray Tubes The video signal is sent to a very specialized type of vacuum tube known as a cathode-ray tube. A **cathode-ray tube (CRT),** or picture tube, is an electronic device that uses electrons to produce images on a screen. A CRT converts video signals into a pattern of light.

At the back end of a CRT are three electron guns, one for each of the primary colors of light—red, blue, and green. The front end of a CRT is the screen that you see. The inside of the screen is coated with fluorescent materials, called phosphors, that glow when they are hit by an electron beam. The phosphors are arranged in clusters of three dots—one for each color. Each cluster is surrounded by dark space. You have seen the phosphors and dark spaces if you completed the Discover activity. The video signal is fed to the electron guns, causing each one to aim at the matching phosphor at the appropriate time. Your eyes combine the three colors to form all of the colors in the images you see.

A black and white television uses a single electron gun. The intensity of the beam is varied to produce a different brightness at each point on the screen. The result is different shades of black, white, and gray.

In order to produce the image, the electron beams must sweep across the entire screen in a zigzag pattern. The beams

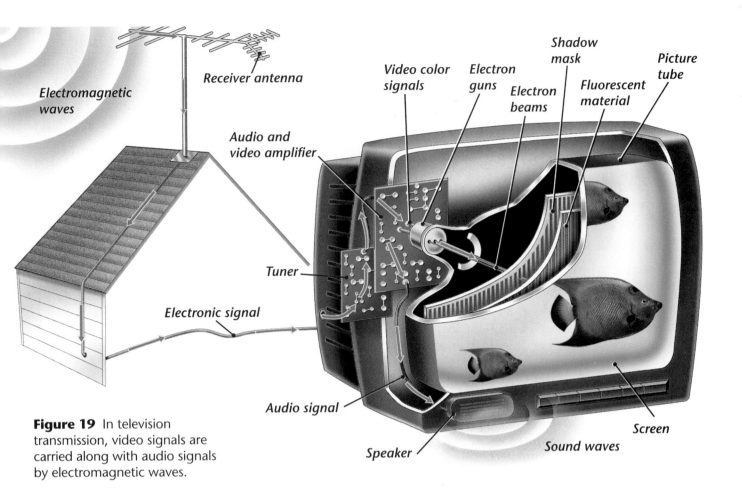

Electromagnetic waves

Receiver antenna

Audio and video amplifier

Video color signals

Electron guns

Shadow mask

Electron beams

Fluorescent material

Picture tube

Tuner

Electronic signal

Audio signal

Speaker

Sound waves

Screen

Figure 19 In television transmission, video signals are carried along with audio signals by electromagnetic waves.

scan across the screen in 525 horizontal lines before returning to the top of the screen. This pattern repeats 30 times each second!

Improved televisions allow broadcasters to transmit twice as many lines per screen. The images can be larger and sharper. These televisions are known as high-definition televisions (HDTV).

Section 2 Review

1. How does a telephone work?
2. What are electromagnetic waves? How can they carry electronic signals?
3. Describe how information is transmitted in radios and televisions.
4. What is a cathode-ray tube? How does it work to create a color television image?
5. **Thinking Critically Making Generalizations** How do you think solid-state devices have affected radios and televisions?

Science at Home

Remote Controls A remote-control device uses electromagnetic waves to program an electronic device—for instance, a television, VCR, radio, or toy—from a distance. Find a device with a remote control. Ask your family members to help you locate the receiver for the remote control on the device. Find out how far away from the device you can stand and still control the device. Find out what objects the waves will travel through. Will they bounce off mirrors? Off walls? Off your hand?

SECTION 3 Computers

DISCOVER

ACTIVITY

How Fast Are You?

1. Write out ten math problems involving the addition or subtraction of two two-digit numbers.

2. Switch lists with a friend.

3. Take turns timing how long it takes each of you to solve the ten problems by hand.

4. Then time how long it takes each of you to solve the ten problems using a calculator. What is the time difference? Is there a difference in accuracy?

Think It Over

Inferring What are the advantages of using an electronic device to complete calculations?

GUIDE FOR READING

◆ How is information stored and processed in a computer?

◆ How is computer hardware different from computer software?

Reading Tip As you read, use the headings to make an outline about how computers work.

Figure 20 You may never have seen an abacus, but these devices can be used to perform complex calculations.

Over two thousand years ago, the first calculator was invented. But it was not what you may think. This calculating device is called an abacus. People use an abacus to count by sliding beads along strings.

In the United States, mechanical adding machines and abacuses have generally been replaced by electronic calculators and computers. Although the development of computers has occurred in less than a century, computers have become commonplace.

What Is a Computer?

A **computer** is an electronic device that stores, processes, and retrieves information. One of the reasons that computers can process and store so much information is that they do not store information in the same form that you see it—numbers, letters, and pictures. **Computer information is represented in the binary system.** The **binary system** uses combinations of just two digits, 0 and 1. Although computers can use analog signals, almost all modern computers are digital.

INTEGRATING MATHEMATICS You may be wondering how large numbers can be represented using only series of 1's and 0's. Begin by thinking about the numbers with which you are more familiar. You are used to using the base-10 number system. Each place value in a number represents the number 10 raised to some power. The digits 1 through 9 are then multiplied by the place value in each position. For example, the number 327 means 3×100 plus 2×10 plus 7×1.

Binary System		
Place Values 8 4 2 1	**Expanded Value**	**Base-10 Number**
1 =	$(1 \times 1) =$ 1 =	1
1 0 =	$(1 \times 2) + (0 \times 1) =$ 2 + 0 =	2
1 1 =	$(1 \times 2) + (1 \times 1) =$ 2 + 1 =	3
1 0 0 =	$(1 \times 4) + (0 \times 2) + (0 \times 1) =$ 4 + 0 + 0 =	4
1 0 1 =	$(1 \times 4) + (0 \times 2) + (1 \times 1) =$ 4 + 0 + 1 =	5
1 0 1 0 =	$(1 \times 8) + (0 \times 4) + (1 \times 2) + (0 \times 1) = 8 + 0 + 2 + 0 =$	10
1 0 1 1 =	$(1 \times 8) + (0 \times 4) + (1 \times 2) + (1 \times 1) = 8 + 0 + 2 + 1 =$	11
1 1 1 1 =	$(1 \times 8) + (1 \times 4) + (1 \times 2) + (1 \times 1) = 8 + 4 + 2 + 1 =$	15

The binary system is similar to the base-10 number system, except that the base number is 2. Notice in Figure 21 that the place values begin with 1, 2, 4, and 8 instead of 1, 10, 100, and 1,000. In the binary system, only the numbers 0 and 1 are multiplied by each place value.

Each 1 or 0 in the binary system is called a **bit,** short for **bi**nary di**git.** Arrangements of eight bits are called **bytes.** Computer memories are rated in kilobytes (one thousand bytes), megabytes (one million bytes), or even gigabytes (one billion bytes).

Figure 21 Each place value in the binary system is double the value to its right. In this table, you see the binary numbers representing the base-10 numbers 1, 2, 3, 4, 5, 10, 11, and 15. *Interpreting Charts What is your age in the binary system?*

✓ *Checkpoint* *What two digits are used in the binary system?*

Computer Memory

There are many ways to record 0's and 1's. The pits and flats on a CD can represent 0's and 1's. CDs can store not just music, but any kind of data. Computers can also use magnetic tapes to store information. Magnetic tapes, such as video and audio tapes, record information by changing the arrangement of magnetic domains. The magnetic domains can be oriented in one direction to represent 1's, and in the opposite direction to represent 0's.

Computers also use integrated circuits, or chips. Chips contain thousands of tiny circuits with transistors that act as switches. A switch in the off position represents a 0 and a switch in the on position represents a 1. One chip may consist of as many as 16 million switches or bits.

Figure 22 Electronic switches are shown in this enlarged view. They are part of a chip that can store over 500,000 bits of information.

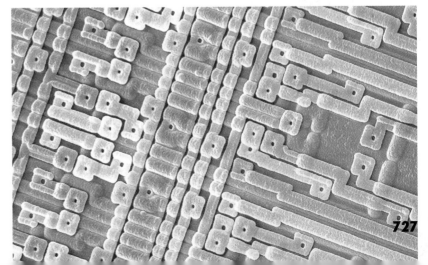

EXPLORING Computer Hardware

A computer system has several basic physical parts that are used to enter data into the computer, process the data, and retrieve information out of the computer.

Input Devices

The computer gathers data by means of input devices such as a keyboard, mouse, scanner, joystick, microphone, light pen, scanner, or touch-sensitive screen.

Modem

A modem, which connects a computer to a telephone line, can serve as both an input and an output device.

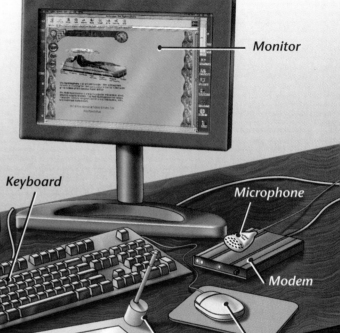

Monitor

Keyboard

Microphone

Modem

Scanner

Mouse

Light pen

Computer Hardware

The physical parts that allow a computer to receive, store, and present information make up the computer's hardware. **Computer hardware** refers to the permanent components of the computer. **Computer hardware includes a central processing unit, input devices, output devices, and memory storage devices.** Identify the different devices as you read *Exploring Computer Hardware.*

The central processing unit serves as the brain of a computer. The **central processing unit,** or CPU, directs the operation of the computer, performs logical operations and calculations, and stores information.

Data are fed to a CPU by an **input device.** There are several different types of input devices. The one most familiar to you is probably the keyboard. Other input devices are shown in *Exploring Computer Hardware.*

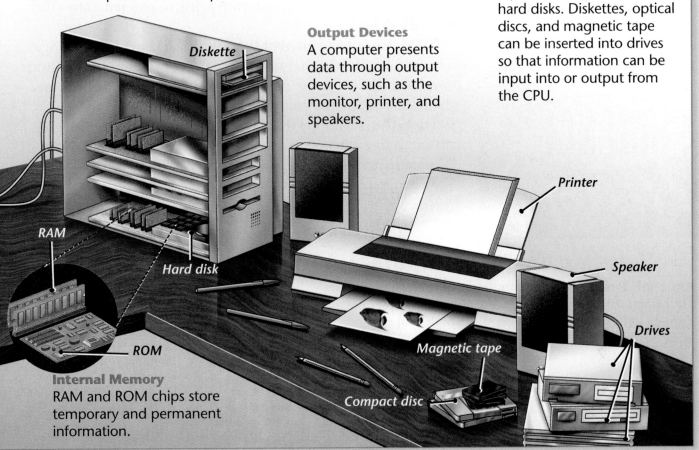

Central Processing Unit (CPU)
The CPU is the control center of the computer. The CPU processes and stores information, and coordinates the functions of the other parts of the computer.

External Memory
Information can be stored on hard disks, diskettes, optical discs, and magnetic tape. All computers use hard disks. Diskettes, optical discs, and magnetic tape can be inserted into drives so that information can be input into or output from the CPU.

Output Devices
A computer presents data through output devices, such as the monitor, printer, and speakers.

Diskette

RAM

Hard disk

Printer

Speaker

ROM

Drives

Internal Memory
RAM and ROM chips store temporary and permanent information.

Magnetic tape

Compact disc

Data from a computer are presented on an **output device.** A computer monitor, on which you view information, is the most familiar output device. Other output devices are shown in *Exploring Computer Hardware.*

Memory Devices

Computers store information in their memory. There are two general types of computer memory, internal and external. Chips on the main circuit board within the CPU are referred to as internal memory. **Random Access Memory (RAM)** is the temporary storage area for data while the computer is operating. Information stored in RAM is lost when the computer is turned off.

Information the computer needs to operate properly is stored in **Read Only Memory (ROM).** The CPU can read these data but cannot change them. Information in ROM is permanently stored and is not lost when the computer is turned off.

Neither RAM nor ROM allow you to save information when you turn your computer off. For that reason, devices outside the main CPU circuit are used to store information. They are called external memory. The most widely used form of external storage is the disk. Information is read from a disk or entered onto a disk by a **disk drive.**

There are several different types of disks. **Hard disks** are rigid magnetic metal disks that stay inside the computer. Information on a hard disk remains in the computer and can be accessed whenever you use the computer.

Diskettes, or floppy disks, are thin, round plastic disks that you can remove from the computer and carry with you. Floppy disks are coated with magnetic material laid in circles. If you have

SCIENCE & History

The Development of Computers

Although some modern computers can fit in the palm of your hand, this wasn't always the case. Computers have come a long way in a relatively short period of time.

1823

The Difference Engine

British mathematician Charles Babbage designed the first computer, called the Difference Engine. It was a mechanical computing device that had more than 50,000 moving parts. For a later computer of Babbage's, Ada Lovelace wrote what is considered the first computer program.

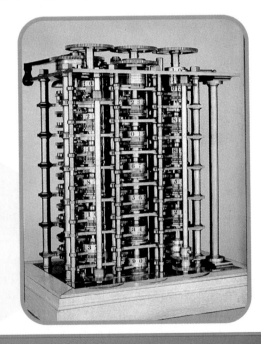

1800   1850

1890

Census Counting Machine

Herman Hollerith constructed a machine that processed information by allowing electric current to pass through holes in punch cards. With Hollerith's machine, the United States census of 1890 was completed in one fourth the time needed for the 1880 census.

used such a diskette, you may be confused by the term *floppy*. This is because the floppy disk is encased in a hard, square plastic case for protection. If you slide the metal portion of the case to the side, you can see the floppy disk inside.

Another type of memory is an optical disc, also called a compact disc. An **optical disc** is a disc on which information is written and read by lasers. Optical discs can hold much greater amounts of information than diskettes. They are commonly used for video games. They also hold reference materials such as encyclopedias, magazines, and videos. Such optical discs are called CD-ROMs (Compact Disc—Read-Only Memory).

✓ *Checkpoint* *What is read-only memory (ROM)?*

In Your Journal

In 1953, there were only about 100 computers in the entire world. Today, there are hundreds of millions of computers in businesses, homes, government offices, schools, and stores. Select one of the early forms of the computer. Write a newspaper article introducing it and its applications to the public.

1946
ENIAC

The first American-built computer was developed by the United States Army. The Electronic Numerical Integrator and Calculator, or ENIAC, consisted of thousands of vacuum tubes and filled an entire warehouse. To change the program, programmers had to rewire the entire machine.

1900   **1950**   **2000**

1939
Binary System

American physicists John V. Atanasoff and Clifford Berry produced a working model of a computer based on the binary system. They recognized that the digits 1 and 0 could be easily represented by electronic components.

1974
Personal Computers

The first personal computer (PC) went on the market. Today's personal computer is 400 times faster than ENIAC, 3,000 times lighter, and several million dollars cheaper.

Computer Software

A computer needs a set of instructions that tell it what to do. **A program is a detailed set of instructions that directs the computer hardware to perform operations on stored information.** Computer programs are called **computer software.** Whenever you use a word processor, solve mathematical problems, or play a computer game, a computer program is instructing the computer to perform in a certain way.

One category of computer software is called the operating system of the computer. An operating system is a set of basic instructions that keep a computer running. Perhaps you have heard of the operating software known as DOS, or disk operating system. Unix is another example of operating software.

A second category of software is usually called applications software. Applications are particular tasks that a computer may carry out. These programs are grouped by their function, such as word processing, graphics, games, or simulations.

✓ *Checkpoint* *What is a computer program?*

Computer Programming

People who program computers are called computer programmers. **Computer programmers** use computer languages that convert input information into instructions that the CPU can understand. You may have heard the names of some computer languages, such as Fortran, Basic, C, and COBOL. Each language is designed for a specific purpose. Fortran, for example, allows users to complete complex calculations. It is not, however, practical for word processing.

Programmers create software by using a step-by-step development process. First, they outline exactly what the program will do. Second, they develop a flowchart. A flowchart is a diagram showing the order of computer actions and data flow. Third, they write the instructions for the computer in a particular language. Complicated programs may contain millions of instructions. And finally, they test the program.

If the program does not work as the programmers intend, they *debug* it by identifying any problems with their logic. The term *bug* was applied to a mysterious malfunction in an early computer. Programmers discovered a moth in a vital electrical switch. Thereafter the programmers referred to problems as bugs and fixing problems as debugging.

Figure 23 Computer programmers develop software with all sorts of applications, from typing simple sentences to using simulators to train pilots and these oil rig operators.

Figure 24 Computers do not always take the form of desktop computers. Computer technology is used in devices as common as cameras and watches.

Computers at Work

Computer hardware and software are not always obvious. Just because you don't see an entire computer setup, you shouldn't assume a computer isn't involved. Do you wear a digital watch? If so, you are wearing a computer. Computer chips are used to control the timing of alarms and displays in digital watches.

Has a photographer ever taken your school picture? Computers and electronic sensors are used to monitor exposures in cameras. At the grocery store, computers are used to enter inventory bar codes into the cash register and add up your purchases. Computer chips are used to regulate engines in cars, monitor heating and cooling systems in buildings, and even to operate the locks on some doors. Look around. Computers are everywhere.

Section 3 Review

1. What is a computer? How does a computer store information?
2. How are computer hardware and software involved in the operation of a computer?
3. How do switches within a computer count to ten using binary code?
4. **Thinking Critically Classifying** Identify each of the following as an input device, output device, or both: keyboard, printer, diskette, scanner, touch-activated screen.

CHAPTER PROJECT

Check Your Progress

Choose a task that you would like to have done by a computer. Consider an activity such as mowing the lawn or watering the crops on a farm. Try to make your computer application original. Develop a series of steps that the computer would follow to complete the task. What input information is required? What is the resulting output from the computer? A flowchart diagram will help other students understand your new invention.

The Penny Computer

Computers can only count to 1! Computers use a binary number system that has only two digits, 0 and 1, to represent numbers. In a computer, a 0 is represented by a switch that is turned off, and a 1 by a switch that is turned on. You will make a model of a computer using pennies instead of switches.

Problem

How can pennies be used to model counting and adding in a computer?

Materials

15 pennies   paper   ruler
binary number table (Figure 22)

Procedure

Part 1 Binary Numbers

1. Review binary numbers. (See Figure 22 in this chapter.)
2. Before you use the computer, you need to learn the rules for counting with the penny code:
   ◆ A heads-up penny represents the digit 1.
   ◆ A tails-up penny represents the digit 0.

16	8	4	2	1
		🪙	🪙	🪙

Figure 1

3. Examine Figure 1. The row of pennies represents a binary number. In your notebook, write the binary number represented by the row of pennies.
4. Convert this binary number to a base-10 number. Write the result in your notebook. Remember that the binary number 101 is equivalent to 5:
$$(1 \times 4) + (0 \times 2) + (1 \times 1) =$$
$$4 \quad + \quad 0 \quad + \quad 1 \quad = 5$$
5. In your notebook, write the binary numbers 110, 111, 1000, 1001, and 10001.
6. Use pennies to represent these five binary numbers. Then convert the five binary numbers to their base-10 equivalents, and record.

Part 2 Adding with Binary Numbers

7. Learn the following rules for binary addition.

$$\begin{array}{ccc} 0 & 1 & 1 \\ +0 & +0 & +1 \\ \hline 0 & 1 & 10 \end{array}$$

The third rule may look odd, but remember that 10 in the binary system is equivalent to the number 2 in the base-10 system. The third rule shows you how to carry a 1 when adding binary numbers.

Figure 2

8. Using a heads-up penny for the digit 1, and a tails-up penny for the digit 0, the addition rules in Step 7 can be represented as shown in Figure 2. The first rule is complete. Use pennies to work out the other two. Copy the results in your notebook.

9. Look at Figure 3. It shows an addition problem done with the computer. Check that the arithmetic is done according to the rules you have learned. (Remember that you may have to carry a 1.)

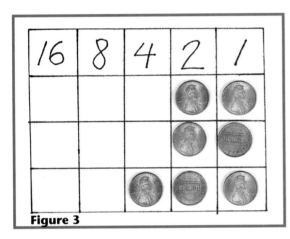

Figure 3

Part 3 Building a Binary Computer

10. Make a blank chart like the one in Figure 3. Be sure that each of the spaces in the three blank rows is large enough for a penny. This chart is your computer.

11. Put three pennies in the first blank row to represent the binary number 110.

12. Put three more pennies in the second row to represent the binary number 101.

13. Add together the two binary numbers. Use pennies to represent the sum.

14. Convert the three rows of pennies to base-10 numbers.

15. Use the base-10 numbers to check that you have done the problem correctly.

16. Next, use your computer to add the binary numbers 11 and 11. You will have to carry a 1 in two places. If you get the result 110, you have carried correctly.

17. Make up three other addition problems for your partner to solve. At least one of the binary numbers in each pair should have more than three digits. You will need to repeat Steps 10–15 each time. Write the problems in your notebook.

Analyze and Conclude

1. For the calculations you performed in Part 3, did you find the same results with the binary and base-10 systems?

2. What is the largest number that can be represented using 5 pennies? Explain.

3. How could you change your computer so you could represent larger numbers than your answer to Question 2? How could you represent 32 or 64 in the binary system? Use pennies to illustrate your answer.

4. **Think About It** In a computer, each on-off switch is called a bit. A byte is made up of 8 bits. How many pennies would be needed to model each byte? A typical personal computer may have a hard disk capacity of 3 gigabytes (3 billion bytes). How many pennies would be needed to model the number of bytes in the hard disk?

More to Explore

Find the rule that describes how your model can be used to double binary numbers. (*Hint:* You know that if you double the base-10 number 9, the answer is 18. What is 9 in binary? What is 18 in binary? Try other examples, and look for a pattern.) What is the relationship between a binary number and twice that number?

SECTION ④ The Information Superhighway

DISCOVER ···ACTIVITY····

How Important Are Computers?

1. Obtain a local or national newspaper.
2. Look through the newspaper for articles that refer to computers, the Internet, the World Wide Web, or the information superhighway.
3. Write down the topics of the articles. For example, was the article about politics, cooking, money, or computers?
4. Create a data table to show your results.

Think It Over

Inferring What can you infer about the kinds of information available through the computer? How much do you think people use information that they obtain through computers?

GUIDE FOR READING

◆ **What are the advantages of a computer network?**

◆ **What is the Internet?**

◆ **How can you use computers safely?**

Reading Tip Before you read, list five things that you know about the Internet. Add to your list after you read the section.

Because of the Internet, the world is at your fingertips! You can send an e-mail message to someone on the other side of the planet. Through the World Wide Web, information is yours for the searching as you prepare a school report. The news, sport scores, travel information, and weather reports are all available at any time. How is this possible? The answer is through the use of a computer connected to a network.

Computer Networks

You have traveled on a network of roads and highways that connects cities and towns. A **computer network** is a group of computers connected by cables or telephone lines. **A computer network allows people in different locations to share information and software.**

Figure 25 This is an artist's view of the information superhighway. *Forming Operational Definitions* How would you define this term?

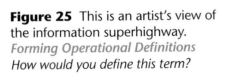

Figure 26 Cables connect computers in a local area network. People all over the world are connected by wide area networks such as the Internet.

There are two types of networks. A set of computers connected in one classroom or office building is known as a **local area network (LAN).** Computers connected across larger distances form a **wide area network (WAN).** In wide area networks, very powerful computers serve as a support connection for hundreds of less powerful computers.

The Internet

The most significant wide area network is the Internet. The **Internet** is a global network that links millions of computers in businesses, schools, and research organizations. **The Internet is a network of host computers that extends around the world.** You might say that the Internet is a network of networks. The Internet, along with other smaller networks, sometimes is called the information superhighway.

The Internet began in 1969 as a military communications system. Its purpose was to link computers used in military work. The links were designed so that communication would continue even if many computers were destroyed. In order for scientists to exchange data through their computers, colleges and universities were later added to the Internet.

Beginning in 1993, businesses were allowed to sell Internet connections to individuals. These businesses are known as Internet service providers (ISPs). With easy access available, the Internet has grown at an incredible rate. Its use for entertainment, shopping, and everyday information gathering completely overshadows its original purpose.

World Wide Web

You have probably seen advertisements for information available on the World Wide Web (WWW). The World Wide Web was developed in 1989. The **World Wide Web** is a system that allows you to display and view files, called pages, on the Internet. A Web page can include text, pictures, video, or sound. Prior to the development of the World Wide Web, Internet users could only view information in the form of words and numbers. Through the World Wide Web, users can look at images similar to those you might see on television or videos. Software programs called search engines allow people to search through the Web for information.

✓ *Checkpoint* *How has the World Wide Web changed the Internet?*

Using Computers Safely

Like any tool, computer networks have their pros and cons. For instance, information is so easy to transfer that it can get into the wrong hands. Networks are designed to protect credit card numbers, medical data, business records, and other information. Networks usually require authorization for you to enter, and have software designed to keep out unwanted users. You may have used a password to enter a local area network.

Another way to protect information is to code, or encrypt it. **Encryption** is a mathematical process of coding information so that only the intended user can read it.

Computer viruses, which are a form of computer vandalism, are another danger of the Internet. **Computer viruses** are programs that interfere with the normal operation of a computer. Much like a living virus, a computer virus enters a computer and reproduces itself. A virus can destroy information or even disable the computer.

Figure 27 Most networks require authorized users to have passwords. Never give your password to anyone you do not know well.

738

Software is available that will detect viruses before they can infect a computer. **When you load a file from a network, you should always run virus-checking software.** Store downloaded programs on a diskette, to protect your hard drive.

One important kind of computer safety is your personal safety. Computer users are not screened. For this reason, be very careful about using chat rooms. **Chat rooms** are a feature of networks that allow two or more users to exchange messages. **You do not know who may be using a chat room, so you should never give out your name, address, or telephone number. Do not respond to offensive messages, and do not accept files from strangers.**

Intellectual Property

A computer program is a piece of intellectual property. **Intellectual property** is an idea, or artistic creation, such as a poem or book. Governments protect intellectual property by granting copyrights to authors and patents to inventors.

When you buy a computer program you are actually buying a license only for yourself to use that program. If a friend copies your program onto another computer, the author receives no payment. If the authors are not paid, it will not be worthwhile for them to improve their programs or to write new ones.

Besides the software that you have to buy, there are thousands of programs known as freeware or shareware which are available through the Internet. **Freeware** is software that the author has decided to let people use at no charge. **Shareware** is software that the author allows people to try out and use for a very low fee. The user pays the fee and registers the software with the author. Then the author usually continues to improve the program and supply registered users with revisions.

Figure 28 The software that a school buys is licensed only for use on computers in the school.

Section 4 Review

1. What is a computer network? Why are networks used?
2. What is the Internet? What are some reasons for using the Internet?
3. What is a chat room?
4. **Thinking Critically Calculating** You receive a free disk with a game on it. There is a computer virus on the disk that doubles in size every time you play the game. How much larger has the virus grown by the time you have played the game ten times?

Science at Home

Computer Age Although computers are commonplace today, this was not always the case. Interview a family member who grew up before computers were common. Prepare a list of questions for the interview. Find out whether that person has used a computer, what he or she thinks about computers, and how computers might have changed his or her life. Ask if the large number of applications for computers has come as a surprise.

SCIENCE AND SOCIETY

When Seeing ISN'T Believing

The combination of computers and photography can make magic. A computer can turn the bits of light, dark, and color in a photo into a code. By using the computer to change the code, a technician can change any part of a photo.

This way of working with photos is called digital manipulation. Fuzzy pictures can be made clearer and sharper. Colors can be brightened or completely changed. Tiny or hidden details can be made easier to see and understand. Old or stained photos can be made to look like new. Objects or people in a photo can even be added, removed, or moved around.

But some people worry that digital manipulation could be used to cheat or harm people. Are there ways to be informed and entertained by digital manipulation without being fooled by it?

The Issues

What Are the Dangers of Manipulated Photos? It's nearly impossible to tell the difference between a digitally changed photo and an unchanged one. Suppose, for example, a photographer has one photo of the mayor hugging her husband and another photo of a well-known criminal. With digital "magic," an unethical person could create a photo of the mayor hugging the criminal. Not only could newspapers, magazines, and TV stations mislead the public, but witnesses might try to use faked photographs in court cases.

How Can People Protect Themselves? Governments could pass laws against changing photographs. Such laws would be hard to enforce, however, because digital manipulation is so hard to detect. Laws might also make it difficult to use digital manipulation for useful purposes. And such laws might violate the right of free speech. Our courts consider photos a kind of speech, or expression.

Another option is for photographers or organizations to police themselves. They could write codes of conduct. The United States armed forces already have a code for photos (for instance, photos taken from military airplanes). Under this code, it is all right to make photos clearer digitally. But it is not all right to add, take away, or move around parts of a photo. Some photographers who work for newspapers have suggested a similar code for themselves.

Should Manipulated Photos Be Marked? One safeguard might be to put a symbol on any digitally manipulated photo. That way viewers would be warned. But opponents point out that nearly every photo seen in newspapers and magazines is changed a little, usually just to make the colors more clear. If every photo had the symbol, people wouldn't be able to see the difference between a photo whose image had been made clearer and one in which something had been faked. People might stop trusting any photo.

You Decide

1. Identify the Problem
In your own words, describe the problems created by digital manipulation of photos.

2. Analyze the Options
List reasons for and against
a. passing a law against changing any photo digitally,
b. letting photographers make their own code of conduct, and
c. marking all digitally manipulated photos with a special symbol.

3. Find a Solution
You run a TV station. Your assistants want to use two digitally changed photos, one in a commercial and one in a news story. Will you let them use one, or both, or neither? Explain.

740

SECTION 1 Electronic Signals and Semiconductors

Key Ideas

◆ Electronics uses electric currents to carry information.

◆ Semiconductors are used to make solid-state devices such as integrated circuits.

Key Terms

electronics
electronic signal
analog signal
digital signal
solid-state component

diode
transistor
integrated circuit
vacuum tube

SECTION 2 Electronic Communication

Key Ideas

◆ Sound is converted into an electronic signal in the transmitter of a telephone.

◆ Electronic signals can be carried over long distances by electromagnetic waves.

Key Term

cathode ray tube (CRT)

SECTION 3 Computers

Key Ideas

◆ Computer hardware includes the central processing unit, input devices, output devices, and memory storage devices.

Key Terms

computer
binary system
bit
byte
computer hardware
central processing unit
input device
output device
random-access
  memory (RAM)

read-only memory
  (ROM)
disk drive
hard disk
diskette
optical disc
computer software
computer
  programmer

SECTION 4 The Information Superhighway

INTEGRATING TECHNOLOGY

Key Ideas

◆ Computers are connected by computer networks. The Internet is a network of host computers that extends around the world.

◆ Safe use of computer networks includes checking for viruses and using chat rooms with caution.

Key Terms

computer network
local area network (LAN)
wide area network (WAN)
Internet
World Wide Web
encryption

computer virus
chat rooms
intellectual property
freeware
shareware

Organizing Information

Flowchart Copy the flowchart about telephone communication onto a sheet of paper. Complete the flowchart by filling in the missing steps. (For more on flowcharts, see the Skills Handbook.)

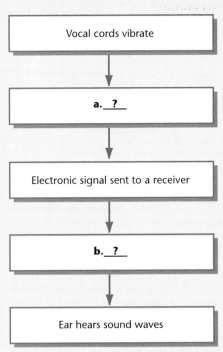

Reviewing Content

 For more review of key concepts, see the Interactive Student Tutorial CD-ROM.

Multiple Choice

Choose the letter of the best answer.

1. A sandwich of 3 layers of semiconductor that is used to amplify an electric signal is known as a(n)
   a. diode.
   b. modem.
   c. transistor.
   d. integrated circuit.

2. A radio speaker
   a. converts sound to an electronic signal.
   b. converts an electronic signal to sound.
   c. places an electronic signal on an electromagnetic wave.
   d. controls the function of an electron gun.

3. An example of a computer output device is a
   a. printer.   b. keyboard.
   c. program.   d. CPU.

4. If you wanted to transfer information from one computer to another you might use a
   a. hard disk.   b. RAM chip.
   c. ROM chip.   d. diskette.

5. A group of computers connected by cables or telephone lines is a
   a. microprocessor.
   b. CPU.
   c. modem.
   d. network.

True or False

If the statement is true, write true. If it is false, change the underlined word or words to make the statement true.

6. A <u>transistor</u> changes alternating current into direct current.

7. Before semiconductors, electronic devices used <u>vacuum tubes</u> to control electric current.

8. A <u>microphone</u> is the part of a television that produces the image.

9. <u>Output devices</u> feed data into a computer.

10. The <u>Internet</u> can be described as a network of computer networks.

Checking Concepts

11. Compare an analog signal with a digital signal.

12. Define each of the following in your own words: diode, transistor, and integrated circuit.

13. Draw an illustration of an electromagnetic wave. Give three examples of electromagnetic waves.

14. Explain how a radio show is broadcast and received.

15. How does a cathode-ray tube create a picture?

16. How is the World Wide Web different from the Internet?

17. **Writing to Learn** Imagine that you have started your own small magazine. Choose a topic for your magazine, such as sports, fashion, science, or cooking. Then write three to four paragraphs describing how a computer and access to the Internet might help you.

Thinking Critically

18. **Comparing and Contrasting** What are some advantages of solid-state devices over vacuum tubes?

19. **Calculating** Each image on a television screen lasts for 1/30th of a second. How many images appear on the screen during a 30-minute program?

20. **Applying Concepts** A computer program is a list of instructions that tells a computer how to perform a task. Write a program that describes the steps involved in some task, such as walking your dog, taking out the trash, setting the table, or playing a game.

21. **Comparing and Contrasting** How do base-10 numbers and binary numbers differ? Explain how you read and write numbers in each system. Give examples.

22. **Making Judgments** Why does a government protect a computer program as the intellectual property of the author?

Applying Skills

Use the illustrations below to answer Questions 23–25.

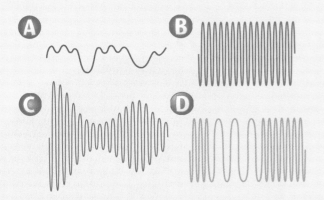

23. Predicting What would the audio signal in part A look like if it were converted to an AM radio signal? Draw a sketch to illustrate your answer.

24. Communicating What is represented in part B? Describe its basic characteristics.

25. Classifying Two radio transmitters send out electronic signals shown as part C and part D. How are the two forms alike and how are they different?

Performance ▼ CHAPTER PROJECT Assessment

Present Your Project Present both the existing computer application and the new one you invented to the class. Provide diagrams of each and describe their operation. You might want to pretend you are trying to sell your new invention to the class. Prepare a poster describing the task that your new application will be doing. Show yourself enjoying the benefits!

Reflect and Record In your journal, discuss what you've learned about computer applications. Think about the new computer application you developed. Is there a way to make it even better or more useful than you already have?

Test Preparation

Use these questions to prepare for standardized tests.

Read the passage. Then answer Questions 26–29.
Jose made a simple computer for a school science project. The only problem was that his computer could read and write only binary numbers. It did not translate to or from base-10 numbers. Jose asked the computer to add the following binary numbers: 100 + 1111 + 110101. The computer's answer was 1001000.

26. What is the base number of the binary system?
  a. 1
  b. 2
  c. 4
  d. 8

27. What is each 1 or 0 in the binary system called?
  a. a bit
  b. a byte
  c. a megabyte
  d. a ram

28. Translate into the base-10 system the numbers Jose added.
  a. 100 + 1,111 + 110,101
  b. 2 + 2,222 + 220,202
  c. 4 + 15 + 53
  d. 6 + 20 + 30

29. Translate the computer's answer into the base-10 system.
  a. 42
  b. 56
  c. 72
  d. 1,001,000

E·D·I·S·O·N—
Genius of Invention

WHAT INVENTOR GAVE US

- *sound recording?*
- *motion pictures?*
- *electric lighting?*

Edison at his workbench

This scene shows New York City in 1881. An electric light high above Madison Square outshines the gas light in the foreground.

In 1881, the electric light in the picture at the left was a novelty. Streets and some homes were lit with gas, while other homes used oil lamps or candles. Thomas Edison was still developing his system of indoor electric lighting.

Electric lights brought with them a system of power distribution which made other uses of electricity possible. If you try to imagine living without any electrical appliances, you will understand the changes in everyday life that Edison started.

Thomas Edison (1847–1931) had almost no schooling. Yet his mind always bubbled with ideas. In addition to his lighting system, Edison invented the phonograph and the movie camera. He also made improvements to the telegraph and telephone. At the time of his death, Edison held 1,093 patents. A patent is a government license protecting an inventor's right to make and sell a product. One of Edison's most important ideas, the first laboratory for industrial research, was never patented.

The Wizard of Menlo Park

Before 1900 most inventors worked alone. Edison, in contrast, depended on a strong team of research co-workers to carry out his ideas. Edison had an unusual ability to inspire those who worked for him. A very hard worker himself, he demanded that everyone on his team also work long hours.

In 1870, he set up a workshop in Newark, New Jersey, to test new ideas and designs. Some of Edison's original team stayed with him for years. They included a Swiss clockmaker, an English engineer, and an American mechanic.

By 1876 Edison had enough money to set up an "invention factory." He chose the small town of Menlo Park, New Jersey. Menlo Park became the world's first industrial research laboratory. Soon a mathematician and a glass blower joined the team.

Edison's team often made improvements on other people's inventions. The light bulb is an example. Other scientists had invented electric lamps, but their light bulbs burned rapidly. The problem was to find a material for the filament that would not overheat or burn out quickly.

The Menlo Park team spent months testing hundreds of materials. First they rolled up each material into a long thin strand. Then they carbonized it, which meant baking it until it turned to charcoal. Then they tested it in a vacuum, or absence of air. Most materials failed in only a few minutes or a few hours. Edison tried platinum, a metallic element, with some success, but then went back to carbonized fibers. The team improved the vacuum inside the bulb. The glass blower tried differently shaped bulbs.

The breakthrough came in 1879. The successful filament was a length of ordinary cotton thread, carefully carbonized. In December, the newspapers carried the headlines: "Success in a Cotton Thread" and "It Makes a Light, Without Gas or Flame."

A light bulb is made of a wire, or filament, inside a glass bulb. Most of the air is removed from the bulb, making a vacuum. Electricity flowing through the wire makes it white hot, so that it glows. Edison's drawing of a light bulb is at the right.

Science Activity

Work together as a team to invent a new electrical device.

♦ What is the problem? What might make your life easier?

♦ What are the solutions? Brainstorm for possible products that use an electrical circuit. Write down all possible ideas.

♦ Evaluate each solution. List the supplies you will need. Note any new skills you should learn. Agree on the best solution.

♦ Plan your design and make a labeled drawing.

Write down the materials you will need and the steps you will use to build your device.

Lighting Manhattan

Edison recognized the value of publicity. Besides being a productive inventor, he knew how to promote himself. He made glowing predictions about his new electric system. Electricity would soon be so cheap, he said, that "only the rich would be able to afford candles."

Edison demonstrated his electric lights in spectacular displays at expositions in Paris and London. These displays led to his setting up companies in France, England, the Netherlands, and other parts of Europe.

When he built his first neighborhood generating station, Edison made a shrewd choice of location. The Pearl Street power station brought light and power to about 2.6 square kilometers of downtown Manhattan. It supplied businesses and factories as well as private homes. The circuits could light 400 light bulbs. Some of those lights were in the offices of J. P. Morgan, the leading banker and financier of the time. Others lights were located in the offices of *The New York Times*. Here's what the *Times* reporter wrote on September 5, 1882.

New York City—Broadway in the 1880s

THE NEW YORK TIMES, September 5, 1882

"Yesterday for the first time The Times Building was illuminated by electricity. Mr. Edison had at last perfected his incandescent light, had put his machinery in order, and had started up his engines, and last evening his company lighted up about one-third of the lower City district in which The Times Building stands. . . .

It was not until about seven o'clock, when it began to grow dark, that the electric light really made itself known and showed how bright and steady it is. . . . It was a light that a man could sit down under and write for hours without the consciousness of having any artificial light about him. There was a very slight amount of heat from each lamp, but not nearly as much as from a gas-burner—one-fifteenth as much as from gas, the inventor says. The light was soft, mellow, and grateful to the eye, and it seemed almost like writing by daylight to have a light without a particle of flicker and with scarcely any heat to make the head ache. . . . The decision was unanimously in favor of the Edison electric lamp as against gas."

Language Arts Activity

The reporter who wrote the newspaper story observed details carefully and used them to write about an event—the first lights in his office. Look back at the story. Now write about the event as Edison would have told it to convince people to buy light bulbs and install electrical power systems. You could make an advertisement. Inform your readers about the product and persuade them to buy it.

Solving Practical Problems

As he grew older, Edison worried that American students were not learning mathematics well enough. To motivate students, he suggested using problems that related to real-life situations. In 1925, when he was 78, he proposed these problems as recorded in his notebooks. Note that light bulbs were called *lamps*. Tungsten is a metal used in light bulbs.

PROBLEM 1

"American power plants now serve 9,500,000 homes. The estimated number of homes in the United States is 21,000,000. What percentage receives electric power?"

PROBLEM 2

"It needs about 280,000,000 tungsten lamps [bulbs] each year to supply the market today. And yet the first lamp factory in the world—the Edison Lamp Works. . .—was not started until 1880, and I was told it would never pay. The output for our first year was about 25,000 globes [bulbs]. How many times that figure would be required for the present market?"

PROBLEM 3

"A household using 21 lamps requires about 7 new lamps each year. What percentage is this?"

PROBLEM 4

"If these lamps had been bought at the retail prices of the first year of the lamp factory, they would have cost $1.25 each. How much would the family save by the decreased prices of today?"

Math Activity

Solve the four math problems that Edison wrote. To solve Problem 4, use 1902 prices. That year, incandescent light bulbs (or lamps) cost $ .30 each.

Electrical Distribution

Electric lighting didn't begin with Edison's light bulb. Before the incandescent bulb, most electric lights were carbon arc lamps. An electric arc flashed between two carbon rods. Carbon arc lamps were used for public places such as railroad stations in both Europe and the United States. But they were too bright and too dangerous for most indoor uses.

Edison found a way to make indoor lighting practical. Along with the light bulb, he had to set up a system to distribute electricity to homes and business. That system included generators, underground cables, junction boxes, and meters.

Local power companies grew slowly. Laying cables to carry power was slow and expensive. In the 1920s, less than half the homes in cities had electricity. And less than 10 percent of rural areas had electricity. Only in 1935 was a program begun to bring power to the countryside.

Social Studies Activity

Look at the recent satellite photo of the United States at night. It shows how electric lights now light up the country from coast to coast. Using a map of the United States, identify the regions that are the brightest. What cities are located there? Which states have the most urban areas? Which have the least? Use an almanac to find out the population of 5 of the largest cities. Compare these data with the total United States population.

History of the phonograph

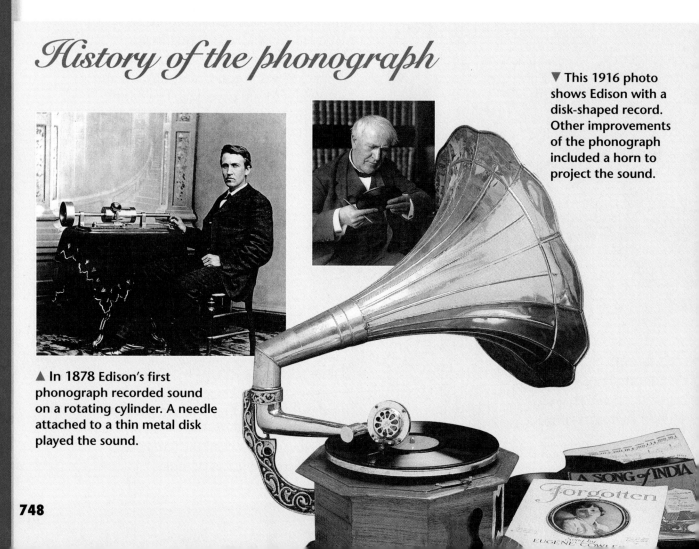

▼ This 1916 photo shows Edison with a disk-shaped record. Other improvements of the phonograph included a horn to project the sound.

▲ In 1878 Edison's first phonograph recorded sound on a rotating cylinder. A needle attached to a thin metal disk played the sound.

A SONG of INDIA

Forgotten

As this satellite image shows, the glow of street lights is visible from space.

By the 1950s, phonographs used electric motors and electronic amplifiers. The quality of sound was better, and the volume could be much greater.

▼ 78 rpm record

◄ 45 rpm records

▲ 33⅓ rpm record

Records played longer as the standard playing speed was reduced from 78 revolutions per minute to 45 and $33\frac{1}{3}$ revolutions per minute.

Modern Times

Many of the inventions that came out of Menlo Park still affect things we do today. Work in pairs to research one of Edison's inventions. Or research another scientist's inventions. Find out how the device changed and improved in the 1900s. Write up your research and present it to the class. If the device is no longer used, explain what has replaced it. Here are a few inventions from which to choose. (Not all of them were Edison's.)

◆ stock ticker
◆ telegraph
◆ phonograph
◆ disk record
◆ voting machine
◆ electric pen and press
◆ typewriter
◆ telephone
◆ automobile
◆ radio transmitter
◆ vacuum tube
◆ mechanical music
◆ linotype

Compact discs are recordings, and they are shaped like phonograph records. But are they related to Edison's invention?

Think Like a Scientist

Although you may not know it, you think like a scientist every day. Whenever you ask a question and explore possible answers, you use many of the same skills that scientists do. Some of these skills are described on this page.

Observing

When you use one or more of your five senses to gather information about the world, you are **observing.** Hearing a dog bark, counting twelve green seeds, and smelling smoke are all observations. To increase the power of their senses, scientists sometimes use microscopes, telescopes, or other instruments that help them make more detailed observations.

It is important to keep careful records of your observations in science class by writing or drawing in a notebook. An observation must be an accurate report of what your senses detect. The information collected through observations is called evidence, or data.

Inferring

When you interpret an observation, you are **inferring,** or making an inference. For example, if you hear your dog barking, you may infer that someone is at your front door. To make this inference, you combine the evidence—the barking dog—and your experience or knowledge—you know that your dog barks when strangers approach— to reach a logical conclusion.

Notice that an inference is not a fact; it is only one of many possible interpretations for an observation. For example, your dog may be barking because it wants to go for a walk. An inference may turn out to be incorrect even if it is based on accurate obser- vations and logical reasoning. The only way to find out if an inference is correct is to investigate further.

Predicting

When you listen to the weather forecast, you hear many predictions about the next day's weather—what the temperature will be, whether it will rain, and how windy it will be. Weather forecasters use observations and knowledge of weather patterns to predict the weather. The skill of **predicting** involves making an inference about a future event based on current evidence or past experience.

Because a prediction is an inference, it may prove to be false. In science class, you can test some of your predictions by doing experiments. For example, suppose you predict that larger paper airplanes can fly farther than smaller airplanes. How could you test your prediction?

ACTIVITY Use the photograph to answer the questions below.

Observing Look closely at the photograph. List at least three observations.

Inferring Use your observations to make an inference about what has happened. What experience or knowledge did you use to make the inference?

Predicting Predict what will happen next. On what evidence or experience do you base your prediction?

Classifying

Could you imagine searching for a book in the library if the books were shelved in no particular order? Your trip to the library would be an all-day event! Luckily, librarians group together books on similar topics or by the same author. Grouping together items that are alike in some way is called **classifying.** You can classify items in many ways: by size, by shape, by use, and by other important characteristics.

Like librarians, scientists use the skill of classifying to organize information and objects. When things are sorted into groups, the relationships among them become easier to understand.

Classify the objects in the photograph into two groups based on any characteristic you choose. Then use another characteristic to classify the objects into three groups.

Making Models

Have you ever drawn a picture to help someone understand what you were saying? Such a drawing is one type of model. A model is a picture, diagram, computer image, or other representation of a complex object or process. **Making models** helps people understand things that they cannot observe directly.

Scientists often use models to represent things that are either very large or very small, such as the planets in the solar system, or the parts of a cell. Such models are physical models—drawings or three-dimensional structures that look like the real thing. Other models are mental models—mathematical equations or words that describe how something works.

These students are using a model rocket to learn about the principles of flight. How can a model help you learn about the full-scale object it represents?

Communicating

Whenever you talk on the phone, write a letter, or listen to your teacher at school, you are communicating. **Communicating** is the process of sharing ideas and information with other people. Communicating effectively requires many skills, including writing, reading, speaking, listening, and making models.

Scientists communicate to share results, information, and opinions. Scientists often communicate about their work in journals, over the telephone, in letters, and on the Internet. They also attend scientific meetings where they share their ideas with one another in person.

On a sheet of paper, write out clear, detailed directions to set a table for dinner. Give your directions to a family member to follow. Was he or she able to follow your directions exactly? How could you have communicated more clearly?

Making Measurements

When scientists make observations, it is not sufficient to say that something is "big" or "heavy." Instead, scientists use instruments to measure just how big or heavy an object is. By measuring, scientists can express their observations more precisely and communicate more information about what they observe.

Measuring in SI

The standard system of measurement used by scientists around the world is known as the International System of Units, which is abbreviated as SI (in French, *Système International d'Unités*). SI units are easy to use because they are based on multiples of 10. Each unit is ten times larger than the next smallest unit and one tenth the size of the next largest unit. The table lists the prefixes used to name the most common SI units.

Common SI Prefixes

Prefix	Symbol	Meaning
kilo-	k	1,000
hecto-	h	100
deka-	da	10
deci-	d	0.1 (one tenth)
centi-	c	0.01 (one hundredth)
milli-	m	0.001 (one thousandth)

Length To measure length, or the distance between two points, the unit of measure is the **meter (m).** One meter is the approximate distance from the floor to a doorknob. Long distances, such as the distance between two cities, are measured in kilometers (km). Small lengths are measured in centimeters (cm) or millimeters (mm). Scientists use metric rulers and meter sticks to measure length.

Common Conversions

1 km = 1,000 m
1 m = 100 cm
1 m = 1,000 mm
1 cm = 10 mm

Liquid Volume To measure the volume of a liquid, or the amount of space it takes up, you will use a unit of measure known as the **liter (L).** One liter is the approximate volume of a medium-sized carton of milk. Smaller volumes are measured in milliliters (mL). Scientists use graduated cylinders to measure liquid volume.

Common Conversion

1 L = 1,000 mL

> **ACTIVITY**
>
> The larger lines on the metric ruler in the picture show centimeter divisions, while the smaller, unnumbered lines show millimeter divisions. How many centimeters long is the block? How many millimeters long is it?

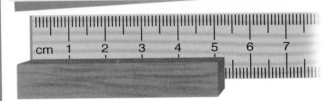

> **ACTIVITY**
>
> The graduated cylinder in the picture is marked in milliliter divisions. Notice that the water in the cylinder has a curved surface. This curved surface is called the *meniscus.* To measure the volume, you must read the level at the lowest point of the meniscus. What is the volume of water in this graduated cylinder?

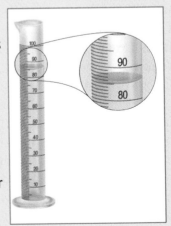

Mass To measure mass, or the amount of matter in an object, you will use a unit of measure known as the **gram (g).** One gram is approximately the mass of a paper clip. Larger masses are measured in kilograms (kg). Scientists use a balance to find the mass of an object.

Common Conversion

1 kg = 1,000 g

The electronic balance displays the mass of a potato in kilograms. **ACTIVITY** What is the mass of the potato? Suppose a recipe for potato salad called for one kilogram of potatoes. About how many potatoes would you need?

Temperature
To measure the temperature of a substance, you will use the **Celsius scale.** Temperature is measured in degrees Celsius (°C) using a Celsius thermometer. Water freezes at 0°C and boils at 100°C.

ACTIVITY
What is the temperature of the liquid in degrees Celsius?

Converting SI Units

To use the SI system, you must know how to convert between units. Converting from one unit to another involves the skill of **calculating,** or using mathematical operations. Converting between SI units is similar to converting between dollars and dimes because both systems are based on multiples of ten.

Suppose you want to convert a length of 80 centimeters to meters. Follow these steps to convert between units.

1. Begin by writing down the measurement you want to convert—in this example, 80 centimeters.
2. Write a conversion factor that represents the relationship between the two units you are converting. In this example, the relationship is *1 meter = 100 centimeters.* Write this conversion factor as a fraction, making sure to place the units you are converting from (centimeters, in this example) in the denominator.

3. Multiply the measurement you want to convert by the fraction. When you do this, the units in the first measurement will cancel out the units in the denominator. Your answer will be in the units you are converting to (meters, in this example).

Example

80 centimeters = ___?___ meters

$$80 \text{ centimeters} \times \frac{1 \text{ meter}}{100 \text{ centimeters}} = \frac{80 \text{ meters}}{100}$$
$$= 0.8 \text{ meters}$$

Convert between the following units. **ACTIVITY**
1. 250 millimeters = _?_ meters
2. 1.5 liters = _?_ milliliters
3. 750 grams = _?_ kilograms

Conducting a Scientific Investigation

In some ways, scientists are like detectives, piecing together clues to learn about a process or event. One way that scientists gather clues is by carrying out experiments. An experiment tests an idea in a careful, orderly manner. Although all experiments do not follow the same steps in the same order, many follow a pattern similar to the one described here.

Posing Questions

Experiments begin by asking a scientific question. A scientific question is one that can be answered by gathering evidence. For example, the question "Which freezes faster—fresh water or salt water?" is a scientific question because you can carry out an investigation and gather information to answer the question.

Developing a Hypothesis

The next step is to form a hypothesis. A **hypothesis** is a possible explanation for a set of observations or answer to a scientific question. Hypotheses are based on your observations and previous knowledge or experience. A hypothesis must be something that can be tested. In science, a hypothesis can take the form of an *If … then …* statement. For example, a hypothesis might be *"If I add salt to fresh water, then the water will take longer to freeze."* A hypothesis worded this way serves as a rough outline of the experiment you should perform.

754

Designing an Experiment

Next you need to plan a way to test your hypothesis. Your plan should be written out as a step-by-step procedure and should describe the observations or measurements you will make.

Two important steps involved in designing an experiment are controlling variables and forming operational definitions.

Controlling Variables In a well-designed experiment, you need to keep all variables the same except for one. A **variable** is any factor that can change in an experiment. The factor that you change is called the **manipulated variable.** In this experiment, the manipulated variable is the amount of salt added to the water. Other factors, such as the amount of water or the starting temperature, are kept constant.

The factor that changes as a result of the manipulated variable is called the responding variable. The **responding variable** is what you measure or observe to obtain your results. In this experiment, the responding variable is how long the water takes to freeze.

An experiment in which all factors except one are kept constant is a **controlled experiment.** Most controlled experiments include a test called the control. In this experiment, Container 3 is the control. Because no salt is added to Container 3, you can compare the results from the other containers to it. Any difference in results must be due to the addition of salt alone.

Forming Operational Definitions
Another important aspect of a well-designed experiment is having clear operational definitions. An **operational definition** is a statement that describes how a particular variable is to be measured or how a term is to be defined. For example, in this experiment, how will you determine if the water has frozen? You might decide to insert a stick in each container at the start of the experiment. Your operational definition of "frozen" would be the time at which the stick can no longer move.

EXPERIMENTAL PROCEDURE

1. Fill 3 containers with 300 milliliters of cold tap water.

2. Add 10 grams of salt to Container 1; stir. Add 20 grams of salt to Container 2; stir. Add no salt to Container 3.

3. Place the 3 containers in a freezer.

4. Check the containers every 15 minutes. Record your observations.

Interpreting Data

The observations and measurements you make in an experiment are called data. At the end of an experiment, you need to analyze the data to look for any patterns or trends. Patterns often become clear if you organize your data in a data table or graph. Then think through what the data reveal. Do they support your hypothesis? Do they point out a flaw in your experiment? Do you need to collect more data?

Drawing Conclusions

A conclusion is a statement that sums up what you have learned from an experiment. When you draw a conclusion, you need to decide whether the data you collected support your hypothesis or not. You may need to repeat an experiment several times before you can draw any conclusions from it. Conclusions often lead you to pose new questions and plan new experiments to answer them.

Is a ball's bounce affected by the height from which it is dropped? Using the steps just described, plan a controlled experiment to investigate this problem. **ACTIVITY**

Thinking Critically

Has a friend ever asked for your advice about a problem? If so, you may have helped your friend think through the problem in a logical way. Without knowing it, you used critical-thinking skills to help your friend. Critical thinking involves the use of reasoning and logic to solve problems or make decisions. Some critical-thinking skills are described below.

Comparing and Contrasting

When you examine two objects for similarities and differences, you are using the skill of **comparing and contrasting.** Comparing involves identifying similarities, or common characteristics. Contrasting involves identifying differences. Analyzing objects in this way can help you discover details that you might otherwise overlook.

> Compare and contrast the two clocks in the photo. First list all the similarities that you see. Then list all the differences.
>
> **ACTIVITY**

Applying Concepts

When you use your knowledge about one situation to make sense of a similar situation, you are using the skill of **applying concepts.** Being able to transfer your knowledge from one situation to another shows that you truly understand a concept. You may use this skill in answering test questions that present different problems from the ones you've reviewed in class.

> You have just learned that water takes longer to freeze when other substances are mixed into it. Use this knowledge to explain why people need a fluid called antifreeze in their car's radiator in the winter.
>
> **ACTIVITY**

Interpreting Illustrations

Diagrams, photographs, and maps are included in textbooks to help clarify what you read. These illustrations show processes, places, and ideas in a visual manner. The skill called **interpreting illustrations** can help you learn from these visual elements. To understand an illustration, take the time to study the illustration along with all the written information that accompanies it. Captions identify the key concepts shown in the illustration. Labels point out the important parts of a diagram or map, while keys identify the symbols used in a map.

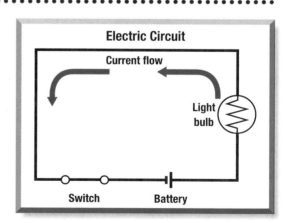

Electric Circuit

Current flow

Light bulb

Switch   Battery

> Study the diagram above. Then write a short paragraph explaining what you have learned.
>
> **ACTIVITY**

Relating Cause and Effect

If one event causes another event to occur, the two events are said to have a cause-and-effect relationship. When you determine that such a relationship exists between two events, you use a skill called **relating cause and effect.** For example, if you notice an itchy, red bump on your skin, you might infer that a mosquito bit you. The mosquito bite is the cause, and the bump is the effect.

It is important to note that two events do not necessarily have a cause-and-effect relationship just because they occur together. Scientists carry out experiments or use past experience to determine whether a cause-and-effect relationship exists.

> **ACTIVITY**
> You are on a camping trip and your flashlight has stopped working. List some possible causes for the flashlight malfunction. How could you determine which cause-and-effect relationship has left you in the dark?

Making Generalizations

When you draw a conclusion about an entire group based on information about only some of the group's members, you are using a skill called **making generalizations.** For a generalization to be valid, the sample you choose must be large enough and representative of the entire group. You might, for example, put this skill to work at a farm stand if you see a sign that says, "Sample some grapes before you buy." If you sample a few sweet grapes, you may conclude that all the grapes are sweet—and purchase a large bunch.

> **ACTIVITY**
> A team of scientists needs to determine whether the water in a large reservoir is safe to drink. How could they use the skill of making generalizations to help them? What should they do?

Making Judgments

When you evaluate something to decide whether it is good or bad, or right or wrong, you are using a skill called **making judgments.** For example, you make judgments when you decide to eat healthful foods or to pick up litter in a park. Before you make a judgment, you need to think through the pros and cons of a situation, and identify the values or standards that you hold.

> **ACTIVITY**
> Should all children and teens be required to take music lessons in school? Explain why you feel the way you do.

Problem Solving

When you use critical-thinking skills to resolve an issue or decide on a course of action, you are using a skill called **problem solving.** Some problems, such as how to convert a fraction into a decimal, are straightforward. Other problems, such as figuring out why your computer has stopped working, are complex. Some complex problems can be solved using the trial and error method—try out one solution first, and if that doesn't work, try another. Other useful problem-solving strategies include making models and brainstorming possible solutions with a partner.

Organizing Information

As you read this textbook, how can you make sense of all the information it contains? Some useful tools to help you organize information are shown on this page. These tools are called *graphic organizers* because they give you a visual picture of a topic, showing at a glance how key concepts are related.

Concept Maps

Concept maps are useful tools for organizing information on broad topics. A concept map begins with a general concept and shows how it can be broken down into more specific concepts. In that way, relationships between concepts become easier to understand.

A concept map is constructed by placing concept words (usually nouns) in ovals and connecting them with linking words. Often, the most general concept word is placed at the top, and the words become more specific as you move downward. Often the linking words, which are written on a line extending between two ovals, describe the relationship between the two concepts they connect. If you follow any string of concepts and linking words down the map, it should read like a sentence.

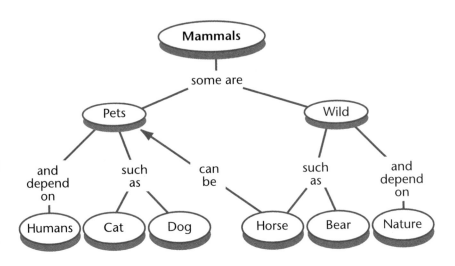

Some concept maps include linking words that connect a concept on one branch of the map to a concept on another branch. These linking words, called cross-linkages, show more complex interrelationships among concepts.

Compare/Contrast Tables

Compare/contrast tables are useful tools for sorting out the similarities and differences between two or more items. A table provides an organized framework in which to compare items based on specific characteristics that you identify.

To create a compare/contrast table, list the items to be compared across the top of a table. Then list the characteristics that will form the basis of your comparison in the left-hand

Characteristic	Baseball	Basketball
Number of Players	9	5
Playing Field	Baseball diamond	Basketball court
Equipment	Bat, baseball, mitts	Basket, basketball

column. Complete the table by filling in information about each characteristic, first for one item and then for the other.

Venn Diagrams

Another way to show similarities and differences between items is with a Venn diagram. A Venn diagram consists of two or more circles that partially overlap. Each circle represents a particular concept or idea. Common characteristics, or similarities, are written within the area of overlap between the two circles. Unique characteristics, or differences, are written in the parts of the circles outside the area of overlap.

To create a Venn diagram, draw two overlapping circles. Label the circles with the names of the items being compared. Write the

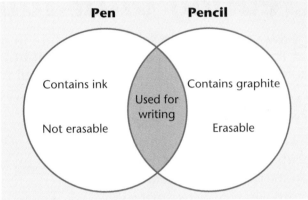

Pen   **Pencil**

Contains ink

Used for writing

Not erasable

Contains graphite

Erasable

unique characteristics in each circle outside the area of overlap. Then write the shared characteristics within the area of overlap.

Flowcharts

A flowchart can help you understand the order in which certain events have occurred or should occur. Flowcharts are useful for outlining the stages in a process or the steps in a procedure.

To make a flowchart, write a brief description of each event in a box. Place the first event at the top of the page, followed by the second event, the third event, and so on. Then draw an arrow to connect each event to the one that occurs next.

Preparing Pasta

Boil water

↓

Cook pasta

↓

Drain water

↓

Add sauce

Cycle Diagrams

A cycle diagram can be used to show a sequence of events that is continuous, or cyclical. A continuous sequence does not have an end because, when the final event is over, the first event begins again. Like a flowchart, a cycle diagram can help you understand the order of events.

To create a cycle diagram, write a brief description of each event in a box. Place one event at the top of the page in the center. Then, moving in a clockwise direction around an imaginary circle, write each event in its proper sequence. Draw arrows that connect each event to the one that occurs next, forming a continuous circle.

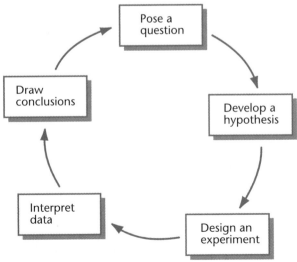

Steps in a Science Experiment

Pose a question

Develop a hypothesis

Design an experiment

Interpret data

Draw conclusions

Creating Data Tables and Graphs

How can you make sense of the data in a science experiment? The first step is to organize the data to help you understand them. Data tables and graphs are helpful tools for organizing data.

Data Tables

You have gathered your materials and set up your experiment. But before you start, you need to plan a way to record what happens during the experiment. By creating a data table, you can record your observations and measurements in an orderly way.

Suppose, for example, that a scientist conducted an experiment to find out how many Calories people of different body masses burn while doing various activities. The data table shows the results.

Notice in this data table that the manipulated variable (body mass) is the heading of one column. The responding variable (for Experiment 1, the number of Calories burned while bicycling) is the heading of the next column. Additional columns were added for related experiments.

CALORIES BURNED IN 30 MINUTES OF ACTIVITY

Body Mass	Experiment 1 Bicycling	Experiment 2 Playing Basketball	Experiment 3 Watching Television
30 kg	60 Calories	120 Calories	21 Calories
40 kg	77 Calories	164 Calories	27 Calories
50 kg	95 Calories	206 Calories	33 Calories
60 kg	114 Calories	248 Calories	38 Calories

Bar Graphs

To compare how many Calories a person burns doing various activities, you could create a bar graph. A bar graph is used to display data in a number of separate, or distinct, categories. In this example, bicycling, playing basketball, and watching television are three separate categories.

To create a bar graph, follow these steps.

1. On graph paper, draw a horizontal, or *x*-, axis and a vertical, or *y*-, axis.
2. Write the names of the categories to be graphed along the horizontal axis. Include an overall label for the axis as well.
3. Label the vertical axis with the name of the responding variable. Include units of measurement. Then create a scale along the axis by marking off equally spaced numbers that cover the range of the data collected.
4. For each category, draw a solid bar using the scale on the vertical axis to determine the

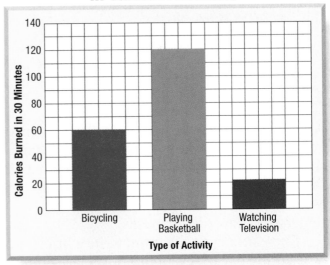

Calories Burned by a 30-kilogram Person in Various Activities

appropriate height. For example, for bicycling, draw the bar as high as the 60 mark on the vertical axis. Make all the bars the same width and leave equal spaces between them.
5. Add a title that describes the graph.

Line Graphs

To see whether a relationship exists between body mass and the number of Calories burned while bicycling, you could create a line graph. A line graph is used to display data that show how one variable (the responding variable) changes in response to another variable (the manipulated variable). You can use a line graph when your manipulated variable is *continuous,* that is, when there are other points between the ones that you tested. In this example, body mass is a continuous variable because there are other body masses between 30 and 40 kilograms (for example, 31 kilograms). Time is another example of a continuous variable.

Line graphs are powerful tools because they allow you to estimate values for conditions that you did not test in the experiment. For example, you can use the line graph to estimate that a 35-kilogram person would burn 68 Calories while bicycling.

To create a line graph, follow these steps.

1. On graph paper, draw a horizontal, or *x*-, axis and a vertical, or *y*-, axis.
2. Label the horizontal axis with the name of the manipulated variable. Label the vertical axis with the name of the responding variable. Include units of measurement.
3. Create a scale on each axis by marking off equally spaced numbers that cover the range of the data collected.
4. Plot a point on the graph for each piece of data. In the line graph above, the dotted lines show how to plot the first data point (30 kilograms and 60 Calories). Draw an imaginary vertical line extending up from the horizontal axis at the 30-kilogram mark. Then draw an imaginary horizontal line extending across from the vertical axis at the 60-Calorie mark. Plot the point where the two lines intersect.

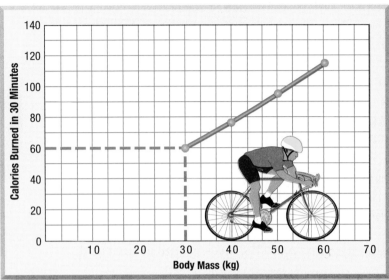

Effect of Body Mass on Calories Burned While Bicycling

5. Connect the plotted points with a solid line. (In some cases, it may be more appropriate to draw a line that shows the general trend of the plotted points. In those cases, some of the points may fall above or below the line. Also, not all graphs are linear and it may be more appropriate to draw a curve to connect the points.)
6. Add a title that identifies the variables or relationship in the graph.

> **ACTIVITY**
> Create line graphs to display the data from Experiment 2 and Experiment 3 in the data table.

> **ACTIVITY**
> You read in the newspaper that a total of 5 centimeters of rain fell in your area in July, 3.5 centimeters fell in August, and 4.5 centimeters fell in September. What type of graph would you use to display these data? Use graph paper to create the graph.

Circle Graphs

Like bar graphs, circle graphs can be used to display data in a number of separate categories. Unlike bar graphs, however, circle graphs can only be used when you have data for *all* the categories that make up a given topic. A circle graph is sometimes called a pie chart because it resembles a pie cut into slices. The pie represents the entire topic, while the slices represent the individual categories. The size of a slice indicates what percentage of the whole a particular category makes up.

The data table below shows the results of a survey in which 24 teenagers were asked to identify their favorite sport. The data were then used to create the circle graph at the right.

Sports That Teens Prefer

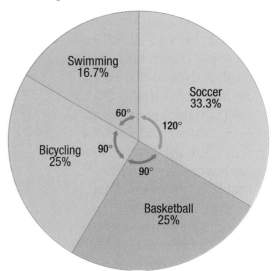

FAVORITE SPORTS

Sport	Number of Students
Soccer	8
Basketball	6
Bicycling	6
Swimming	4

To create a circle graph, follow these steps.

1. Use a compass to draw a circle. Mark the center of the circle with a point. Then draw a line from the center point to the top of the circle.
2. Determine the size of each "slice" by setting up a proportion where x equals the number of degrees in a slice. (NOTE: A circle contains 360 degrees.) For example, to find the number of degrees in the "soccer" slice, set up the following proportion:

$$\frac{\text{students who prefer soccer}}{\text{total number of students}} = \frac{x}{\text{total number of degrees in a circle}}$$

$$\frac{8}{24} = \frac{x}{360}$$

Cross-multiply and solve for x.

$$24x = 8 \times 360$$
$$x = 120$$

The "soccer" slice should contain 120 degrees.

3. Use a protractor to measure the angle of the first slice, using the line you drew to the top of the circle as the 0° line. Draw a line from the center of the circle to the edge for the angle you measured.
4. Continue around the circle by measuring the size of each slice with the protractor. Start measuring from the edge of the previous slice so the wedges do not overlap. When you are done, the entire circle should be filled in.
5. Determine the percentage of the whole circle that each slice represents. To do this, divide the number of degrees in a slice by the total number of degrees in a circle (360), and multiply by 100%. For the "soccer" slice, you can find the percentage as follows:

$$\frac{120}{360} \times 100\% = 33.3\%$$

6. Use a different color to shade in each slice. Label each slice with the name of the category and with the percentage of the whole it represents.
7. Add a title to the circle graph.

ACTIVITY

In a class of 28 students, 12 students take the bus to school, 10 students walk, and 6 students ride their bicycles. Create a circle graph to display these data.

Laboratory Safety

Safety Symbols

These symbols alert you to possible dangers in the laboratory and remind you to work carefully.

Safety Goggles Always wear safety goggles to protect your eyes in any activity involving chemicals, flames or heating, or the possibility of broken glassware.

Lab Apron Wear a laboratory apron to protect your skin and clothing from damage.

Breakage You are working with materials that may be breakable, such as glass containers, glass tubing, thermometers, or funnels. Handle breakable materials with care. Do not touch broken glassware.

Heat-resistant Gloves Use an oven mitt or other hand protection when handling hot materials. Hot plates, hot glassware, or hot water can cause burns. Do not touch hot objects with your bare hands.

Heating Use a clamp or tongs to pick up hot glassware. Do not touch hot objects with your bare hands.

Sharp Object Pointed-tip scissors, scalpels, knives, needles, pins, or tacks are sharp. They can cut or puncture your skin. Always direct a sharp edge or point away from yourself and others. Use sharp instruments only as instructed.

Electric Shock Avoid the possibility of electric shock. Never use electrical equipment around water, or when the equipment is wet or your hands are wet. Be sure cords are untangled and cannot trip anyone. Disconnect the equipment when it is not in use.

Corrosive Chemical You are working with an acid or another corrosive chemical. Avoid getting it on your skin or clothing, or in your eyes. Do not inhale the vapors. Wash your hands when you are finished with the activity.

Poison Do not let any poisonous chemical come in contact with your skin, and do not inhale its vapors. Wash your hands when you are finished with the activity.

Physical Safety When an experiment involves physical activity, take precautions to avoid injuring yourself or others. Follow instructions from your teacher. Alert your teacher if there is any reason you should not participate in the activity.

Animal Safety Treat live animals with care to avoid harming the animals or yourself. Working with animal parts or preserved animals also requires caution. Wash your hands when you are finished with the activity.

Plant Safety Handle plants in the laboratory or during field work only as directed by your teacher. If you are allergic to certain plants, tell your teacher before doing an activity in which those plants are used. Avoid touching harmful plants such as poison ivy, poison oak, or poison sumac, or plants with thorns. Wash your hands when you are finished with the activity.

Flames You may be working with flames from a lab burner, candle, or matches. Tie back loose hair and clothing. Follow instructions from your teacher about lighting and extinguishing flames.

No Flames Flammable materials may be present. Make sure there are no flames, sparks, or other exposed heat sources present.

Fumes When poisonous or unpleasant vapors may be involved, work in a ventilated area. Avoid inhaling vapors directly. Only test an odor when directed to do so by your teacher, and use a wafting motion to direct the vapor toward your nose.

Disposal Chemicals and other laboratory materials used in the activity must be disposed of safely. Follow the instructions from your teacher.

Hand Washing Wash your hands thoroughly when finished with the activity. Use antibacterial soap and warm water. Lather both sides of your hands and between your fingers. Rinse well.

General Safety Awareness You may see this symbol when none of the symbols described earlier appears. In this case, follow the specific instructions provided. You may also see this symbol when you are asked to develop your own procedure in a lab. Have your teacher approve your plan before you go further.

Science Safety Rules

To prepare yourself to work safely in the laboratory, read over the following safety rules. Then read them a second time. Make sure you understand and follow each rule. Ask your teacher to explain any rules you do not understand.

Dress Code

1. To protect yourself from injuring your eyes, wear safety goggles whenever you work with chemicals, burners, glassware, or any substance that might get into your eyes. If you wear contact lenses, notify your teacher.
2. Wear a lab apron or coat whenever you work with corrosive chemicals or substances that can stain.
3. Tie back long hair to keep it away from any chemicals, flames, or equipment.
4. Remove or tie back any article of clothing or jewelry that can hang down and touch chemicals, flames, or equipment. Roll up or secure long sleeves.
5. Never wear open shoes or sandals.

General Precautions

6. Read all directions for an experiment several times before beginning the activity. Carefully follow all written and oral instructions. If you are in doubt about any part of the experiment, ask your teacher for assistance.
7. Never perform activities that are not assigned or authorized by your teacher. Obtain permission before "experimenting" on your own. Never handle any equipment unless you have specific permission.
8. Never perform lab activities without direct supervision.
9. Never eat or drink in the laboratory.
10. Keep work areas clean and tidy at all times. Bring only notebooks and lab manuals or written lab procedures to the work area. All other items, such as purses and backpacks, should be left in a designated area.
11. Do not engage in horseplay.

First Aid

12. Always report all accidents or injuries to your teacher, no matter how minor. Notify your teacher immediately about any fires.
13. Learn what to do in case of specific accidents, such as getting acid in your eyes or on your skin. (Rinse acids from your body with lots of water.)
14. Be aware of the location of the first-aid kit, but do not use it unless instructed by your teacher. In case of injury, your teacher should administer first aid. Your teacher may also send you to the school nurse or call a physician.
15. Know the location of emergency equipment, such as the fire extinguisher and fire blanket, and know how to use it.
16. Know the location of the nearest telephone and whom to contact in an emergency.

Heating and Fire Safety

17. Never use a heat source, such as a candle, burner, or hot plate, without wearing safety goggles.
18. Never heat anything unless instructed to do so. A chemical that is harmless when cool may be dangerous when heated.
19. Keep all combustible materials away from flames. Never use a flame or spark near a combustible chemical.
20. Never reach across a flame.
21. Before using a laboratory burner, make sure you know proper procedures for lighting and adjusting the burner, as demonstrated by your teacher. Do not touch the burner. It may be hot. Never leave a lighted burner unattended. Turn off the burner when not in use.
22. Chemicals can splash or boil out of a heated test tube. When heating a substance in a test tube, make sure that the mouth of the tube is not pointed at you or anyone else.
23. Never heat a liquid in a closed container. The expanding gases produced may blow the container apart.
24. Before picking up a container that has been heated, hold the back of your hand near it. If you can feel heat on the back of your hand, the container is too hot to handle. Use an oven mitt to pick up a container that has been heated.

Using Chemicals Safely

25. Never mix chemicals "for the fun of it." You might produce a dangerous, possibly explosive substance.

26. Never put your face near the mouth of a container that holds chemicals. Many chemicals are poisonous. Never touch, taste, or smell a chemical unless you are instructed by your teacher to do so.

27. Use only those chemicals needed in the activity. Read and double-check labels on supply bottles before removing any chemicals. Take only as much as you need. Keep all containers closed when chemicals are not being used.

28. Dispose of all chemicals as instructed by your teacher. To avoid contamination, never return chemicals to their original containers. Never simply pour chemicals or other substances into the sink or trash containers.

29. Be extra careful when working with acids or bases. Pour all chemicals over the sink or a container, not over your work surface.

30. If you are instructed to test for odors, use a wafting motion to direct the odors to your nose. Do not inhale the fumes directly from the container.

31. When mixing an acid and water, always pour the water into the container first and then add the acid to the water. Never pour water into an acid.

32. Take extreme care not to spill any material in the laboratory. Wash chemical spills and splashes immediately with plenty of water. Immediately begin rinsing with water any acids that get on your skin or clothing, and notify your teacher of any acid spill at the same time.

Using Glassware Safely

33. Never force glass tubing or thermometers into a rubber stopper or rubber tubing. Have your teacher insert the glass tubing or thermometer if required for an activity.

34. If you are using a laboratory burner, use a wire screen to protect glassware from any flame. Never heat glassware that is not thoroughly dry on the outside.

35. Keep in mind that hot glassware looks cool. Never pick up glassware without first checking to see if it is hot. Use an oven mitt. See rule 24.

36. Never use broken or chipped glassware. If glassware breaks, notify your teacher and dispose of the glassware in the proper broken-glassware container. Never handle broken glass with your bare hands.

37. Never eat or drink from lab glassware.

38. Thoroughly clean glassware before putting it away.

Using Sharp Instruments

39. Handle scalpels or other sharp instruments with extreme care. Never cut material toward you; cut away from you.

40. Immediately notify your teacher if you cut your skin when working in the laboratory.

Animal and Plant Safety

41. Never perform experiments that cause pain, discomfort, or harm to animals. This rule applies at home as well as in the classroom.

42. Animals should be handled only if absolutely necessary. Your teacher will instruct you as to how to handle each animal species brought into the classroom.

43. If you know that you are allergic to certain plants, molds, or animals, tell your teacher before doing an activity in which these are used.

44. During field work, protect your skin by wearing long pants, long sleeves, socks, and closed shoes. Know how to recognize the poisonous plants and fungi in your area, as well as plants with thorns, and avoid contact with them. Never eat any part of a plant or fungus.

45. Wash your hands thoroughly after handling animals or the cage containing animals. Wash your hands when you are finished with any activity involving animal parts, plants, or soil.

End-of-Experiment Rules

46. After an experiment has been completed, turn off all burners or hot plates. If you used a gas burner, check that the gas-line valve to the burner is off. Unplug hot plates.

47. Turn off and unplug any other electrical equipment that you used.

48. Clean up your work area and return all equipment to its proper place.

49. Dispose of waste materials as instructed by your teacher.

50. Wash your hands after every experiment.

Using a Laboratory Balance

The laboratory balance is an important tool in scientific investigations. You can use a balance to determine the masses of materials that you study or experiment with in the laboratory.

Different kinds of balances are used in the laboratory. One kind of balance is the triple-beam balance. The balance that you may use in your science class is probably similar to the balance illustrated in this Appendix. To use the balance properly, you should learn the name, location, and function of each part of the balance you are using.

The Triple-Beam Balance

The triple-beam balance is a single-pan balance with three beams calibrated in grams. The back, or 100-gram, beam is divided into ten units of 10 grams each. The middle, or 500-gram, beam is divided into five units of 100 grams each. The front, or 10-gram, beam is divided into ten major units of 1 gram each. Each of these units is further divided into units of 0.1 gram. What is the largest mass you could find with a triple-beam balance?

The following procedure can be used to find the mass of an object with a triple-beam balance:

1. When no object is on the pan, and the riders are at zero, the pointer should be at zero.
2. Place the object on the pan.
3. Move the rider on the middle beam notch by notch until the horizontal pointer drops below zero. Move the rider back one notch.
4. Move the rider on the back beam notch by notch until the pointer again drops below zero. Move the rider back one notch.
5. Slowly slide the rider along the front beam until the pointer stops at the zero point.
6. The mass of the object is equal to the sum of the readings on the three beams.

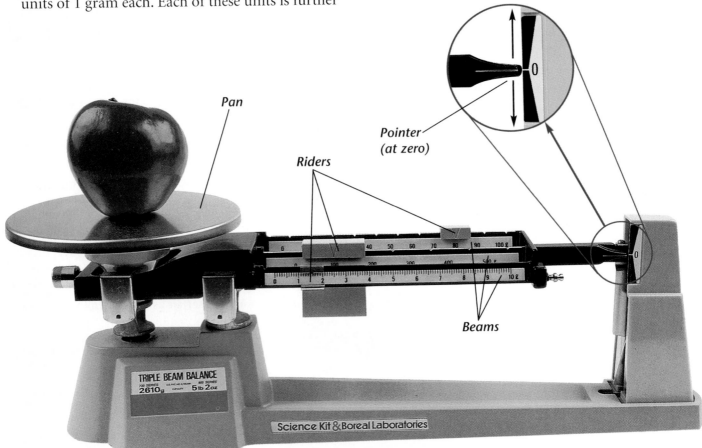

Triple-Beam Balance

List of Chemical Elements

Name	Symbol	Atomic Number	Atomic Mass†
Actinium	Ac	89	227.028
Aluminum	Al	13	26.982
Americium	Am	95	(243)
Antimony	Sb	51	121.75
Argon	Ar	18	39.948
Arsenic	As	33	74.922
Astatine	At	85	(210)
Barium	Ba	56	137.327
Berkelium	Bk	97	(247)
Beryllium	Be	4	9.012
Bismuth	Bi	83	208.980
Bohrium	Bh	107	(262)
Boron	B	5	10.811
Bromine	Br	35	79.904
Cadmium	Cd	48	112.411
Calcium	Ca	20	40.078
Californium	Cf	98	(251)
Carbon	C	6	12.011
Cerium	Ce	58	140.115
Cesium	Cs	55	132.905
Chlorine	Cl	17	35.453
Chromium	Cr	24	51.996
Cobalt	Co	27	58.933
Copper	Cu	29	63.546
Curium	Cm	96	(247)
Dubnium	Db	105	(262)
Dysprosium	Dy	66	162.50
Einsteinium	Es	99	(252)
Erbium	Er	68	167.26
Europium	Eu	63	151.965
Fermium	Fm	100	(257)
Fluorine	F	9	18.998
Francium	Fr	87	(223)
Gadolinium	Gd	64	157.25
Gallium	Ga	31	69.723
Germanium	Ge	32	72.61
Gold	Au	79	196.967
Hafnium	Hf	72	178.49
Hassium	Hs	108	(265)
Helium	He	2	4.003
Holmium	Ho	67	164.930
Hydrogen	H	1	1.008
Indium	In	49	114.818
Iodine	I	53	126.904
Iridium	Ir	77	192.22
Iron	Fe	26	55.847
Krypton	Kr	36	83.80
Lanthanum	La	57	138.906
Lawrencium	Lr	103	(260)
Lead	Pb	82	207.2
Lithium	Li	3	6.941
Lutetium	Lu	71	174.967
Magnesium	Mg	12	24.305
Manganese	Mn	25	54.938
Meitnerium	Mt	109	(266)
Mendelevium	Md	101	(258)
Mercury	Hg	80	200.659
Molybdenum	Mo	42	95.94

Name	Symbol	Atomic Number	Atomic Mass†
Neodymium	Nd	60	144.2
Neon	Ne	10	20.180
Neptunium	Np	93	237.048
Nickel	Ni	28	58.69
Niobium	Nb	41	92.906
Nitrogen	N	7	14.007
Nobelium	No	102	(259)
Osmium	Os	76	190.23
Oxygen	O	8	15.999
Palladium	Pd	46	106.42
Phosphorus	P	15	30.974
Platinum	Pt	78	195.08
Plutonium	Pu	94	(244)
Polonium	Po	84	(209)
Potassium	K	19	39.098
Praseodymium	Pr	59	140.908
Promethium	Pm	61	(145)
Protactinium	Pa	91	231.036
Radium	Ra	88	226.025
Radon	Rn	86	(222)
Rhenium	Re	75	186.207
Rhodium	Rh	45	102.906
Rubidium	Rb	37	85.468
Ruthenium	Ru	44	101.07
Rutherfordium	Rf	104	(261)
Samarium	Sm	62	150.36
Scandium	Sc	21	44.956
Seaborgium	Sg	106	(263)
Selenium	Se	34	78.96
Silicon	Si	14	28.086
Silver	Ag	47	107.868
Sodium	Na	11	22.990
Strontium	Sr	38	87.62
Sulfur	S	16	32.066
Tantalum	Ta	73	180.948
Technetium	Tc	43	(98)
Tellurium	Te	52	127.60
Terbium	Tb	65	158.925
Thallium	Tl	81	204.383
Thorium	Th	90	232.038
Thulium	Tm	69	168.934
Tin	Sn	50	118.710
Titanium	Ti	22	47.88
Tungsten	W	74	183.85
Ununbium	Uub	112	(272)
Ununhexium	Uuh	116	*
Ununnilium	Uun	110	(269)
Unununium	Uuu	111	(272)
Ununoctium	Uuo	118	*
Ununquadium	Uuq	114	*
Uranium	U	92	238.029
Vanadium	V	23	50.942
Xenon	Xe	54	131.29
Ytterbium	Yb	70	173.04
Yttrium	Y	39	88.906
Zinc	Zn	30	65.39
Zirconium	Zr	40	91.224

†Numbers in parentheses give the mass number of the most stable isotope.

*Newly discovered

Periodic Table of the Elements

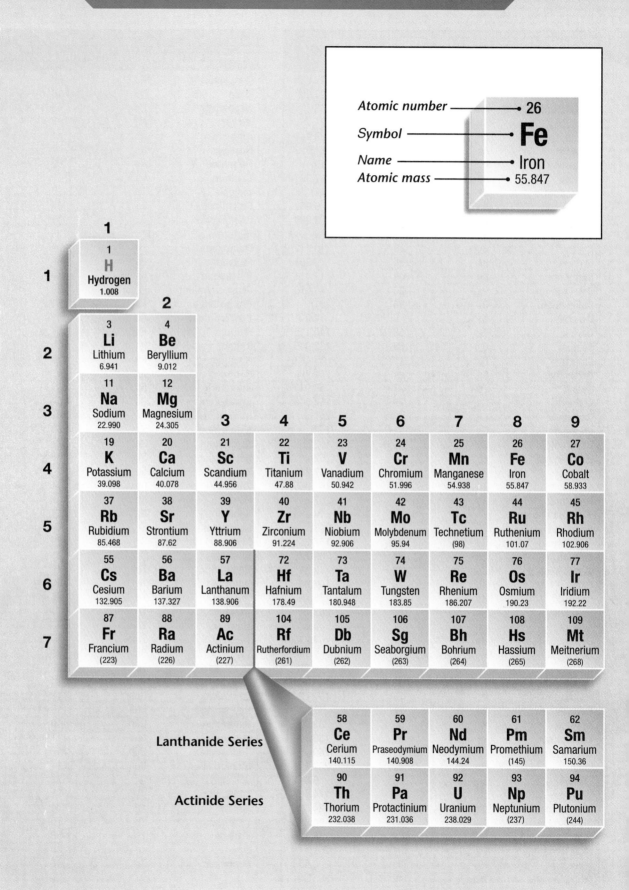

Atomic number —— 26
Symbol —— **Fe**
Name —— Iron
Atomic mass —— 55.847

1

1
H
Hydrogen
1.008

2

3	4
Li	**Be**
Lithium	Beryllium
6.941	9.012

11	12
Na	**Mg**
Sodium	Magnesium
22.990	24.305

3   **4**   **5**   **6**   **7**   **8**   **9**

19	20	21	22	23	24	25	26	27
K	**Ca**	**Sc**	**Ti**	**V**	**Cr**	**Mn**	**Fe**	**Co**
Potassium	Calcium	Scandium	Titanium	Vanadium	Chromium	Manganese	Iron	Cobalt
39.098	40.078	44.956	47.88	50.942	51.996	54.938	55.847	58.933

37	38	39	40	41	42	43	44	45
Rb	**Sr**	**Y**	**Zr**	**Nb**	**Mo**	**Tc**	**Ru**	**Rh**
Rubidium	Strontium	Yttrium	Zirconium	Niobium	Molybdenum	Technetium	Ruthenium	Rhodium
85.468	87.62	88.906	91.224	92.906	95.94	(98)	101.07	102.906

55	56	57	72	73	74	75	76	77
Cs	**Ba**	**La**	**Hf**	**Ta**	**W**	**Re**	**Os**	**Ir**
Cesium	Barium	Lanthanum	Hafnium	Tantalum	Tungsten	Rhenium	Osmium	Iridium
132.905	137.327	138.906	178.49	180.948	183.85	186.207	190.23	192.22

87	88	89	104	105	106	107	108	109
Fr	**Ra**	**Ac**	**Rf**	**Db**	**Sg**	**Bh**	**Hs**	**Mt**
Francium	Radium	Actinium	Rutherfordium	Dubnium	Seaborgium	Bohrium	Hassium	Meitnerium
(223)	(226)	(227)	(261)	(262)	(263)	(264)	(265)	(268)

Lanthanide Series

58	59	60	61	62
Ce	**Pr**	**Nd**	**Pm**	**Sm**
Cerium	Praseodymium	Neodymium	Promethium	Samarium
140.115	140.908	144.24	(145)	150.36

Actinide Series

90	91	92	93	94
Th	**Pa**	**U**	**Np**	**Pu**
Thorium	Protactinium	Uranium	Neptunium	Plutonium
232.038	231.036	238.029	(237)	(244)

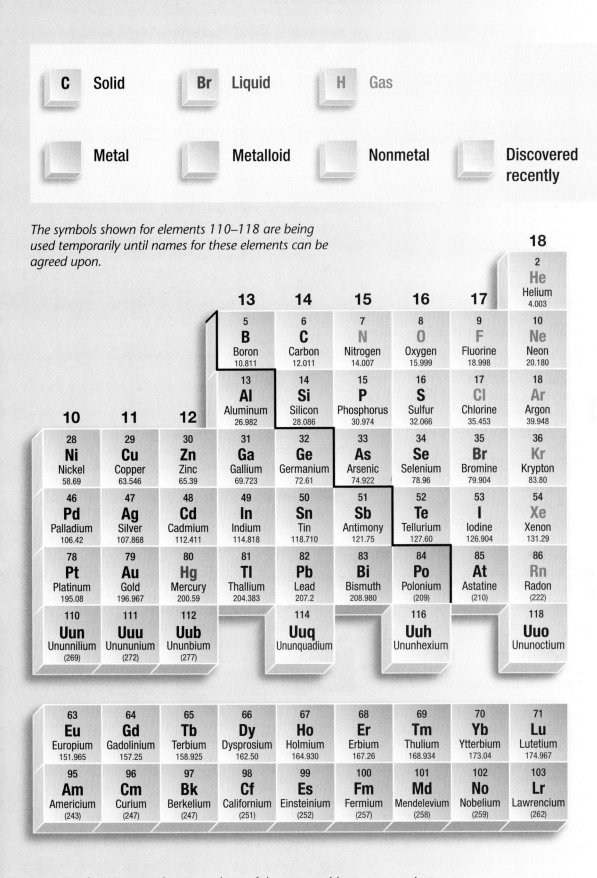

C Solid Br Liquid H Gas

Metal Metalloid Nonmetal Discovered recently

The symbols shown for elements 110–118 are being used temporarily until names for these elements can be agreed upon.

18
2 **He** Helium 4.003

13

| 5 **B** Boron 10.811 | 6 **C** Carbon 12.011 | 7 **N** Nitrogen 14.007 | 8 **O** Oxygen 15.999 | 9 **F** Fluorine 18.998 | 10 **Ne** Neon 20.180 |

14 15 16 17

| 13 **Al** Aluminum 26.982 | 14 **Si** Silicon 28.086 | 15 **P** Phosphorus 30.974 | 16 **S** Sulfur 32.066 | 17 **Cl** Chlorine 35.453 | 18 **Ar** Argon 39.948 |

10 11 12

28 **Ni** Nickel 58.69	29 **Cu** Copper 63.546	30 **Zn** Zinc 65.39	31 **Ga** Gallium 69.723	32 **Ge** Germanium 72.61	33 **As** Arsenic 74.922	34 **Se** Selenium 78.96	35 **Br** Bromine 79.904	36 **Kr** Krypton 83.80
46 **Pd** Palladium 106.42	47 **Ag** Silver 107.868	48 **Cd** Cadmium 112.411	49 **In** Indium 114.818	50 **Sn** Tin 118.710	51 **Sb** Antimony 121.75	52 **Te** Tellurium 127.60	53 **I** Iodine 126.904	54 **Xe** Xenon 131.29
78 **Pt** Platinum 195.08	79 **Au** Gold 196.967	80 **Hg** Mercury 200.59	81 **Tl** Thallium 204.383	82 **Pb** Lead 207.2	83 **Bi** Bismuth 208.980	84 **Po** Polonium (209)	85 **At** Astatine (210)	86 **Rn** Radon (222)
110 **Uun** Ununnilium (269)	111 **Uuu** Unununium (272)	112 **Uub** Ununbium (277)		114 **Uuq** Ununquadium		116 **Uuh** Ununhexium		118 **Uuo** Ununoctium

| 63 **Eu** Europium 151.965 | 64 **Gd** Gadolinium 157.25 | 65 **Tb** Terbium 158.925 | 66 **Dy** Dysprosium 162.50 | 67 **Ho** Holmium 164.930 | 68 **Er** Erbium 167.26 | 69 **Tm** Thulium 168.934 | 70 **Yb** Ytterbium 173.04 | 71 **Lu** Lutetium 174.967 |
| 95 **Am** Americium (243) | 96 **Cm** Curium (247) | 97 **Bk** Berkelium (247) | 98 **Cf** Californium (251) | 99 **Es** Einsteinium (252) | 100 **Fm** Fermium (257) | 101 **Md** Mendelevium (258) | 102 **No** Nobelium (259) | 103 **Lr** Lawrencium (262) |

Mass numbers in parentheses are those of the most stable or common isotope.

Glossary

A

absolute zero The temperature at which no more energy can be removed from matter. (p. 438)

acceleration The rate at which velocity changes. (p. 302)

acid A substance that tastes sour, reacts with metals and carbonates, and turns blue litmus red. (p. 192)

acid rain Rainwater that is more acidic than normal rainwater. (p. 202)

acoustics The study of how well sounds can be heard in a particular room or hall. (p. 516)

actinides A group of elements in the second row of the rare earth elements in the periodic table. (p. 94)

activation energy The minimum amount of energy needed to start a chemical reaction. (p. 161)

actual mechanical advantage The mechanical advantage that a machine provides in a real situation. (p. 383)

air resistance The fluid friction experienced by objects falling through air. (p. 327)

alcohol A substituted hydrocarbon that contains one or more hydroxyl groups. (p. 224)

alkali metal An element in Group 1 of the periodic table. (p. 91)

alkaline earth metal An element in Group 2 of the periodic table. (p. 92)

alloy A substance made of two or more elements, at least one of which is a metal, that has the properties of metal. (p. 255)

alpha particle A form of nuclear radiation consisting of two protons and two neutrons. (p. 267)

alternating current (AC) Current consisting of charges that move back and forth in a circuit. (p. 684)

amino acid One of 20 kinds of organic compounds that are the building blocks of proteins. (p. 231)

ammeter A device used to measure electric current. (p. 658)

amorphous solid A solid made up of particles that are not arranged in a regular pattern. (p. 48)

amplitude The maximum distance the particles of a medium move away from their rest positions as a wave passes through the medium. (p. 477)

amplitude modulation (AM) Method of transmitting radio signals by changing the amplitude of the waves. (p. 555)

analog signal An electronic signal in which the current is varied smoothly. (p. 711)

angle of incidence The angle between an incoming wave and an imaginary line drawn perpendicular to the surface of the barrier or new medium. (p. 482)

angle of reflection The angle between a reflected wave and an imaginary line drawn perpendicular to the surface of the barrier. (p. 482)

antinode A point of maximum amplitude on a standing wave. (p. 486)

Archimedes' principle The rule that the buoyant force on an object is equal to the weight of the fluid displaced by that object. (p. 359)

armature The moving part of an electric motor, consisting of dozens or hundreds of loops of wire wrapped around an iron core. (p. 679)

atom The smallest particle of an element. (p. 19)

atomic mass The average mass of one atom of an element. (p. 82)

atomic mass unit (amu) A unit of measurement for the mass of particles in atoms. (p. 77)

atomic number The number of protons in the nucleus of an atom. (p. 77)

aurora A glowing region produced by the interaction of charged particles from the sun and atoms in the atmosphere. (p. 626)

B

balanced forces Equal forces acting on an object in opposite directions. (p. 314)

base A substance that tastes bitter, feels slippery, and turns red litmus blue. (p. 197)

battery A combination of two or more electrochemical cells in series. (p. 700)

beats The regular changes in loudness of a sound when two sounds of different frequencies are played together. (p. 517)

Bernoulli's principle The rule that a stream of fast-moving fluid exerts less pressure than the surrounding fluid. (p. 366)

beta particle An electron that is given off by a nucleus during radioactive decay. (p. 267)

bimetallic strip A strip made of two different metals that expand at different rates. (p. 454)

binary system The number system that uses combinations of just two digits, 0 and 1. (p. 726)

bioluminescence Light produced by organisms as a result of a chemical reaction. (p. 551)

bit Each 1 or 0 in the binary system. (p. 727)

boiling Vaporization that occurs on and below the surface of a liquid. (p. 67)

boiling point The temperature at which a substance changes from a liquid to a gas. (p. 67)

Boyle's law The relationship between the pressure and volume of a gas at constant temperature; when volume increases, pressure decreases. (p. 54)

brushes The contact points connected to a current source and the commutator of a motor. (p. 679)

buoyant force The upward force exerted by a fluid on a submerged object. (p. 359)

byte An arrangement of eights bits. (p. 727)

camera Optical instrument that uses lenses to focus light and record an image of an object. (p. 593)

carbohydrate An energy-rich organic compound made of the elements carbon, hydrogen, and oxygen. (p. 228)

carboxyl group A group of atoms, —COOH, found in organic acids. (p. 225)

catalyst A material that increases the rate of a chemical reaction by lowering the activation energy. (p. 164)

cathode ray tube (CRT) A vacuum tube that uses electrons to produce images on a screen. (p. 724)

cellulose A complex carbohydrate with which plants build strong stems and roots. (p. 230)

Celsius scale The temperature scale on which zero and 100 are the temperatures at which water freezes and boils. (p. 437)

central processing unit (CPU) The part of a computer that directs the operation of the computer. (p. 728)

centripetal force A force that causes an object to move in a circle. (p. 339)

ceramic A hard, crystalline solid made by heating clay and other mineral materials to high temperatures. (p. 260)

change of state The physical change of matter from one state to another. (p. 450)

Charles's law The relationship between the temperature and volume of a gas at constant pressure; when temperature increases, volume increases. (p. 56)

chat room A network feature that allows two or more users to exchange messages. (p. 739)

chemical bond The force that holds two atoms together. (p. 34)

chemical change A change in matter that produces new substances. (p. 23)

chemical digestion The process that changes large food molecules into smaller molecules. (p. 206)

chemical energy The potential energy stored in chemical compounds. (p. 412)

chemical equation A short, easy way to show a chemical reaction, using symbols instead of words. (p. 152)

chemical reaction A process in which substances undergo chemical changes. (p. 23)

chemistry The study of the properties of matter and how matter changes. (p. 19)

cholesterol A waxy lipid found in all animal cells. (p. 232)

circuit breaker A safety device that uses an electromagnet to shut off a circuit when the current gets too high. (p. 669)

cochlea A fluid-filled cavity behind the inner ear. (p. 521)

coefficient A number placed in front of a chemical formula in an equation that indicates how many atoms or molecules of each reactant and product are involved in a reaction. (p. 156)

colloid A mixture with small undissolved particles that do not settle out. (p. 181)

combustion A rapid reaction between oxygen and fuel that produces thermal energy. (p. 168)

commutator A device that controls the direction of the flow of current through an electric motor. (p. 679)

compass A device with a magnetized needle that can spin freely (p. 622)

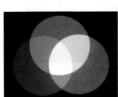 

complementary colors Any two colors that combine to form white light or black pigment. (p. 584)

complex carbohydrate A substance consisting of long chains of simple carbohydrates. (p. 229)

composite A combination of two or more substances that creates a new material. (p. 248)

compound A substance made of two or more elements chemically combined. (p. 20)

compound machine A device that combines two or more simple machines. (p. 396)

compression The part of a longitudinal wave where the particles of the medium are close together. (p. 475)

computer An electronic device that stores, processes, and retrieves information. (p. 726)

computer hardware The permanent components of a computer. (p. 728)

computer network A group of computers connected by cables or telephone lines. (p. 736)

computer programmer A person who uses computer languages to convert input information into instructions that a computer can understand. (p. 732)

computer software A detailed set of instructions that directs the computer hardware to perform operations on stored information. (p. 732)

F

Fahrenheit scale The temperature scale on which 32 and 212 are the temperatures at which water freezes and boils. (p. 437)

family Elements in the same vertical column of the periodic table; also called a group. (p. 86)

farsightedness Condition that causes a person to see nearby objects as blurry. (p. 590)

fatty acid An organic compound that is part of a fat or an oil. (p. 232)

ferromagnetic material A material that is strongly attracted to a magnet, and which can be made into a magnet. (p. 617)

fluid Any substance that can flow and easily change shape. (p. 348)

fluid friction Friction that occurs as an object moves through a fluid. (p. 325)

fluorescent lights Lights that glow when an electric current causes ultraviolet waves to strike a coating inside a tube. (p. 549)

focal point The point at which rays of light meet, or appear to meet, after being reflected (or refracted) by a mirror (or a lens). (p. 573)

force A push or pull exerted on an object. (p. 312)

formula A combination of symbols that shows the ratio of elements in a compound. (p. 20)

fossil fuels Materials such as coal that are burned to release their chemical energy. (p. 423)

free fall The motion of a falling object when the only force acting on it is gravity. (p. 326)

freeware Software that the author has decided to let others use free of charge. (p. 739)

freezing The change in state from a liquid to a solid. (p. 66)

freezing point The temperature at which a substance changes from a liquid to a solid. (pp. 182, 452)

frequency The number of complete waves that pass a given point in a certain amount of time. (p. 480)

frequency modulation (FM) Method of transmitting radio signals by changing the frequency of the waves. (p. 556)

friction A force that one surface exerts on another when the two rub against each other. (p. 324)

fuel A material that releases energy when it burns. (p. 168)

fulcrum The fixed point around which a lever pivots. (p. 389)

fullerene A form of the element carbon that consists of carbon atoms arranged in a repeating pattern similar to the surface of a soccer ball. (p. 217)

fuse A safety device with a thin metal strip that will melt if too much current flows through it. (p. 668)

G

galvanometer A device that uses the rotation of a loop of wire in a magnetic field to measure small amounts of current. (p. 677)

gamma radiation A form of nuclear radiation consisting of high-energy waves. (p. 267)

gamma rays Electromagnetic waves with the shortest wavelengths and highest frequencies. (p. 546)

gas A state of matter with no definite shape or volume. (p. 49)

gears Two or more wheels linked together by interlocking teeth. (p. 396)

glass A clear, solid material with no crystal structure, created by heating sand to a very high temperature. (p. 262)

glucose A sugar found in the body; the monomer of many complex carbohydrates. (p. 229)

graph A diagram that shows how two variables are related. (p. 58)

graphite A form of the element carbon in which carbon atoms form flat layers. (p. 216)

gravitational potential energy Potential energy that depends on the height of an object. (p. 411)

gravity The force that pulls objects toward Earth. (p. 326)

grounded Term used to describe a circuit that allows charges to flow directly from the circuit to the ground connection. (p. 667)

group Elements in the same vertical column of the periodic table; also called a family. (p. 86)

H

half-life The length of time needed for half the atoms of a radioactive isotope sample to decay. (p. 268)

halogen family The elements in Group 17 of the periodic table. (p. 102)

hard disk The rigid magnetic metal disk that remains inside the computer and holds information that can be accessed whenever the computer is on. (p. 730)

heat The movement of thermal energy from one substance to another. (p. 439)

heat engine A device that converts thermal energy into mechanical energy. (p. 455)

hertz (Hz) Unit of measurement for frequency. (p. 480)

hologram A three-dimensional photograph formed by the interference between two laser beams. (p. 598)

hydraulic system A system that multiplies force by transmitting pressure from a small surface area through a confined fluid to a larger surface area. (p. 356)

hydrocarbon An organic compound that contains only the elements carbon and hydrogen. (p. 220)

hydrogen ion A positively charged ion (H⁺) formed of a hydrogen atom that has lost its electron. (p. 198)

hydroxide ion A negatively charged ion (OH⁻) made of oxygen and hydrogen. (p. 199)

hydroxyl group A group of atoms, —OH, found in alcohols. (p. 224)

hypothesis A possible explanation for observations that relate to a scientific question; must be testable. (p. 6)

ideal mechanical advantage The mechanical advantage that a machine would have without friction. (p. 383)

illuminated Word used to describe an object that can be seen because it reflects light. (p. 548)

image A copy of an object formed by reflected or refracted rays of light. (p. 572)

incandescent lights Lights that glow when a filament inside them gets hot. (p. 548)

inclined plane A simple machine consisting of a flat surface with one end higher than the other. (p. 387)

independent variable *See* **manipulated variable.**

index of refraction The measure of how much a ray of light bends when it enters a new medium. (p. 576)

indicator A compound that changes color when in contact with an acid or a base. (p. 194)

induction The movement of electrons to one part of an object caused by the electric field of another object. (p. 648)

inertia The tendency of a moving object to continue in a straight line or a stationary object to remain in place. (p. 316)

inference A logical interpretation based on observations and prior knowledge. (p. 5)

infrared rays Electromagnetic waves with higher frequencies and shorter wavelengths than radio waves. (p. 541)

infrasound Sound waves with frequencies below 20 Hz. (p. 506)

inhibitor A material that decreases the rate of a reaction. (p. 165)

input device A device, such as a keyboard, that feeds data to a computer. (p. 728)

input force The force exerted on a machine. (p. 379)

insulator A material that does not easily transfer thermal energy or electric current between its particles. (pp. 443, 630)

integrated circuit An electrical circuit manufactured on a tiny slice of semiconductor, or chip. (p. 715)

intellectual property A story, poem, computer program, or similar product whose ownership is legally protected. (p. 739)

intensity The amount of energy per second carried through a unit area by a wave. (p. 504)

interference The interaction between waves that meet. (p. 484)

internal combustion engine An engine that burns fuel inside cylinders within the engine. (p. 456)

International System of Units (SI) A system of measurement based on multiples of ten and on established measures of mass, length, and time. (p. 25)

Internet A global computer network that links millions of computers in businesses, schools, and research organizations. (p. 737)

ion An atom or group of atoms that is electrically charged. (p. 115)

ionic bond The attraction between two oppositely charged ions. (p. 115)

iris The ring of colored muscle around the pupil of the eye. (p. 588)

isomer One of a number of compounds that have the same molecular formula but different structures. (p. 222)

isotope An atom with the same number of protons and different number of neutrons from other atoms of the same element. (p. 266)

joule A unit of work equal to one newton-meter. (p. 377)

Kelvin scale The temperature scale on which zero is the temperature at which no more energy can be removed from matter. (p. 437)

kinetic energy Energy that an object has because of its motion. (p. 409)

lanthanides A group of elements in the first row of the rare earth elements in the periodic table. (p. 94)

larynx Two folds of tissue that make up the human voice box. (p. 595)

laser A device that produces coherent light. (p. 595)

law of conservation of energy The rule that energy cannot be created or destroyed. (p. 420)

law of conservation of momentum The rule that the total momentum of objects in an interaction does not change. (p. 336)

lens A curved piece of glass or other transparent material that is used to refract light. (p. 578)

lever A simple machine consisting of a rigid object that pivots about a fixed point. (p. 389)

lightning rod A metal rod on a building connected to a grounding wire in order to protect the building. (p. 668)

linear Term used to describe a relationship between variables whose graph is a straight line. (p. 306)

lipid An energy-rich compound made of carbon, oxygen, and hydrogen; fats, oils, waxes, and cholesterol are lipids. (p. 232)

liquid A state of matter that has a definite volume but no definite shape. (p. 48)

local area network (LAN) A set of computers connected in one office building or classroom. (p. 737)

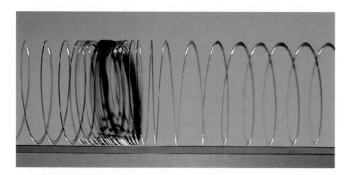

longitudinal wave A wave that moves the medium parallel to the direction in which the wave travels. (p. 474)

loudness Perception of the intensity of a sound. (p. 505)

luminous Word used to describe an object that can be seen because it emits light. (p. 548)

machine A device that changes the amount of force exerted or the direction in which force is exerted. (p. 378)

magnetic A characteristic of those metals that are attracted to magnets and can be made into magnets. (p. 90)

magnetic declination The angle between geographic north and the north to which a compass needle points. (p. 624)

magnetic domain A region in which the magnetic fields of all atoms are lined up in the same direction. (p. 617)

magnetic field The region around a magnet where the magnetic force is exerted. (p. 615)

magnetic field lines Lines that map out the magnetic field around a magnet. (p. 615)

magnetic pole The ends of a magnetic object, where the magnetic force is strongest. (p. 613)

magnetic resonance imaging (MRI) A process that uses radio waves to form pictures of the inside of the human body. (p. 541)

magnetism The force of attraction or repulsion of magnetic materials. (p. 613)

magnetosphere The region of Earth's magnetic field shaped by the solar wind. (p. 625)

malleable A term used to describe material that can be pounded or rolled into shape. (p. 89)

manipulated variable The one factor that a scientist changes during an experiment; also called independent variable. (p. 6)

mass A measure of how much matter is in an object. (p. 25)

mass number The sum of the protons and neutrons in the nucleus of an atom. (p. 266)

mechanical advantage The number of times the force exerted on a machine is multiplied by the machine. (p. 381)

mechanical digestion The physical process that tears, grinds, and mashes large food particles into smaller ones. (p. 207)

mechanical energy Kinetic or potential energy associated with the motion or position of an object. (p. 412)

mechanical wave A wave that requires a medium through which to travel. (p. 473)

medium Material through which a wave travels. (p. 473)

melting The change from the solid to the liquid state of matter. (p. 65)

melting point The temperature at which a substance changes from a solid to a liquid. (p. 48)

metalloid An element that has some of the characteristics of metals and some of the characteristics of nonmetals. (p. 103)

microscope Optical instrument that forms enlarged images of tiny objects. (p. 593)

microwaves Radio waves with the shortest wavelengths and the highest frequencies. (p. 539)

middle ear The space behind the eardrum. (p. 521)

mineral A naturally occurring solid that has a crystal structure and a definite chemical composition; a simple element, which is not organic, that is needed by the body. (pp. 128, 235)

mirage An image of a distant object caused by refraction of light as it travels through air of varying temperature. (p. 577)

mixture Two or more substances that are mixed together but not chemically combined. (p. 20)

molecular compound A compound consisting of molecules of covalently bonded atoms. (p. 122)

molecular formula A combination of chemical symbols that represent the elements in each molecule of a compound. (p. 221)

molecule A combination of two or more atoms that are bonded together. (p. 34)

momentum The product of an object's mass and its velocity. (p. 335)

monomers Small, carbon-based molecules that make up the links in a polymer chain. (p. 226)

motion The state in which one object's distance from another is changing. (p. 283)

music A set of tones and overtones combined in ways that are pleasing to the ear. (p. 512)

nearsightedness Condition that causes a person to see distant objects as blurry. (p. 590)

neon lights Glass tubes filled with neon that produce light. (p. 550)

net force The overall force on an object when all the individual forces acting on an object are added together. (p. 314)

neutralization A reaction between an acid and a base. (p. 202)

neutron Small uncharged particle in the nucleus of an atom. (p. 76)

newton (N) A unit of measure that equals the force required to accelerate one kilogram of mass at a rate of one meter per second per second. (p. 321)

noble gas An element in Group 18 of the periodic table. (p. 102)

node A point of zero amplitude on a standing wave. (p. 486)

noise A mixture of sound waves with no pleasing timbre and no identifiable pitch. (p. 513)

nonlinear Term used to describe a relationship between variables whose graph is not a straight line. (p. 306)

nonmetal An element that lacks most of the properties of metals. (p. 96)

nonpolar The description of a covalent bond in which electrons are shared equally, or of a molecule containing nonpolar bonds or polar bonds that cancel out. (p. 124)

nonrenewable resource A natural resource that cannot be replaced if used up. (p. 689)

nuclear energy The potential energy stored in the nucleus of an atom. (p. 413)

nuclear fusion The process in which smaller nuclei combine into larger nuclei, forming heavier elements and releasing energy. (p. 107)

nuclear radiation Particles and energy produced during radioactive decay. (p. 267)

nuclear reaction A reaction involving the particles in the nucleus of an atom that can change one element into another element. (p. 266)

nucleic acid A very large organic compound made up of carbon, oxygen, hydrogen, nitrogen, and phosphorus; examples are DNA and RNA. (p. 234)

nucleotide One of several organic molecules that are the monomers of nucleic acids. (p. 234)

nucleus The central core of an atom containing protons and usually neutrons. (p. 76)

nutrient A substance that provides energy or raw materials that the body needs in order to grow, repair worn parts, or function properly. (p. 228)

objective Lens that gathers light from an object and forms a real image. (p. 592)

observation Using one or more of the five senses to gather information. (p. 5)

Ohm's law The rule that resistance equals voltage divided by current. (p. 658)

opaque Term used to describe a material that reflects or absorbs all light that strikes it. (p. 570)

optic nerve Short, thick nerve that carries signals from the eye to the brain. (p. 589)

optical disc A disc on which information is written and read by lasers. (p. 731)

optical fiber Long, thin strand of glass or plastic that can carry light for long distances without allowing the light to fade out; can be used for transmitting messages (pp. 263, 598)

organic acid A substituted hydrocarbon that contains one or more carboxyl groups (—COOH) of atoms. (p. 225)

organic compounds Most compounds that contain carbon. (p. 219)

output device A device, such as a monitor, that presents data from a computer. (p. 729)

output force The force exerted on an object by a machine. (p. 379)

parallel circuit An electric circuit with several paths for the current to take. (p. 664)

pascal (Pa) A unit of pressure equal to one newton per square meter. (p. 347)

Pascal's principle The rule that when force is applied to a confined fluid, the increase in pressure is transmitted equally to all parts of the fluid. (p. 355)

period A horizontal row of elements in the periodic table. (p. 87)

periodic table An arrangement of the elements in order of atomic number, in which elements with similar properties are grouped in columns. (p. 83)

permanent magnet A magnet made of material that keeps its magnetism. (p. 618)

pH scale A range of values from 0 to 14 that expresses the concentration of hydrogen ions in a solution. (p. 200)

photoelectric effect The movement of electrons in a substance when light is shined on it. (p. 537)

photon A tiny particle or packet of light energy. (p. 537)

physical change A change that alters the form or appearance of a substance but does not make the material into another substance. (p. 22)

physical science The study of matter, energy, and the changes that matter and energy undergo. (p. 4)

pigment An opaque substance used to color other materials. (p. 584)

pitch Perception of the frequency of a sound. (p. 506)

plane mirror A flat mirror that produces an upright, virtual image the same size as the object. (p. 572)

plasma A state of matter in which atoms are stripped of their electrons and the nuclei are packed closely together. (p. 106)

plastic A synthetic polymer that can be molded or shaped. (p. 247)

plate One of the major pieces that make up Earth's upper layer. (p. 296)

polar The description of a covalent bond in which electrons are shared unequally, or of a molecule containing polar bonds that do not cancel out. (p. 123)

polarized light Light that vibrates in only one direction. (p. 536)

polyatomic ion An ion that is made of more than one atom. (p. 117)

polymer A large, complex molecule built from smaller molecules bonded together. (p. 226)

potential difference The difference in electrical potential between two places. (p. 655)

potential energy Energy that is stored and held in readiness. (p. 410)

power The rate at which work is done or the rate at which one form of energy is converted into another. (pp. 426, 691)

precipitate A solid that forms from a solution during a chemical reaction. (p. 145)

pressure The force exerted on a surface divided by the total area over which the force is exerted; also the force of a gas's outward push divided by the area of the walls of the container. (pp. 53, 347)

primary colors Three colors that can be used to make any other color. (p. 583)

primary wave A longitudinal seismic wave. (p. 491)

product A substance formed as a result of a chemical reaction. (p. 154)

projectile An object that is thrown. (p. 326)

protein An organic compound that is a polymer made of amino acids. (p. 231)

proton Small, positively charged particle in the nucleus of an atom. (p. 76)

pulley A simple machine consisting of a grooved wheel around which is wrapped a rope, chain, or cable. (p. 394)

pupil The hole through which light enters the eye. (p. 588)

radar A system of detecting reflected radio waves. (p. 540)

radiation The transfer of energy by electromagnetic waves. (p. 442)

radiation therapy A process in which radioactive elements are used to destroy unhealthy cells. (p. 270)

radio waves Electromagnetic waves with the longest wavelengths and lowest frequencies. (p. 539)

radioactive dating The process of determining the age of an object using the half-life of one or more radioactive isotopes. (p. 268)

radioactive decay The process in which the atomic nuclei of unstable isotopes release fast-moving particles and energy. (p. 266)

random-access memory (RAM) The temporary storage area for data while the computer is operating. (p. 729)

rarefaction The part of a longitudinal wave where the particles of the medium are far apart. (p. 475)

ray Straight line used to represent a light wave. (p. 571)

reactant A substance that enters into a chemical reaction. (p. 154)

read-only memory (ROM) The permanent storage area for data in the computer. (p. 729)

real image An inverted image formed where rays of light meet. (p. 573)

rechargeable battery A battery in which the products of the electrochemical reaction can be changed back into reactants to be reused. (p. 701)

reference point A place or object used for comparison to determine if an object is in motion. (p. 284)

reflecting telescope A telescope that uses one or more mirrors to gather light from distant objects. (p. 592)

reflection The bouncing back of a wave when it hits a surface through which it cannot pass. (p. 482)

refracting telescope A telescope that uses convex lenses to gather and focus light. (p. 592)

refraction The bending of waves as they enter a different medium. (p. 483)

regular reflection Reflection that occurs when parallel rays of light hit a smooth surface and all reflect at the same angle. (p. 571)

renewable resource A natural resource that can be replaced in nature at a rate close to the rate at which it is used. (p. 689)

replacement A reaction in which one element replaces another in a compound, or in which two elements in different compounds trade places. (p. 159)

resistance The opposition to the movement of electric charges flowing through a material. (p. 632)

resistor A device in an electric circuit that uses electrical energy as it interferes with the flow of electric charge. (p. 632)

resonance The increase in the amplitude of vibration that occurs when external vibrations match the object's natural frequency. (p. 486)

responding variable The factor that changes as a result of changes to the manipulated, or independent, variable in an experiment; also called dependent variable. (p. 6)

retina The layer of cells that lines the inside of the eyeball. (p. 589)

RNA *RiboNucleic Acid*; a compound that, with DNA, determines the order of amino acids in a protein. (p. 234)

rods Cells on the retina that detect dim light. (p. 589)

rolling friction Friction that occurs when an object rolls over a surface. (p. 325)

············ **S** ············

salt An ionic compound that can form from the neutralization of an acid with a base. (p. 203)

satellite Any object that travels around another object in space. (p. 339)

saturated hydrocarbon A hydrocarbon in which all the bonds between carbon atoms are single bonds. (p. 223)

saturated solution A mixture that contains as much solute in it as possible at a given temperature. (p. 186)

science A way of learning about the natural world through observations and logical reasoning; leads to a body of knowledge. (p. 4)

scientific inquiry Another term for the ongoing process of discovery in science. (p. 4)

scientific law A statement that describes what scientists expect to happen every time under a particular set of conditions. (p. 9)

scientific theory A well-tested idea that explains and connects a wide range of observations. (p. 9)

screw A simple machine that consists of an inclined plane wrapped around a central cylinder to form a spiral. (p. 389)

secondary color Any color produced by combining equal amounts of any two primary colors. (p. 583)

secondary wave A transverse seismic wave. (p. 491)

seismic wave A wave produced by an earthquake. (p. 491)

seismograph Instrument used to detect and measure earthquakes. (p. 492)

semiconductor A substance that can conduct electricity under some conditions. (p. 103)

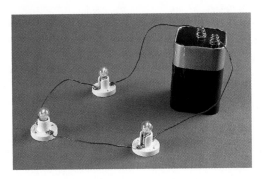

series circuit An electric circuit with only one path for the current to take. (p. 663)

shareware Software that the author allows others to try out and use for a low fee. (p. 739)

short circuit An electrical connection that allows current to take an unintended path. (p. 666)

sliding friction Friction that occurs when one solid surface slides over another. (p. 325)

slip rings The parts of a generator that rotate with the armature and make contact with the brushes. (p. 685)

slope The steepness, or slant, of a line on a graph. (p. 291)

sodium vapor lights Light bulbs containing solid sodium plus neon and argon gas. (p. 550)

solar wind Streams of electrically charged particles flowing at high speeds from the sun's corona. (p. 625)

solenoid A current-carrying coil of wire with many loops that acts as a magnet. (p. 637)

solid A state of matter that has a definite volume and a definite shape. (p. 47)

solid-state component Part of a circuit in which a signal is controlled by a solid material. (p. 714)

solubility A measure of how well a solute can dissolve in a solvent at a given temperature. (p. 186)

solute The part of a solution present in a lesser amount and dissolved by the solvent. (p. 179)

solution A very well-mixed mixture, having the same properties throughout. (p. 179)

solvent The part of a solution that is present in the largest amount and dissolves a solute. (p. 179)

sonar A system of detecting reflected sound waves. (p. 525)

sonogram An image formed by an ultrasound machine. (p. 527)

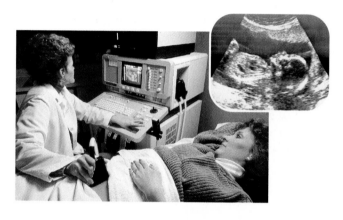

sound A disturbance that travels through a medium as a longitudinal wave. (p. 498)

specific heat The amount of thermal energy required to raise the temperature of one kilogram of a substance by one kelvin. (p. 444)

spectroscope An instrument used to view the different colors of light produced by different sources. (p. 548)

speed The distance an object travels in one unit of time. (p. 286)

standing wave A wave that appears to stand in one place, even though it is really two waves interfering as they pass through each other. (p. 485)

starch A complex carbohydrate in which plants store energy. (p. 230)

states The three forms (solid, liquid, and gas) in which matter exists. (p. 450)

static discharge The loss of static electricity as electric charges move off an object. (p. 648)

static electricity A buildup of charges on an object. (p. 647)

step-down transformer A transformer that decreases voltage. (p. 693)

step-up transformer A transformer that increases voltage. (p. 693)

structural formula A description of a molecule that shows the kind, number, and arrangement of atoms. (p. 222)

sublimation The change in state from a solid directly to a gas without passing through the liquid state. (p. 68)

subscript A number in a chemical formula that tells the number of atoms in a molecule or the ratio of elements in a compound. (p. 153)

substituted hydrocarbon A hydrocarbon in which one or more hydrogen atoms have been replaced by atoms of other elements. (p. 224)

superconductor A material that has no electrical resistance. (p. 633)

supernova An explosion that breaks apart a massive star. (p. 108)

supersaturated solution A mixture that has more dissolved solute than is predicted by its solubility at the given temperature. (p. 188)

surface wave A wave that occurs at the surface between two mediums. (p. 475)

suspension A mixture in which particles can be seen and easily separated by settling or filtration. (p. 186)

symbol Usually one- or two-letter set of characters that is used to identify an element. (p. 20)

synthesis A chemical reaction in which two or more simple substances combine to form a new, more complex substance. (p. 157)

synthetic A material that is manufactured. (p. 226)

telescope An optical instrument that forms enlarged images of distant objects. (p. 592)

temperature The measure of the average kinetic energy of the particles in a substance. (p. 52)

tendon A band of connective tissue that attaches a muscle to a bone. (p. 400)

terminal The part of an electrode above the surface of the electrolyte. (p. 699)

terminal velocity The maximum velocity a falling object achieves. (p. 327)

thermal energy The total energy of a substance's particles due to their movement or vibration. (p. 64)

thermal expansion The expansion of matter when it is heated. (p. 453)

thermogram An image that shows regions of different temperatures in different colors. (p. 543)

thermostat A device that regulates temperature. (p. 454)

third prong The round prong of a plug which connects the metal shell of an appliance to the safety grounding wire of a building. (p. 667)

timbre The overall quality of a sound. (p. 511)

total internal reflection The complete reflection of light by the inside surface of a medium. (p. 600)

tracer A radioactive isotope that can be followed through the steps of a chemical reaction or industrial process. (p. 269)

transformer A device that increases or decreases voltage. (p. 692)

transistor A device that either amplifies an electronic signal or switches current on and off. (p. 714)

transition metal An element in Groups 3 through 12 of the periodic table. (p. 92)

translucent Term used to describe a material that scatters light as it passes through. (p. 570)

transparent Term used to describe a material that transmits light. (p. 570)

transverse wave A wave that moves the medium in a direction perpendicular to the direction in which the wave travels. (p. 474)

trough The lowest part of a transverse wave. (p. 474)

tsunami A surface wave on the ocean caused by an underwater earthquake. (p. 491)

tungsten-halogen lights Bulbs containing a tungsten filament and a halogen gas that produce light. (p. 551)

turbine A circular device with many blades that is turned by water, wind, steam, or tides. (p. 685)

ultrasound Sound waves with frequencies above 20,000 Hz. (p. 506)

ultraviolet rays Electromagnetic waves with frequencies higher than visible light, but lower than X-rays. (p. 544)

unbalanced force A nonzero net force that changes an object's motion. (p. 314)

unsaturated hydrocarbon A hydrocarbon in which one or more of the bonds between carbon atoms is double or triple. (p. 223)

unsaturated solution A mixture in which more of the same solute can be dissolved. (p. 186)

vacuum tube A sealed glass tube from which most of the air has been removed. (p. 716)

valence electrons The electrons that are farthest away from the nucleus of an atom and involved in chemical reactions. (p. 79)

Van Allen belts Two doughnut-shaped regions 1,000–25,000 kilometers above Earth that contain electrons and protons traveling at high speeds. (p. 625)

vaporization The change from the liquid to the gaseous state of matter. (p. 66)

variable Any factor that can change in an experiment. (p. 6)

vary inversely A term used to describe the relationship between two variables whose graph forms a curve that slopes downward from left to right. (p. 61)

velocity Speed in a given direction. (p. 289)

vibration A repeated back-and-forth or up-and-down motion. (p. 473)

virtual image An upright image formed where rays of light appear to meet or come from. (p. 572)

viscosity The resistance of a liquid to flowing. (p. 49)

visible light Electromagnetic radiation that can be seen with the unaided eye. (p. 544)

vitamin An organic compound that serves as a helper molecule in a variety of chemical reactions in the body. (p. 235)

voltage The difference in electrical potential between two places. (p. 655)

voltage source A device, such as a battery or a generator, that creates a potential difference in an electric circuit. (p. 656)

voltmeter A device used to measure voltage, or potential difference. (p. 658)

volume The amount of space that matter occupies. (p. 25)

wave A disturbance that transfers energy from place to place. (p. 472)

wavelength The distance between the crest of one wave and the crest of the next. (p. 479)

wedge A simple machine consisting of a device that is thick at one end and tapers to a thin edge at the other. (p. 388)

weight A measure of the force of gravity on an object. (p. 25)

wet cell An electrochemical cell in which the electrolyte is a liquid. (p. 700)

wheel and axle A simple machine consisting of two circular or cylindrical objects that are fastened together and rotate about a common axis. (p. 392)

wide area network (WAN) A system of computers connected across large distances. (p. 737)

work The product of force and distance when a force is used to move an object. (p. 374)

World Wide Web A system that allows the displaying of text, pictures, video, and sound on the Internet. (p. 738)

X-rays Electromagnetic waves with higher frequencies than ultraviolet rays, but shorter than gamma rays. (p. 545)

absolute zero 438
abutments 463
acceleration 302–306
  forces and, 318–319
  graphing, 306
acetic acid 34, 225
acetylene (ethyne) 223
AC generator 684–685
acid-base reactions 202–203
acid rain 158, 202
acids 138
  formulas, 198
  important, 193
  properties of, 192–194
  in solution, 198–199
  strengths of, 200
  uses of, 195
acoustics 516
actinides 84, 94
action and reaction 332–334
activation energy 161, 162
actual mechanical advantage 383
air, density of 363
air conditioner 458
airplane wings 367
air pressure (atmospheric pressure) 349, 350–351, 368
  boiling point and, 67
air resistance 327
air traffic controllers 289
alcohols 224–225
alkali metals 91
alkaline earth metals 92
alloys 91, 255, 256–259
alpha decay 266, 267
alpha particle 267
alternating current (AC) 683–684, 695, 714
aluminum 93
aluminum alloys 257
amalgam 258, 259
amine group 231
amino acids 208, 231, 233
ammeter 648, 663
amorphous solids 48
Ampère, André Marie 629
ampere (amp or A) 629
amplifiers 715
amplitude 722
  of waves, 476, 477–478
amplitude modulation (AM) 555–556, 722
AM radio 555–556
amylase 207
analog signals 711, 712
analog thermometers 711
angle of incidence 482
angle of reflection 482
animal polymers 246
antacids 204–205
antifreeze 183
antinodes 486
anvil (bone) 521
applications software 732
applying concepts, skill of 756
arch bridge 462, 463
Archimedes' principle 359

architect 13
area of rectangle 347
armature 679
artificial sweeteners 238
ascorbic acid 235
Asimov, Isaac 34
aspartame 238
astronauts, gravity and 329
Atanasoff, John V. 731
atmospheric pressure (air pressure) 67, 349, 350–351, 368
atomic mass 77, 82, 84, 86
atomic mass unit (amu) 77
atomic nuclei 106–107
atomic number 83, 85, 266
atomizer 368
atoms 19, 31–35, 76–80
  electrons in, 77–80
audiologist 13
audio signal 723
aurora 626
automation 397
average speed 287
ax 388

Babbage, Charles 730
bakelite 248
balanced forces 314, 315
balanced pressures 349–350
bar graphs 760
barium 82
bases 138, 196, 197, 199, 200
  acid-base reactions, 202–203
bats, echolocation in 527
batteries 697–704
  dead and rechargeable, 701
  disposal of, 704
beam bridges 463
beats 517
Bell, Alexander Graham 718
bends, the 188
benzene 172
Benz tricycle car 288
Bernoulli, Daniel 366
Bernoulli's principle 365–368
Berry, Clifford 731
beryllium 107, 108
beta decay 266, 267
beta particle 267
bicarbonate ion 208
bimetallic strips 454
binary system 726–727, 731, 734–735
bioluminescence 551
bird wings 367
bits 727
blast furnace 40
blind spots 589
body, human
  acids in, 195
  electric current in, 669
  machines in, 400–402
Bohr, Niels 79
boiling 67
boiling point 452
  air pressure and, 67

  of molecular compounds, 122
  of solutions, 182, 183
bonds. *See* **chemical bonds**
bones, levers consisting of muscles and 400–402
boron oxide 253
Boyle, Robert 54
Boyle's Law 54, 60, 61
brain, optic nerve and 589
brass 91, 258, 259
brass instruments 512–513, 515
bridges 462–469
  balance of forces in, 463
  geometry of, 468
bromine 102, 224
bronze 144, 256, 258, 259
Bronze Age 255
Brooklyn Bridge 464–467
brushes 679
buoyancy 359–362, 364
butane 220, 222
butyric acid 225
bytes 727

cable television 557
  networks, 723
calcium 82, 92
calcium carbonate 194
calculation 753
Calder, Alexander 390
California gold rush 36, 37
cameras 528, 593–594, 597
car, hydraulic brake system of 356–357
carbohydrates 228–230
  complex, 229–230, 233
  simple, 229
carbon
  atom and bonds of, 214, 215, 218, 223, 245
  atomic number, 215
  electron dot diagram, 122
  isotopes, 266
  in living things, 227–238
carbon arc lamps 748
carbonates, acid reactions with 194
carbon chemistry 214–238
  nuclear fusion in sun and carbon production, 107, 108
carbon family 100
carbonic acid 202
carbon steel 258
carboxyl group 225
careers in physical science 12–13
carrier signal 723
carrier wave 722
Cartesian diver 362
catalase 166
catalysts 164–165
  enzymes, 165, 166–167, 207–208
cathode-ray tubes (CRT) 724–725
cause and effect, relating 757
CD-ROM (Compact Disc—Read-Only Memory) 731
cellular telephones 557, 559
celluloid 248
cellulose 229–230, 233, 246

Celsius scale 437, 753
converting degrees to kelvins, 59
census counting machine 730
centimeter (cm) 285
central processing unit (CPU) 729
centripetal force 339
ceramics 260–262
Chadwick, James 79
changes in matter 22–23, 45
changes in properties 145, 146
changes in state 64–70, 450–453
energy and, 64–65, 68
identifying substances through, 69
between liquid and gas, 66–67, 452–453
between liquid and solid, 64–66, 451–452
charcoal 100
charges. See electric charges
Charles, Jacques 56
Charles's Law 56–57, 59, 60
chat rooms 739
chemical bonds 34, 112–133, 161
chemical reactions and, 148–149
covalent bonds, 121–125
crystal chemistry and, 128–130
ionic bonds, 114–119
valence electrons and formation of, 79–80
chemical digestion 206–207
chemical energy 412, 417, 424
in batteries, 698–703
chemical equations 152–159
balancing, 155–157
conservation of mass and, 154–155
chemical reactions 23, 142–175
chemical bonds and, 148–149
classifying, 157–159
controlling, 160–165
evidence for, 144–147, 150–151
fire and fire safety, 168–171, 764
hazardous substances and, transporting, 172
observing, 144–149
obtaining elements from compounds by, 37–39, 40
rates of, 162–165
reactants and products in, 154
on small scale, 148
starting, 161–162
chemical researcher 13
chemicals, laboratory safety with 765
chemistry 19
chips, integrated circuit 715, 727
chlorine 102, 224
chlorofluorocarbons (CFCs) 1–2
chloroform 69
cholesterol 232–233
chromium 90
Chunnel 393
circle graphs 762
circuit breakers 668, 669
circuits. See electric circuits
circular motion 304, 339
citric acid 225
clarinet 515
Clarke, Mary Stetson 137
classification 751

clay 260–261
cleaners, ultrasonic 528
cloud of electrons 79
coal 247, 248–249, 423, 688
cobalt 253, 270
cochlea 521, 523
coefficient 156
coherent waves 595
Colgate, William 136
colloids 181
color(s) 581–586
changing, 146, 586
chemical reaction and, 146
combining, 583–585
of objects, 581–583
of visible spectrum, 544, 549, 577
colored light, objects in 582–583
color filters 583, 586
Columbus, Christopher 622
combustion 425, 455–456
fire as result of, 168–169
heat engines, 455–457
communication(s) 9, 751
electromagnetic waves and, 720–722
electronic, 718–725
through glass, 263–264
optical fibers in, 600
radio and, 554–556, 562–564, 723
telephones and, 557–558, 559, 560, 718–720
television and, 557, 723–725
wireless, 554–564
communication satellites 559, 560–561, 723
communication technology 533
commutator 679
compact disc (CD) 596–597, 599, 712–713, 727
compare/contrast tables 758
comparing and contrasting 756
compass 622
complementary colors 584
complex carbohydrates 229–230, 233
composites 248–250
compound machines 396
compounds 20, 33. See also chemical bonds
carbon, 213, 219–226, 245
chemical reaction to break down, 37–39, 40
as electrically neutral, 115
formulas for, 153
ionic, 117–119
model, 113
of nonmetals, 99
solubility of, 187
compression force 462, 463
compressions 475, 477, 478
sound and, 499
compression stroke 457
computer languages 732
computer networks 736–737
computer programmers 732
computers 715, 726–735
binary system, 726–727, 731, 734–735
hardware, 728–731
history of, 730–731
making model of, 734–735

memory in, 727
programming, 732
software, 732
uses of, 733
computer viruses 738–739
concave mirrors 573
concentration 163, 184–185
concept maps 758
conclusions, drawing 8, 755
Concorde aircraft 277
condensation 67, 452–453
conduction 440
charging by, 647, 649
conduction electrons 630
conductivity, electrical
of ionic compound, 119
of molecular compounds, 123
solutions and, 181
conductivity tester 119, 126–127
conductors 443–444, 448, 630
metals as, 90
superconductors, 633
cones of eye 589
Conrad, Frank 539
conservation
of charge, law of, 648
of energy, law of, 420–421
of mass, 154–155
of momentum, law of, 336–337
conserving (saving) energy 421
constant ratios 33
constant speed 286–287
constructive interference 484, 487, 516
controlled experiment 6, 755
convection 440, 441
convection current 441
conversion factor 298–299
converter 714
convex lens 589
convex mirrors 574
copper 37–39
copper chloride, isolating copper from 38–39
cordless telephones 558
cornea 588
corrosion 90
covalent bonds 121–125
of carbon, 216, 245
electron sharing in, 121
properties of molecular compounds, 122–123
unequal electron sharing, 123–124
crankshaft 456, 457
crests 474, 477, 722
antinodes, 486
critical thinking 756–757
cross-linkages 758
crystal chemistry 128–130
bonding in mineral crystals, 129–130
comparing crystals, 130
ionic compounds as crystals, 118, 120
mineral properties, 128–129
crystalline solids 48
cubic centimeter 25, 27
cubit 26

cyclamate 238
cycle diagrams 759
cylinder 456, 457

Daguerre, Louis-Jacques-Mandé 597
Dalton, John 32–33, 78
Darden, Christine Mann 276–279
data 5, 750
    collecting, 7, 59, 61
    interpreting, 7, 755
data tables 760
DC generators 685. *See also* **direct current**
    (DC)
debugging 732
decibels (dB) 505
decimal notation 26
decomposition 158
Democritus 32
density 28–29, 30, 362–364
    of medium, speed of sound and, 501
dependent (responding) variable 6, 755
depth, fluid pressure and 351
destructive interference 485, 486, 487, 516
detergents 125, 135, 136
diabetes 238
diamond 214, 216
diatomic molecules 99
diesel engine 456
difference engine 730
diffraction 483–484, 486
    sound and, 500
diffuse reflection 571
digestion 206–208
digital manipulation 740
digital signals 712
digital thermometers 711
dilute solution 184
dimmer switch 660–661
diodes 714
direct current (DC) 683–684, 695, 714
    DC generator, 685
direction of force 313–314, 315
    changing, 302, 303, 380, 381
    work and, 374
dirigibles 162
disk drive 730
diskettes 730–731
dissonance 513
distance
    describing, 284–285
    multiplying, 380, 381
    of plate motion, calculating, 297–298
distilled water 178
DNA (deoxyribonucleic acid) 234
dolphins, echolocation used by 526
Doppler, Christian 508
Doppler effect 508–509, 540, 541
double bond 122, 223
dredges 37
dress code for laboratory 764
drum, vibration of 498–499
dry cells 700
dry ice 69
ductile material 89
dynamite 165

ear 520–523
ear canal 520–521
eardrum 521
Earth
    elements from, 36–40
    gravitational pull of, 329
    magnetic field of, 623, 625, 626–627
    motion of, 283
    plate tectonics and motion on, 296–299
    satellites in orbit around, 340
earthquakes 490, 491–492
echo 482, 524
echolocation 526–527
Edison, Thomas 549, 606, 632, 695–696,
    744–749
Edison Electric Light Company 695
efficiency of machines 382–385
effort force. *See* **input force**
Einstein, Albert 421, 537
elasticity of medium 501
elastic potential energy 411, 414–415
electrical conductivity. *See* **conductivity,**
    electrical
electrical distribution 748
electrical energy 413, 417, 424, 630
    batteries for, 697–704
    conversion to mechanical energy, 676–677
    mechanical energy converted to, 425
electrical energy audit 675
electrical engineer 12
electrical potential 654
electrical resistance. *See* **resistance**
electrical safety 666–670
    fuses and circuit breakers, 668–669
    grounding, 666, 667–668
electric charges 628–629, 643–670. *See*
    also **electrical safety; electric circuits**
    detecting, 651
    electric field surrounding, 645–646
    interactions between, 645
    static charge, 646–651
    transferring, 647–648, 649
    types of, 644–646
    in versorium, 652–653
electric circuits 630, 662–665
    circuit measurements, 654–659
    household circuits, 665
    parallel circuits, 663–664
    series circuits, 663
electric current 628–629, 643
    alternating and direct, 683–684, 694–696,
        714
    conductors and insulators and, 630
    electric circuits and, 630, 631
    generators for producing, 684–685
    induction of, 682–683
    magnetic field produced by, 629
    as means of carrying information, 710
    resistance and, 632–633, 657
    turbines and, 425, 685
electric discharge through gases 550
electric fields 535, 645–646, 721
electric generators 684–685
electric induction. *See* **induction**
electricity, generating 688–689

electricity, uses of 674–707
    electric motors, 678–681
    galvanometers, 677–678, 682–683
    motion and, 676–681
electric motors 678–681
electric power, using 690–696
    history of, 694–695
    paying for, 692
    transformers and, 692–696
electric shocks 666, 669–670
electrochemical cells 699–703
    combining, 700
    wet cells and dry cells, 700, 702–703
electrodes 38–39, 699
electrolysis 38–39
electrolyte 699, 700
electromagnetic energy 413, 417, 632
electromagnetic induction 683
electromagnetic radiation 535
    as waves vs. particles, 536–537
electromagnetic spectrum 538–548
    gamma rays, 539, 543, 546, 547
    infrared rays, 539, 541–543
    radio waves, 480, 539–541, 542
    ultraviolet rays, 1, 539, 543, 544–545
    visible light, 538, 539, 543, 544, 548–553
    X-rays, 539, 543, 545
electromagnetic waves 473, 533–564,
    720–722
    amplitude and frequency modulation,
        555–556, 722
    bioluminescence, 551
    defined, 535
    electric field, 535, 721
    electromagnetic radiation, 535, 536–537
    electromagnetic spectrum, 538–548
    food irradiation and, 547
    magnetic field, 535, 615–616, 618, 721
    nature of, 534–537
    polarized light, 536–537
    speed of, 536, 538
    wireless communication, 554–564
electromagnetism 628–638, 695
    electric current and magnetic fields in,
        628–633
electromagnets 636–638
    increasing strength of, 638
    solenoids, 636–637
electron beam in cathode-ray tubes
    724–725
electron dot diagram 80, 122
electron guns 724
electronic keyboard 515
Electronic Numerical Integrator and
    Calculator (ENIAC) 731
electronics 708–740
    computers, 715, 726–735
    electricity versus, 710
    electronic communication, 718–725
    electronic signals, 711–713
    information superhighway and, 736–740
    past and future of, 716
    semiconductors in, 713, 714
    solid-state components, 714–715, 716
electronic signals 711–713

electrons 76, 628, 630, 632, 644–645
    attractions between, 124–125
    role of, 77–80
    valence. *See* **valence electrons**
electron sharing in covalent bonds 121
    unequal, 123–124
electron spin 616–617
electron transfer in ionic bonds 114–115
electroscope 651
elements 19–20, 81–88, 616
    from Earth, 36–40
    list of chemical, 767
    patterns in, 81–82
    periodic table of, 82–88, 768–769
    from stars, 106–108
    from sun, 107–108
    symbols for, 20, 84
elevation, fluid pressure and 350–351
e-mail 736
encryption 738
end-of-experiment rules 765
endothermic reaction 147, 162
energy 408–425. *See also* **electrical energy;
    thermal energy**
    activation, 161, 162
    changes in, 147
    changes in state and, 64–65, 68
    conservation of, 420–421
    conserving (saving), 421
    energy conversion, 416–419, 422–425
    forms of, 412–413
    fossil fuels, 422–425, 687, 689
    geothermal, 687, 688
    kinetic, 409–410, 418–419, 436–437
    nature of, 408–409
    nuclear, 413, 686
    potential, 409, 410–411, 414–415,
        418–419, 654
    power and, 428–429
    waves and, 472–473
energy conversion 416–419
    fossil fuels and, 422–425
energy-efficient buildings 448
energy recovery ventilation 448
energy resources 686–689
enzymes 165, 207–208
    temperature and action of, 166–167
Escher, M.C. 420
esters 225
etching 193
ethane 221, 222, 224
ethanol 69, 224–225
ethene (ethylene) 223
ethyne (acetylene) 223
evaporation 66
exhaust stroke 457
exothermic reaction 147, 162
experiments 754–755
    designing, 6, 755
    laboratory safety and, 763–765
external combustion engines 456
external memory 729
eye 588–589
eyeglasses 589–590, 596
eyepiece 592, 593

Fahrenheit, Gabriel 27
Fahrenheit scale 437
family (group) in periodic table 85, 86
Fantastic Voyage (Asimov) 34
Faraday, Michael 694
Farrington, Frank 466
farsightedness 590
fats 232
fatty acids 138, 232
fax machines 720
Federal Aid Highway Act 289
Federal Communications Commission
    (FCC) 555
ferromagnetic material 617
fiberglass 249, 250, 443
filters, objects seen through 583
fire 168–171
    common sources of, 170
    controlling, 169–170
    home fire safety, 170–171
    laboratory fire safety, 764
    understanding, 168–170
fire extinguisher 171
fire triangle 169
first aid 764
fixed pulleys 395
flashlight, building 634–635
flight 365
    Bernoulli's principle and, 366, 367
floating forces in fluids 358–364
    buoyancy, 359–361, 362, 364
    density, 362–364
floppy disks 730–731
flowcharts 759
fluid friction 325
fluid pressure 348–353
    balanced, 349
    Bernoulli's principle and, 365–368
    transmission of, 354–357
    variations in, 350–351
fluids 348
    forces in. *See* **forces in fluids**
fluorescent light 548, 549
fluorine 102, 224
fluorite 129
FM radio 556
focal point 573
food
    acids and, 195
    bases and, 196
    irradiation of, 547
    nutrients in. *See* **nutrients from foods**
force pumps 355
forces 310–340
    acceleration and, 318–319
    action and reaction, 332–334
    balanced, 314, 315
    changes in mass and, 322
    defined, 312–313
    friction. *See* **friction**
    gravity, 25, 326–329
    momentum, 335–337
    multiplying, 356–357, 379–380, 381
    orbiting satellites and, 338–340
    pressure and, 347

    unbalanced, 313–314, 315, 323
forces in fluids 344–371
    Bernoulli's principle and, 365–368
    floating and sinking, 358–364
    fluid pressure, 348–353
    transmission of pressure in fluid, 354–357
formic acid 225
formula 20
fossil fuels 422–425
    energy from, 422–425, 687, 689
    formation of, 423–425
    uses of, 425
fossils, radioactive dating of 268
four-color printing 585
four-stroke engines 456, 457
Franklin, Benjamin 645, 668
freefall 326
freeware 739
freezing 66, 452
freezing point 452
    solutes and lower, 182
French horn 515
freon 224
frequency 722
    Doppler effect, 508–509, 540, 541
    of electromagnetic waves, 538–539
    of sound, 506–507
    ultrasonic, 526–528
    of waves, 476, 480
frequency modulation (FM) 556, 722
    FM radio, 556
friction 323–325, 336
    charging by, 647, 649
    conservation of energy and, 420–421
    control of, 325
    efficiency of machines and, 382
    measuring, 330–331
    mechanical advantage without, 383
    uses of, 325
fuel
    combustion of, 168
    fossil fuels, 422–425, 687, 689
fulcrum 389, 391, 401
Fuller, Buckminster 217
fullerene 217
fundamental tone 511
fuses 668

galena 128
Galileo, Galilei 316, 596
Galvani, Luigi 698
galvanometers 677–678, 682–683
gamma decay 266, 267
gamma radiation 267, 269–270
gamma rays 539, 543, 546, 547
gas behavior 51–61
    graphing, 58–61
    pressure-temperature relationship, 54–55
    pressure-volume relationship, 53–54,
        60–61, 62–63
    volume-temperature relationship, 56–57,
        59–60
gases 49–50, 68, 450
    changes between liquids and, 66–67,
        452–453

changes between solids and, 68–69
chemical reaction and production of, 146
electric discharge through, 550
measuring, 52–53
solubility of, 188
gasoline 220
gasoline engine 456
gears 396
generalizations, making 757
generators 684–685
geodesic domes 217
geographic poles 624
geosynchronous satellite orbits 559
geothermal energy 687, 688
germanium 103
Gilbert, William 623
glass 262–264
glassblowing 262–263
glassware in laboratory, safety in using 765
glaze on ceramics 261
Global Positioning System (GPS) 561
global warming 689
glucose 228, 229, 233
glycerin 138
glycerol 138, 232
gold 36–37, 90, 253, 256, 257
density of, 29, 37
Goodyear, Charles 248
gram (g) 25, 753
graphic organizers 758–759
graphite 96–97, 216
graphing 58, 760–762
gas behavior, 58–61
motion, 290, 291–293
gravitational potential energy 411, 414–415
gravity 326–329
air resistance and, 327
freefall and, 326
projectile motion, 326–327
universal gravitation, 328–329
weight and, 25, 327
Green, Andy 502
grounding wires 666, 667–668

half-life 268, 272
halite 118, 129–130
halogen compounds 224
halogen family 102
halogen light bulbs 551
hammer (bone) 521
hard disks 730
hardware, computer 728–731
hard water 135
harp 514
Hazardous Materials Transportation Act (1975, 1994) 172
hazardous substances, transporting 172
hearing 520–523
loss of, 522, 523
mechanism of, 520–521
range of, 506
hearing aids 522
heart, force pumps in 355
heat 439, 440
conductors and insulators of, 443–444, 448

movement of, 442
nature of, 439–445
specific, 444–445
uses of, 455–458
heat engines 455–457
heat lamps 542
heat transfer 440–442, 446–447
direction of, 442
methods of, 440–442
helium 102, 107
hemoglobin 93
Henry, Joseph 694
Hero's engine 352
Hertz, Heinrich 480, 558
hertz (Hz) 480, 555
high-definition televisions (HDTV) 725
high-density polyethylene (HDPE) 247
Hindenburg (airship) 161
Hollerith, Herman 730
holograms and holography 598, 599
horsepower 430
household circuits 665
Hubble Space Telescope 284, 597
humidity, static discharge and 648–650
hydrangea flowers as indicators 194
hydraulic systems 356–357
hydrocarbons 220–221, 223–225
carbon chains in, 220, 222
formulas of, 221
properties of, 221
saturated and unsaturated, 223
substituted, 224–225
hydroelectric power 686, 688
hydrogen 102–103
nuclear fusion in sun, 107–108
in plasma state, 106
hydrogen ions 198–199, 200
pH scale to measure concentration of, 200–201
hydrogen peroxide 166
hydroxide ions 199, 200
hydroxyl group 224
hypothesis 6, 754

ice 46
density of, 363
freezing to form, 66
melting, 65, 70
ideal mechanical advantage 383
of compound machine, 396
of inclined plane, 387
of lever, 390
of pulley, 395
of wheel and axle, 394
ignition 457
illumination 548
image 572, 573
incandescent light 548–549, 552–553
incisors 402
inclined plane 386, 387–388, 392, 393, 398–399
independent (manipulated) variable 6, 755, 761
index of refraction 576
indicators 177

acid reactions with, 177, 194
base reactions with, 177, 197
measuring pH with, 201
indoor air pollution 448
induction 694
charging by, 647, 648, 649, 650
of electric current, 682–683
industry
acids used by, 195
bases used in, 196
radioactive isotopes used in, 269–270
X-rays used in, 545
inertia 316–317
infection, hearing loss due to 522
inference 6, 750
information superhighway 736–740
computer networks in, 736–737
digital manipulation, 740
intellectual property and, 739
Internet, 9, 737
protection in, 738–739
World Wide Web, 736, 738
infrared camera 542–543
infrared rays 539, 541–543
infrasound 506, 526
inhibitors 165
inner ear 520, 521
input devices 728
input force 379–380, 391, 401
instruments, musical 512–515
insulators 443–444, 448, 630
intake stroke 457
integrated circuits 715, 727
intellectual property 739
intensity of sound wave 504–505
interference 484–485, 487
sound and, 516–517
internal combustion engines 456
internal memory 729
International Bureau of Weights and Measures 27
International System of Units (SI) 7, 25, 285, 752
converting SI units, 753
Internet 9, 737
Internet service providers (ISPs) 737
interpreting illustrations 756
Interstate Highway System 289
iodine 224
ion 115
ionic bonds 114–119
electron transfer and, 114–115
forming, 115, 116
naming ionic compounds, 117
polyatomic ions, 117
properties of ionic compounds, 118–119
ionic crystal 129–130
ionic solids in water 180
ion implantation 256
ionosphere 556
iris 588
iron 93, 108
alloys, 257
blast furnace to extract, 40
Iron Peacock, The (Clarke) 137

irradiation of food 547
isobutane 222
isomers 222
isotopes 266
  half-life of, 268, 272
  radioactive decay and, 267–268
  using radioactive, 269–270

Jansen, Hans and Zacharias 596
jaundice 544
joule (J) 377, 409
judgments, making 757
juggling, energy conversion in 418

kaleidoscope 569
kelvins 59
Kelvin scale 437–438
kevlar 249
keyboard 728
kilogram (kg) 317
kilogram-meters per second (kg-m/s) 335
kilohertz (kHz) 555
kilometer 285
kilowatt-hour (kWh) 692
kilowatts (kW) 427, 692
kinetic energy 409–410
  calculating, 410
  conversion of potential energy to, 418–419
  temperature and, 436–437
Krakatau volcano 490

labels 756
laboratory balance 766
laboratory safety 11, 763–765
  rules, 764–765
  symbols, 763
landfills, radioactive wastes in 271
lanthanides 84, 94
larynx 499
lasers 594–598, 599, 731
lava, viscosity of 49
lead 93, 362–363
lead oxide 253
Leblanc, Nicolas 136
length, measuring 752
lens(es) 578–579
  camera, 593, 594
  concave, 578
  convex, 578–580
  correcting vision, 589–590
  of eye, 589
  microscope, 593
  telescope, 592
levers 384–385, 386, 389–391, 393
  classes of, 391
  in human body, 400–402
light 569–600. See also electromagnetic
     waves
  color and, 581–586
  lenses and, 578–579
  reflection of, 571–574
  refraction of, 575–577
  vision and, 587–590
light, using 591–600
  cameras, 528, 593–594, 597

holography, 598, 599
lasers, 594–598, 599, 731
microscopes, 593, 596
optical fibers, 263–264, 598–600, 719
optical instruments, history of, 596–597
telescopes, 592, 596, 597
light amplification 595
light bulb 429, 552–553, 632, 745
light-emitting diode (LED) 717
light-emitting polymers (LEP) 249
lighting, types of 548–553
lightning 650
lightning rods 668
lignin 249
limestone 194, 253
linear relationship 306
line graphs 761
lines, electric 665
lipids 232–233
liquids 48–49, 68, 450
  liquid-gas changes of state, 66–67, 452–453
  solid-liquid changes of state, 65–66, 68, 451–452
  sound in, 499–500
liquid volume, measuring 752
liter (L) 25, 27, 752
litmus 194, 197
litmus test 199
load 463
local area network (LAN) 737
longitudinal waves 474–475
  amplitude of, 478
  diagram of, 477
  sound and, 498–500
  wavelength of, 479
loudness 504–505
Lovelace, Ada 730
low-density polyethylene (LDPE) 247
lubricant, graphite as 216
luminosity 548
lye 137

macaws 281
machines 373, 378–402. See also work
  automation and, 397
  changing direction and, 380, 381
  compound, 396
  defined, 378–379
  efficiency of, 382–385, 387–388, 390, 394–395
  in human body, 400–402
  multiplying distance and, 380, 381
  multiplying force and, 379–380, 381
  simple, 386–402
Mack, Robert 276
maglev train (magnetically levitating
     train) 612, 614
Magnesia, Greece 613
magnesium 92, 108
magnesium chloride 115
magnesium oxide 148–149, 157
magnetic declination 623–625
magnetic domains 617
magnetic field(s) 535, 615–616, 618, 721
  around solenoid, 637

of Earth, 623, 625, 626–627
produced by electric current, 629
magnetic field lines 615
magnetic metals 90
magnetic poles 613–614, 619, 645
  of Earth, 623–624
  interactions between, 614
magnetic resonance imaging (MRI) 541
magnetic tapes 727
magnetism 611–627
  breaking magnets, 619
  destroying magnets, 619
  of Earth, 622–627
  electron spin and, 616–617
  interaction of electricity and, 676–677
  making magnets, 618
  nature of, 612–621
magnetite 613, 618
magnetosphere 625–626
Maiman, Theodore 597
malic acid 225
malleable material 89
manipulated (independent) variable 6, 755
  continuous, 761
Marconi, Guglielmo 558
mass 24–25, 317
  atomic, 77, 82, 84, 86
  of atoms of each element, 33
  changes in, 322
  conservation of, 154–155
  measuring, 753
  units of, 25, 317
  velocity and, 409–410
  weight vs., 327
mass number 266
matter 16–43
  changes in, 22–23, 45
  conservation of energy and, 421
  density of, 28–29, 30
  elements from Earth, 36–40
  kinds of, 19–22
  mass of, 24–25
  measuring, 24–30
  particles of, 31–35
  properties of, 18–19
  states of, 22, 46–50
  volume of, 25–27
Maxwell, James Clerk 558
measurement(s) 24–30, 752–753
  common units and conversions, 28, 284–285, 298–299
  of concentration, 185
  of gases, 52–53
  of matter, 24–30
  of momentum, 335
  systems developed through history, 26–27
mechanical advantage 381, 390, 394–395
  actual and ideal, 383
mechanical digestion 206
mechanical energy 412, 417, 424
  conversion to thermal energy, friction and, 420–421
  electrical energy converted to, 676–677
  thermal energy converted to, 425, 455–457
mechanical waves 473

medicine
  gamma rays used in, 546
  optical fibers in, 600
  radioactive isotopes used in, 270
  ultrasound in, 527
medium 473
  speed of sound and, 500–501
megahertz (MHz) 555
melting 68, 70, 451
melting point 48, 65
  of ionic compound, 119
  of metals, 90
  of molecular compounds, 122
memory in computers 727
  storage devices, 728, 729–731
Mendeleev, Dimitri 82, 83, 88
mental models 751
mercury 90
metalloids 103
metals 89–94, 255
  acid reactions with, 193
  in aircraft, 257
  alloys, 91, 255, 256–259
  as conductors, 630
  contamination from, cleaning up, 95
  ionic bonds between nonmetals and,
    114–119
  in periodic table, 85, 91–94
  properties of, 89–90, 255
meter (m) 285, 752
methane 220, 221, 222, 224
methanol 224
mica 129
microphone 728
microscopes 593, 596
microwaves 539–540, 542
middle ear 520, 521
mid-ocean ridge 627
milk 213
milliliter (mL) 25, 27
millimeter (mm) 285
minerals 128, 235
  crystal structure of, 129–130
  properties of, 128–129
mirages 577
mirrors 572–574
mixtures 20–22
  alloys, 91, 255, 256–259
models, making 751
modem 728
molars 402
molecular compounds 122–123
molecular crystal 130
molecular formula 221
molecular solids in water 181
molecules 34, 233, 348
Molina, Mario xxii–3, 4, 5, 9
momentum 335–337
monitor 728
monomers 226, 245
monounsaturated oils 232
Moon
  gravitational pull of, 329
  orbit of Earth, 304
Morgan, J.P. 746

Morse code 710
motion 276–306. *See also* **forces**
  acceleration and, 302–306
  calculating speed of, 286–287, 294–295
  circular, 304, 339
  describing, 282–285
  electricity and, 676–681
  energy of (kinetic energy), 409–410
  graphing, 290, 291–293
  Newton's first law of, 316–319, 323
  Newton's second law of, 320–321
  Newton's third law of, 311, 332–334, 338
  of particles in solid, 47
  periodic, 471
  plate tectonics, 296–299
  projectile, 326–327
  recognizing, 283–284
  satellite, 339
  sonic booms and, 276–279
  velocity of, describing, 288–291
  vibration, 473
  work and, 374
motors, electric 678–681
mouth, pH and digestion in 207
movable pulleys 395
movies 604–609
  models used in, 607
  motion in, 606
  point of view in, 605
muscles, levers consisting of bones and
    400–402
music 497, 512–515, 518–519
musical instruments 512–515
musical notes 518–519
musician 12

Nagaoka, Hantaro 78
National Aeronautics and Space
    Administration (NASA) 276, 278
national road, construction of 288
natural gas 688
nearsightedness 590
Needleman, Kathy 276
negative ion 115
neon light 548, 550
net force 314
neutralization 202, 203
neutrons 76, 77, 78, 107
Newton, Isaac 316, 321, 335, 340
newton (N) 321
Newton's laws of motion
  first law, 316–319, 323
  second law, 320–321
  third law, 311, 332–334, 338
Niagara Falls 416, 418–419
Nicéphore Niepce, Joseph 597
nickel alloys 257
nickel-cadmium (NiCad) batteries 701, 704
nitrogen 122
nitrogen family 100–101
nitrogen fixation 100
nitroglycerin 165
Nobel, Alfred 165
noble gases 102
nodes 486

noise 513, 523
noise pollution 523
nonlinear relationship 306
nonmetals 98–103
  chemical properties of, 99
  compounds of, 99
  covalent bonds between, 121–125
  families of, 100–103
  ionic bonds between metals and, 114–119
  in periodic table, 85
  physical properties of, 99
nonpolar compounds 189, 220
nonpolar covalent bond 124
nonpolar molecules 124, 125
nonrenewable resource 689
Northern Lights 626
nuclear energy 413, 686
nuclear fission 413
nuclear fusion 107–108, 413, 423
nuclear power 270, 688
nuclear radiation 267
nuclear reactions 266
nucleic acids 234
nucleotides 233, 234
nucleus, nuclei 76, 77, 616–617
  collisions of, 106–107
nutrients from foods 228–237
  carbohydrates, 228–230, 233
  lipids, 232–233
  nucleic acids, 234
  proteins, 230–231, 233, 246
nylon 247, 249

objective 592, 593
observation 5, 750
ocean
  bioluminescence in, 551
  echolocation in, 526
Oersted, Hans Christian 628, 694
Office of Noise Abatement and Control 523
Ohm, Georg 648
Ohm's law 658–659
oil (petroleum) 220, 247, 248–249, 688
oils (food) 232
opaque material 570
operating system, computer 732
operational definition 755
optical disc 731
optical fiber 263–264, 598–600, 719
optical instruments, history of 596–597
optic nerve 589
orbiting satellites 338–340
  lift-off of, 338–339
  location of, 340
  motion of, 339–340
organic acids 224, 225
organic compounds 219–220, 227, 245.
    See also **nutrients from foods**
  esters, 225
  hydrocarbons, 220–221, 223–225
  isomers, 222
  polymers, 226
  properties of, 220
organizing information 758–759
outer ear 520–521

output devices 728, 729
output force 379–380, 391, 401
overtone 511
oxygen 108, 122, 169
oxygen family 101
ozone 101
ozone layer xxii–3
cycle of ozone destruction, 1
ozone hole and, 2

packaging with polymers 252–253
pagers 558–559
panning 37
paraffin wax 220
parallel circuits 663–664
particles
in gas, 50
in liquid, 49
in solid, 47–48
in solutions, 180–181
particles of matter 31–35
atoms, 19, 31–35, 76–80
molecules, 34, 233, 348
Pascal, Blaise 355
Pascal's principle 355
hydraulic systems based on, 356–357
pascal (Pa) 347
patent 744
path of least resistance 657
pendulum 10, 419
pepsin 208
perchloroethylene 224
percussion instruments 513
periodic motion 471
periodic table 82–88, 768–769
fitting alien elements in, 104–105
of Mendeleev, 83
metals in, 85, 91–94
modern, 83
organization of, 86–87
period (row of periodic table) 84, 87
permanent magnet 618
persistence of vision 606
personal computer (PC) 731
petroleum jelly 221
petroleum (oil) 220, 247, 248–249, 688
pewter 258
pH
acid-base reactions and, 202
in digestive system, 207–208
pH scale, 200–201
phenylketonuria (PKU) 238
phonograph, history of 748–749
phosphors 724
phosphorus 101
photocopier, static charge in 648
photoelectric effect 537
photograph 594
digital manipulation of, 740
photons 537, 595
photosynthesis 423
physical change 22, 23
physical models 751
physical science 4
careers in, 12–13

in daily life, 11
piano 507
pigments 20, 584–585
Pioneer Zephyr 289
piston 456, 457
pitch 506–507
Doppler effect and change in, 508–509
pits and flats in CD 712
plane mirrors 572
plant polymers 246
plasma 106
plastic 213, 244, 247
disadvantages of using, 250–251
grocery bags, 254
recycling, 251
plastic wrap, static charge in 648
plates 296–297
plate tectonics 296–299
speed of plates, 297–299
polar compounds 189
polar covalent bond 123
polarized light 536–537
polar molecules 124, 125
pole vault, energy conversion in 418, 419
pollution control officer 12
polyatomic ions 117
polymers 226, 243–254
carbon compounds forming, 245
composites and, 248–250
development of, 248–249
disadvantages of, 250–251
natural, 246
packaging of, 252–253
starch and cellulose, 229–230, 233
synthetic, 226, 247
polypropylene (PP) 247
polystyrene (PS) 247
polytetrafluoroethylene 247
polyunsaturated oils 232
polyvinyl chloride (PVC) 247
positive ion 115
potassium 90, 91
potassium nitrate 203
potential difference 655
potential energy 409, 410–411, 414–415
conversion to kinetic energy, 418–419
electrical potential, 654
types of, 411, 414–415
pottery. *See* ceramics
power 426–430
calculating, 426–427
electric, 690–696
energy and, 428–429
horsepower, 430
power plants 425
power ratings 691
power stroke 457
precipitate 145, 146
prediction 750
pressure(s) 346–348
balanced, 349–350
calculating, 347–348
fluid, 348–357
force and, 347
of gas, 53

solubility of gases and, 188
temperature and, 54–55
volume and, 53–54, 60–61, 62–63
primary colors 583, 584, 585
primary waves (P waves) 491, 492
prisms 576
problem solving 757
products 154
programming, computer 732
projectile 326
satellite as, 340
projectile motion 326–327
Prokofiev, Sergei 513
propane 220, 221, 222
properties, changes in 145, 146
proteins 230–231, 233, 246
protons 76, 77, 78, 616–617, 628, 644–645
pulleys and pulley systems 386, 392, 394–395
pupil of eye 588
pyrite 36

qualitative data 7
quantitative data 7
quartz 130
questions, posing 5, 754

radar 540–541, 720
radiation 1, 440, 442
electromagnetic, 535, 536–537
radiation therapy 270
radio 554–556
building crystal, 562–564
transmission and reception of, 723
radioactive dating 268
radioactive decay 266–267, 268
radioactive elements 265–272
half-life of, 268, 272
isotopes, 266
nuclear reactions, 266
radioactive decay, 266–267, 268
using, 269–271
radioactive wastes 270, 271
radio waves 480, 539–541, 542
magnetic resonance imaging (MRI), 541
microwaves, 539–540, 542
radar, 540–541, 720
rainbows 577
ramp, wheelchair-access 398–399
Random Access Memory (RAM) 729–730
rare earth elements 94
rarefactions 475, 477, 478, 499
ratio 33, 153
reactants 154, 163
Read Only Memory (ROM) 729–730
real image 573
receiver, telephone 720
rechargeable battery 701
recording information, electromagnets and 638
rectangle, area of 347
recycling 251
reed of woodwind instruments 513
reference point 284
reflecting telescope 592

reflection 482, 487, 571–574
  diffuse, 571
  mirrors, 572–574
  regular, 571
  of sound waves, 524
refracting telescope 592
refraction 483, 486
  of light, 575–577
refrigerators 458
relativity, theory of 421
renewable resource 689
replacement 159
resistance 632–633, 656–657
  in human body, 669–670
  Ohm's law and, 658–659
  parallel circuit and, 664
  series circuit and, 663
resistance force. See output force
resistors 631, 632, 658–659
resonance 486–487, 507
responding (dependent) variable 6, 755
retina 589
rise 292
RNA (ribonucleic acid) 234
rocks, radioactive dating of 268
rods of eye 589
Roebling, Emily Warren 466
Roebling, John Augustus 465, 466
Roebling, Washington 466
rolling friction 325
Rowland, Sherwood 1
run 292
rust 99
Rutherford, Ernest 79

saccharin 238
safety
  electrical, 666–670
  fire, 170–171, 764
  laboratory, 11, 763–765
safety symbols 763
saliva 207
salt 203
  table salt (sodium chloride), 99, 116,
    118, 120
saponification 138
satellites 339
  communication, 559, 560–561, 723
  location, 340
  orbiting, 338–340
satellite telephone systems 560
saturated fats 232
saturated hydrocarbons 223
saturated solution 186
scanner 599, 728
science 4
science fiction movies 608–609
science safety rules 764–765
scientific inquiry 4, 5–8, 754–755
scientific law 9
scientific theory 9
scientist, thinking like 5, 750–751
screws 386, 389
scuba divers 188
scum 135

search engines 738
sea stars, water vascular system of 357
secondary colors 583, 584
secondary waves (S waves) 491, 492
seesaws, properties of 384–385
seismic waves 490–492
seismographs 492
selenium 253
semiconductors 103, 713, 714
series circuits 663
shareware 739
sharp instruments, using 765
shininess of metals 89
shocks, electric 666, 669–670
short circuit 666
silicon 103, 108, 713
silk 246
simple machines 386–402
  inclined plane, 386, 387–388, 392, 393,
    398–399
  levers, 384–385, 386, 389–391, 393,
    400–402
  pulley, 386, 392, 394–395
  screws, 386, 389
  wedge, 386, 388, 392, 402
  wheel and axle, 386, 392–394
sinking forces in fluids 358–364
  buoyancy, 359–361, 362, 364
  density, 362–364
slide projector 583
sliding friction 325
slippery feel of bases 197
slip rings 685
slope 291, 292–293
small intestine, pH and digestion in 208
soap 125, 134–141
  chemistry of, 138
  in colonial times, 137
  development of, 136
  how it works, 135
  recipe for, 140
  soapmaking, 137, 139
  uses of, 134
sodium 90, 91
  bonding with chlorine, 115, 116
sodium carbonate 253
sodium chloride 99, 116
  crystal shape of, 118, 120
sodium vapor lights 548, 550
software 732
solar energy 686, 688
solar wind 625
solder 258, 259
solenoids 636–637
solids 47–48, 68, 450
  changes between gases and, 68–69
  changes between liquid and, 65–66, 68,
    451–452
  sound in, 499–500
  types of, 48
solid-state components 714–715, 716
solubility 186–189
solutes 179, 182–183
solutions 178–183
  acids in, 198–199

  bases in, 199
  colloids, 181
  concentrated, 184
  dilute, 184
  dissolving times in, 190–191
  particles in, 180–181
  saturated and unsaturated, 186
  solutes and, 179, 182–183
  solvents and, 179–180
  suspensions and, 178–179
  without water, 180
solvents 179–180
  solubility in, 186–189
  solutes and freezing/boiling points of,
    182–183
sonar 524
Sonic Boom Group (NASA) 276
sonic booms 276–279, 509
  research on, 278–279
sonogram 527
sound 497–528
  applications of, 524–528
  canceling, 516
  combining waves of, 510–519
  Doppler effect, 508–509, 540, 541
  frequency and pitch, 506–507, 508–509
  hearing, 520–523
  intensity and loudness, 504–505
  interference and, 516–517
  longitudinal waves and, 498–500
  music, 497, 512–515, 518–519
  nature of, 498–503
  noise, 513, 523
  properties of, 504–509
  quality of, 511
  speed of, 279, 500–502, 503
sound barrier, breaking 277, 502, 509
sound recordings 712–713
sour taste 192–193
Southern Lights 626
space, gamma rays given off in 546
sparks 650
specific heat 444–445
spectroscope 548, 549
spectrum, electromagnetic. See
  electromagnetic spectrum
speed
  calculating, 286–287, 294–295, 300–301
  decreasing, 302, 303
  of Earth's plates, 297–299
  of electromagnetic waves, 536, 538
  increasing, 302, 303
  of sound, 279, 500–502, 503
  of transportation, 288–289
  velocity and, 288–289
  of waves, 476, 480–481
spider web 242–243, 246
spoilers 367
spotlights 583
sprinkler systems, spinning 352–353
Sputnik 559, 608
squid, motion of 333
stainless steel 91, 256, 258
standing wave 485, 511, 518
starch 229–230, 233

stars, elements from 106–108
states of matter 22, 46–50. *See also*
    changes in state; gases; liquids; solids
  plasma, 106
  thermal energy and, 449–454
static charge 646–651
static cling 648
static discharge 648–650
static electricity 647, 649
steam engines 456
steel 258
step-down transformer 693, 695–696
step-up transformer 693, 695–696
sterling silver 258
stimulated emission 595
stirrup (bone) 521
stomach, pH and digestion in 207–208
stringed instruments 512, 514
stroke of piston 456, 457
strontium 82
structural formula 222, 223
styrene 172
sublimation 68–69
submarine, density of 363
subscript 153, 221, 222
substituted hydrocarbons 224–225
sugars 229
sulfur 101, 128
sulfuric acid 158
Sun
  elements from, 107–108
  as energy source, 423, 424
  nuclear fusion in, 107–108
  temperature in core of, 106
sunlight, overexposure to 545
superconducting materials 716
superconductors 633
superfund law 95
supernova 108
supersaturated solution 188
supersonic aircraft and flight 277, 278–279, 502
surface area, rate of chemical reaction and 164
surface waves 474, 475, 491–492
surgery, laser 597, 599
suspension bridges 464–467
suspensions 178–179
Sutter, John 36
sweeteners, artificial 238
symbols 152
  of elements, 20, 84
  safety, 763
synthesis 157–158
synthetic polymers 226, 247
Système International. *See* International System of Units (SI)

table salt. *See* sodium chloride
tap water 178
tar 244
technetium-99 270
technology, communication 533. *See also* electronics
teeth, expansion properties of 453

teflon (polytetrafluoroethylene) 247
telephones 557–558, 559, 560, 718–720
telescopes 592, 596, 597
television 557, 723–725
television satellites 561
temperature 52, 435–438. *See also* **thermal energy**
  Celsius scale, 437, 753
  chemical reaction and, 146, 147, 163–164
  enzyme action and, 166–167
  Fahrenheit scale, 437
  of gas, 52
  Kelvin scale, 437–438
  measuring, 753
  of medium, speed of sound and, 501
  pressure and, 54–55
  solubility changes and, 187–188
  volume and, 56–57, 59–60
temperature scales 437–438
temporary magnets 618
tendons 400
terminal 699
terminal velocity 327
Tesla, Nikola 695–696
TGV 289
thallium-201 270
thermal energy 64–65, 412, 417, 424, 438–458, 632
  changes of state and, 68
  combustion of fossil fuels for, 425
  friction converting mechanical energy to, 420–421
  heat transfer, 440–442, 446–447
  nature of heat, 439–445
  states of matter and, 449–454
  uses of heat, 455–458
thermal expansion 453–454
thermogram 436, 543
thermometers 453, 711
thermos bottles 444
thermostats 454
third prong 667
Thomson, J.J. 78
thorium 94, 265
thrust 339
tidal energy 687, 688
timbre 511
tin 93
Titanic, sinking of 358
titanium 256
titanium alloys 257
total internal reflection 600
tourmaline 129
tracers 269, 270
transcontinental railroad 288
transistors 714–715, 716
transition metals 92–93
translucent material 570
transmitter of telephone 719
transparent material 570
transportation, speed of 288–289
transverse waves 474
  amplitude of, 477
  diagram of, 476–477
  wavelength of, 479

trash 250–251
trichloroethane 224
Trifid Nebula 591
triode tubes 716
triple-beam balance 766
triple bonds 223
troughs 474, 477, 486, 722
truss bridges 468
tsunamis 491
tungsten halogen light 548, 551
turbines 425, 685

Ultra High Frequency (UHF) television 557
ultrasound 506, 526–528
ultraviolet (UV) rays 1, 539, 543, 544–545
unbalanced forces 313–314, 315, 323
U.S. Food and Drug Administration (FDA) 238
universal gravitation 328–329
universal product code (UPC) 599
universal solvent 179
unsaturated fatty acids 232
unsaturated hydrocarbons 223
unsaturated solution 186
uranium 94, 265, 270

vacuum tube 716
valence electrons 79–80, 88
  in alkali metals, 91
  in alkaline earth metal, 92
  transfer of, 115
valine 231
Van Allen, J.A. 625
Van Allen belts 625
vaporization 66–67, 68, 452
variables 6, 755
velocity 335
  calculating change in, 304
  describing, 288–291
  mass and, 409–410
  terminal, 327
venn diagrams 759
ventilation 448
versorium 652–653
Very High Frequency (VHF) television 557
vibration 473. *See also* **sound**
  resonance, 486–487
  sound from, 498–499
violin 514
virtual images 572, 573, 578, 579
viscosity 49
visible light 538, 539, 543, 544
  colors of visible spectrum, 544, 549, 577
  fluorescent light, 548, 549
  incandescent light, 548–549, 552–553
  neon light, 548, 550
  production of, 548–553
  sodium vapor lights, 548, 550
  tungsten halogen light, 548, 551
vision 587–590
  correction of, 589–590
  human eye and, 588–589
  persistence of, 606
vitamins 189, 235, 236–237, 544
vocal cords, frequency of sound and 506

voice-over 605
Volta, Alessandro 698–699, 700
voltage 655–656
 of household circuits, 665
 transformer and changing, 693–694, 696
voltage source 656
voltmeter 648, 664
volume 25–27
 buoyancy and density and, 364
 of gas, 52
 liquid, measuring, 752
 pressure and, 53–54, 60–61, 62–63
 temperature and, 56–57, 59–60

Waste Isolation Pilot Plant (WIPP) 271
water 178
 density of, 28
 identifying, through changes of state, 69
 ionic solids in, 180
 molecular solids in, 181
 molecules, 34
 properties of, 19
 solutions without, 180
 as solvent, 179
waterfall, energy conversion in 416, 418–419
water vapor 68
water vascular system 357
Watt, James 427, 430, 691
wattage 429
watt (W) 427, 691

wave(s) 471–492. *See also* **electromagnetic**
 waves; sound
 amplitude of, 476, 477–478
 diffraction of, 483–484, 486
 energy and, 472–473
 frequency of, 476, 480
 interactions of, 482–489
 interference and, 484–485, 487
 nodes and antinodes, 486
 properties of, 476–481
 reflection of, 482, 487
 refraction of, 483, 486
 resonance, 486–487
 seismic, 490–492
 speed of, 476, 480–481
 types of, 474–475
 wavelength of, 476, 479, 480, 538–539
wave diagrams 476–477
wavelength 476, 479
 calculating, 480
 of electromagnetic waves, 538–539
wedge 386, 388, 392, 402
weight 25, 327
Westinghouse, George 696
wet cells 700, 702–703
whales, echolocation used by 526
wheel and axle 386, 392–394
wheelchair-access ramp 398–399
white light 582, 583
wide area network (WAN) 737
wind 408
wind energy 687, 688

wings, Bernoulli's principle and 367
wireless communication 554–564
 cellular telephones, 557, 559
 communication satellites, 559, 560–561, 723
 cordless telephones, 558
 history of, 558–559
 pagers, 558–559
 radio and television, 554–557, 562–564, 723–725
wood 249
wood's metal 258
woodwind instruments 513, 515
wool 246
work 374–377. *See also* **machines**
 calculating, 376–377
 meaning of, 374–376
 power and, 426–430
 SI unit of, 377
 as transfer of energy, 408–409
World Wide Web 736, 738
Wright, Wilbur and Orville 365

xenon-133 270
X-rays 539, 543, 545

Yeager, Chuck 502
Yingxian Pagoda 393

zippers 388
zoetrope 606

Acknowledgments

Staff Credits

The people who made up the *Life, Earth, and Physical Science* team—representing design services, editorial, editorial services, electronic publishing technology, manufacturing & inventory planning, marketing, marketing services, market research, online services & multimedia development, production services, product planning, project office, publishing processes—are listed below. Bold type denotes core team members.

Carolyn Belanger, Barbara Bertell, Kristen Braghi, **Roger Calado, Jonathan Cheney, Lisa Clark,** Ed Cordero, Patricia Cully, Patricia Dambry, **Kathleen Dempsey,** Jim Fellows, Joel Gendler, Robert Graham, Joanne Hudson, Don Manning, Brent McKenzie, Paul W. Murphy, **Cindy Noftle,** Julia Osborne, **Caroline M. Power,** Shelley Ryan, **Robin Santel,** Helen Young

Additional Credits

Peggy Bliss, Barnard Gage, Julia Gecha, Adam Goldberg, Jessica Gould, Anne Jones, Dorothy Kavanaugh, Toby Klang, Jay Kulpan, Jeanne Maurand, Tania Mlawer, Shilo McDonald, Carolyn McGuire, Danny Marcus, Angela Sciaraffa

Illustrations

Annie Bissett: 134, 135b, 135t, 138
Peter Brooks: 25m, 30, 38, 62, 70, 96, 104, 218, 236, 620, 634, 702, 717
Morgan Cain & Associates: 1, 3, 35tl, 35, 39, 47l, 47r, 48, 50, 53, 54, 55, 56, 59t, 60b, 66, 68b, 77t, 78tl, 78tr, 78br, 79b, 79t, 84b, 84t, 85t, 86, 87, 92b, 92t, 93b, 93t, 94t, 94b, 99, 100t, 100b, 101l, 101r, 102tl, 102tr, 102b, 103, 107, 108, 116t, 118, 125tl, 129, 149l, 149m, 149r, 152, 156tl, 156tm, 156tr, 165, 171, 180, 182, 200, 211t, 215m, 215b, 216b, 216t, 217, 233bl, 233br, 233tr, 266t, 266b, 267, 275b, 309b, 328, 339, 343, 348l, 348r, 355, 356b, 359t, 362t, 368tl, 371tl, 379, 394, 395, 405t, 436, 437, 441t, 444, 450tl, 450tm, 450tr, 454, 458, 461, 463t, 463b, 464, 477t, 477m, 477b, 478, 479t, 482b, 485, 486b, 491, 499m, 505t, 505b, 511t, 517tr, 525, 542–543, 561, 567, 615t, 616, 617, 619, 636bm, 637b, 637tr, 638t, 641, 645, 646bl, 646br, 647tr, 651, 656, 657, 665, 673, 723, 752l, 752r, 753l, 753tr, 756b, 768t, 768–769b, 769m, 769t
Corel Corp.: 572
Kathleen Dempsey: 503, 518, 552, 562, 580, 586, 748
DFL Group: 558m
John Edwards & Associates: 73bl, 201, 336–337, 340, 349, 356tl, 356tr, 410, 417, 456, 457bl, 457t, 473, 474t, 475, 483, 484, 495, 499t, 508, 509, 513, 562b, 563tl, 563tr, 563b, 564tl, 624t, 625, 685, 696tr
Julia Gecha: 111, 116
Geosystems: 624b
Andrea Golden: 606t, 125tr, 469t
Jared Lee: 115, 161, 183, 500, 520b, 534b, 775
MapQuest.com, Inc.: 297
Martucci Studio: 58, 59b, 60t, 61, 68t, 80, 88, 116ml, 116mr, 116b, 121, 122tr, 124, 133, 162, 169, 175, 215tm, 265, 275t, 290t, 290m, 290b, 306tl, 306tr, 347, 364, 451
Matt Mayerchak: 41, 109, 131, 173, 207t, 245m, 307, 369br, 431br, 459br, 493, 529, 565, 639br, 671br, 741, 759t
Fran Milner: 207b, 588t, 603
Albert Molnar: 738b
Ortelius Design: 26t, 26br, 27tl, 27tr, 27bl, 27br, 298, 392t, 392b, 393t, 393m, 393b, 558t, 558b, 559t, 559m, 559b, 596bl, 596tr, 597
Matthew Pippin: 278, 424t, 424b, 486–487t
Precision Graphics: 535, 548, 555, 556, 571m, 571b, 573tr, 573b, 574tl, 574tr, 576t, 577br, 578t, 579b, 579t, 579m, 585l, 589t, 590, 592l, 592r, 593t, 594, 595t, 595b, 598t, 600t, 600b, 677t, 677bl, 677br, 678, 682b, 683, 684, 693t, 693b, 698l, 699t, 699b, 700t, 705r, 707, 710, 713, 714t, 714b, 722t, 743
PU: 589b
Rob Schuster: xi, 367t
Nancy Smith: 150, 166, 190, 252, 272, 294, 300, 318, 330, 352, 360, 384, 398, 414, 428, 446, 652, 660, 734
JB Woolsey Associates: 7, 43, 211b, 269, 309t, 327tl, 327tr, 333b, 357, 367, 371br, 405b, 536, 537tr, 539, 540, 560l, 627, 649b, 649m, 655, 662t, 663tr, 664t, 673b, 719, 722b, 725, 728–729

Photography

Photo Research Sue McDermott, Toni Michaels, Paula Wehde
Cover image Cosmo Condina/Tony Stone Images

Front Matter: Page i, ii, Cosmo Condina/Tony Stone Images; **iiil,** Courtesy of Michael J. Padilla, Ph.D.; **iiir,** Courtesy of Martha Cyr, Ph.D. and Ioannis Miaoulis, Ph.D; **viiit,** Doug Martin/Photo Researchers; **viiib,** Darryl Torcklet/Tony Stone Images; **ixt,** Superstock; **ixm,** Russ Lappa; **ixb,** Charles D. Winters/Photo Researchers; **xt,** Robert Maier/Animals Animals, **xb,** George Disario/The Stock Market; **xi,** Addison Geary/Stock Boston; **xi background,** Russ Lappa; **xiit,** Index Stock Imagery; **xiib,** Richard Pasley/Stock Boston; **xiii,** Bill Horsman/Stock Boston; **xiii inset,** Dr. Jeremy Burgess/Science Photo Library/Photo Researchers; **xivt,** Ken Eward/Science Source/Photo Researchers; **xivb,** Lawrence Migdale/Tony Stone Images; **xvt, b,** Richard Haynes; **xvit,** Mark C. Burnett/Photo Researchers; **xvib, xviit&b,** Richard Haynes; **xviim,** Benn Mitchell/The Image Bank; **xviiit,** Spencer Grant/Index Stock Imagery; **xviiimt,** Syracuse/Dick Blume/The Image Works; **xviiimb,** Bob Torrez/Tony Stone Images; **xviiib,** NASA; **xix,** Richard Haynes; **xx,** Russ Lappa; **xxi,** John Henley/The Stock Market; **xxi inset,** Ken Whitmore/Tony Stone Images; **xxiit,** Joe Towers/The Stock Market; **xxiib,** Bourg/Liaison International; **1,** Leonard Lessin/Peter Arnold; **2t,** NASA; **2–3 b,** NASA.

Introduction to Physical Science
Page 4t, Dave Bjorn/Tony Stone Images; **4b,** Bob Shaw/The Stock Market; **5t,** Aaron Haupt/Stock Boston; **5bl,** Bruce Henderson/Stock Boston; **5br,** Index Stock Imagery; **6,** David Howell/The Image Works; **7,** Russ Lappa; **8t,** D'Andrea/Index Stock Imagery; **8b,** Ilene Perlman/Stock Boston; **9,** John Brooks/Liaison Agency; **9 inset,** Megna/Peticolas/Fundamental Photographs; **10,** Russ Lappa; **11,** Richard Haynes; **12l,** Ben Osborne/Tony Stone Images; **12tr,** Michael Newman/PhotoEdit; **12br,** Kaluzny Thatcher/Tony Stone Images; **13tl,** Robin L. Sachs/PhotoEdit; **13tr,** Tryy Vine/Tony Stone Images; **13bl,** Peter Menzel/Stock Boston; **13br,** Index Stock Imagery; **14,** Aaron Haupt/Stock Boston.

Chapter 1
Pages 16–17, Superstock; **18,** Russ Lappa; **19,** Tim Hauf/Visuals Unlimited; **20l,** Ken Lucas/Visuals Unlimited; **20r,** Yoav Levy/PhotoTake; **21tl,** Michael Fogden/DRK Photo; **21tr,** Glenn M. Oliver/Visuals Unlimited; **21bl,** Richard Megna/Fundamental Photographs; **21bml,** Goivaux Communication/Phototake; **21bmr,** Charles D. Winters/Photo Researchers; **21br,** Ken Lucas/Visuals Unlimited; **22,** Lawrence Migdale/Tony Stone Images; **23,** Richard Megna/Fundamental Photographs; **24t,** Richard Haynes; **24b,** Mark Thayer; **25l,** Russ Lappa; **25r,** Richard Haynes; **26, 27t,** Corbis-Bettmann; **27b,** The Granger Collection, NY; **28,** Ken Lucas/Tony Stone Images; **31 both,** 1998, The Art Institute of Chicago; **32,** Rich Treptow/Visuals Unlimited; **33,** Chuck Feil/Uniphoto; **34,** SCI-VU-IBMRL/Visuals Unlimited; **35,** Ken Eward/Science Source/Photo Researchers; **36t,** Russ Lappa; **36b,** Corbis-Bettmann; **37t,** Helga Lade/Peter Arnold; **37bl,** E.R. Degginger/Animals Animals/Earth Scenes; **37br,** Charles D. Winters/Photo Researchers; **38,** Aron Haupt/David R. Frazier Photo Library; **40,** Heine Schneebeli/Science Photo Library/Photo Researchers; **41,** Corbis-Bettmann.

Chapter 2
Pages 44–45, Milton Rand/Tom Stack & Associates; **46t,** Richard Haynes; **46b,** Shambroom/Photo Researchers; **47,** Darryl Torckler/Tony Stone Images; **48t,** Superstock; **48b,** Russ Lappa; **49,** Tsutomu Nakayama/Uniphoto; **50,** Tomas Muscionoco/The Stock Market; **51,** A. Ramey/Stock Boston; **52,** John D. Cunningham/Visuals Unlimited; **53, 54,** Richard Haynes; **55,** Ken Ross/FPG International; **57l,** Michelle Bridwell/PhotoEdit; **57r,** Rudi Von Briel/PhotoEdit; **62,** Russ Lappa; **63, 64t,** Richard Haynes; **64b,** Russ Lappa; **65,** Doug Martin/Photo Researchers; **66,** The Granger Collection, NY; **67,** Martin Dohrn/Science Photo Library/Photo Researchers; **69,** Charles D. Winters/Photo Researchers; **70,** Russ Lappa; **71,** Darryl Torckler/Tony Stone Images.

Chapter 3
74–75, Roy King/Superstock; **76, 77 both, 78 both, 79t,** Russ Lappa; **79b,** Frank Cezus/FPG International; **81 both,** Russ Lappa; **82,** Jo Prater/Visuals Unlimited; **82 inset,** Peter L. Chapman/Stock Boston; **83 both,** The Granger Collection, NY; **87,** Russ Lappa; **89,** Nubar Alexanian/Stock Boston; **90tl,** Russ Lappa; **90tr,** Stephen Frisch/Stock Boston; **90bl,** Charles D. Winters/Photo Researchers; **91,** Jeremy Scott/International Stock; **92l,** Claire Paxton & Jacqui Farrow/Science Photo Library/Photo Researchers; **92r,** David Noton/International Stock; **93,** Russ Lappa; **94,** Steve Wanke/Uniphoto; **95,** Bob Daemmrich/Stock Boston; **96,** Russ Lappa; **97 both,** Richard Haynes; **98,** Tom Brakefield/The Stock Market; **99,** Lawrence Migdale/Science Source/Photo Researchers; **100l,** Charles D. Winters/Photo Researchers; **100r,** Mark Gibson/Visuals Unlimited; **101,**

Novovitch/Liaison International; **102t,** Michael Dalton/Fundamental Photographs; **102b,** Stephen Frisch/Stock Boston; **103,** Roger Du Buisson/The Stock Market; **105,** Francois Gohier/Photo Researchers; **106,** David Nunuk/Science Photo Library/Photo Researchers; **107,** NASA; **108,** Space Telescope Science Institute.

Chapter 4
Pages 112–113, Ken Eward/Science Source/Photo Researchers; **114t,** Russ Lappa; **114b,** Arthur Gurmankin & Mary Morina/Visuals Unlimited; **116tl,** Lawrence Migdale/Photo Researchers; **116tr,** Richard Megna/Fundamental Photographs; **116b, 117,** Russ Lappa; **118,** M. Claye/Jacana/Photo Researchers; **119,** Richard Megna/Fundamental Photographs; **121,** Russ Lappa; **123,** George Disario/The Stock Market; **126, 127,** Richard Haynes; **128l,** Gary Retherford/Photo Researchers; **128r, 129l, m,** Paul Silverman/Fundamental Photographs; **129r,** Ken Lucas/Visuals Unlimited; **130t,** Breck P. Kent/Animals Animals/Earth Scenes; **130b,** Russ Lappa; **131l,** George Disario/The Stock Market; **131r,** Paul Silverman/ Fundamental Photographs; **134t,** E. Lettau/FPG International; **134m,** C.Gail Shumway/FPG International; **134b,** Tilly Arthur/FPG International; **135,** Spencer Grant/PhotoEdit; **136,** The Granger Collection, NY; **137,** Corbis-Bettmann; **140–141,** Russ Lappa.

Chapter 5
Pages 142–143, Kunio Owaki/The Stock Market; **144,** Steve Elmore/The Stock Market; **145,** Brian Sytnyk/Masterfile; **146t,** Charles D. Winters/Photo Researchers; **146ml,** Wood Sabold/International Stock; **146mr,** Ken O'Donaghue; **146bl,** Russ Lappa; **146br,** Steven Needham/Envision; **147t,** Michael Newman/PhotoEdit; **147b,** Mark Wagner/Tony Stone Images; **148l,** Russ Lappa; **148r,** J. Sulley/The Image Works; **149 both,** Richard Megna/Fundamental Photographs; **151,** Richard Haynes; **152, 154 all,** Russ Lappa; **155,** John D. Cummingham/Visuals Unlimited; **157 both,** E.R. Degginger; **158,** Donald Johnson/Tony Stone Images; **159t,** Russ Lappa; **159b,** Charles D. Winters/Photo Researchers; **160t,** Richard Haynes; **160b,** Simon Norfolk/Tony Stone Images; **163t both,** Richard Megna/Fundamental Photographs; **163b,** Russ Lappa; **164,** AP/Wide World Photos; **166,** Russ Lappa; **167, 168t,** Richard Haynes; **168b,** Patrick Donehue/Photo Researchers; **169,** Dorothy Littell/Stock Boston; **170 all,** Russ Lappa; **172,** Dede Gilman/Photo Network; **173,** Steve Elmore/The Stock Market.

Chapter 6
Page 176–177, Minolta Corp.; **178,** Michael Newman/PhotoEdit; **179t, m,** Russ Lappa; **179b,** Leonard Lessin/Peter Arnold; **181,** Runk/Schoenberger/Grant Heilman Photography; **184,** Russ Lappa; **185t,** Tim Laman/Index Stock Imagery; **185m,** Randy Ury/The Stock Market; **185b,** Mike & Carol Werner/Stock Boston; **186,** Russ Lappa; **187,** Dan McCoy/Rainbow; **188t,** Russ Lappa; **188b,** Eric Simmons/Stock Boston; **189,** John Elk III/Stock Boston; **190,** Russ Lappa; **191,** Richard Haynes; **192t,** Russ Lappa; **192b,** Lawrence Migdale/Photo Researchers; **193 both,** Russ Lappa; **194,** Bob Krist/The Stock Market; **195tl, m,** Russ Lappa; **195tr,** David Young-Wolff/PhotoEdit; **195bl,** Mark C. Burnett/Stock Boston; **195br,** Russ Lappa; **196br,** B. Daemmrich/The Image Works; **196 the rest,** Russ Lappa; **197,** P. Aprahamian/Science Photo Library/Photo Researchers; **198,** Russ Lappa; **199t,** L. S. Stepanowicz/Visuals Unlimited; **199b,** Tom Pantages; **201,** Richard Haynes; **202t,** Jenny Hager/The Image Works; **202b,** Russ Lappa; **203,** George Ranalli/Photo Researchers; **204,** Russ Lappa; **205,** Richard Haynes; **206,** Cleo Photography/Photo Researchers; **208,** Russ Lappa; **209,** P. Aprahamian/Science Photo Library/Photo Researchers.

Chapter 7
Pages 212–213, James Schnepf/Liaison Agency; **214,** Vision Agenzia Fotografica/Photo Researchers, Inc.; **216t,** Martin Rogers/Tony Stone Images; **216b,** Russ Lappa; **217,** Richard Pasley/Stock Boston; **218,** Russ Lappa; **219t,** Richard Haynes; **219b,** Bob Daemmrich/Stock Boston; **220l,** Frank Oberle/Tony Stone Images; **220m,** William Taufic/The Stock Market; **220r,** Jeffery Mark Dunn/Stock Boston; **221,** Matthew Naythons/Stock Boston; **222,** David J. Sams/Stock Boston; **223l,** Russ Lappa; **223r,** Novosti/Photo Researchers; **224,** John Edwards/Tony Stone Images; **225t,** R.J. Erwin/Photo Researchers; **225b, 226l,** Russ Lappa; **226r,** Daniel McDonald/Stock Boston; **227t,** Russ Lappa; **227b,** Kenneth Chen/Envision; **228,** Tony Freeman/PhotoEdit; **229, 230 both, 231, 232t,** Russ Lappa; **232b,** Cabisco/Visuals Unlimited; **234l,** Joe McDonald/Visuals Unlimited; **234r,** David Parker/Science Photo Library/Photo Researchers; **235, 236,** Russ Lappa; **237,** Richard Haynes; **238,** Mike Mazzaschi/Stock Boston; **239,** Richard Pasley/Stock Boston.

Chapter 8
Pages 242–243, Larry Ulrich/DRK Photo; **244,** John Terence Turner/FPG International; **245,** Russ Lappa; **246tl,** Tom Tracey/The Stock Market; **246tr,** Inga Spence/Visuals Unlimted; **246b,** William Whitehurst/The Stock Market; **248t,** Leonard Lessin/Peter Arnold; **248bl,** Corbis-Bettmann; **248br,** Terry Wild Studio/

Uniphoto; **249tl,** David Young-Wolff/PhotoEdit; **249tr,** Nick Colaneri/Uniax Corporation; **249b,** Jeffry W. Myers/The Stock Market; **250l,** Bob Torrez/Tony Stone Images; **250r,** David J. Sams/Tony Stone Images; **251l,** Dennis O'Clair/Tony Stone Images; **251r,** Richard Hutchings/Photo Researchers; **252,** Daemmrich/Uniphoto; **253,** Richard Haynes; **254,** Tom Smith/Photo Researchers; **255t,** Russ Lappa; **255b,** Bachmann/PhotoEdit; **256l,** Richard Haynes; **256r,** Diana Calder/The Stock Market; **257m,** AP Photo/Boeing handout/Wide World; **257tl inset,** Peter Gridley/FPG International; **257bl inset,** De Malglaive E./Liaison Agency; **257br inset,** Pratt & Whitney/Liaison Agency; **259l,** William Hopkins; **259r,** Marc Pokempner/Tony Stone Images; **260t,** Russ Lappa; **260b,** M. Borchi White Star/Photo Researchers; **261t,** Daniel Aubry/The Stock Market; **261bl,** Mark Richards/PhotoEdit; **261br,** Dan McCoy/Rainbow; **262 both,** James L. Amos/Peter Arnold; **263,** D. Young-Wolff MR/PhotoEdit; **264,** Ted Horowitz/The Stock Market; **265,** Jan Van Der Straet/Granger Collection, NY; **268,** T.A. Wiewandt/DRK Photo; **270l,** Jean-Perrin/CNRI/Science Photo Library/Photo Researchers; **270r,** Alfred Pasieka/Science Photo Library/Photo Researchers; **271 both,** Pat Cunningham/Liaison Agency; **276t,** Rob Trubia/ Westlight; **276b,** Courtesy of Christine Darden; **277t,** HO/AP/Wide World Photos; **277b,** Uniphoto; **279l,** AP/Wide World Photos; **279r,** Courtesy of Christine Darden.

Chapter 9
Pages 280–281, Frans Lanting/Minden Pictures; **282t,** Richard Haynes; **282bl,** Bob Abraham/The Stock Market; **282br,** Roy Morsch/The Stock Market; **283t,** D. Roundtree/Image Bank; **283b,** Steve Maslowshi/Photo Researchers; **284,** NASA; **285l,** Chuck Zsymanski/International Stock; **285r,** Robert Maier/Animals Animals; **286,** Mike Agliolo/International Stock; **287,** John Kelly/The Image Bank; **288,** National Motor Museum, Beaulieu, England; **289t,** Topham/The Image Works; **289b,** David Barnes/The Stock Market; **290,** Marc Romanelli/The Image Bank; **291,** A.T. Willet/The Image Bank; **295,** Richard Haynes; **296t,** Russ Lappa; **296b,** Image Makers/The Image Bank; **299, 300,** Richard Haynes; **301,** Lou Jones/The Image Bank; **302t,** Richard Haynes; **302b,** Mike Hewitt/Allsport; **303t,** Yann Guichaoua/Agence Vandystadt/Allsport; **303m,** Tim DeFrisco/ Allsport; **303b,** Tracy Frankel/The Image Bank; **304,** Addison Geary/Stock Boston; **305,** Corel Corp.; **307,** Mike Agliolo/International Stock.

Chapter 10
Pages 310–311, David Stoecklein/The Stock Market; **312t,** Russ Lappa; **312bl,** Calimberti/Liaison Agency; **312br,** Alain Ernoult/The Image Bank; **313,** Richard Thom/Visuals Unlimited; **314,** Elisabeth Weiland/Photo Researchers; **315 all,** Richard Haynes; **316,** Bilderberg/The Stock Market; **317t,** Russ Lappa; **317b, 319, 320, 322,** Richard Haynes; **323,** Russ Lappa; **324t,** Jan Hinsch/Science Photo Library/ Photo Researchers; **324b,** B & C Alexander/Photo Researchers; **325tl,** The Photo Works/Photo Researchers; **325tr,** Welzenbach/The Stock Market; **325b,** Russ Lappa; **326t,** Jack Novak/Superstock; **326bl,** Megna/Peticolas/Fundamental Photographs; **326br,** Richard Megna/Fundamental Photographs; **329,** NASA; **330,** Richard Haynes; **331,** Ken O'Donoghue; **332t,** Richard Haynes; **332b,** Ed Young/Science Photo Library/Photo Researchers; **333,** Bob Woodward/The Stock Market; **334l,** Syracuse/Dick Blume/The Image Works; **334r,** Michael Devin Daly/The Stock Market; **336,** Russ Lappa; **338t,** Richard Haynes; **338b,** Corel Corp.; **339,** Jeff Hunter/The Image Bank.

Chapter 11
Pages 344–345, Rana Clamitans/Visuals Unlimited; **346t,** Richard Haynes; **346bl,** Chlaus Lotscher/ Stock Boston; **346br,** Milton Feinberg/Stock Boston; **350 both,** Richard Megna/Fundamental Photographs; **351,** Russ Lappa; **352,** Benn Mitchell/ The Image Bank; **353,** Russ Lappa; **354t,** Richard Haynes; **354b,** Chris Sheridan/ Monkmeyer; **357l,** Stuart Westmorland/Photo Researchers; **357r,** Andrew Mertiner/Photo Researchers; **358,** Ken Marshall/Madison Press Limited; **359,** Russ Lappa; **361,** Richard Haynes; **362,** Russ Lappa; **363,** Runk/Schoenberger/Grant Heilman Photography, Inc.; **365t,** Richard Haynes; **365b,** Mercury Archives/The Image Bank; **366,** Patti McConville/The Image Bank; **368t,** Russ Lappa; **368b,** Richard Haynes; **369l,** Chlaus Lotscher/Stock Boston; **369r,** Milton Finberg/Stock Boston.

Chapter 12
Pages 372–373, Belinda Banks/Tony Stone Images; **374 all,** Richard Haynes; **375t,** David A. Jentz/Photo Network; **375b,** Fotopic/Omni-Photo Communications; **377,** Stephen McBrady/PhotoEdit; **378t,** Richard Haynes; **378b, 379,** Skjold/PhotoEdit; **380,** Siegfried Tauquer/Leo De Wys; **381t,** David Young-Wolff/PhotoEdit; **381b,** Richard Haynes; **382,** Russ Lappa; **385, 386t,** Richard Haynes; **386b,** Russ Lappa; **387,** John Akhtar/Vivid Images Phtg., Inc.; **388t,** Tony Freeman/PhotoEdit; **388b, 389,** Russ Lappa; **390,** Museum of Modern Art-NYC, NY/© FPG International 1991; **391t,** Russ Lappa; **391l,** Jerry Wachter/ Photo Researchers; **391r,** Elliott Smith/International Stock; **392t,** Sylvain Grandadam/Tony Stone Images; **392b,** Gerard Champion/The Image Bank; **393t,** Jeffrey Aaronson/

Network Aspen; **393b,** G.B. Archives/Sygma; **394,** John Elk/Stock Boston; **396t,** David R. Frazier; **396b,** Tony Freeman/PhotoEdit; **397,** Jeff Smith/The Image Bank; **398,** Cleo Freelance Photo/New England Stock; **399,** Richard Haynes; **400 both,** Russ Lappa; **401 all,** Richard Haynes; **402t,** Ken Karp; **402bl, br,** Richard Haynes.

Chapter 13
Pages 406–407, Chris Rogers/The Stock Market; **408t,** Richard Haynes; **408b,** Charles Doswell III/Tony Stone Images; **409,** Zigy Kaluzny/Tony Stone Images; **411,** J. MacPherson/The Stock Market; **412l,** John Shaw/Tom Stack & Associates; **412m,** Paul Silverman/Fundamental Photographs; **412r,** Daniel Cox/Allstock/ PNI; **412–413,** James Balog/Tony Stone Images; **413m,** William L. Wantland/Tom Stack & Associates; **413r,** Howard Sochurek/The Stock Market; **414, 415, 416t,** Richard Haynes; **416b,** Ken Straiton/The Stock Market; **418t,** Dr. Harold E. Edgerton/ The Harold E. Edgerton 1992 Trust; **418b,** Jon Chomitz; **419l,** Richard Megna/ Fundamental Photographs; **419r,** Russ Lappa; **420,** "Waterfall" by M.C. Escher, ©1998, Cordon Art-Baarn-Holland. All Rights Reserved; **421,** Courtesy of the Archives, California Institute of Technology; **422t,** Russ Lappa; **422b,** Ludek Pesek/Photo Researchers; **423,** Bryan Peterson/The Stock Market; **426,** Russ Lappa; **427,** Bill Bachmann/Photo Researchers; **429,** Richard Haynes; **430,** The Granger Collection, NY; **431,** Dr. Harold E. Edgerton/The Harold E. Edgerton 1992 Trust; **433,** Globus, Holway & Lobel/The Stock Market.

Chapter 14
Pages 434–435, Alfred Pasieka/Peter Arnold; **436, 438, 439t,** Russ Lappa; **439b,** Michael Mancuso/Omni-Photo Communications; **440,** Stephen L. Saks/ Photo Researchers; **441,** Ken O'Donoghue; **442t,** Tom Campbell/Liaison Agency; **442b,** Richard Haynes; **443l,** Wayne Lynch/DRK Photo; **443r,** Gay Bumgarner/ Tony Stone Images; **445,** Mike Mazzaschi/Stock Boston; **447,** Richard Haynes; **448,** Andy Sacks/Tony Stone Images; **449t,** Richard Haynes; **449b,** Wayne Eastep/ Tony Stone Images; **450tl,** Runk/Schoenberger/Grant Heilman Photography; **450tr,** Jack Reznicki/The Stock Market; **450b,** Jan Halaska/Photo Researchers; **452,** R. Knolan Benfield, Jr./Visuals Unlimited; **453,** Richard Choy/ Peter Arnold; **455t,** Richard Haynes; **455b,** Larry Ulrich/DRK Photo; **457,** Xenophon A. Beake/ The Stock Market; **459,** Wayne Lynch/DRK Photo; **462t,** IFA/Peter Arnold; **462–463m,** John Higginson/Tony Stone Images; **462–463b,** Chris Warren/ International Stock; **464–465,** Bob Kramer/Stock Boston; **465t,** Joseph Pobereskin/Tony Stone Images; **465b,** Richard Haynes; **466tl,** Corbis-Bettmann; **466tm, tr,** The Granger Collection, NY; **466b, 467,** Corbis-Bettmann; **468–469,** Richard Weiss/Peter Arnold.

Chapter 15
Pages 470–471, Jim Pickerell/Folio, Inc.; **472t,** Richard Haynes; **472b,** Rob Gilley/Adventure Photo & Film; **474,** Richard Megna/Fundamental Photographs; **476t,** Richard Haynes; **476b,** Chris Cole/Duomo; **479, 482, 488, 489,** Richard Haynes; **490,** Lynette Cook/Science Photo Library/Photo Researchers; **492,** Andrew Ratkino/Tony Stone Images; **492 inset,** Russell D. Curtis/Photo Researchers.

Chapter 16
Pages 496–497, Bob Kramer/Index Stock Imagery; **498,** Richard Haynes; **499,** Russell D. Curtis/Photo Researchers; **501,** Russ Lappa; **502t,** The Granger Collection, NY; **502b,** Eric Risberg/AP/Wide World Photos; **503, 504,** Richard Haynes; **506,** Matt Bostick; **507t,** Mark C. Burnett/Stock Boston; **507b,** Martin Bough/Fundamental Photographs; **510t,** Richard Haynes; **510–511b,** Cosmo Condina/Tony Stone Images; **512,** Michael Newman/PhotoEdit; **513,** Stanley Rowin/Index Stock Imagery; **514–515t,** Doug Martin/Photo Researchers; **514m,** Spencer Grant/Index Stock Imagery; **514b,** Nancy Brown/The Stock Market; **515m,** PhotoDisc, Inc.; **515b,** Index Stock Imagery; **516,** David Ball/The Stock Market; **517,** Neil Nissing/FPG International; **518–519, 520,** Richard Haynes; **522,** Stephen Frisch/Stock Boston; **523,** Michael Newman/PhotoEdit; **525,** Corbis; **526t,** Mitch Reardon/Photo Researchers; **526b,** Francois Gohier/Photo Researchers; **527t,** Merlin D. Tuttle, Bat Conservation International/Photo Researchers; **527b,** Charles Gupton/The Stock Market; **527b inset,** Telegraph Color Library/FPG International; **528 all,** Richard Megna/Fundamental Photographs.

Chapter 17
Pages 532–533, Alex Bartel/Science Photo Library/Photo Researchers; **534, 537t,** Richard Haynes; **537b,** Russ Lappa; **538,** Richard Haynes; **540,** Matthew McVay/Tony Stone Images; **541tl,** Jim Roshan; **541tr,** Eric Miller/Liaison Agency; **541b,** Vecto Verso/Leo de Wys; **543,** Alfred Pasieka/Science Photo Library/ Photo Researchers; **544t,** Fundamental Photographs; **544b,** Ron Sutherland/Science Photo Library/Photo Researchers; **545,** RNHRD NHS Trust/Tony Stone Images; **546,** Alfred Pasieka/Science Photo Library/Photo Researchers; **547,** Nordion/ Visuals Unlimited; **549,** Bill Horsman/Stock Boston; **550t,** 98 Kunio Owaki/The Stock Market; **550b,** Phil Degginger; **551t,** Aneal E. Vohra/Unicorn Stock Photos;

551b, Charles Seaborn/Tony Stone Images; **553,** Richard Haynes; **555,** Russ Lappa; **558,** Bruce Forster/Tony Stone Images; **559,** AP/Wide World Photos; **560,** David Ducros/Science Photo Library/Photo Researchers; **564,** Richard Haynes.

Chapter 18
Pages 568–569, Arthur Gurmankin/Mary Morina/Visuals Unlimited; **570t,** Russ Lappa; **570b,** Andy Levin/Photo Researchers; **571l,** Coco McCoy/Rainbow; **571m,** Michael A. Keller Studios LTD./The Stock Market; **571r,** Skip Moody/ Rainbow; **572 both,** Corel Corp.; **575t,** Richard Haynes; **575b,** Russ Lappa; **576,** Photo Researchers; **577t,** John Kieffer/Peter Arnold; **577b,** John M. Dunay IV/ Fundamental Photographs; **578 both,** David Parker/Photo Researchers; **579,** Richard Megna/Fundamental Photographs; **580,** Russ Lappa; **581t,** Richard Haynes; **581b,** David Young-Wolff/PhotoEdit; **582t,** Breck P. Kent; **582b,** Grant Heilman Photography; **583 both,** Michael Dalton/Fundamental Photographs; **584l,** Ralph C. Eagle/Photo Researchers; **584r,** Russ Lappa; **584r inset,** Jerome Wexler/Photo Researchers; **585,** Russ Lappa; **586,** Richard Haynes; **587,** John Coletti/Stock Boston; **588 both,** L.V. Bergman & Associates; **591t,** Richard Haynes; **591b,** Camerique, Inc./Index Stock Imagery; **593t,** Richard T. Nowitz/ Photo Researchers; **593b,** Jan Hinsch/Science Photo Library/Photo Researchers; **596t,** Corbis; **596b,** Scala/Art Resource, NY; **597t,** Grant Heilman Photography; **597b,** Corbis; **598,** Blair Seitz/Photo Researchers; **599tl,** Jon Goell/Index Stock Imagery; **599tr,** Bob Daemmrich/Stock Boston; **599ml,** E.R. Degginger; **599mr,** Grant Heilman Photography; **599mt inset,** Spencer Grant/Photo Researchers; **599mb inset,** Will & Deni Mcintyre/Photo Researchers; **599bl,** E. R. Degginger; **604l,** Everett Collection, Inc.; **604r, 605t,** Russ Lappa; **605b,** Hans W. Silvester/ Rapho/Liaison Agency; **606,** Russ Lappa; **607l,** TITANIC © 1997 Twentieth Century Fox Film Corporation and Paramount Pictures Corporation. All rights reserved.; **607r,** Photofest; **607b,** Russ Lappa; **608tl,** The Kobal Collection; **608tr,** Photofest; **608–609b,** Russ Lappa; **609t,** The Kobal Collection.

Chapter 19
Pages 610–611, Dick Durrance II/The Stock Market; **612t,** Richard Haynes; **612b,** Marcello Bertinetti/Photo Researchers; **613t,** Paul Silverman/Fundamental Photographs; **613b,** Russ Lappa; **614 both, 615l,** Richard Megna/Fundamental Photographs; **615r,** Phil Degginger/Color-Pic, Inc.; **616 both,** Richard Megna/ Fundamental Photographs; **618t,** Russ Lappa; **618b,** Richard Haynes; **620,** Aaron Rezny/The Stock Market; **621 both,** Richard Haynes; **622t,** Russ Lappa; **622bl, br,** Sisse Brimberg/National Geographic Image; **623,** National Geographic Society/ NGS Image; **626,** Lionel F. Stevenson/Photo Researchers; **628t,** Russ Lappa; **628b,** Corbis-Bettmann; **629tl, tm, tr,** Russ Lappa; **629b,** Richard Megna/ Fundamental Photographs; **630,** Fred McKinney/FPG International; **631 background,** Corel Corp.; **631 inset, 632l,** Russ Lappa; **632r,** Richard Megna/ Fundamental Photographs; **633,** AT&T Bell Labs/Science Photo Library/Photo Researchers; **634,** Kevin Cruff/FPG International; **635, 636t,** Richard Haynes; **636b, 637,** Richard Megna/Fundamental Photographs; **639,** Lionel F. Stevenson/ Photo Researchers.

Chapter 20
Pages 642–643, Telegraph Colour Library/FPG International; **644t,** Richard Haynes; **644b,** Mark C. Burnett/Photo Researchers; **647,** Hank Morgan/ Rainbow; **648,** Russ Lappa; **649 both,** Richard Haynes; **650,** Richard Kaylin/Tony Stone Images; **652, 653,** Richard Haynes; **654t,** Russ Lappa; **654b,** Craig Tuttle/The Stock Market; **657, 658,** Russ Lappa; **659,** M. Antman/The Image Works; **660,** Mark Burnett/Stock Boston; **661,** Richard Haynes; **662,** James Dwyer/Stock Boston; **663, 664, 666,** Russ Lappa; **667t,** Joel Page/AP Wide World Photos; **667b,** Russ Lappa; **668,** Armen Kachaturian/Liaison Agency; **669l,** Russ Lappa; **669r,** M. Antman/The Image Works; **670,** Ross Harrison Koty/Tony Stone Images; **671,** Russ Lappa.

Chapter 21
Pages 674–675, John Henley/The Stock Market; **676t,** Russ Lappa; **676b,** Jon Chomitz; **679, 681t,** Russ Lappa; **681b,** Telegraph Colour Library/FPG International; **682,** Richard Haynes; **686t,** Peter Menzel/Stock Boston; **686b,** Martin Rogers/ Tony Stone Images; **687t,** Adam Woolfitt/Woodfin Camp & Associates; **687m,** Roger Ball/The Stock Market; **687b,** Stephen J. Krasemann/ Photo Researchers; **689,** Alison Wright/Stock Boston; **690t,** Russ Lappa; **690b,** Frank Siteman/Stock Boston; **692l,** Toni Michaels; **692r,** B. Daemmrich/The Image Works; **693,** Russ Lappa; **694t,** The Granger Collection, NY; **694b,** Corbis-Bettmann; **695t,** The Granger Collection, NY; **695bl, br,** Corbis-Bettmann; **696,** Montes De Oca, Art 1998/FPG International; **697t,** Russ Lappa; **697b,** William Johnson/Stock Boston; **698,** J-L Charmet/Science Photo Library/Photo Researchers; **701,** Jose Pelaez/ The Stock Market; **702t,** David Barnes/Tony Stone Images; **702b,** Russ Lappa; **703,** Richard Haynes; **704,** David R. Frasier/Tony Stone Images; **705,** Peter Menzel/ Stock Boston.

Chapter 22
Pages 708–709, Tim Davis/Photo Researchers; **711tl,** Bob Daemmrich/Stock Boston; **711tr,** Bill Horsman/Stock Boston; **711b, 712,** Russ Lappa; **712 inset,** Dr. Jeremy Burgess/Science Photo Library/Photo Researchers; **713t,** Russ Lappa; **713t inset,** Dr. Jeremy Burgess/Science Photo Library/Photo Researchers; **713b,** Russ Lappa/Photo Researchers; **714 both,** Russ Lappa; **715,** Manfred Kage /Peter Arnold; **715 inset,** Charles Falco/Photo Researchers; **716,** Ken Whitmore/ Tony Stone Images; **717,** Russ Lappa; **718l,** B. Daemmrich/The Image Works; **718r,** Camerique/Archive Photos; **720t,** Russ Lappa; **720b,** Richard Pasley/Stock Boston; **721,** Craig Tuttle/The Stock Market; **721 inset,** Telegraph Colour Library/ FPG International; **724,** I. Maier, Jr./The Image Works; **726t,** Richard Haynes; **726b,** L. Dematteis/The Image Works; **727,** Andrew Syred/Science Photo Library/ Photo Researchers; **730t,** The Granger Collection, NY; **730b,** Corbis-Bettmann; **731t,** AP/Wide World Photos; **731b,** Camilla Smith/Rainbow; **732,** David Parker/ Science Photo Library/Photo Researchers; **733, 734 all, 735,** Russ Lappa; **736,** Sanford/Asliolo/International Stock; **737tl,** AP Photo/Kamran Jebreili; **737tr,** Russ Lappa; **737m,** NASA; **737bl,** Bob Daemmrich/Stock Boston; **737br,** AP Photo/ Rick Bethem; **739,** Russ Lappa; **740,** Andrew Oliney & TSI Imaging/Tony Stone Images; **744t,** Art Resource, NY; **744b,** The Granger Collection, NY; **745 all,** U.S. Dept. of the Interior National Park Service Edison National Historic Site; **746–747,** AP/Wide World Photos; **748l, m,** U.S. Dept. of the Interior National Park Service Edison National Historic Site; **748r,** Brooks/Brown/Photo Researchers; **749t,** U.S. Geological Survey/Science Photo Library/Photo Researchers; **749bl,** Topham/ The Image Works; **749bm,** Russ Lappa; **749br,** Michael Simpson/FPG International.

Skills Handbook
Page 750, Mike Moreland/Photo Network; **751t,** Russ Lappa; **751m,** Jeff Greenberg/Omni-Communications; **751b,** Russ Lappa; **754,** Richard Haynes; **756 both, 757,** PhotoDisc, Inc.

Glossary
Page 771l, Ralph C. Eagle/Photo Researchers; **771r,** Russ Lappa; **771r inset,** Jerome Wexler/Photo Researchers; **772,** Stephen L. Saks/Photo Researchers; **776,** Richard Megna/Fundamental Photographs; **779,** Russ Lappa; **780,** Charles Gupton/The Stock Market; **780 inset,** Telegraph Color Library/FPG International.